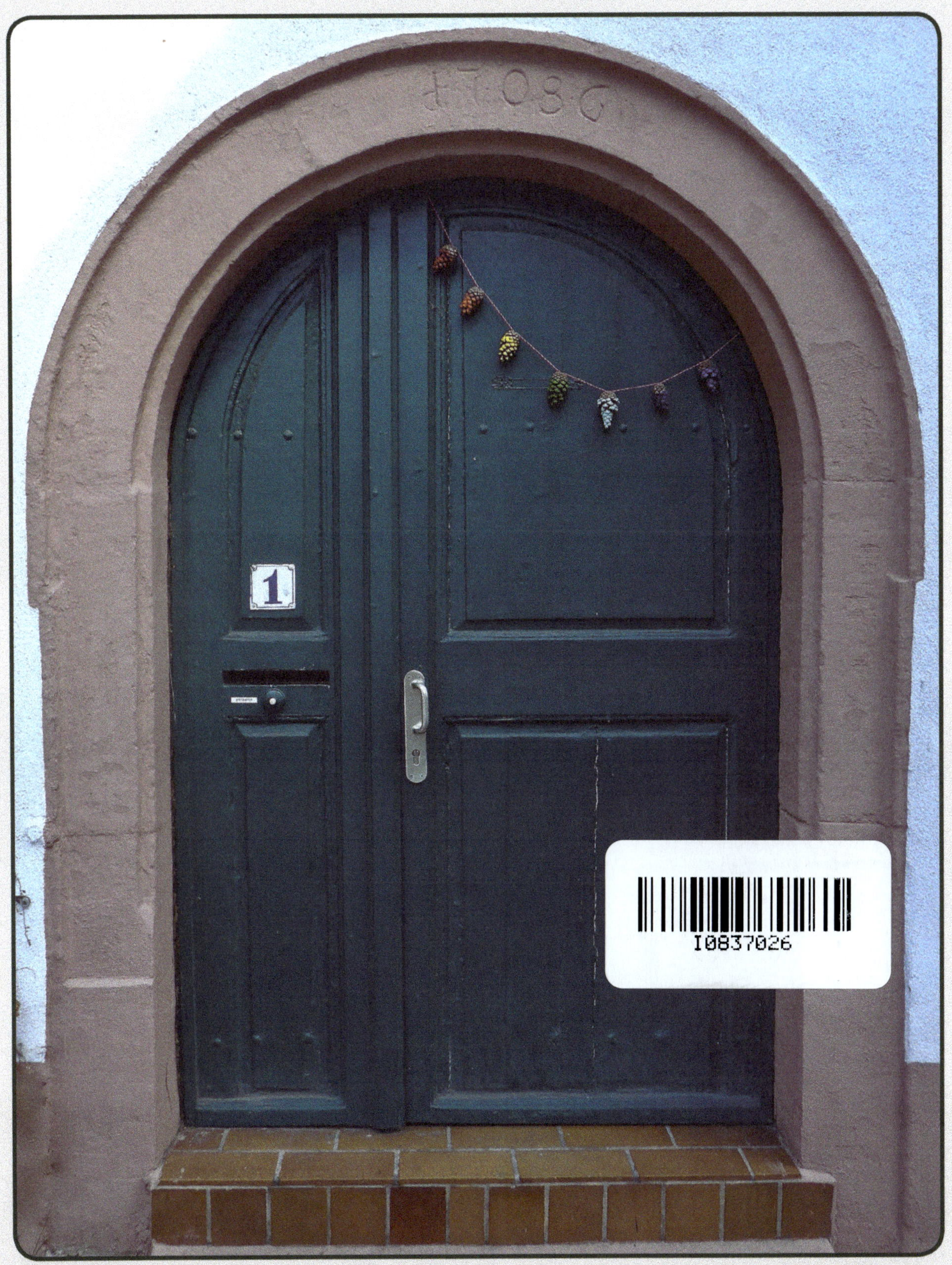

Windows into the Beauty of Flowers & Nature
ISBN-10: 1-941184-17-0
ISBN-13: 978-1-941184-17-2



Cover design by Zita Ballinger Fletcher.
Front and back cover photos by Noël-Marie Fletcher.

Inside front photo: Pine cones ready for a doorway dance.



Cataloging-in-Publication data for this book is available from the Library of Congress.

Library of Congress Control Number: 2017950785

Fletcher & Co. Publishers LLC
www.fletcherpublishers.com

First Edition
Printed in the United States of America

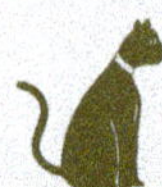

# Windows into the Beauty of Flowers & Nature

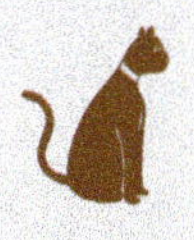

by

Noël-Marie Fletcher

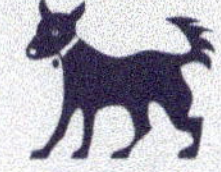

Fletcher & Co. Publishers
www.fletcherpublishers.com

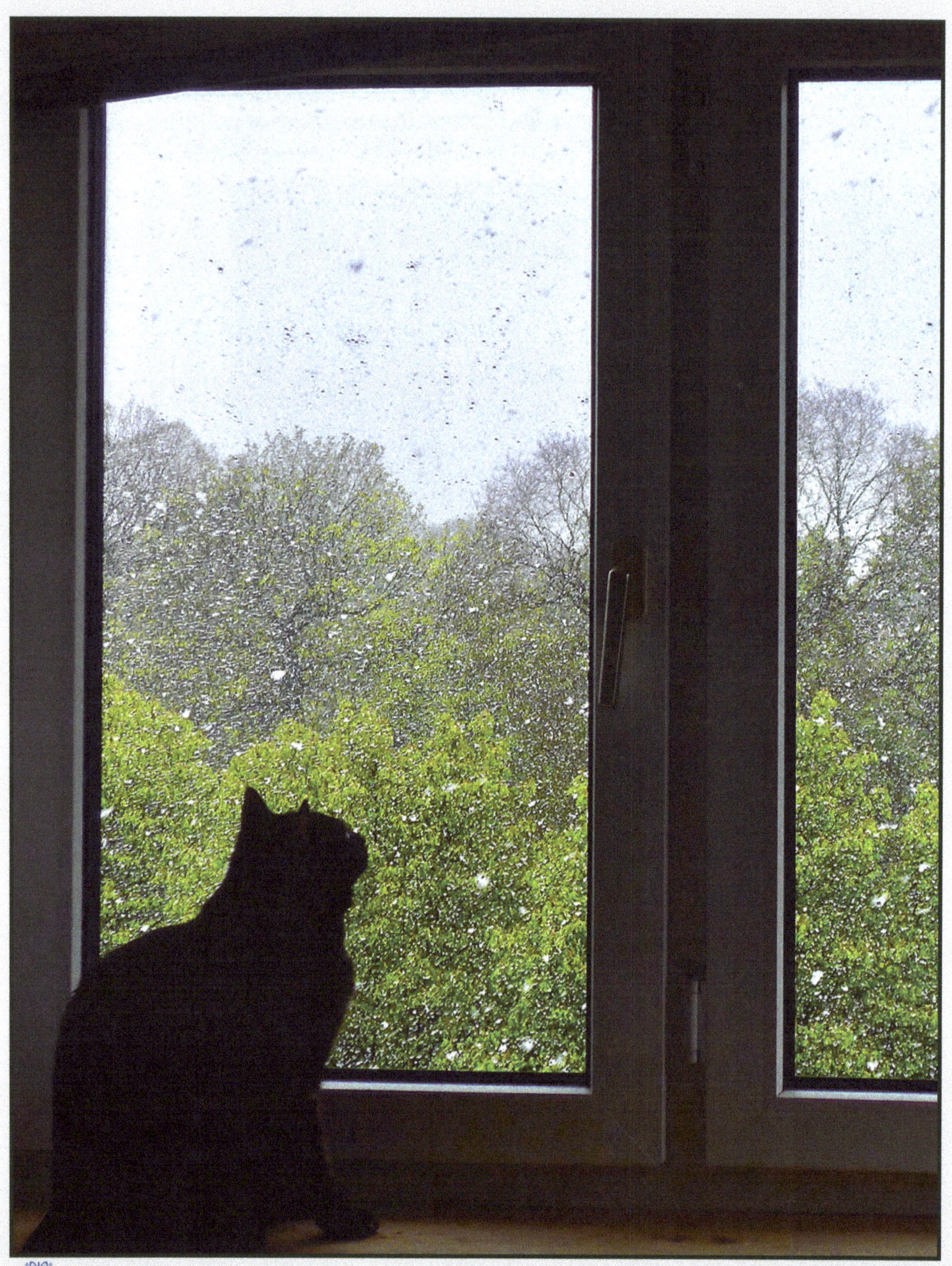

Georgie watches snowflakes fall from the sky one spring morning in Germany.

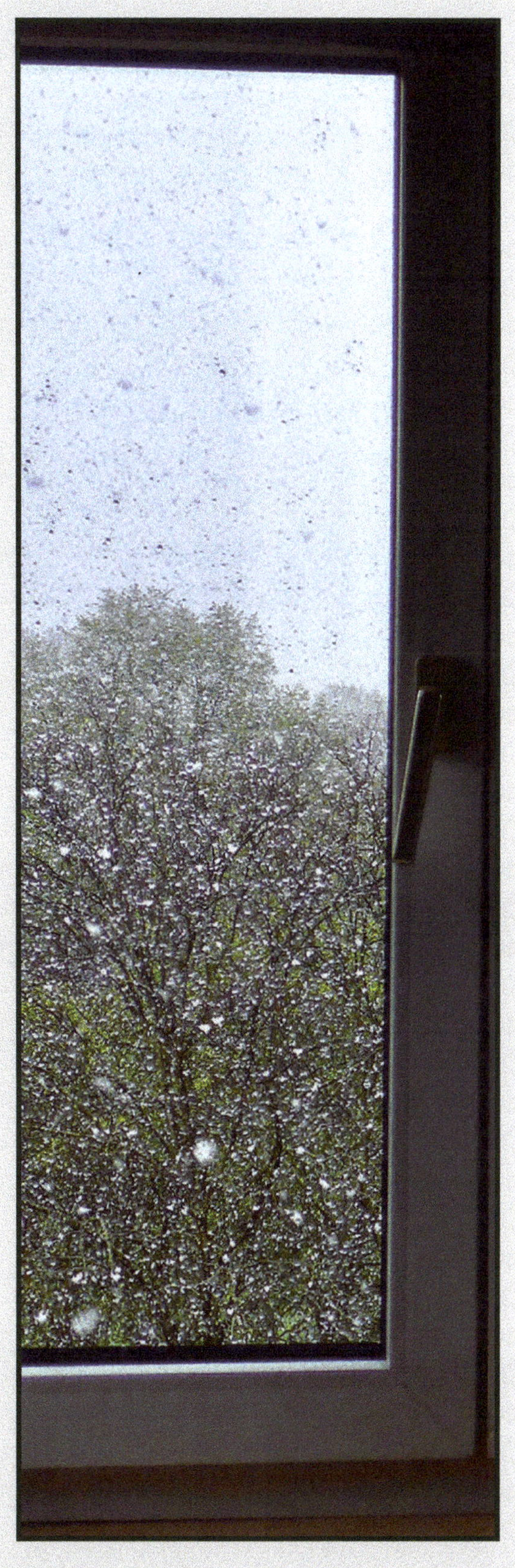

As you open these pages, you will peer through windows into moments that reveal the beauty and wonder in the lives of plants and creatures.

I snapped these photos during my comings and goings over the last few years. I keep a camera handy – in my purse, in my pocket while walking my dog, and even on my car dashboard while driving around town. Interspersed are my freehand pen/ink and pastel artwork of a subject contained within each chapter.

The windows open views into settings where I lived during the past few years – from sunny Southern California to tropical central Florida, the majestic deserts of New Mexico, and lastly to Bavaria, Germany, rich in medieval culture and wondrous forest greenbelts.

Upon moving to Germany, I discovered how its people have a special connection with nature and appreciation for its beauty. This is expressed in many ways, but especially in bringing nature to their windows and entry ways through decorative flowers and shrubs, which are shown among these pages.

What you will see are things that caught my eye and made me stop in my tracks to take a closer look.

Sometimes, I was struck by the vivid colors of a flower blossom on a breezy summer's day. Or, I noticed a tiny insect trying to cross the road at the same time as me, but facing enormous challenges to get from one place to another without being stepped on or run over by a car or bicycle. I've often thought about how all these different life forms occupy the same space as me during a given moment and how easy it can be to get so wrapped up in your own world you forget you're part of something larger and marvelous.

You, too, can observe the beauty of flowers and nature through the windows of your life if you are willing to open them.

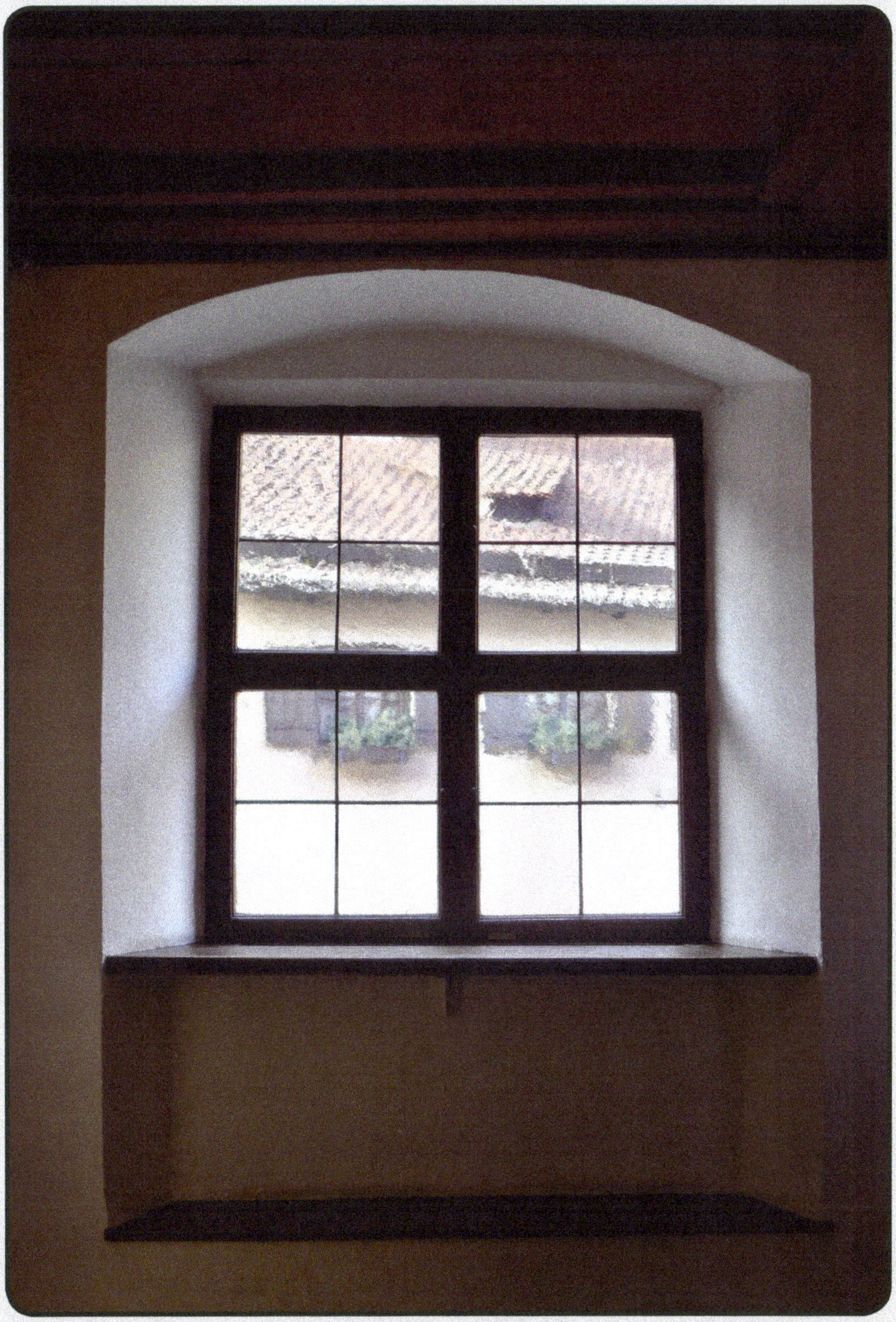

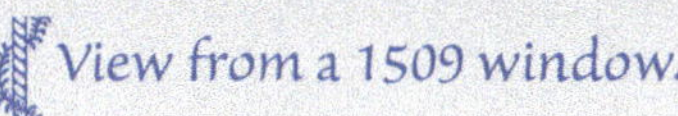

View from a 1509 window.

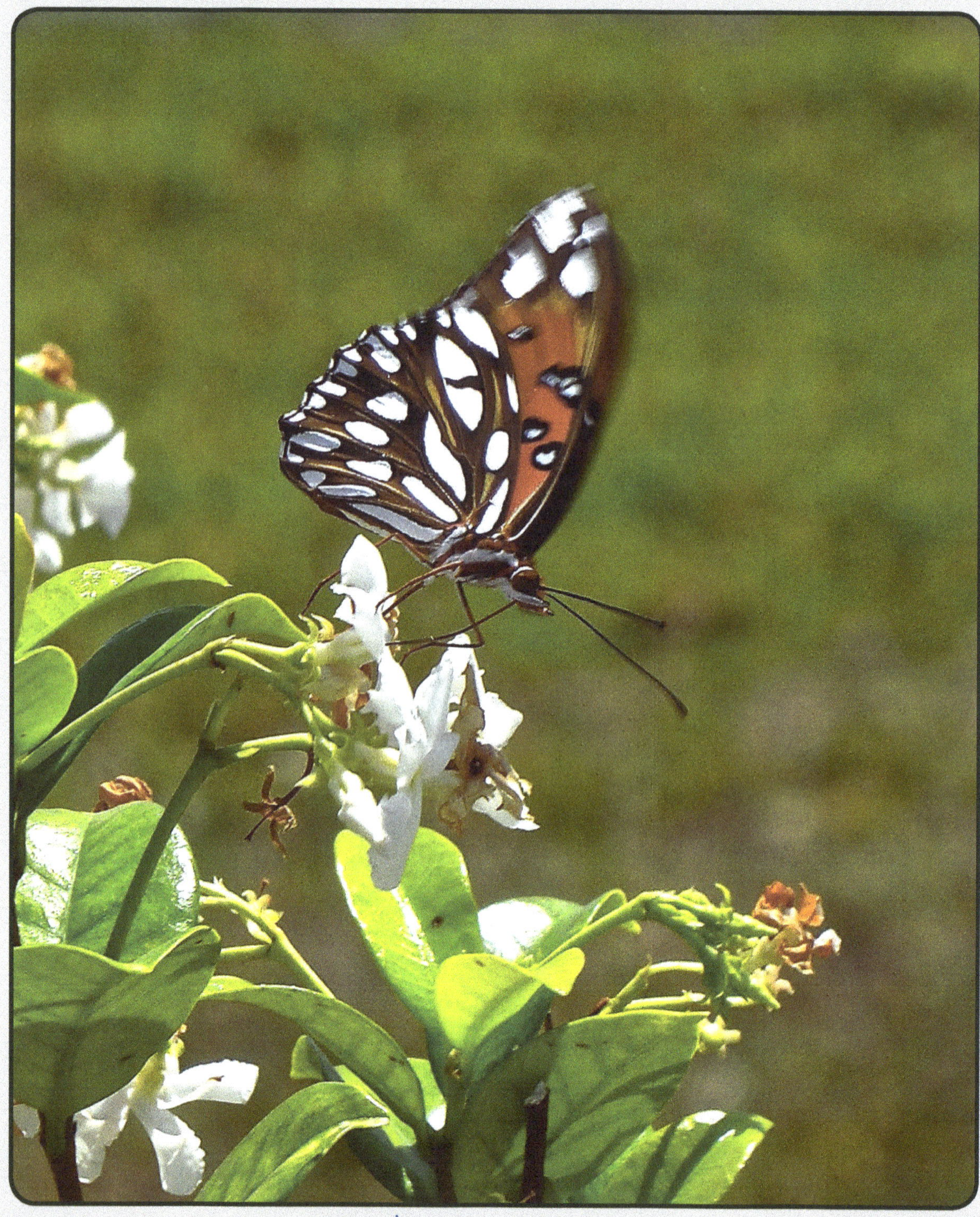

Fluttering landing.

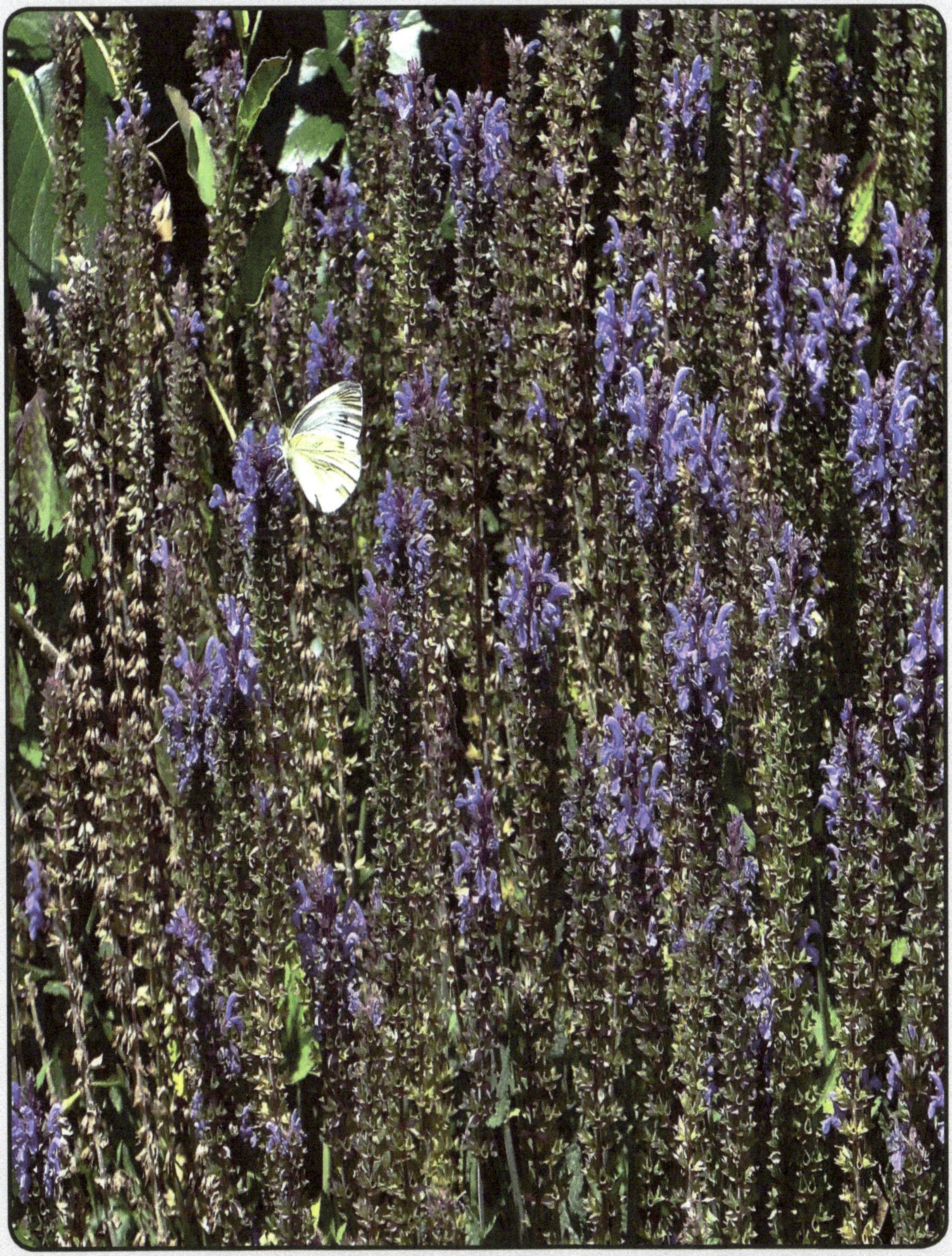

Riding a flower stalk.

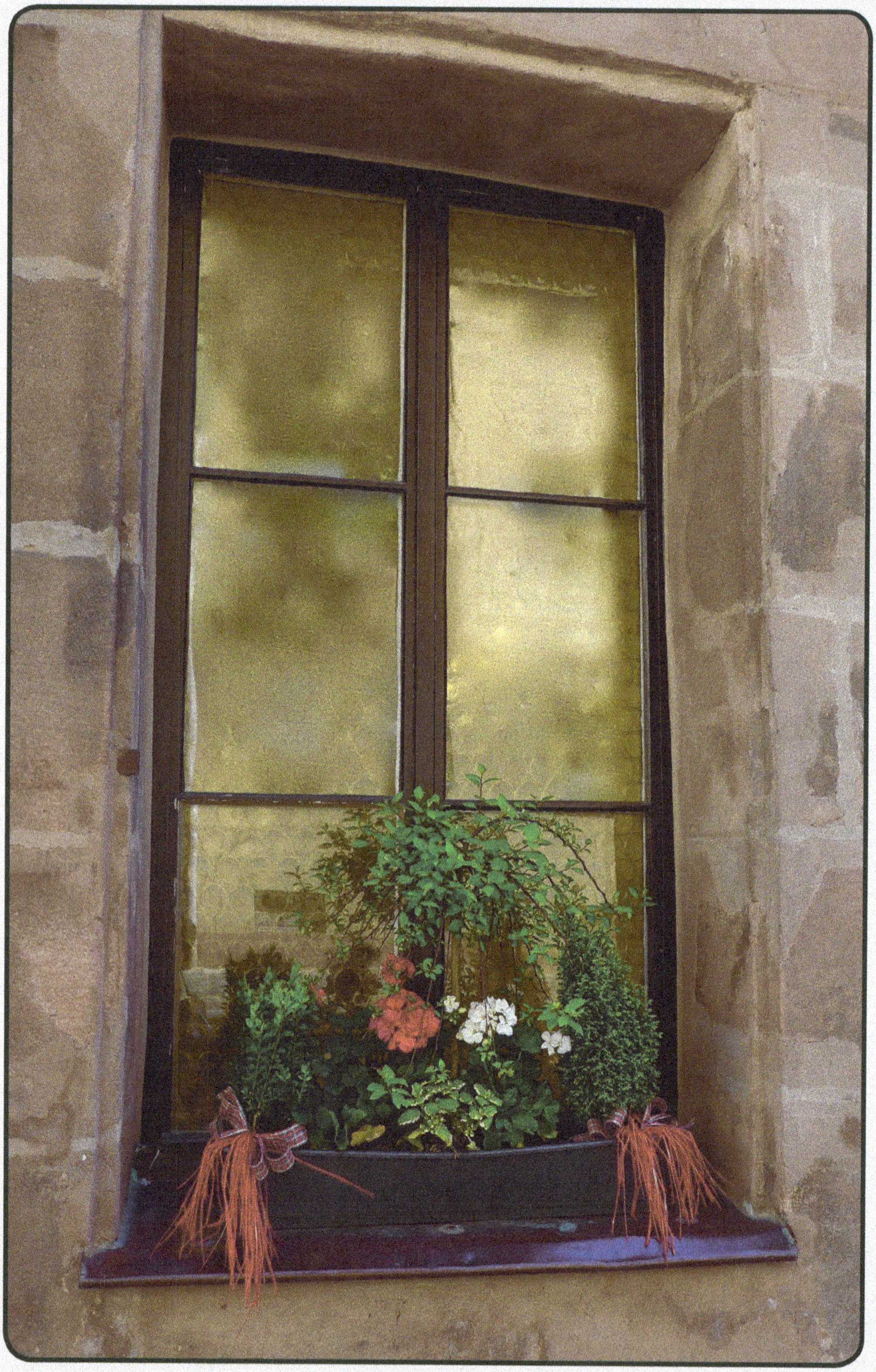

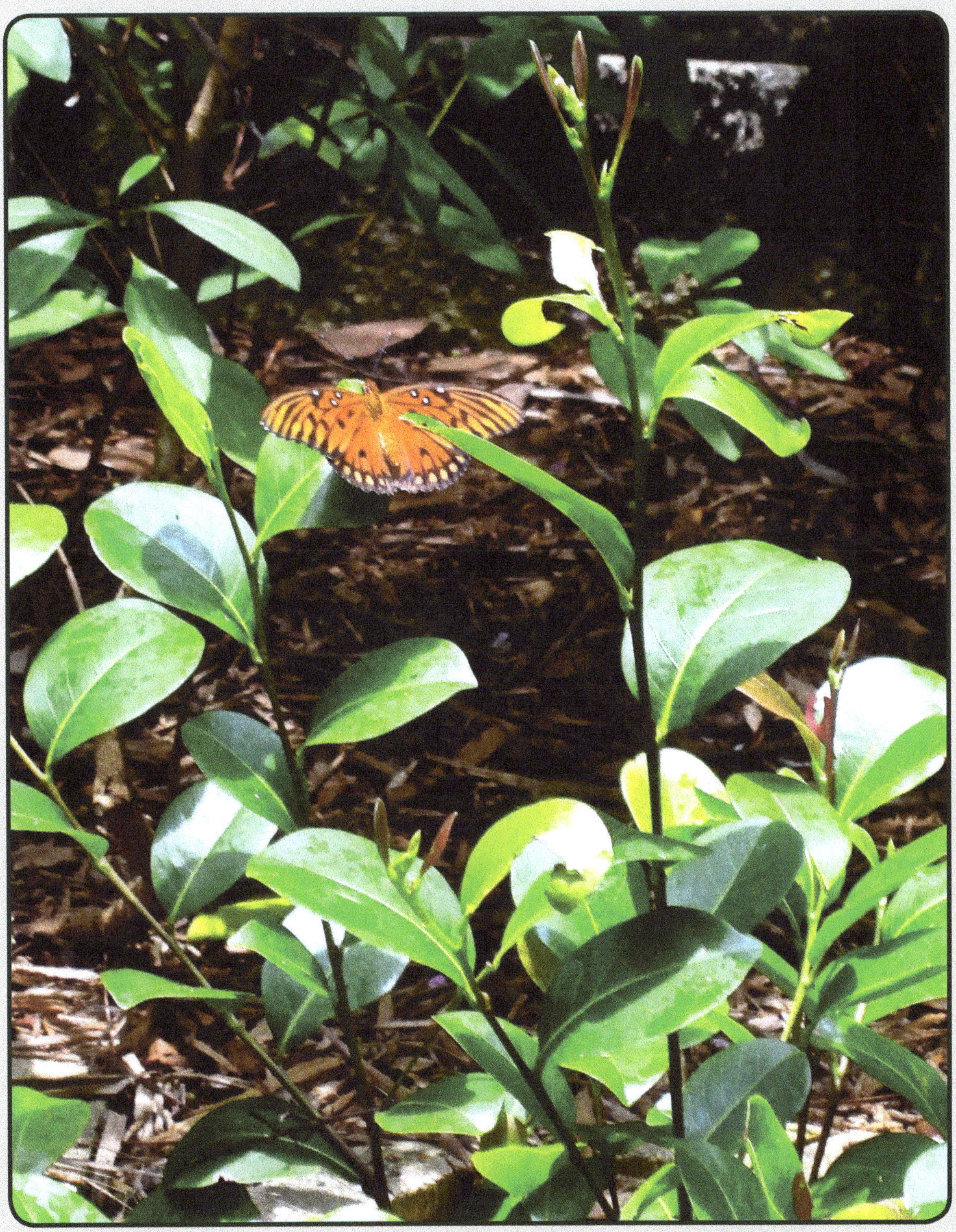

Butterfly perch.

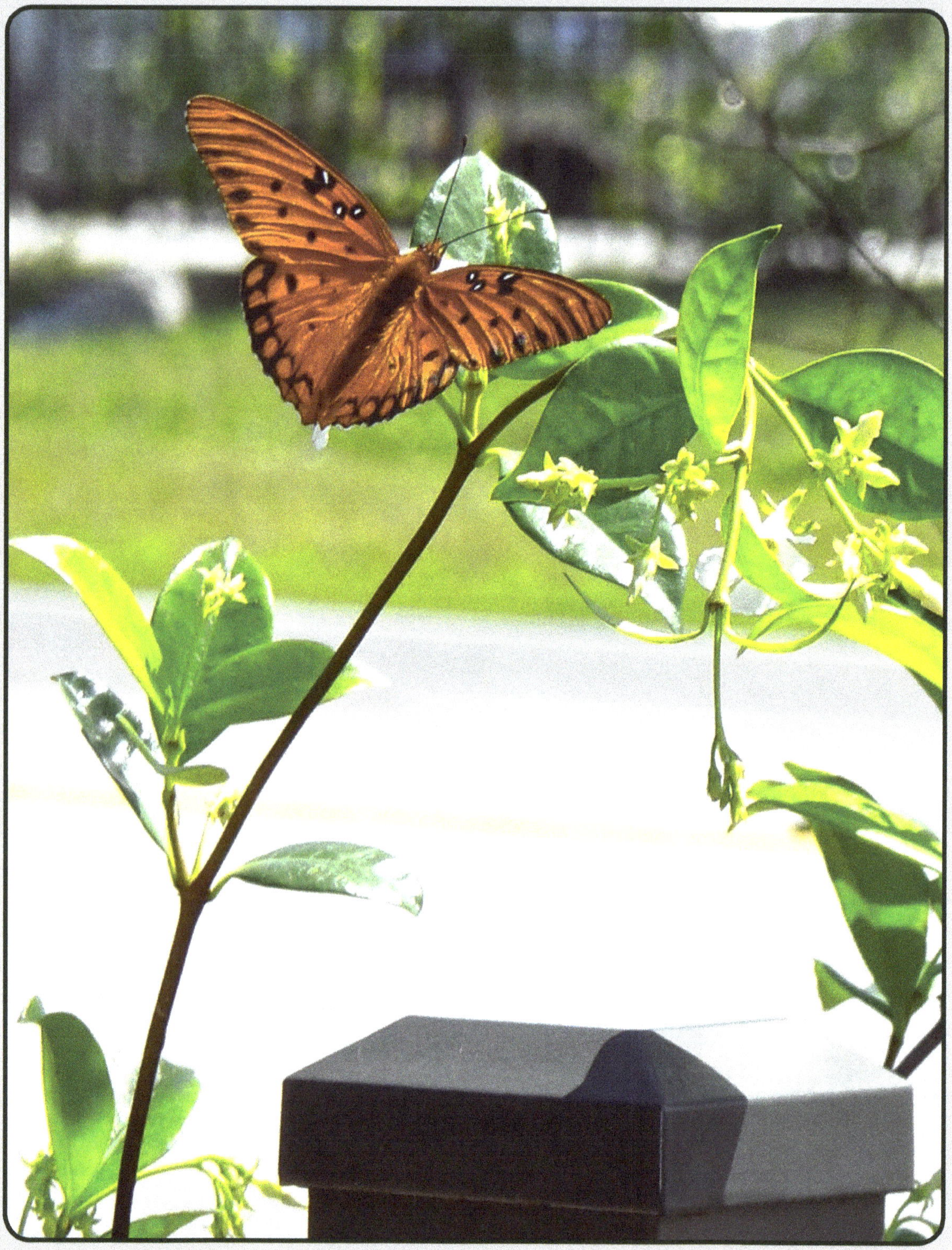

A butterfly and vine.

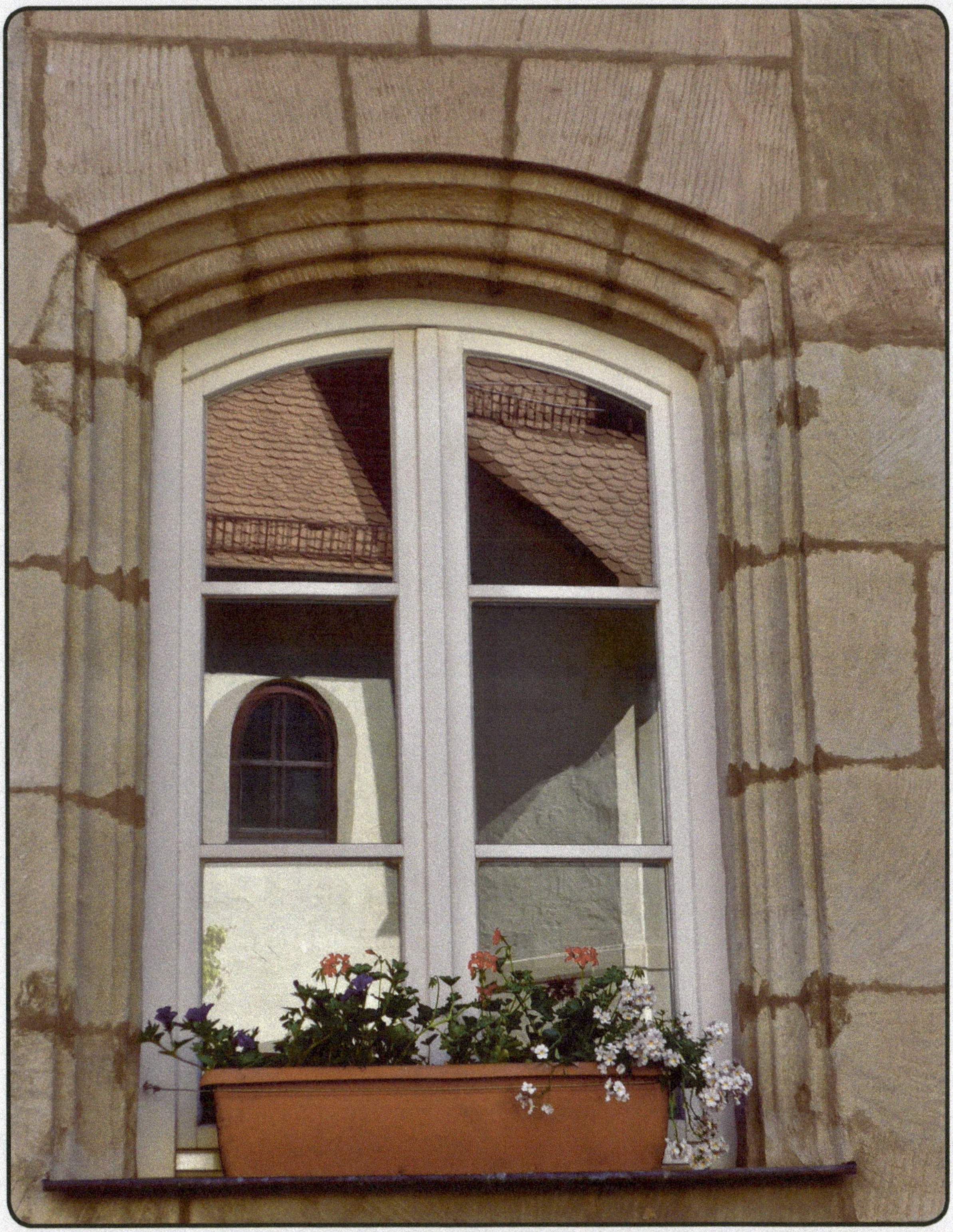

Reflections above a flower box.

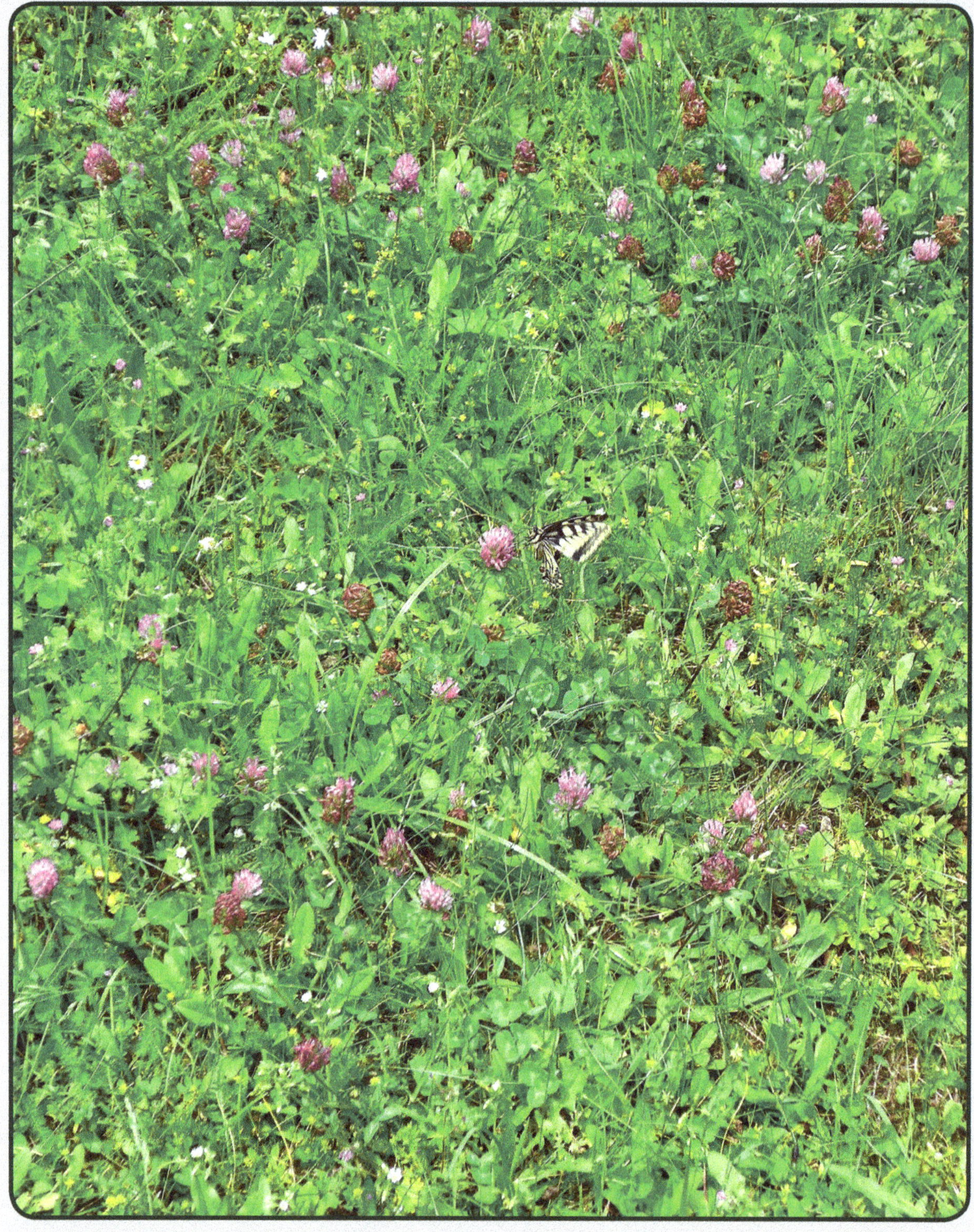

Bavarian butterfly series.

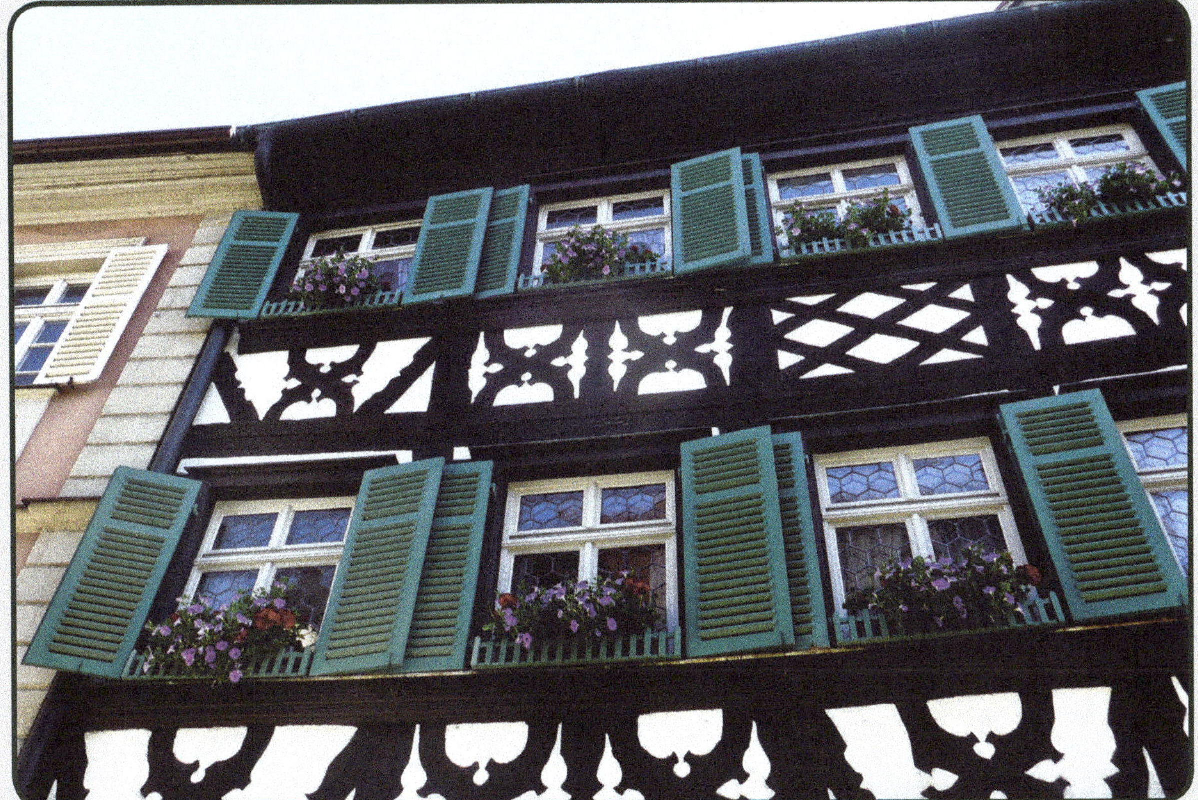

Floral life in old building in Franconia.

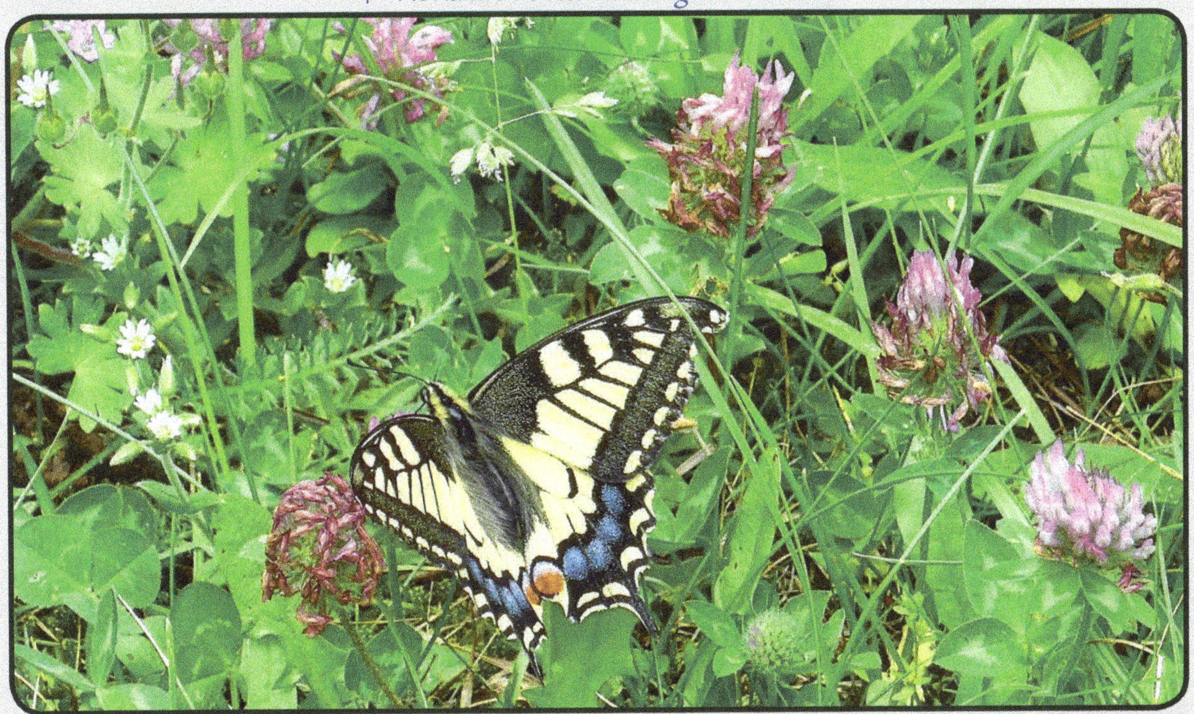

Painted wings.

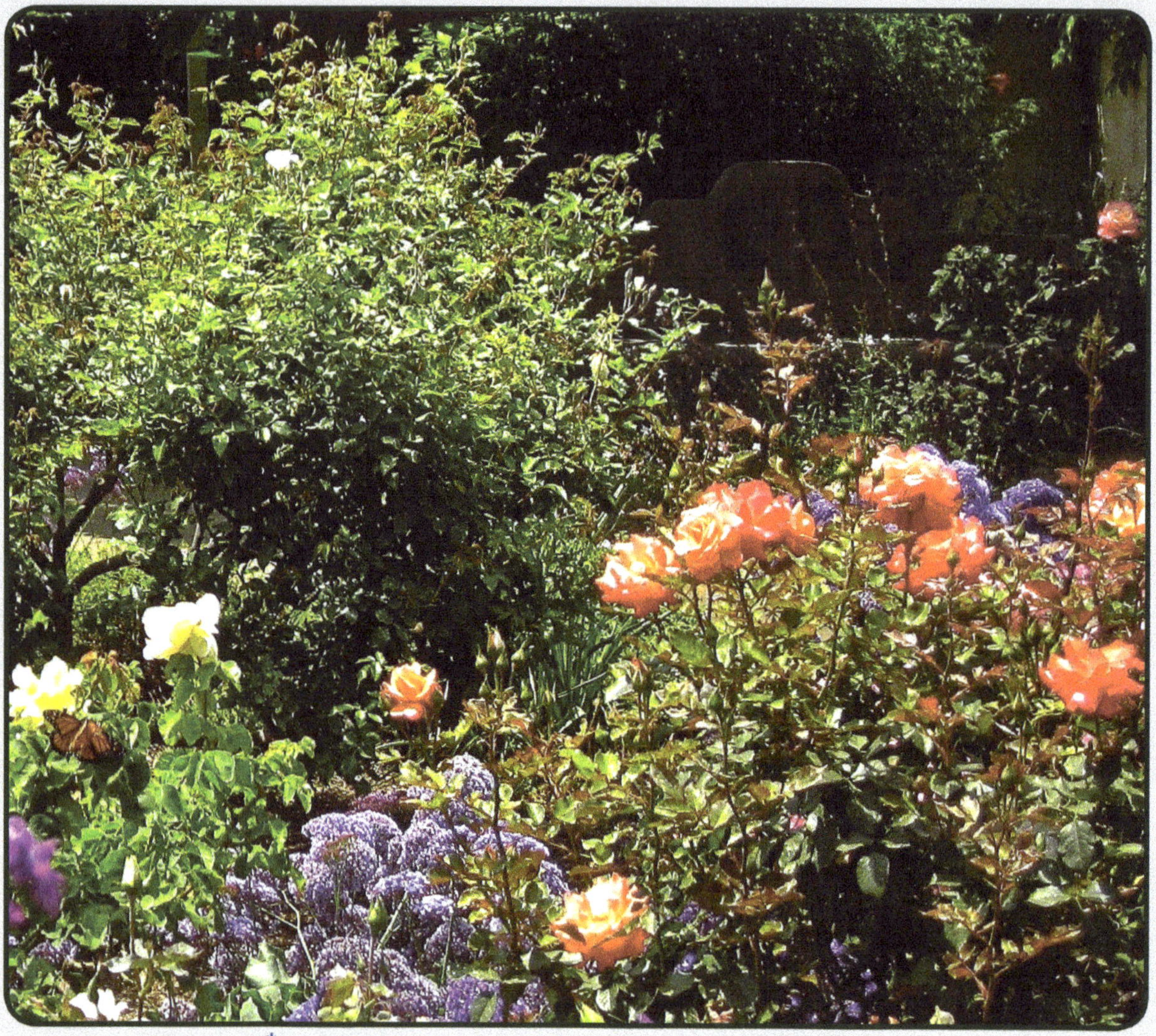

Hidden butterfly in the San Diego de Alcalá Mission.

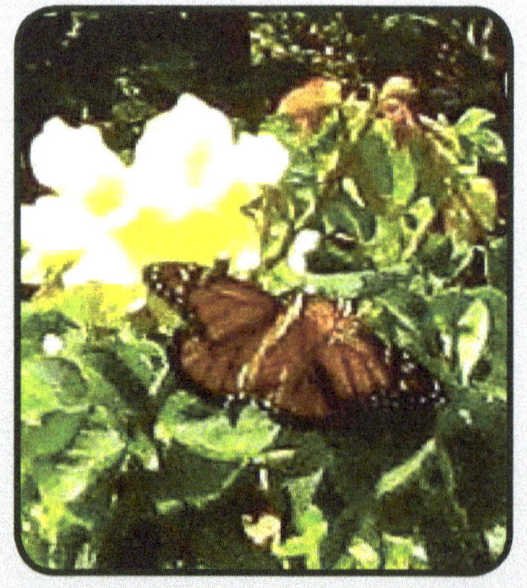

Built in 1769 by the Spanish explorers, this was the first Franciscan mission in California and an important settlement that helped launch other Spanish communities along the Pacific coastline and in central California.

Closeup of the butterfly.

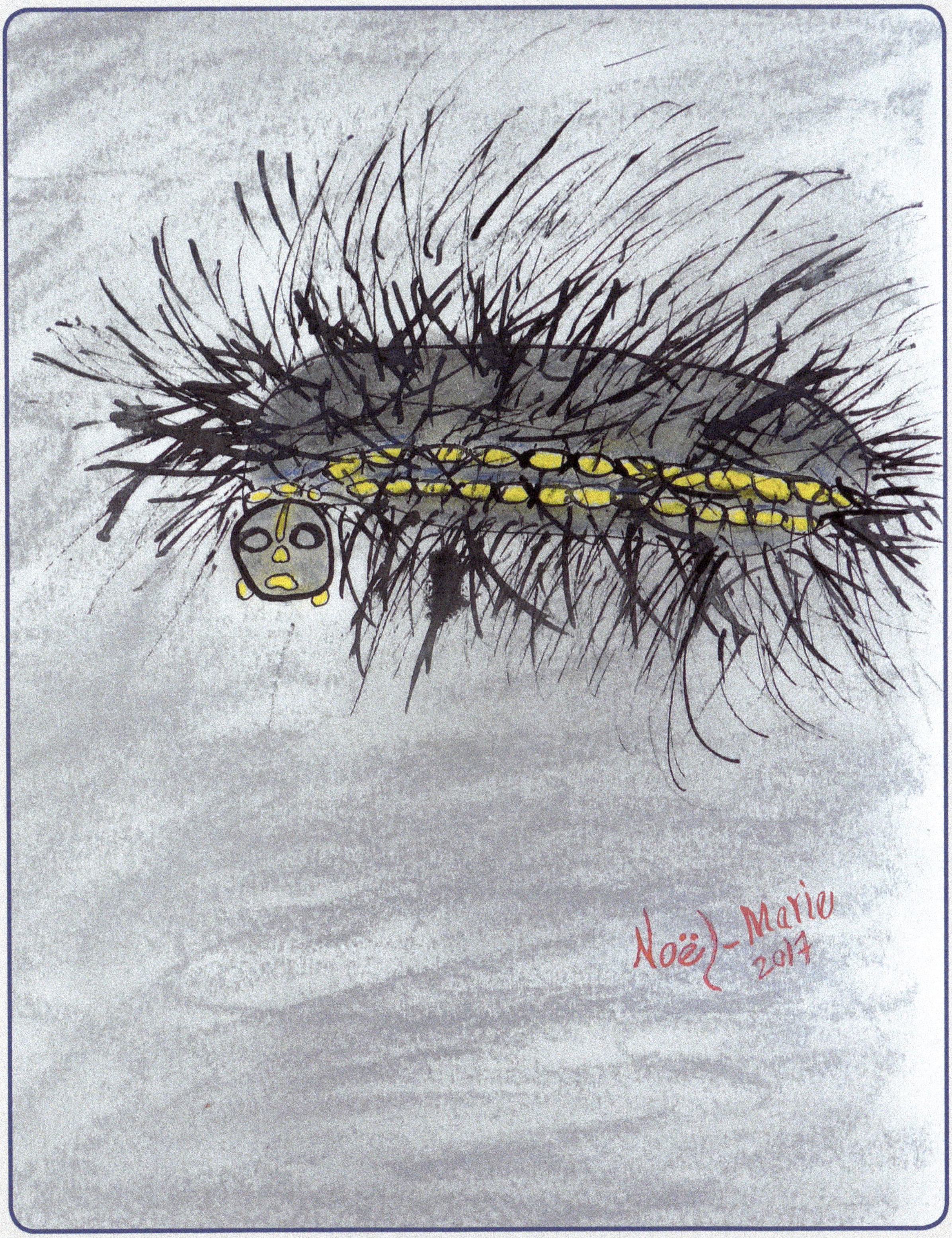

New Mexican salt marsh caterpillar.

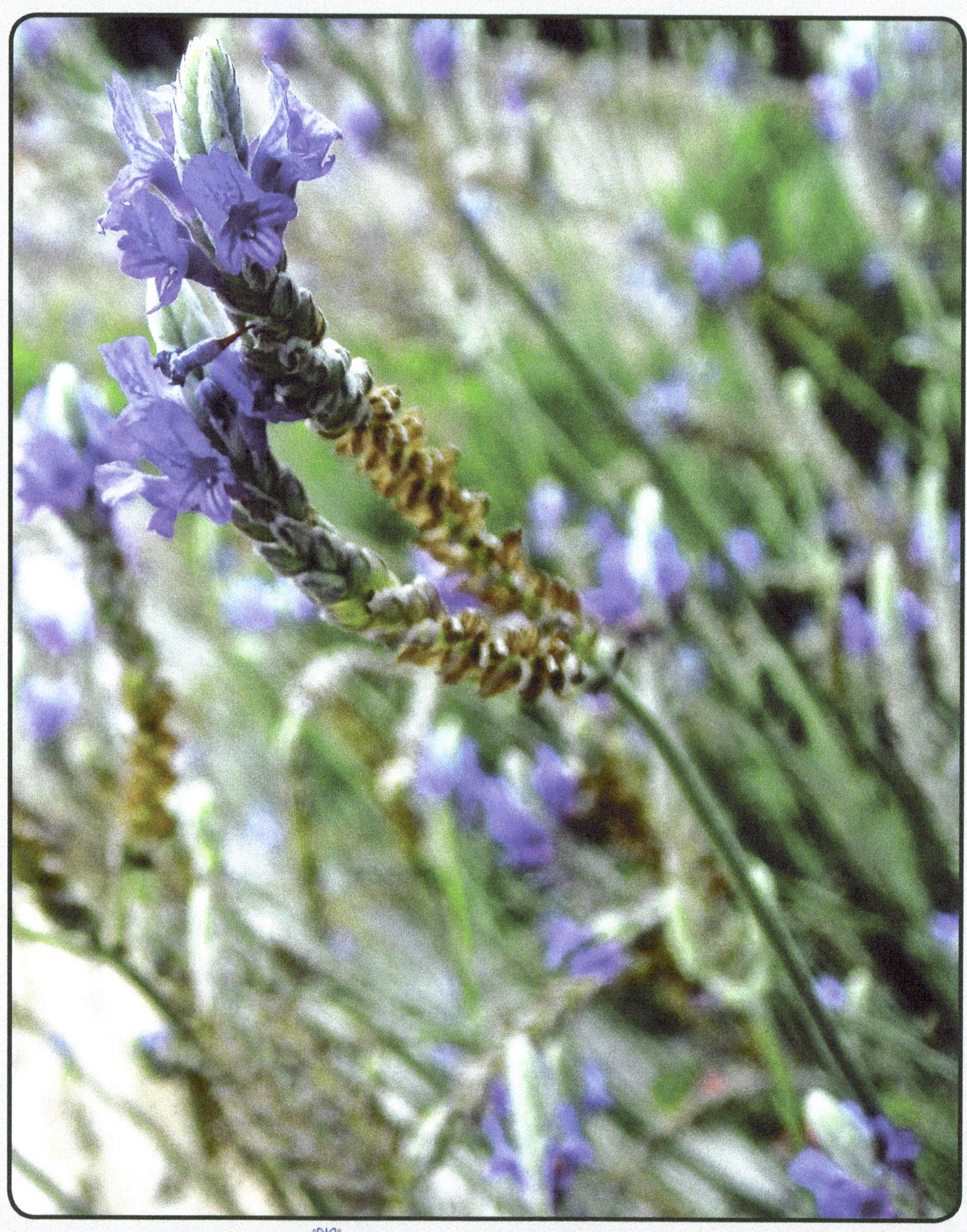

Stem crowned with azure bells.

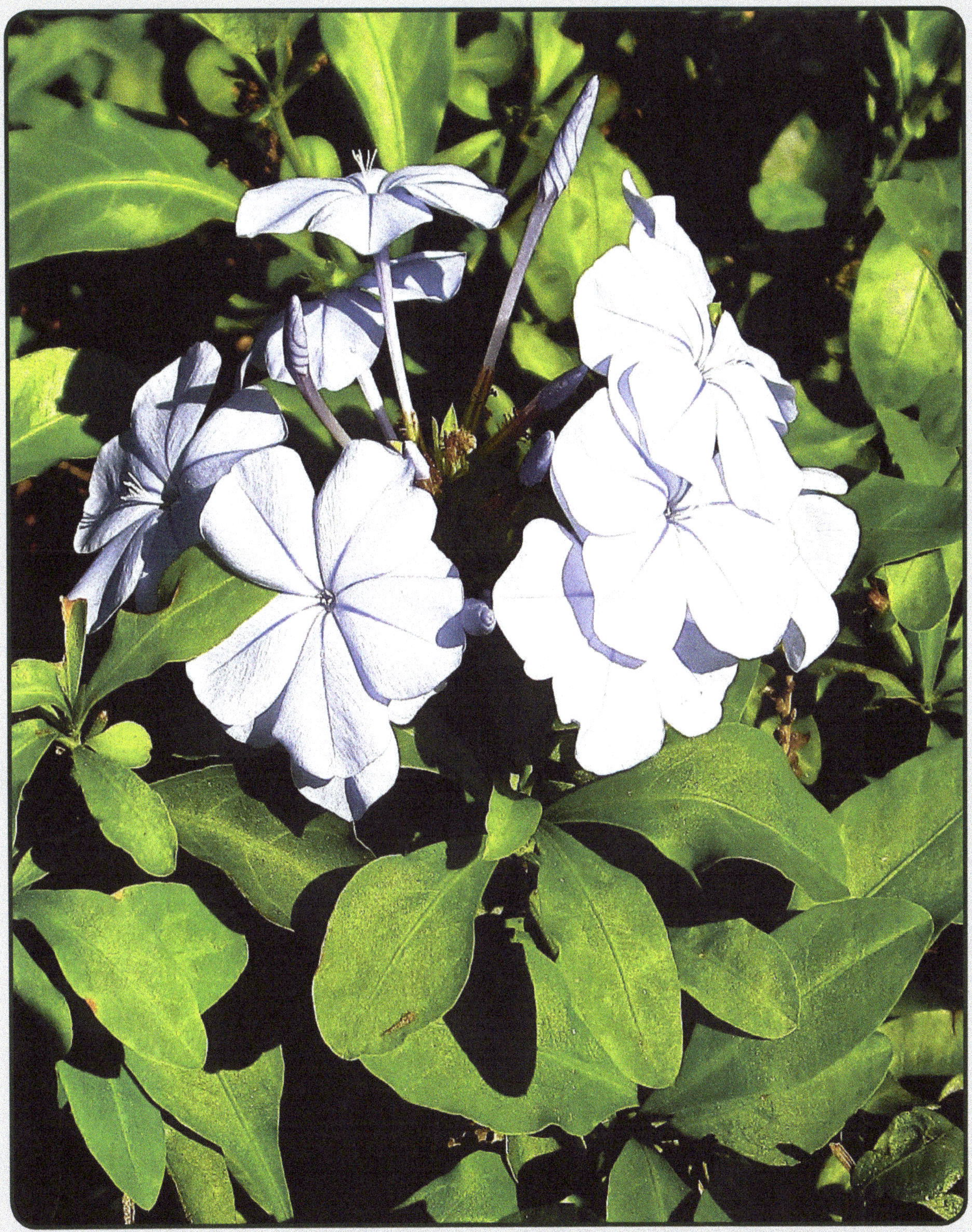

Ready to unfurl blossom.

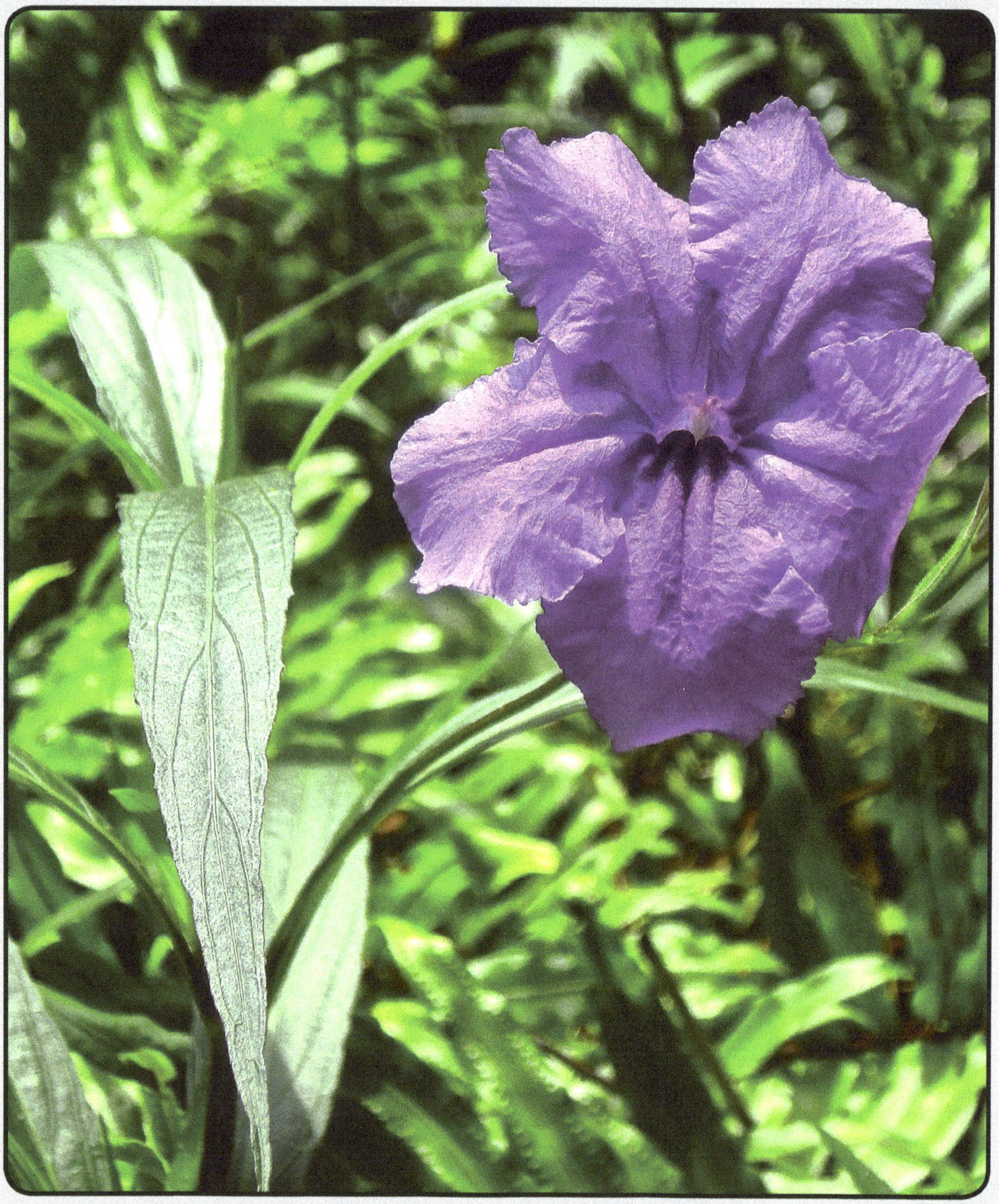

Japanese washi rice-paper petal.

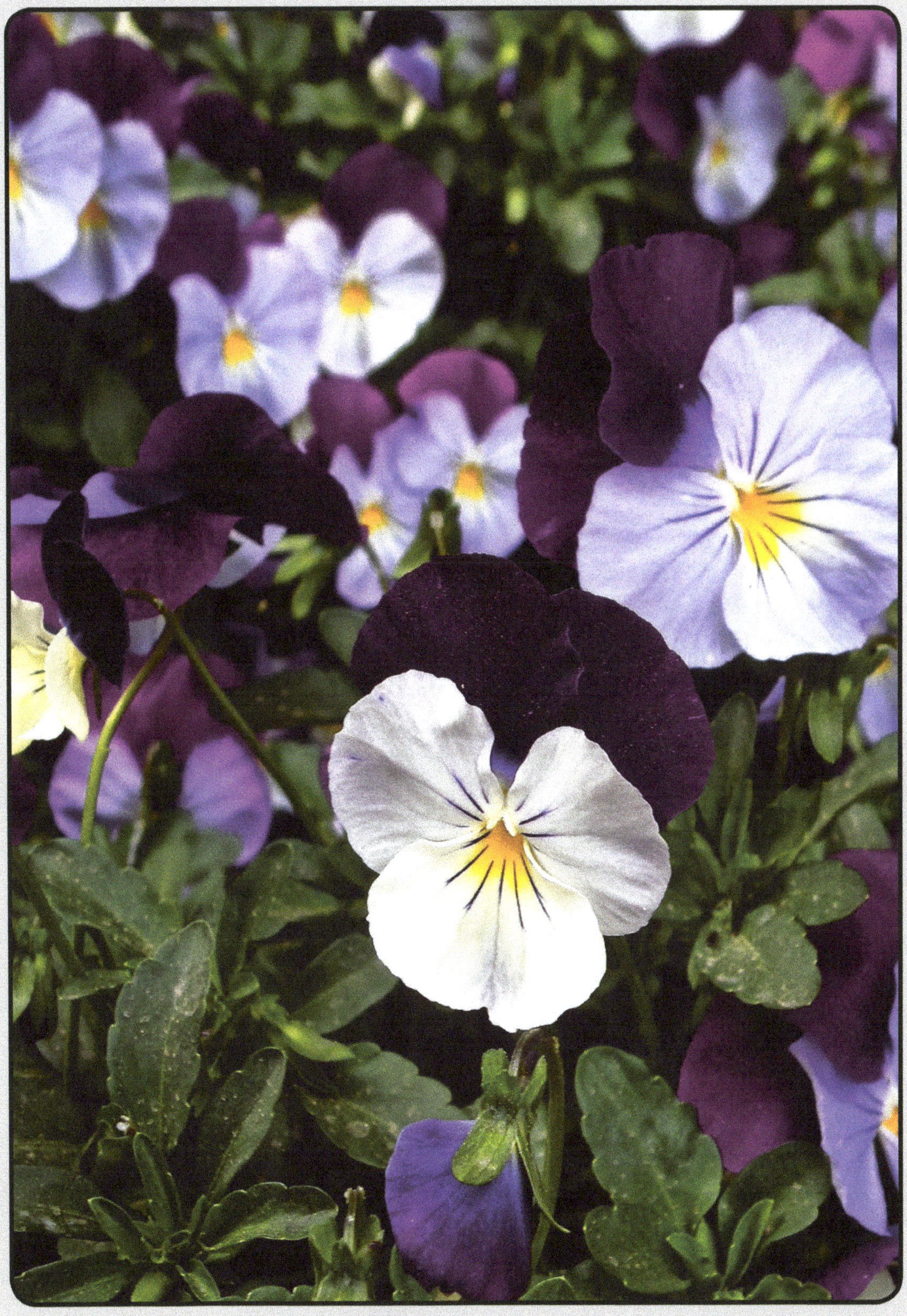

Pansy faces.

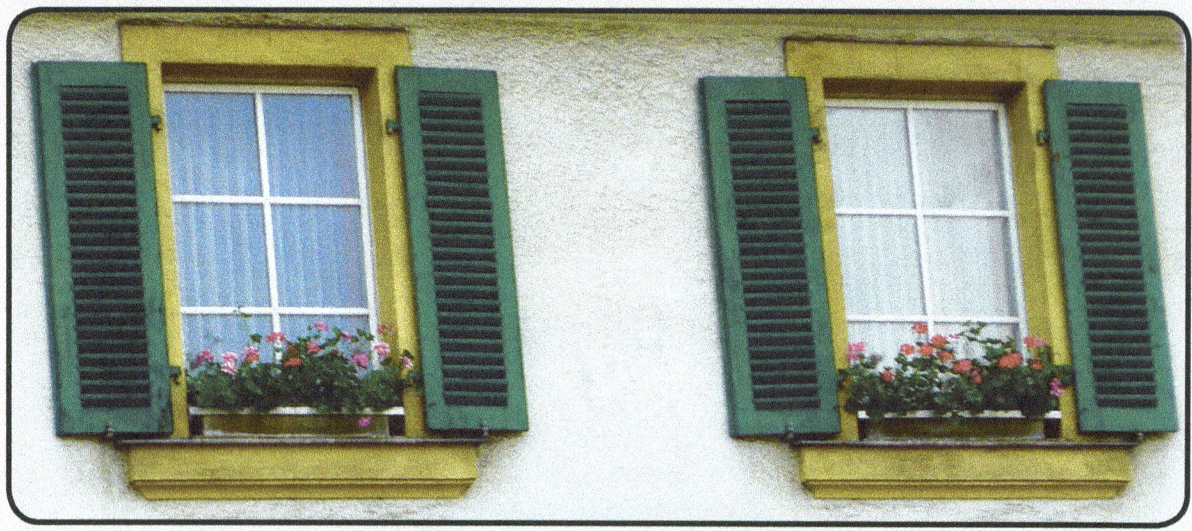

*Greeting the morning.*

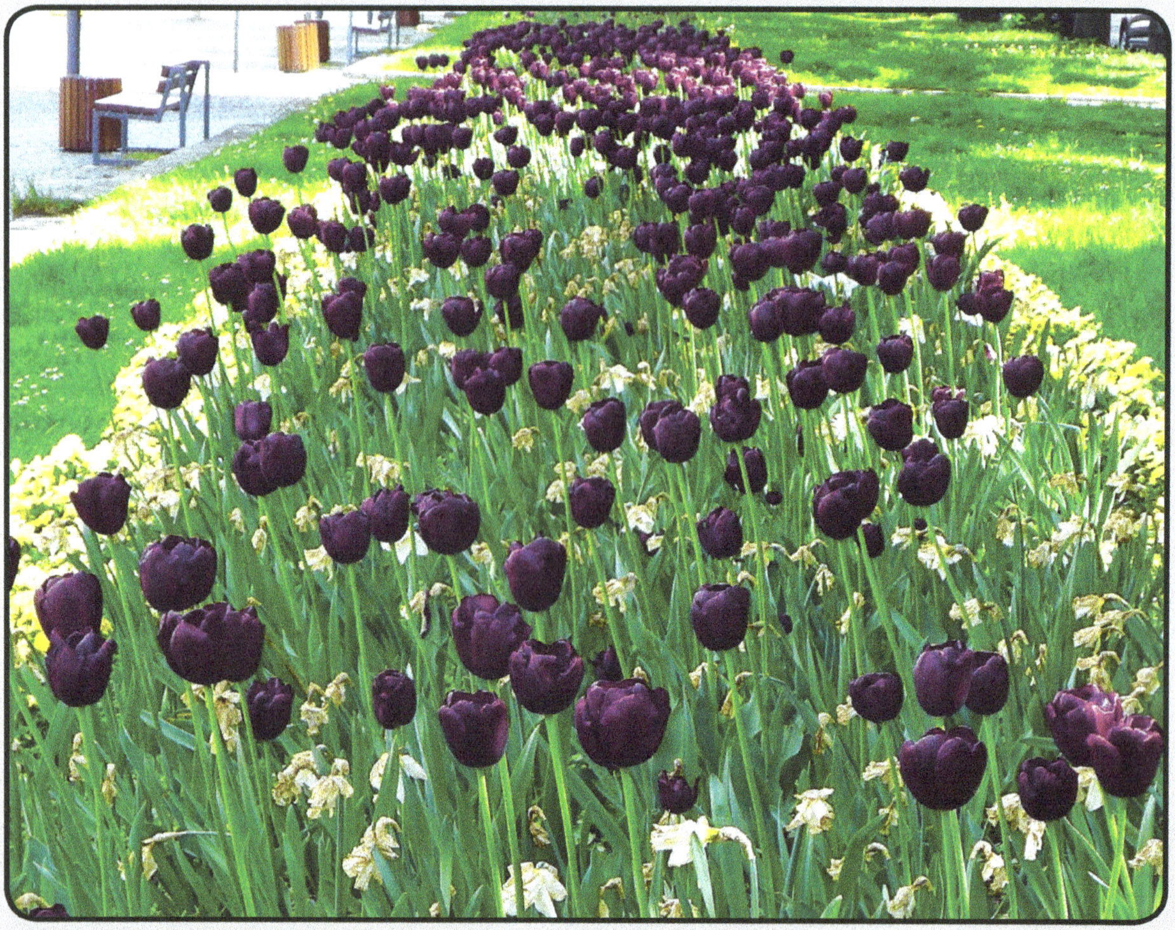

*Purple promenade.*

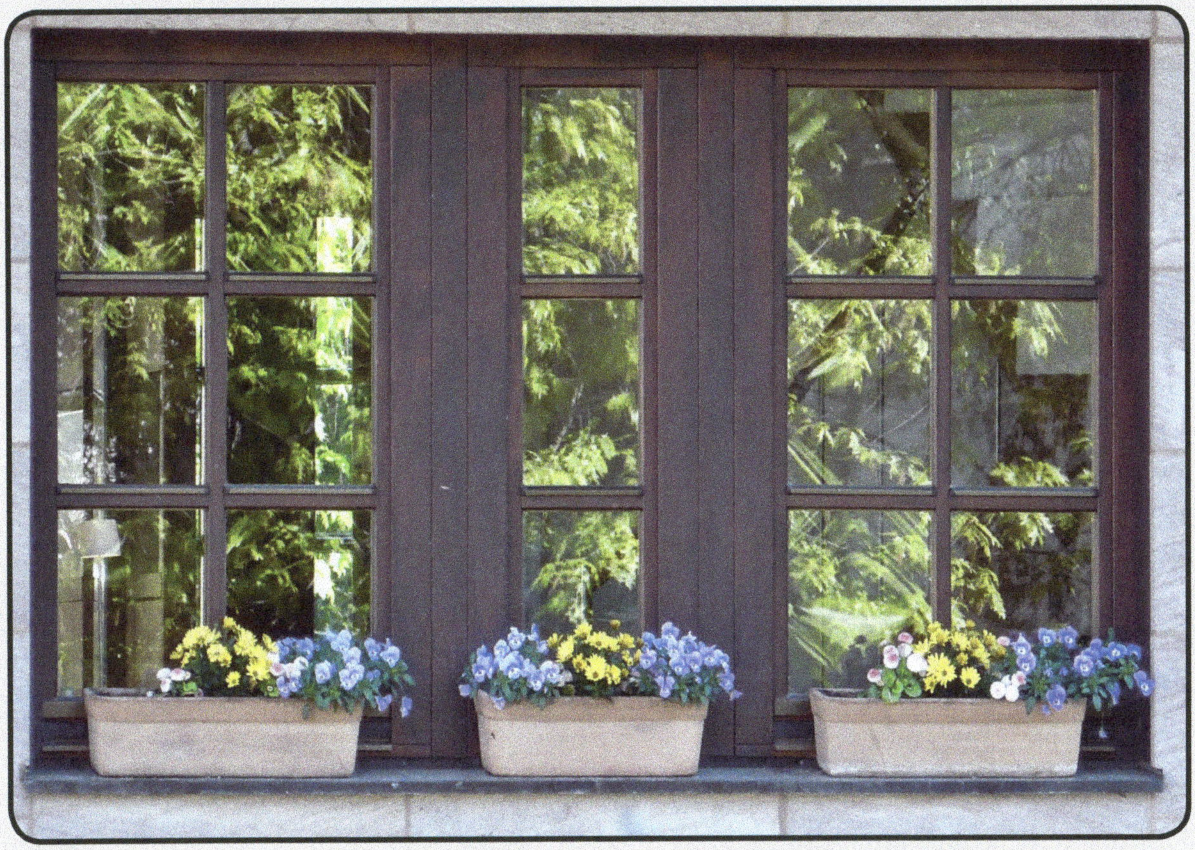

Festive window.

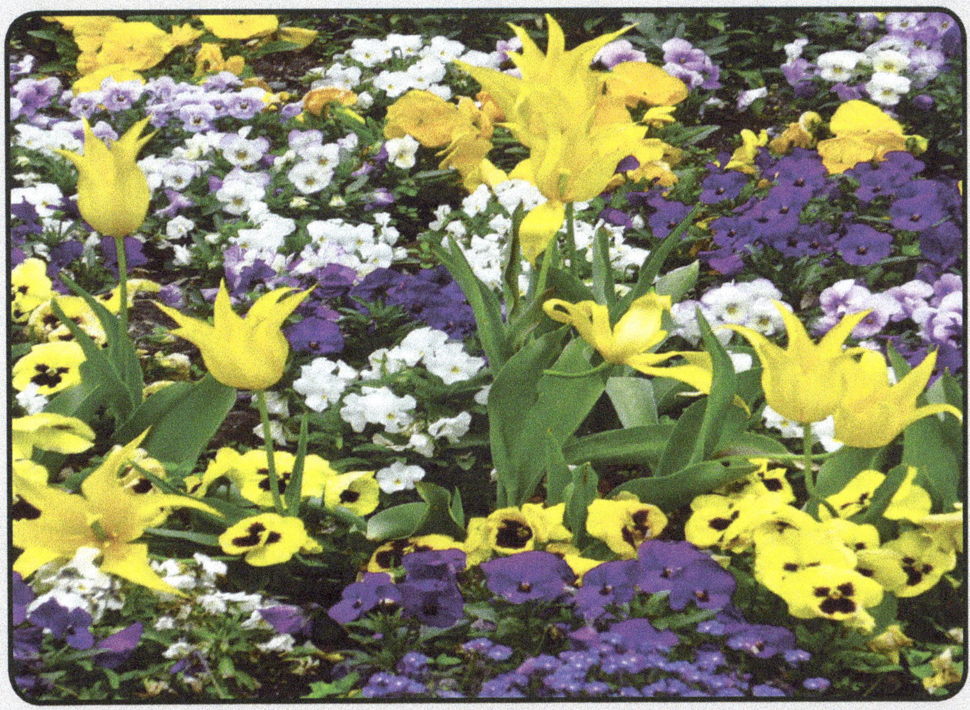

Splendor.

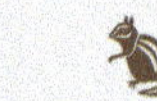

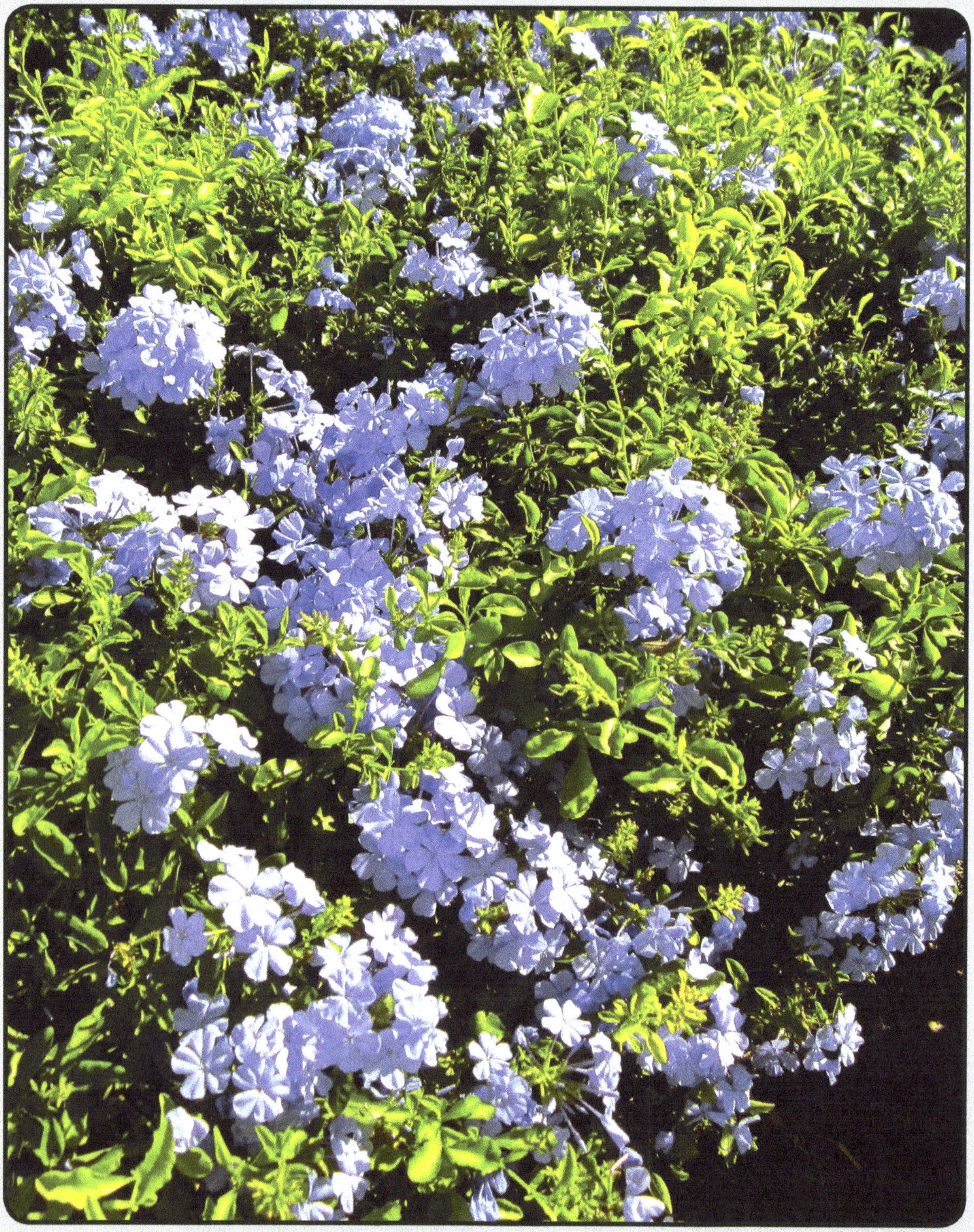

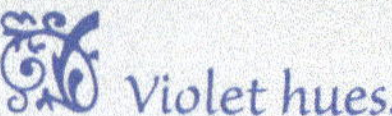

Violet hues.

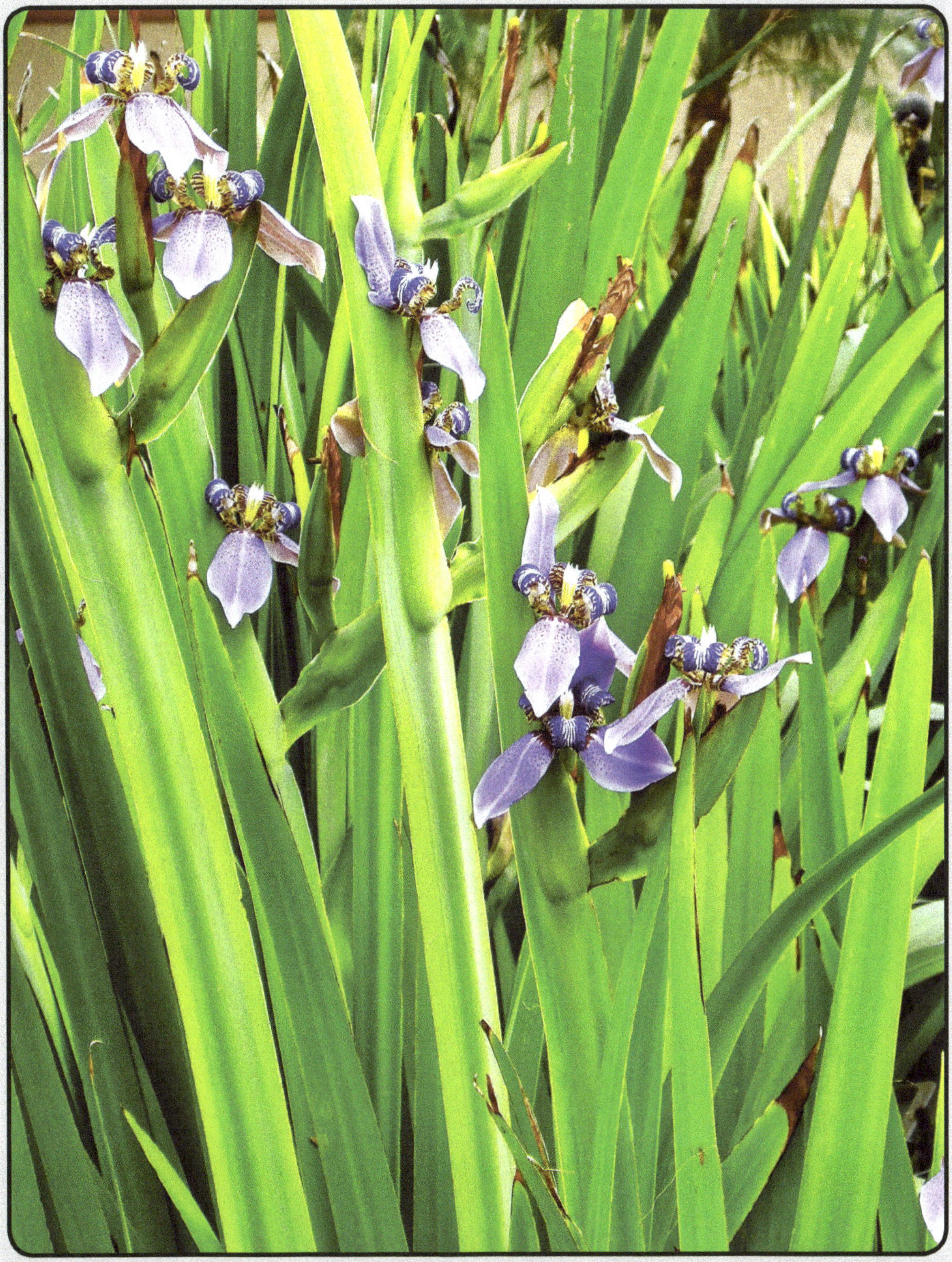

Iris crowns.

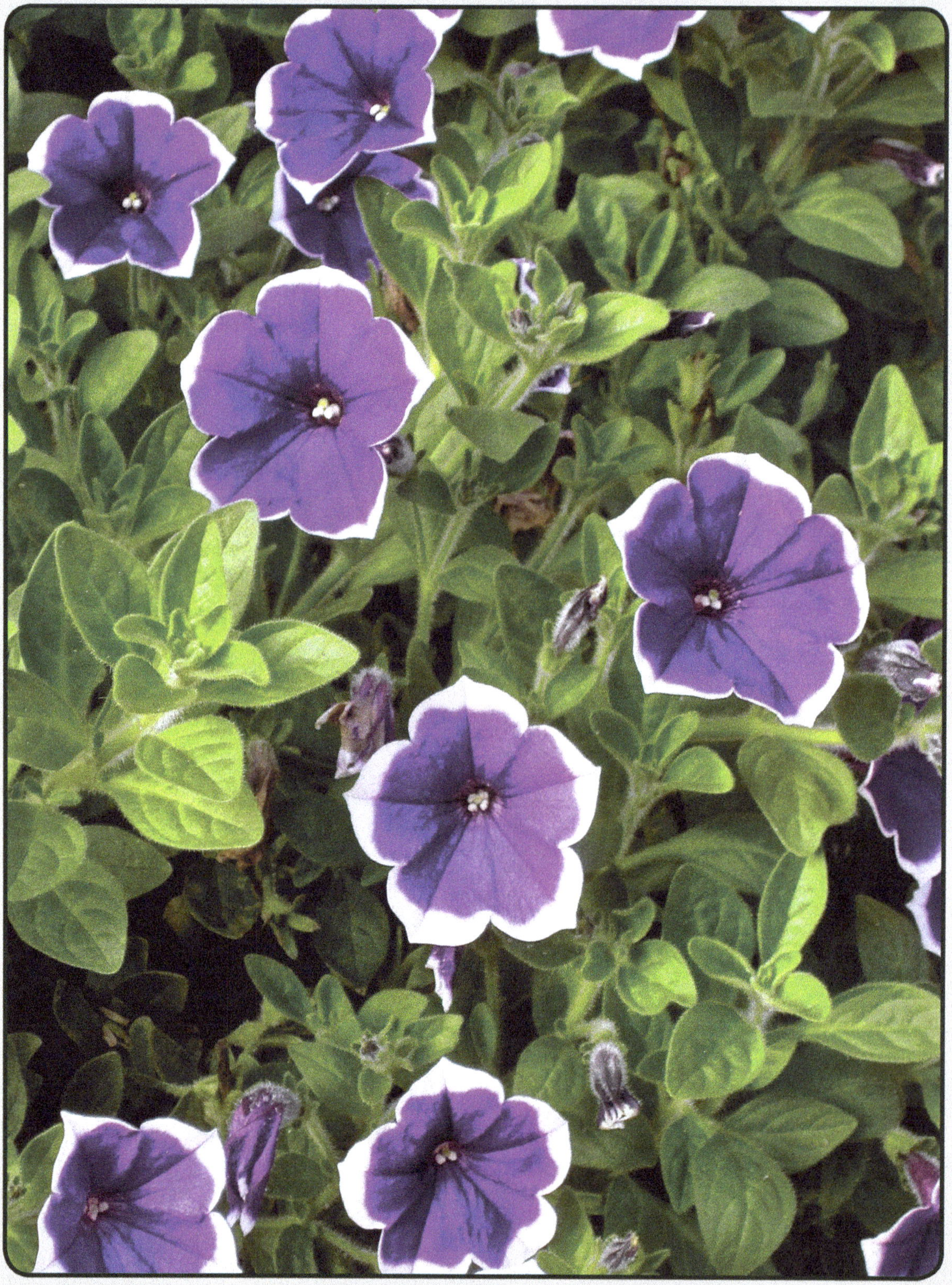

Parasols.

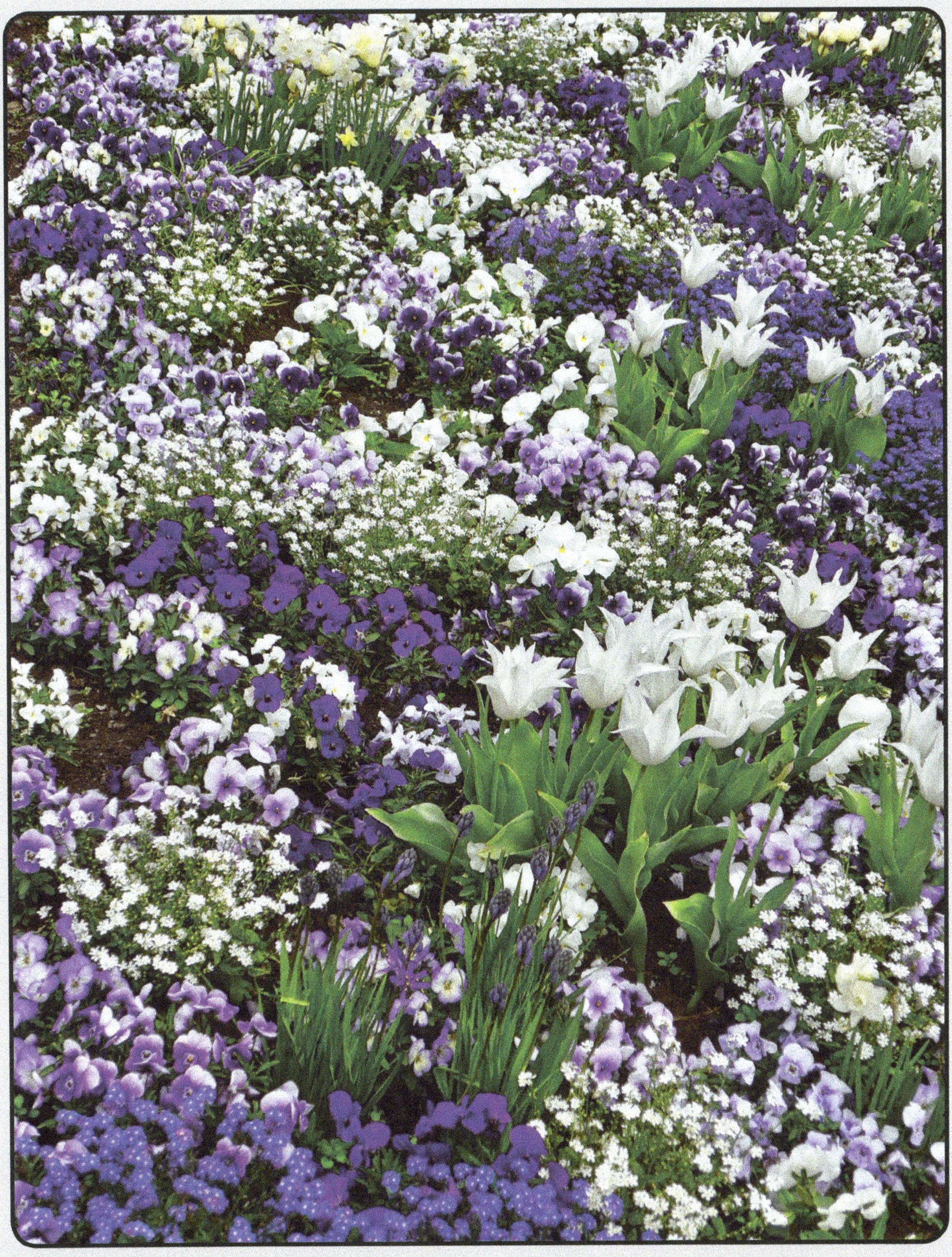

✳ Village of the whites, blues and purples.

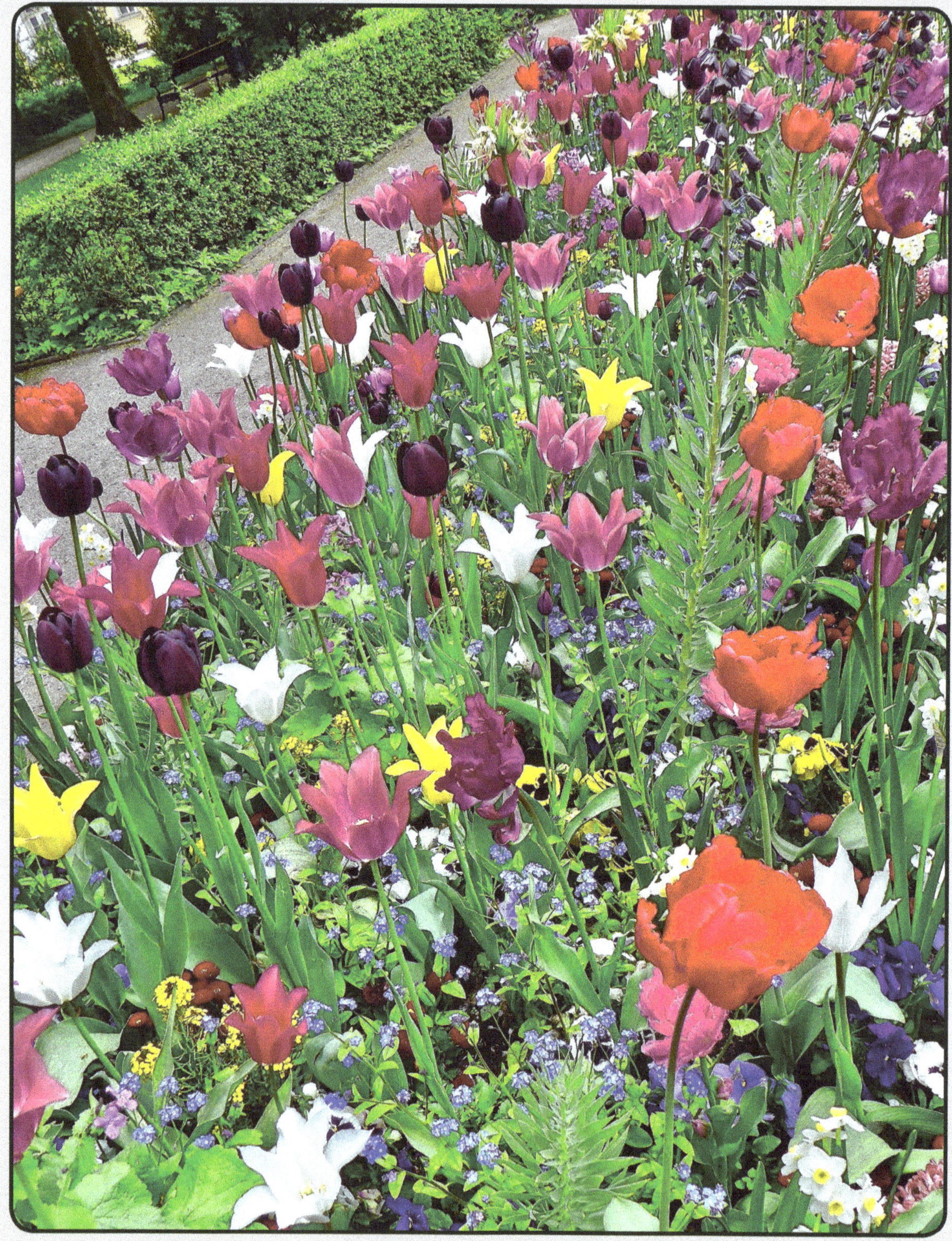

Reaching for the sky.

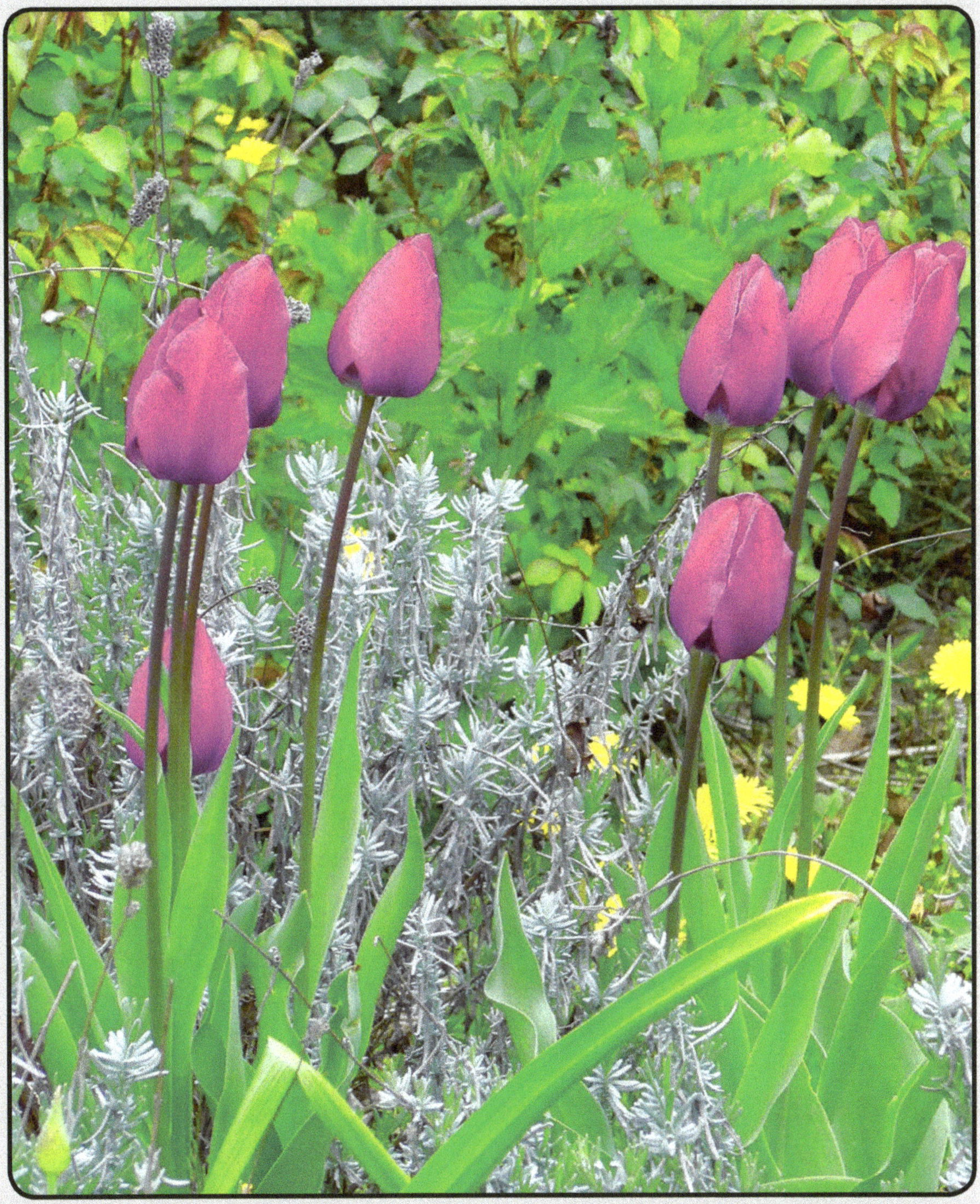

Graceful.

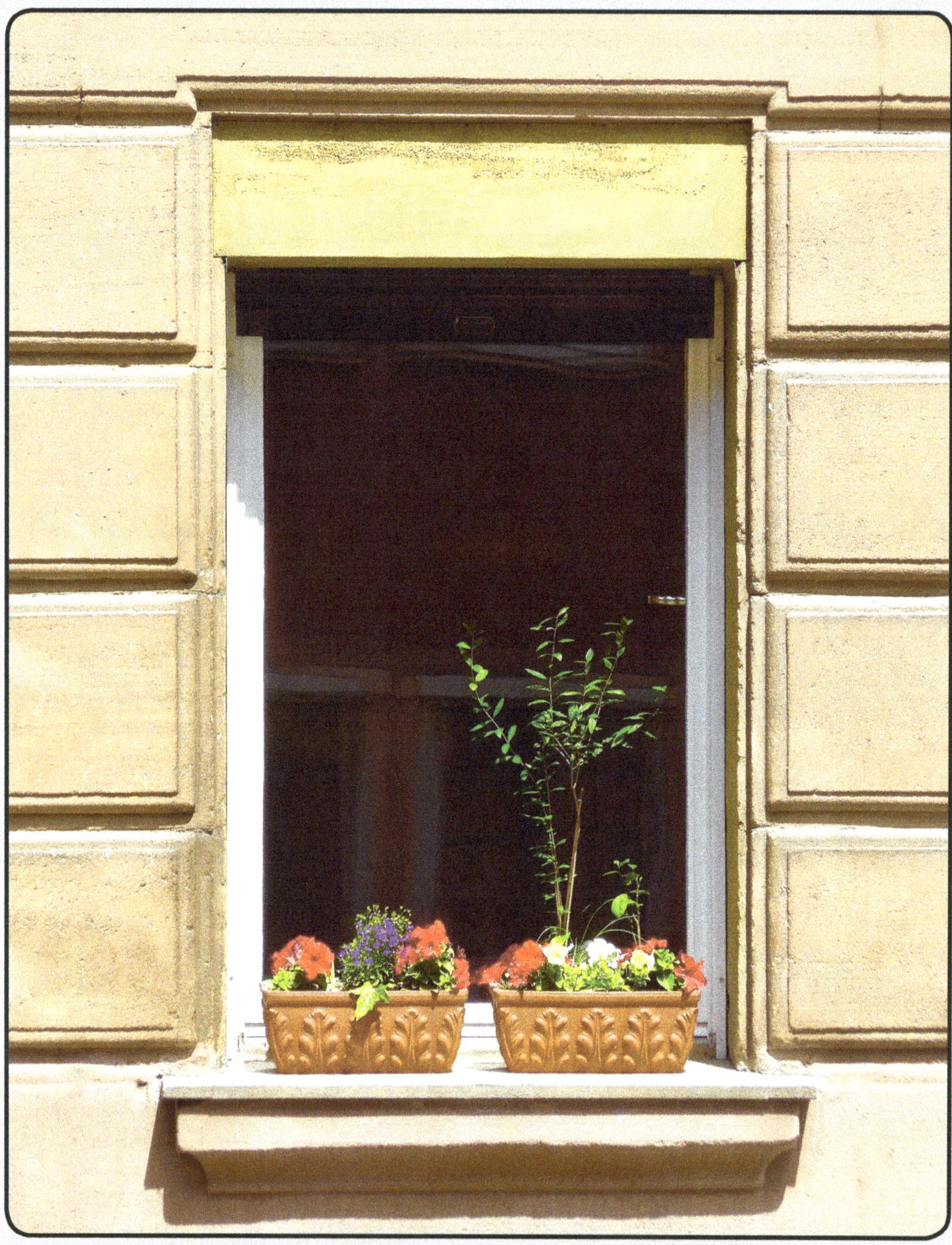

Color splash.

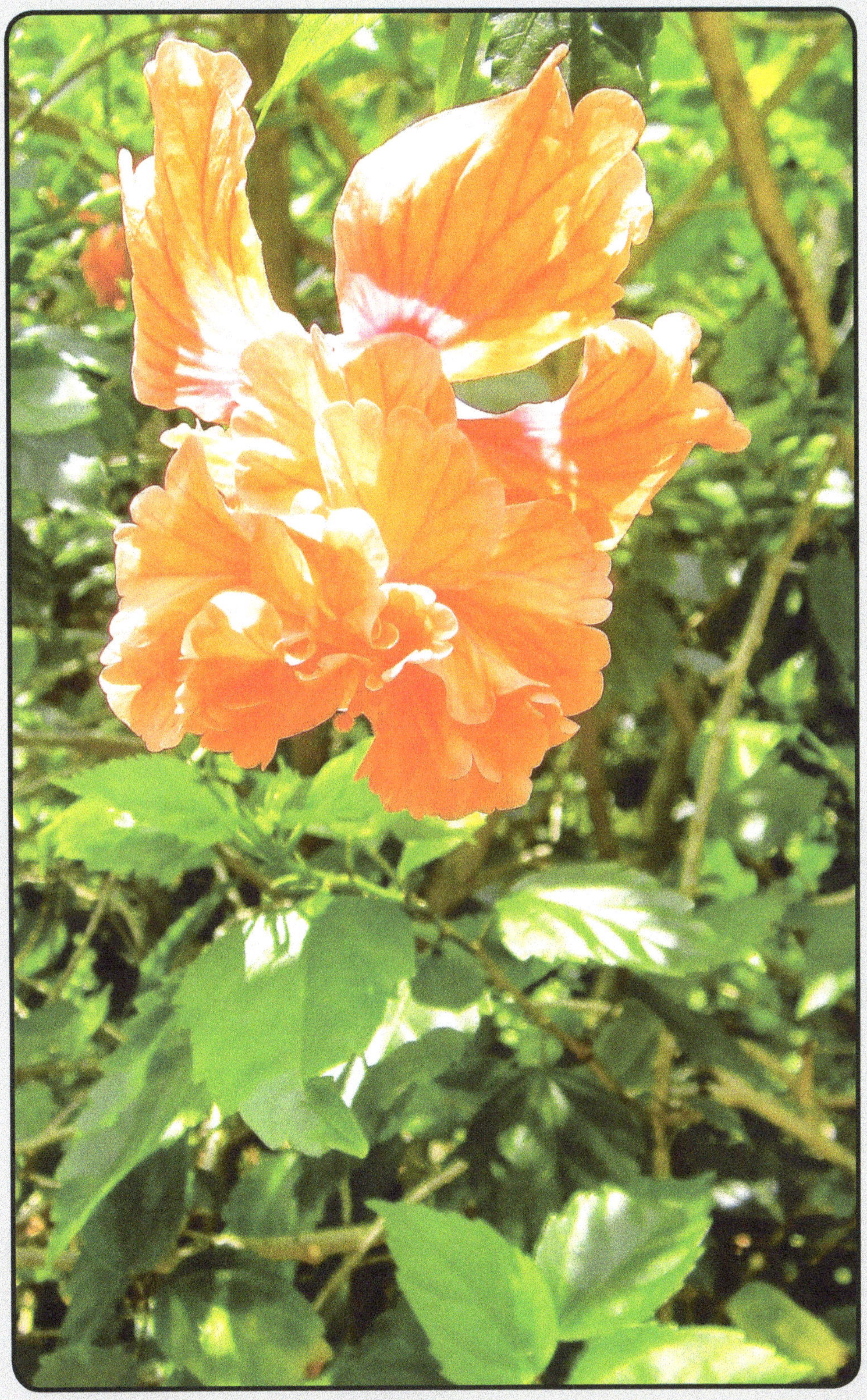

Heaven sent.

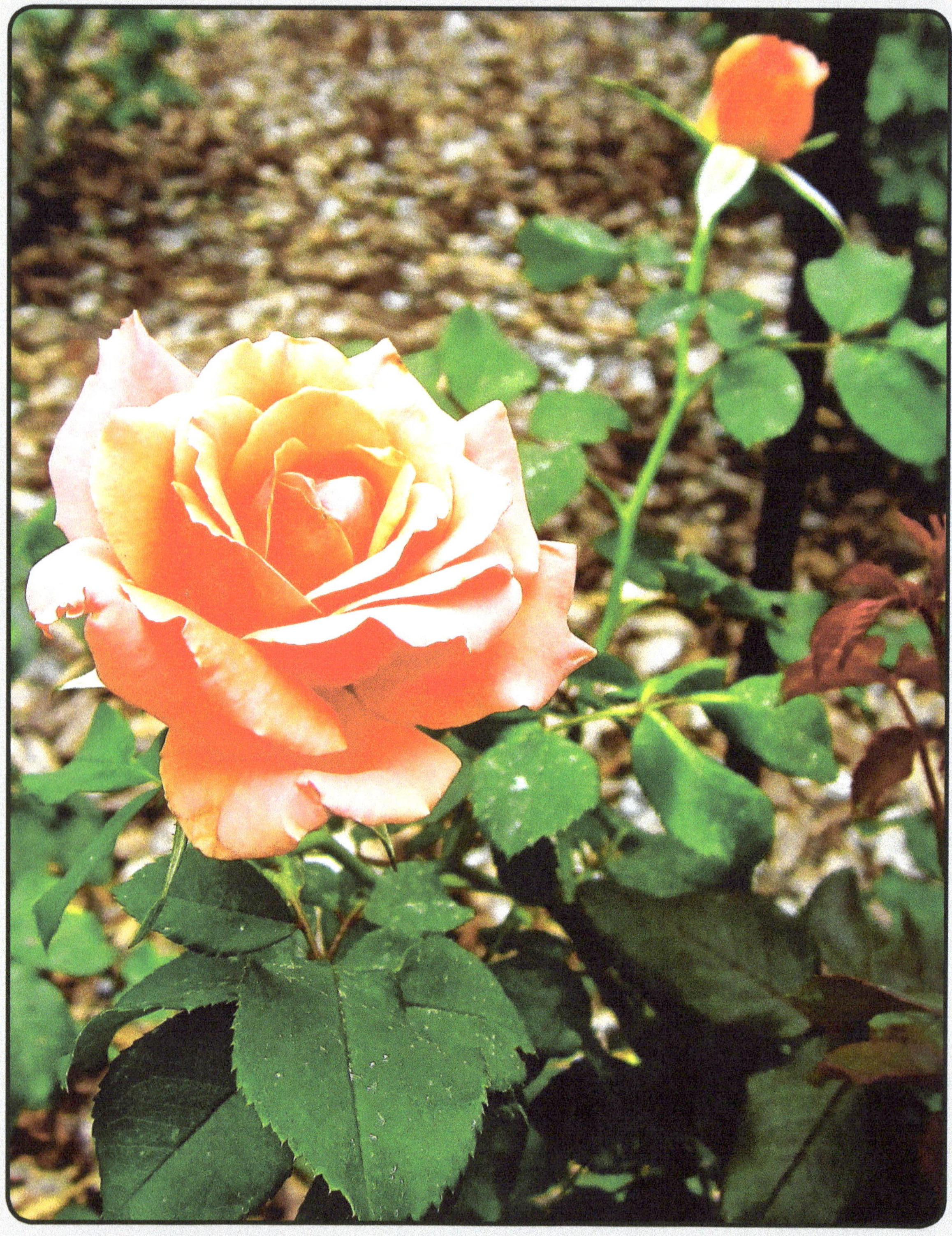

Coral delicacy.

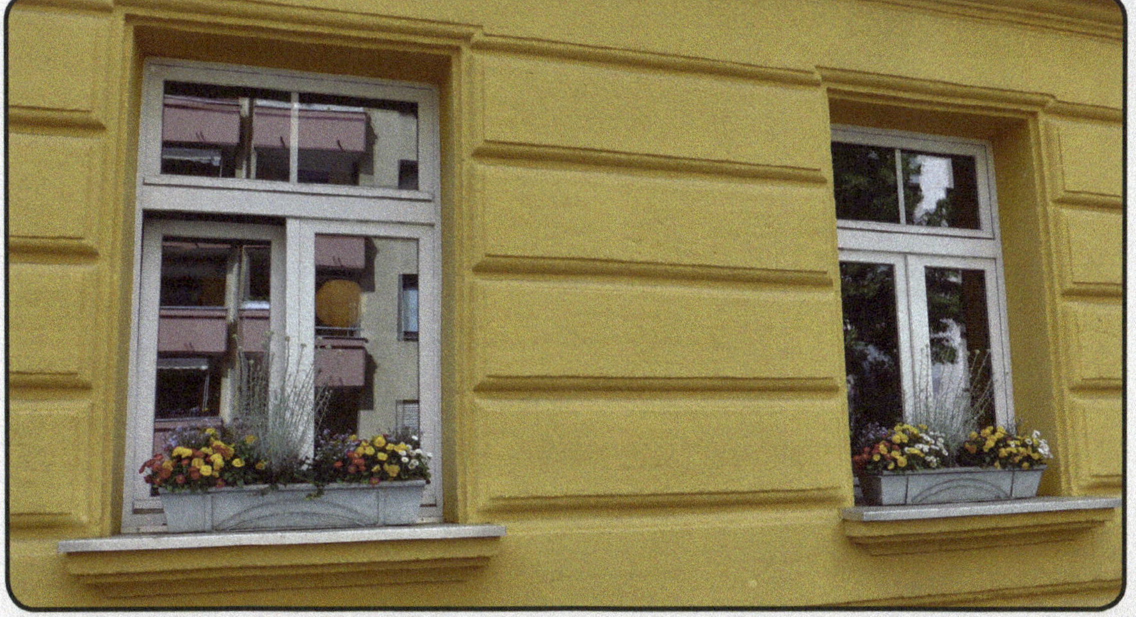

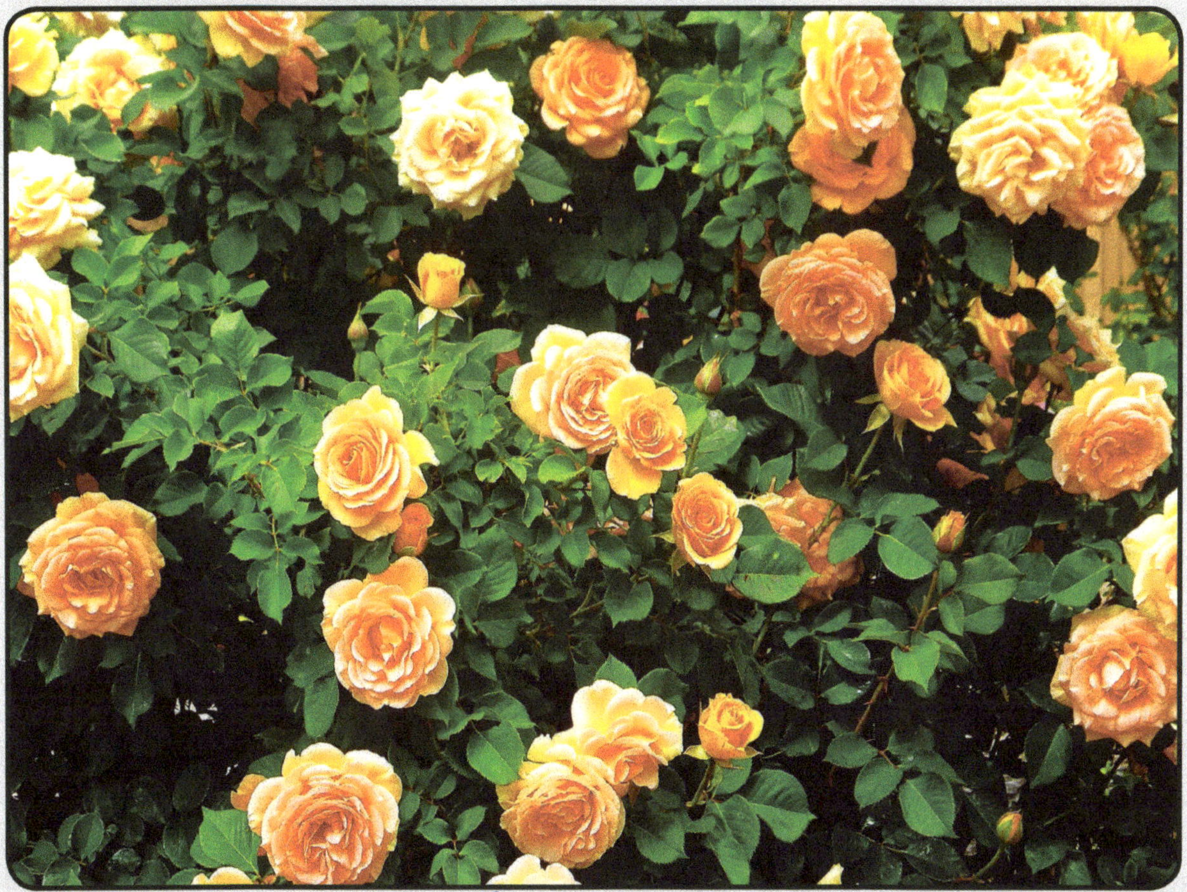

❀ Aromatic wall.

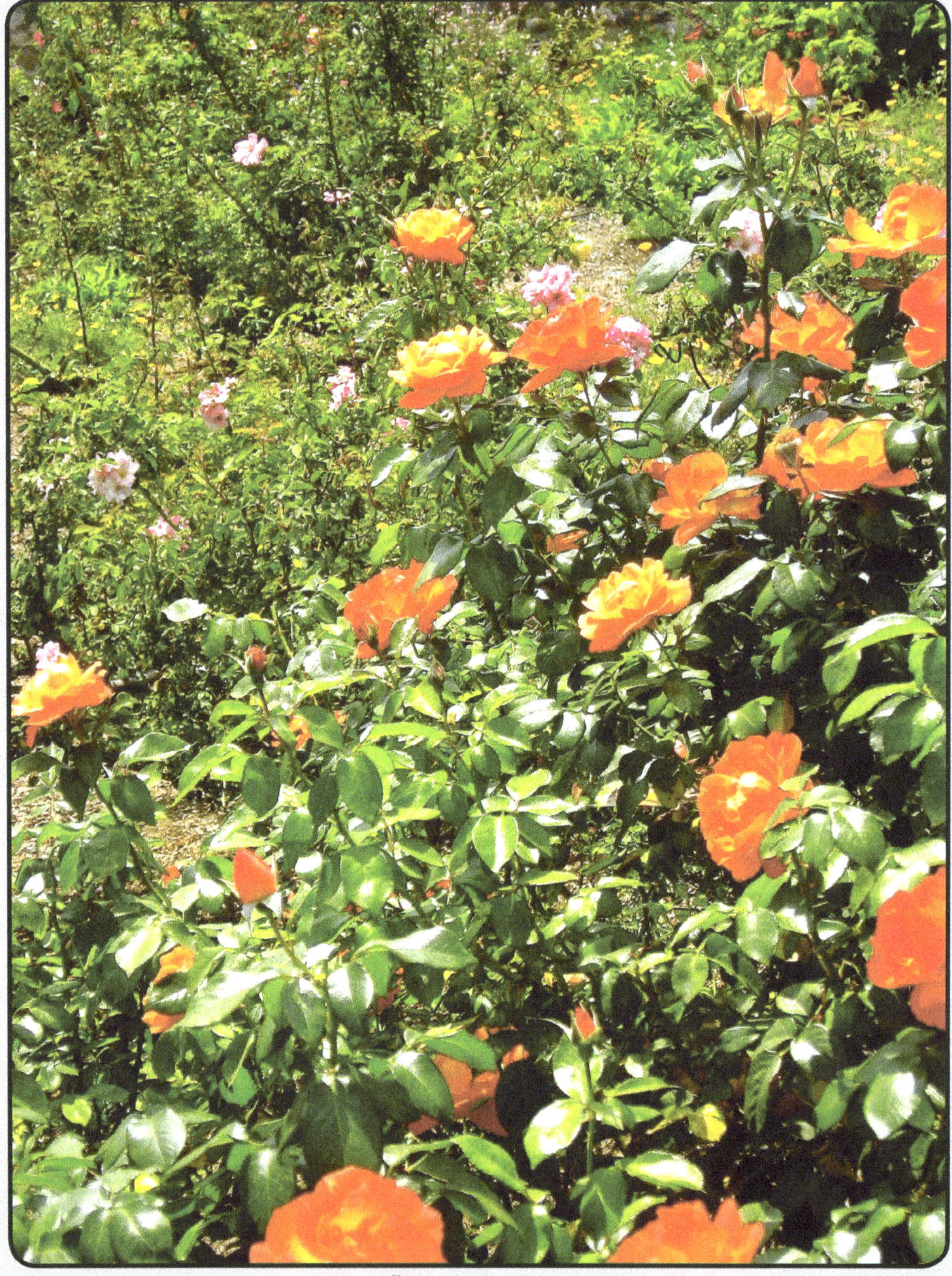

Floral embers.

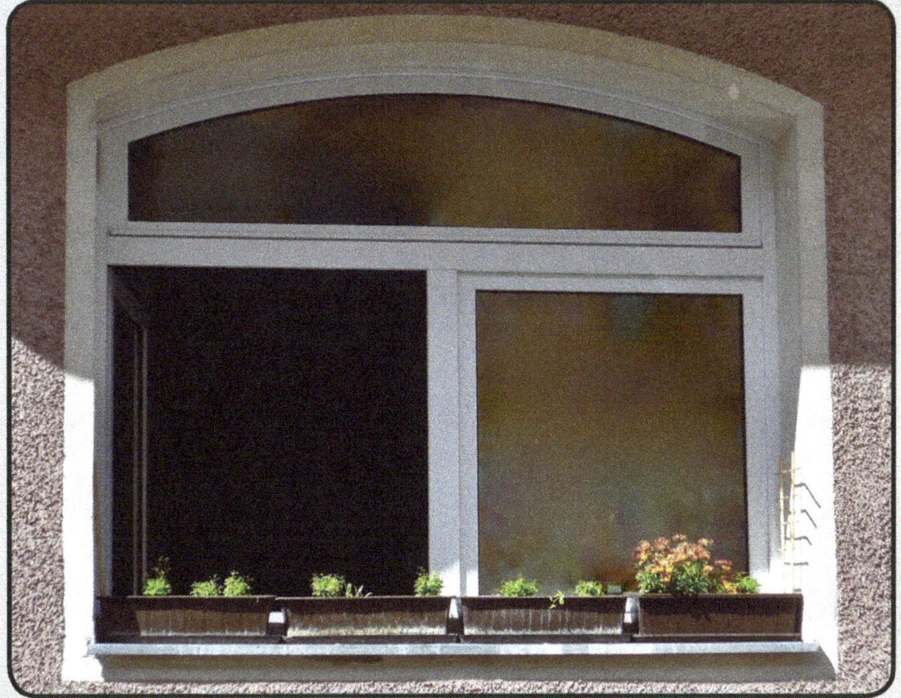

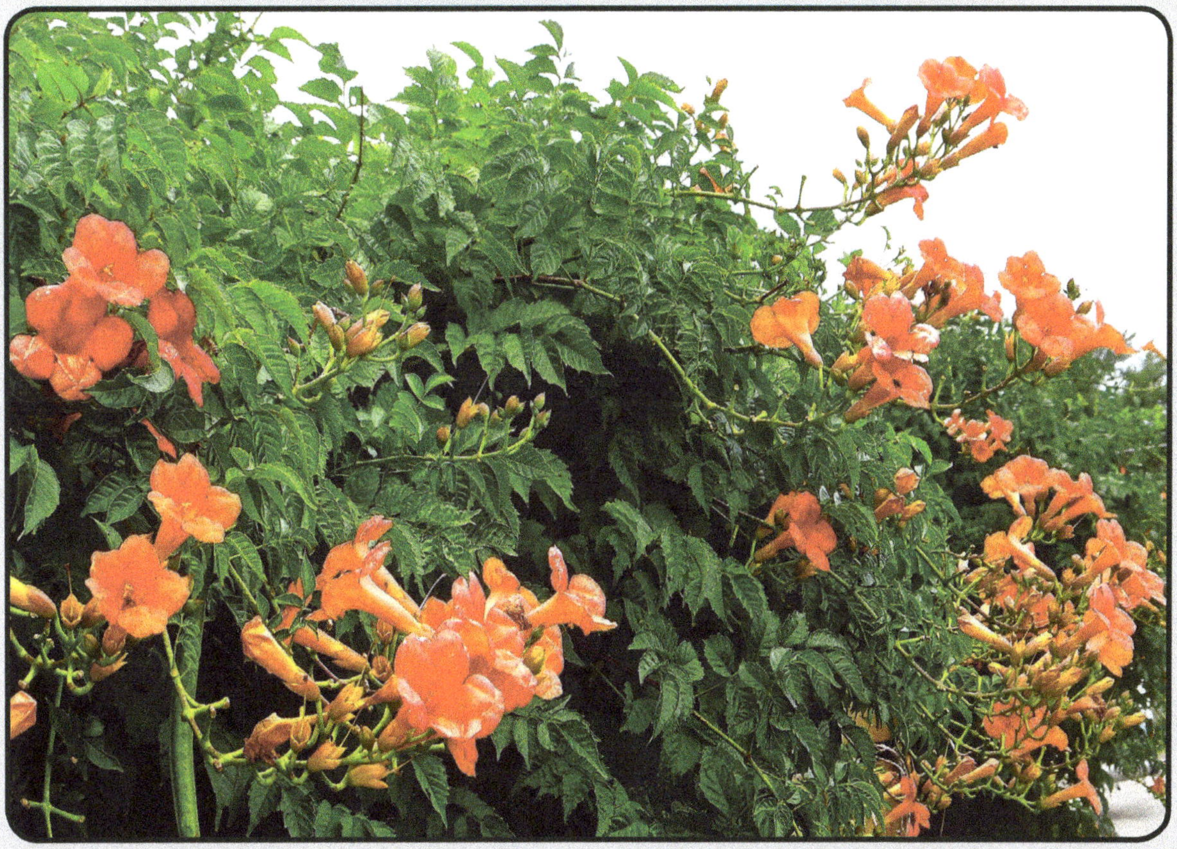

Trumpet blasts.

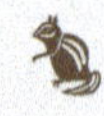

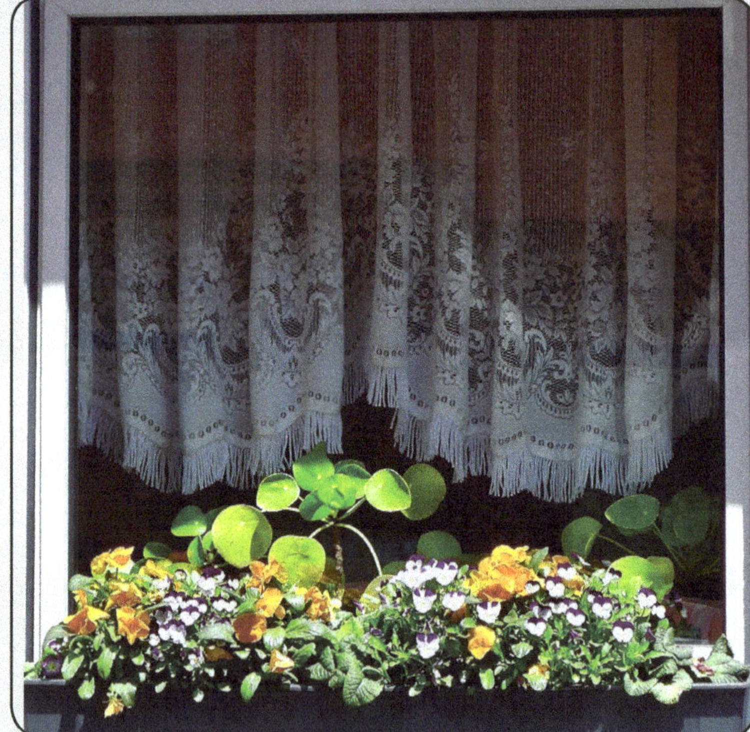

Blossoms and old lace.

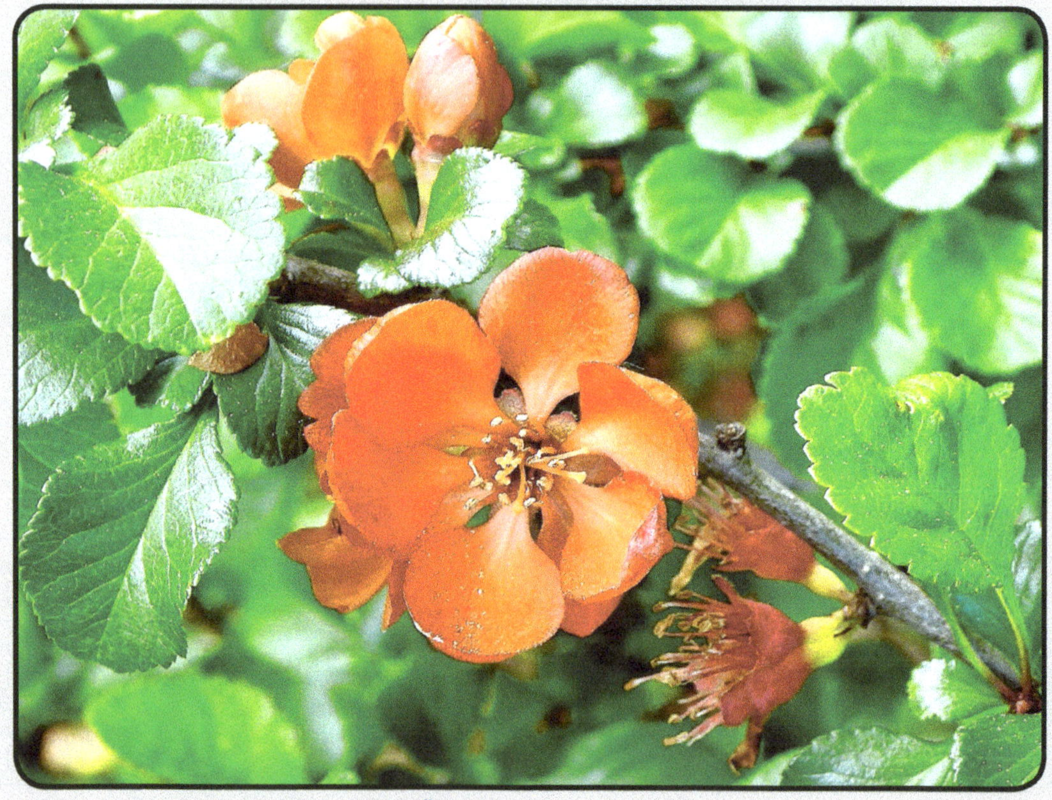

Cupped hands.

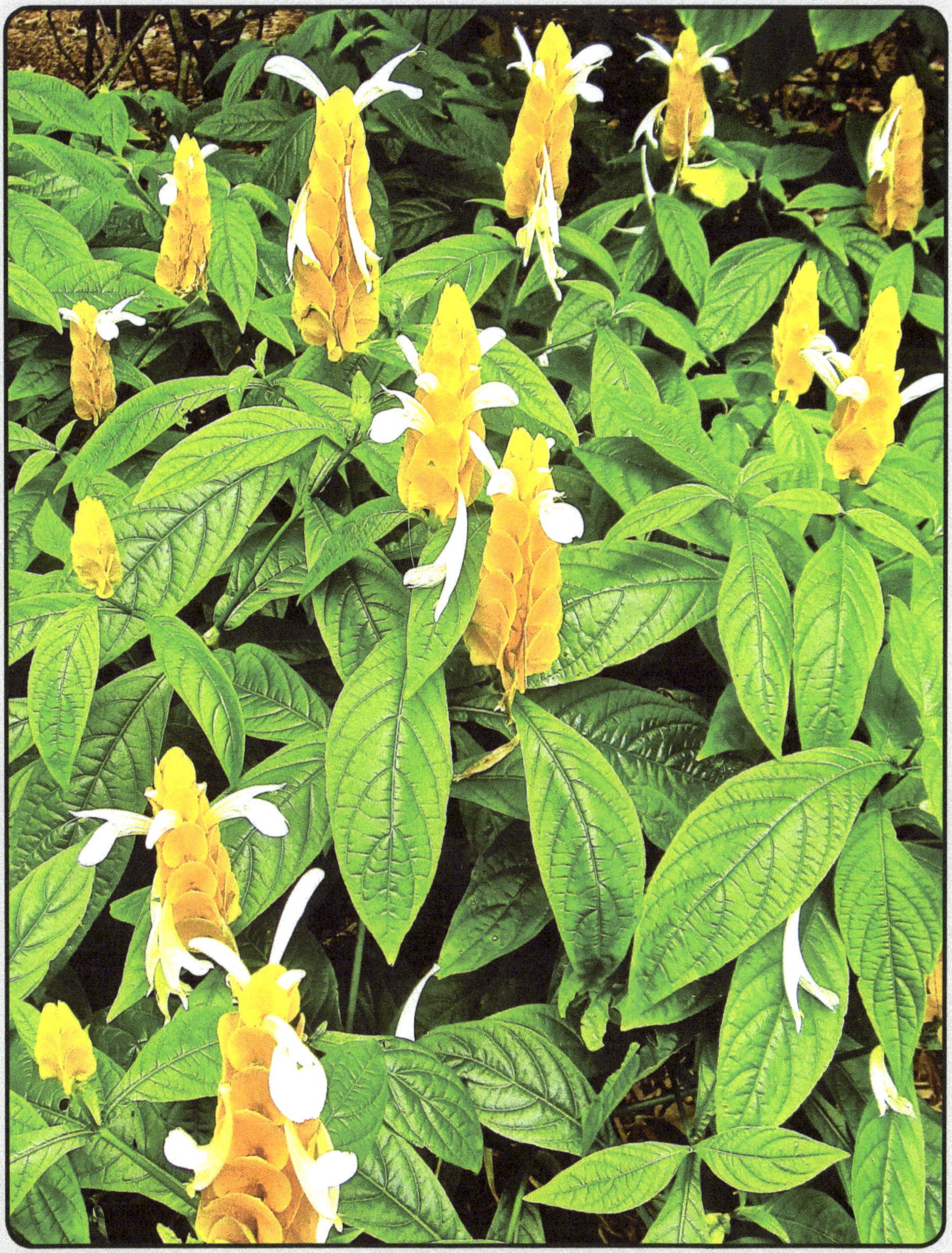

Golden pagodas.

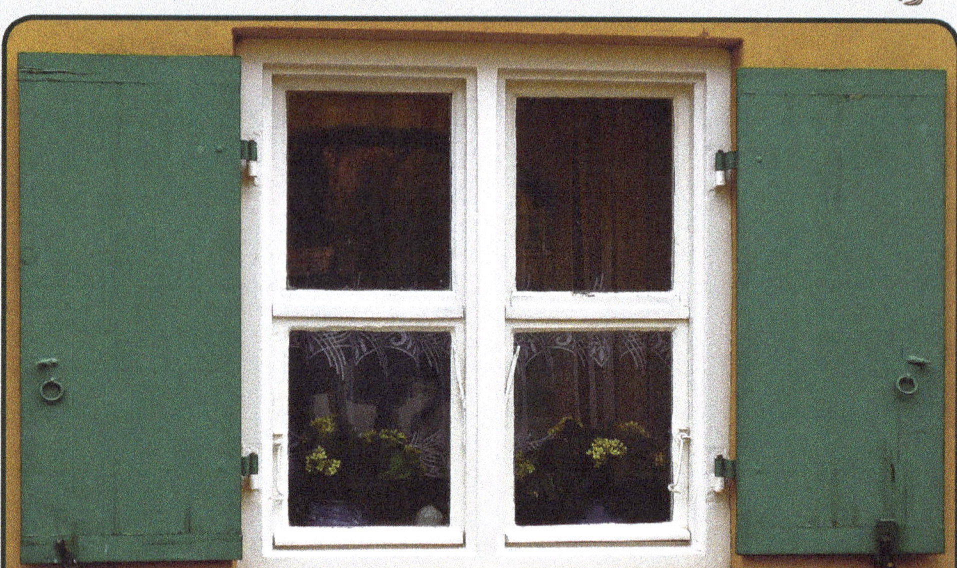

Plants peering out.

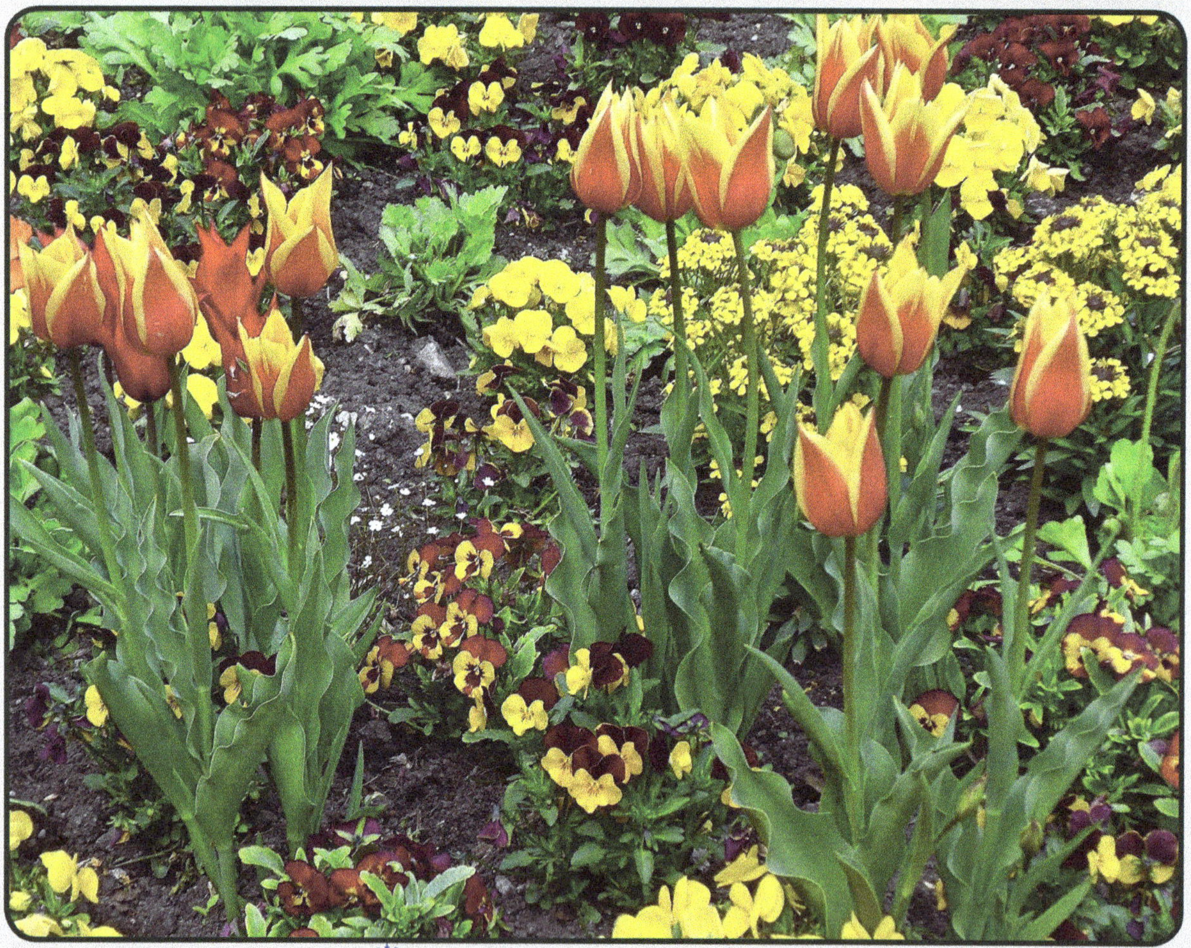

A village of the big and small.

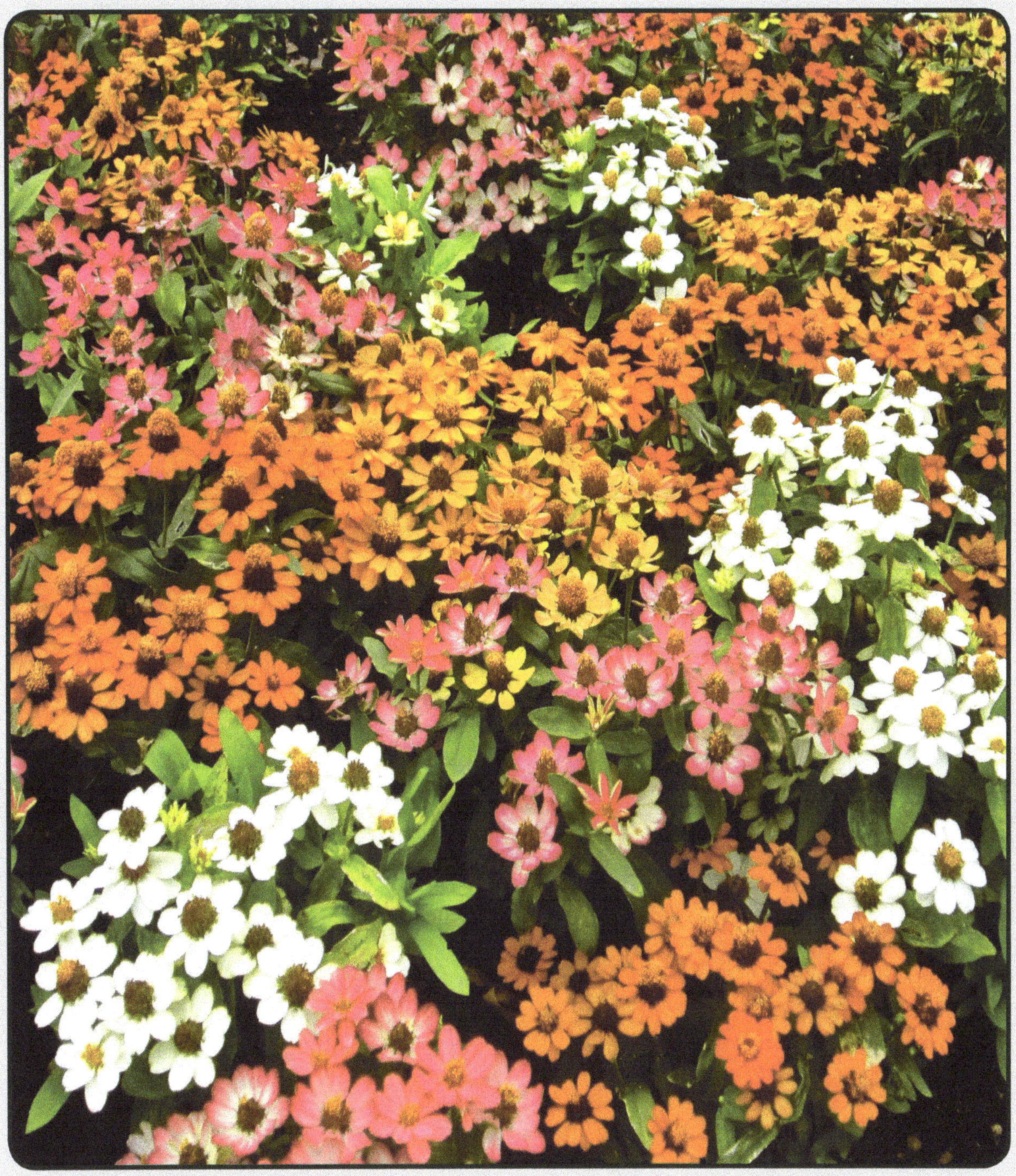

❀ An array of many smiles.

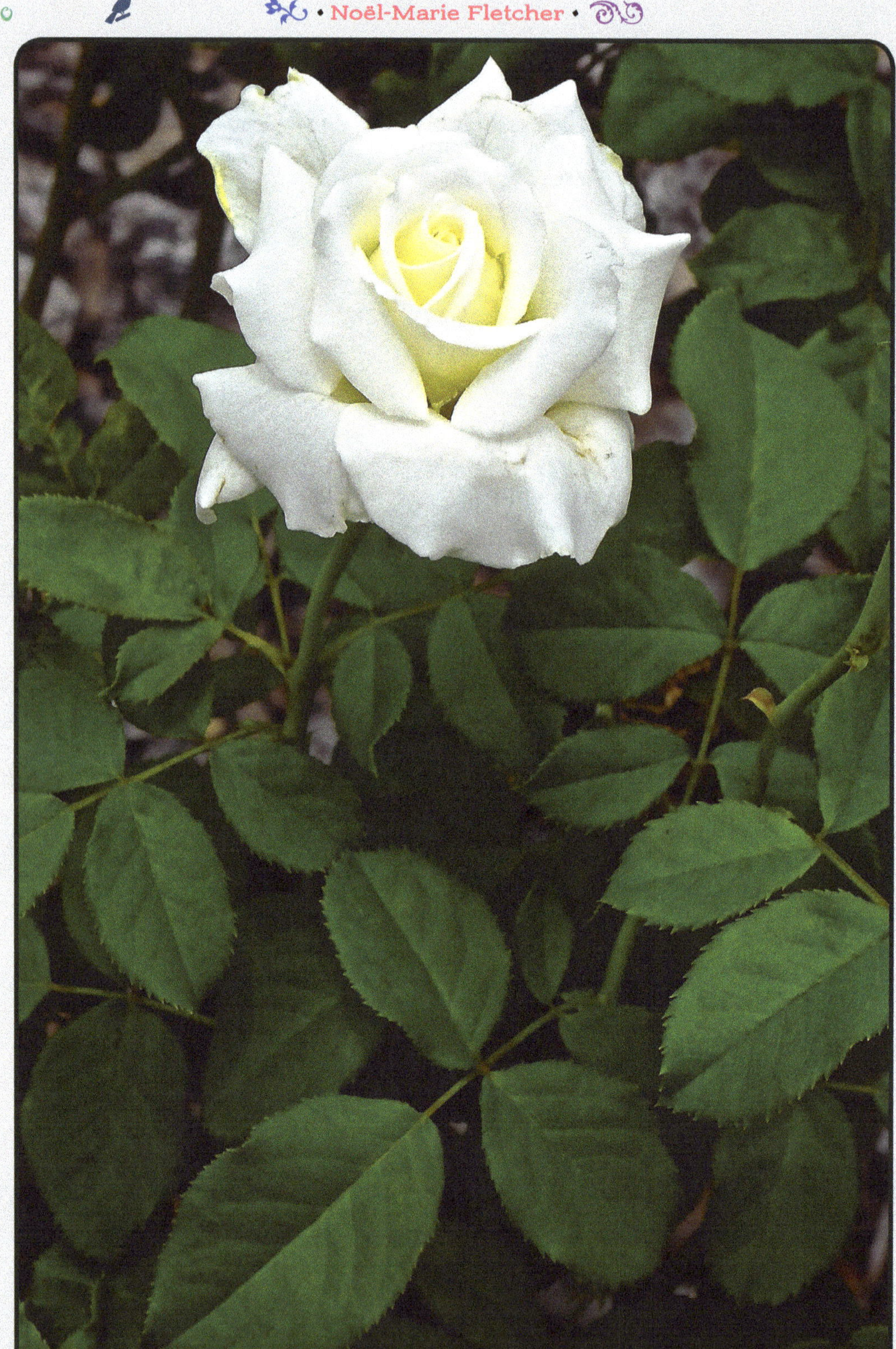

Inner glow.

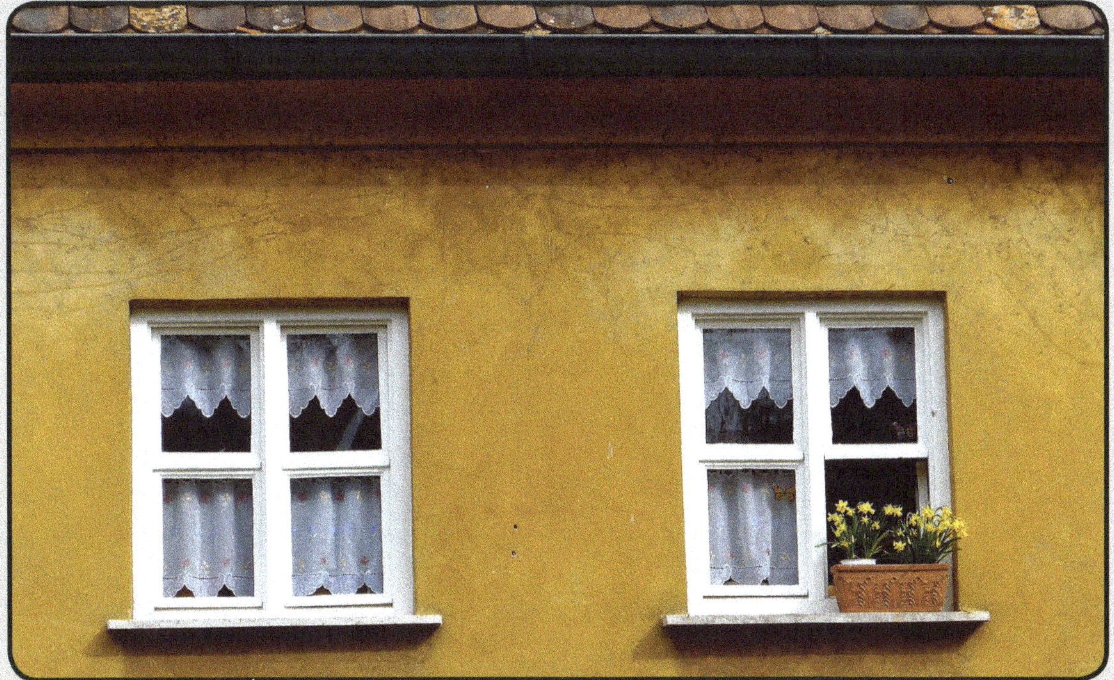

Daffodils in Germany.

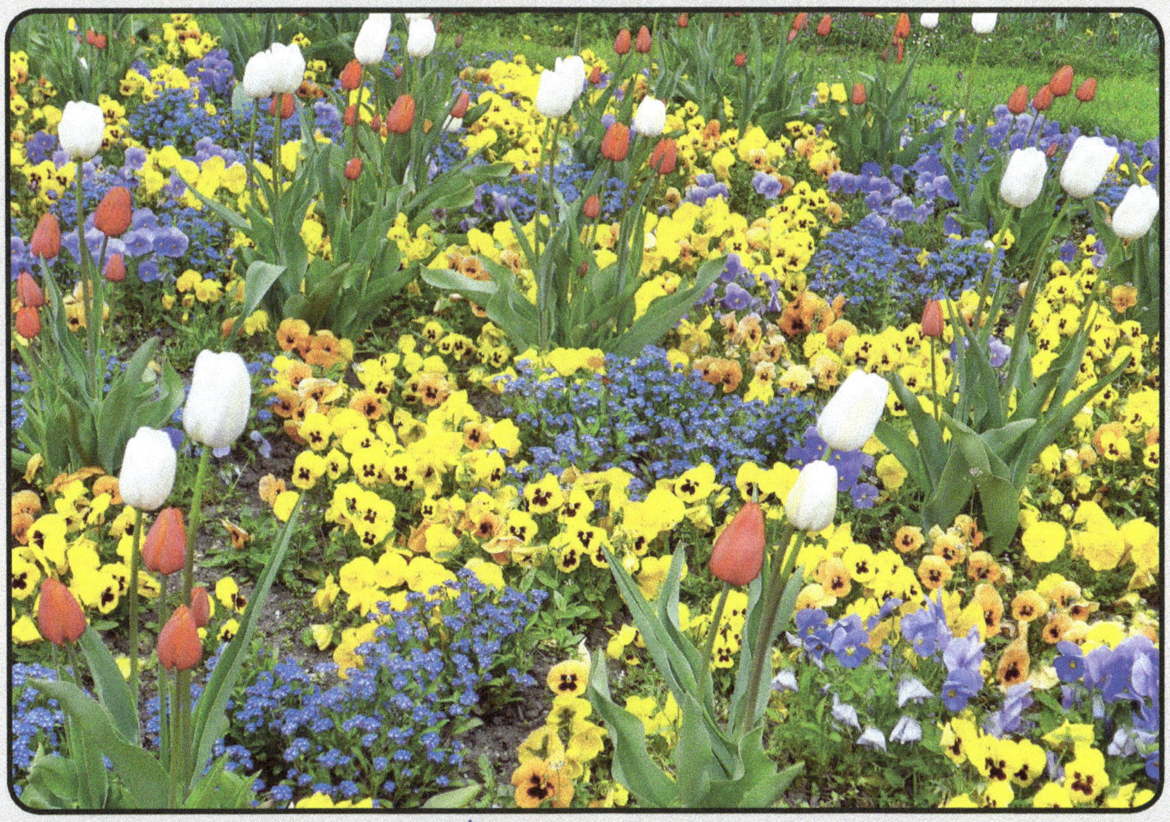

Rejoicing in spring.

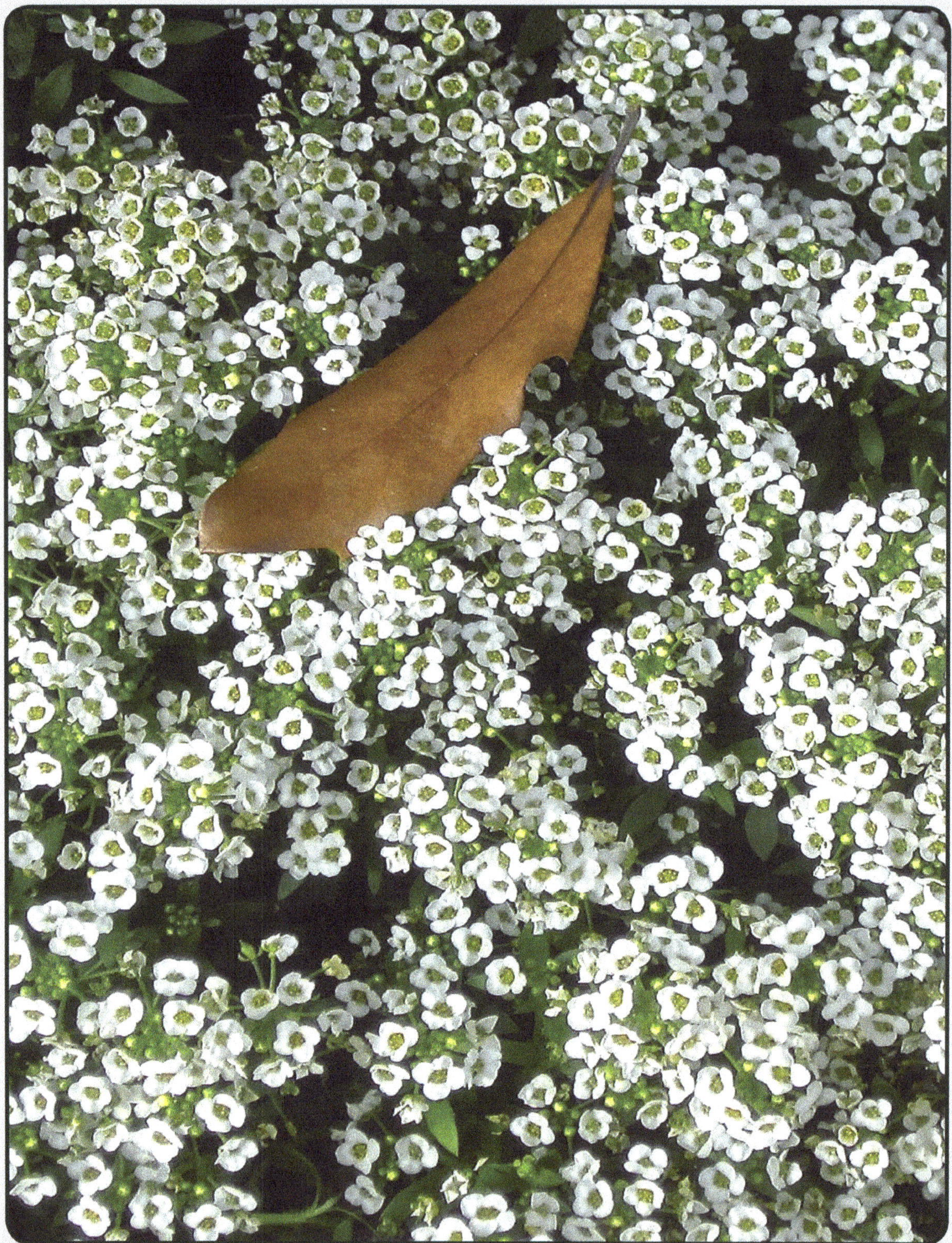

Gulliver's leaf.

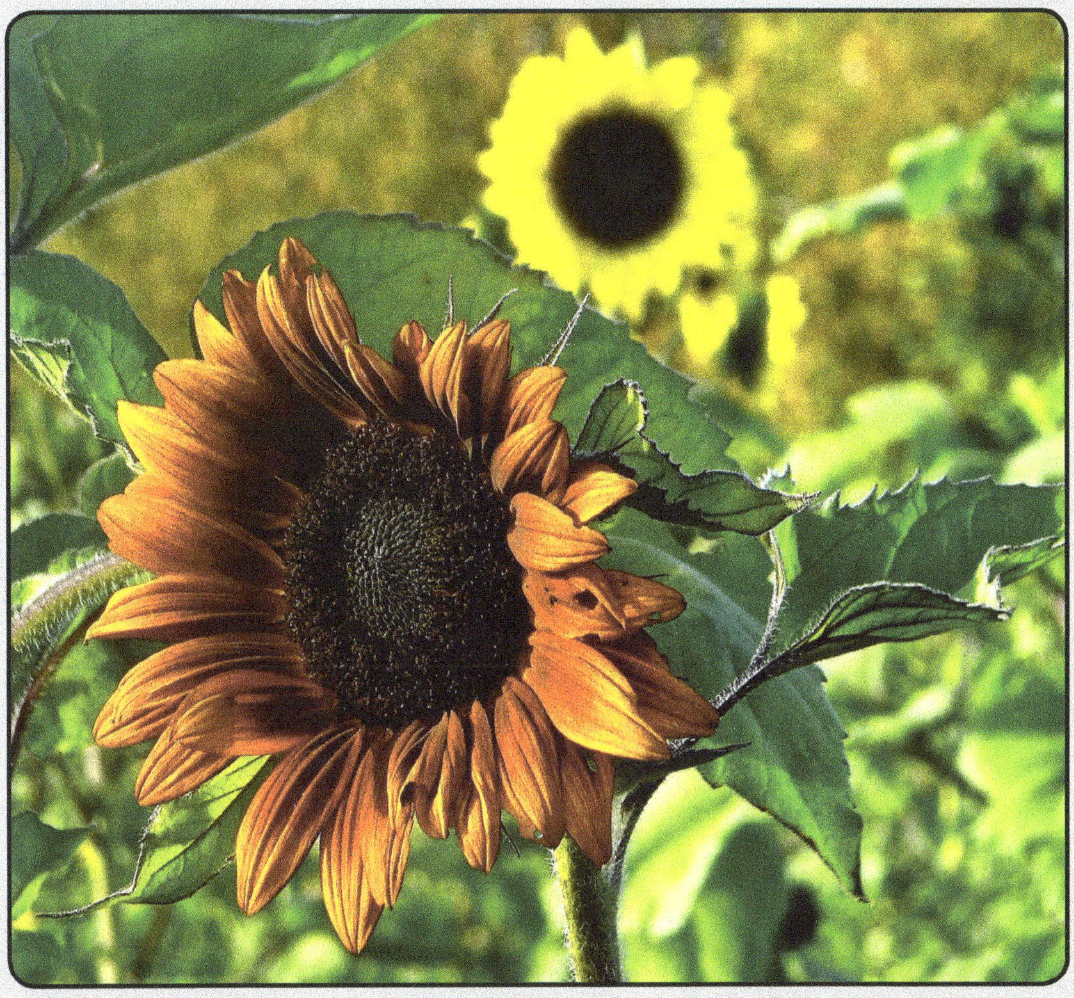

Rust.

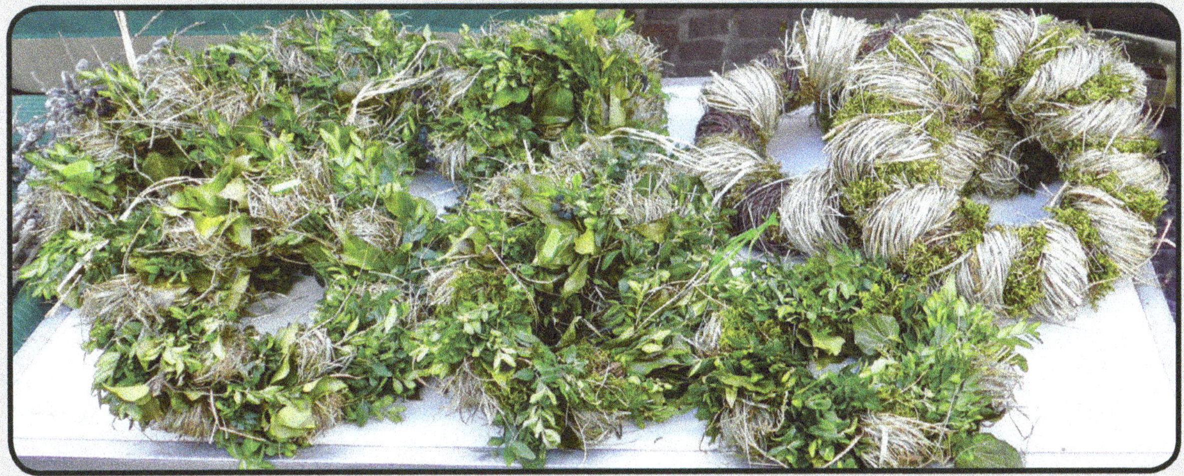

Bavarian wreaths.

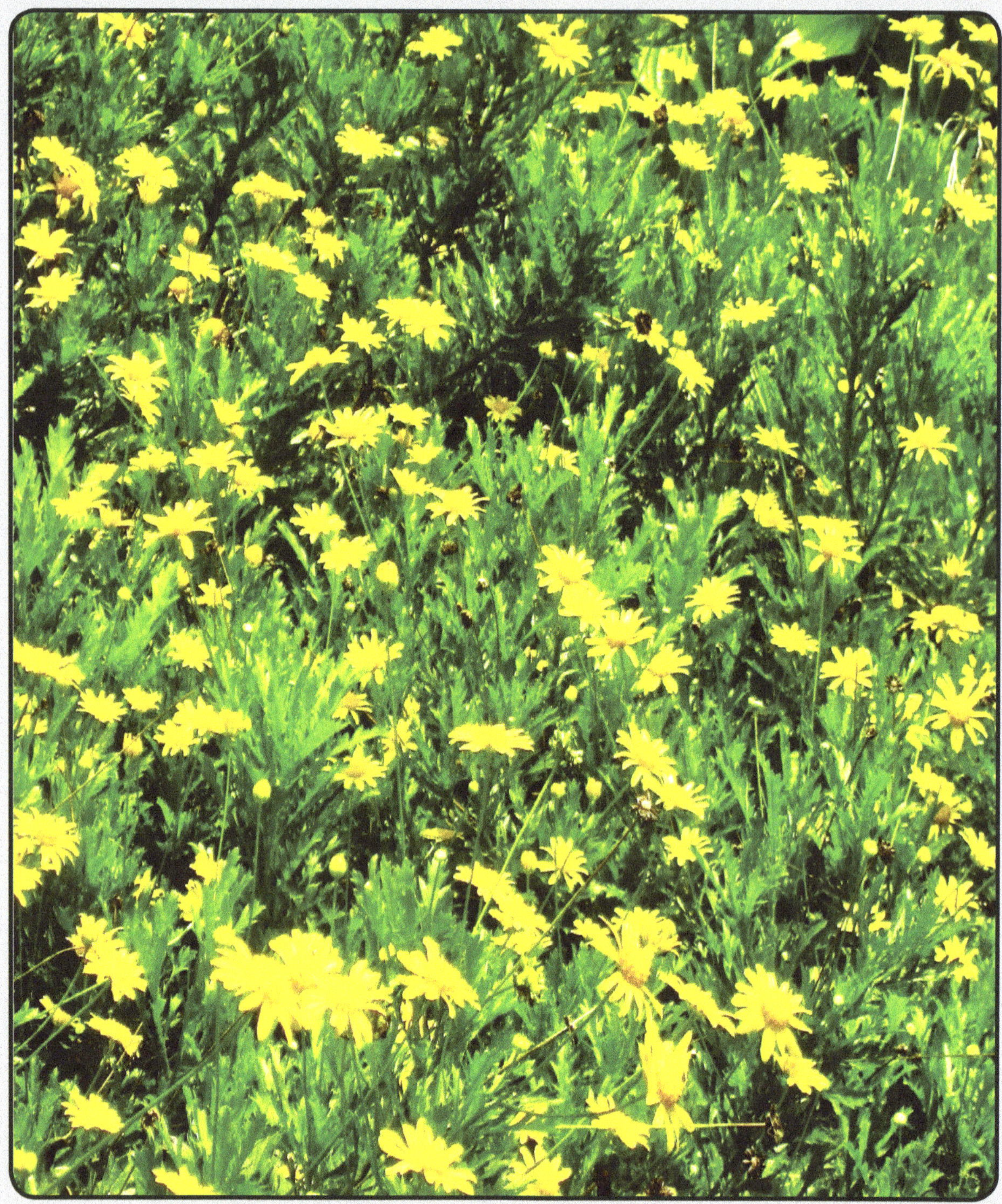

Lemon brilliance.

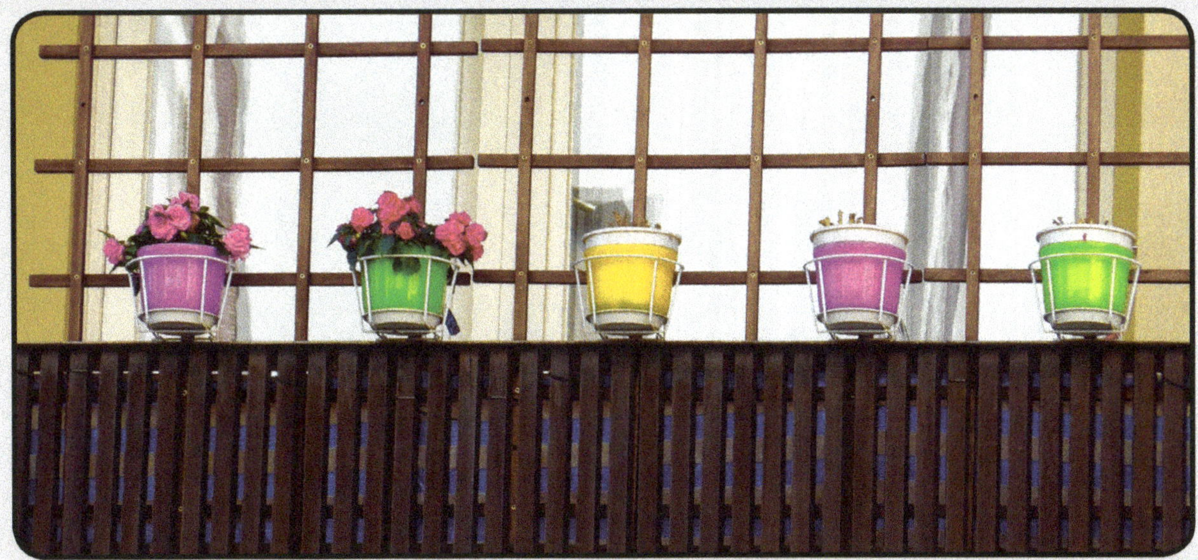

Primary colors.

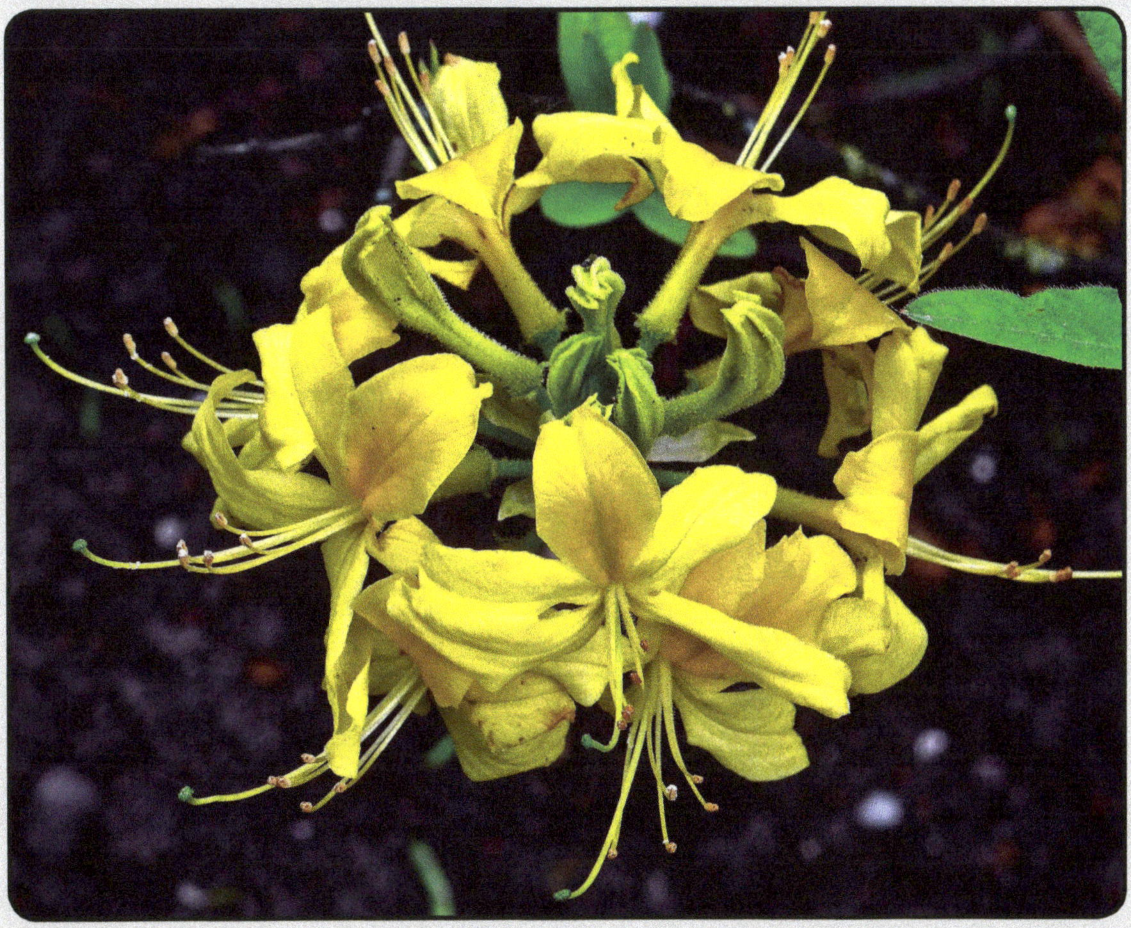

Star bouquet.

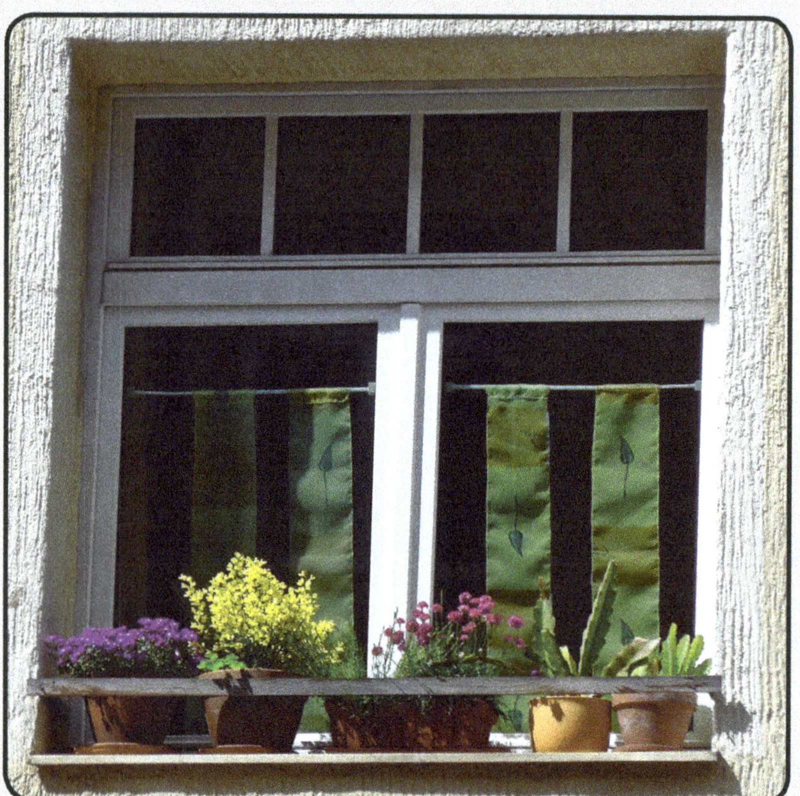

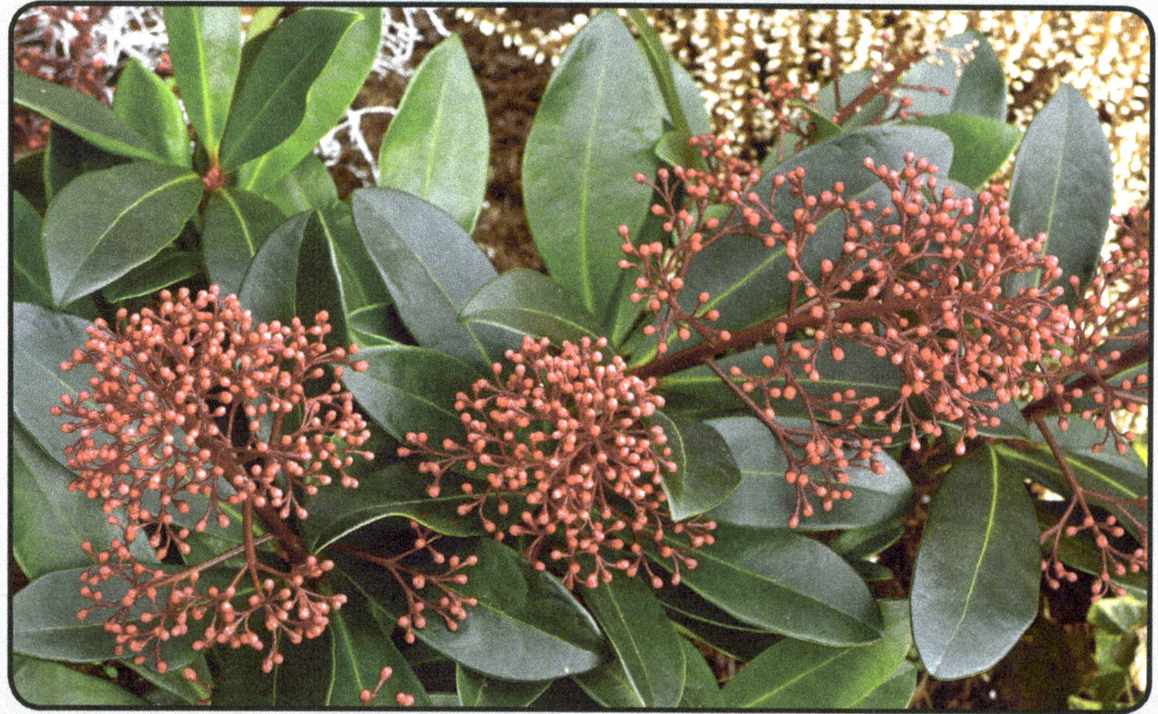

Berry wands.

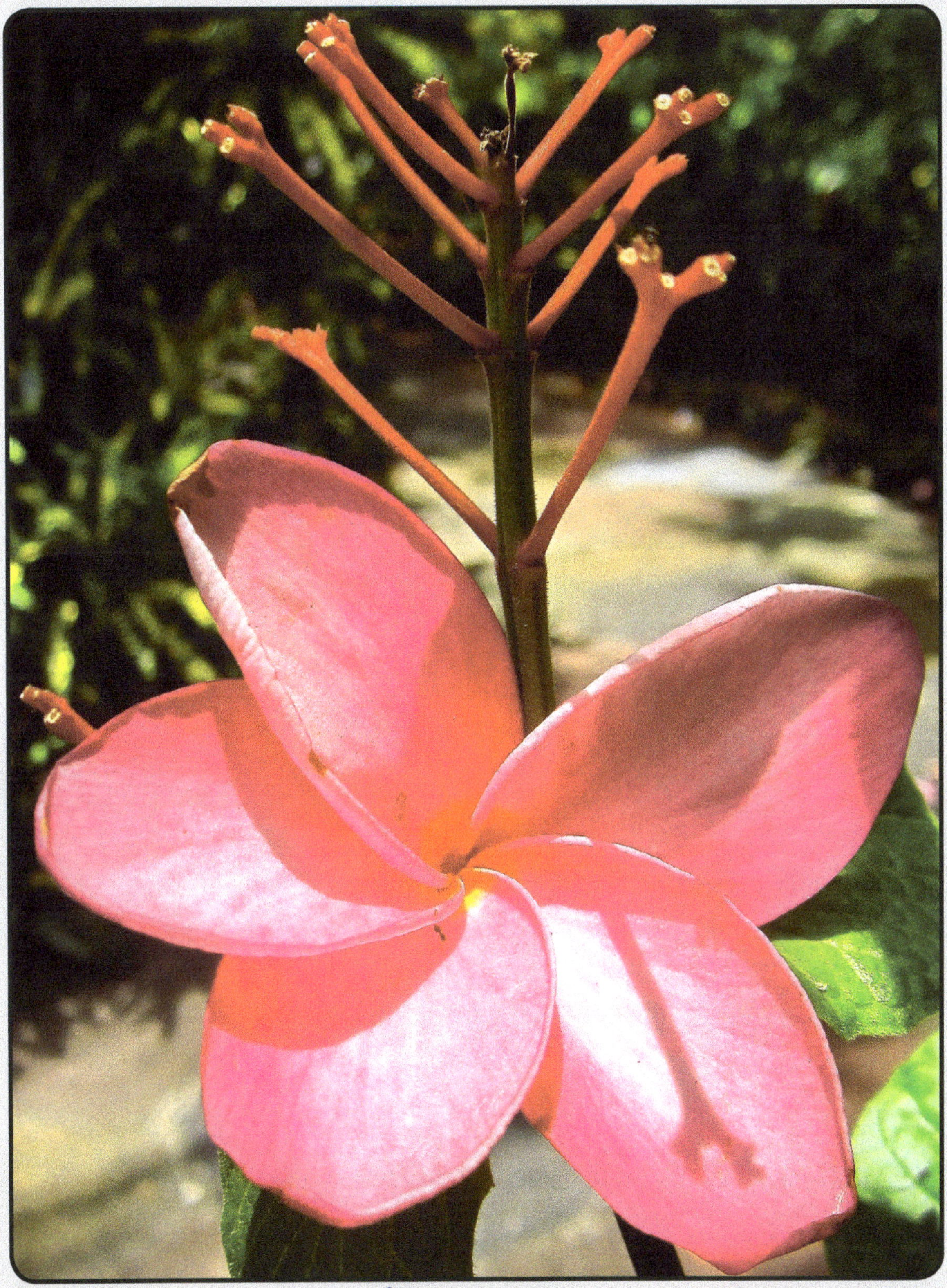

Nature's pinwheel.

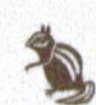

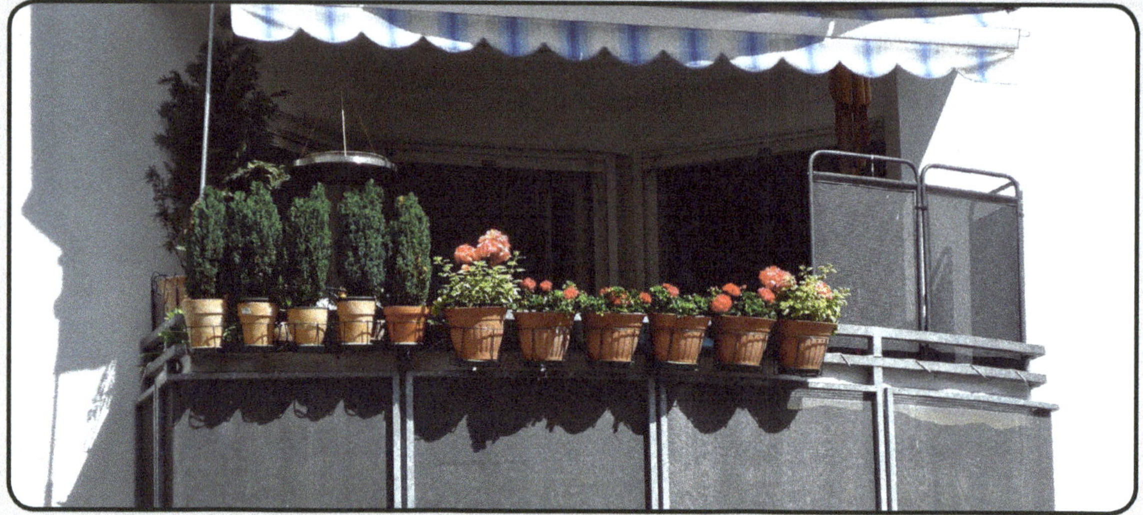

Trees to the left.

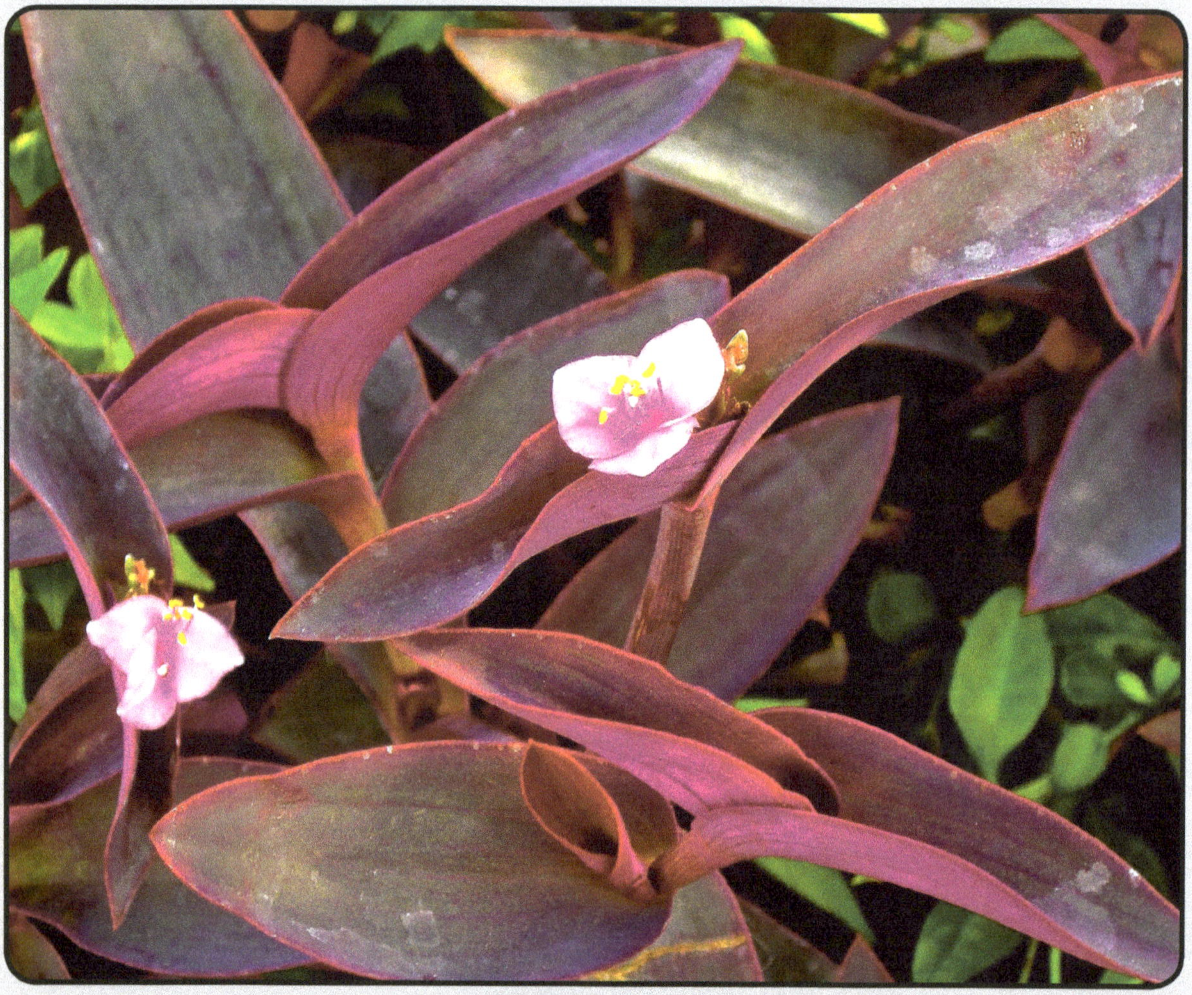

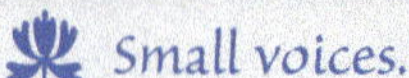

Small voices.

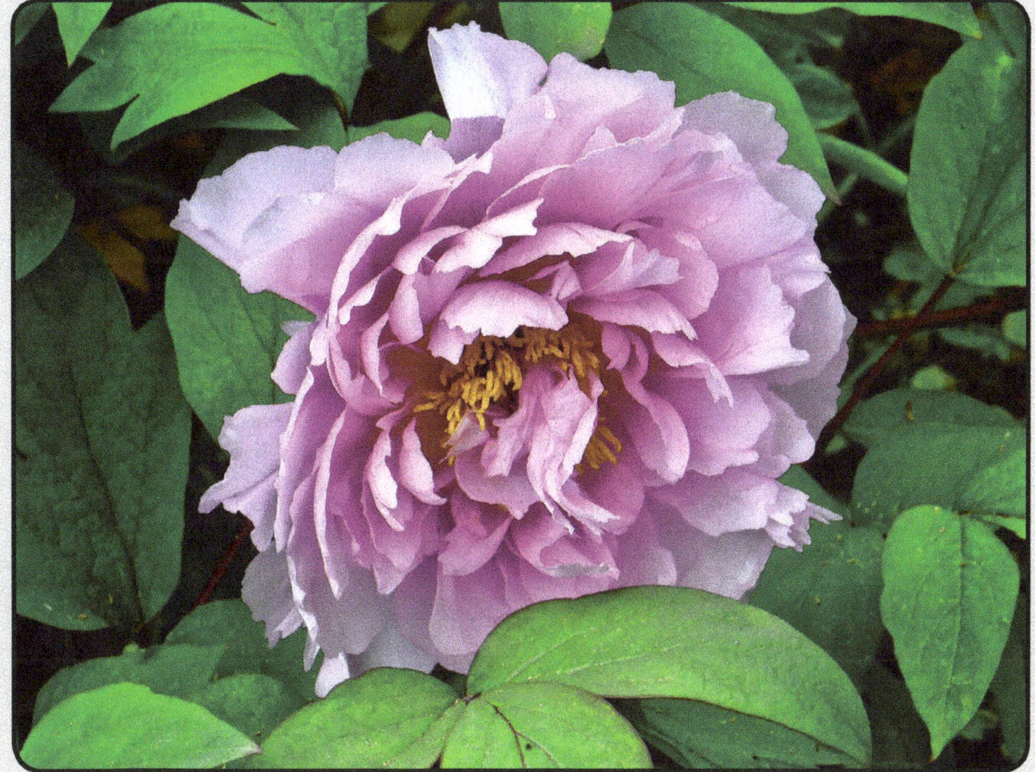

Scalloped edges.

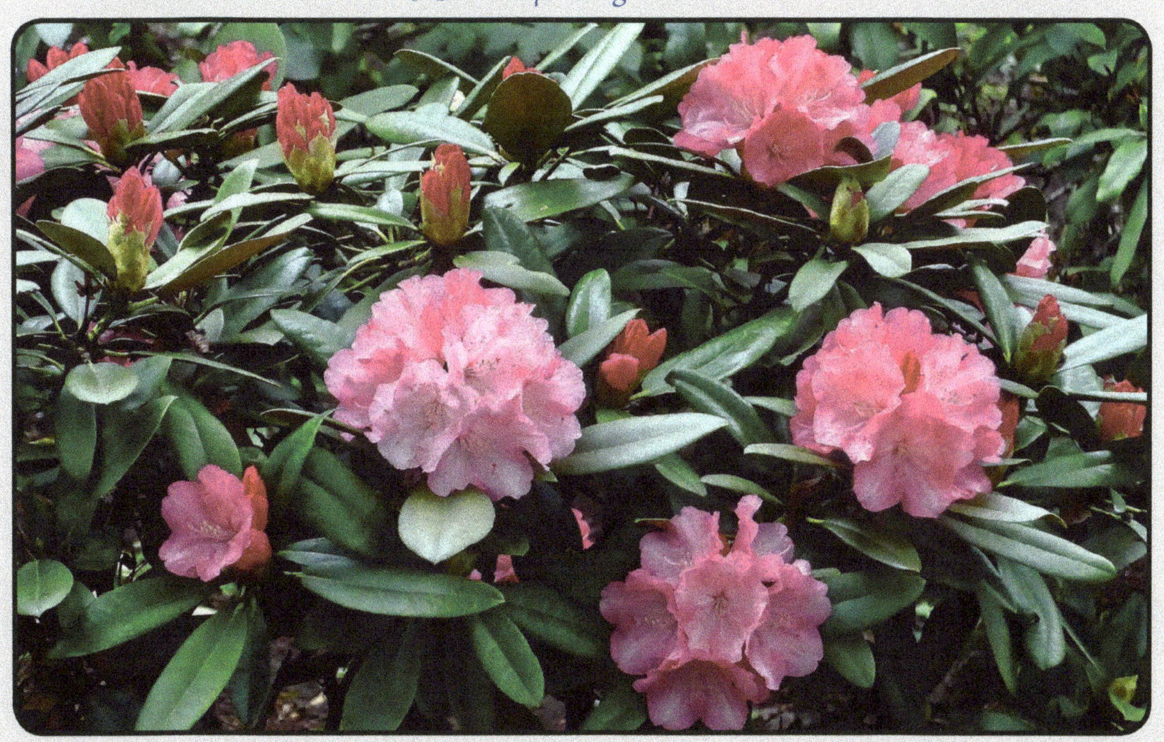

Pom-poms.

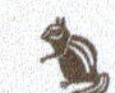

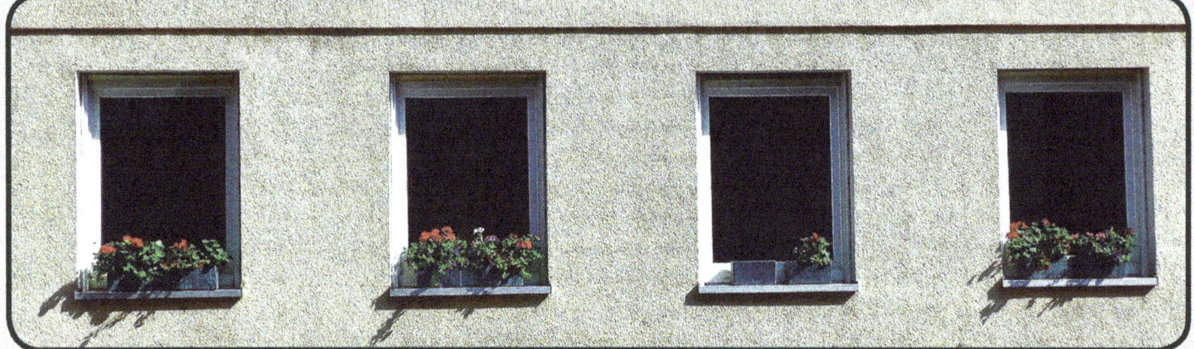

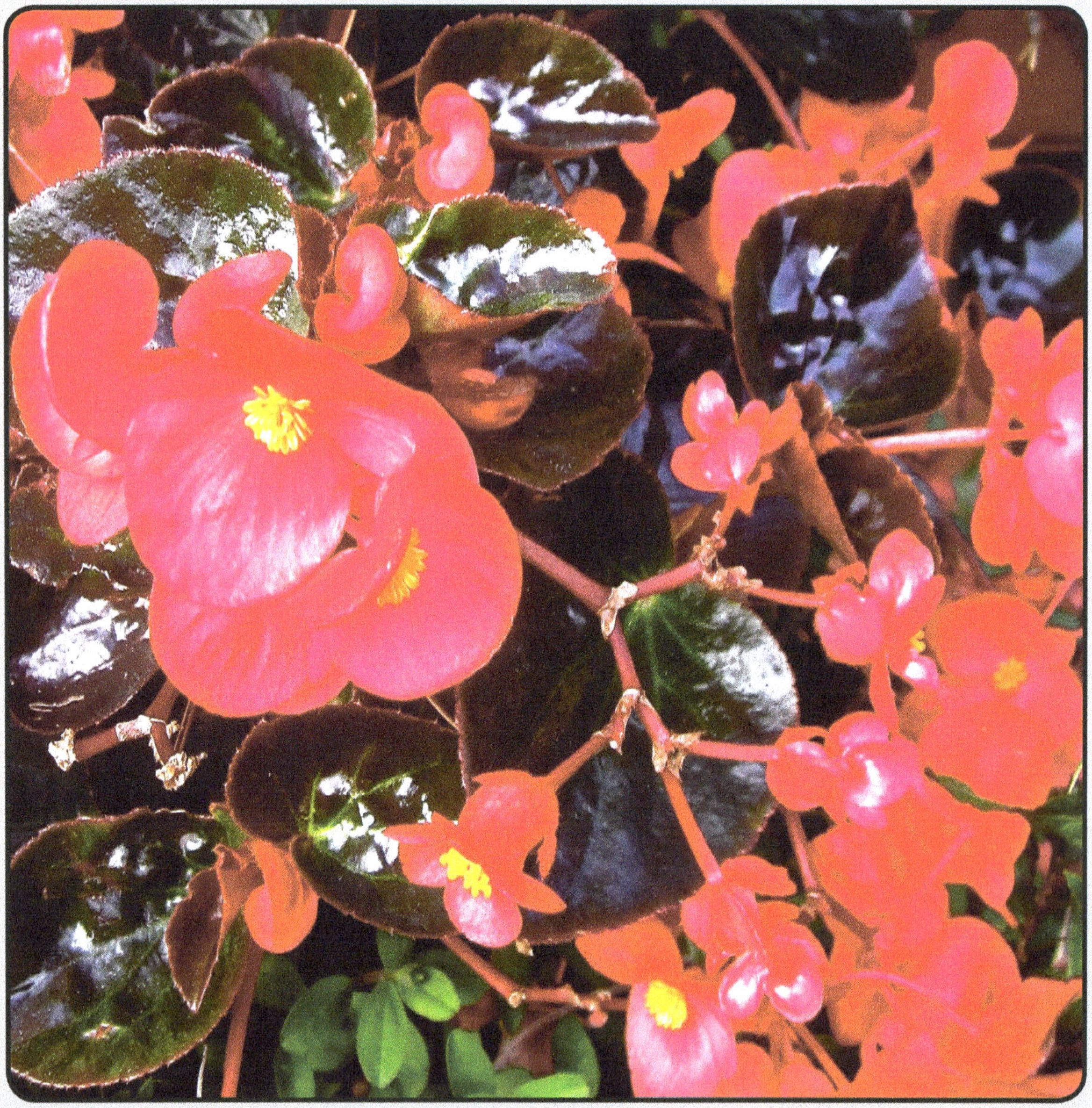

Dashes of yellow.

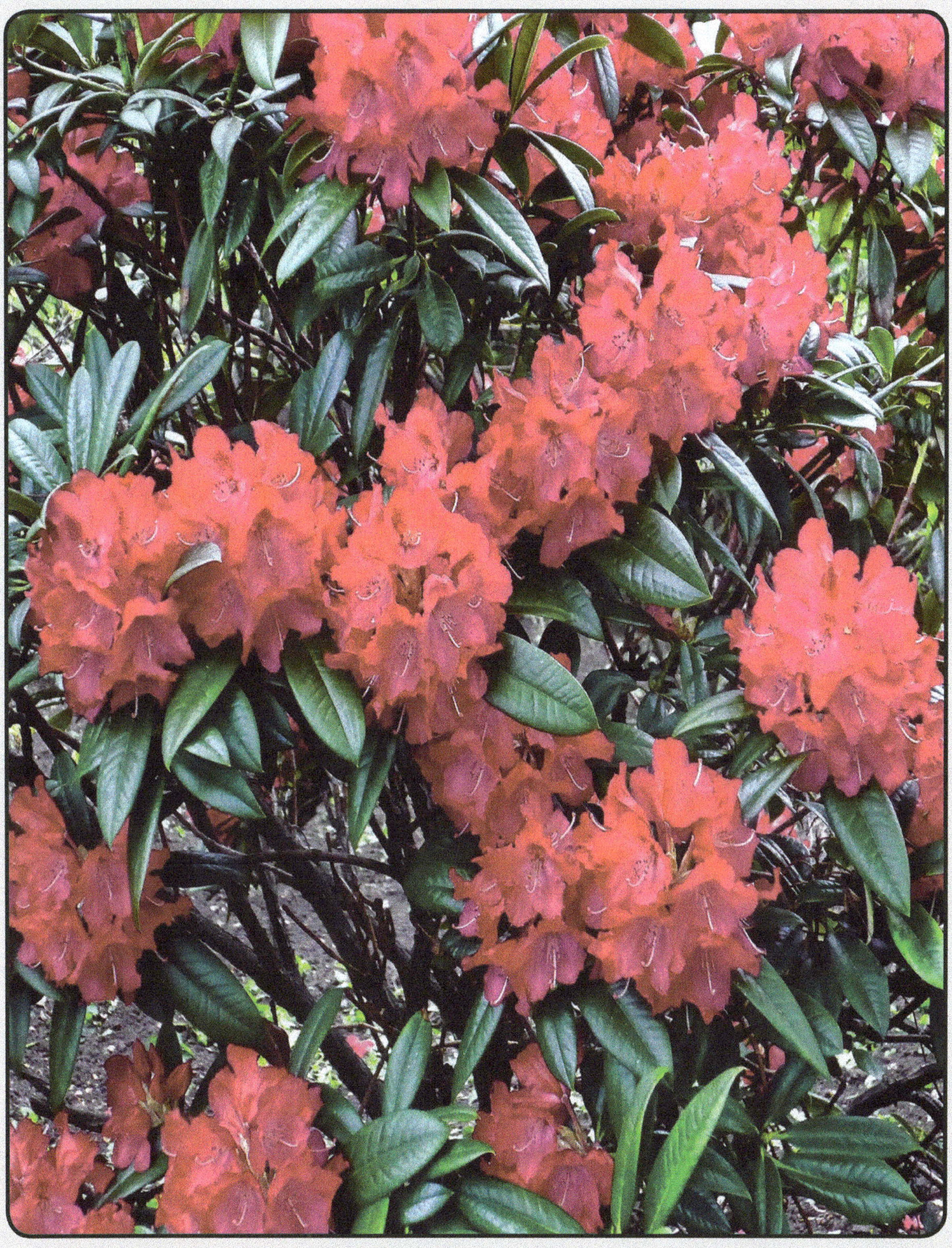

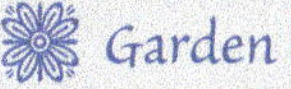

Garden lei.

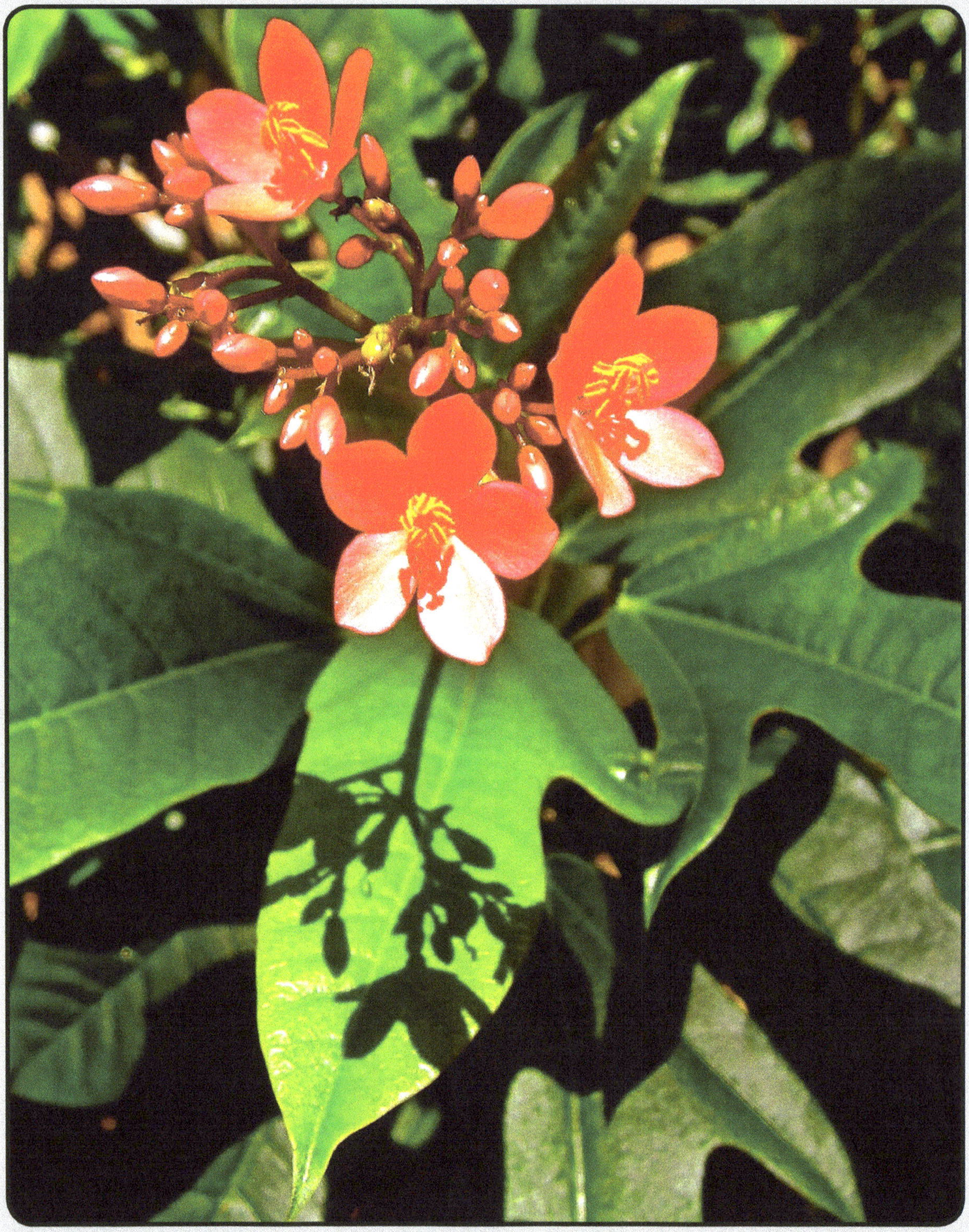

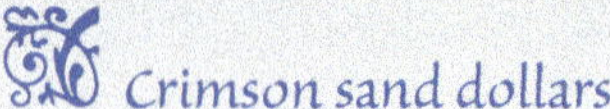

Crimson sand dollars.

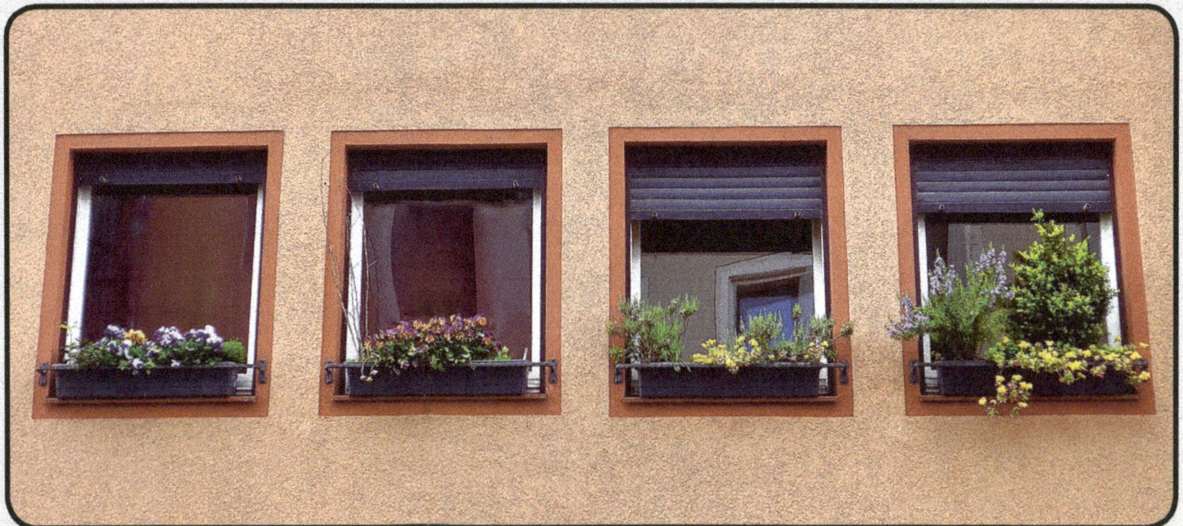

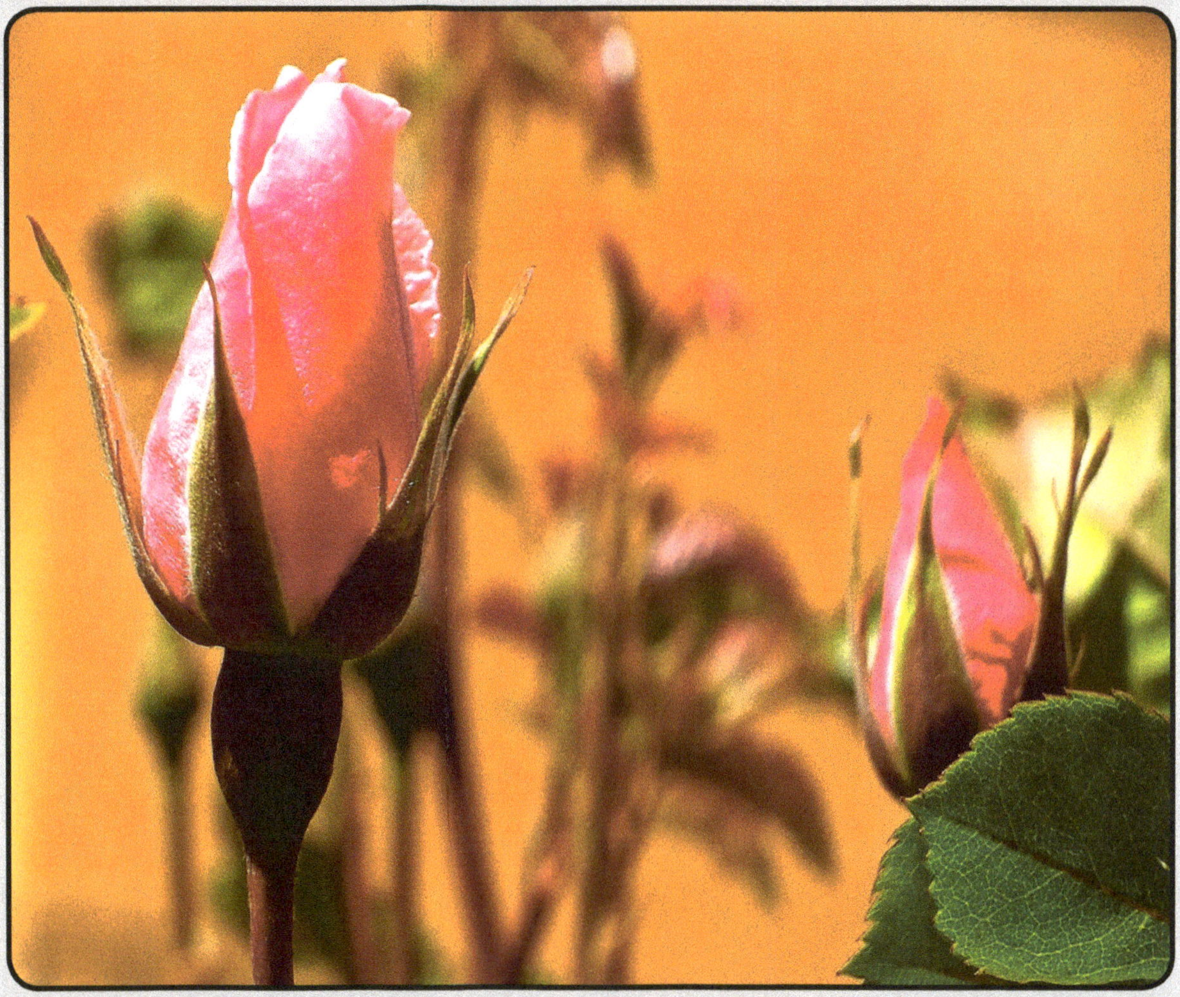

Floral scepters.

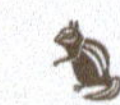

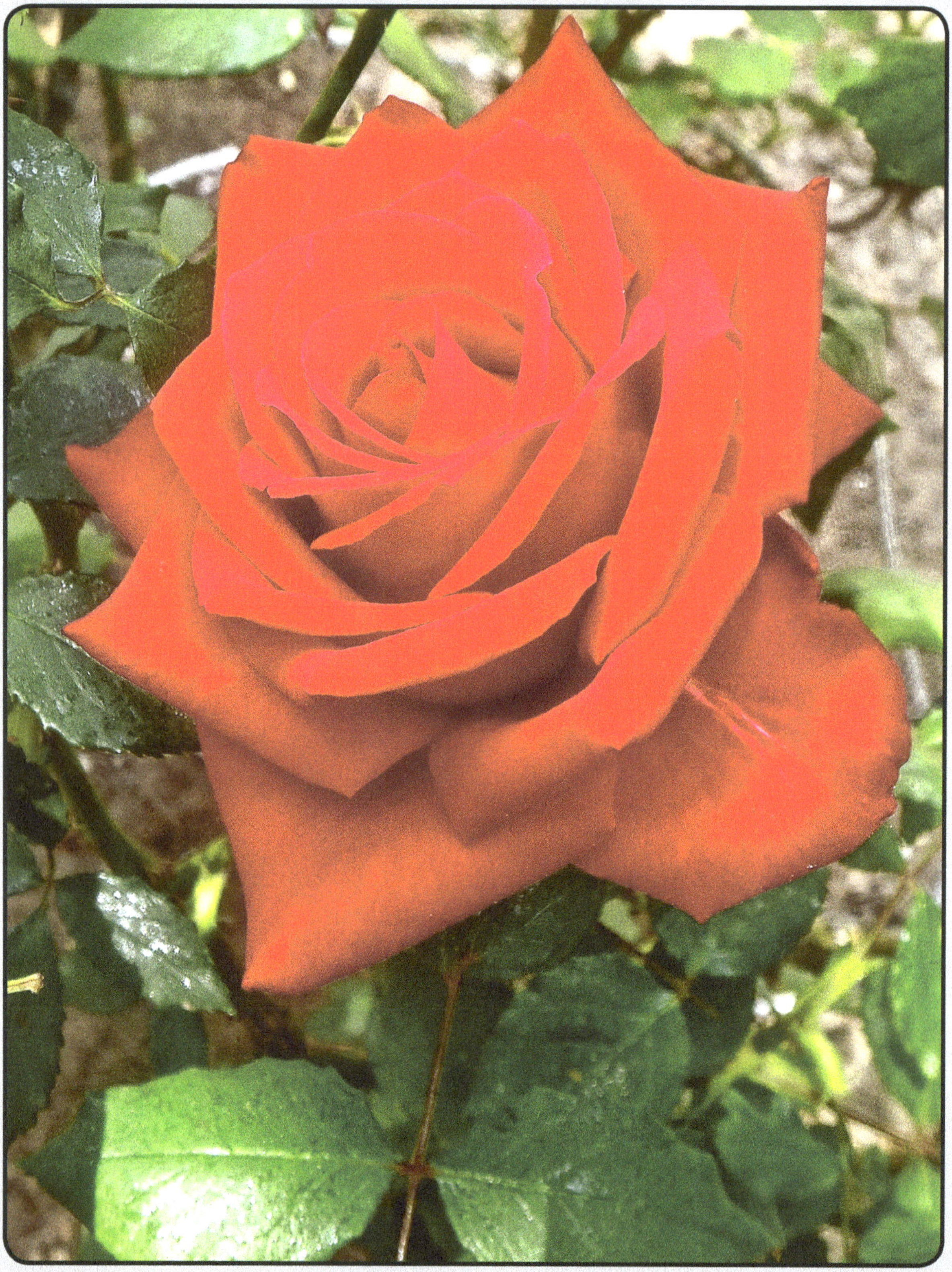

Crimson perfection.

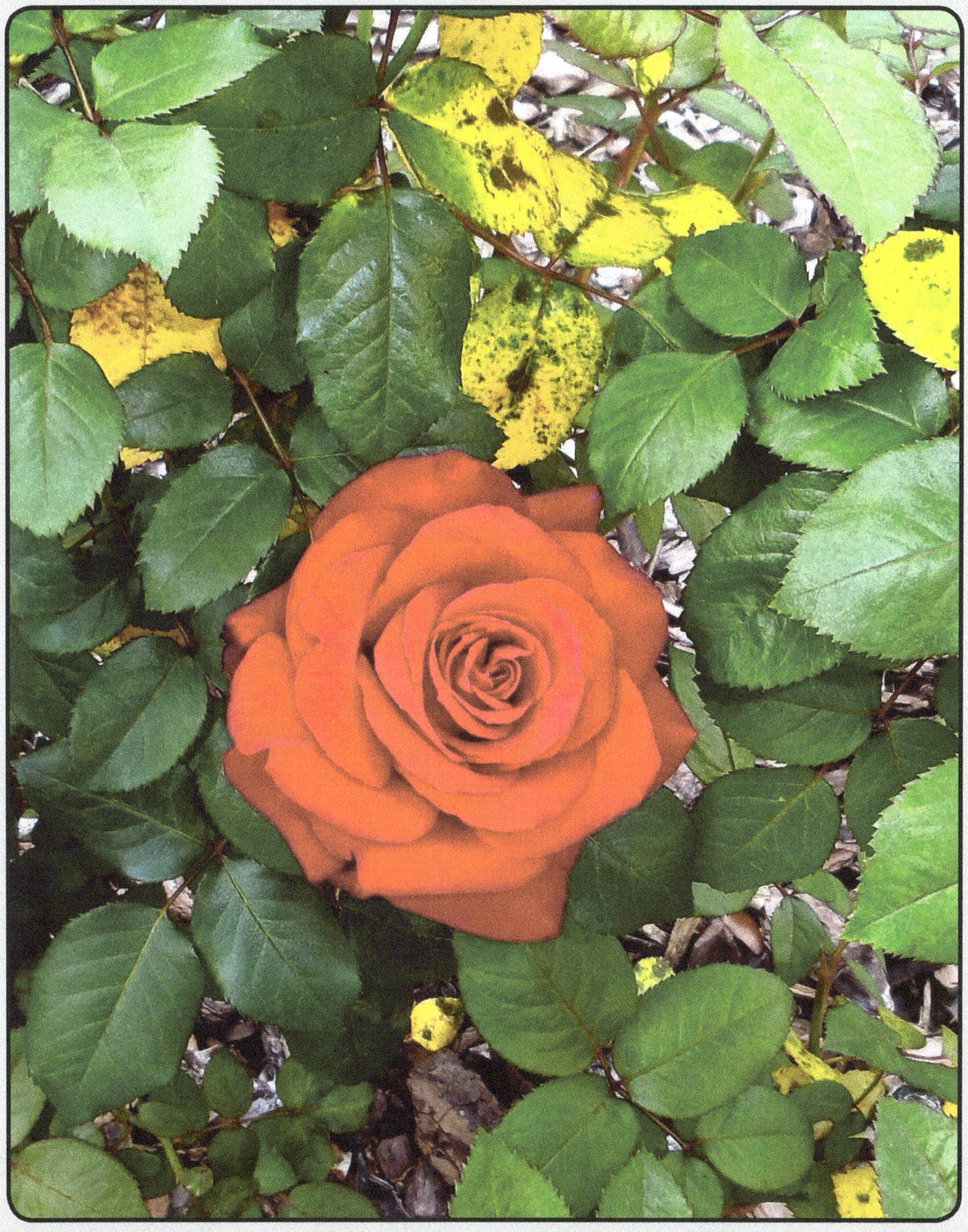

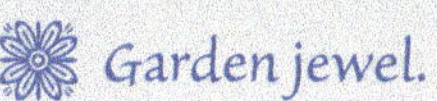

Garden jewel.

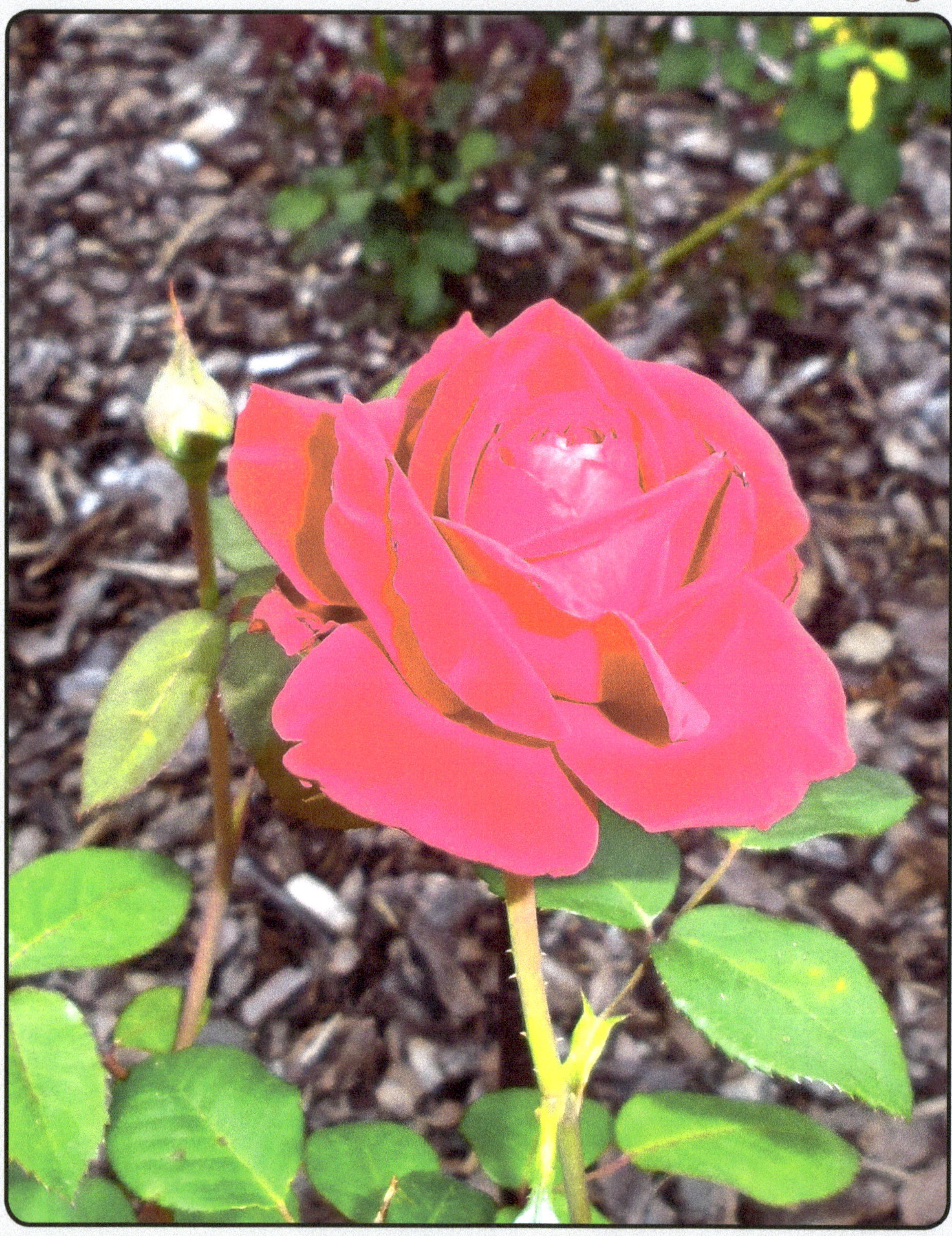

Ruby velvet.

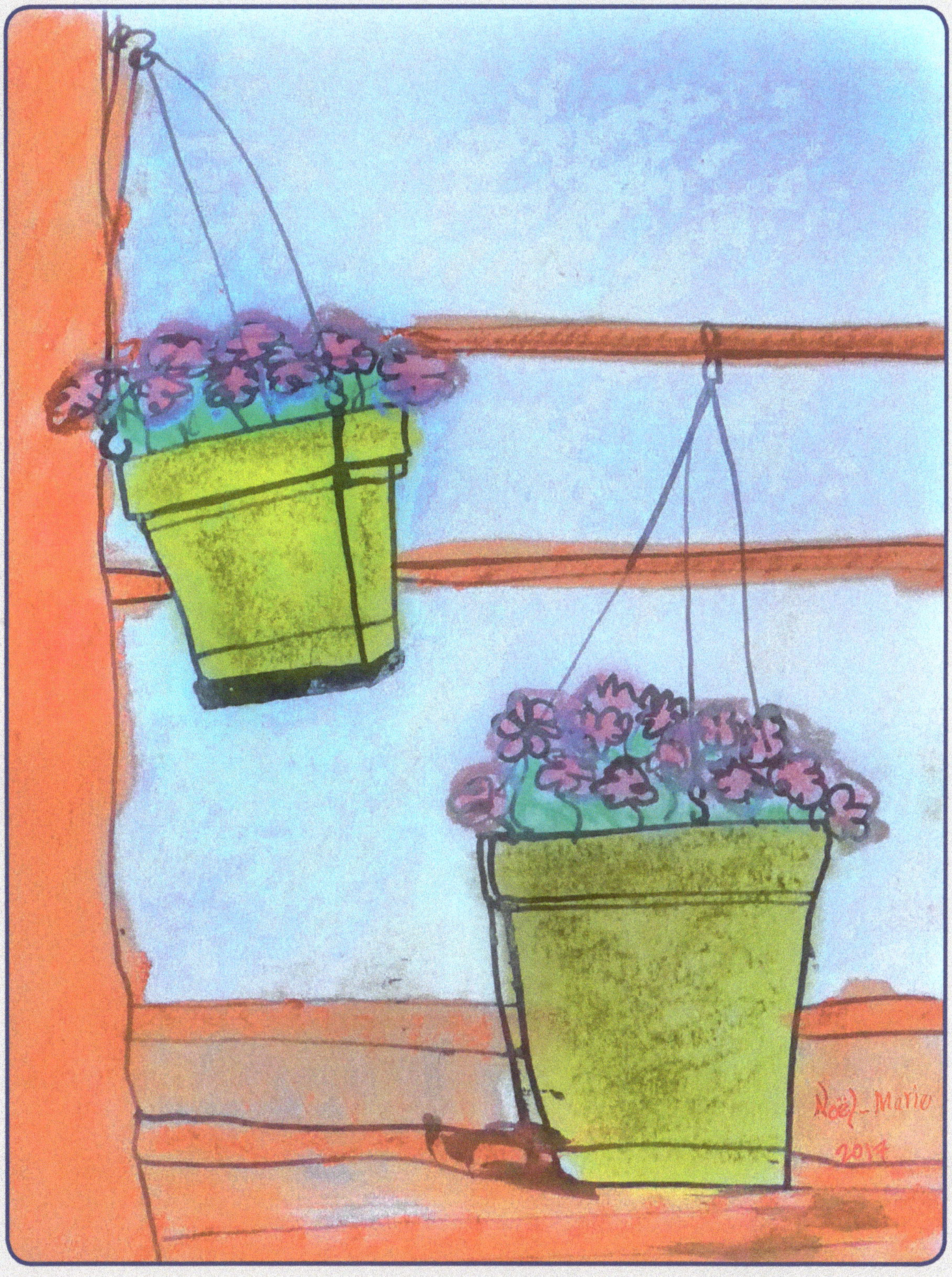

Baskets of blossoms.

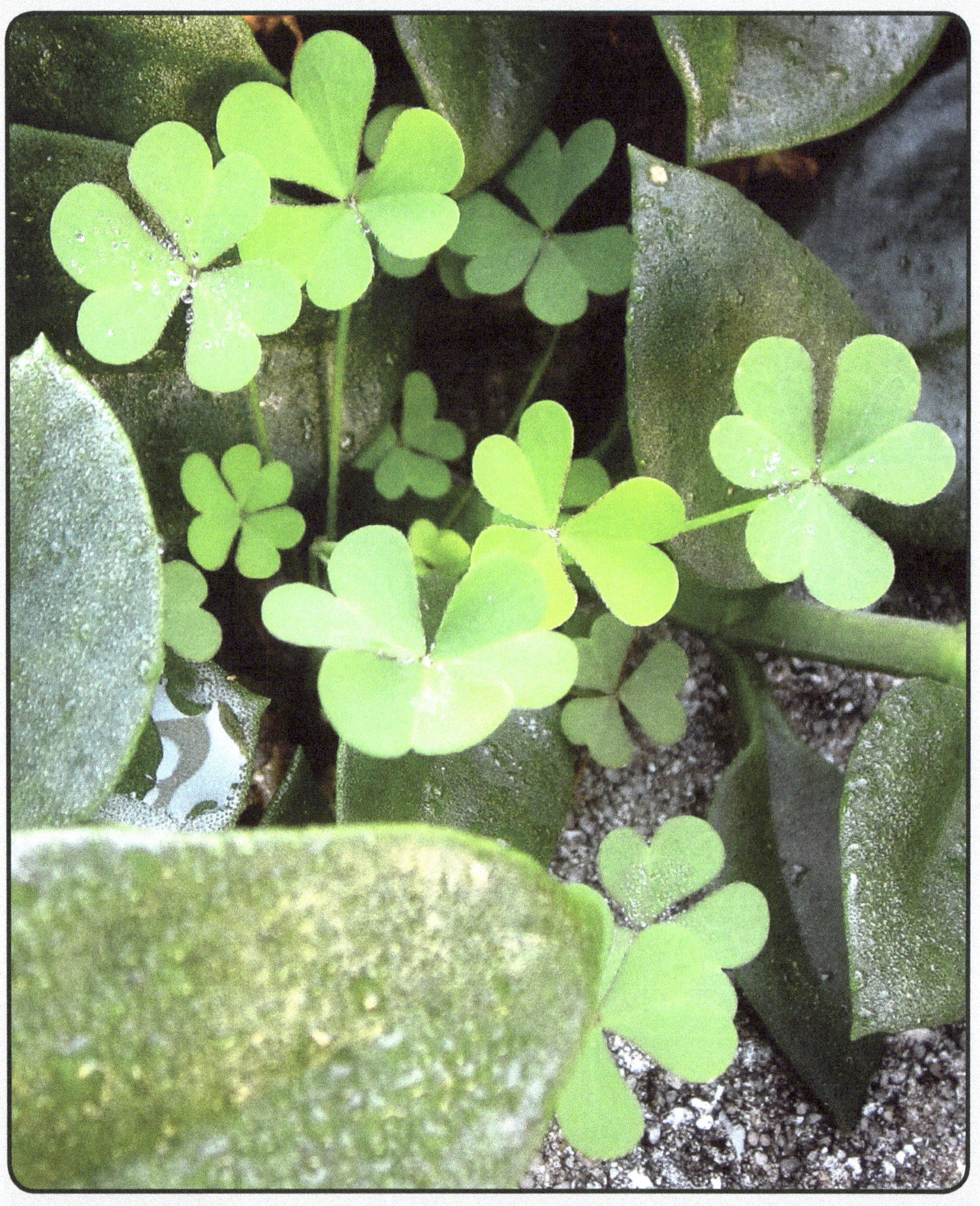

Lucky leaves.

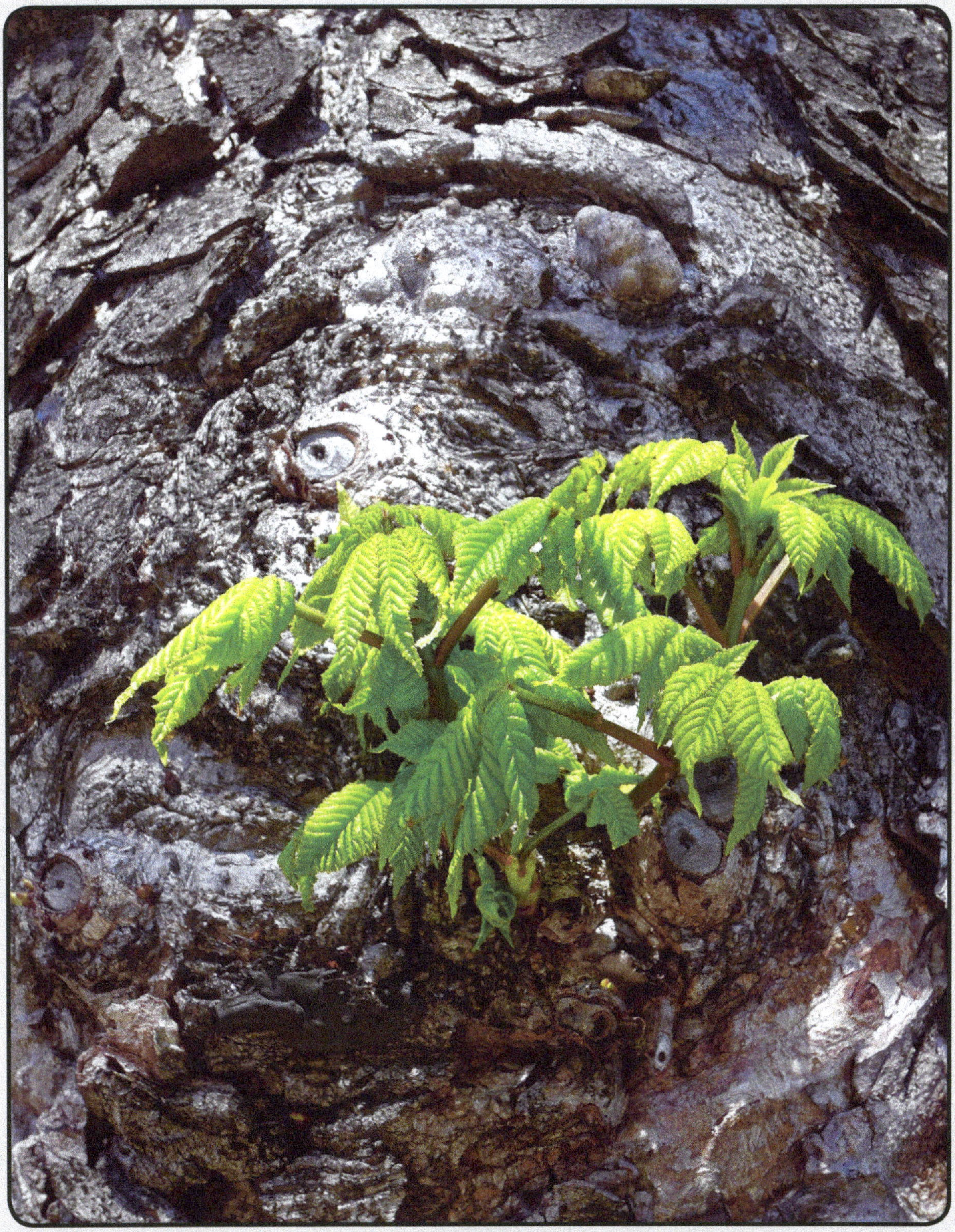

Tree node.

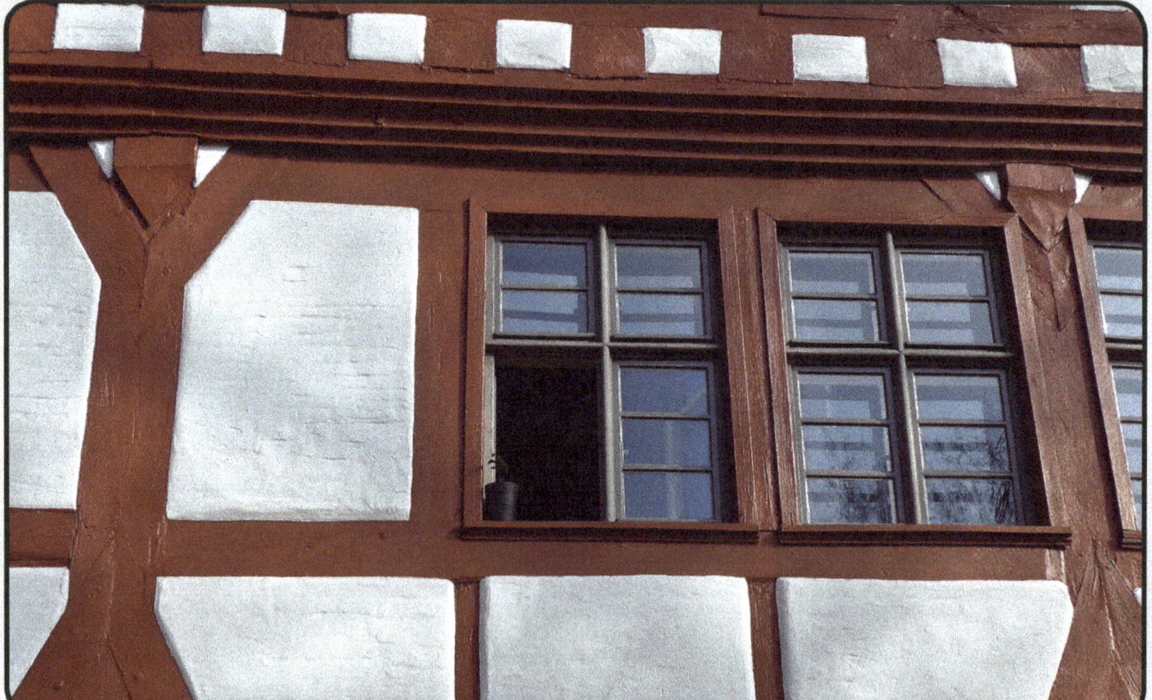

Wishful thinking.

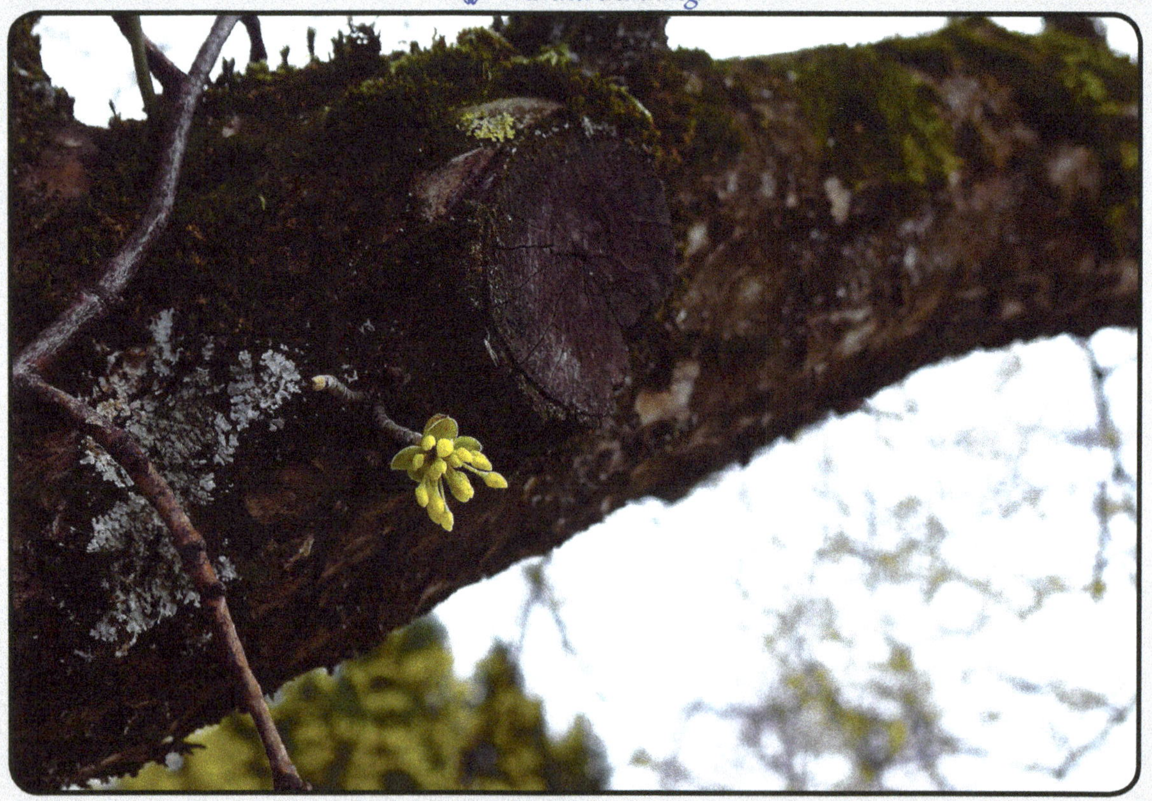

Bark spark.

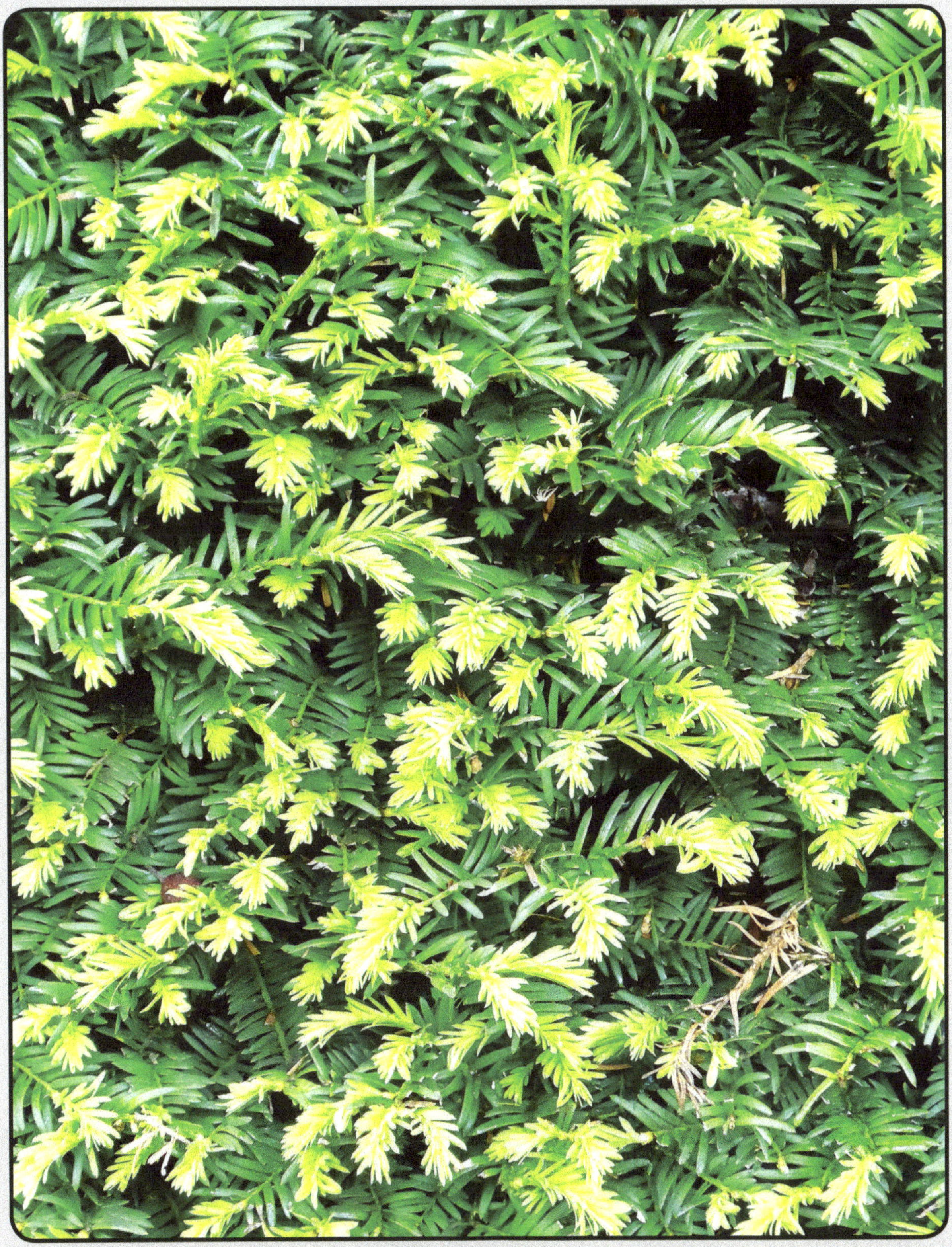

Shades of green.

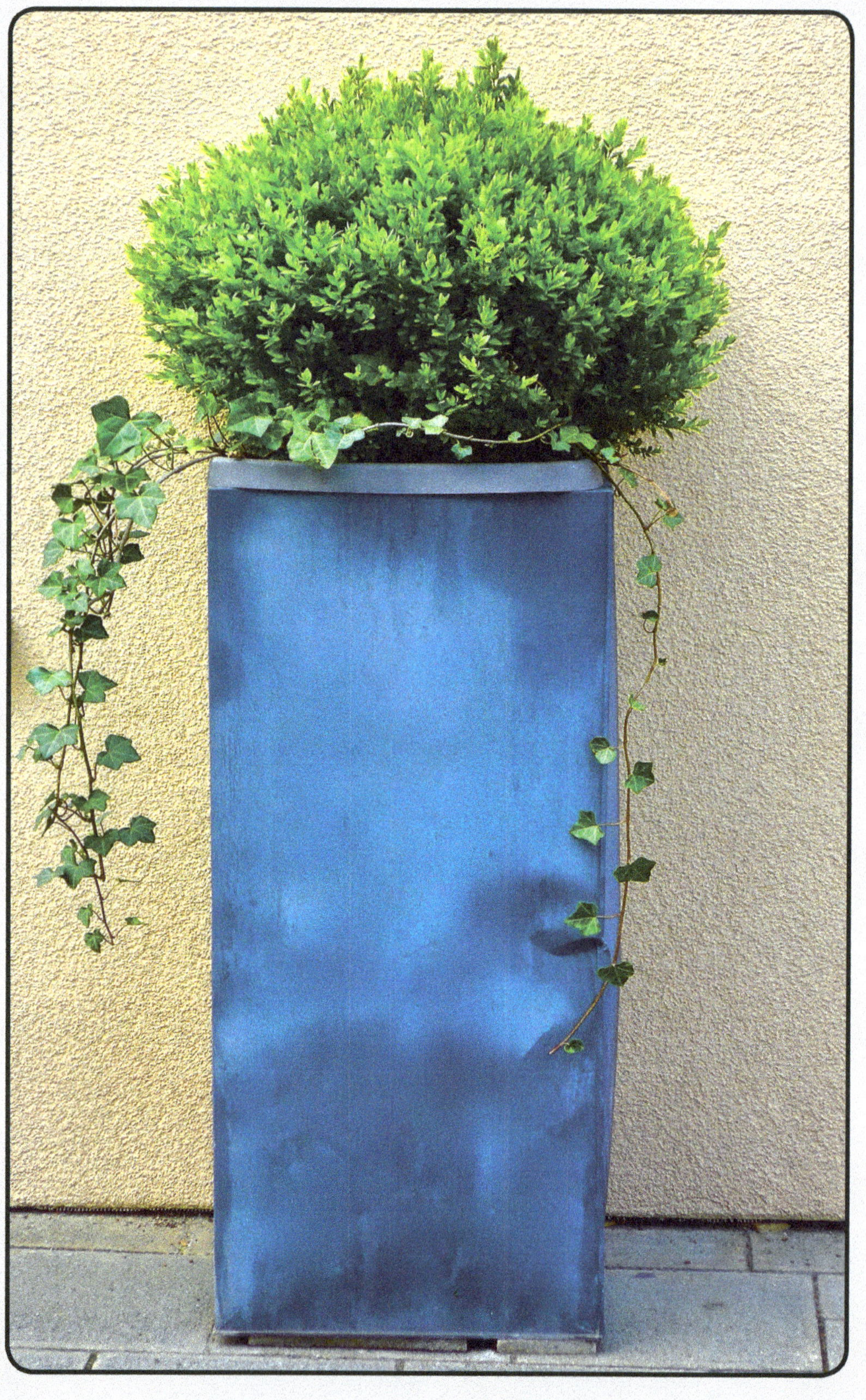

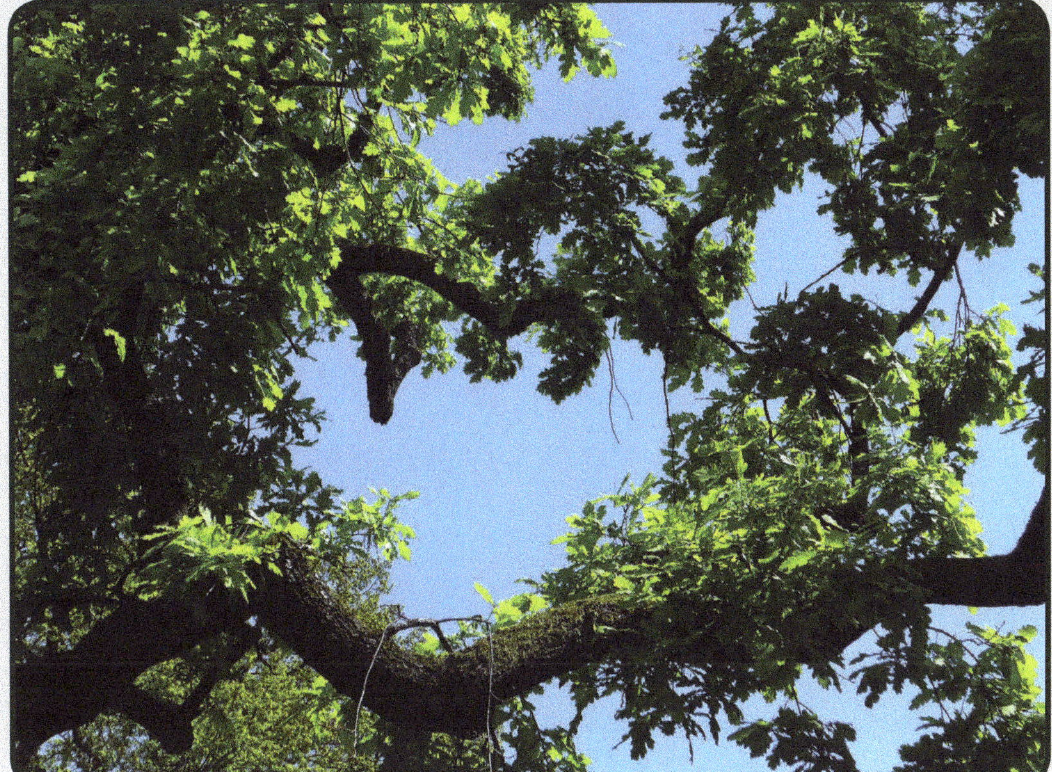

Place of rest.

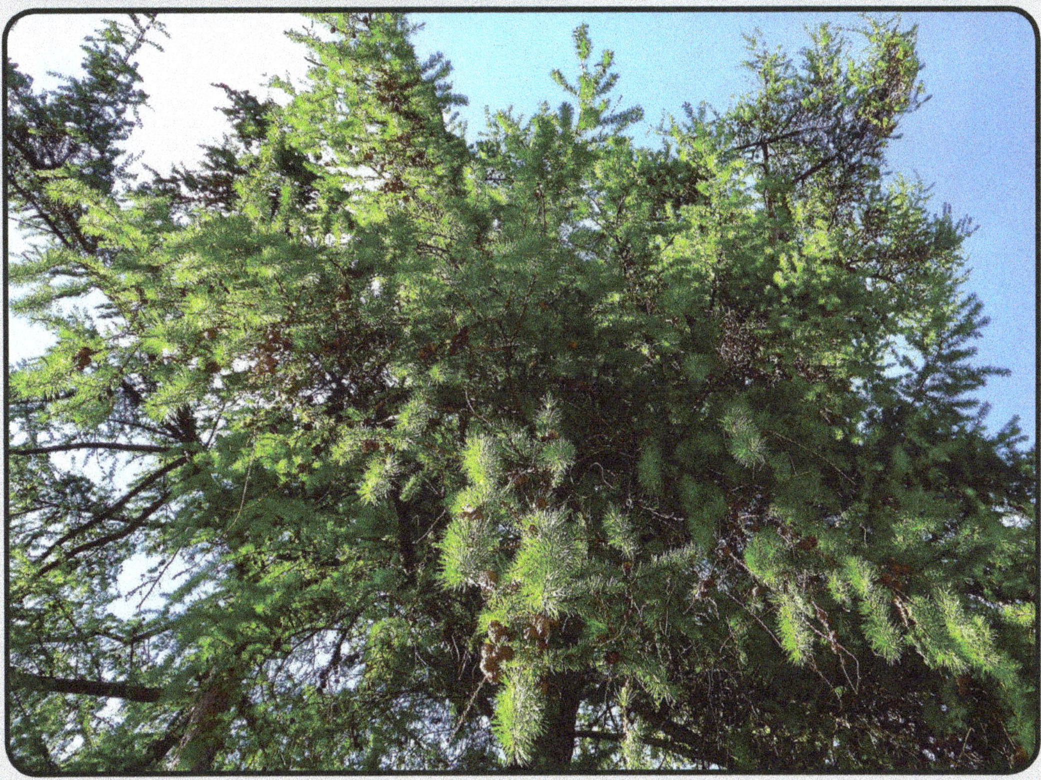

Upward gaze.

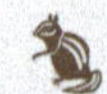

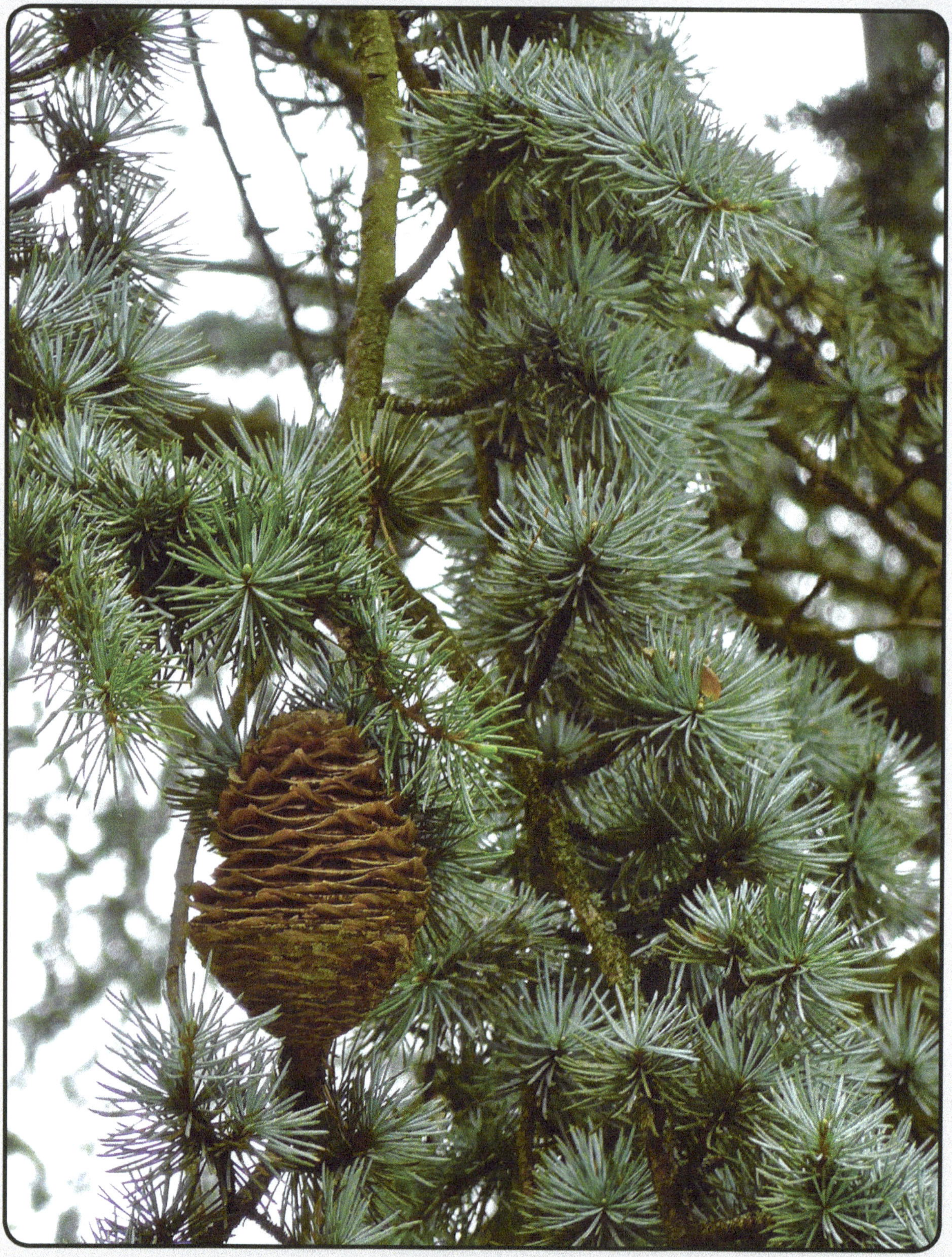

Nature's rattle.

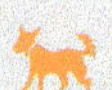

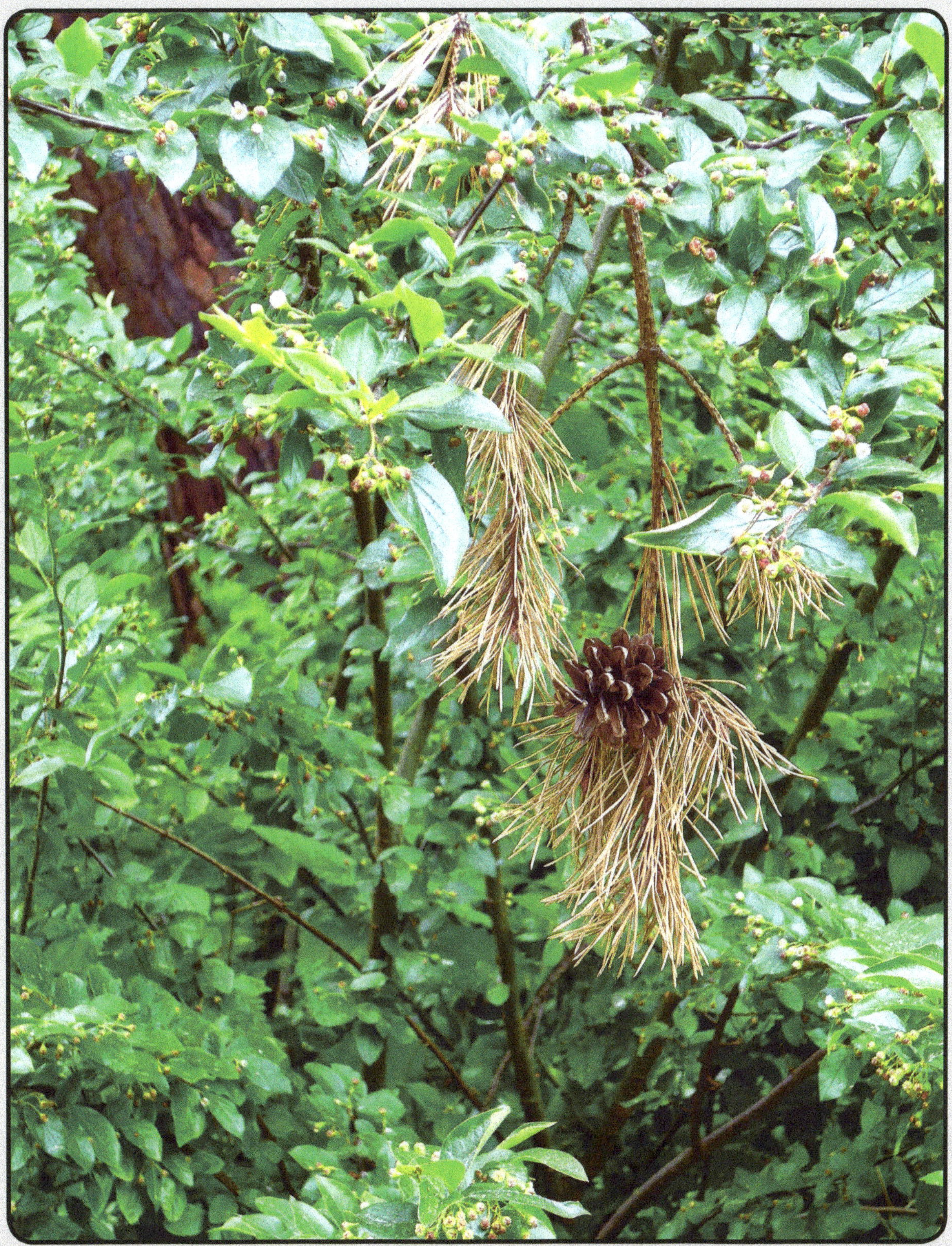

Fallen branch in a graveyard.

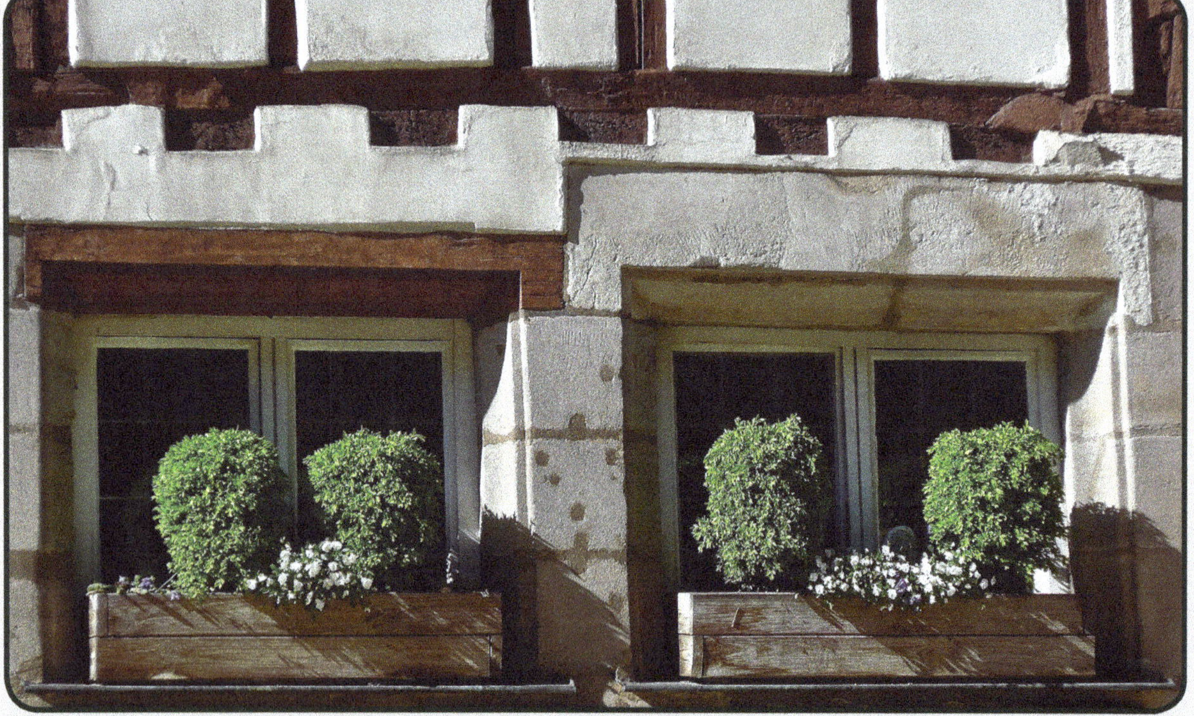

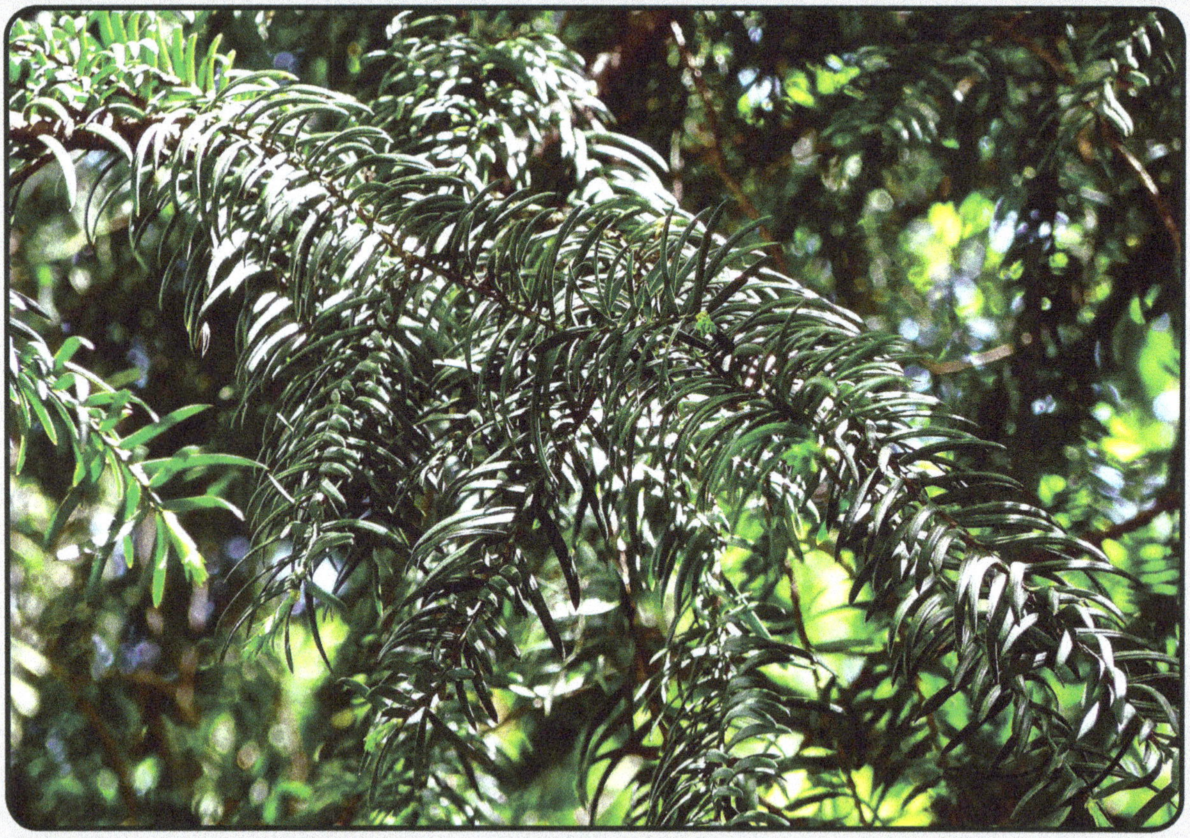

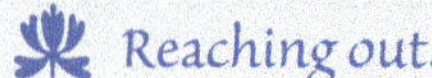
Reaching out.

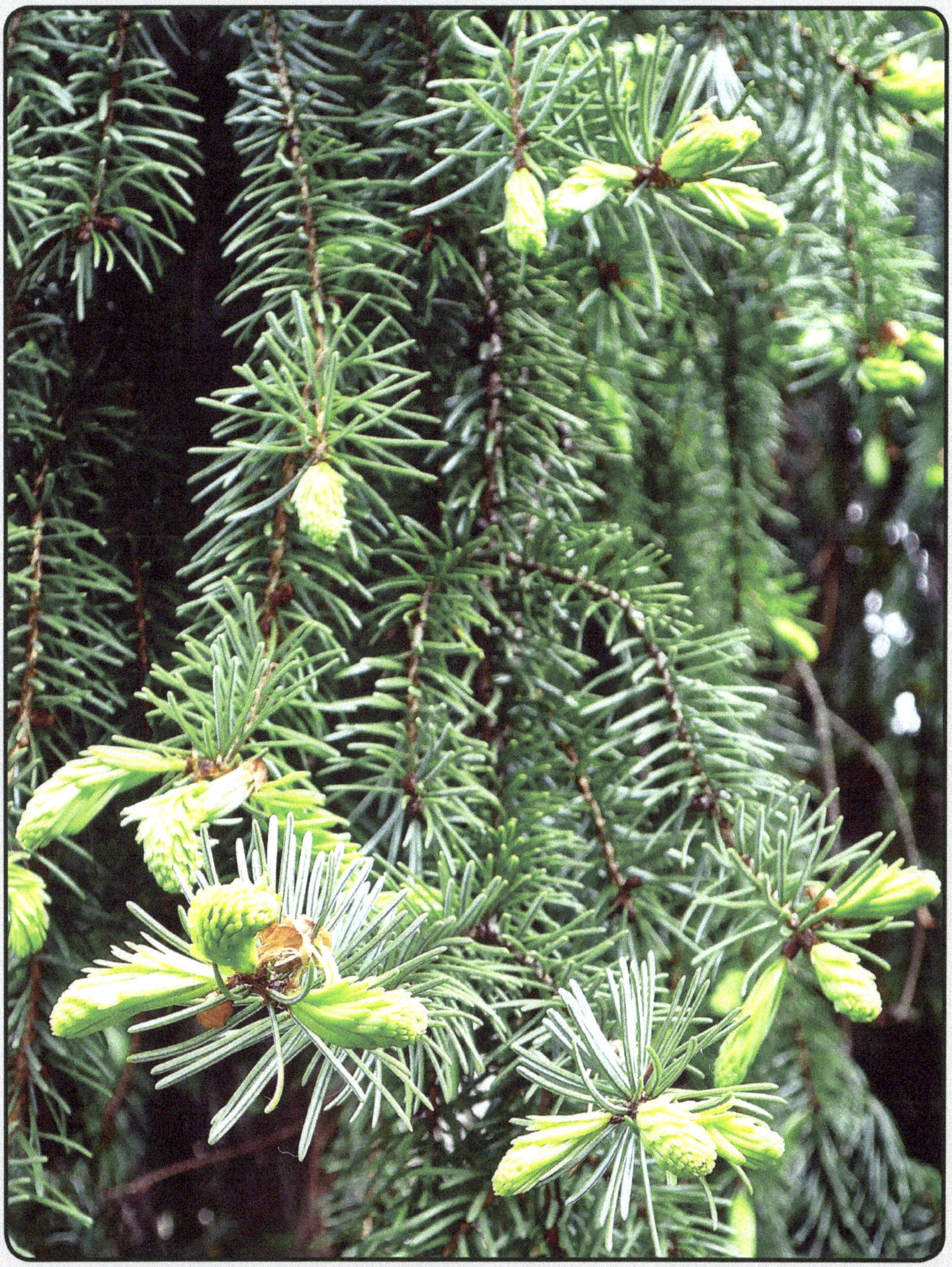

 Ornaments.

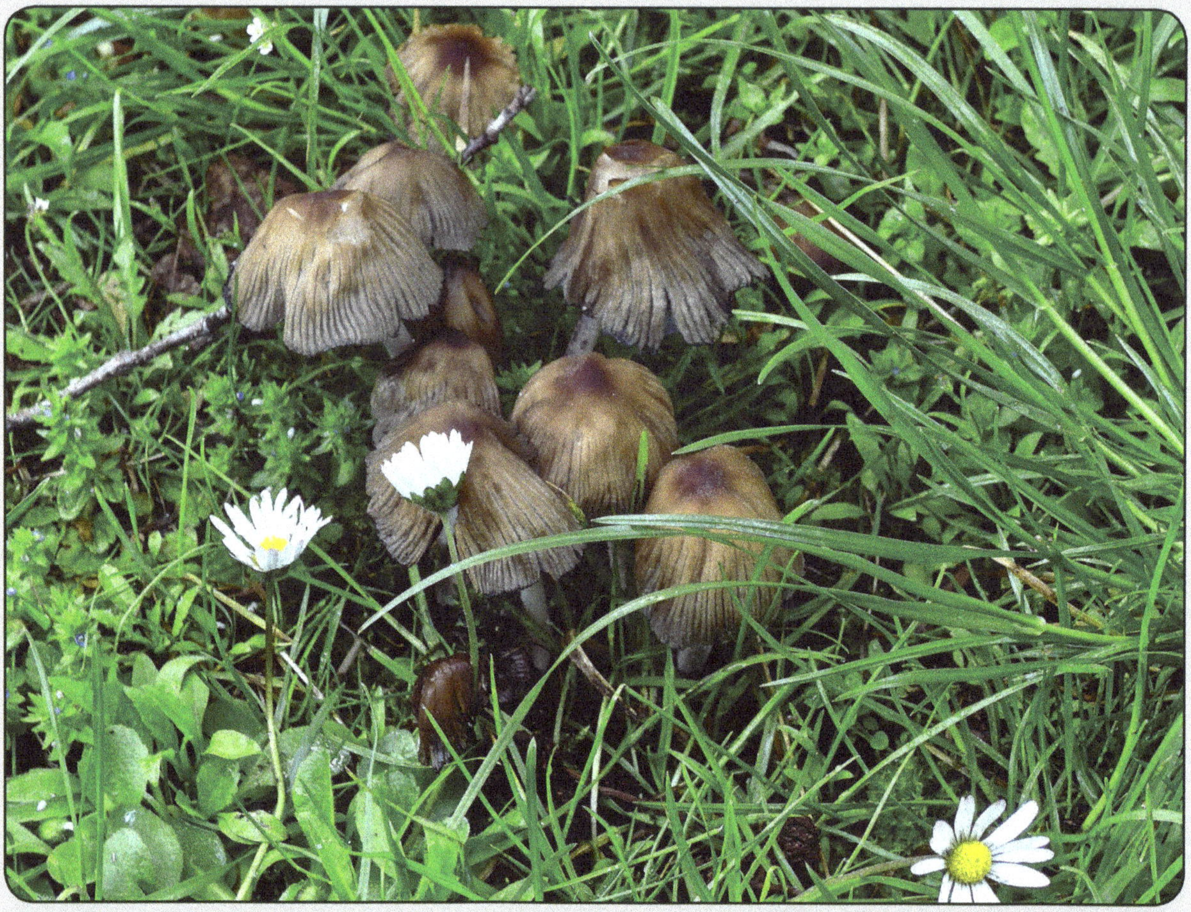

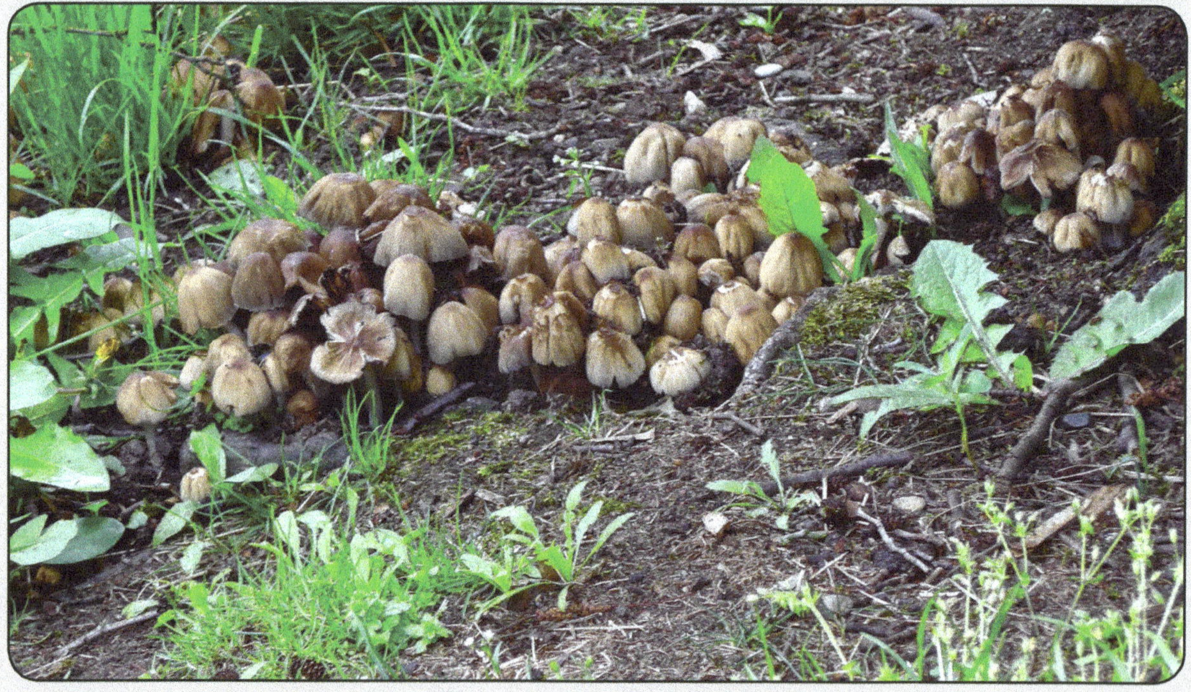

Mushroom village series.

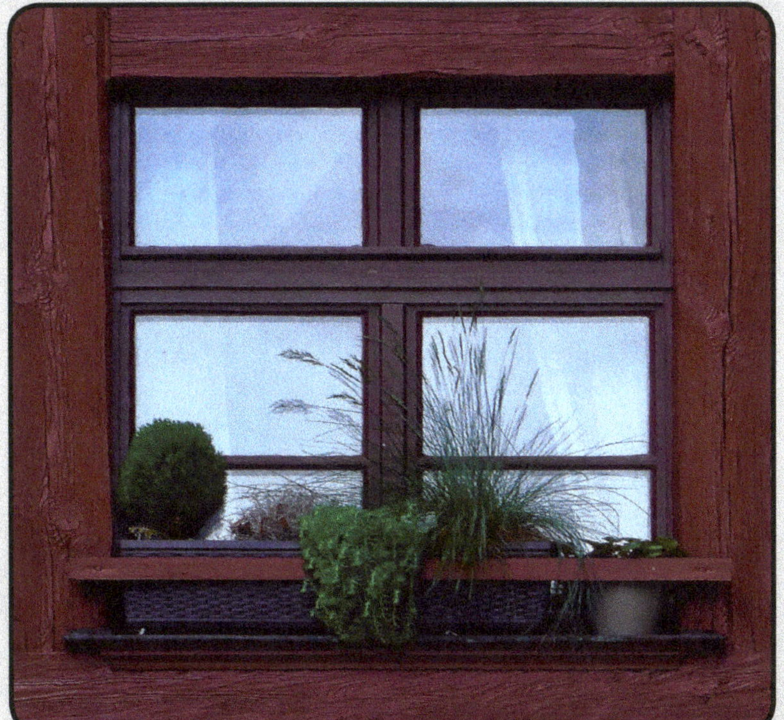

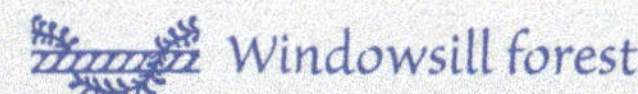

Windowsill forest.

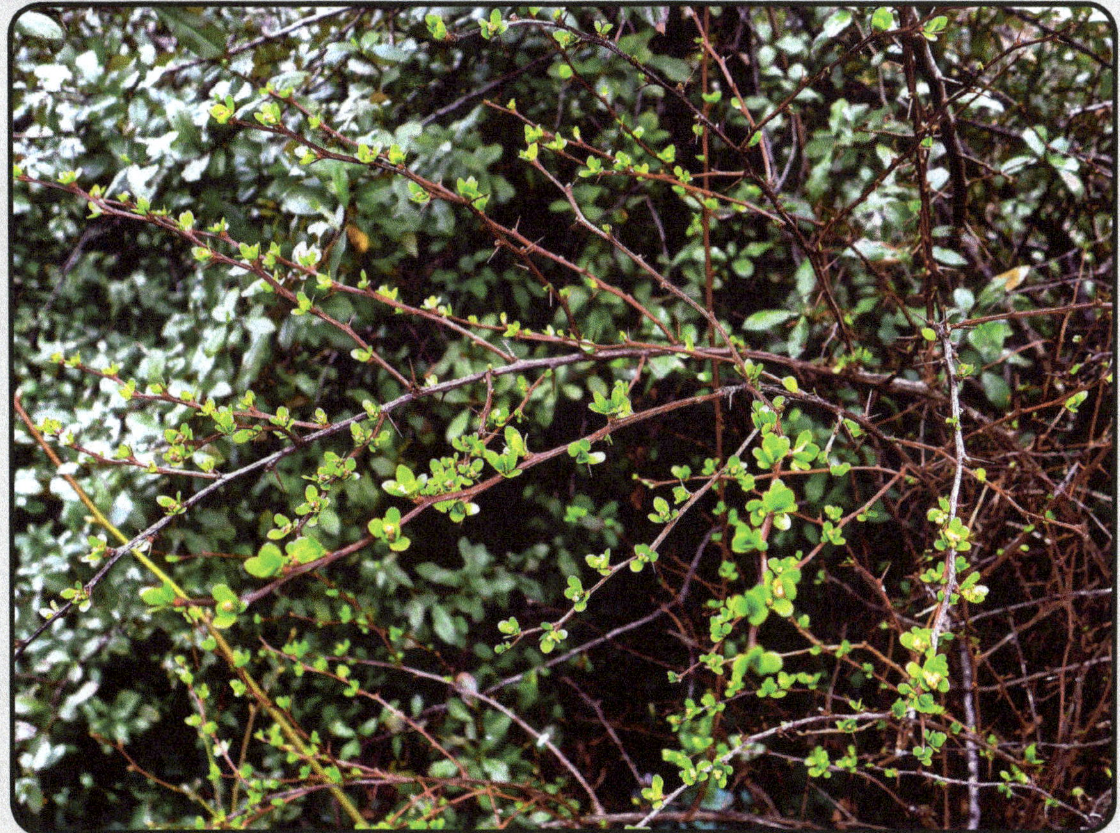

Crimson thicket.

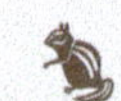

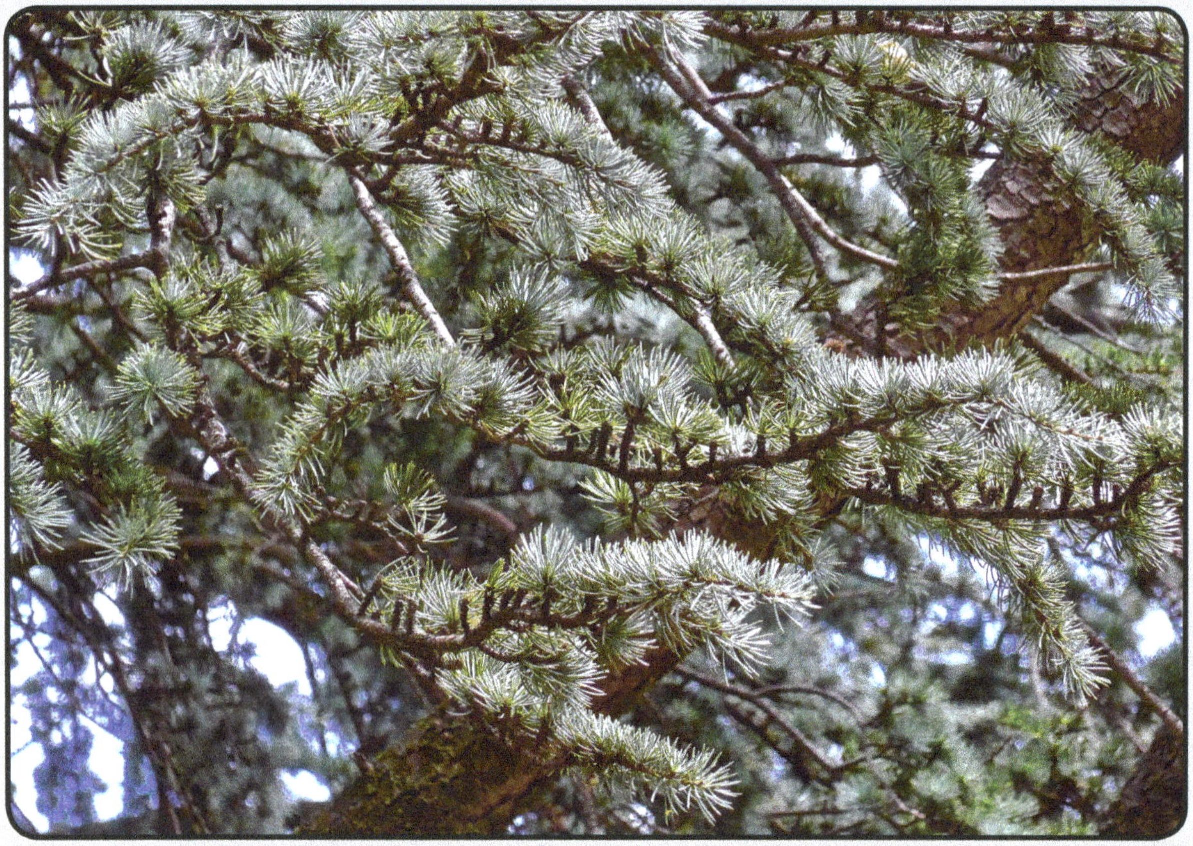

Silver fox.

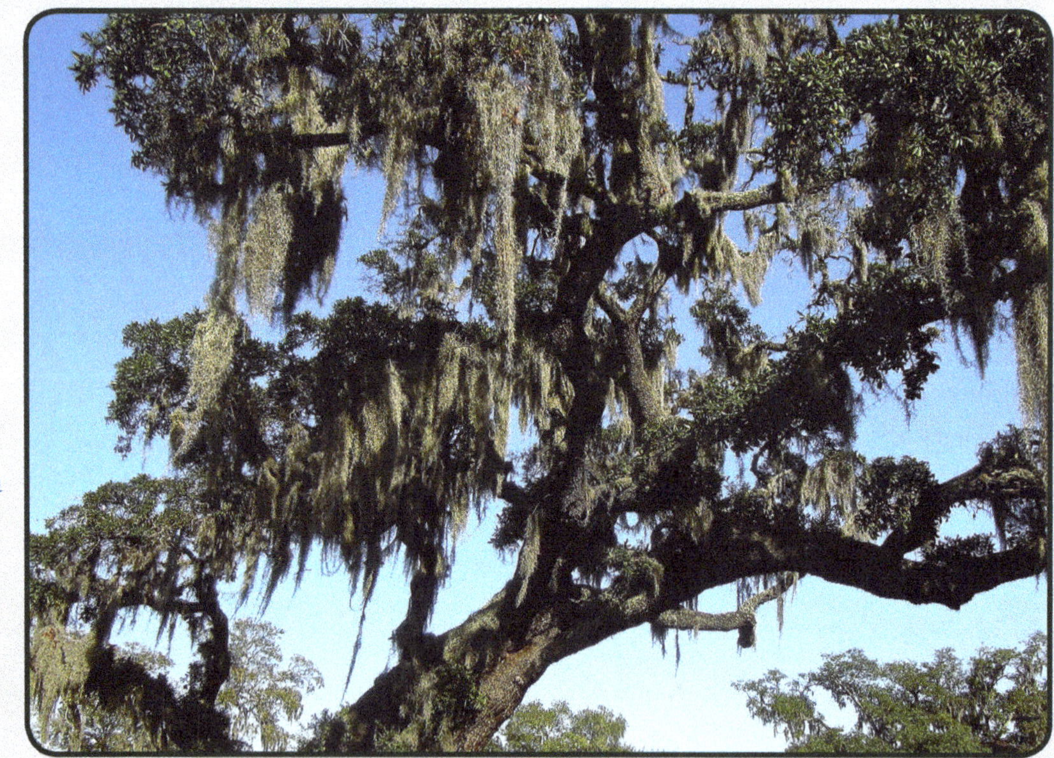

Spanish mane.

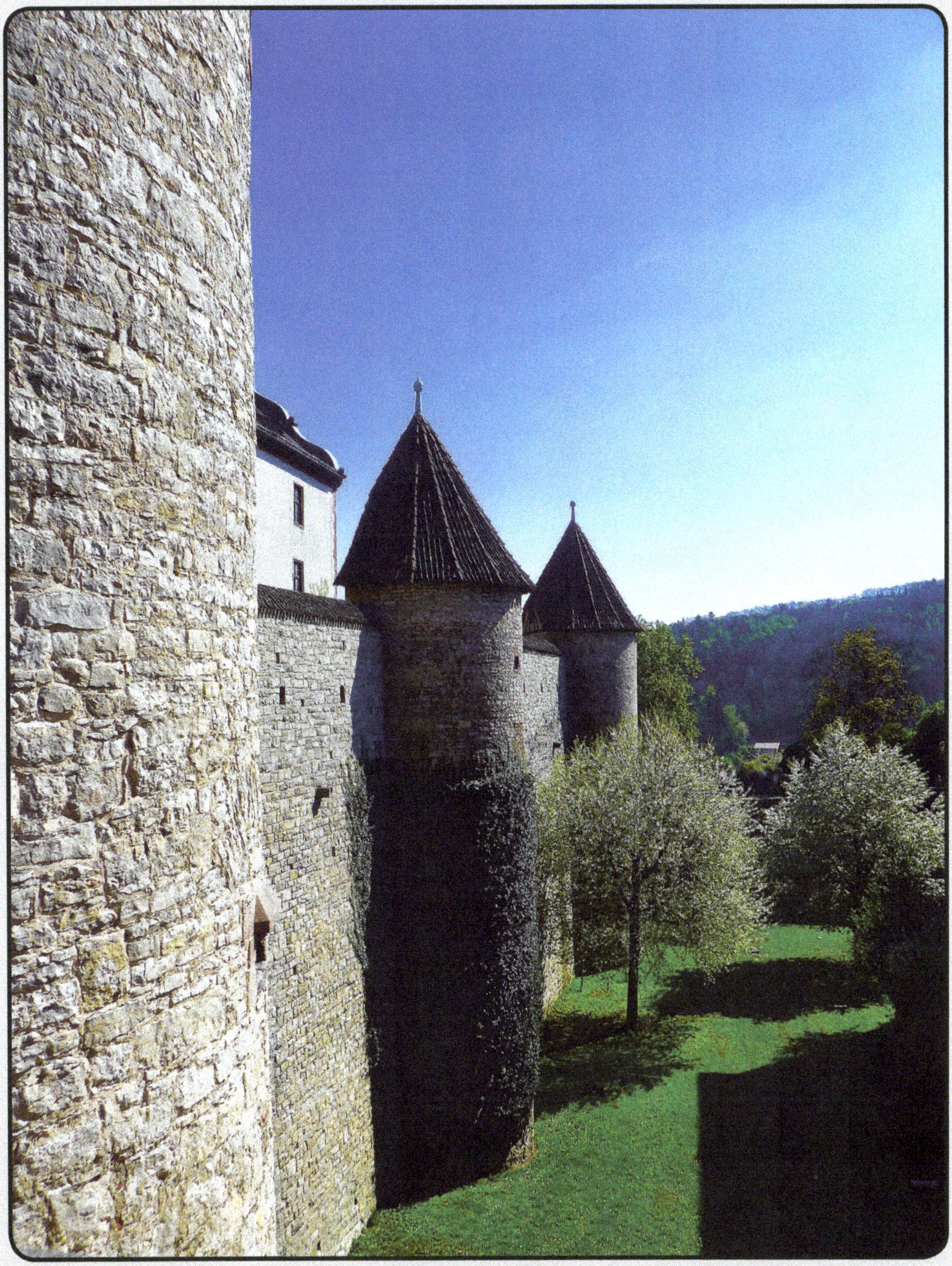

Arbor moat.

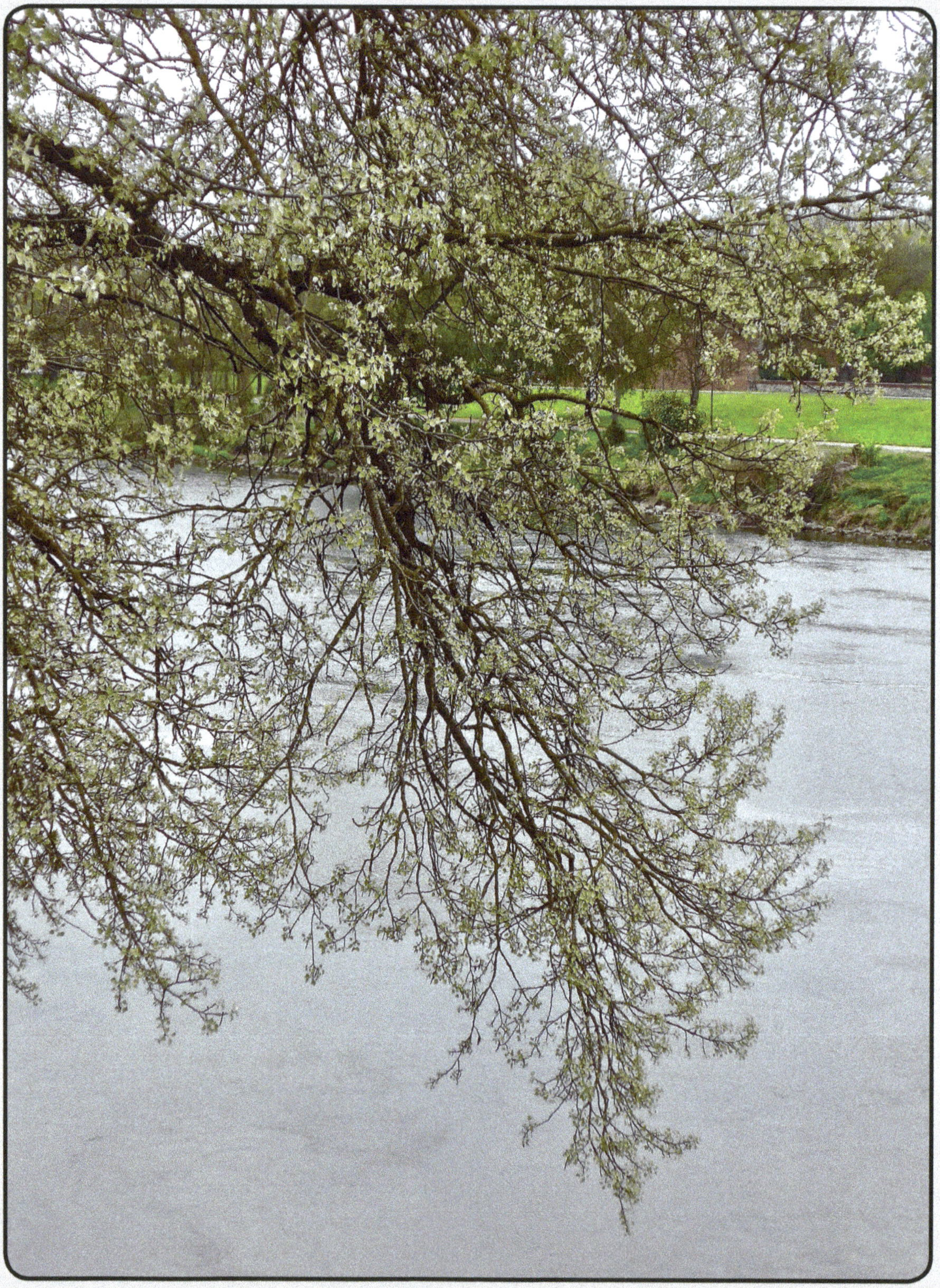

Lace leaves.

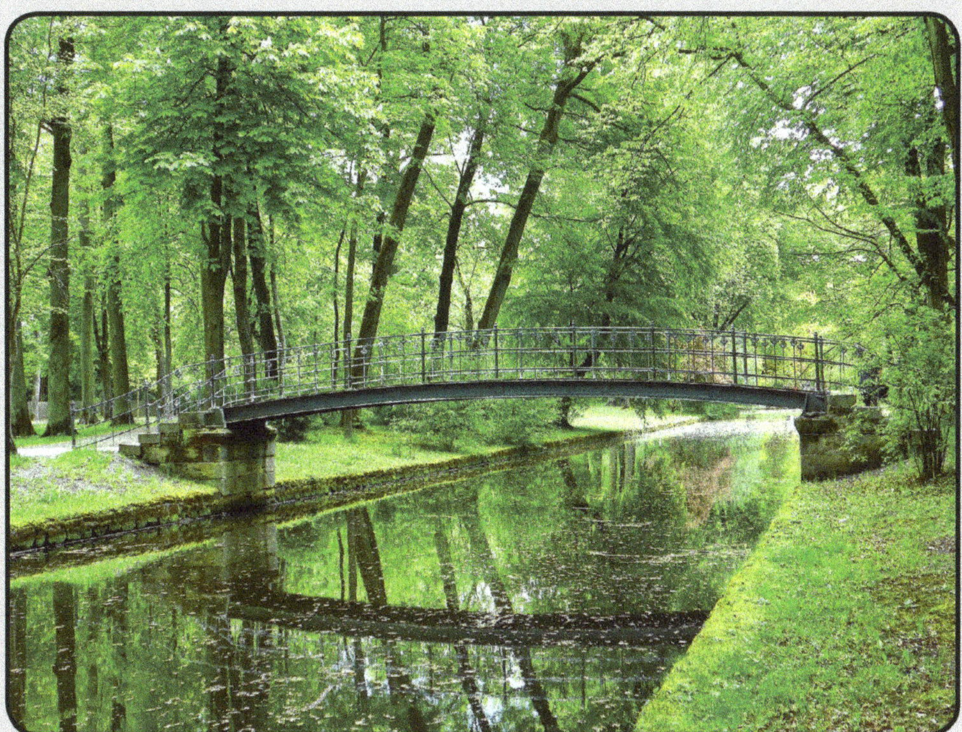

Tranquility.

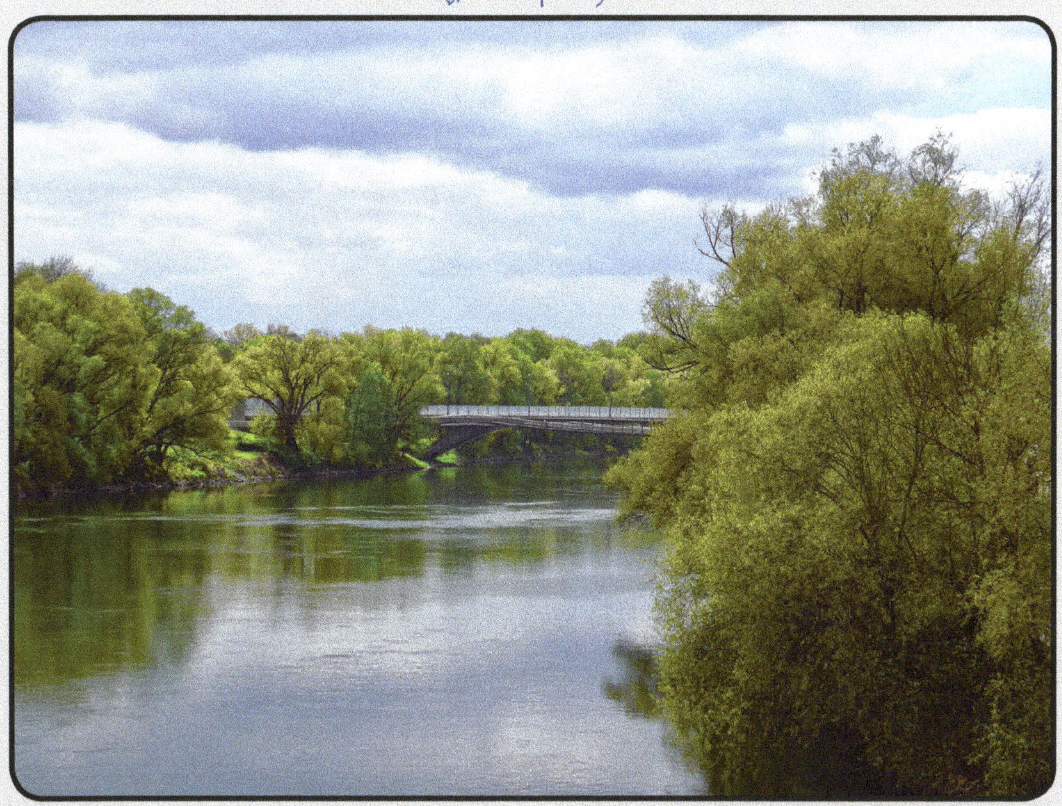

Danube reflections.

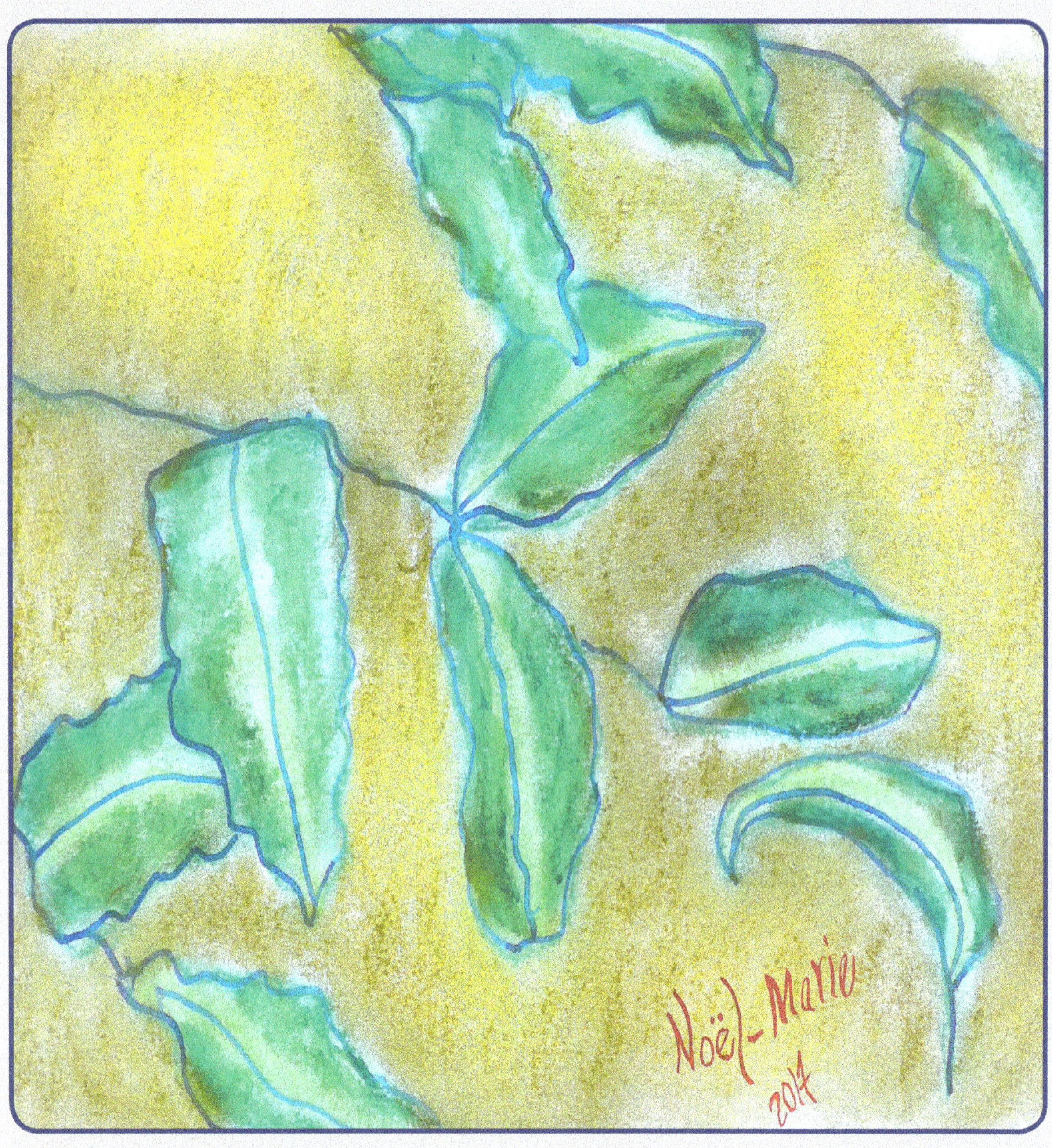


Study in teal.

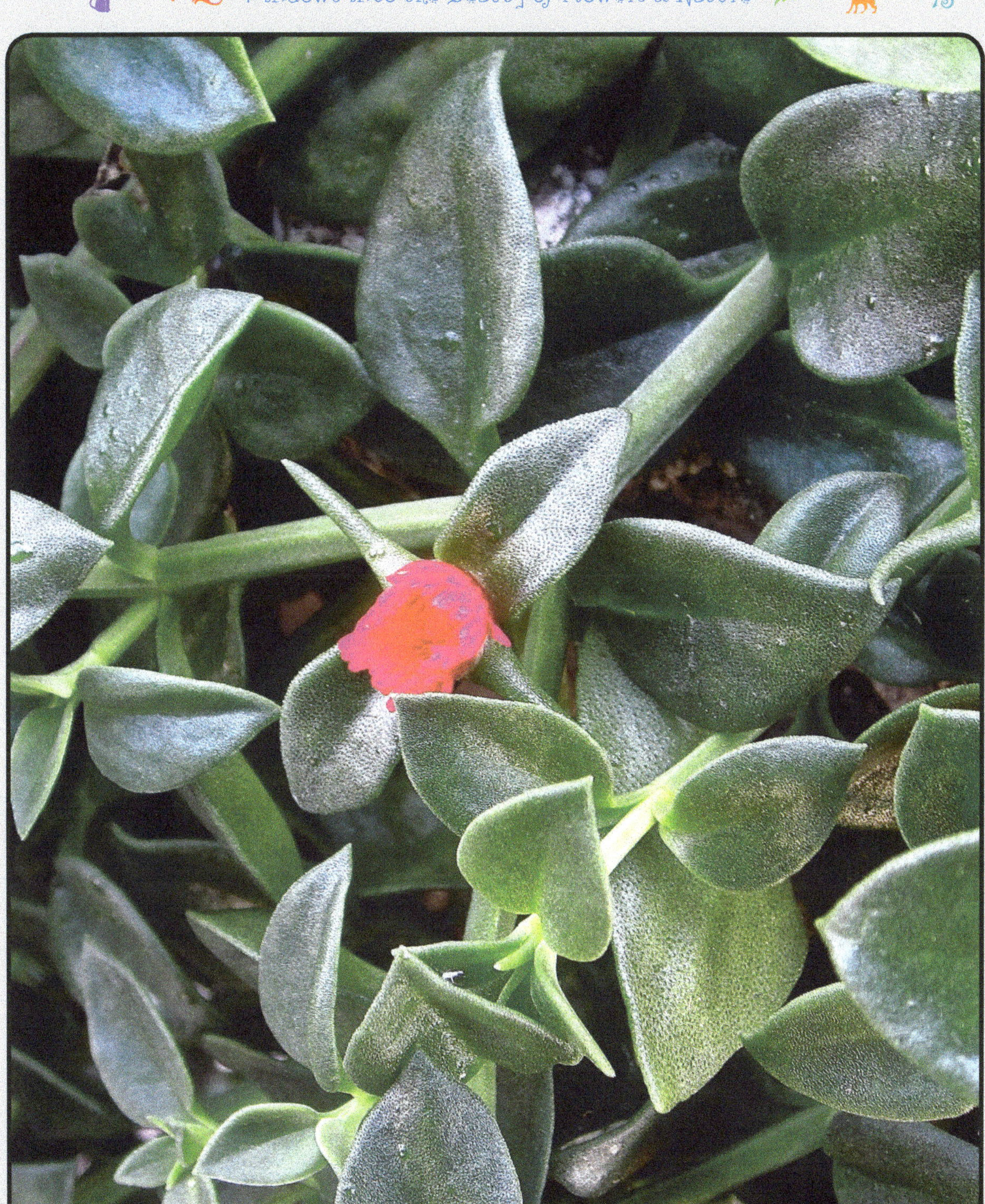

Tiny voice.

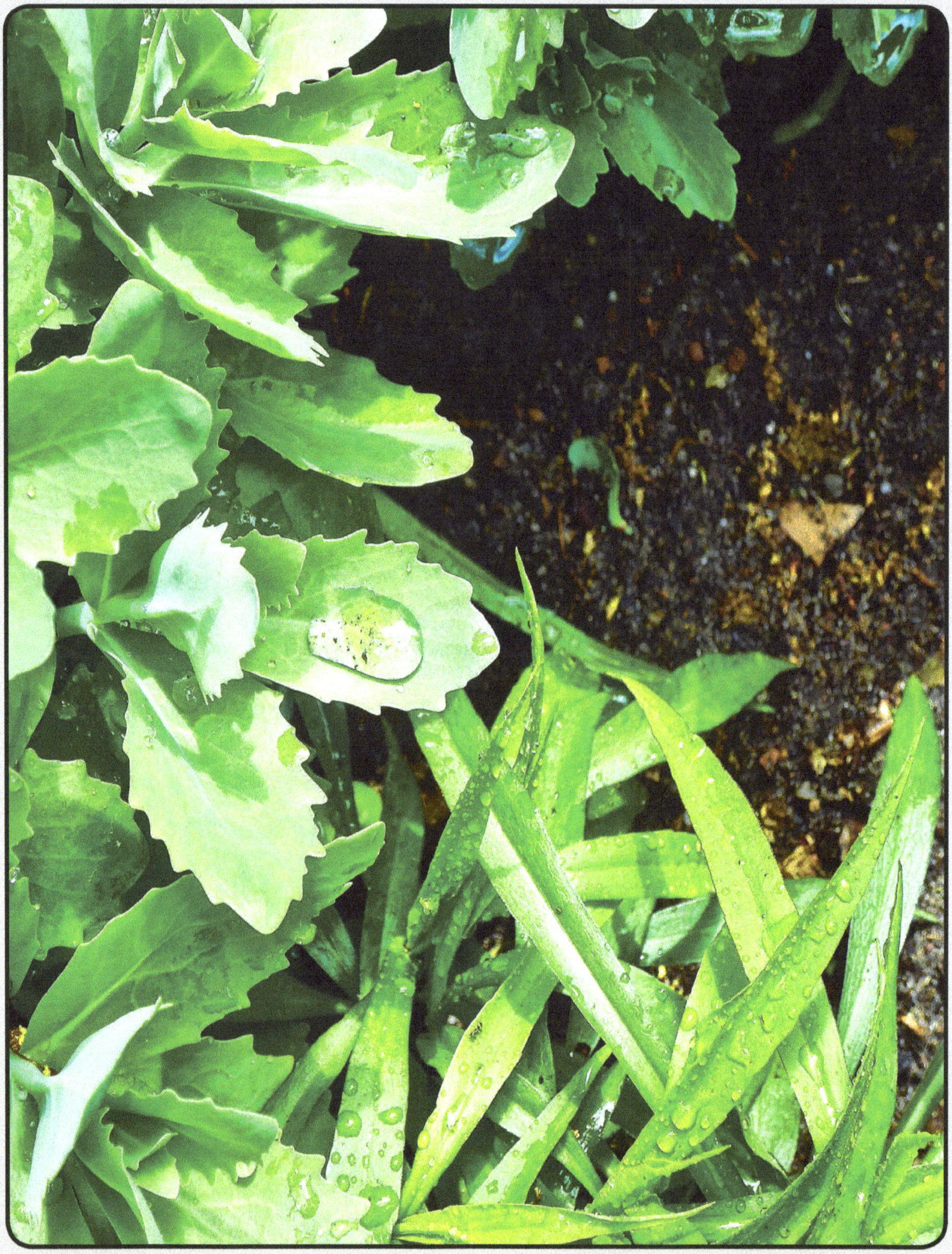

A realm within a rain droplet.

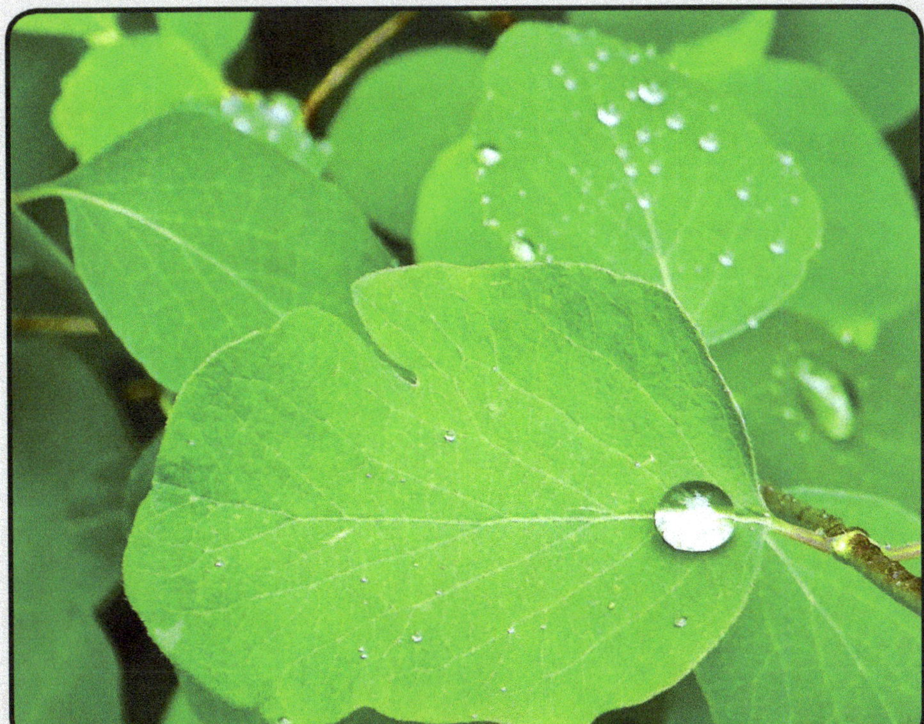

Teardrop.

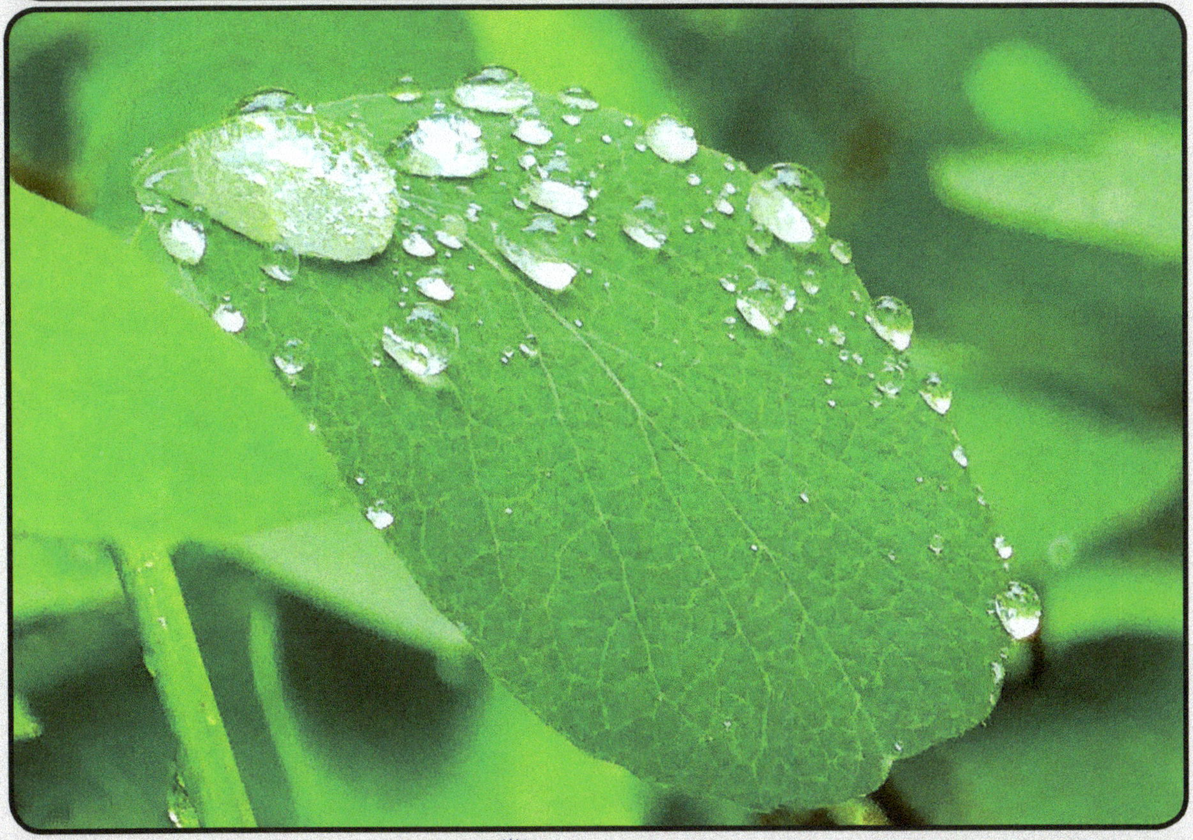

Priceless jewels.

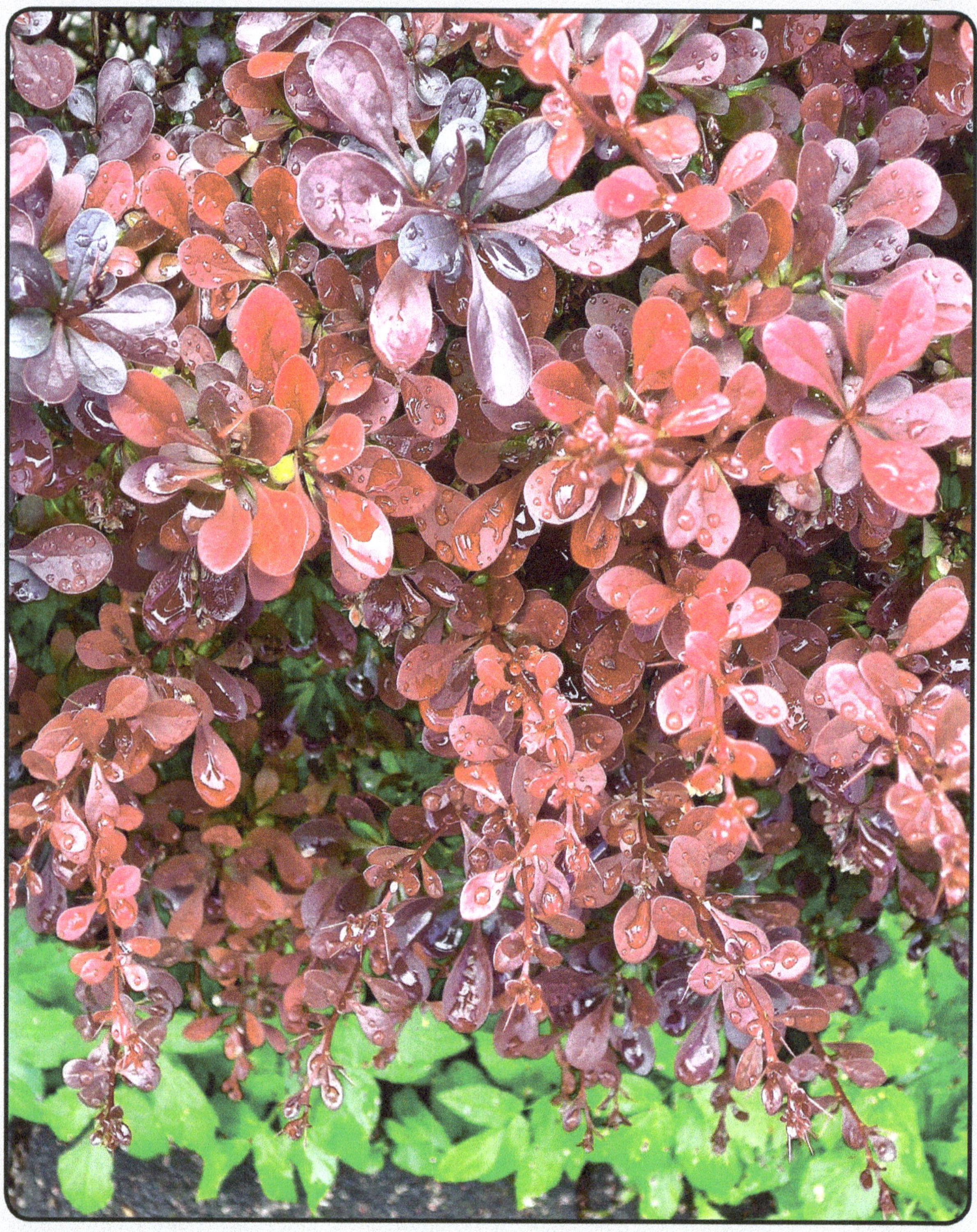

Ruby crystals.

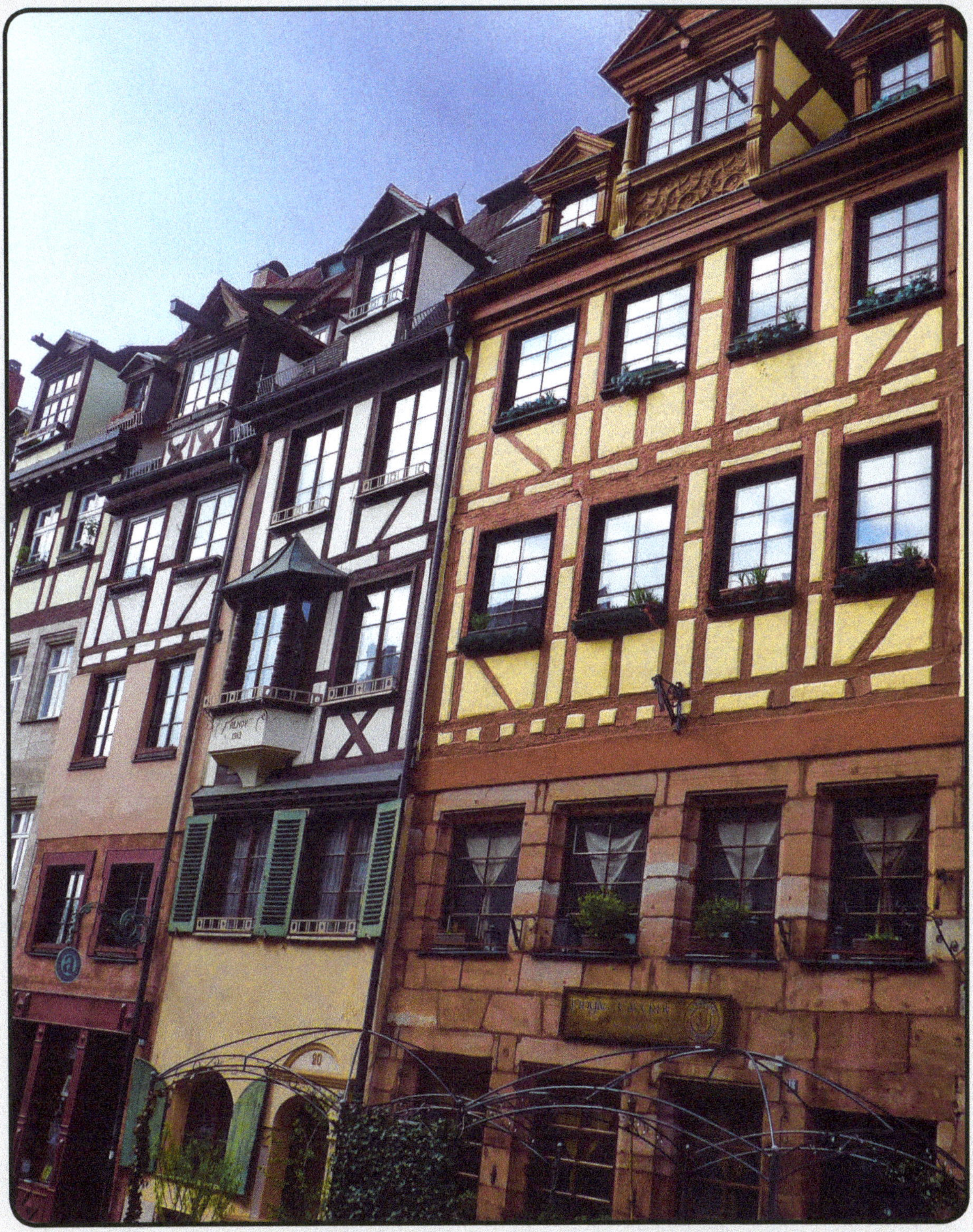

Nürnberg window shrubbery.

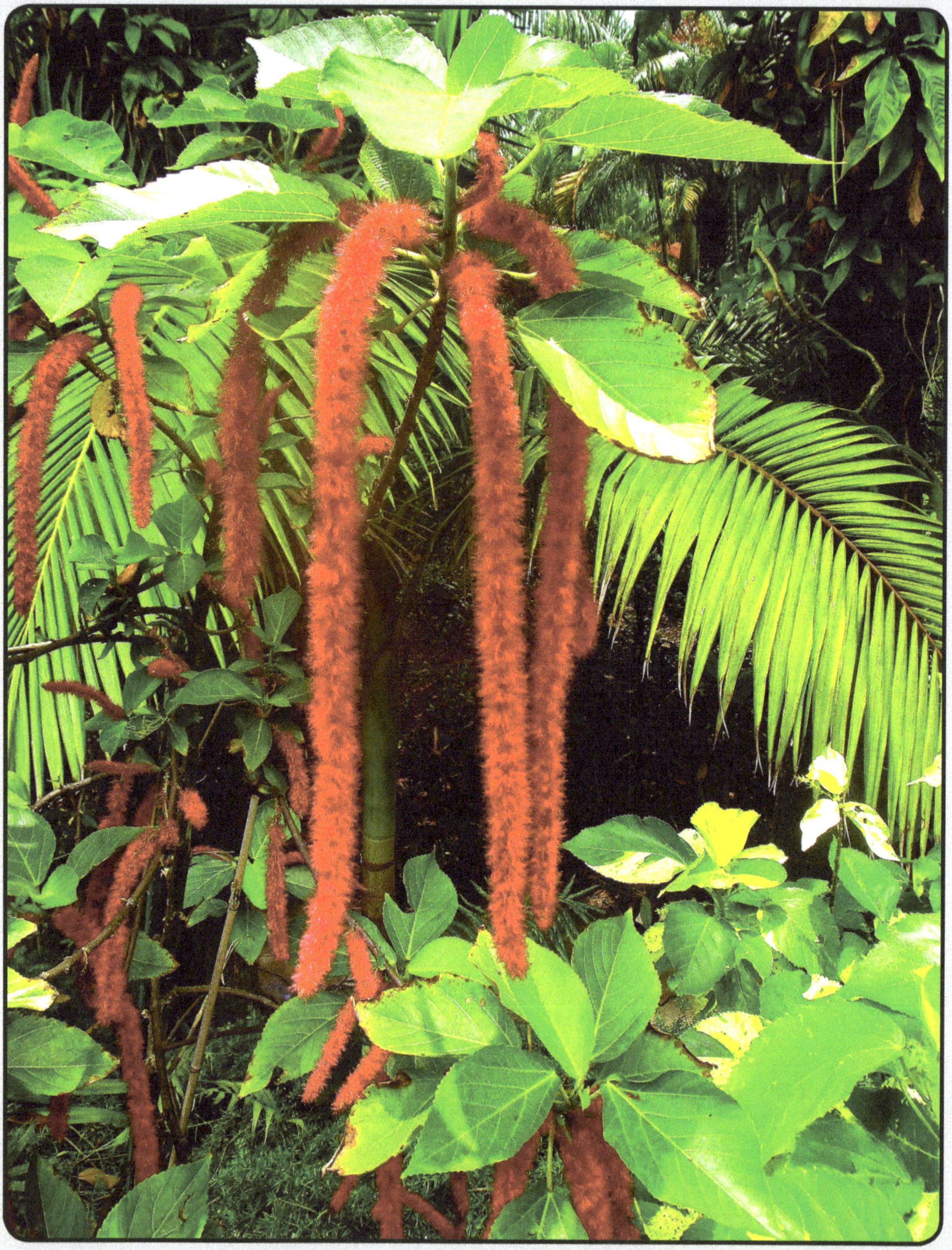

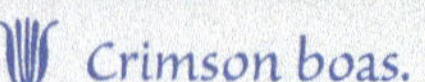

Crimson boas.

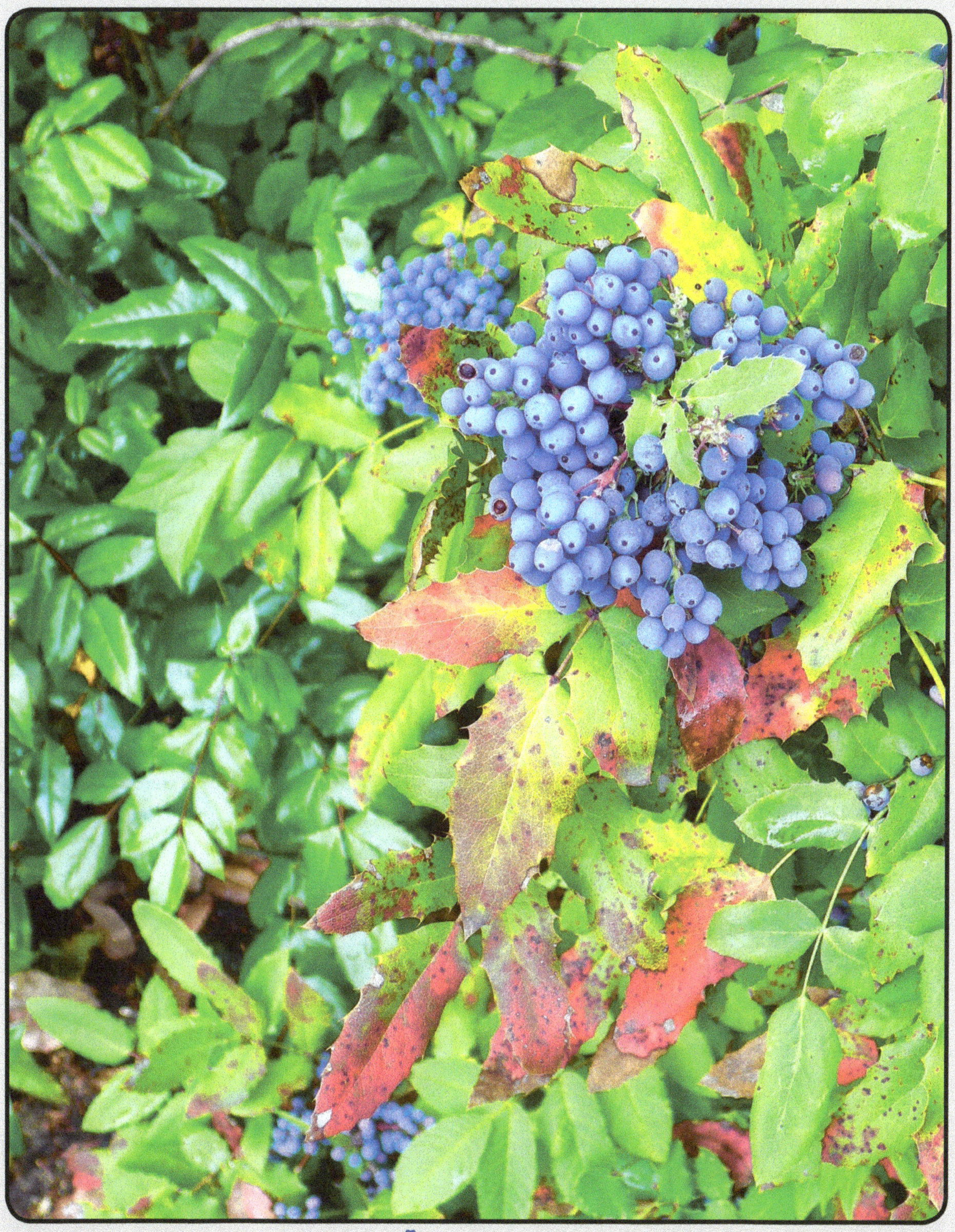

Concord hues.

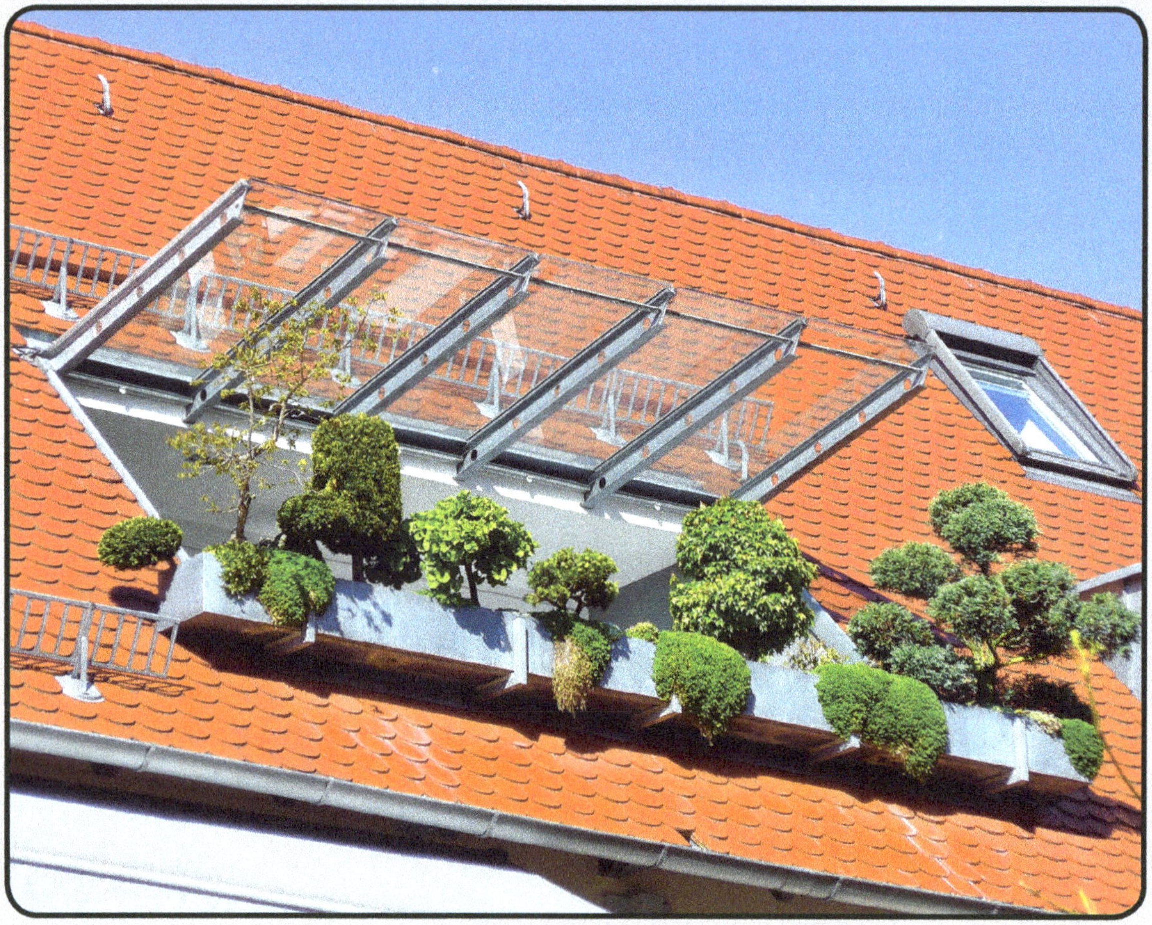

Rooftop forest.

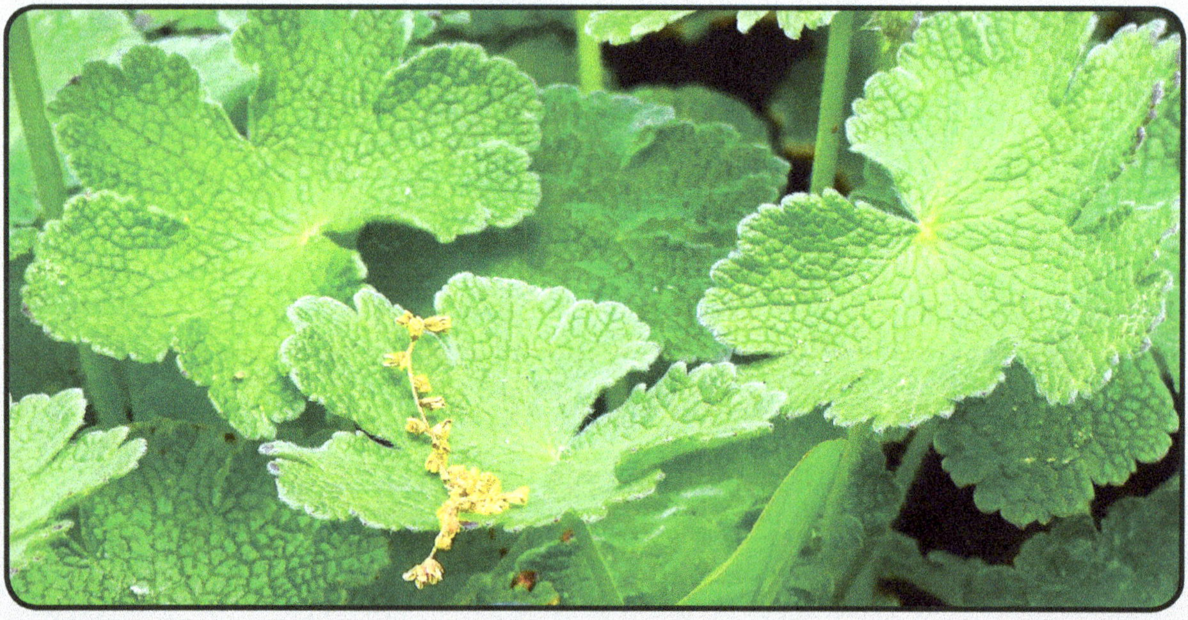

Fairy bracelet.

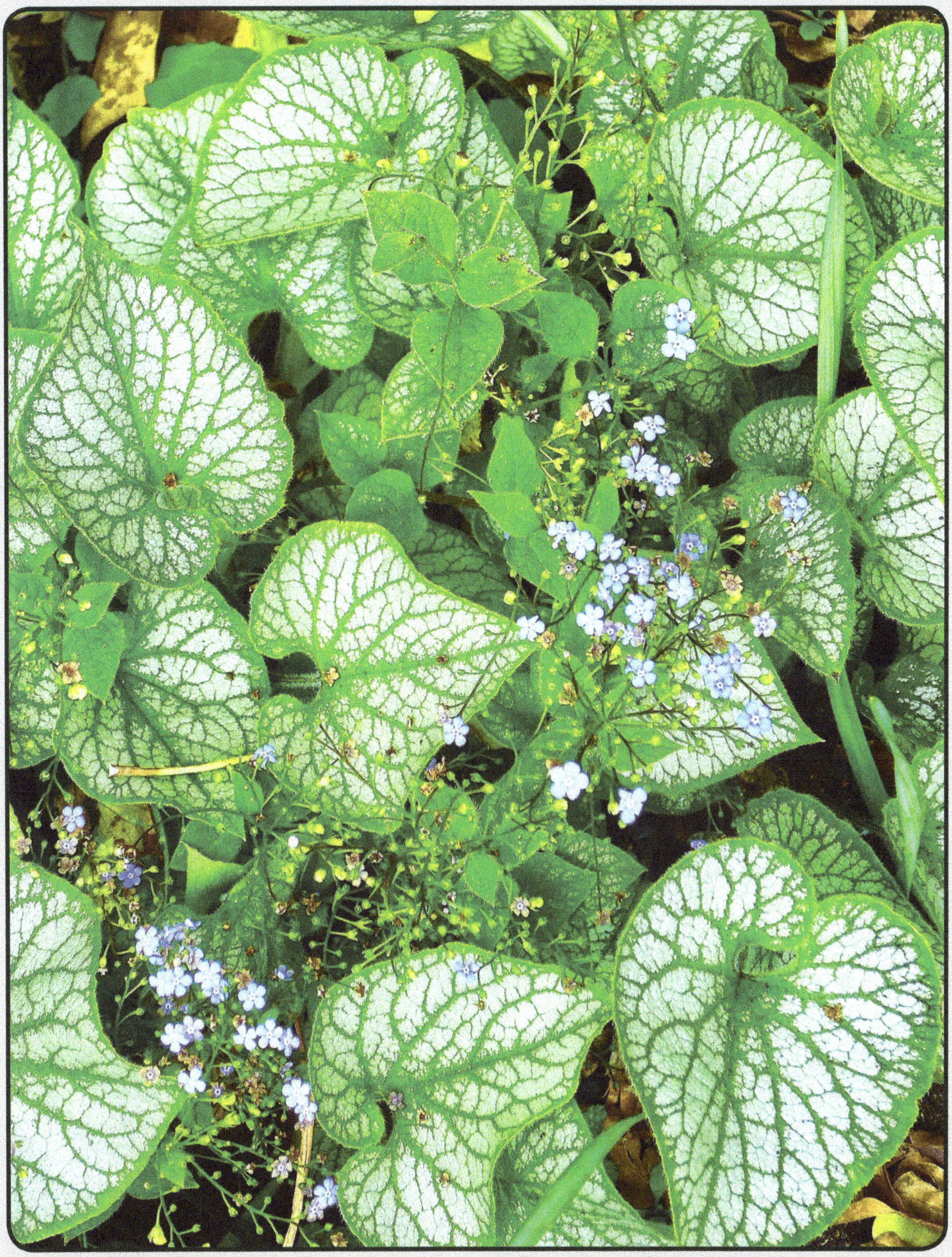

❀ Bouquet of hearts.

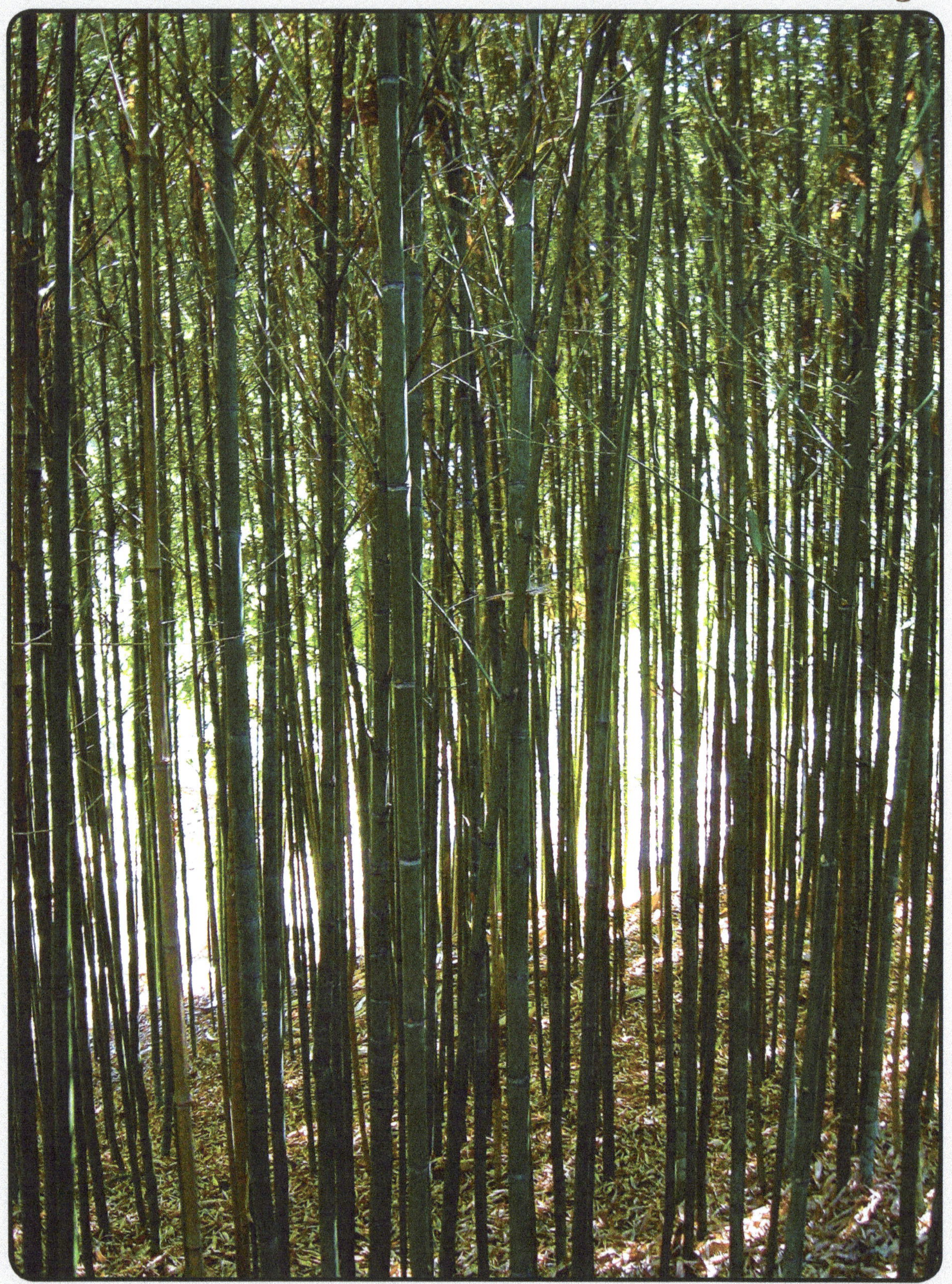

Panda's delight.

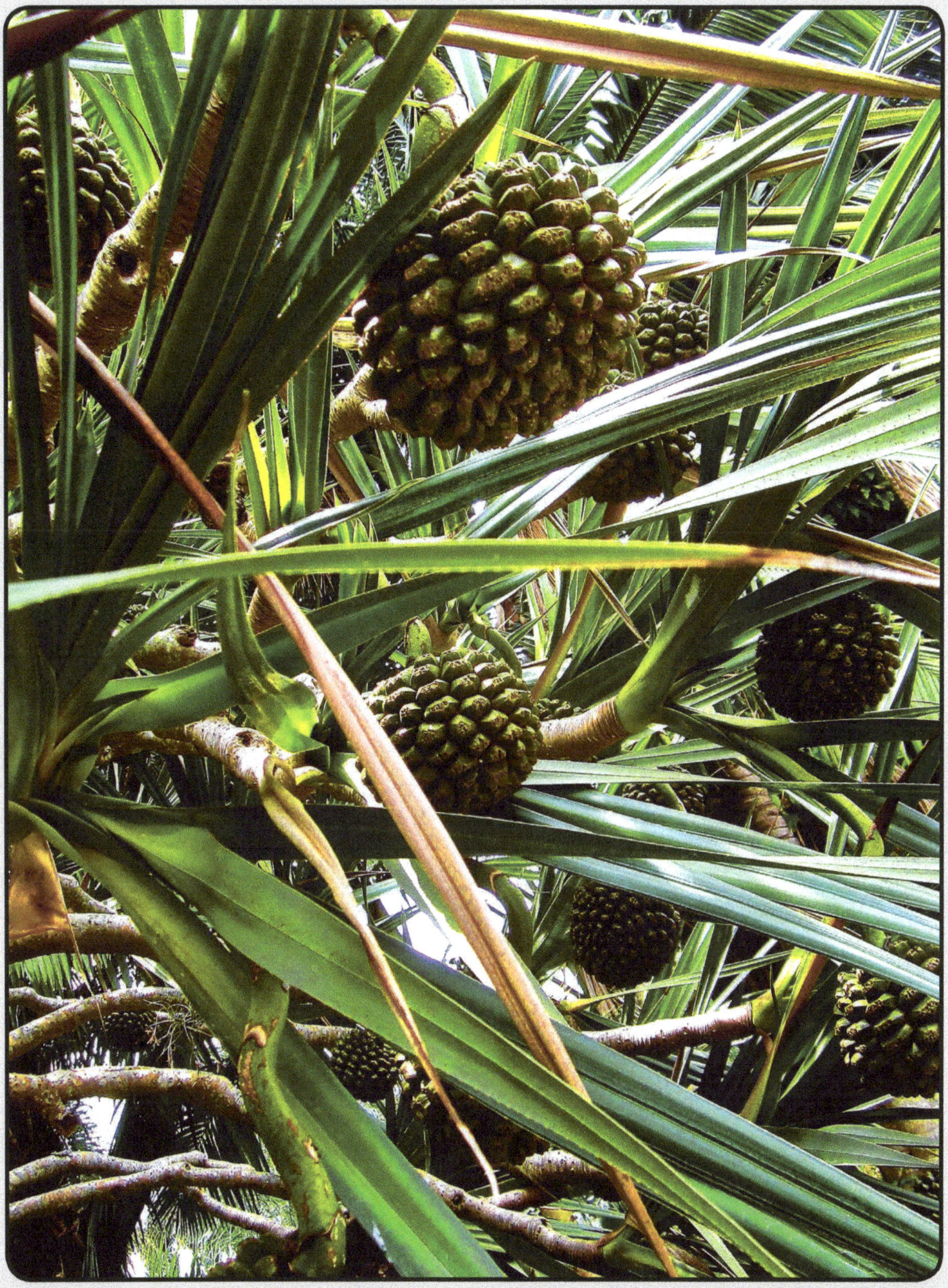

Tropical pine cones.

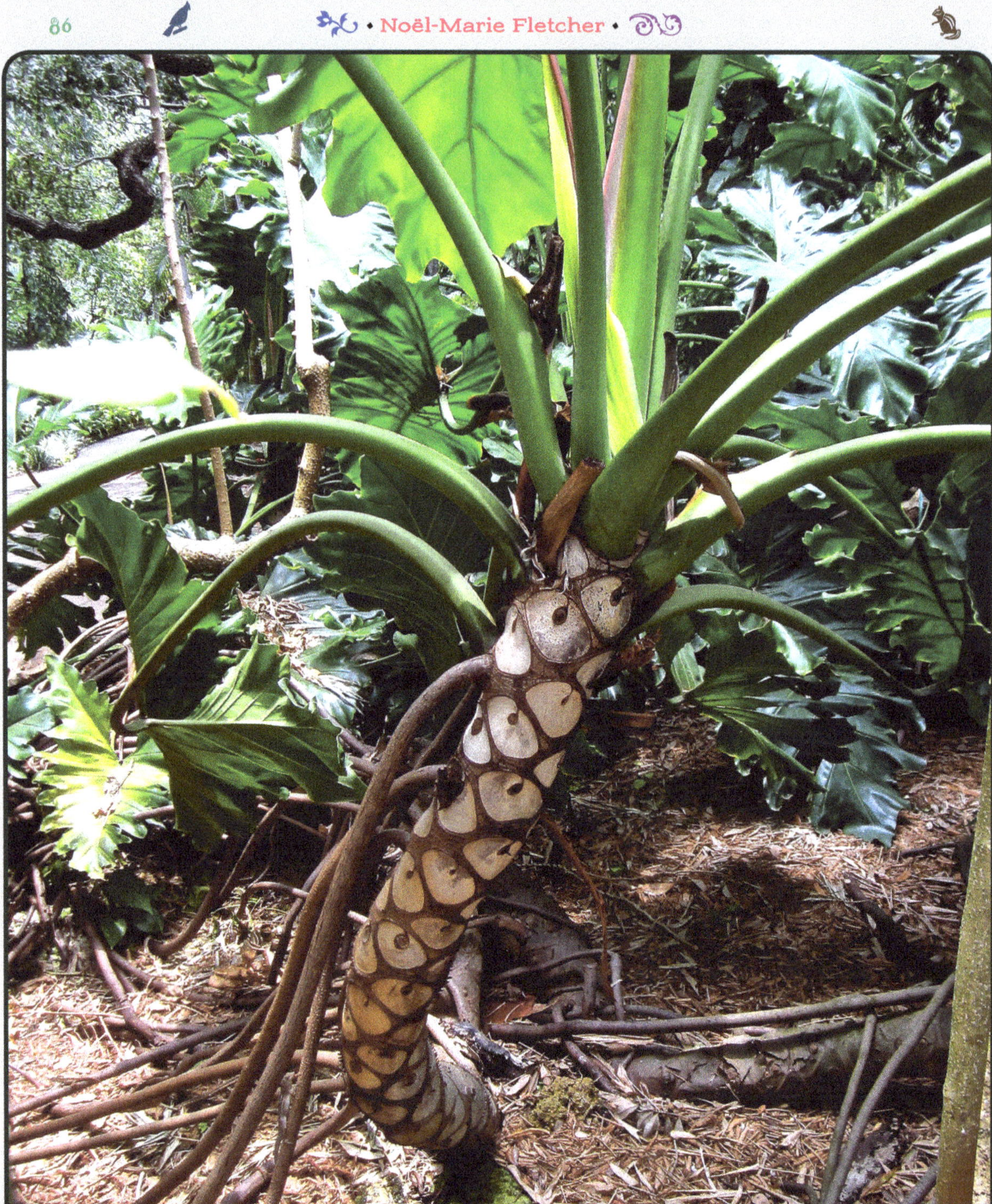

Bark eyes.

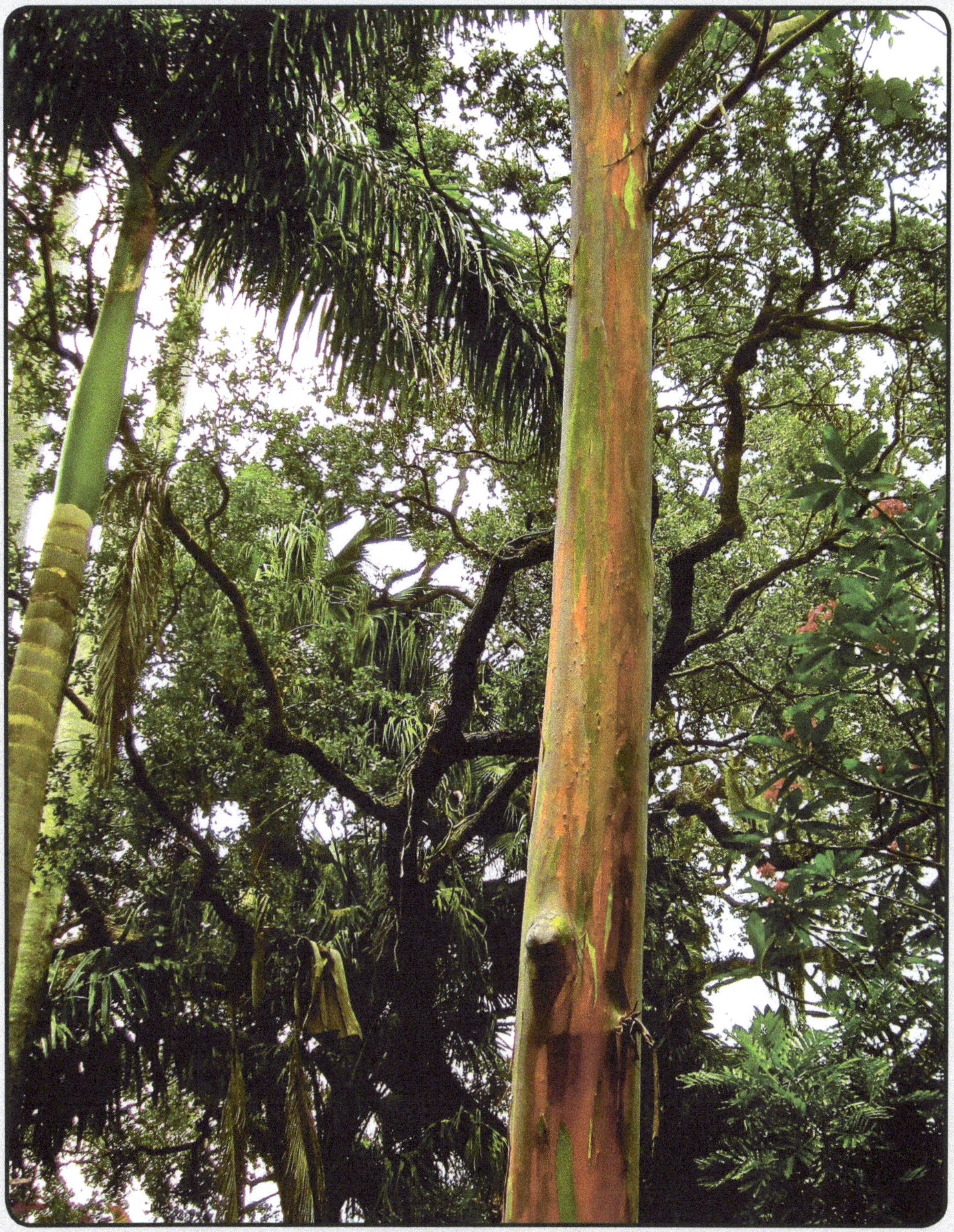

Psychedelic wood.

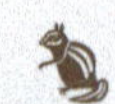

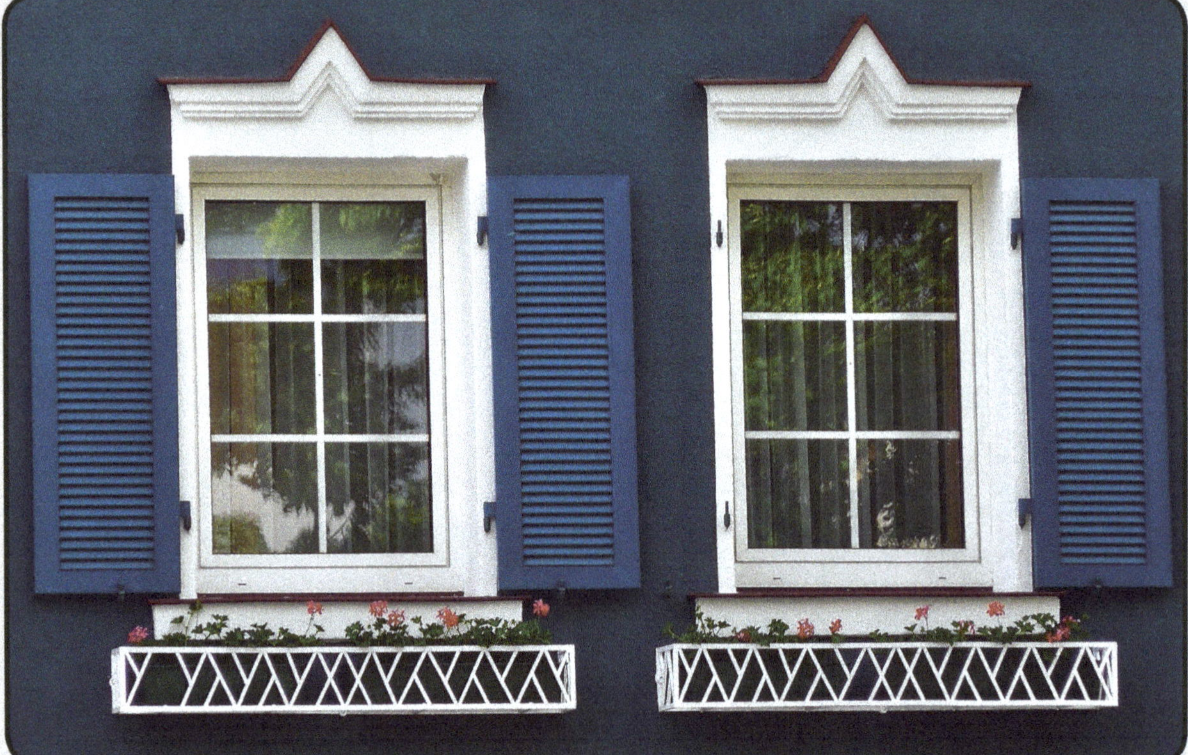

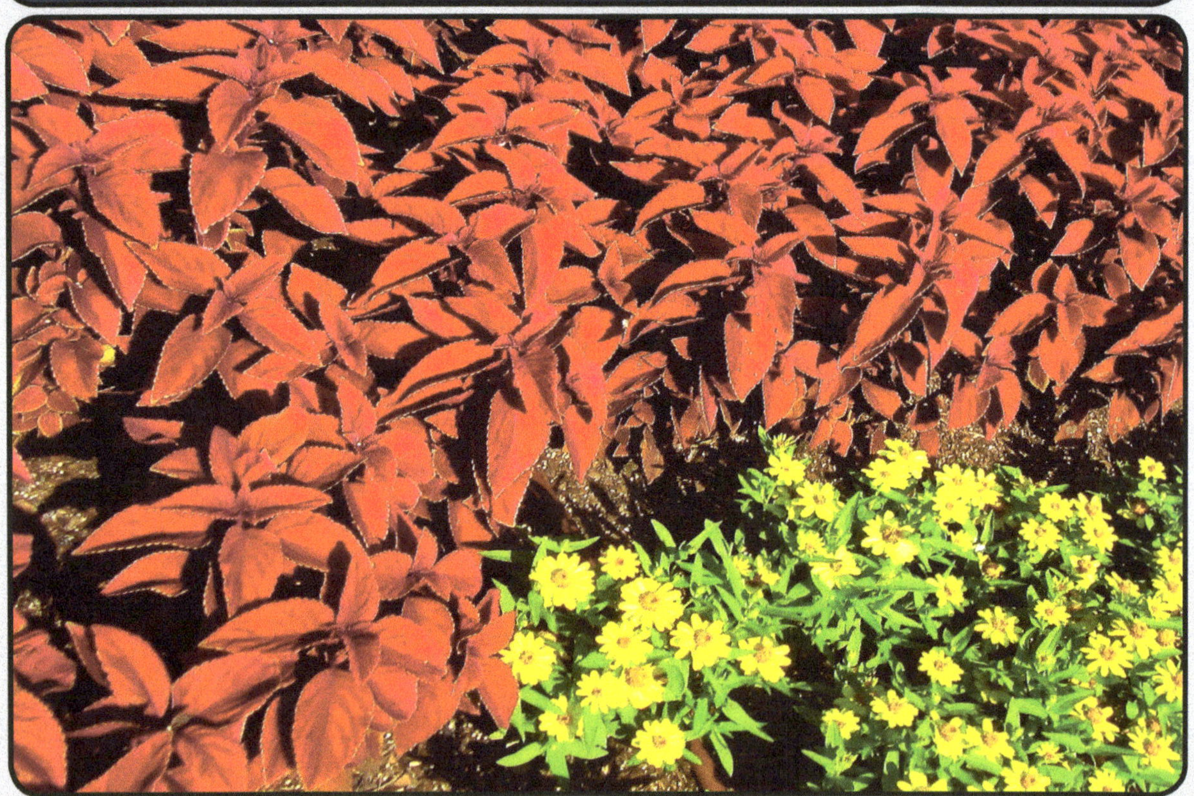

Christmas in spring.

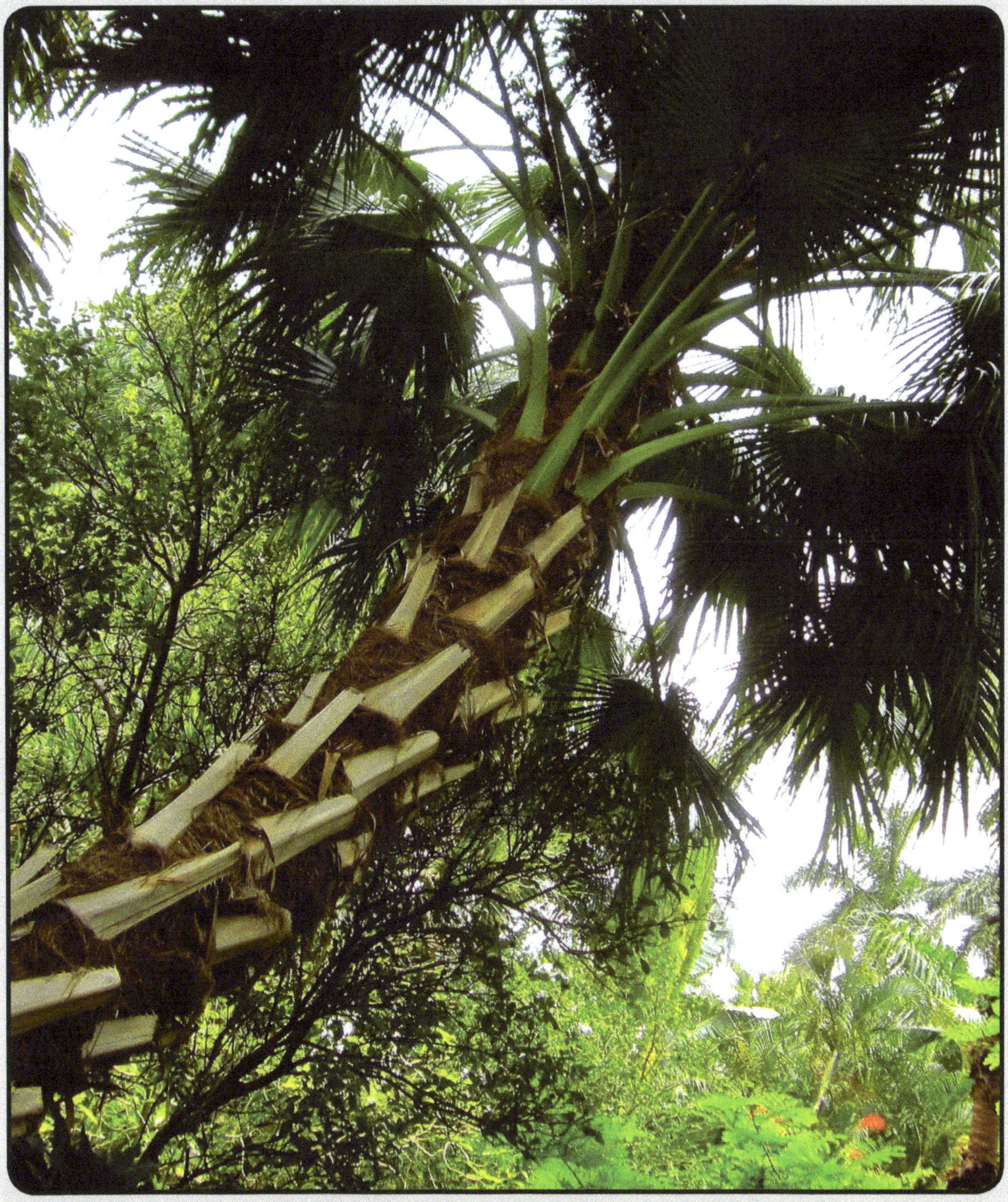

Ready to climb.

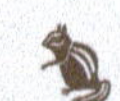

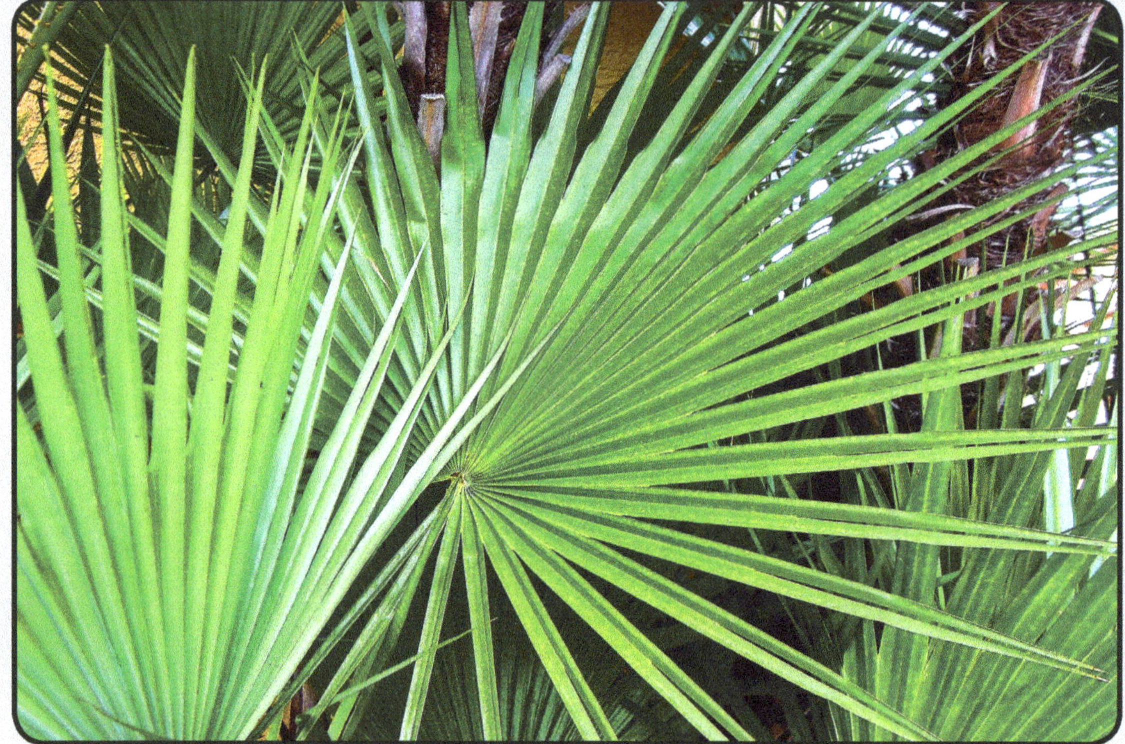

Florida uchiwa.

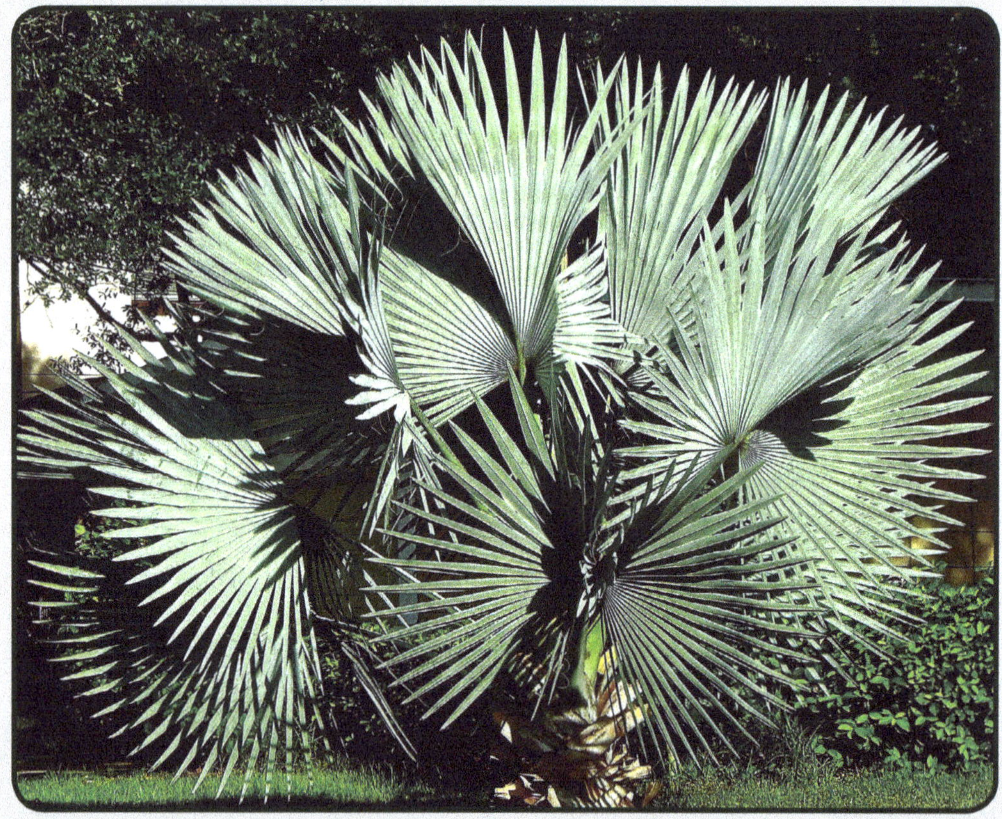

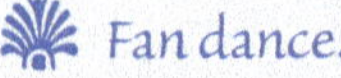

Fan dance.

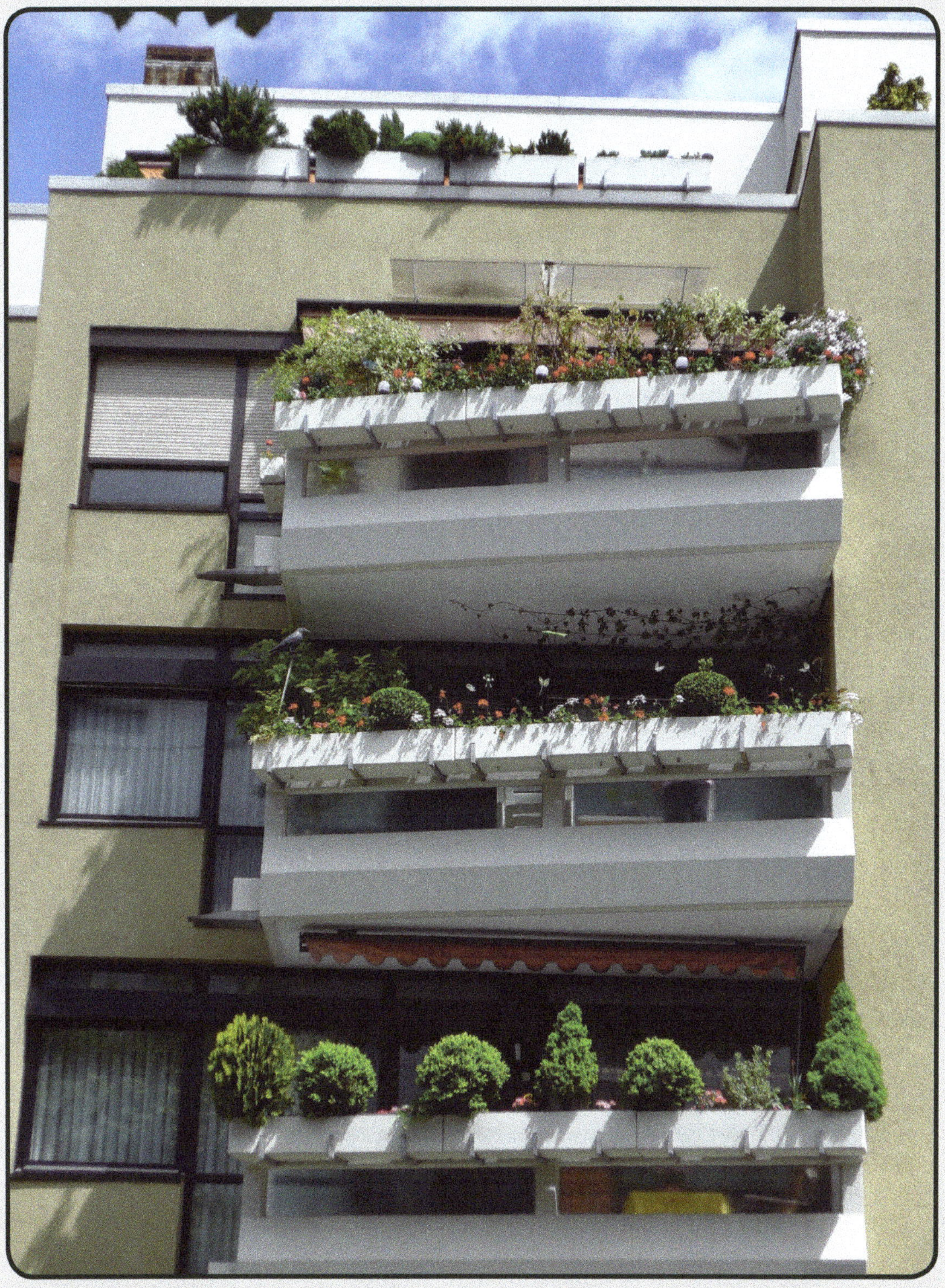

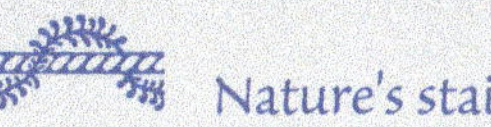 Nature's stairway.

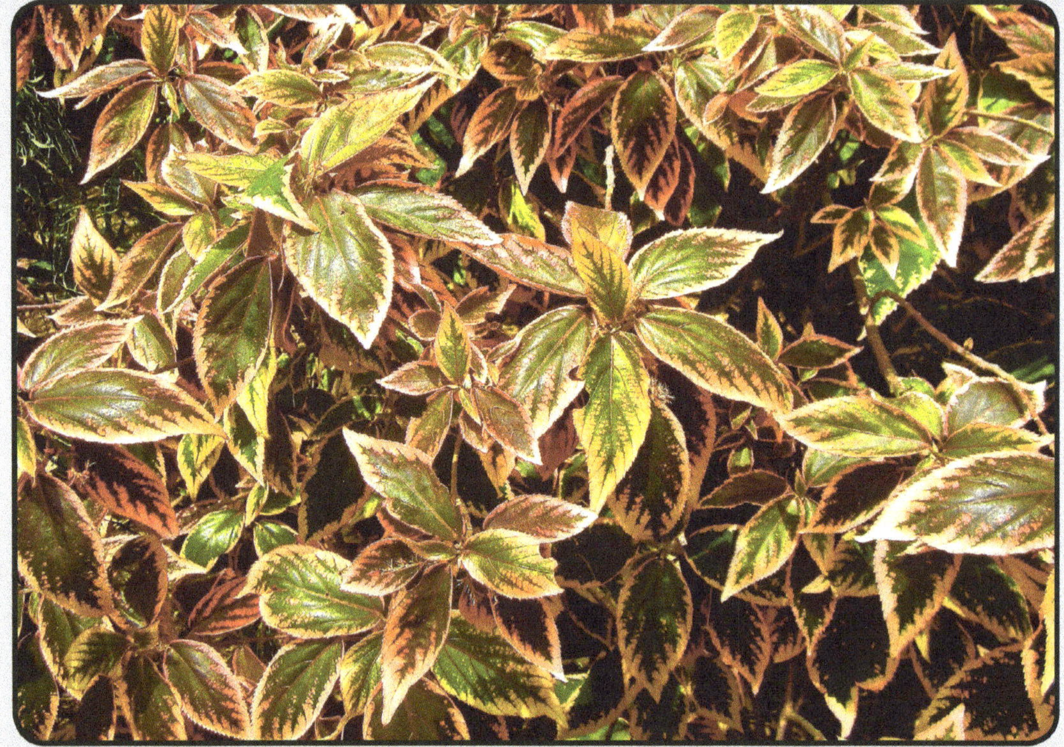

Garden stars.

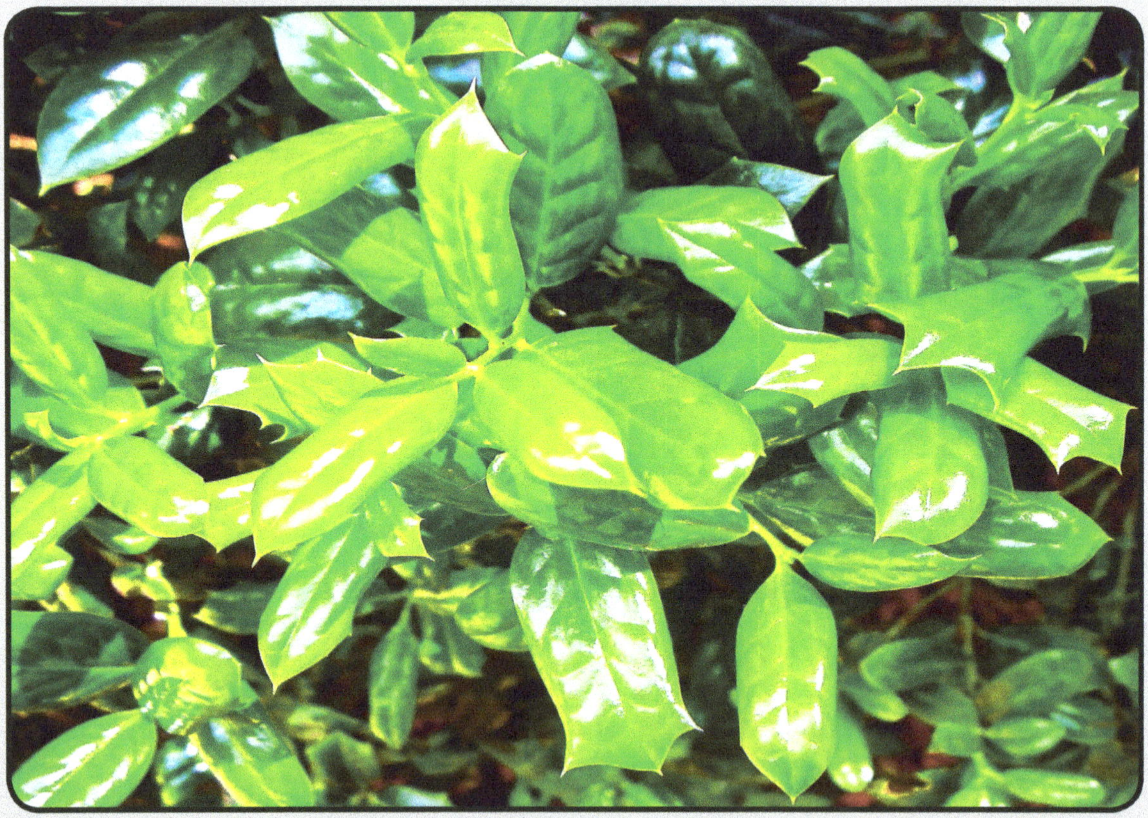

Reflections.

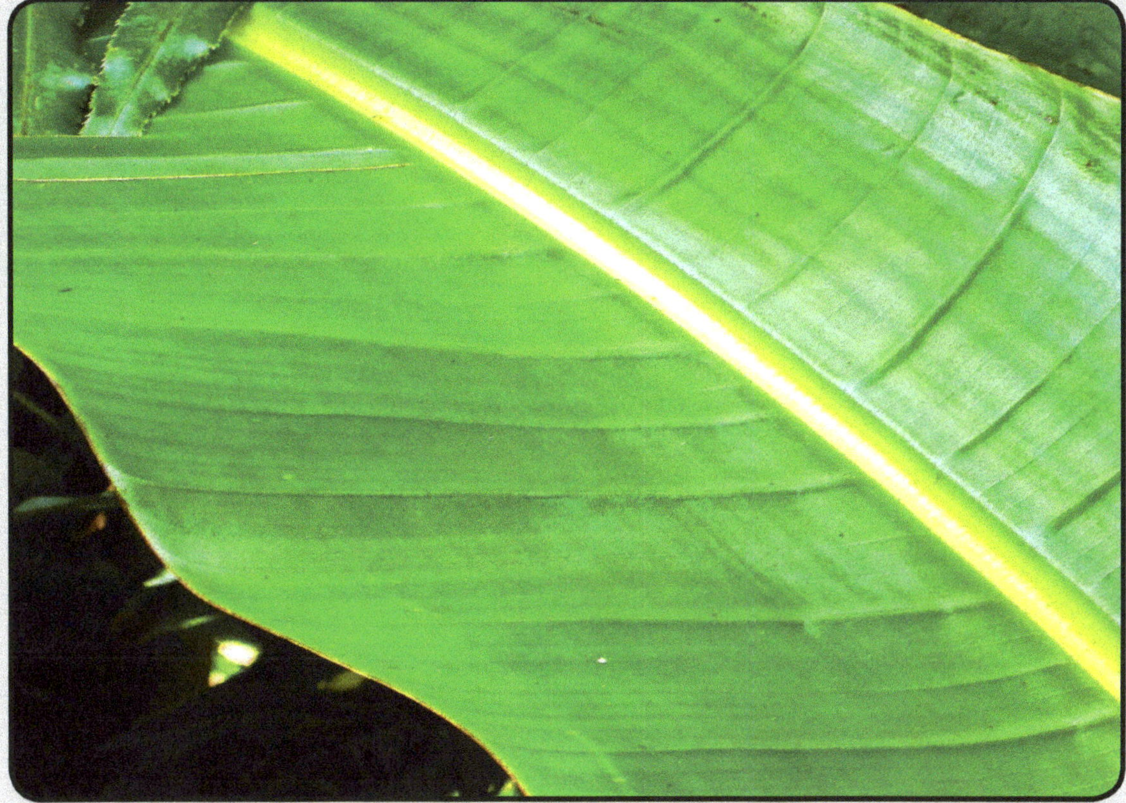

Symmetry.

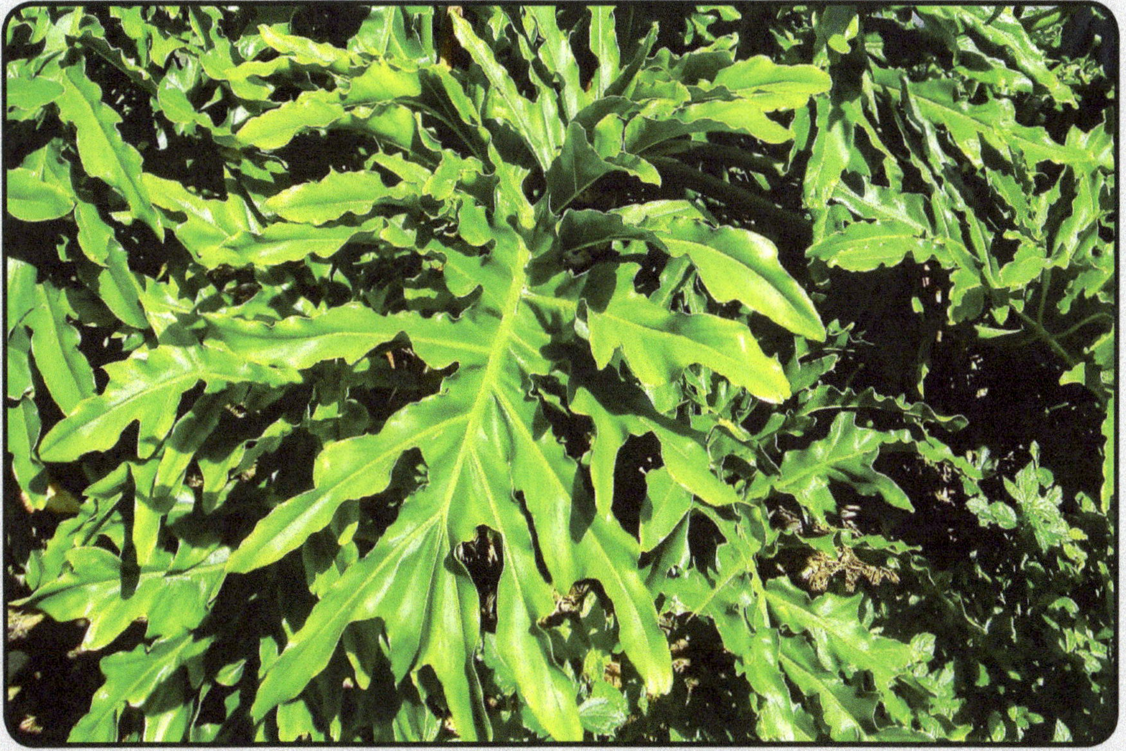

Ragged edges.

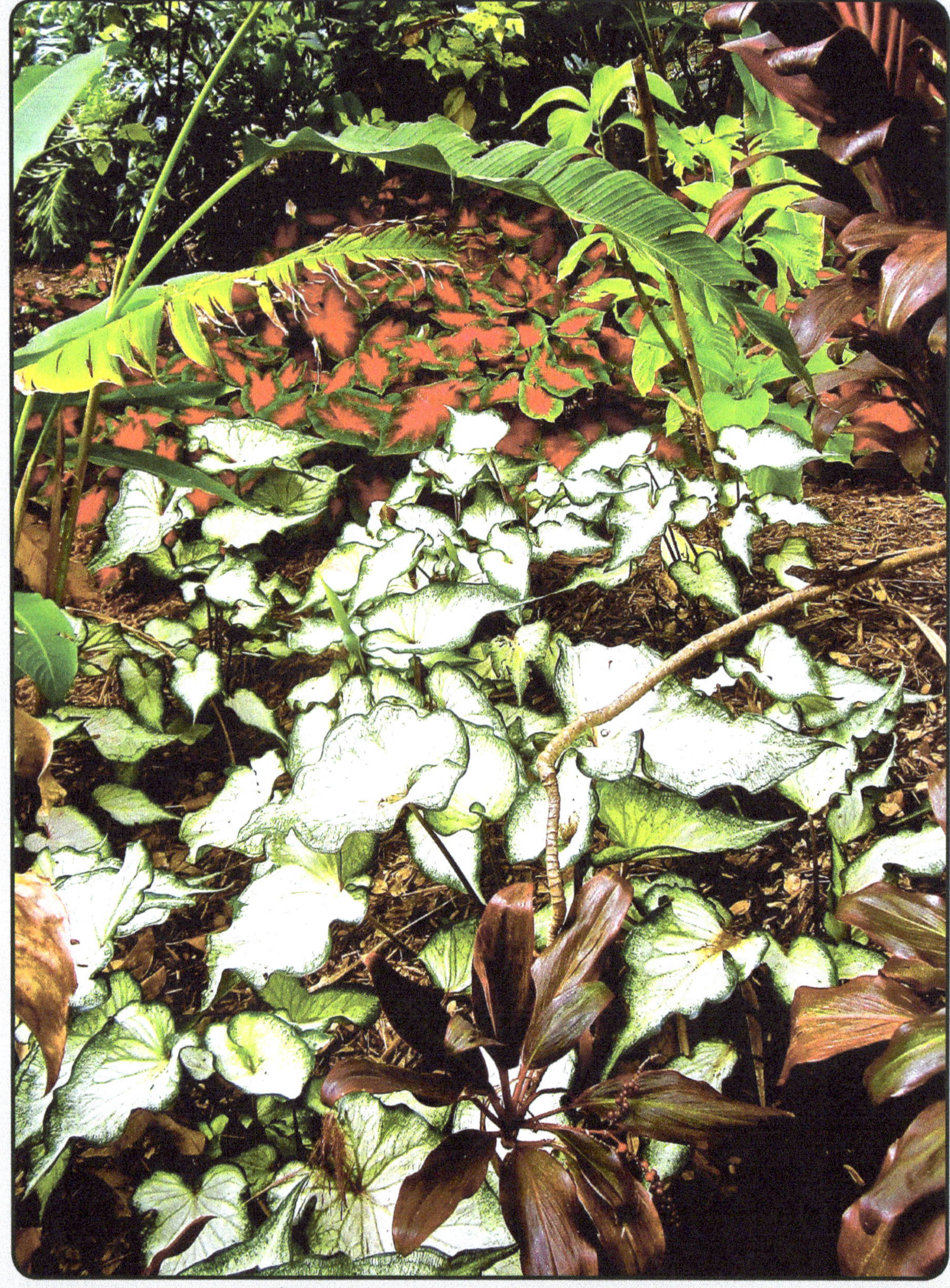

✻ Contest between the white and the red.

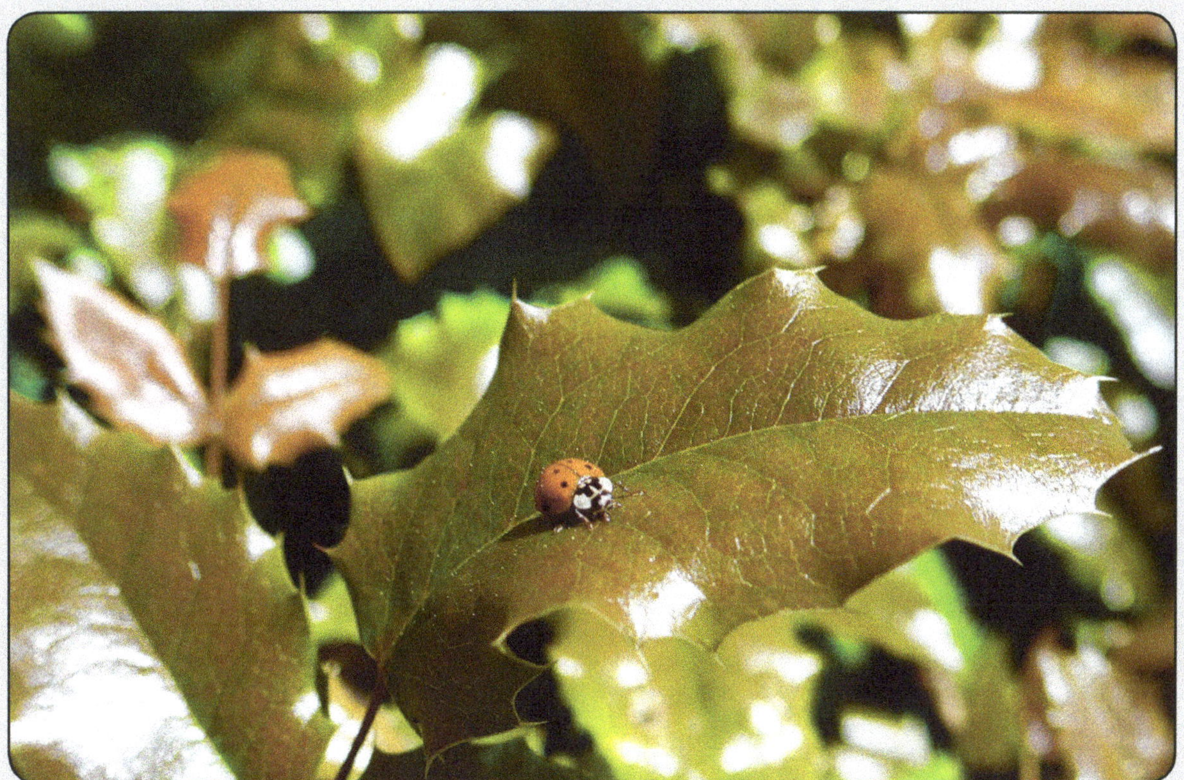

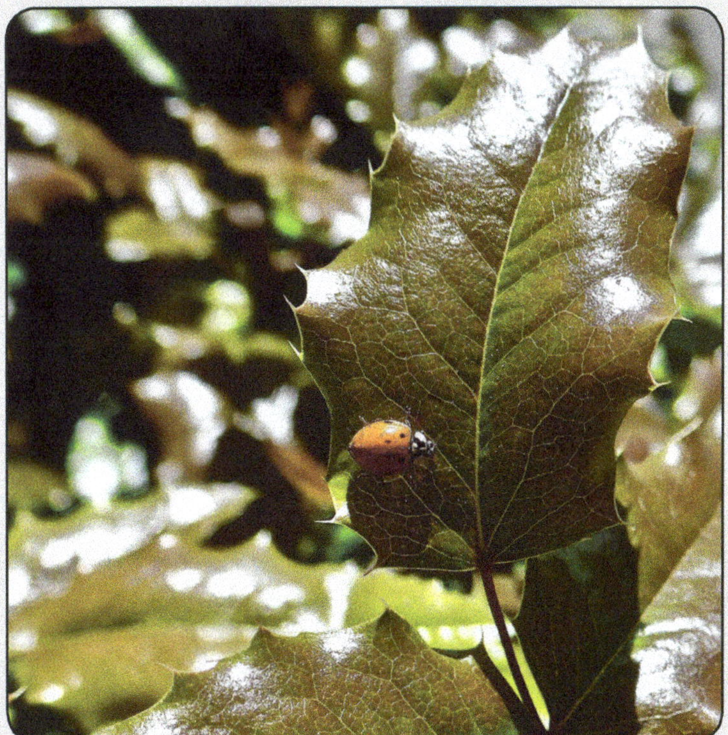

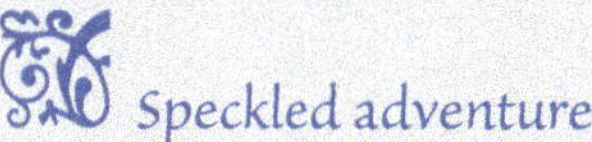

Speckled adventure.

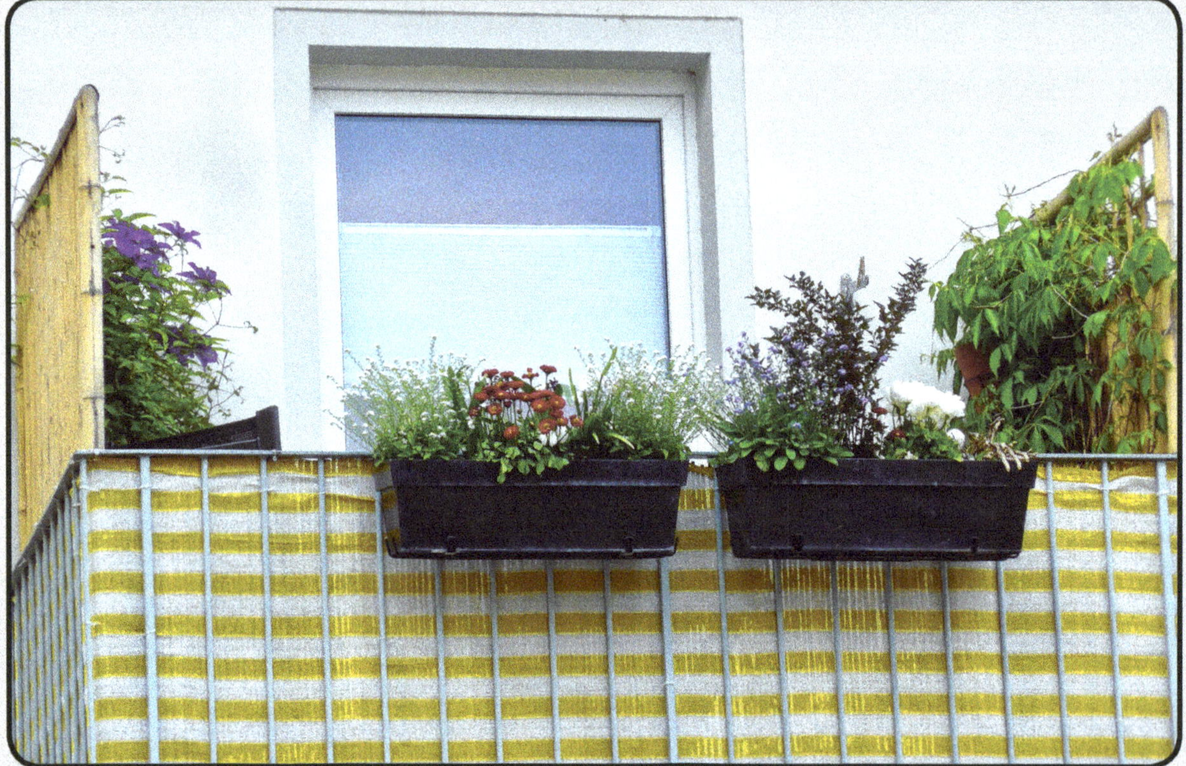

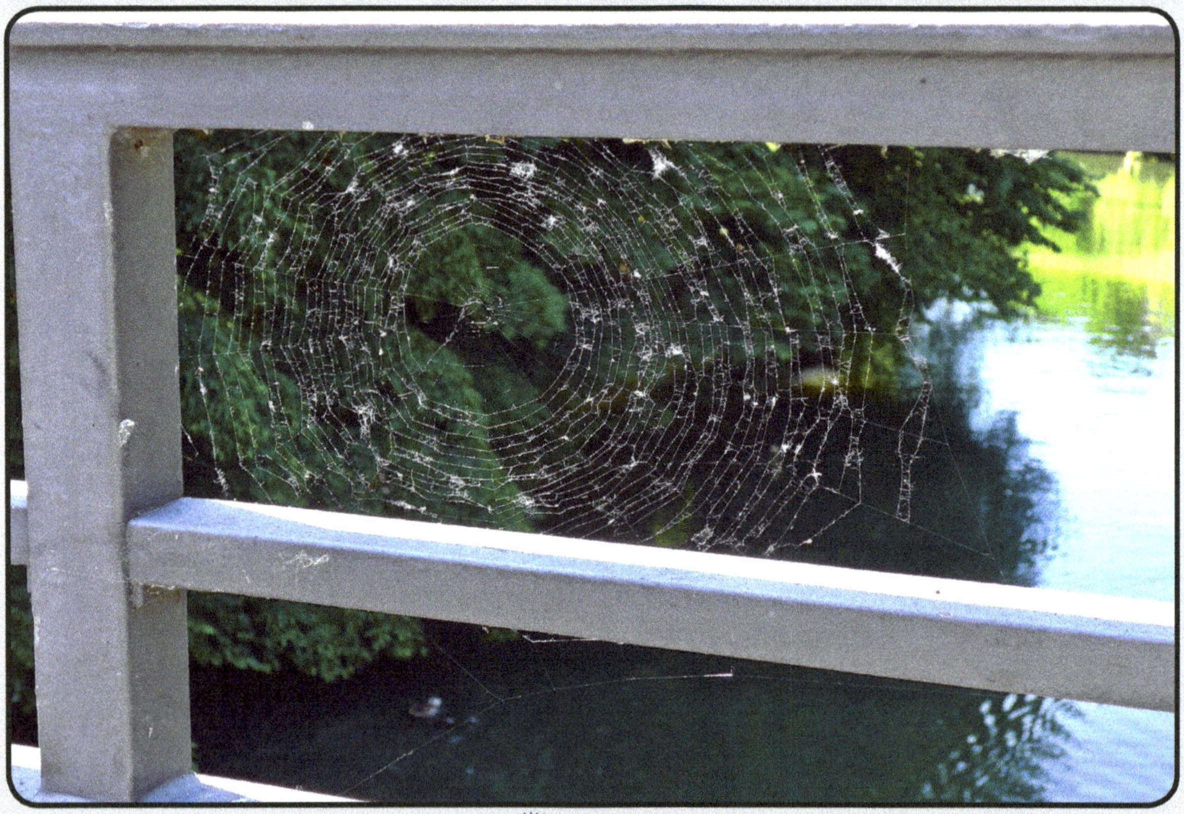

Bridge trap.

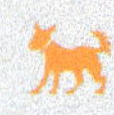

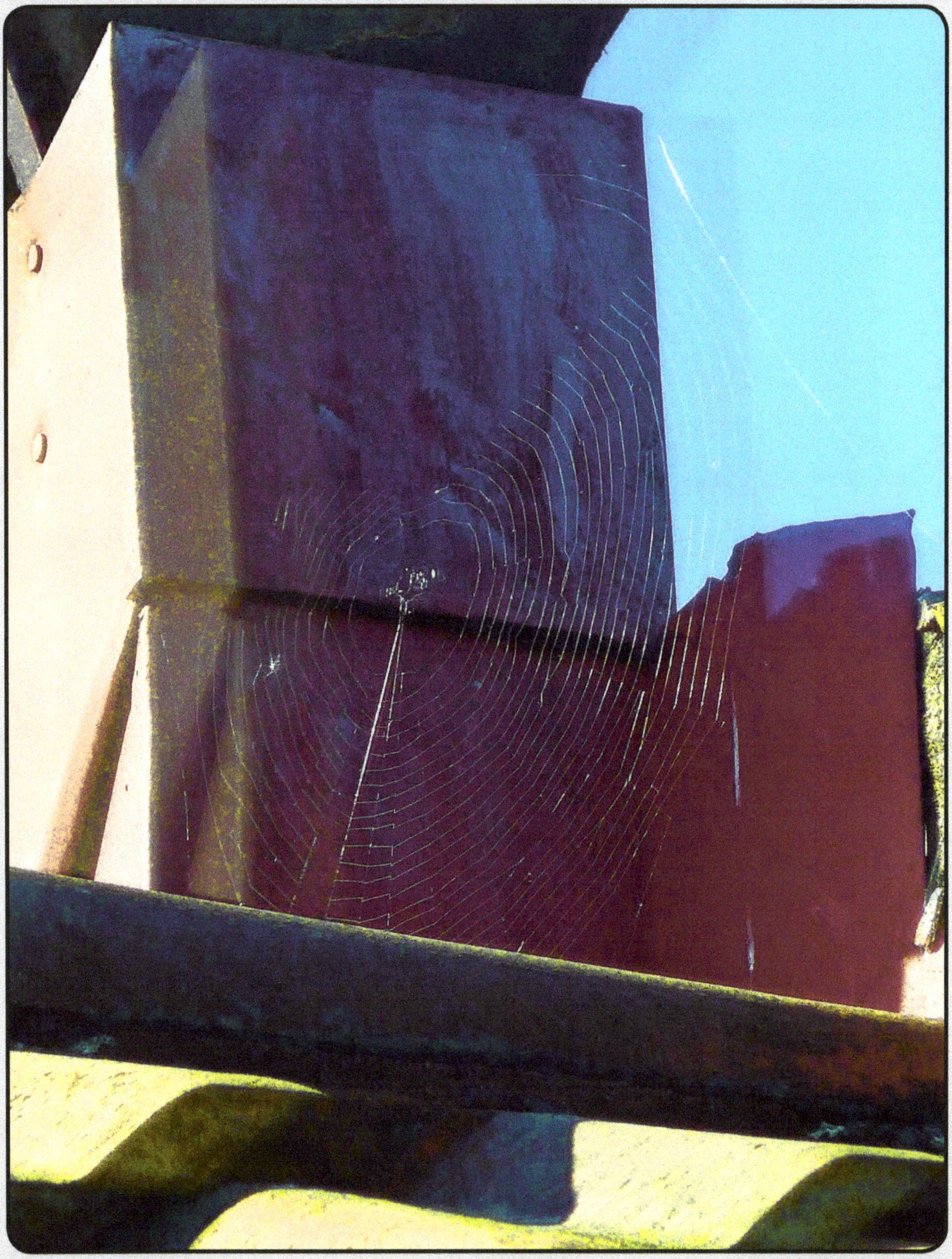

Rooftop weaver.

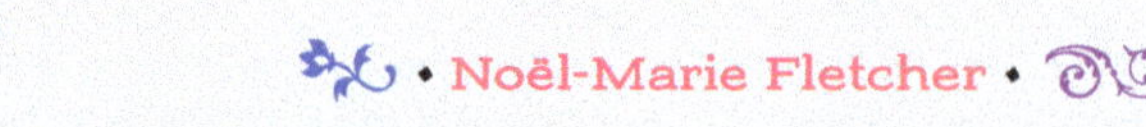

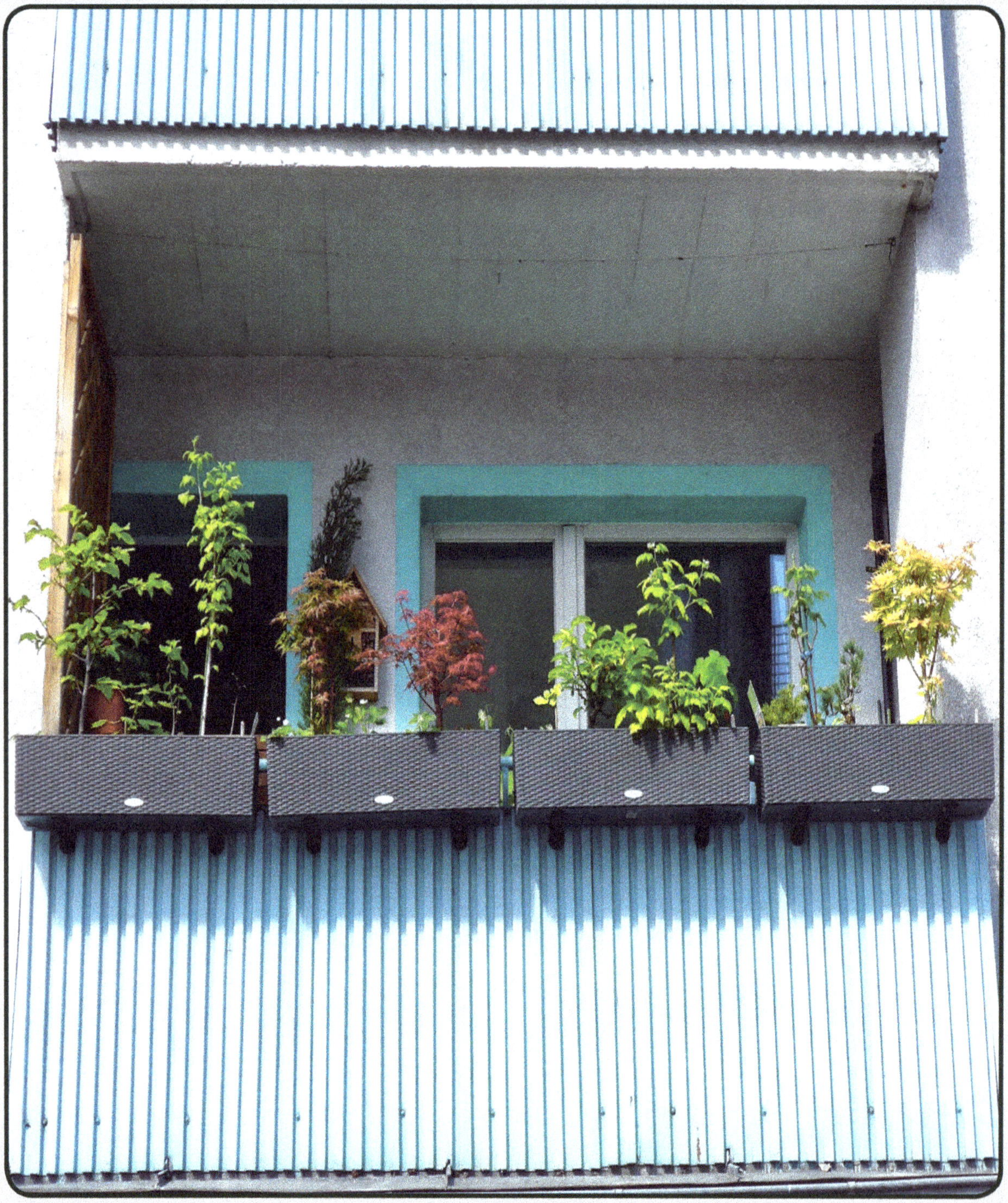

German apartment arbor.

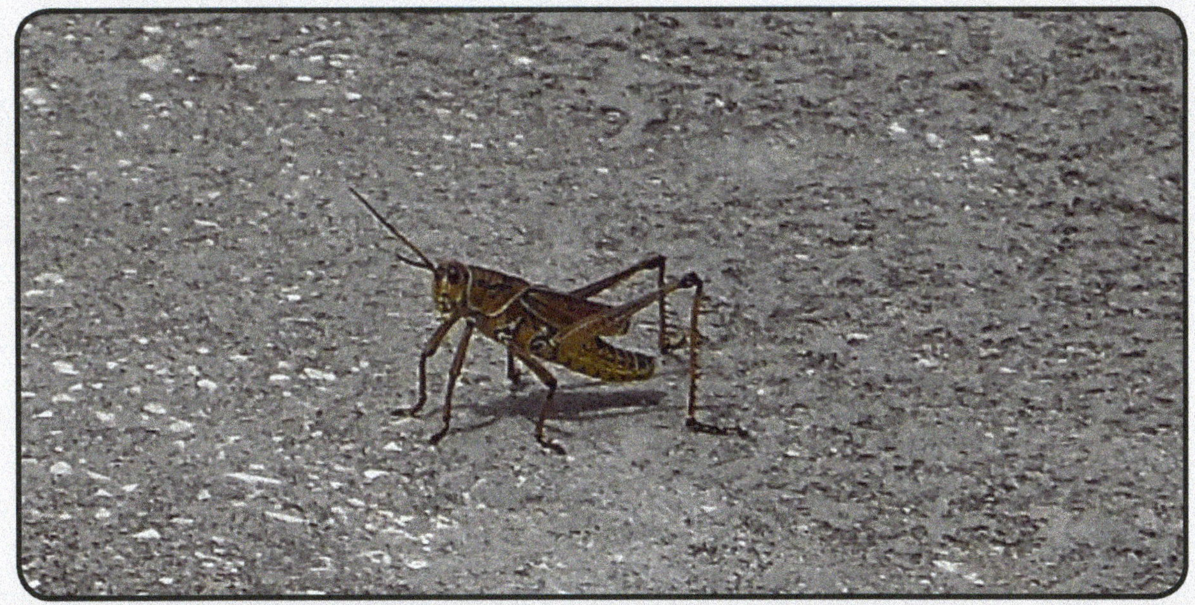

A grasshopper's journey over the tarmac in central Florida.

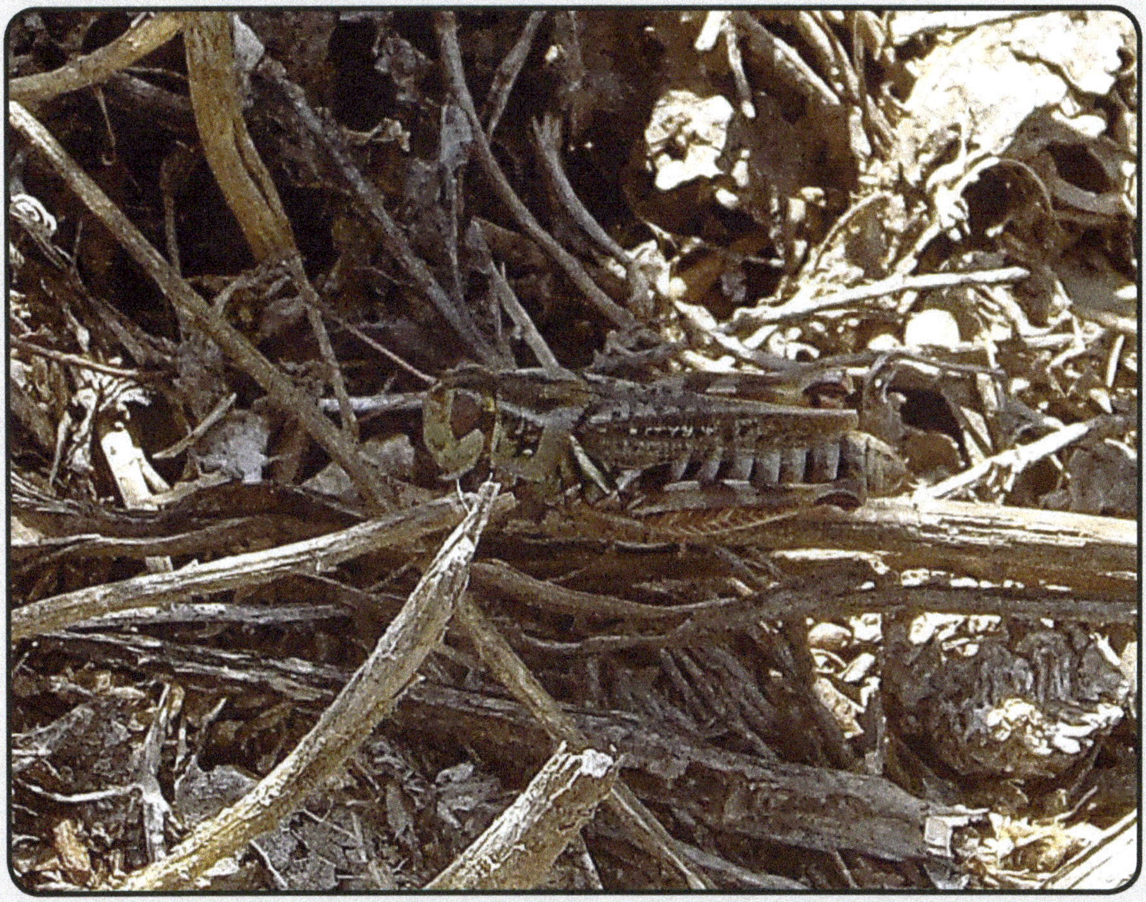

Hidden observer in the high desert.

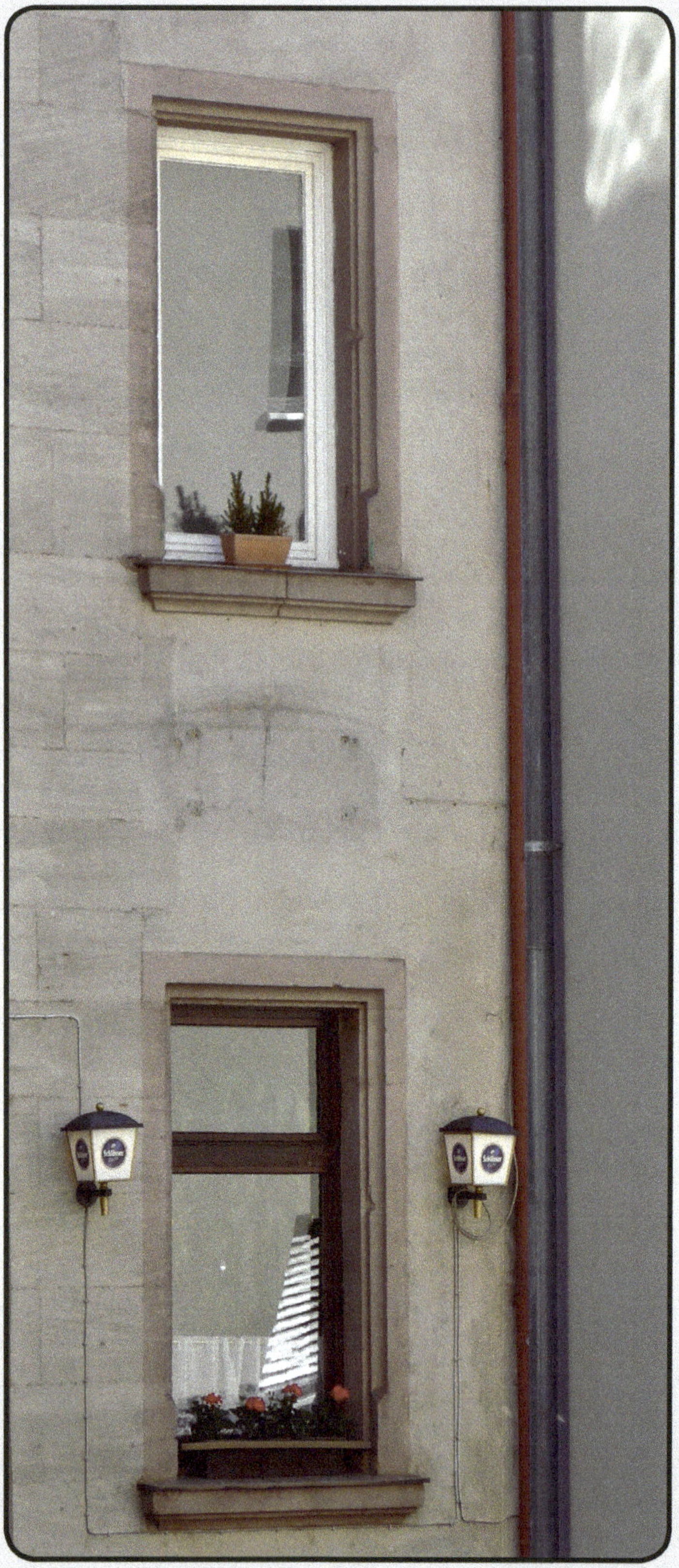

Travels of a brave Bavarian firebug.

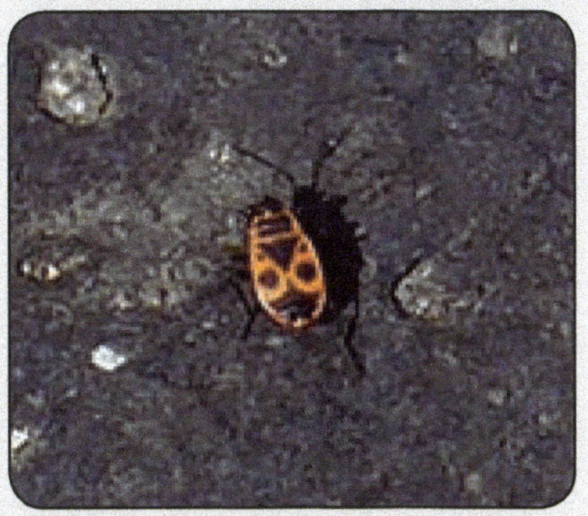

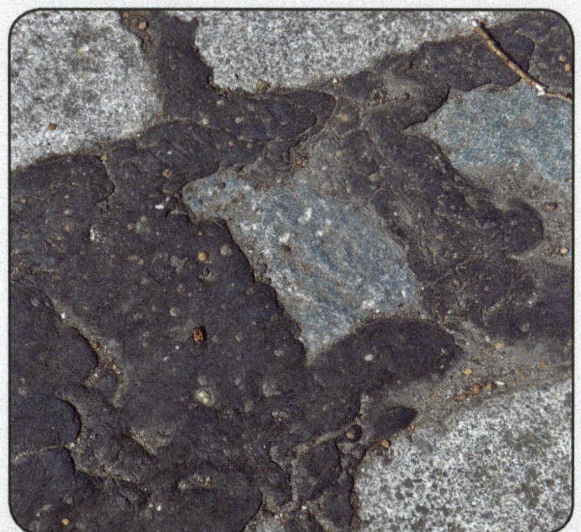

The firebug boldly marched through a busy street, passing speeding cars, whirring bicycle wheels, and stepping shoes.

Its little legs passed a grocery store along its journey to an unknown destination.

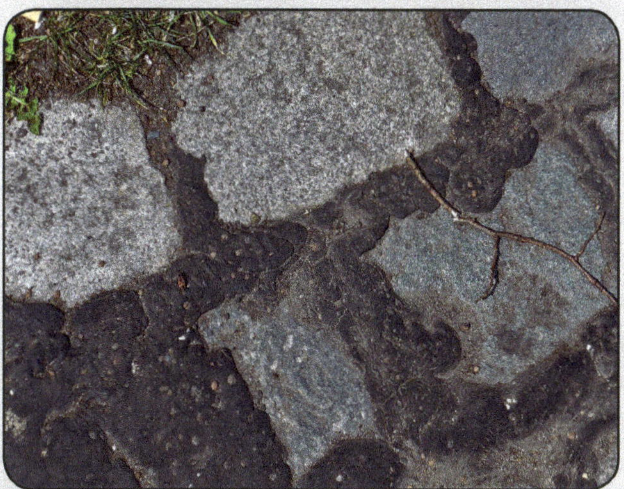

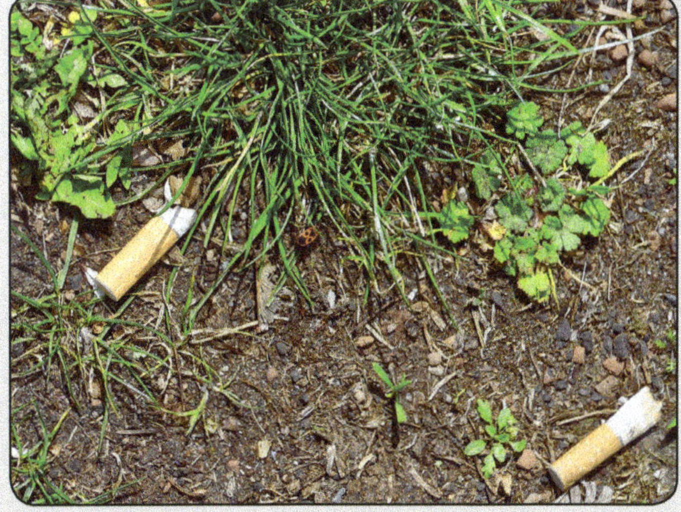

The firebug continued its solitary trek in relative peace when it finally reached a patch of ground – only to navigate around two discarded cigarette butts and trash.

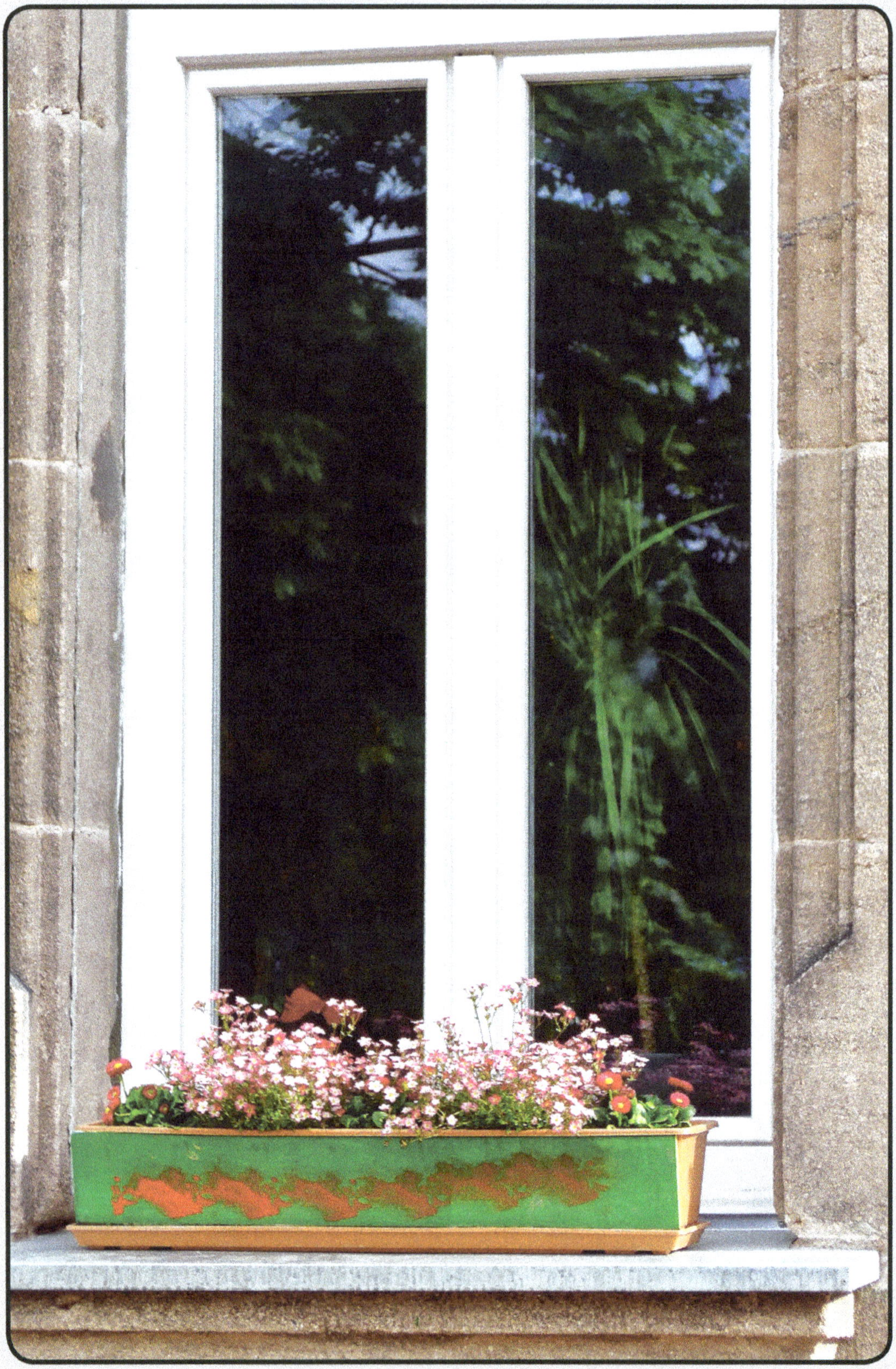

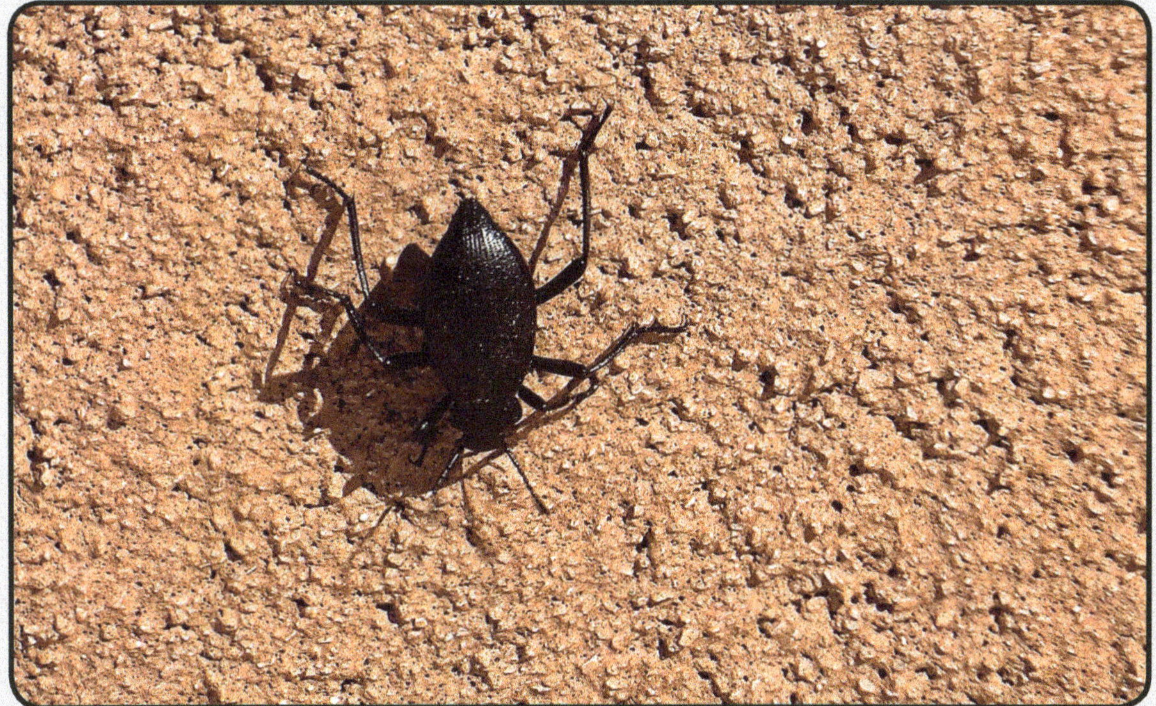

Downward dog pose on a wall by a Santa Fe stink bug.

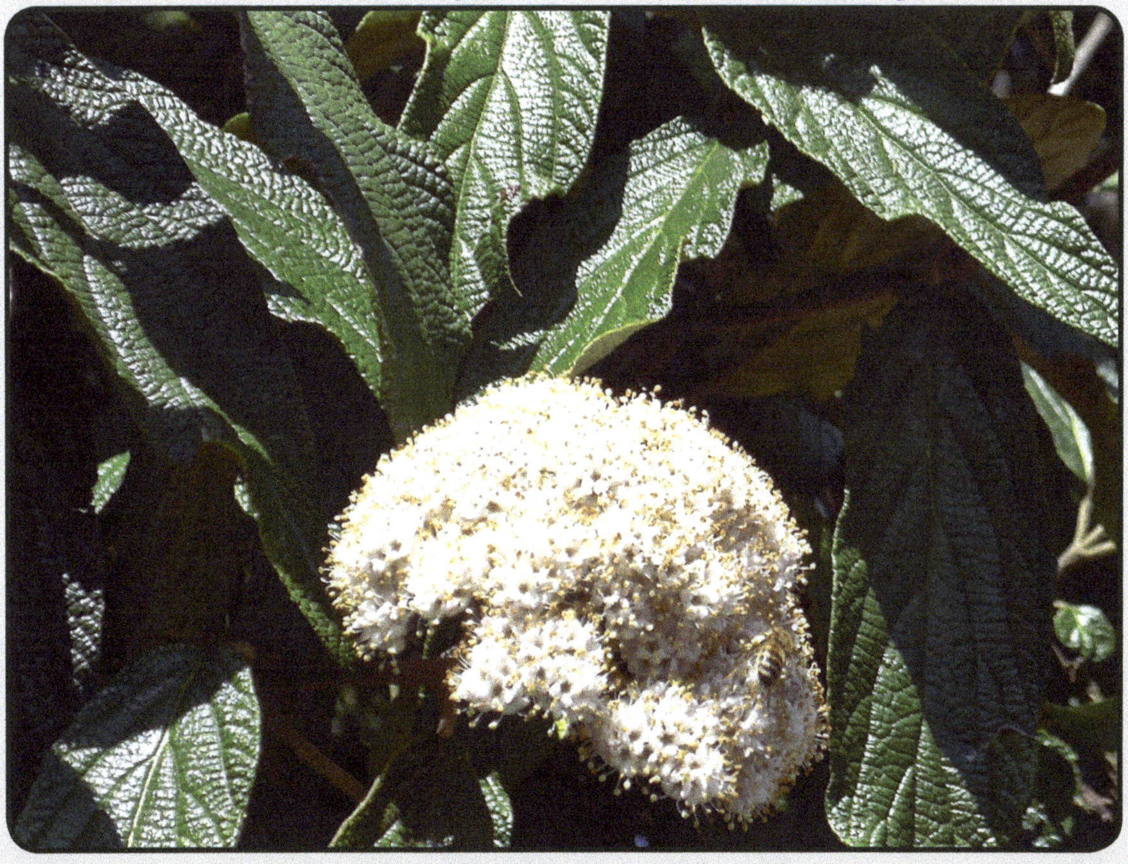

The honey bee and the snow cone.

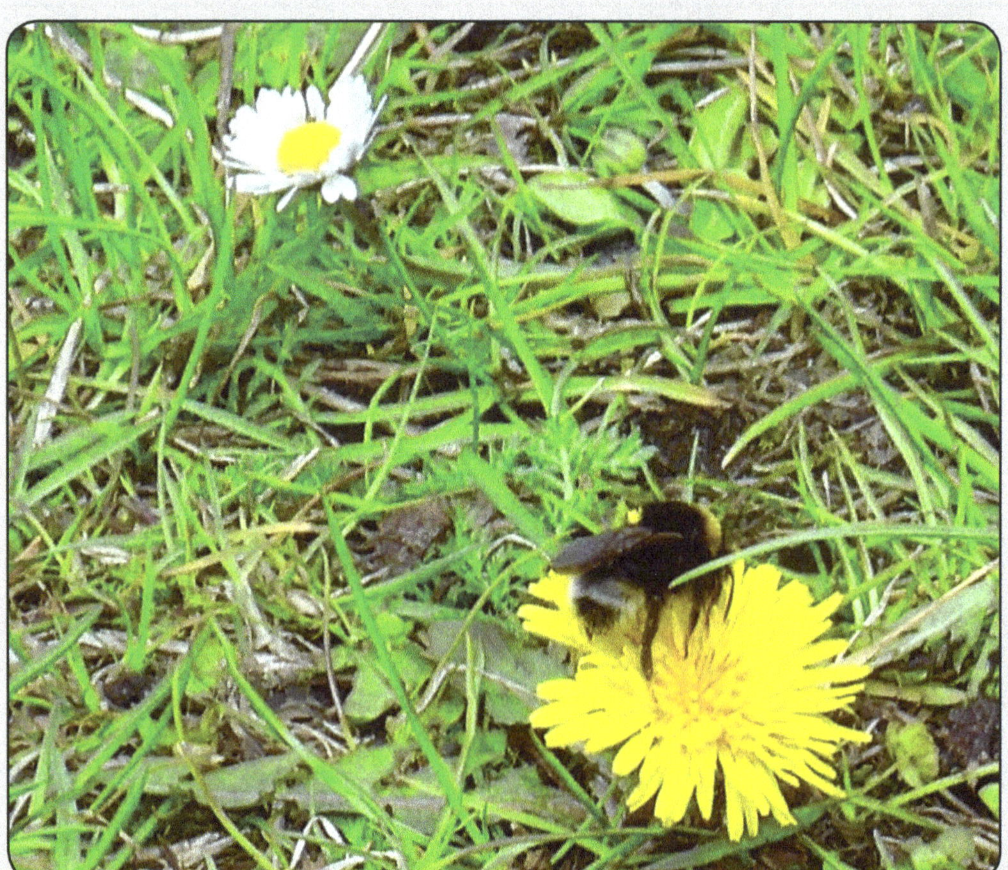

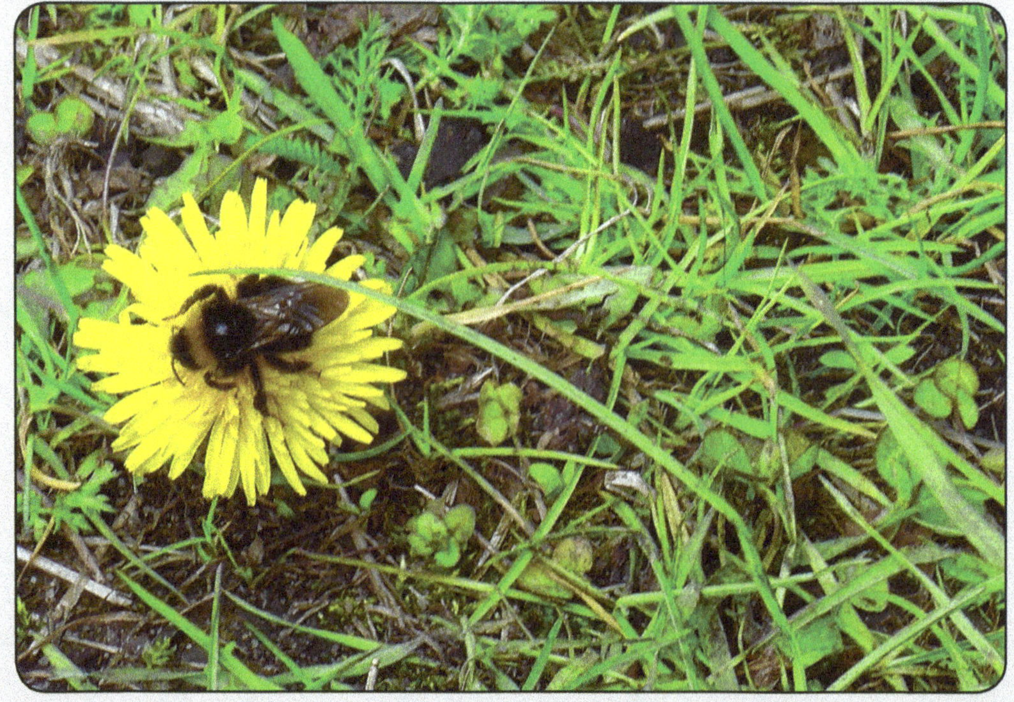

* Can't get enough.

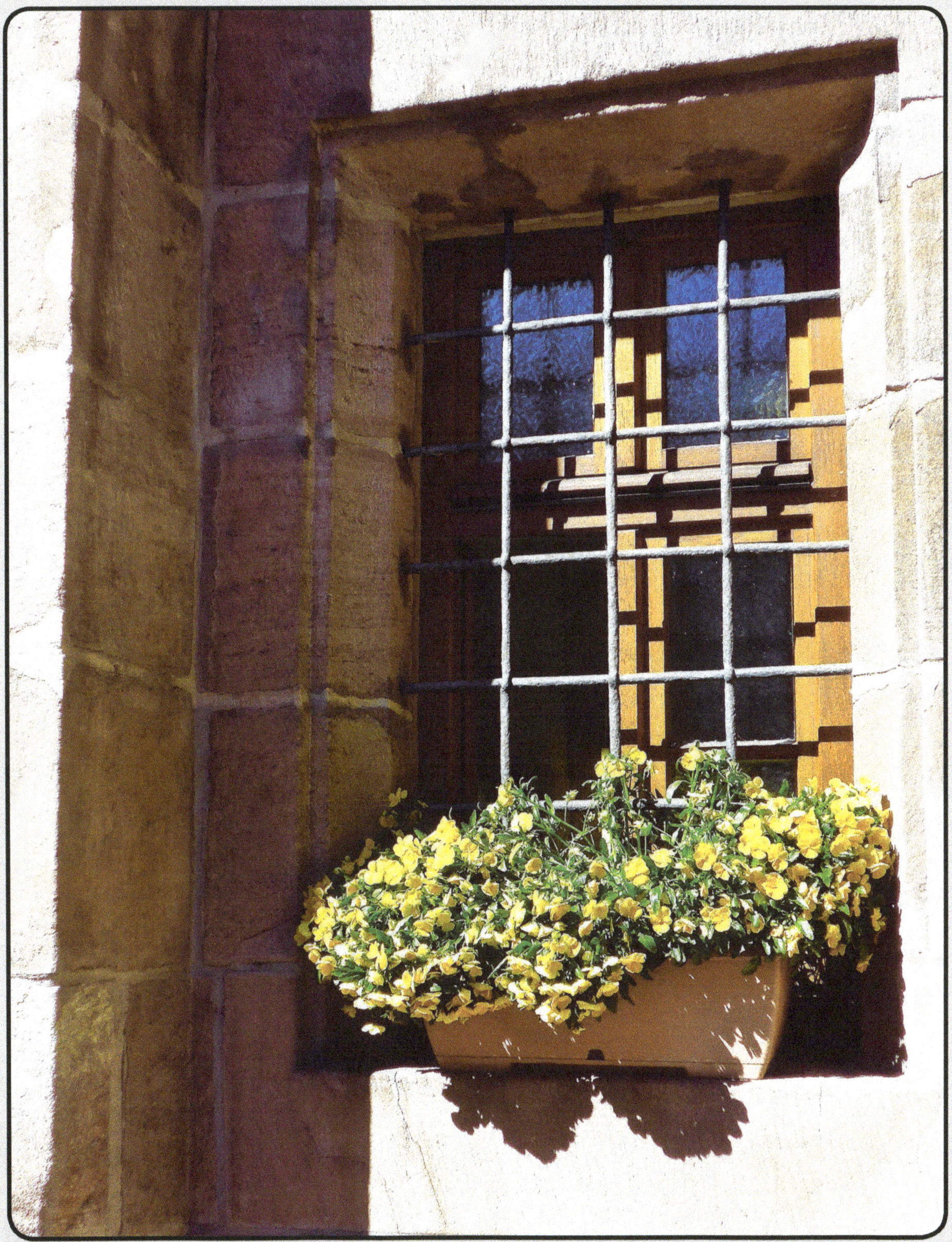

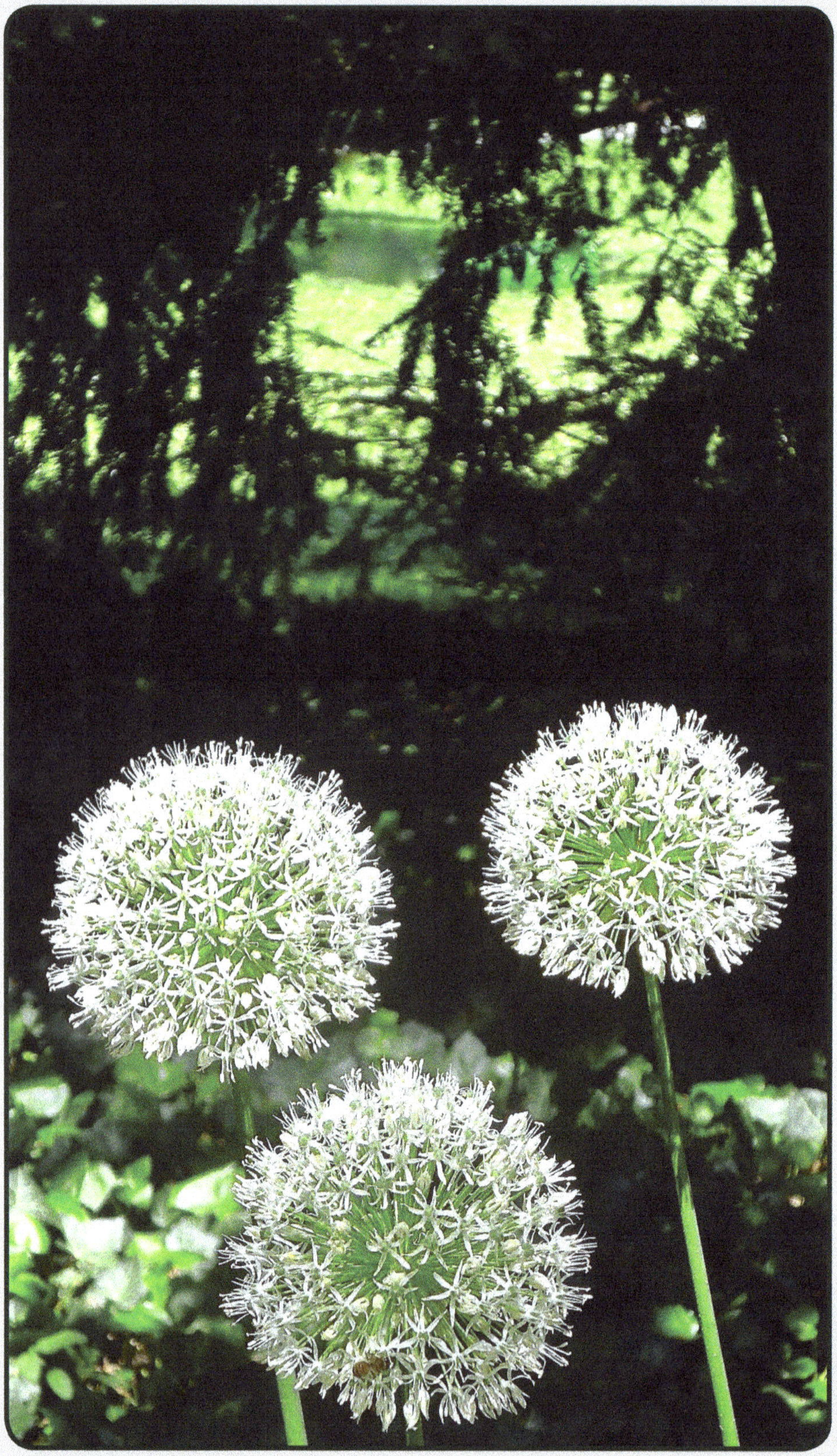

A bee tastes snowballs.

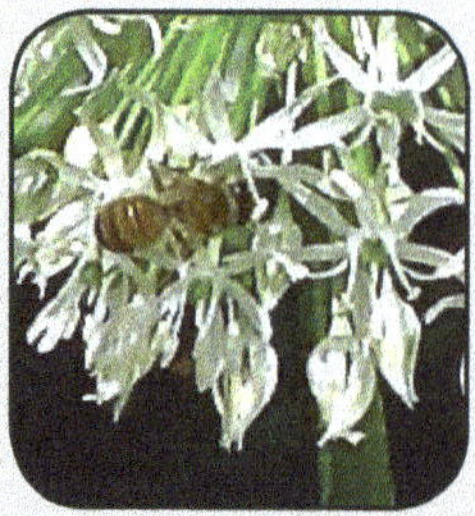

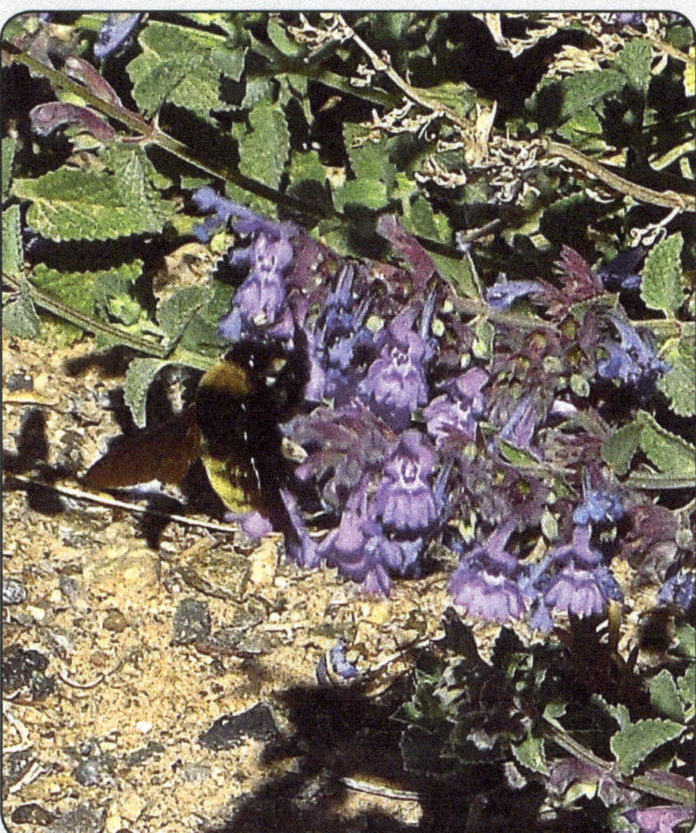

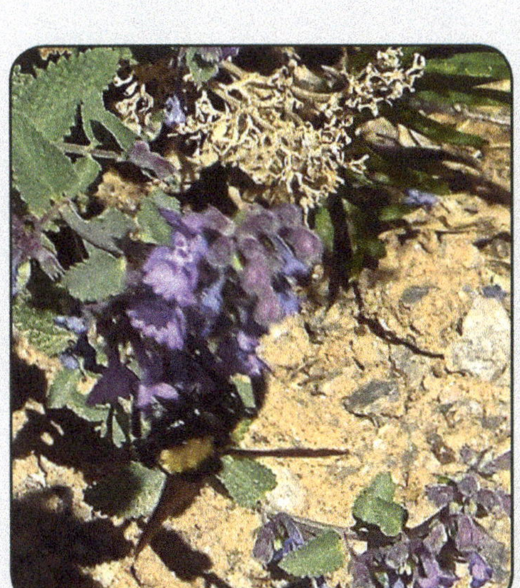

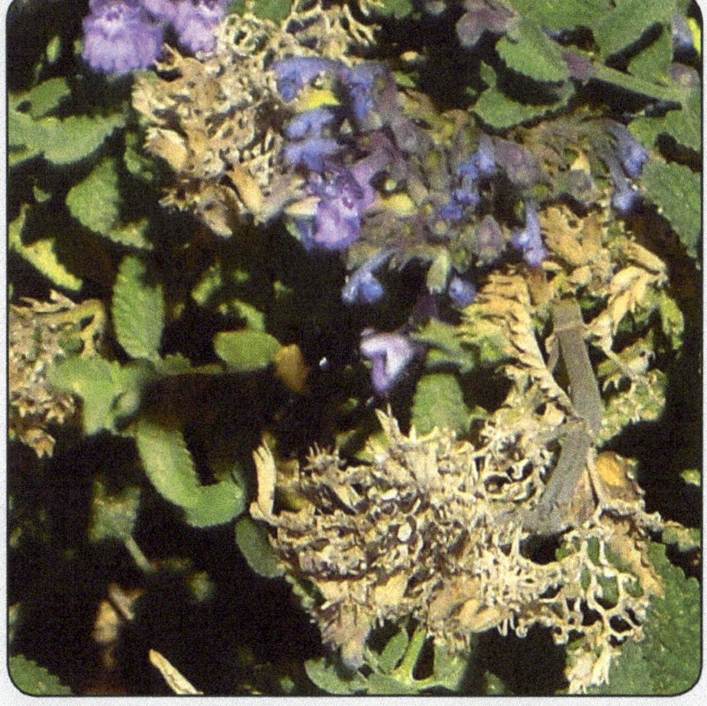

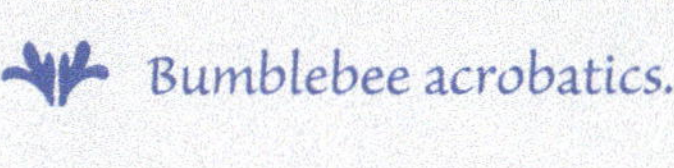
Bumblebee acrobatics.

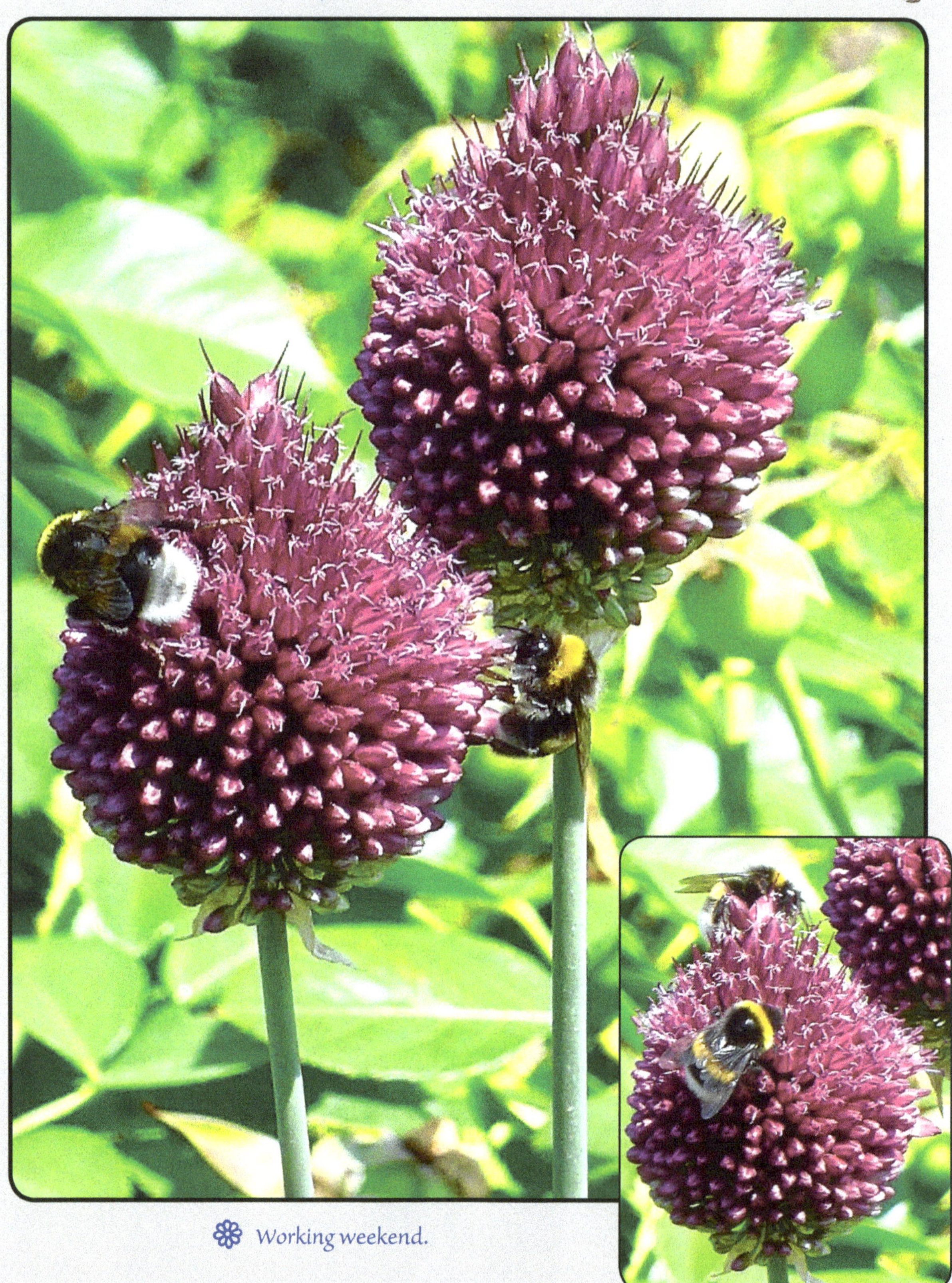

Working weekend.

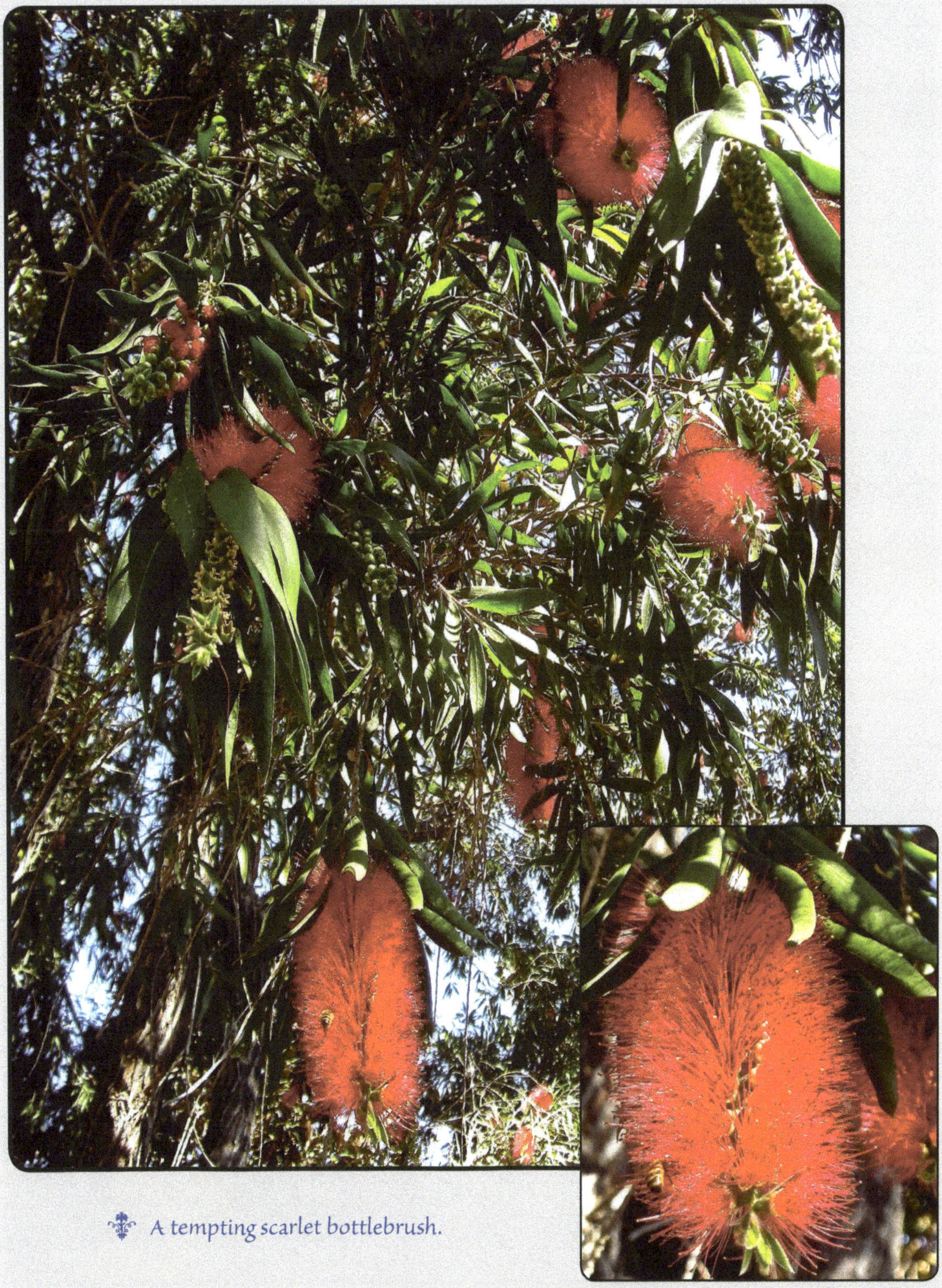

A tempting scarlet bottlebrush.

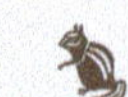

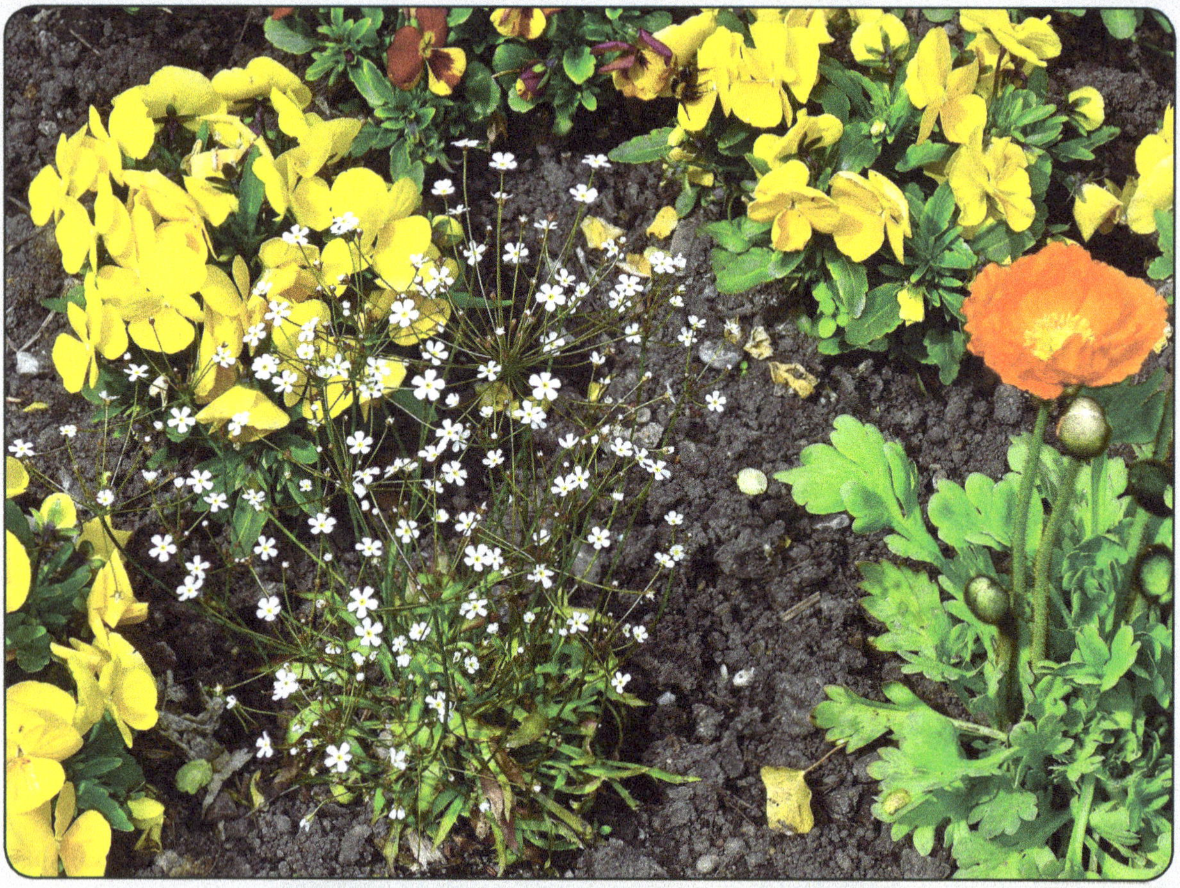

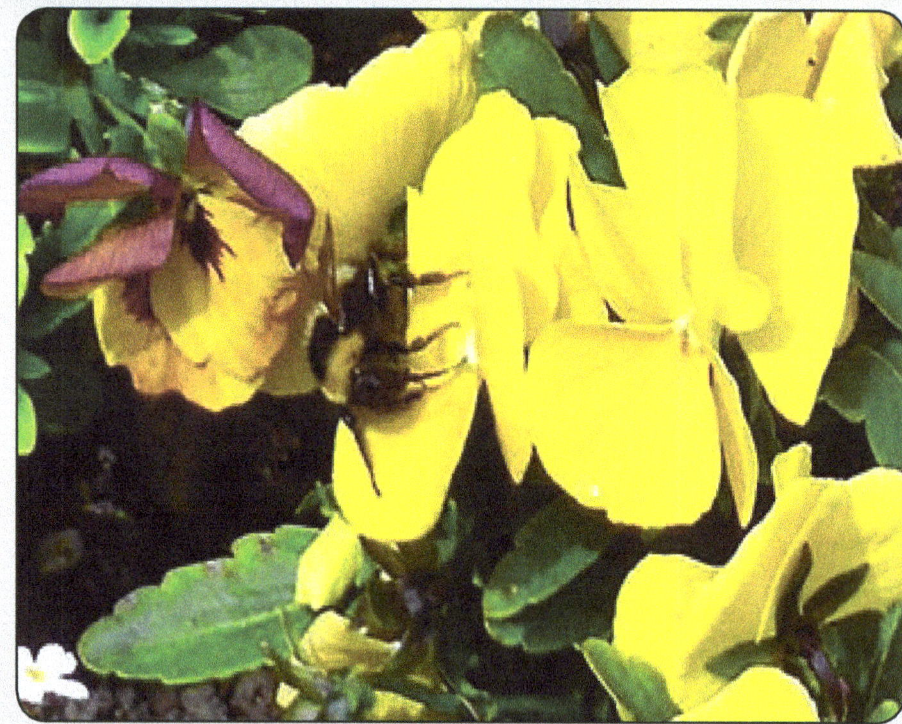

Lemony leaves.

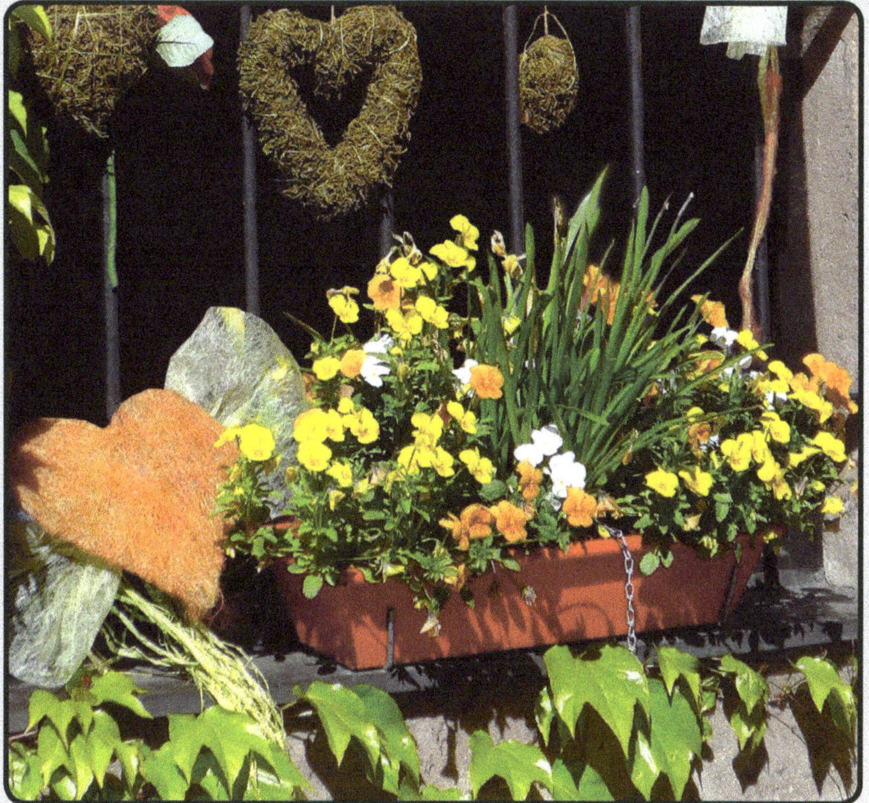

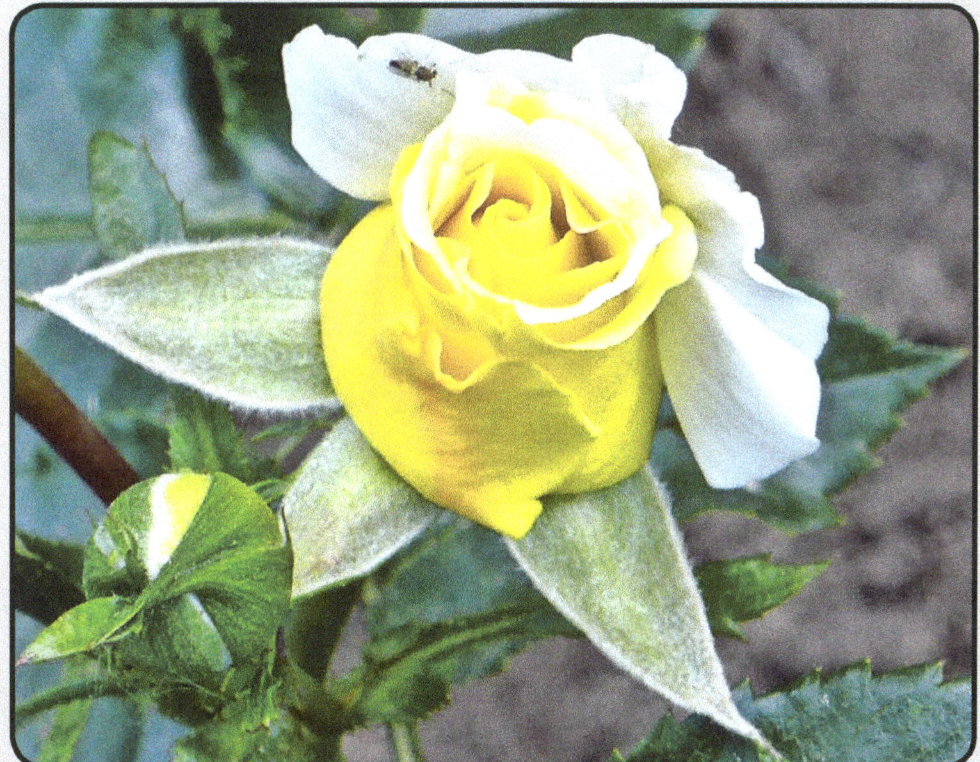

Creeping along.

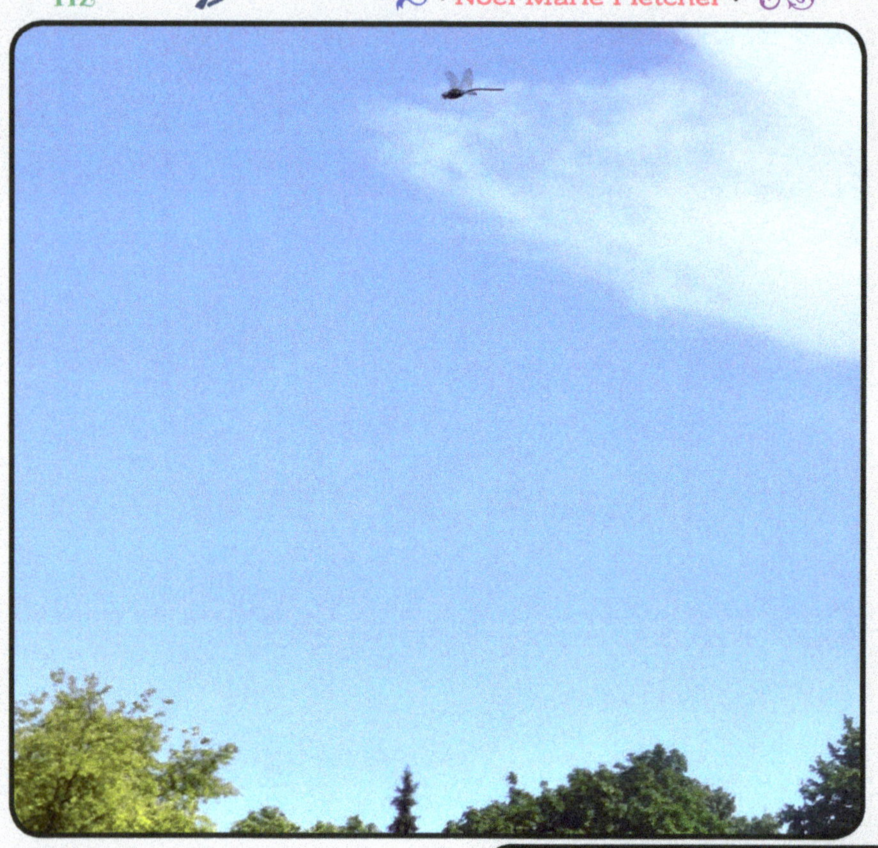

Flight of the dragonfly.

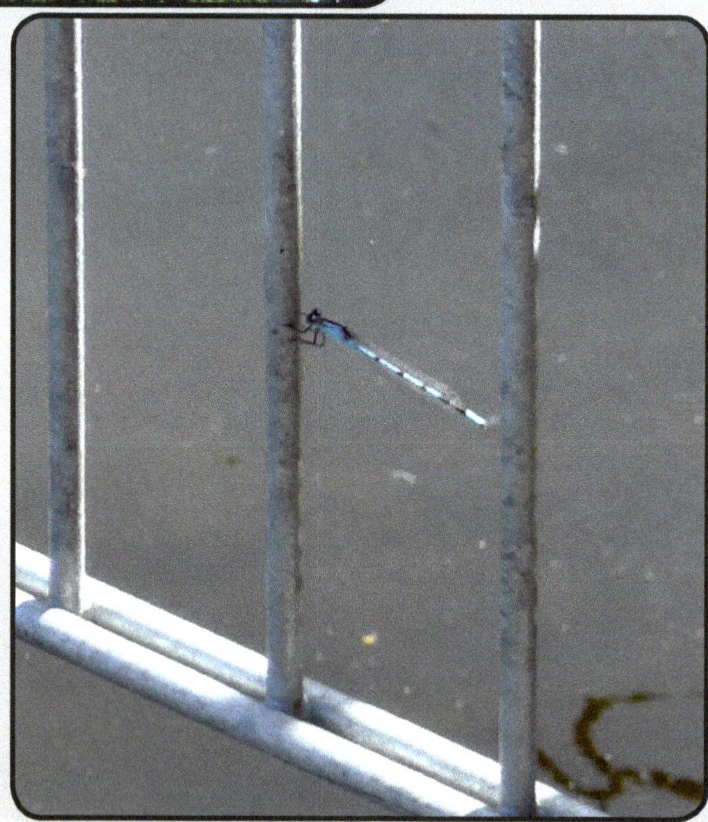

Ascent of the turquoise traveler.

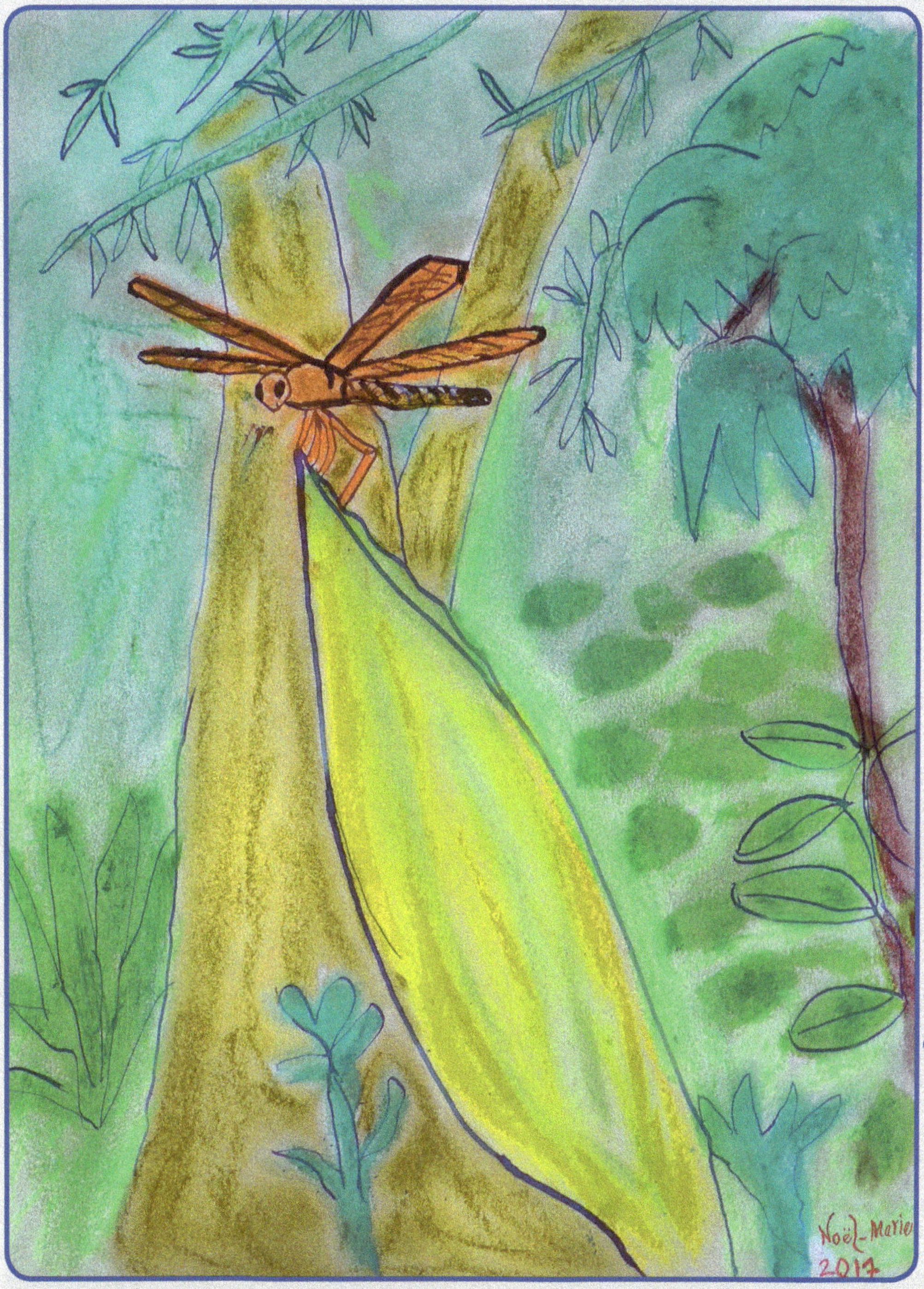

Southern California dragonfly.

In New Mexico, dragonflies are often depicted in Native American art motifs on jewelry and pottery since the insects are seen as important signs of water in barren terrains there.

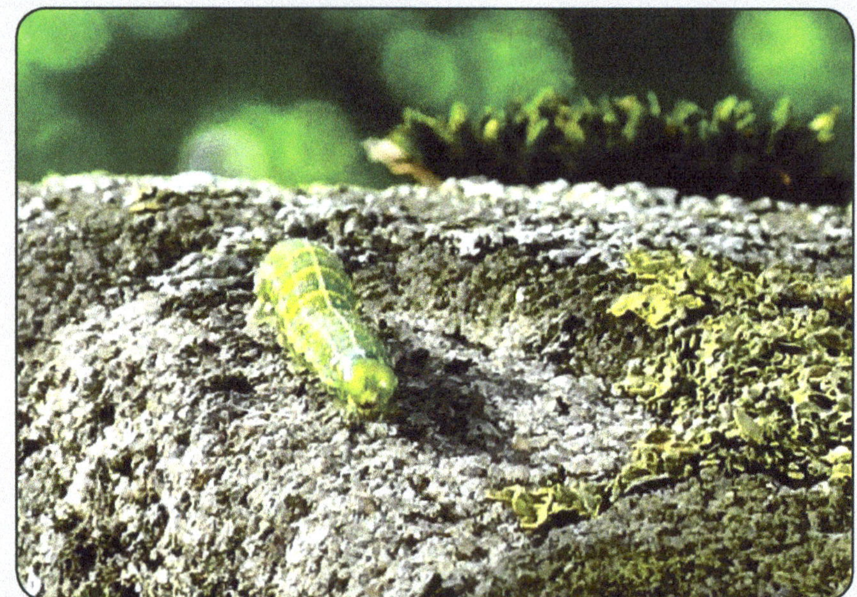

All smiles.

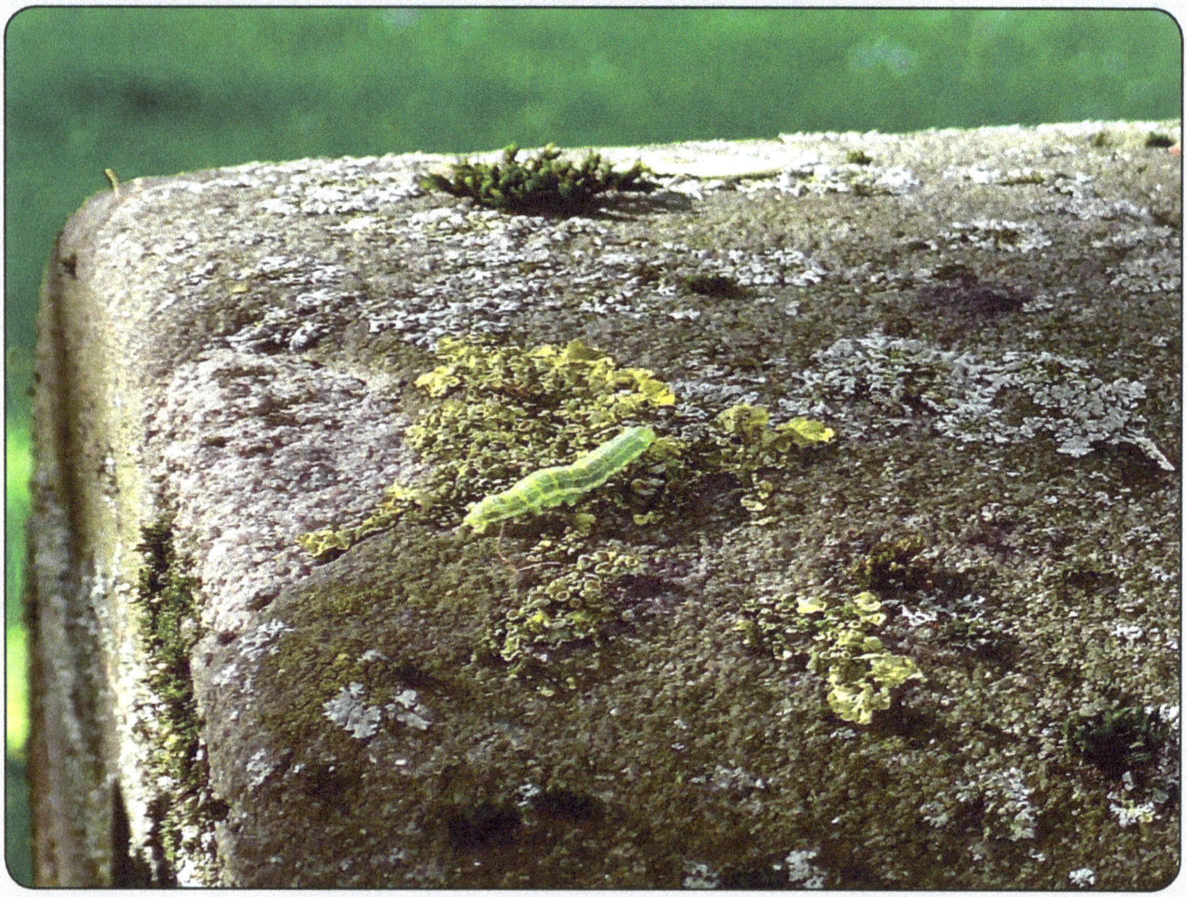

Shuffling along.

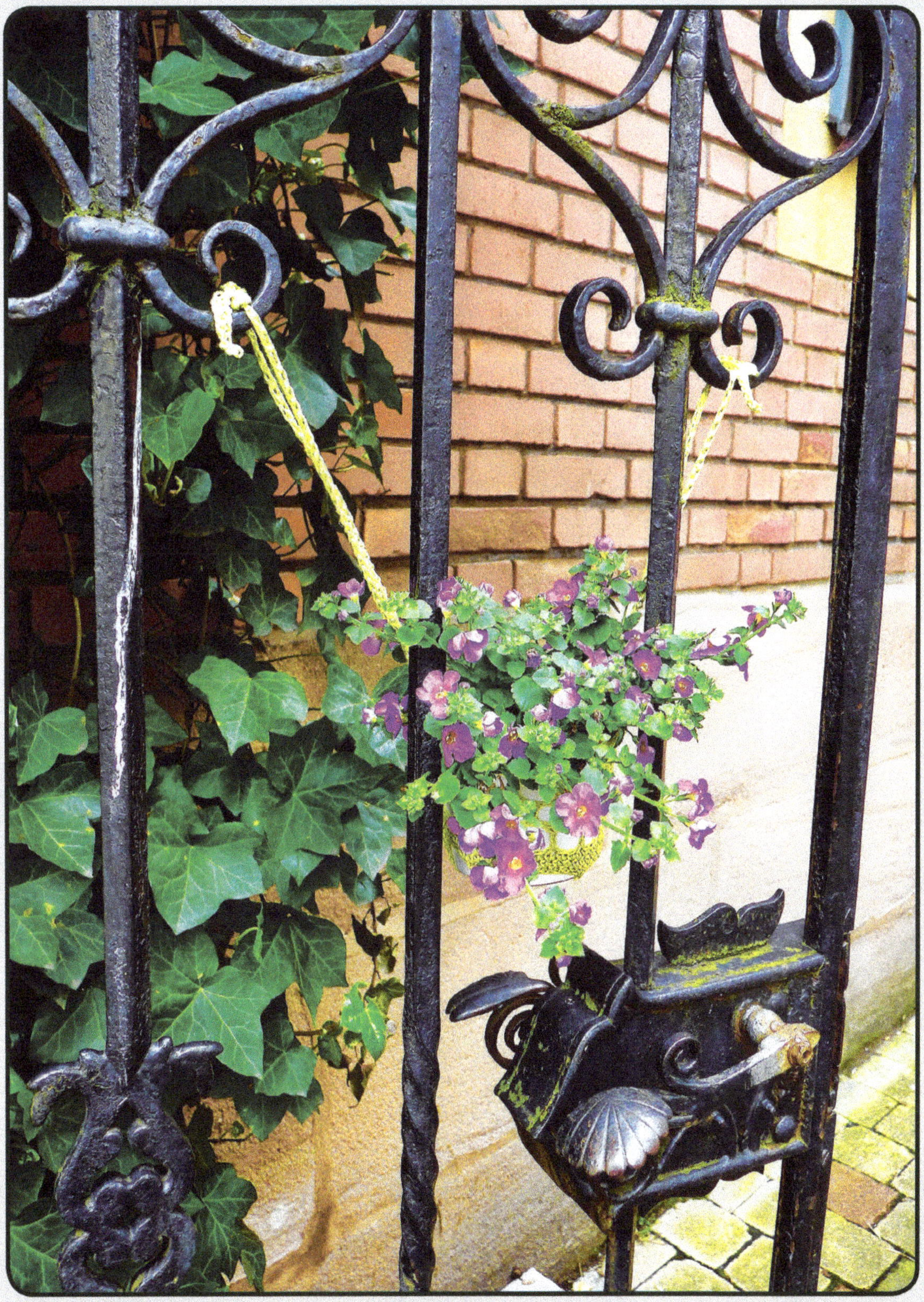

Gate basket.

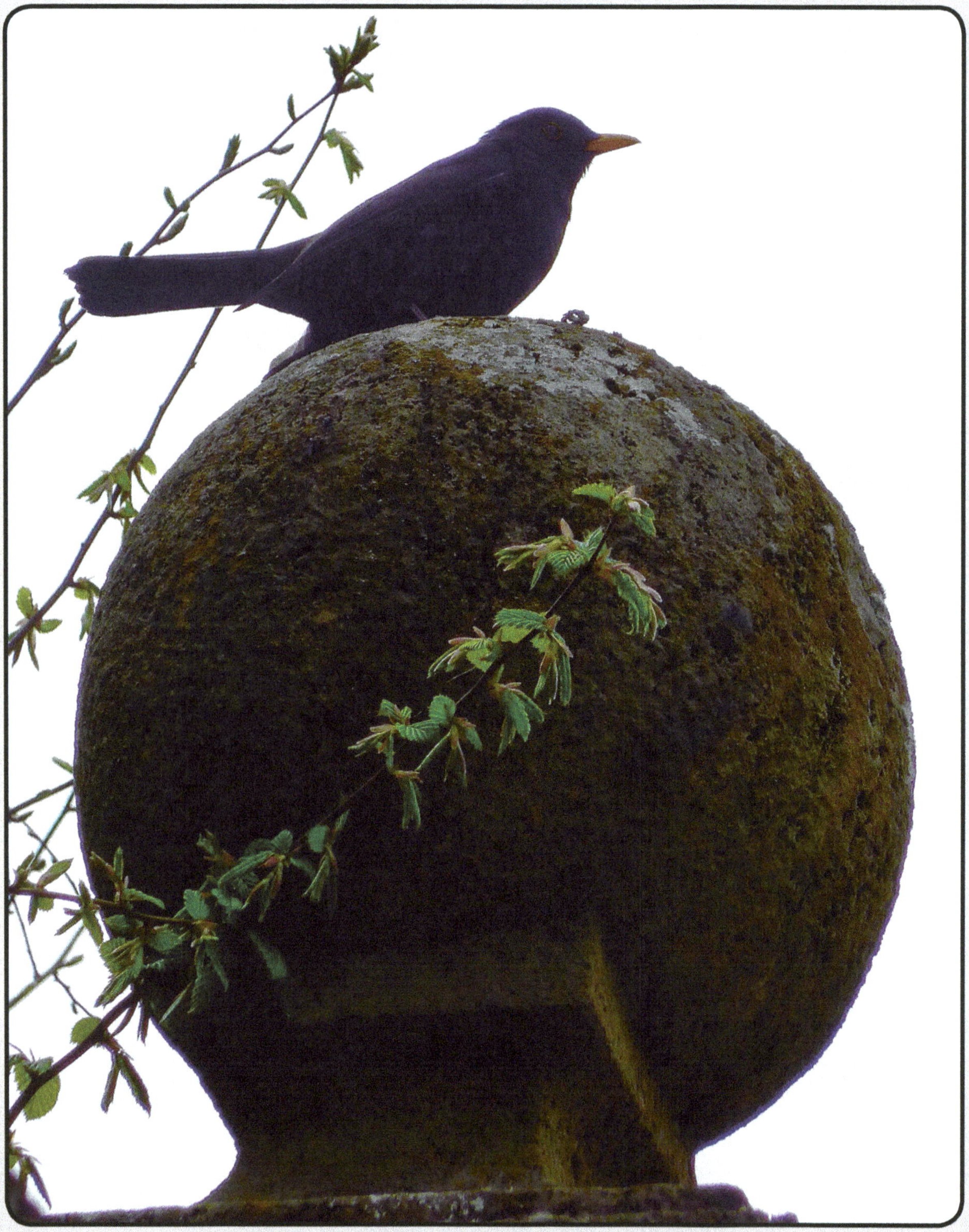

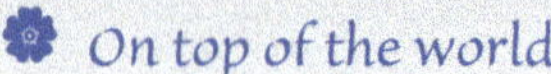

On top of the world.

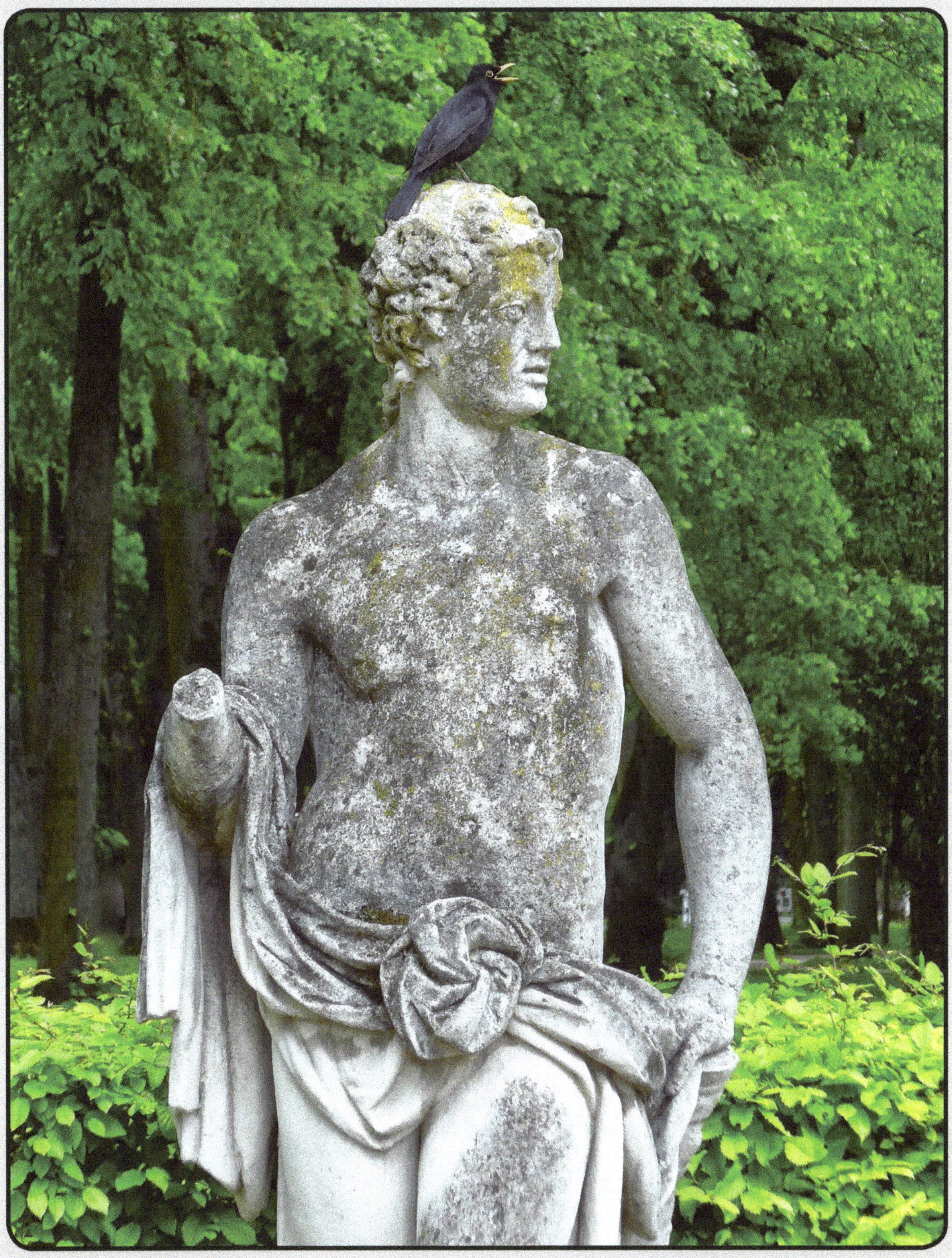

Singing a happy song.

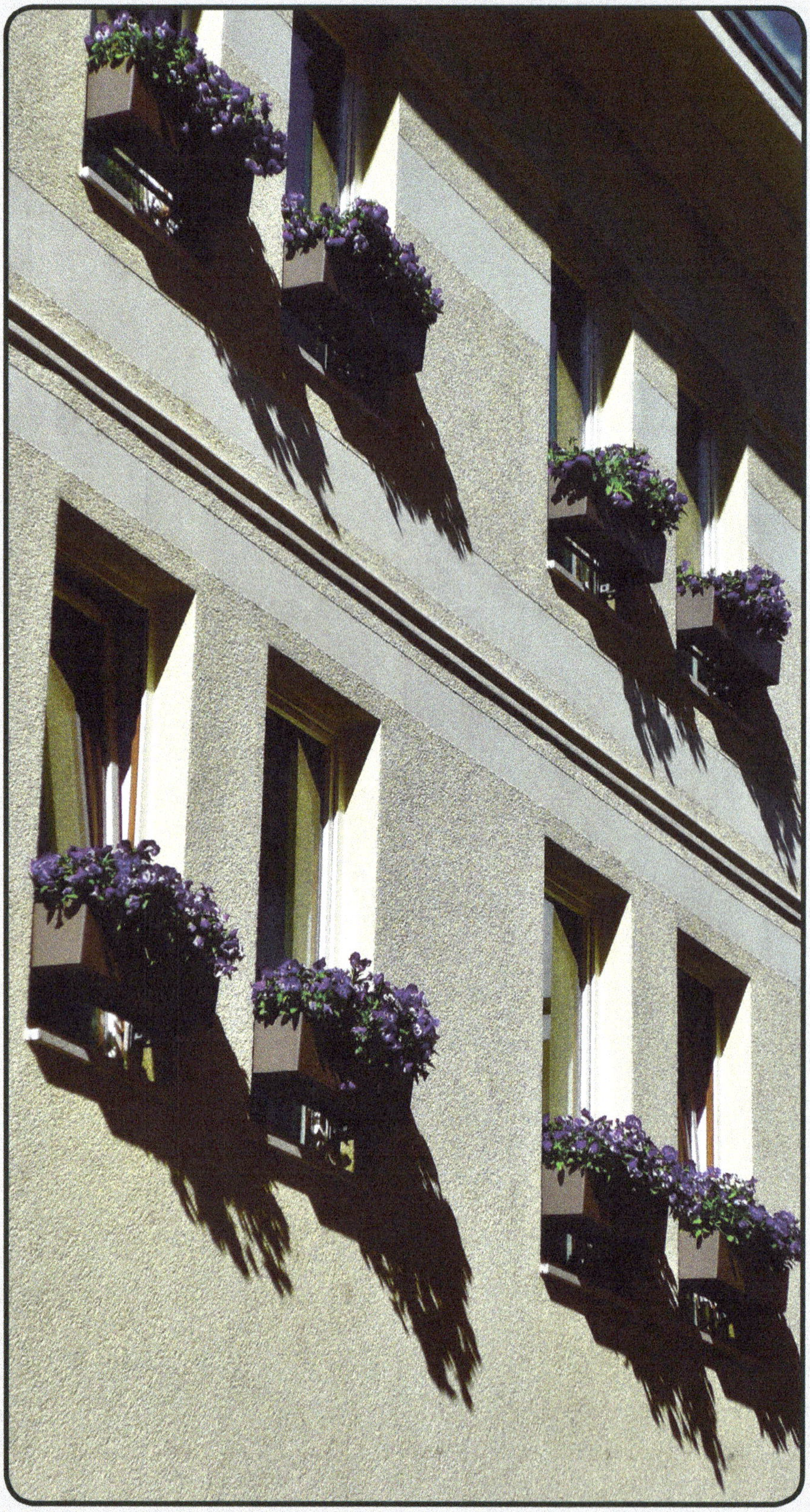

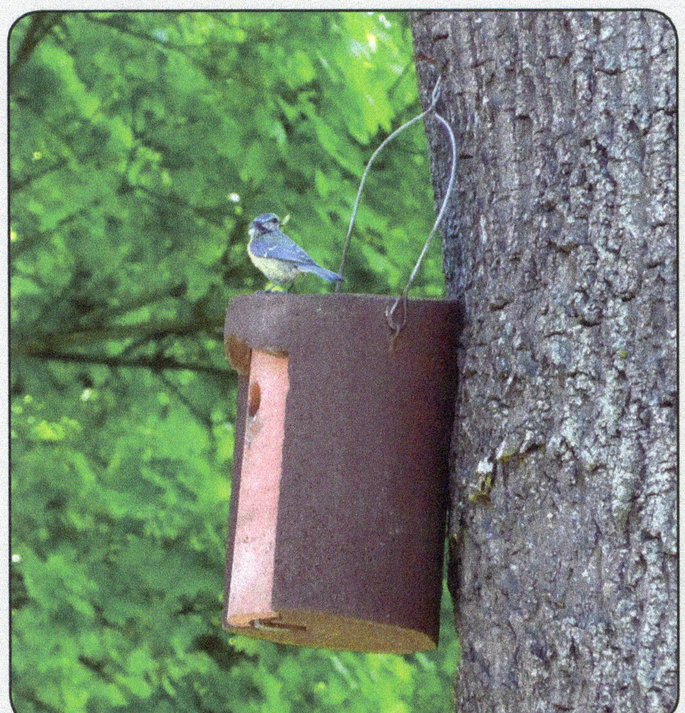

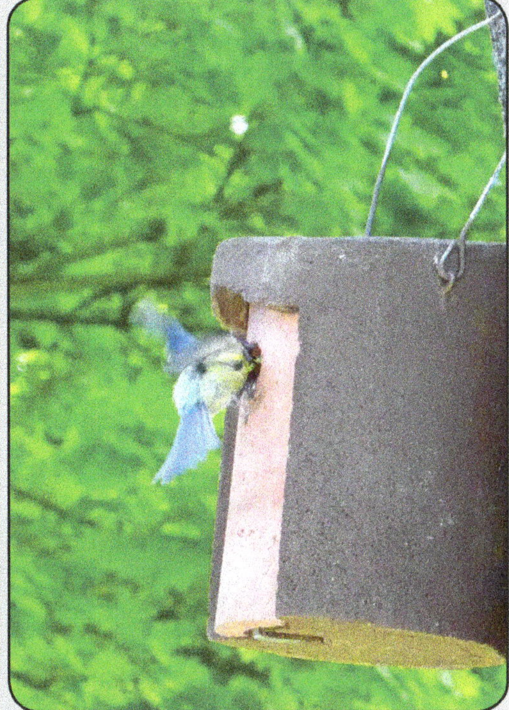

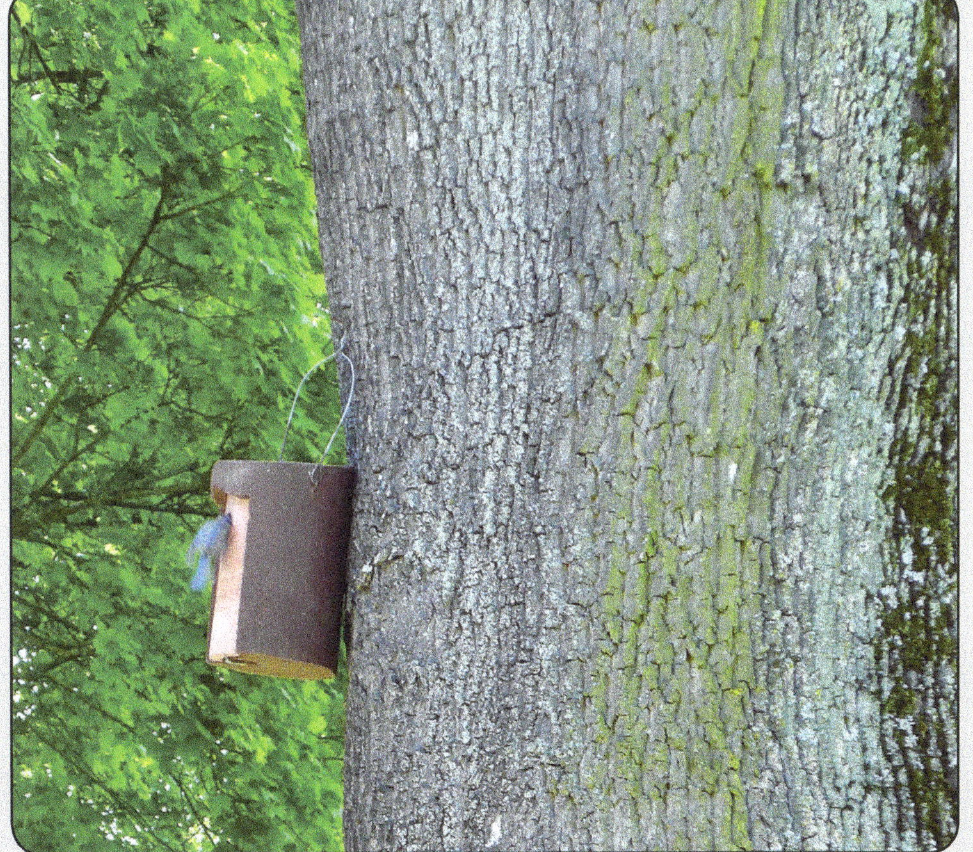

Checking up on the children.

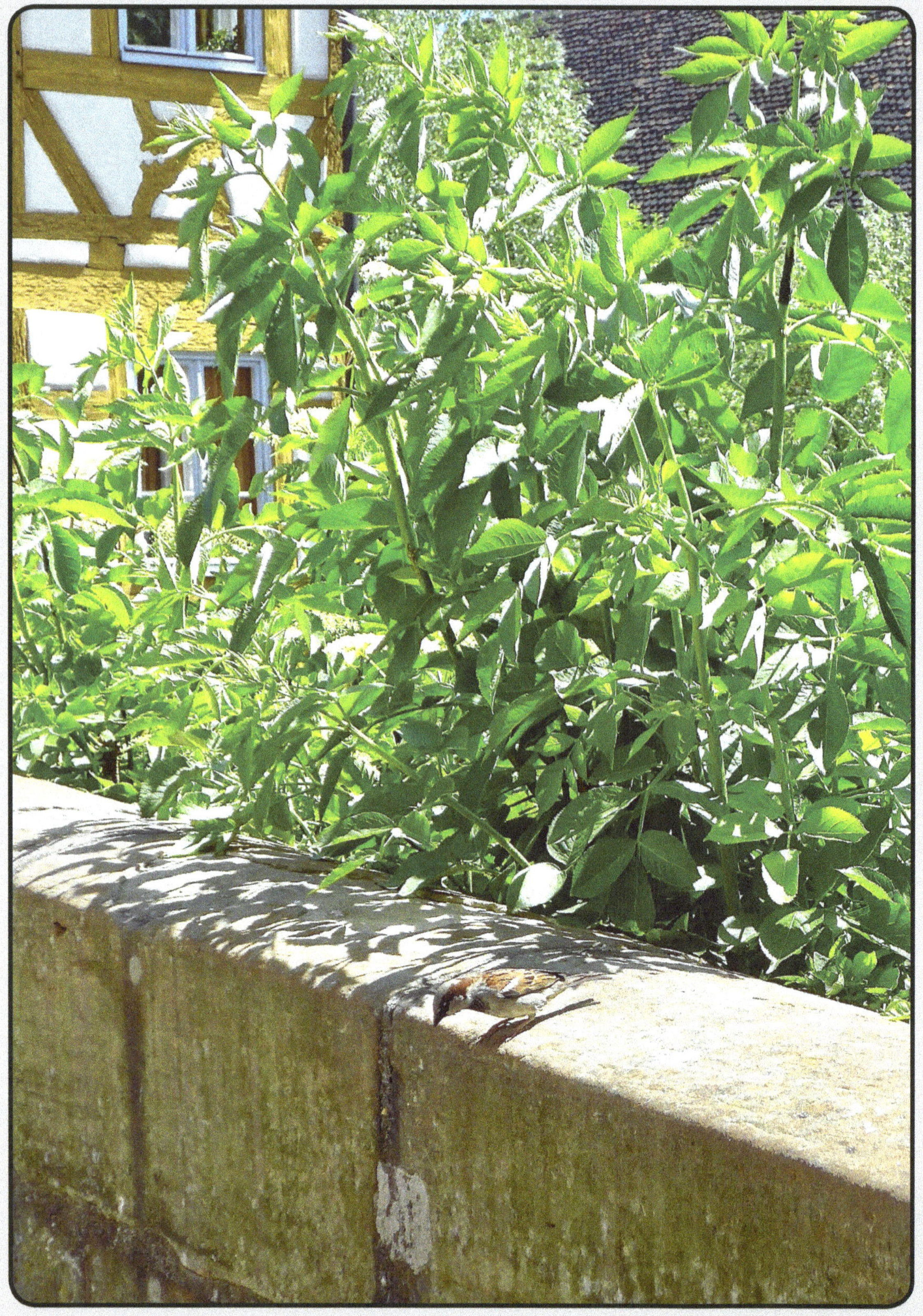

It's a long way down.

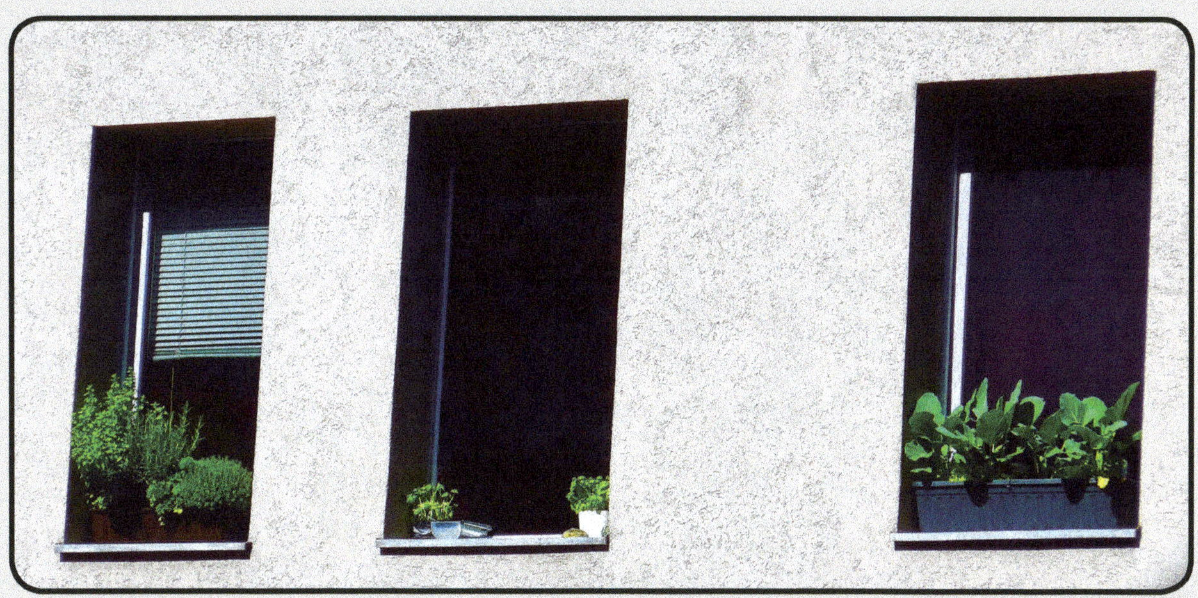

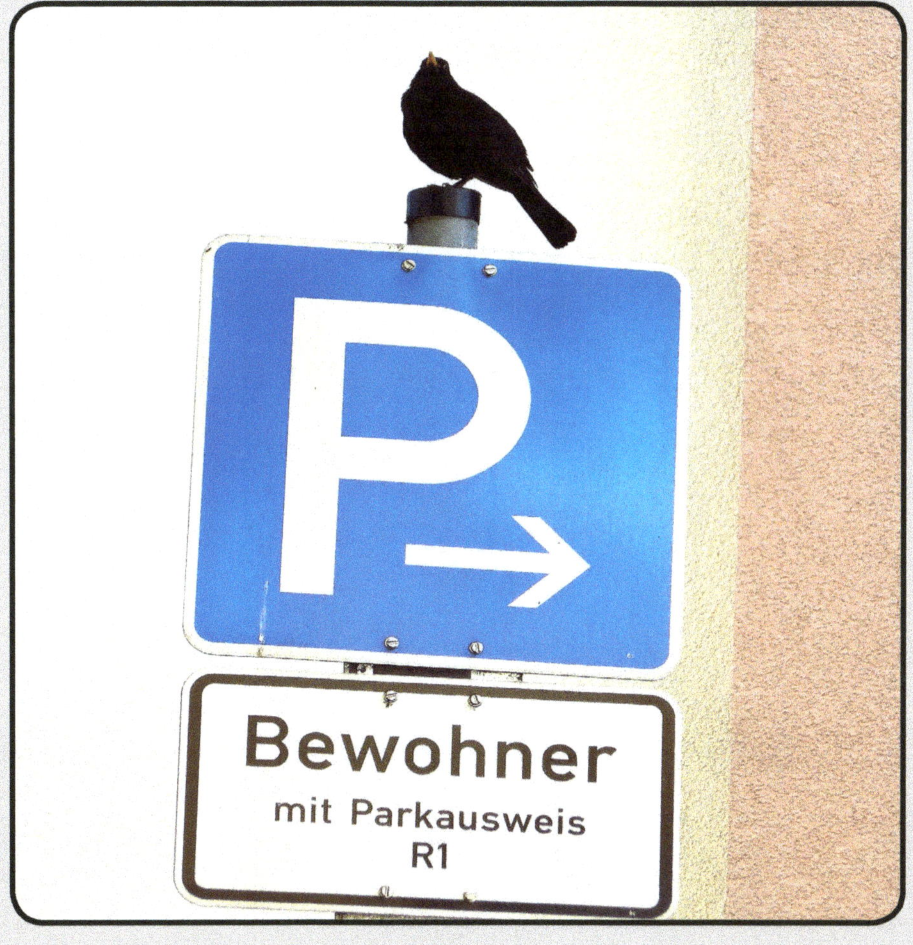


No need for a parking permit.

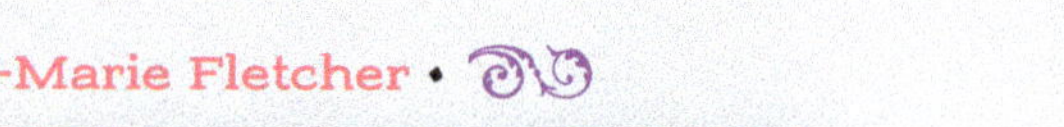

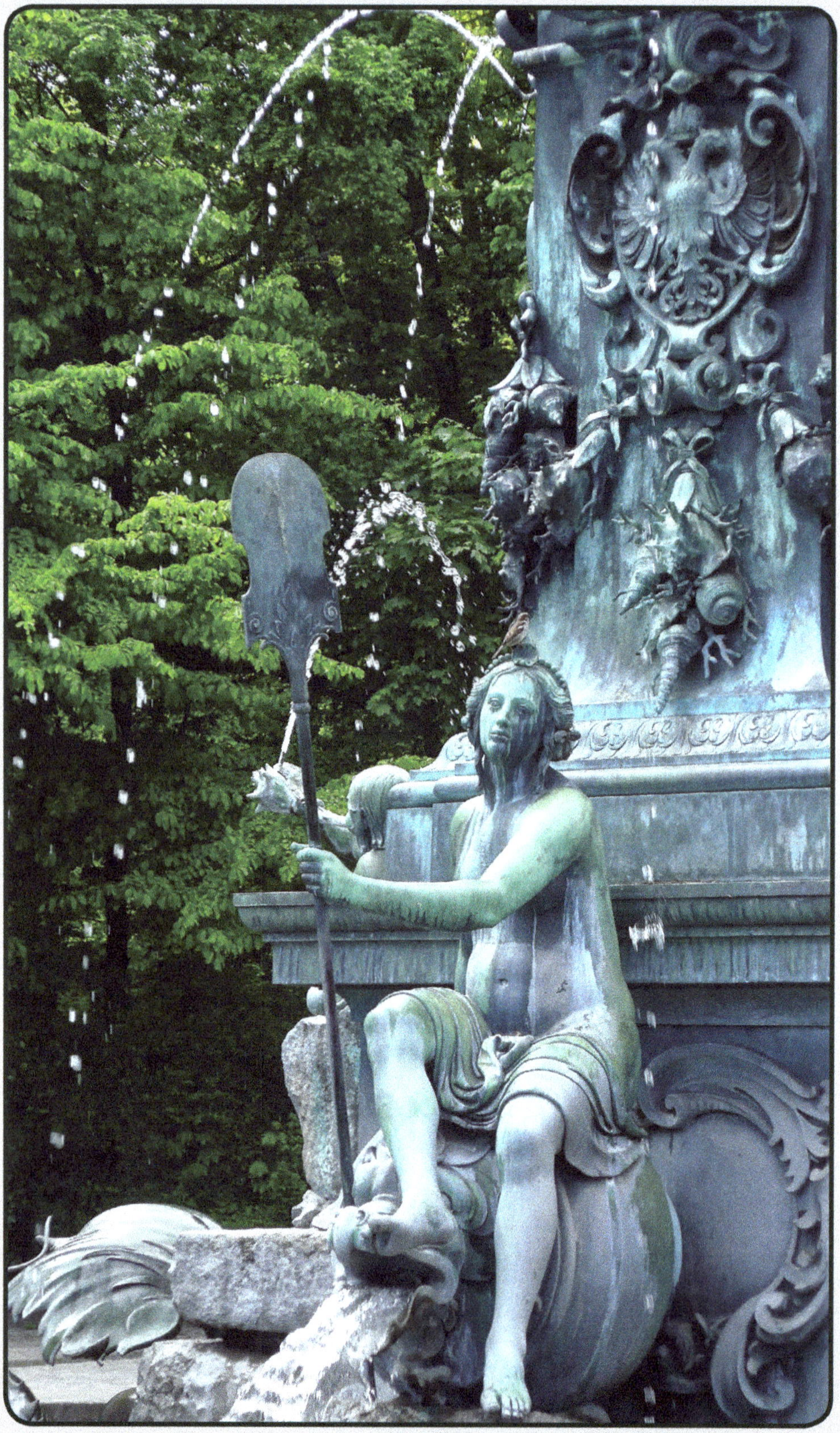

Fount of knowledge.

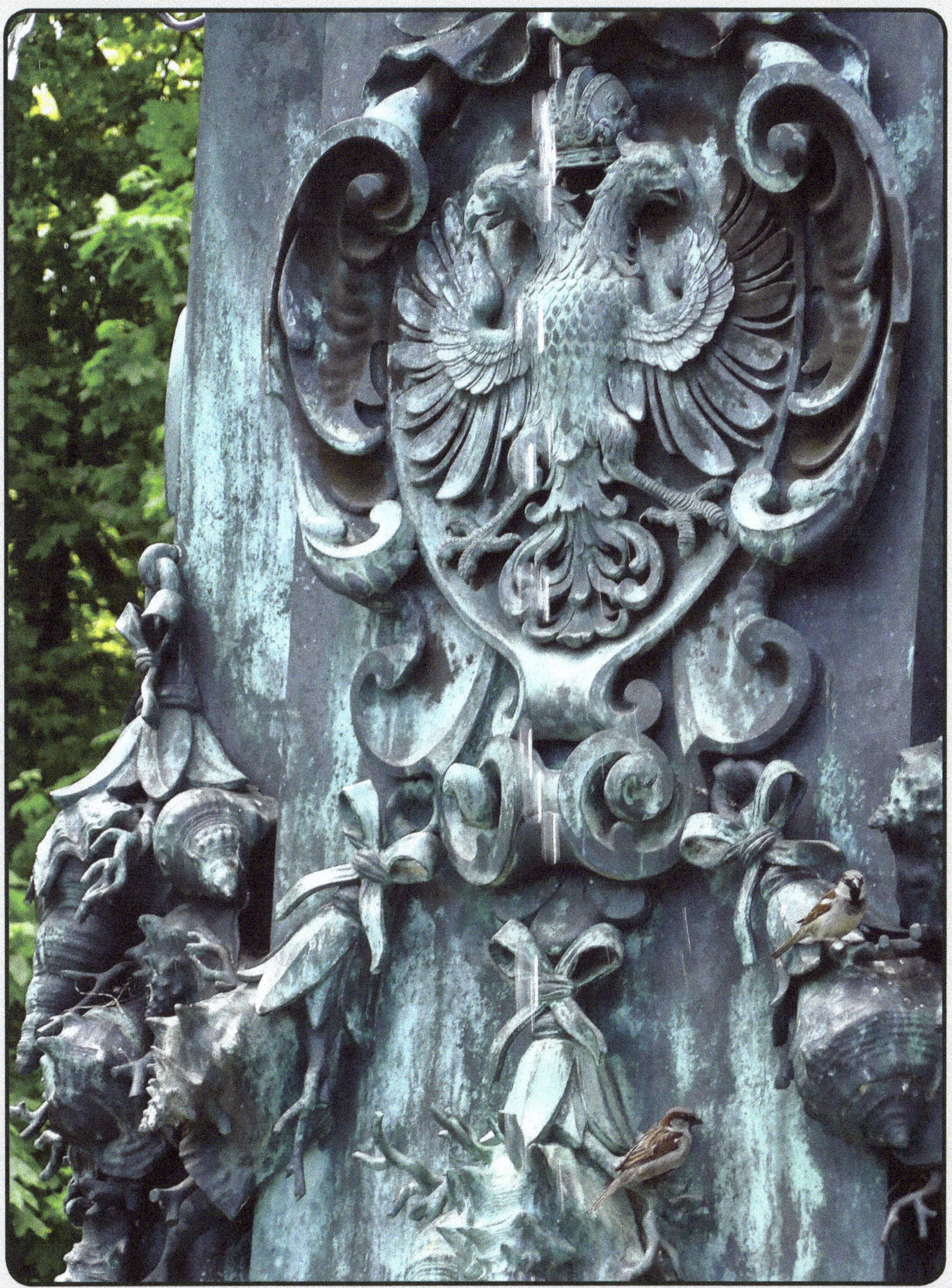

Resting places beneath falling droplets.

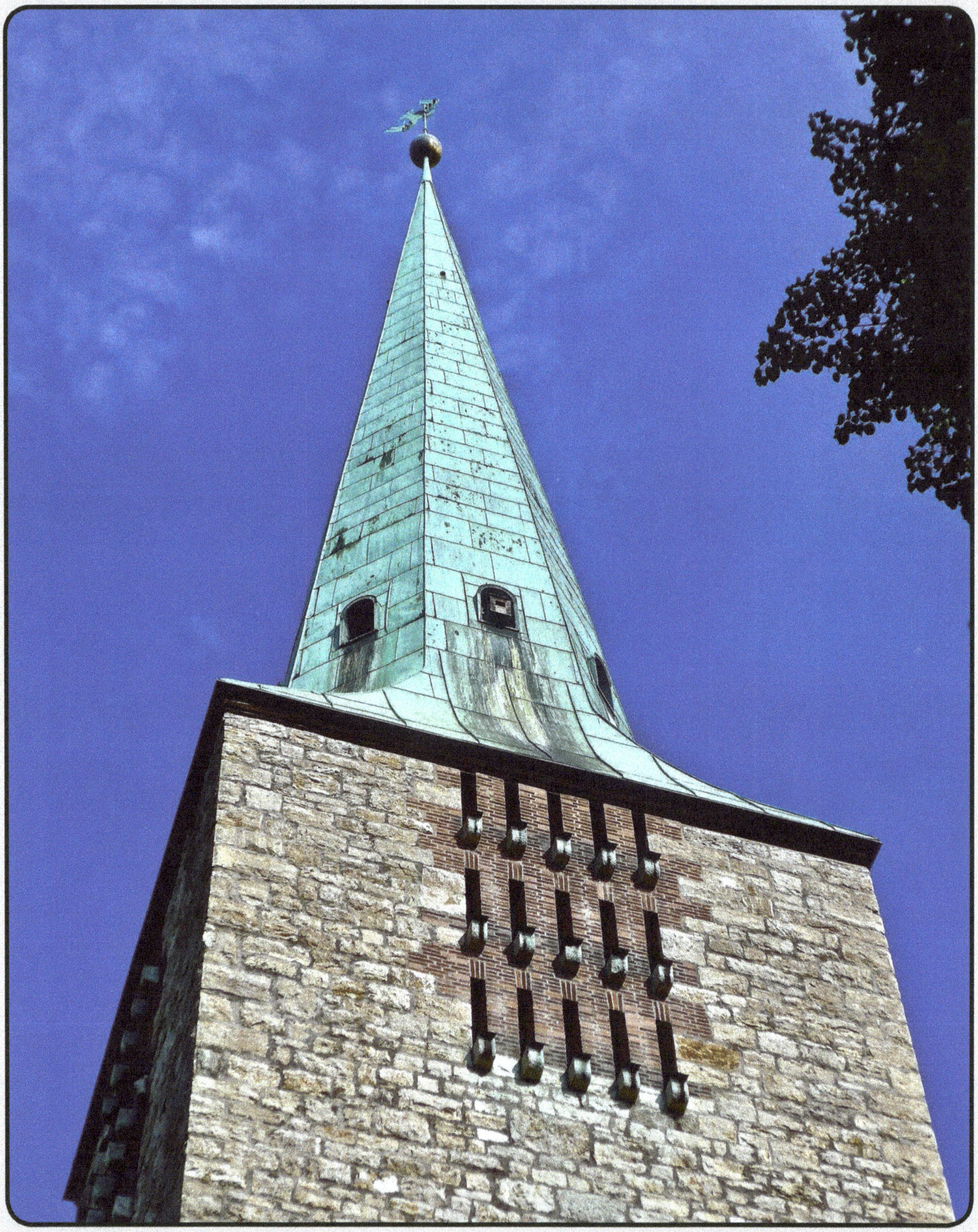

Bird abodes in house of worship in Germany.

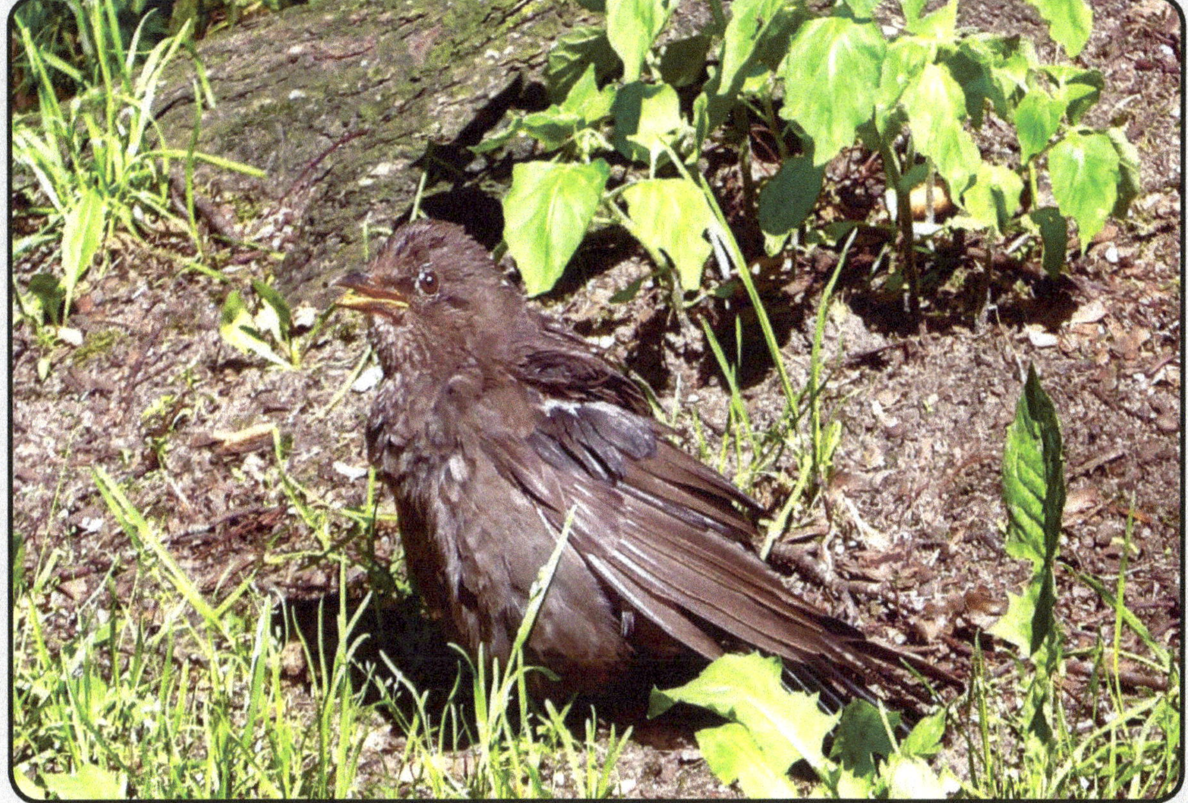

Smiling for the camera.

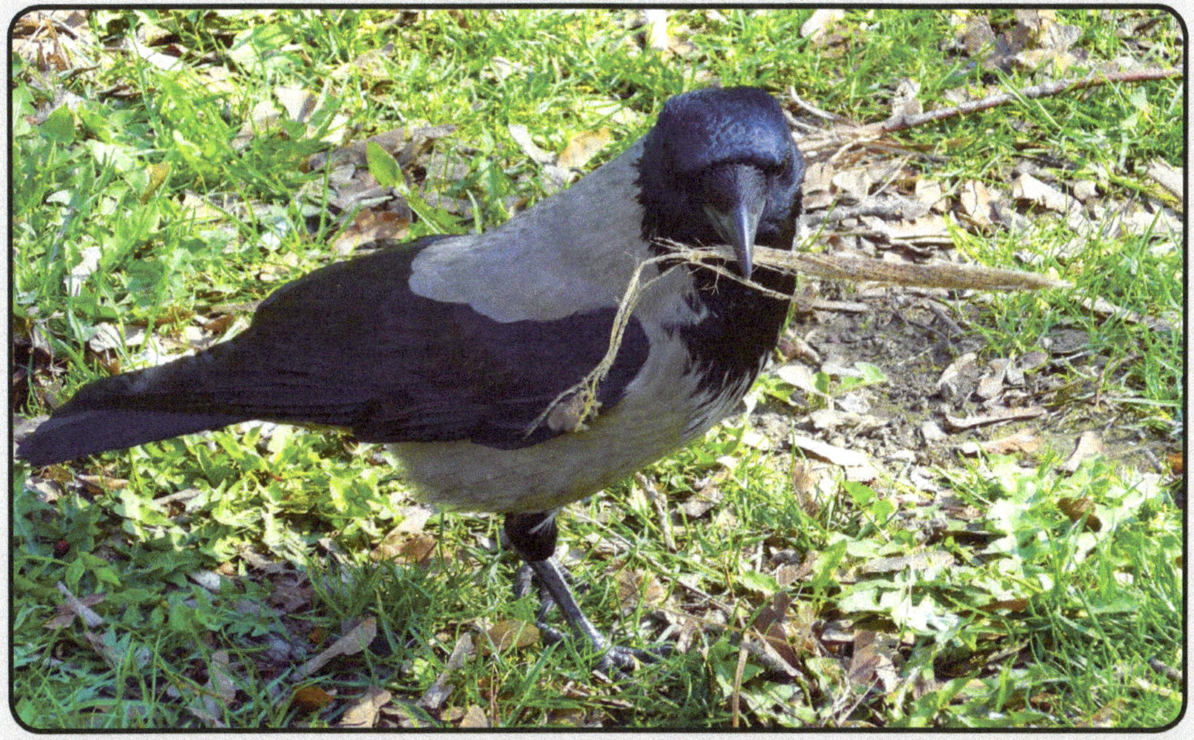

Hooded crow shops at park in Vienna.

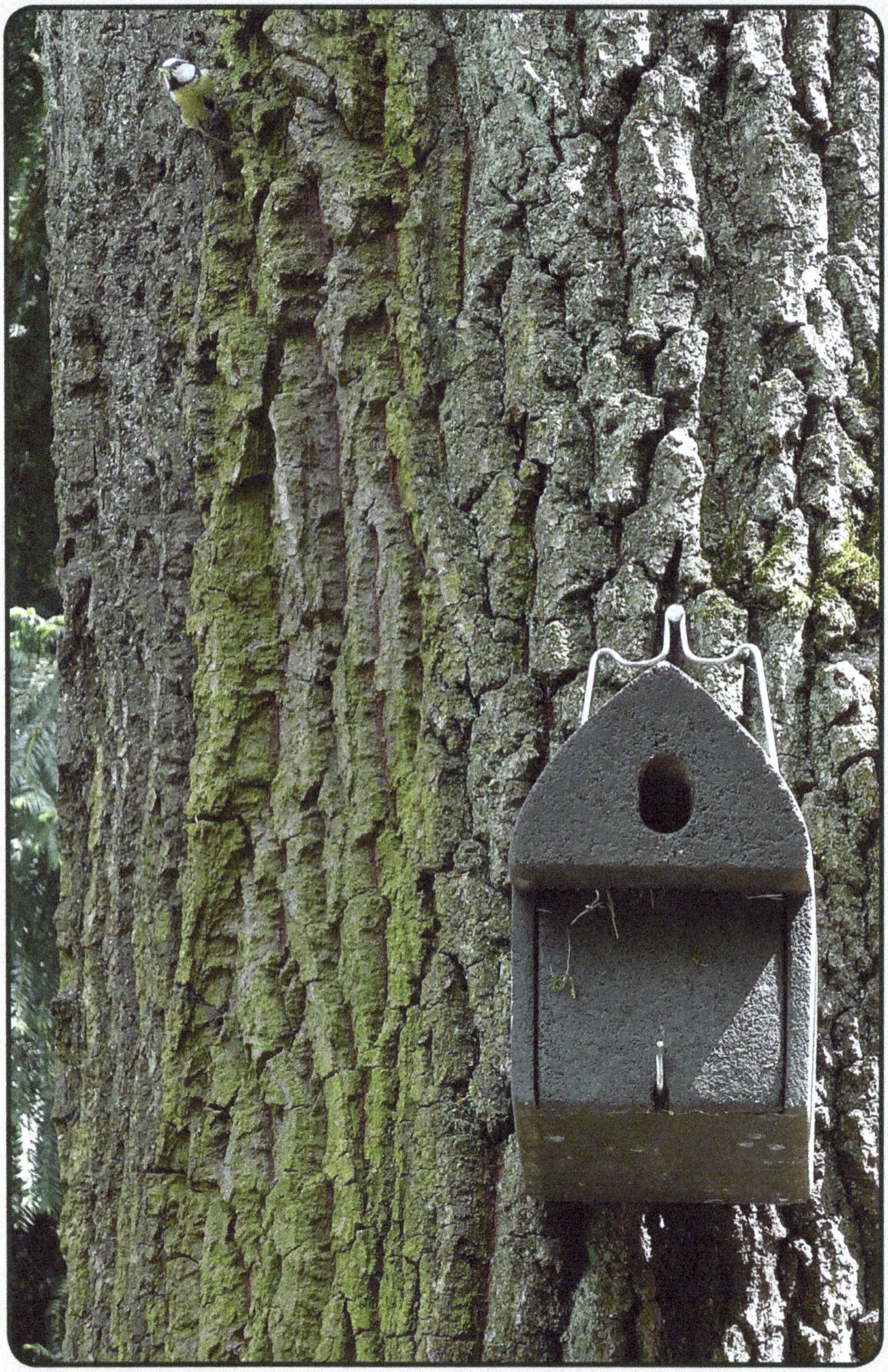

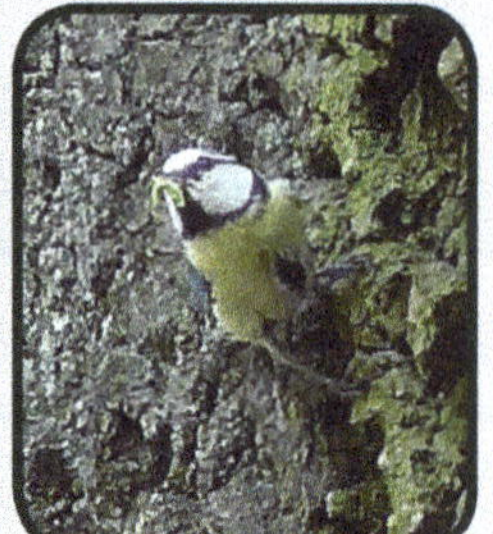

Closeup of the bird watching me while clutching onto the tree, upper left of larger photo.

Protecting the nest series. On the opposite page, the bird ventures inside to check that the chirping little ones are okay before leaving out the front door to patrol outside.

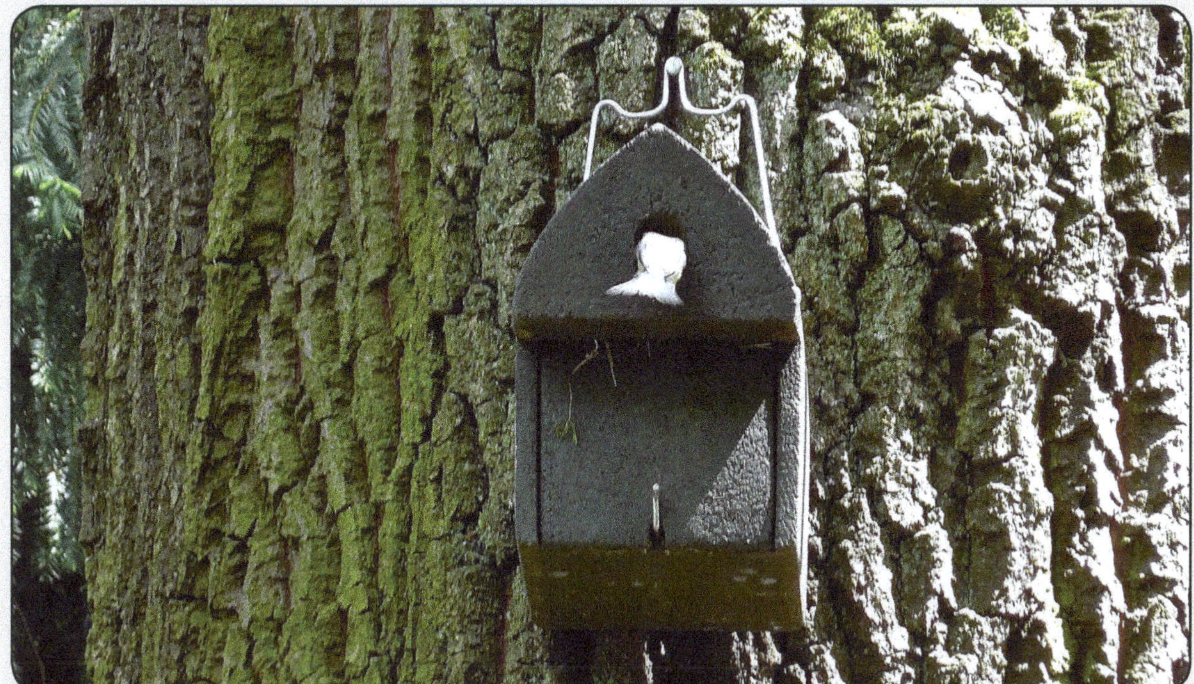

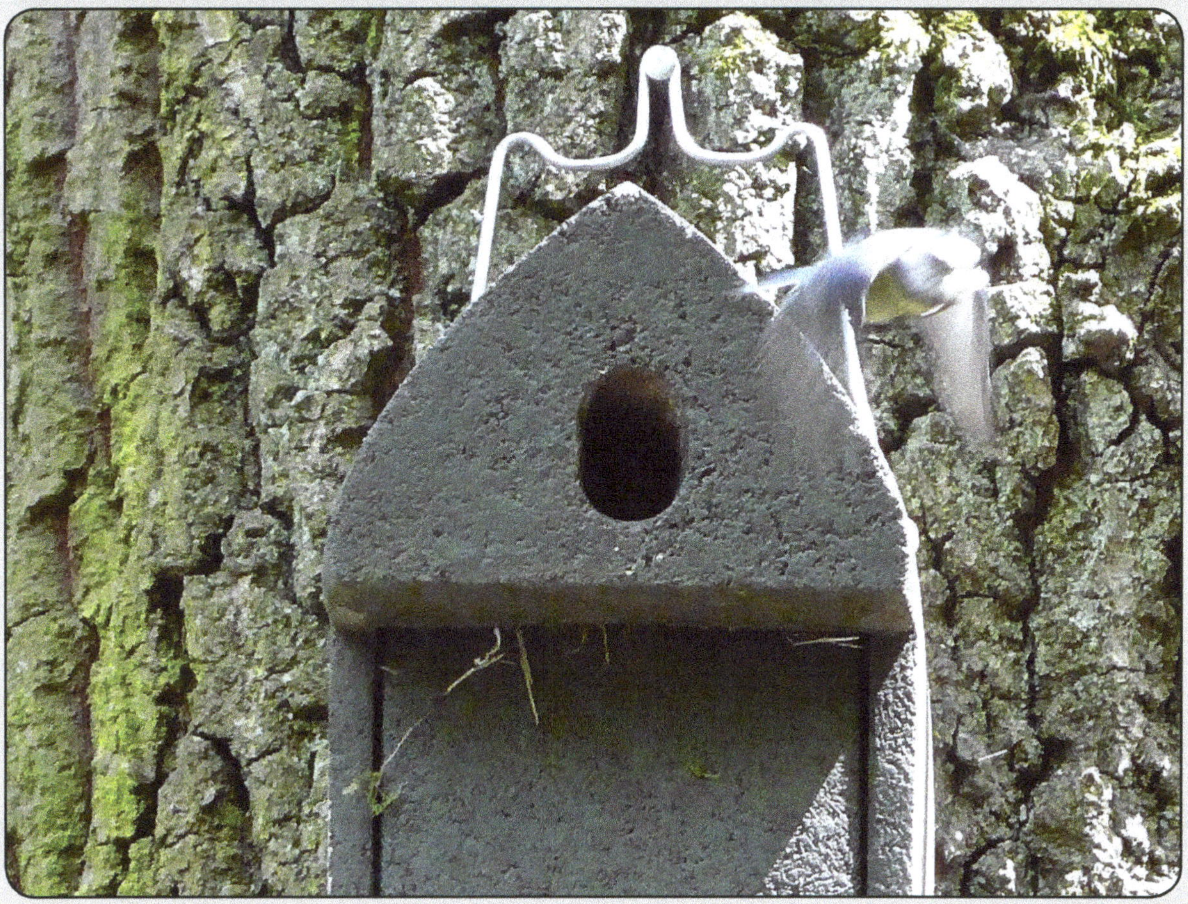

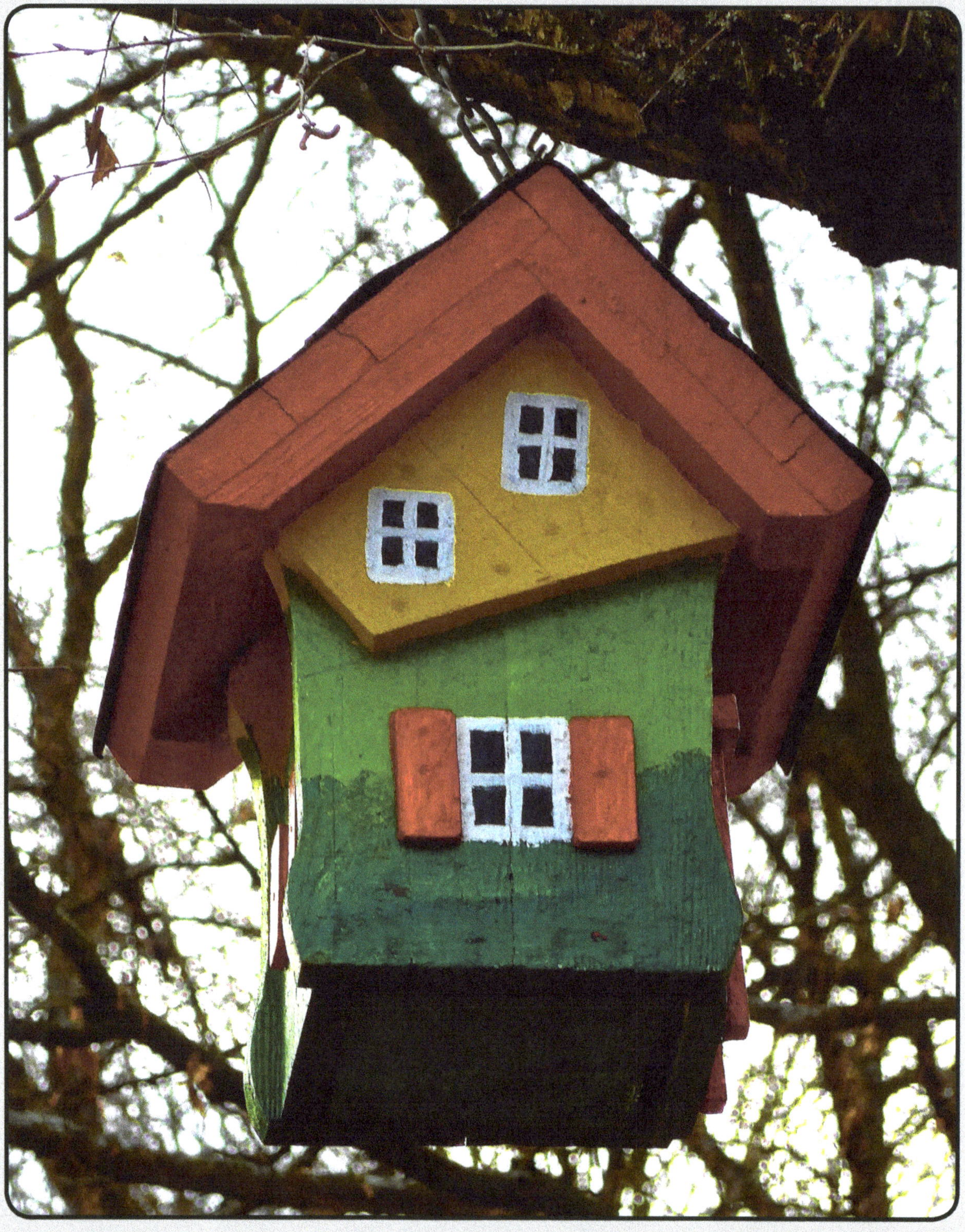

Bird house Bavarian style.

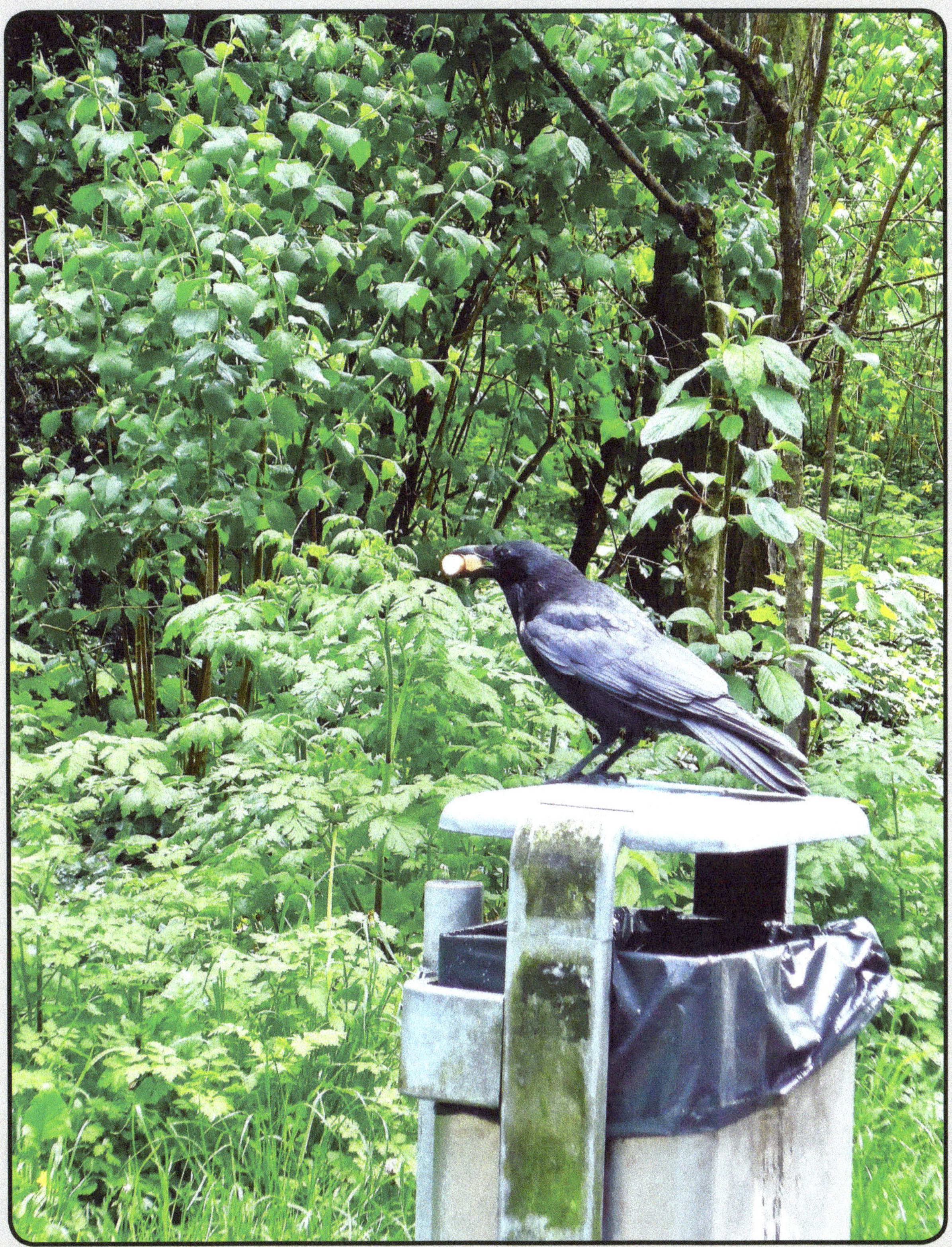

One man's garbage is this bird's treasure.

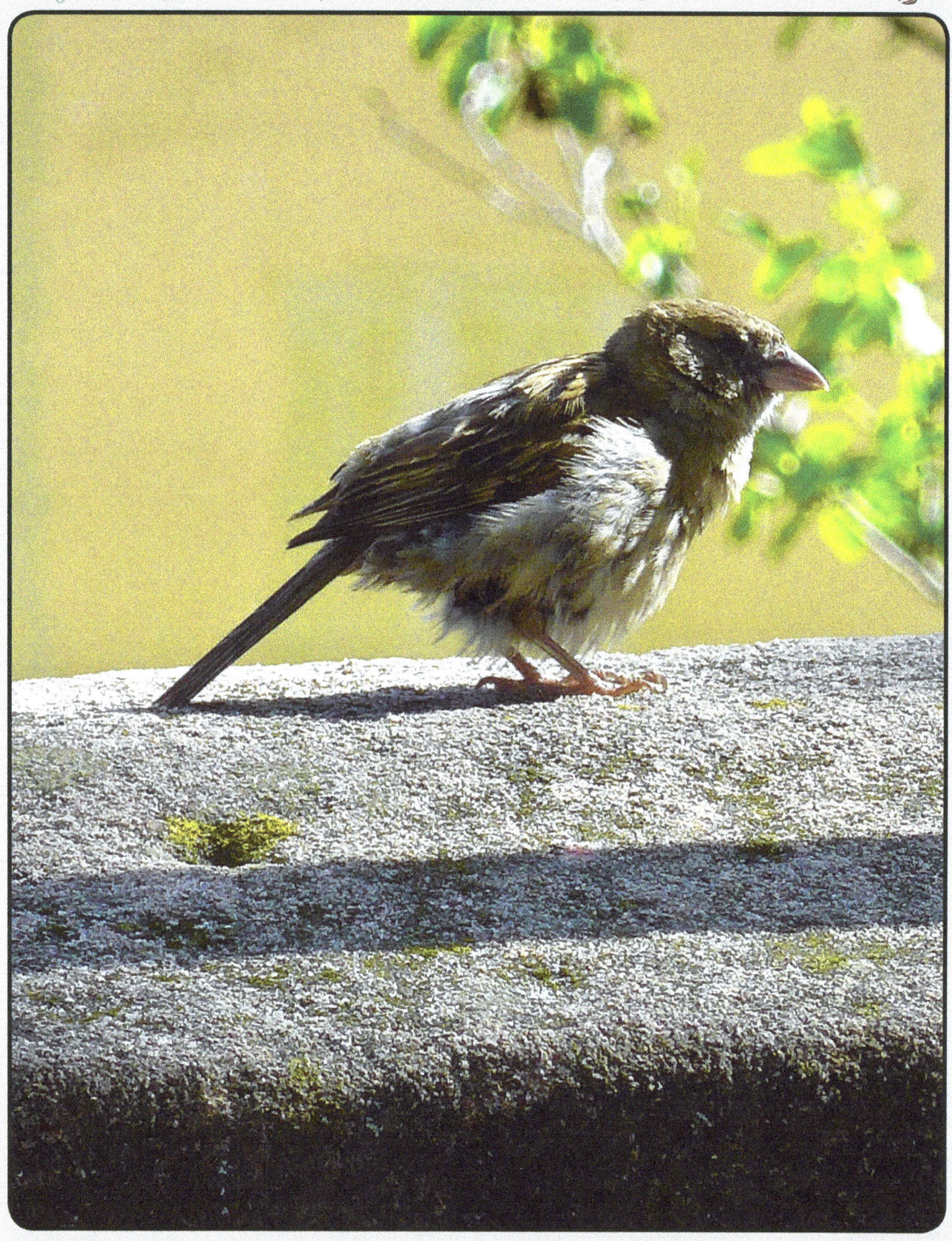

Midday sunbath series.

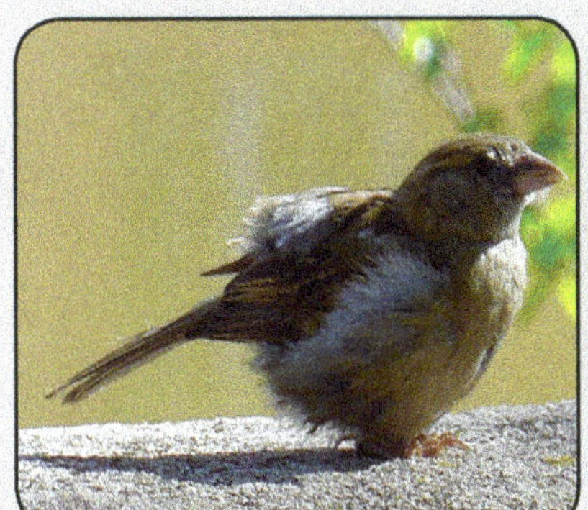
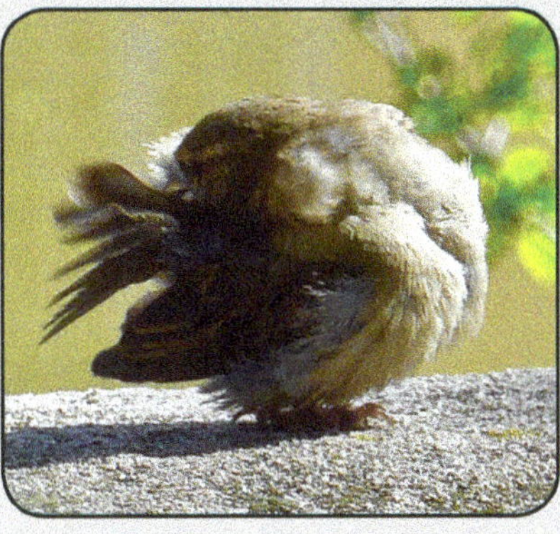
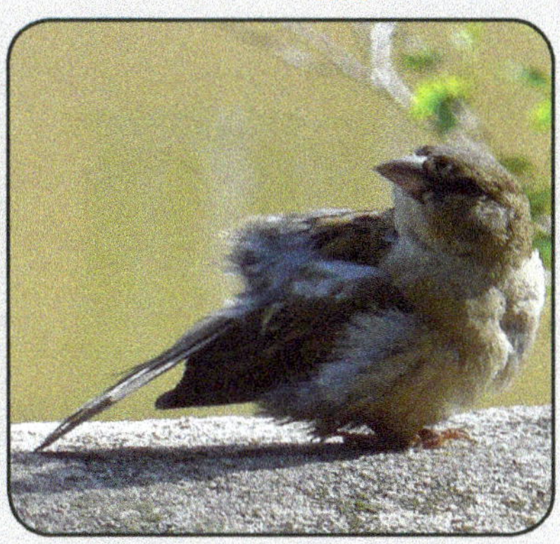
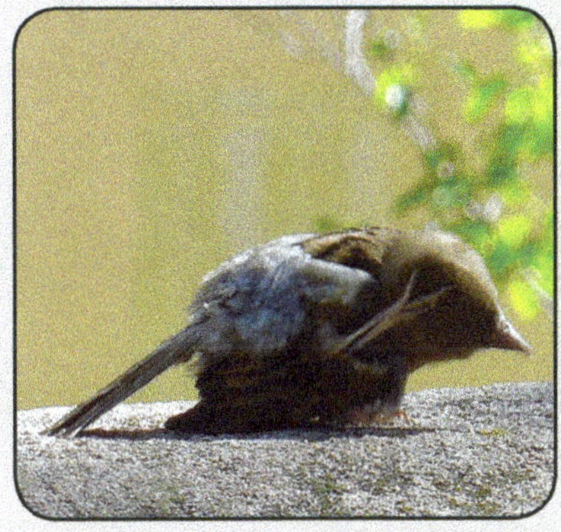
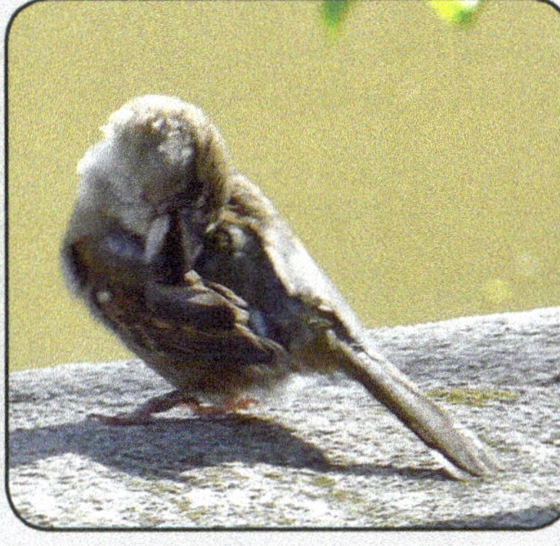
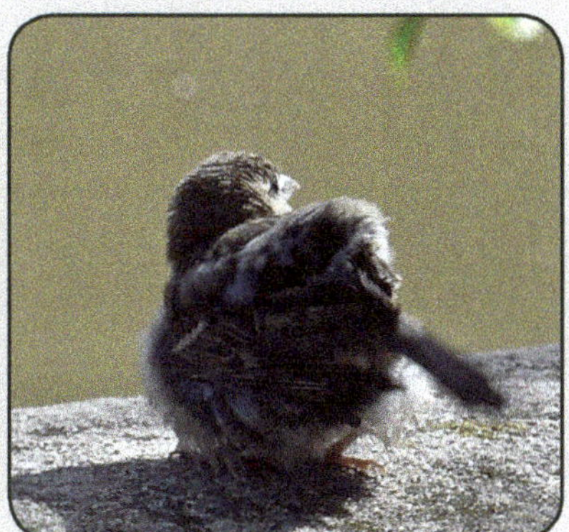
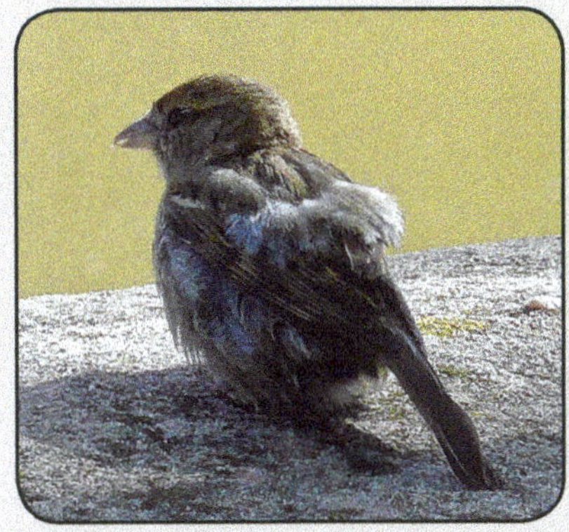
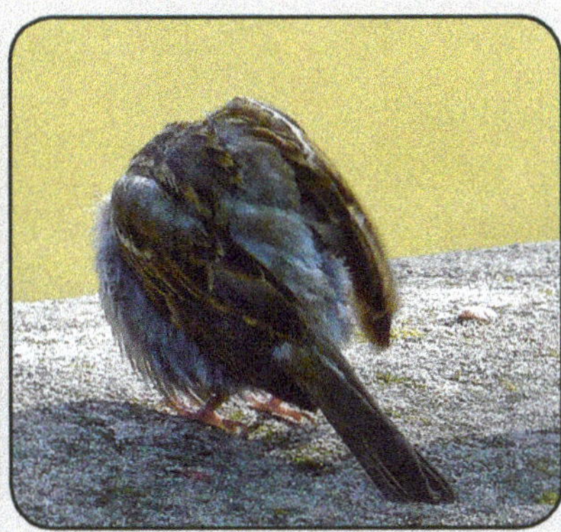
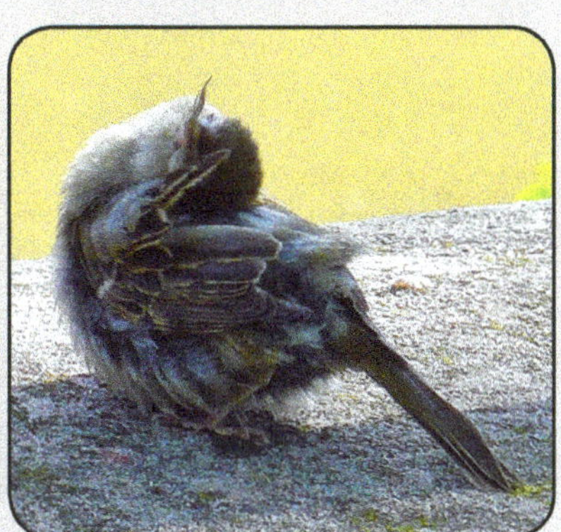
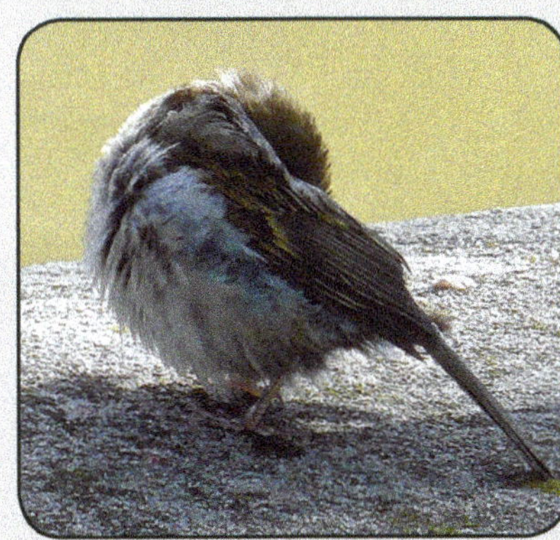
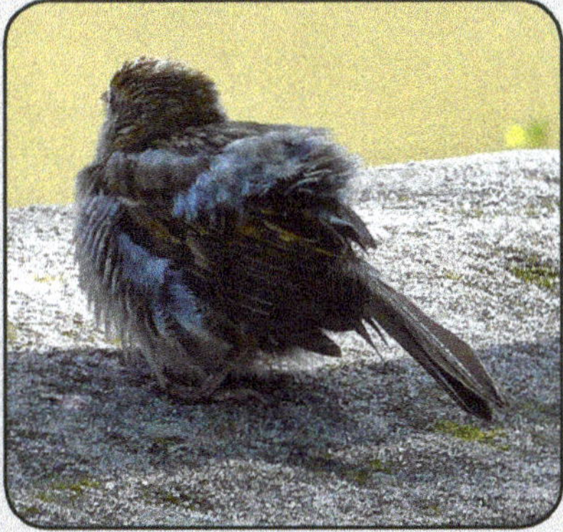
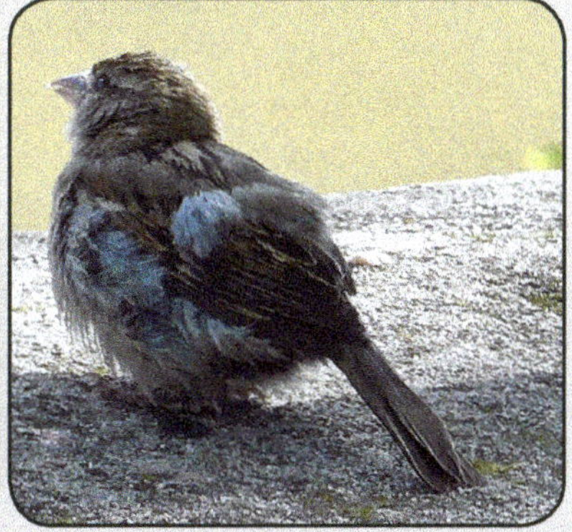

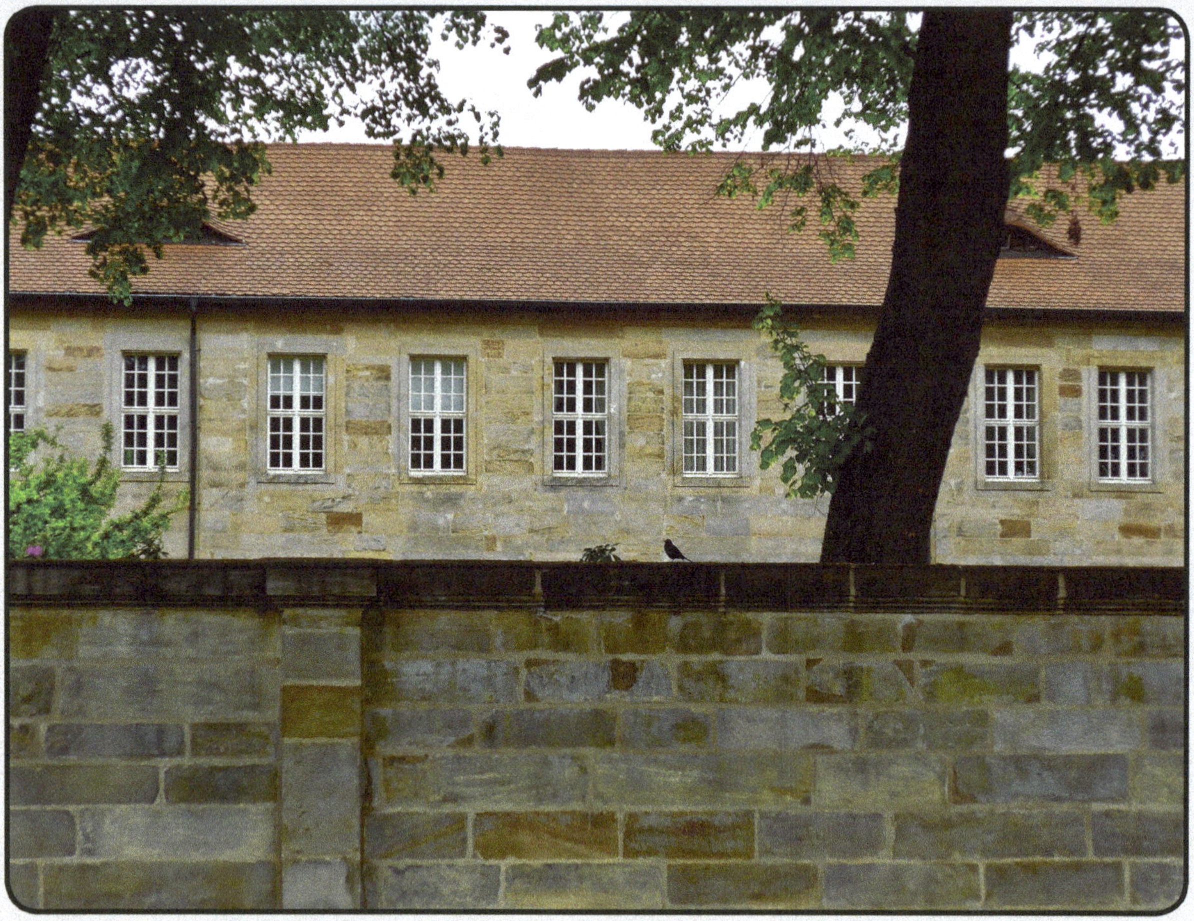

Singing a happy tune at the New Palace in Bayreuth, Germany.

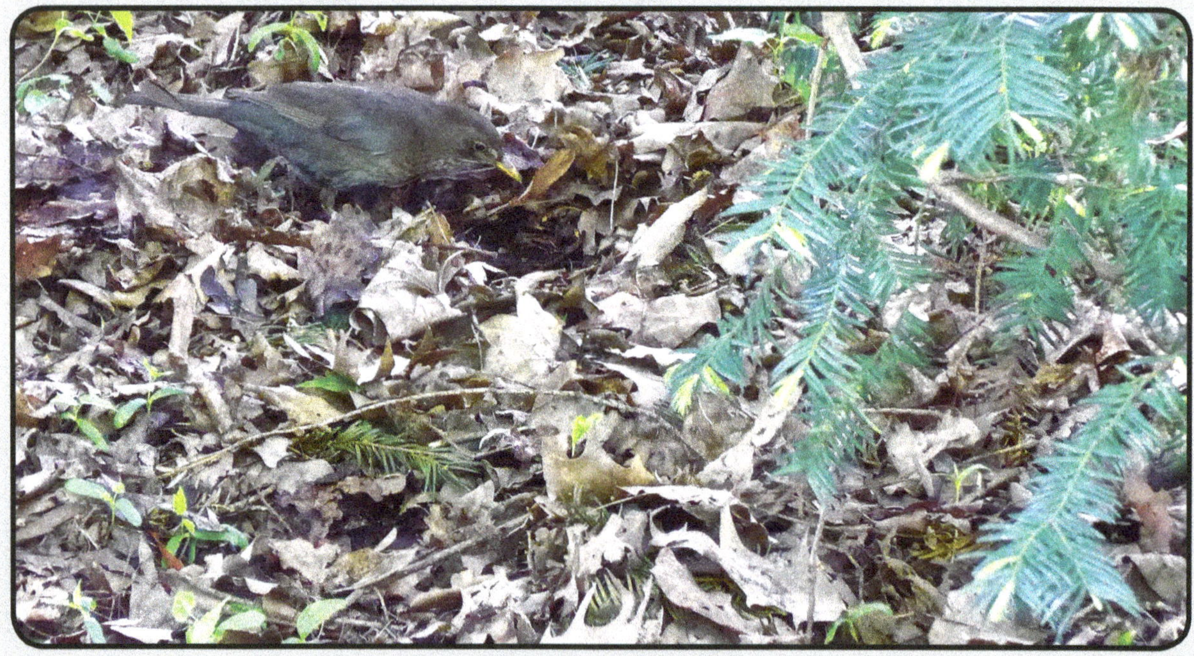

Any goodies under there?

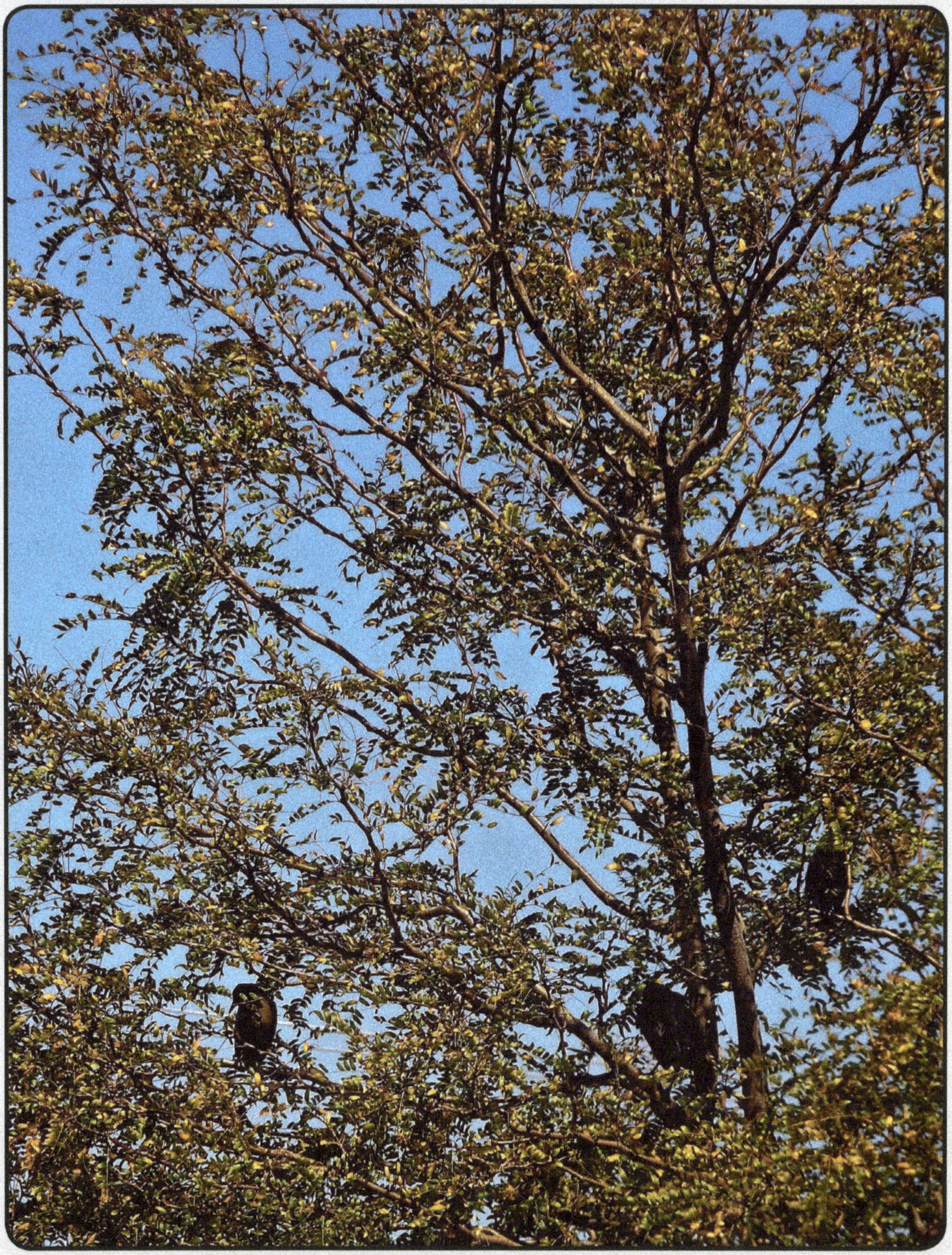

Gazing down at grocery store patrons.

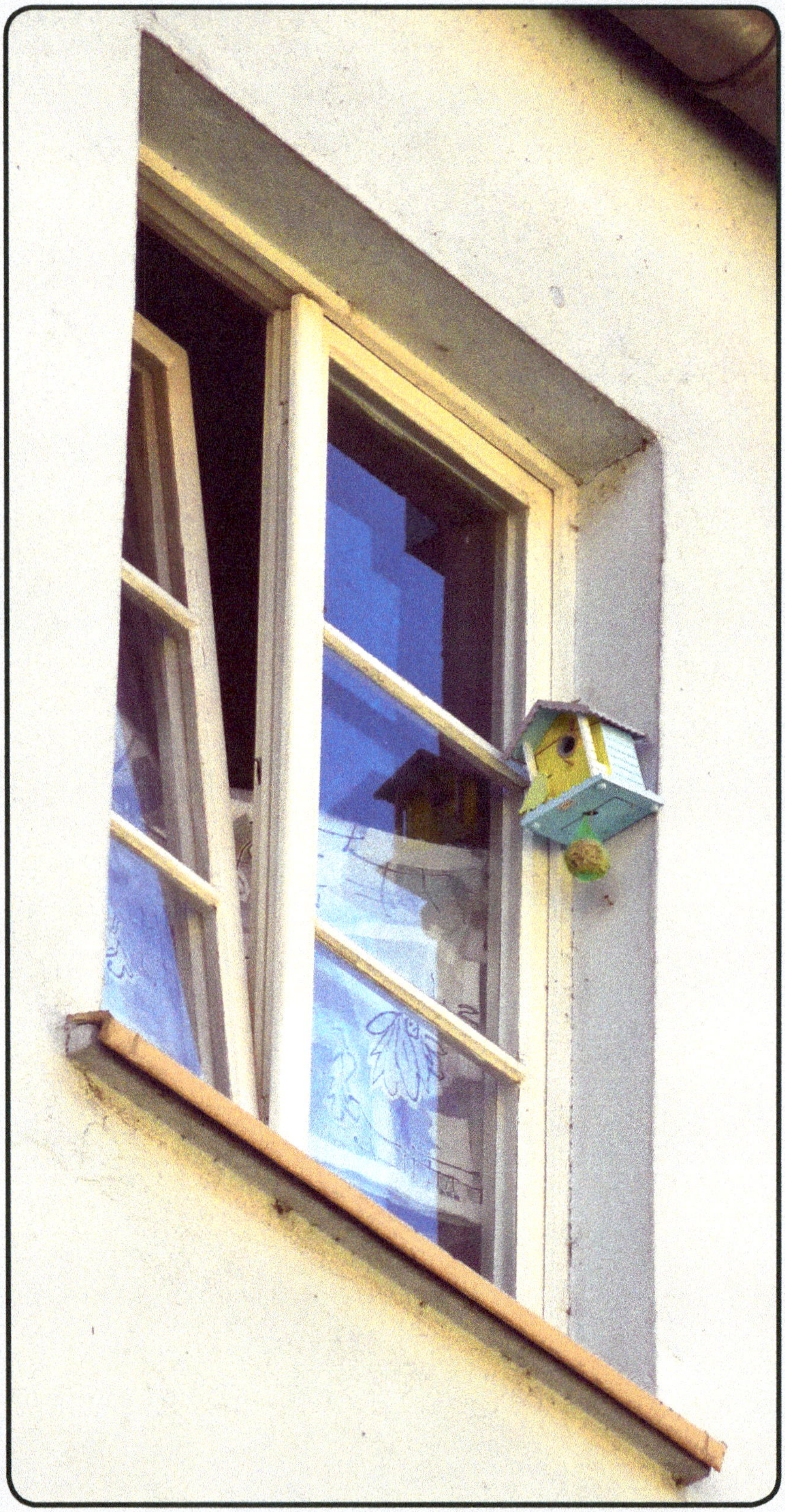

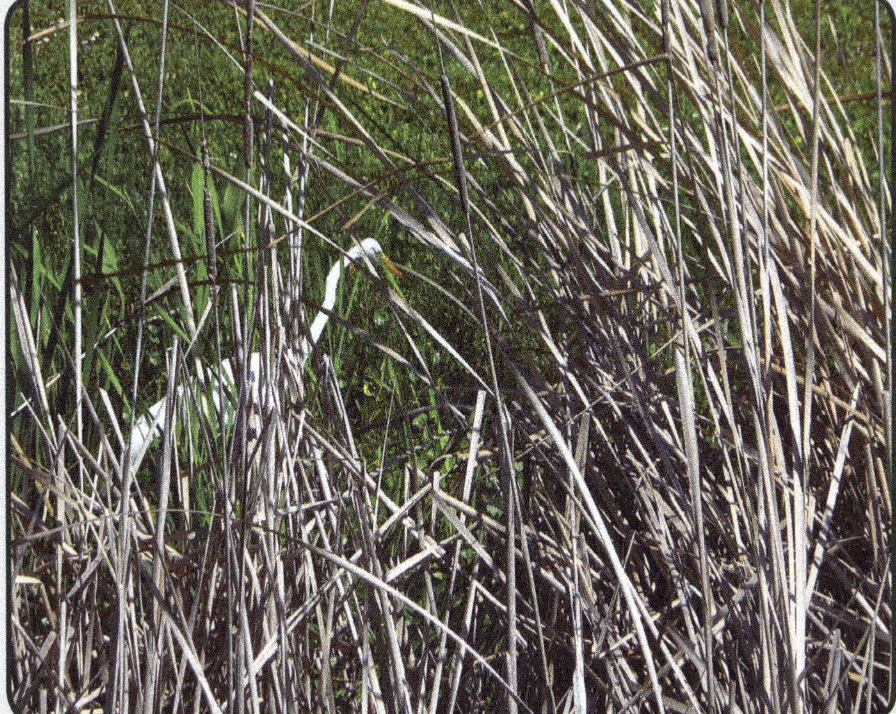

A stroll through the reeds in Florida.

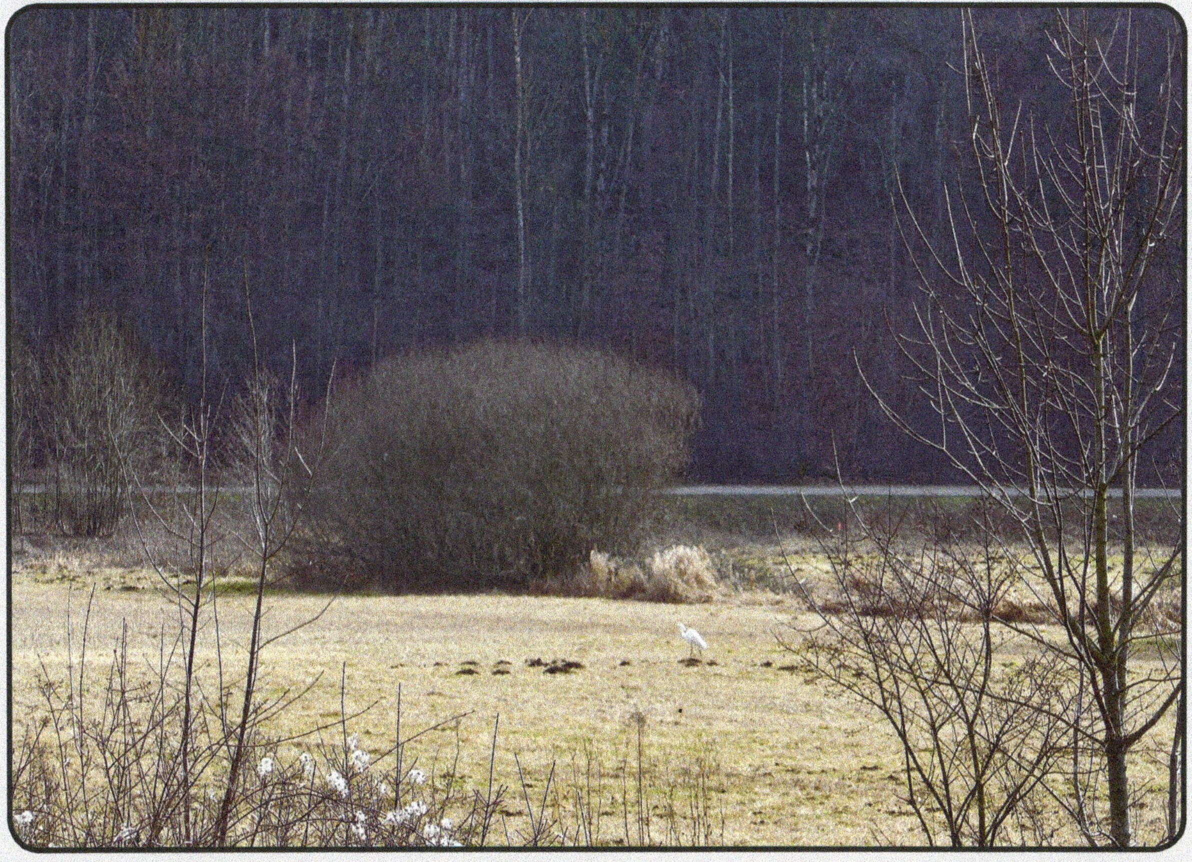

Swabian crane.

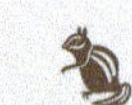

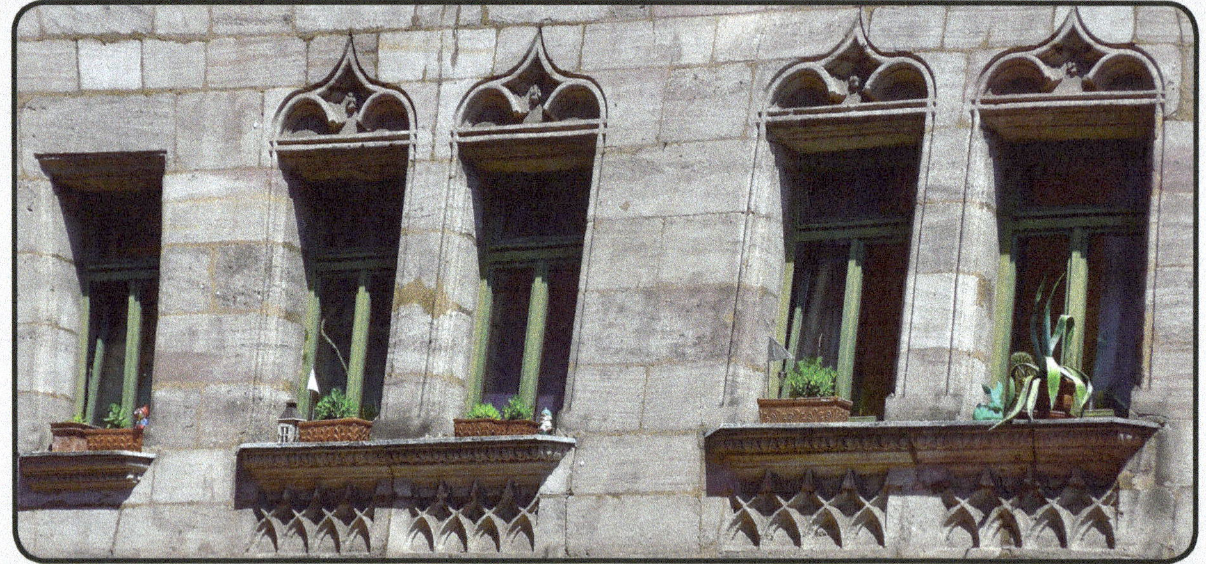

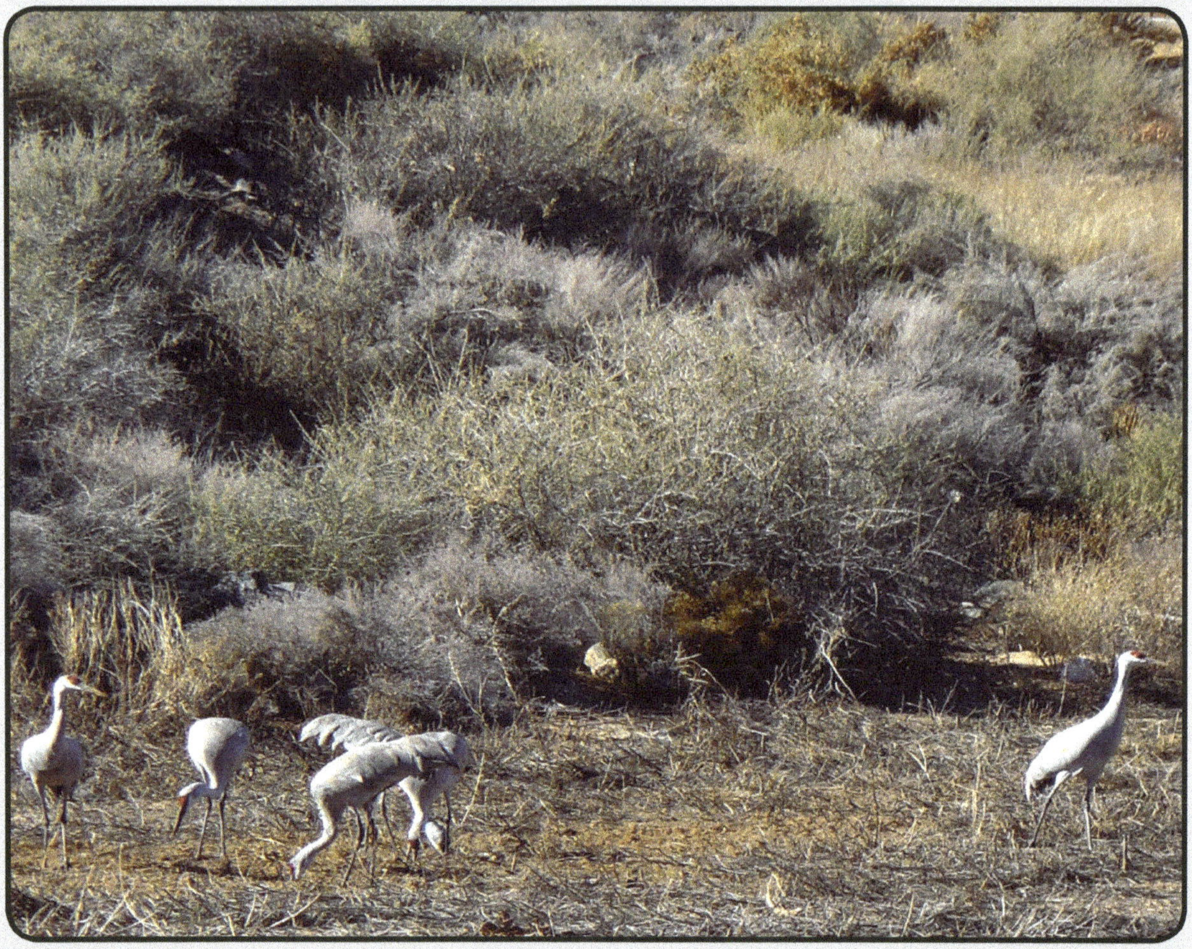

Migratory sandhill cranes forage for lunch near baseball fields.

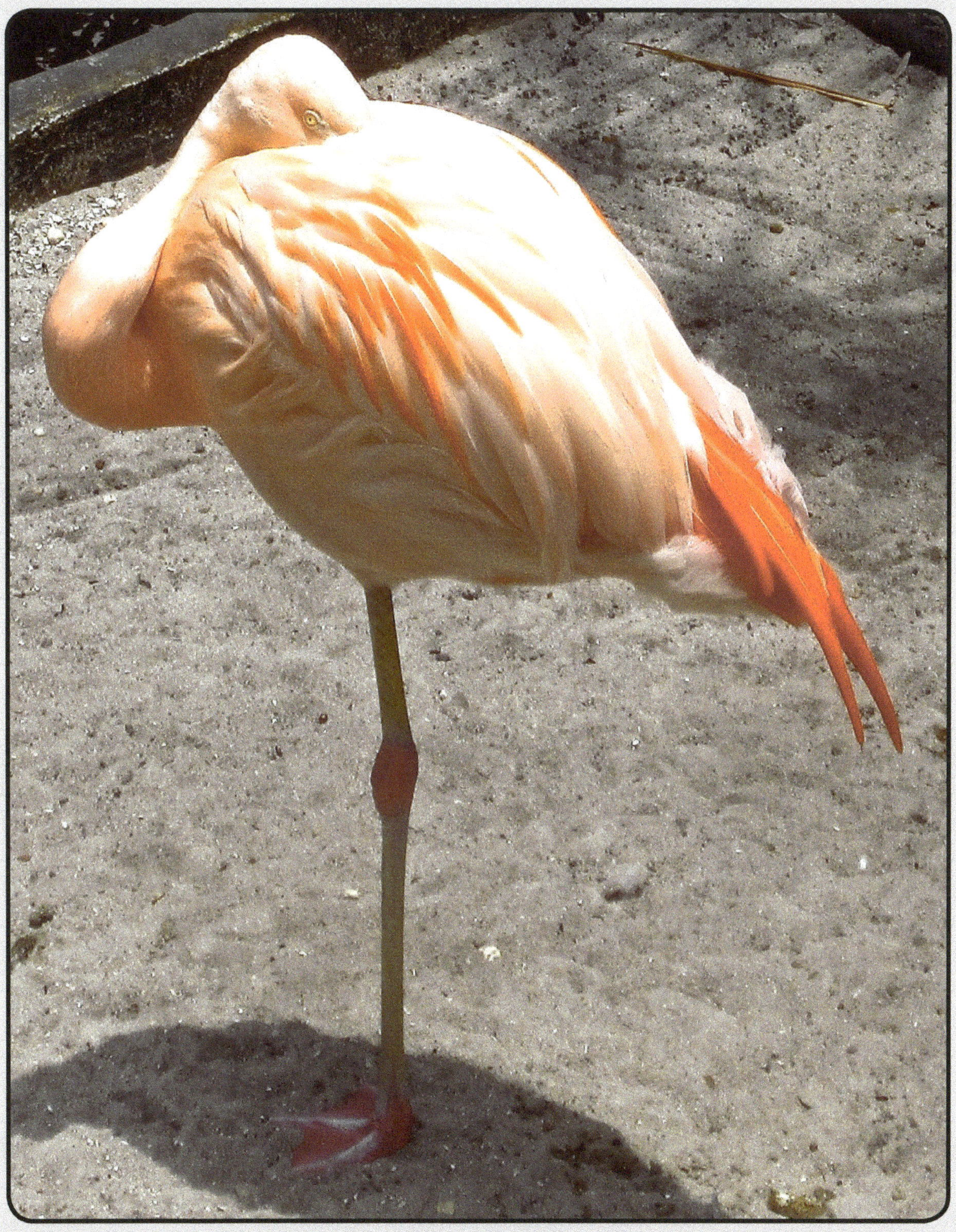

Flamingo stare.

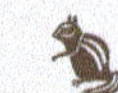

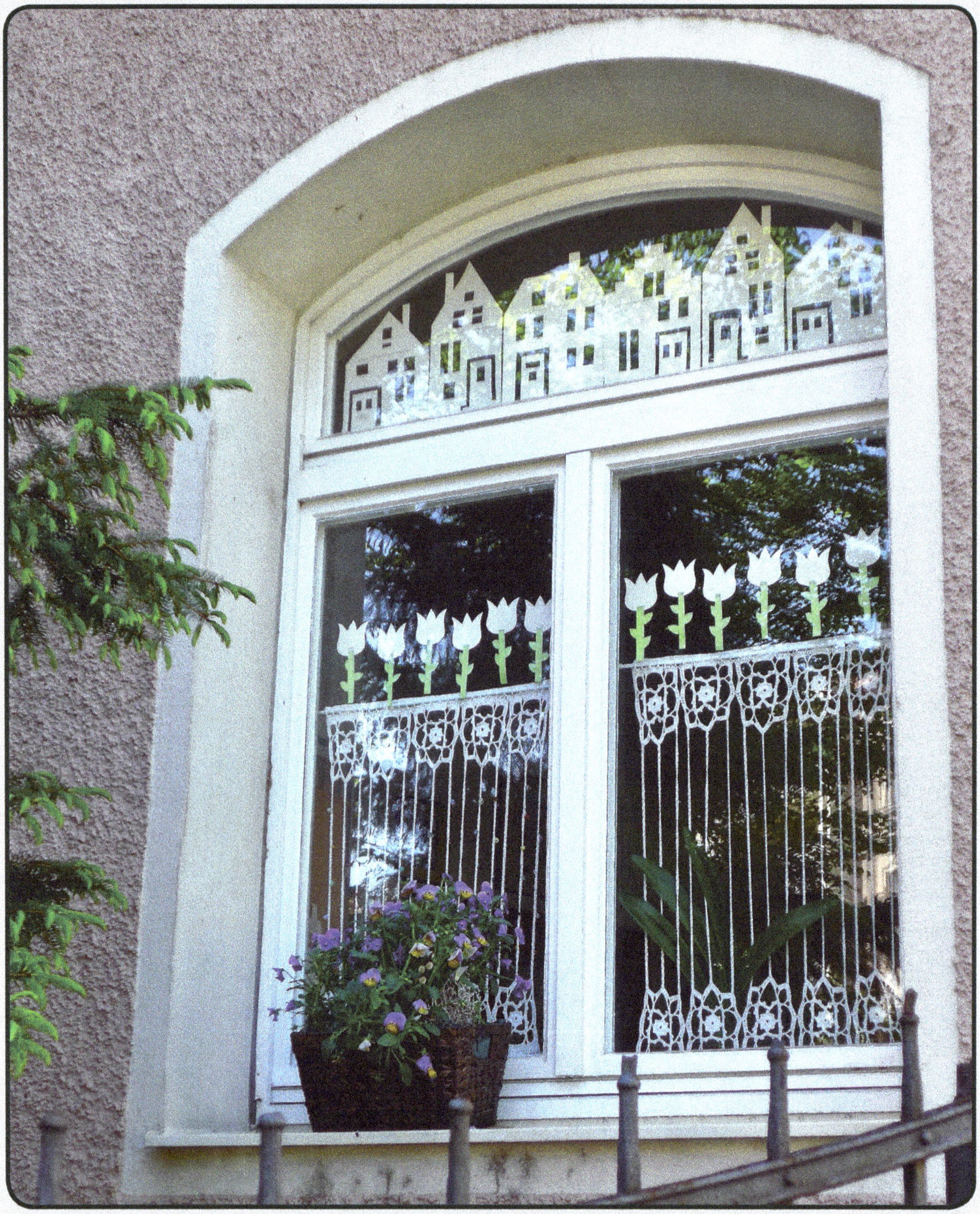

Paper garden in window city.

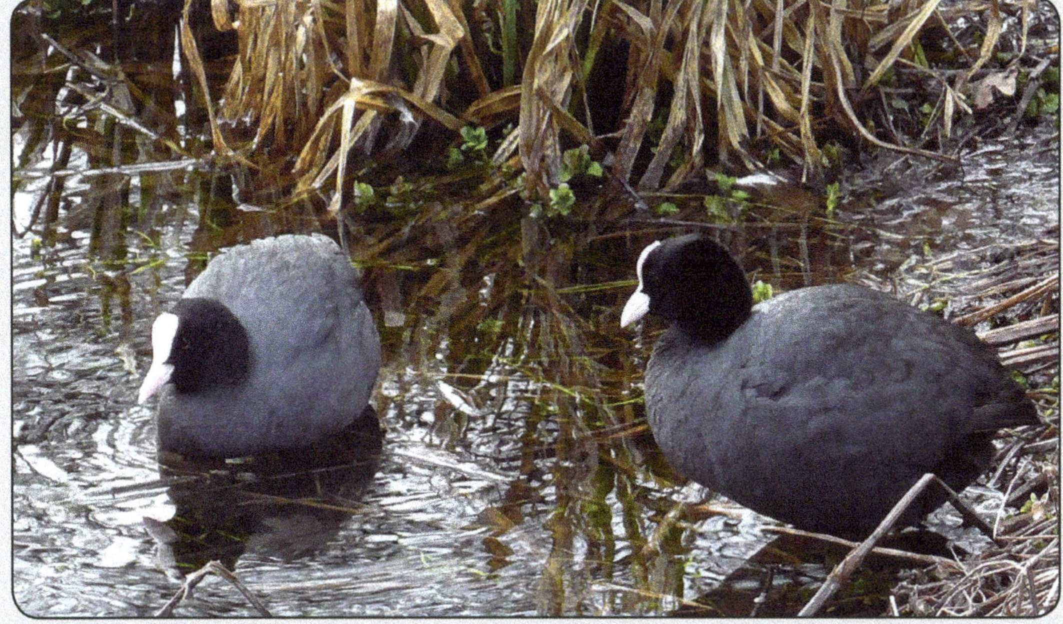

Bird business.

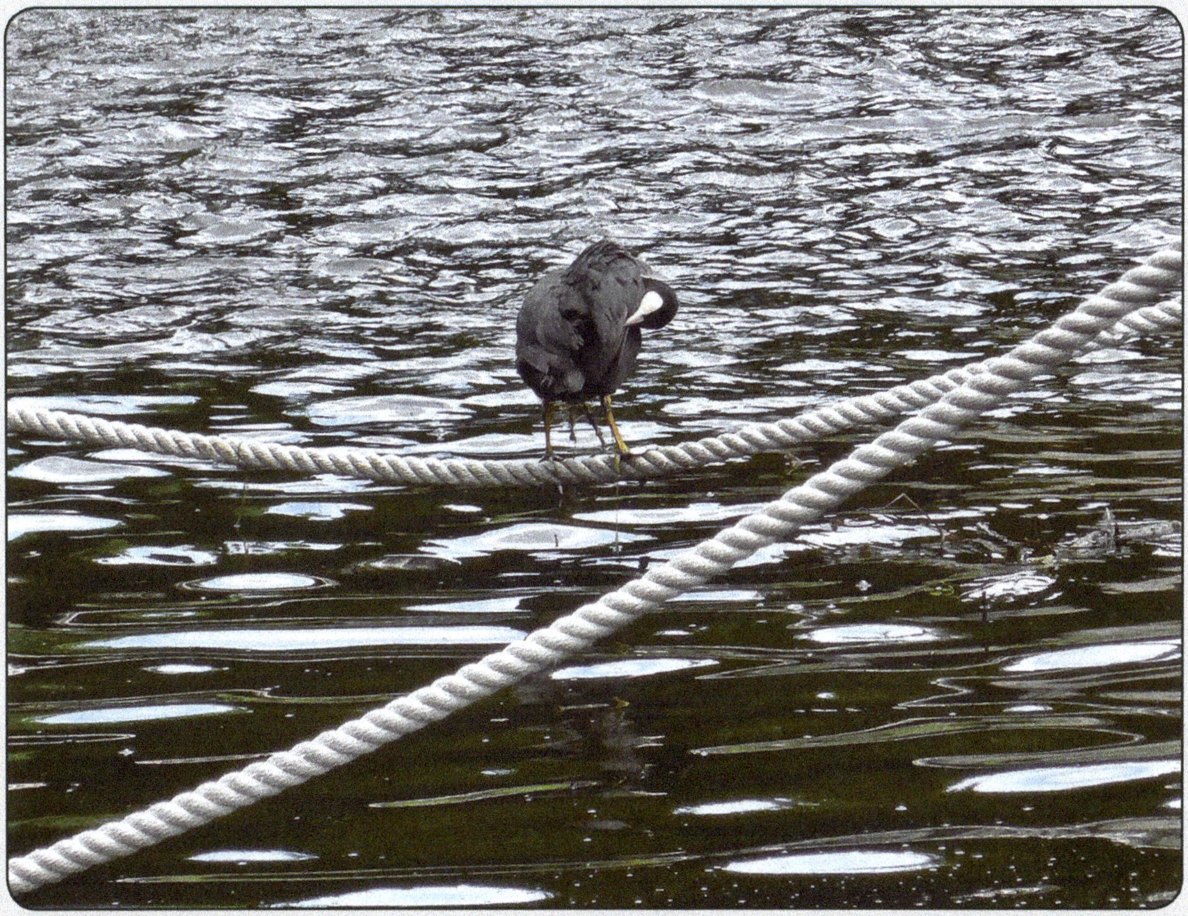

Coot on a rope.

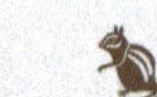

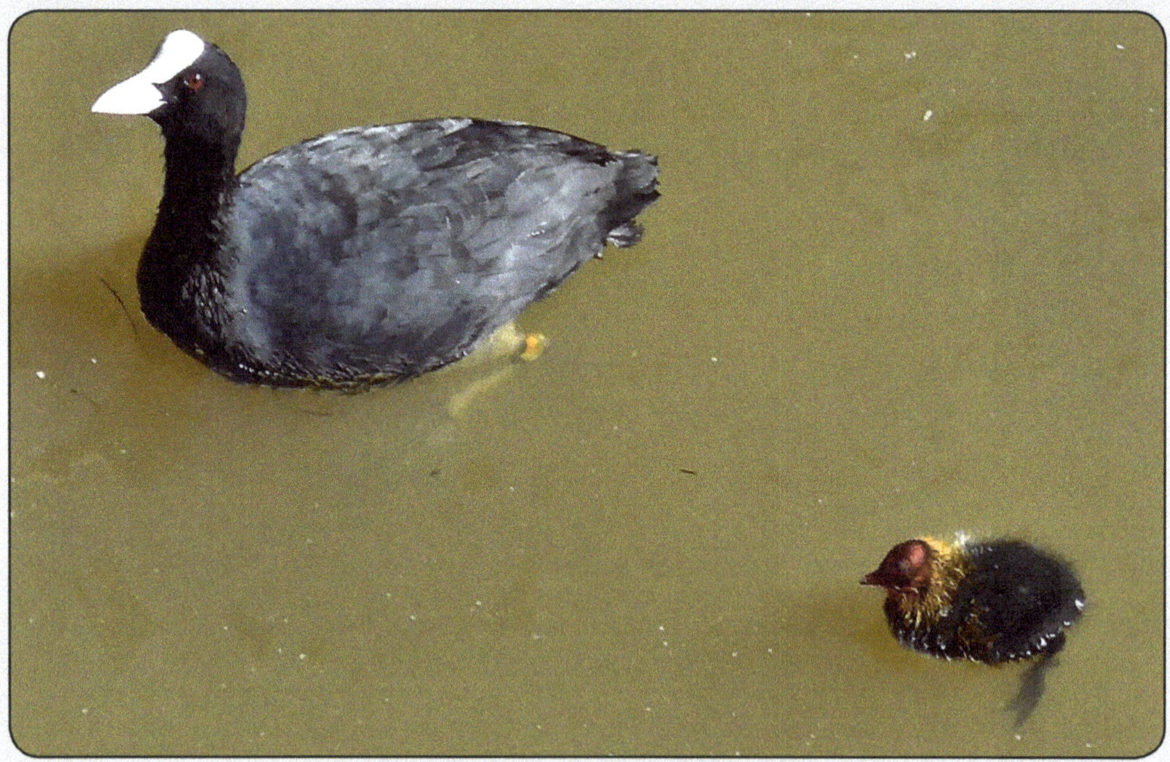

❀ Coot baby swim lessons in the Altstadt.

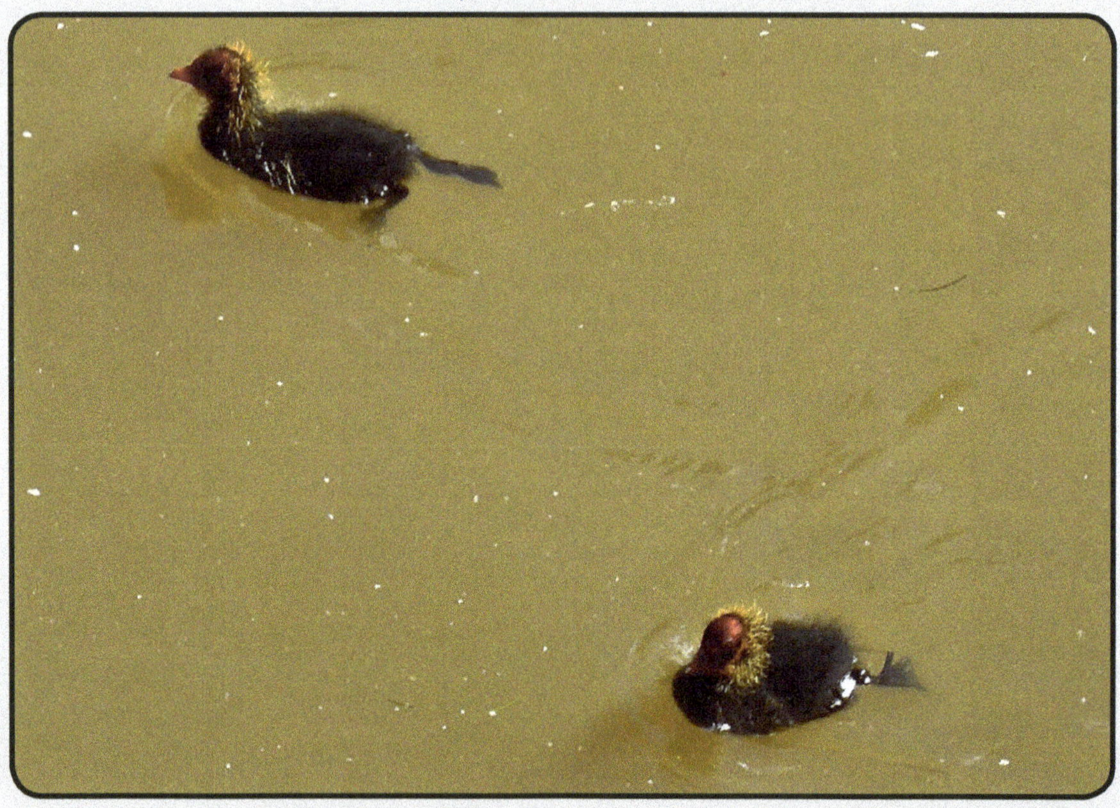

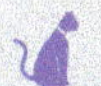

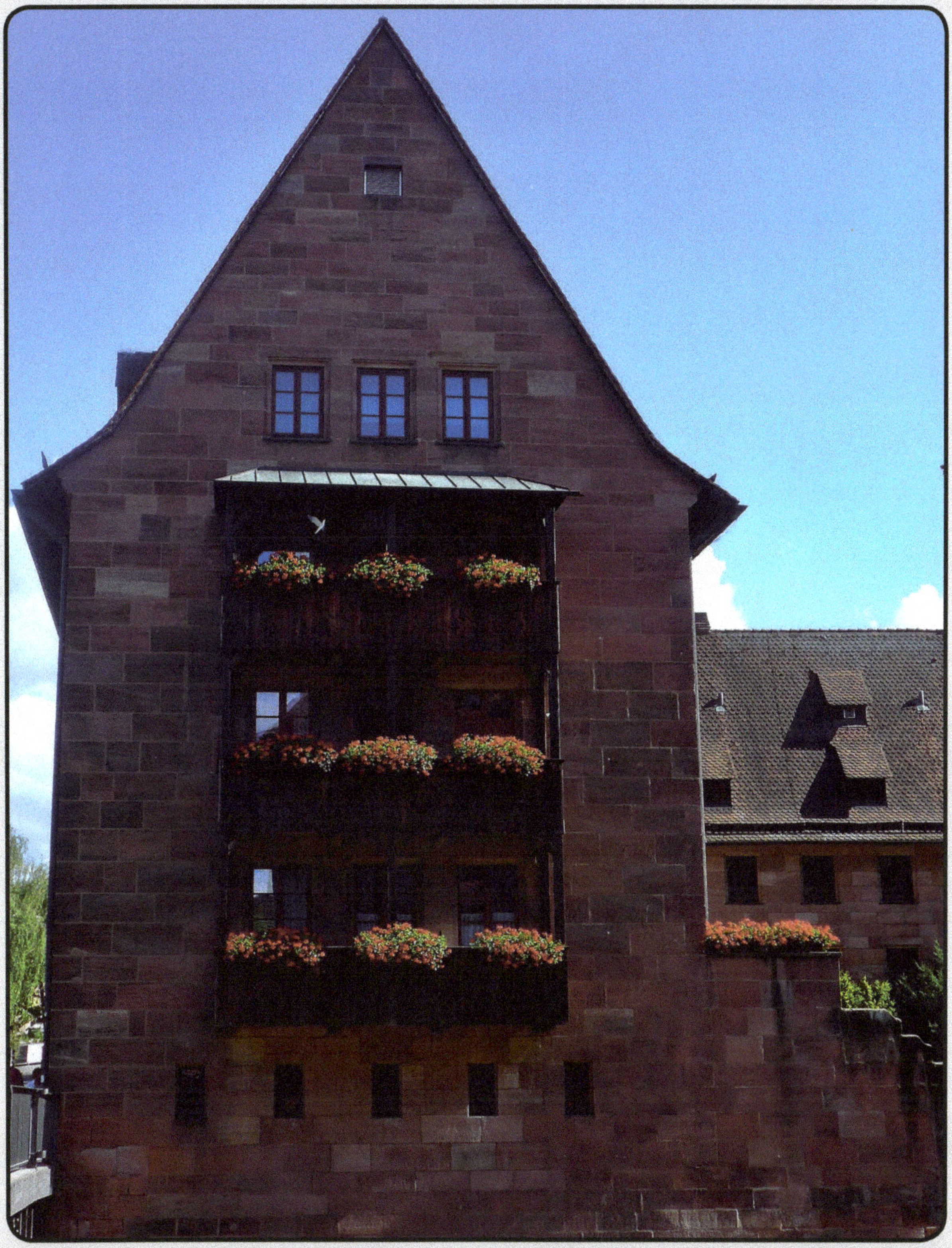

Franconian floral splendor.

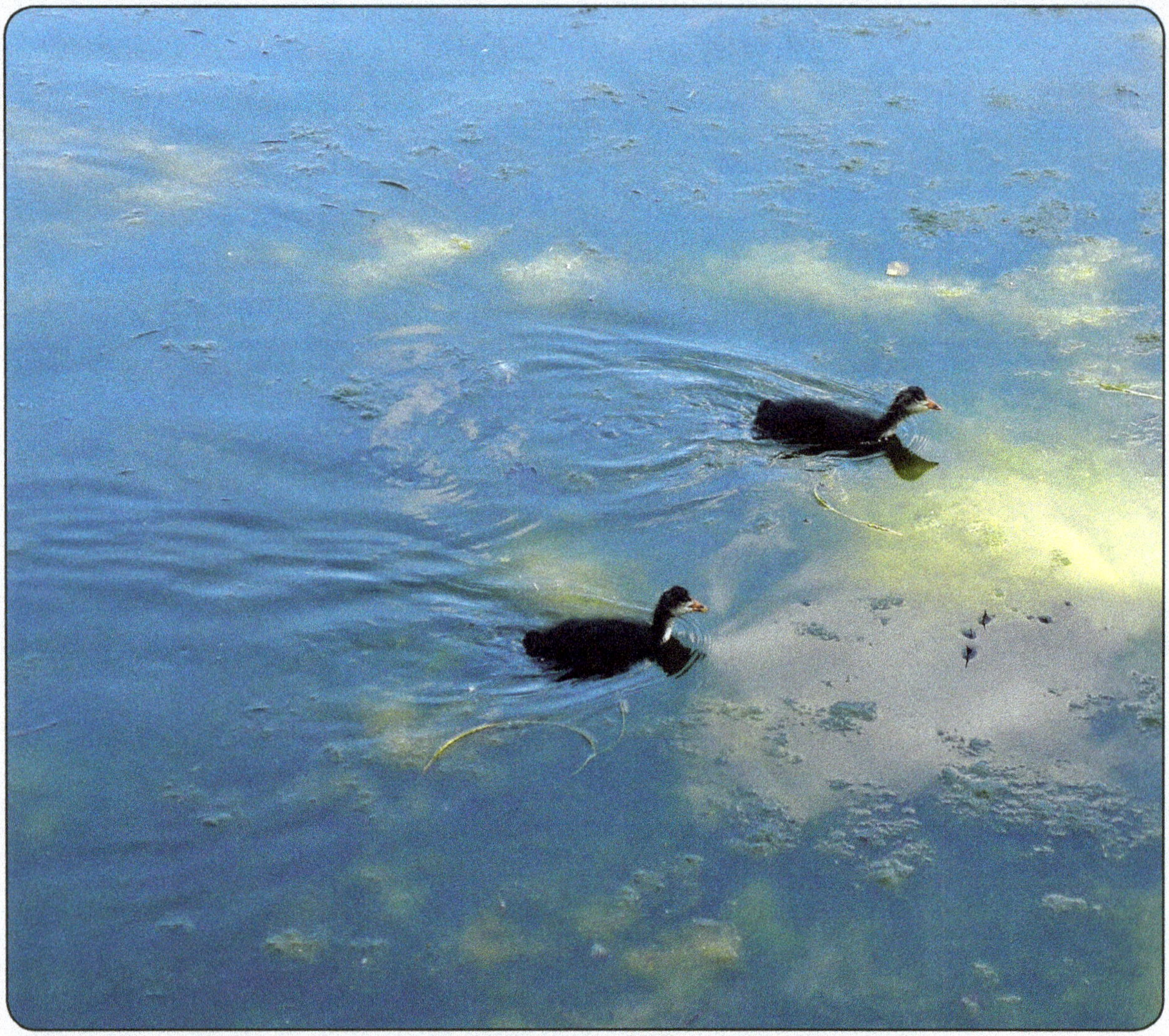

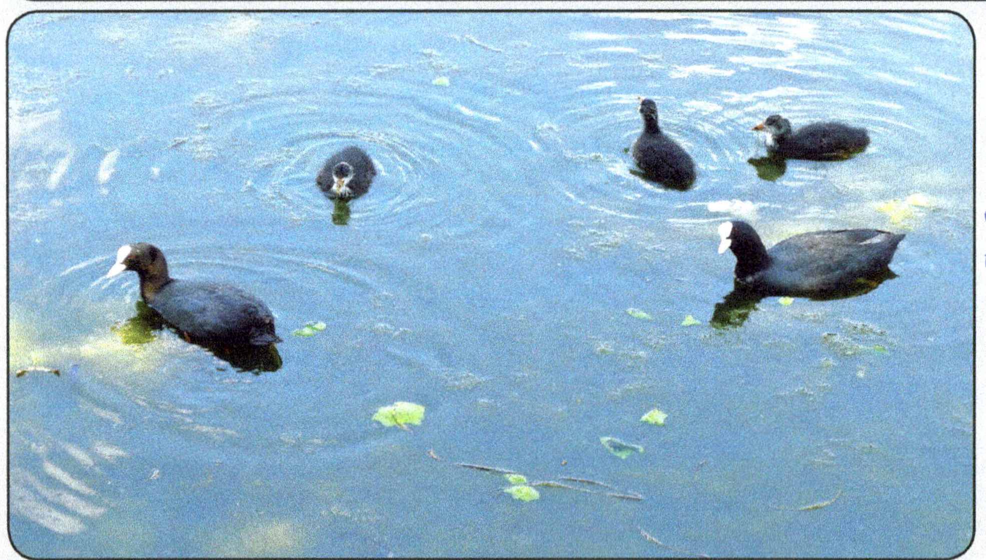

Family outing for brunch series.

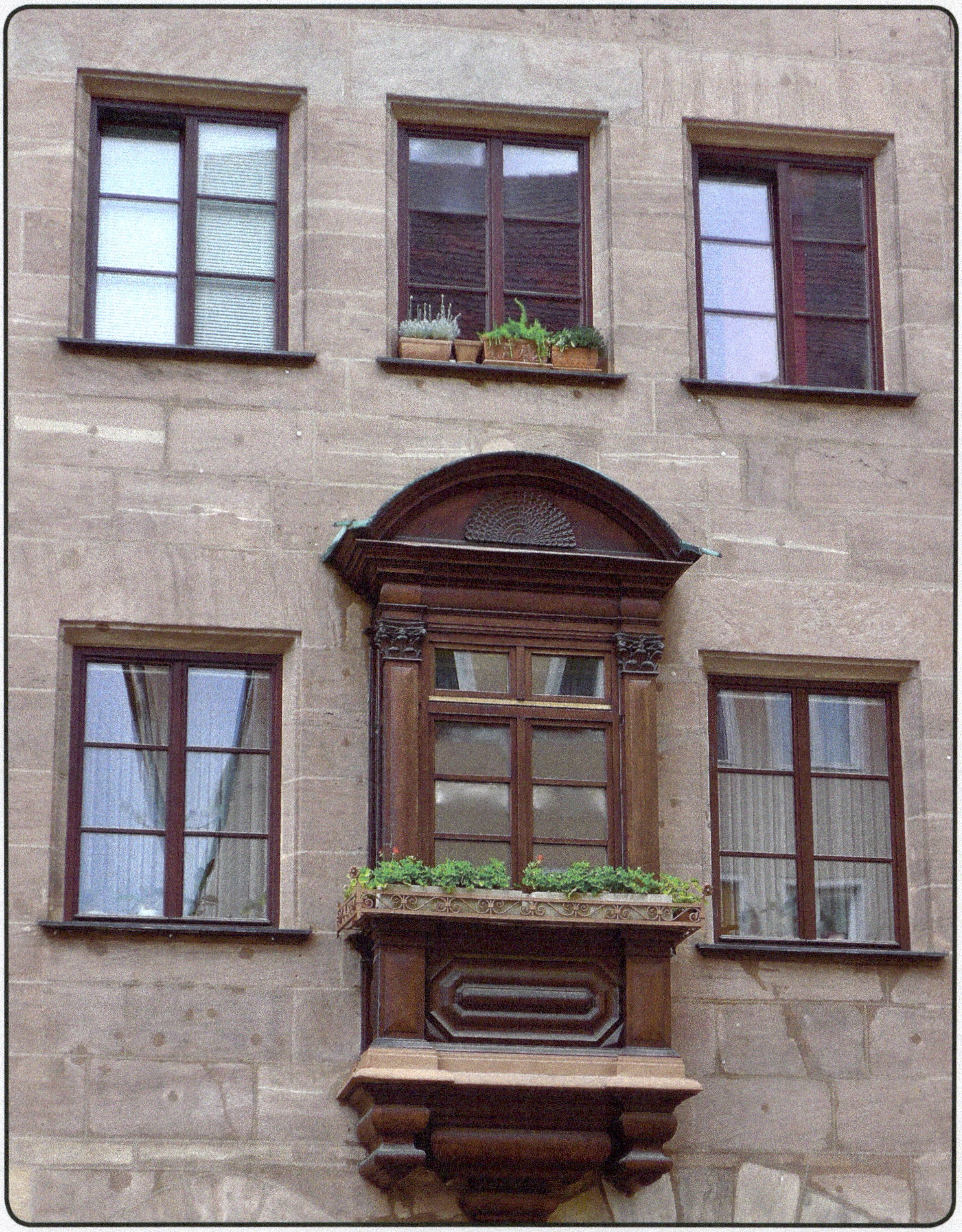

Fancy Franconian window boxes.

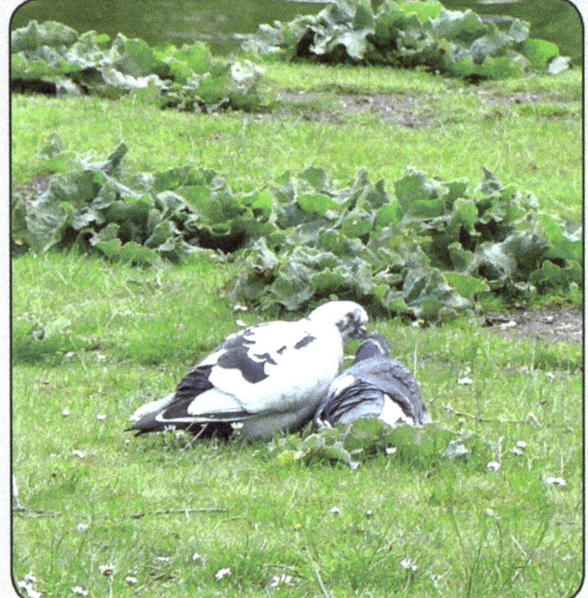

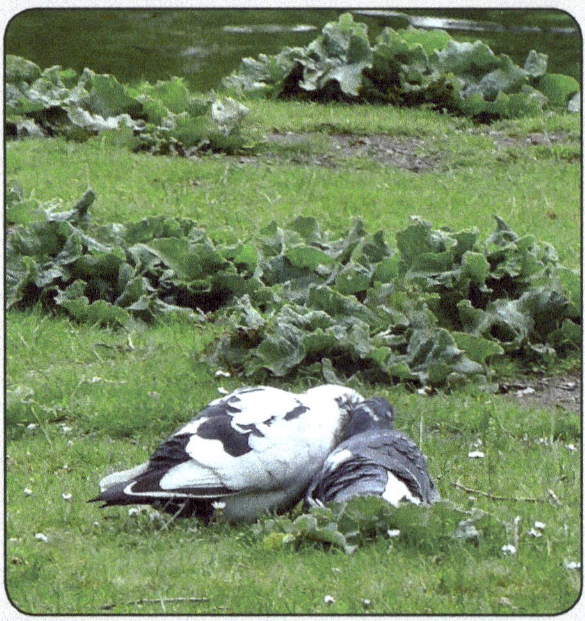

Pigeon romance at park.

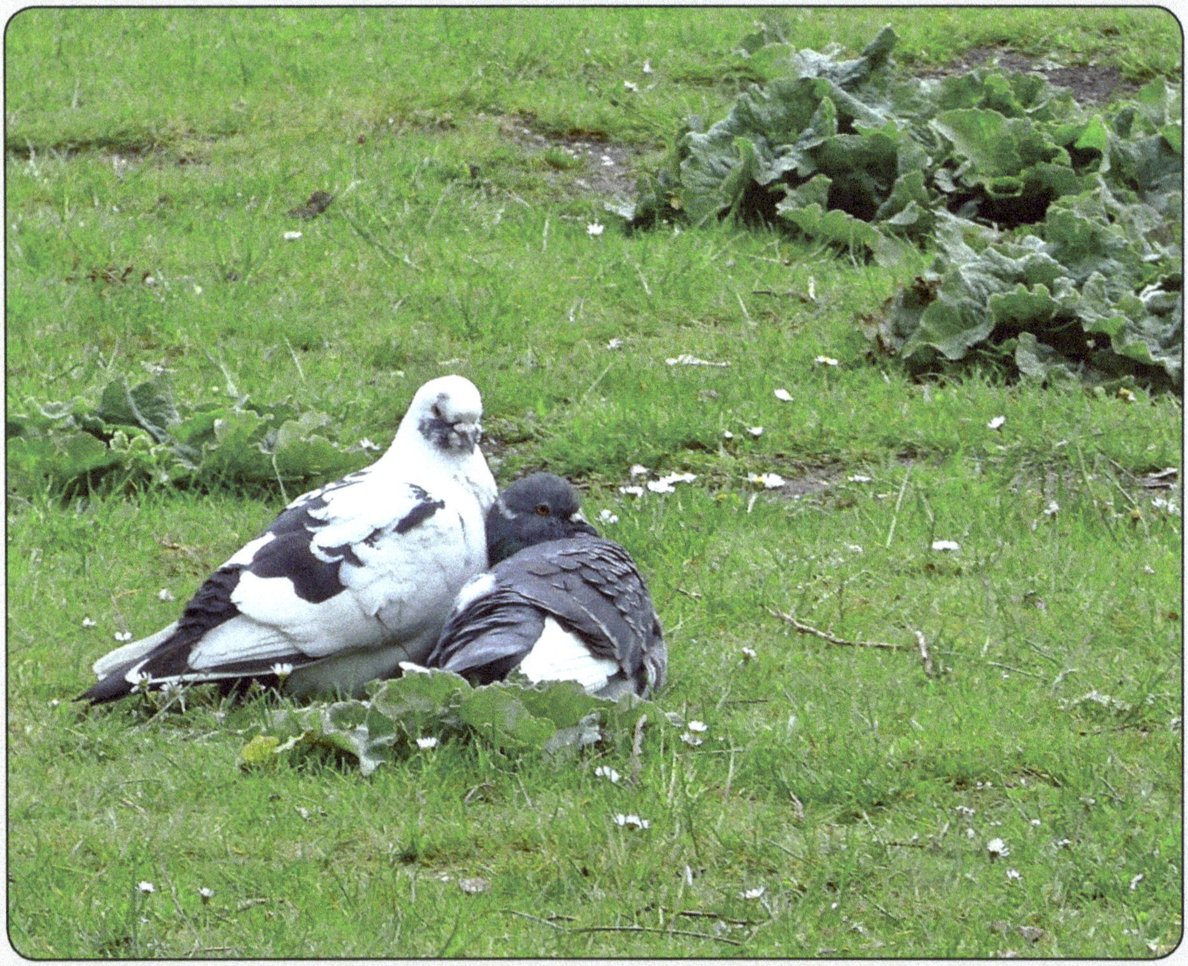

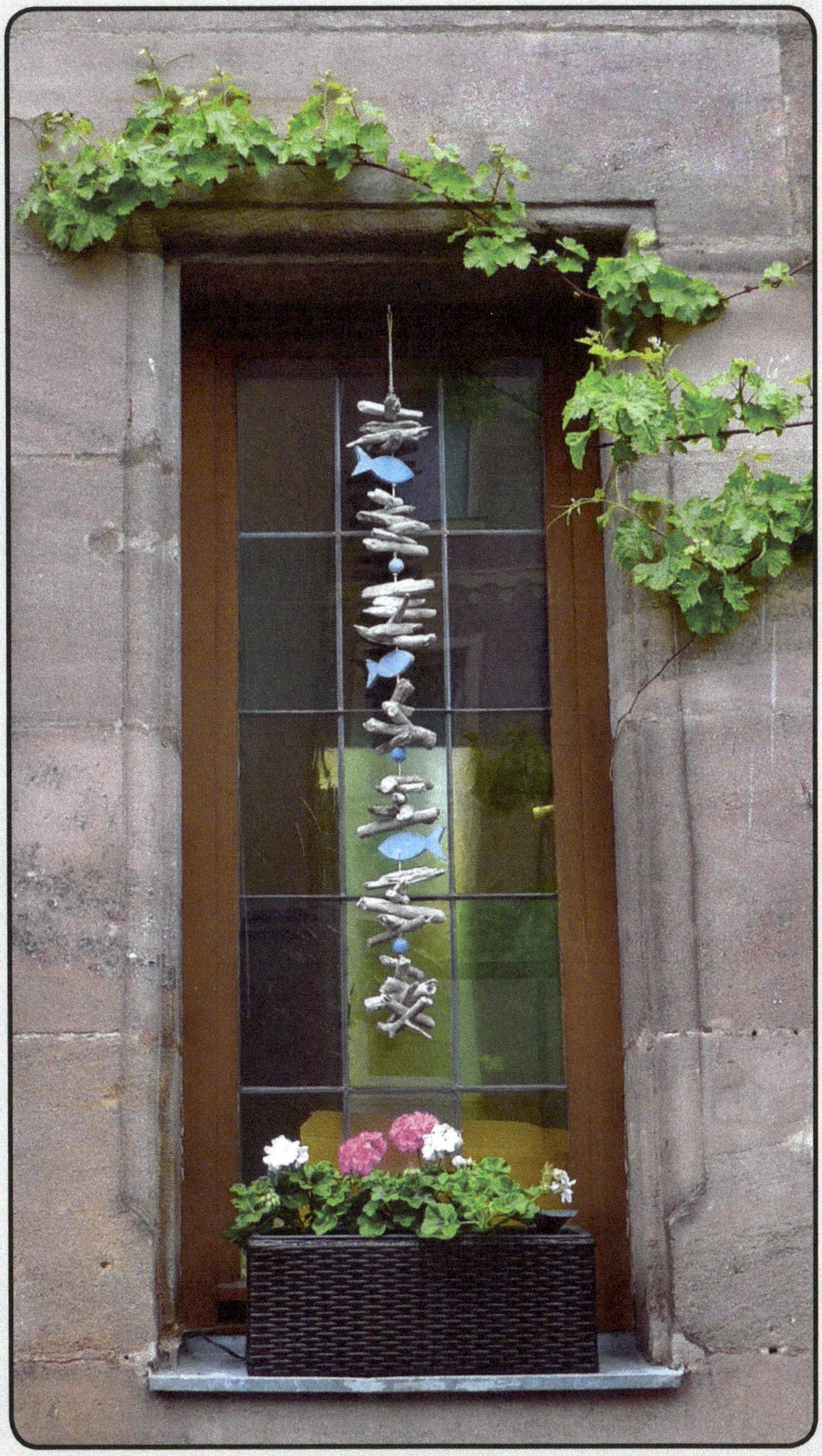

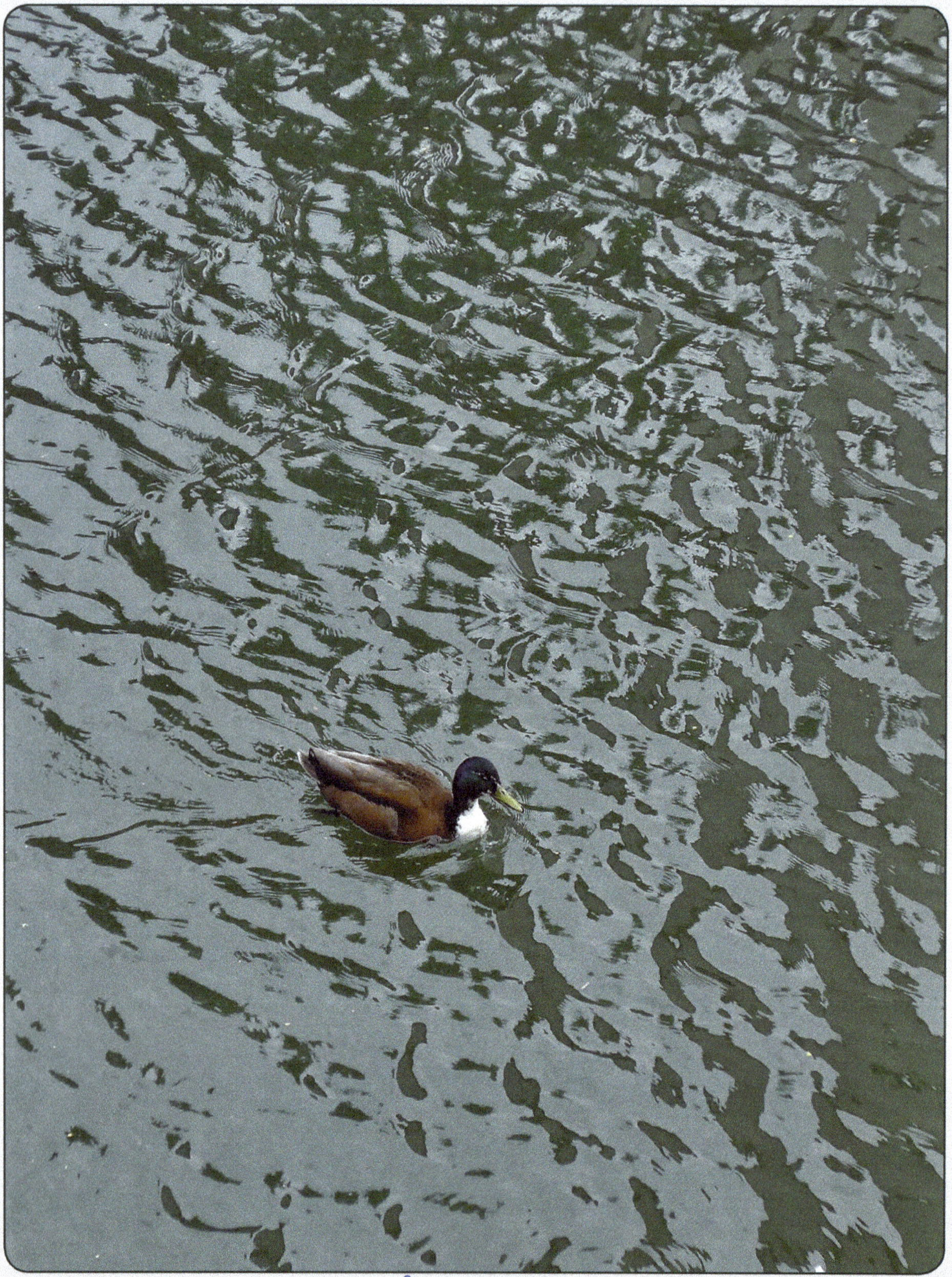

Duck voyage.

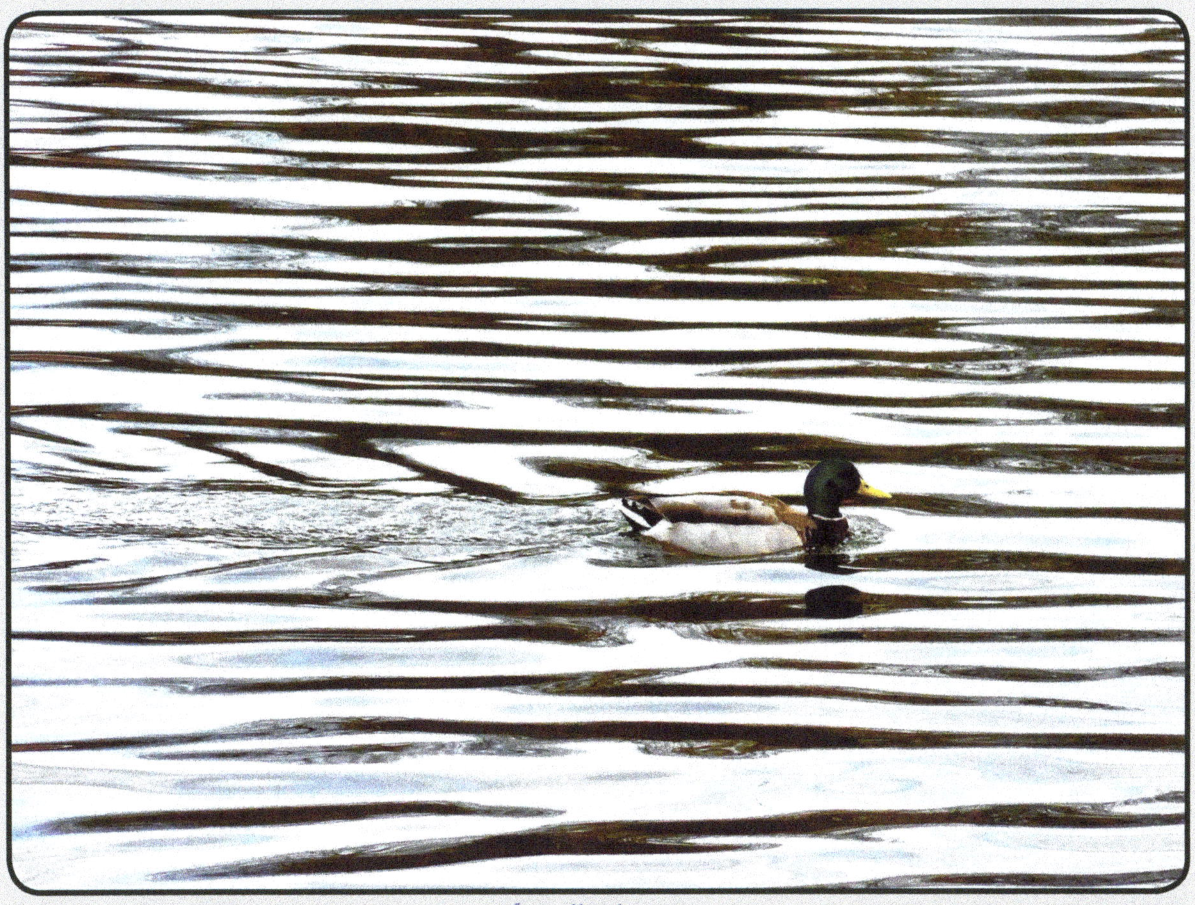

Mallard motor.

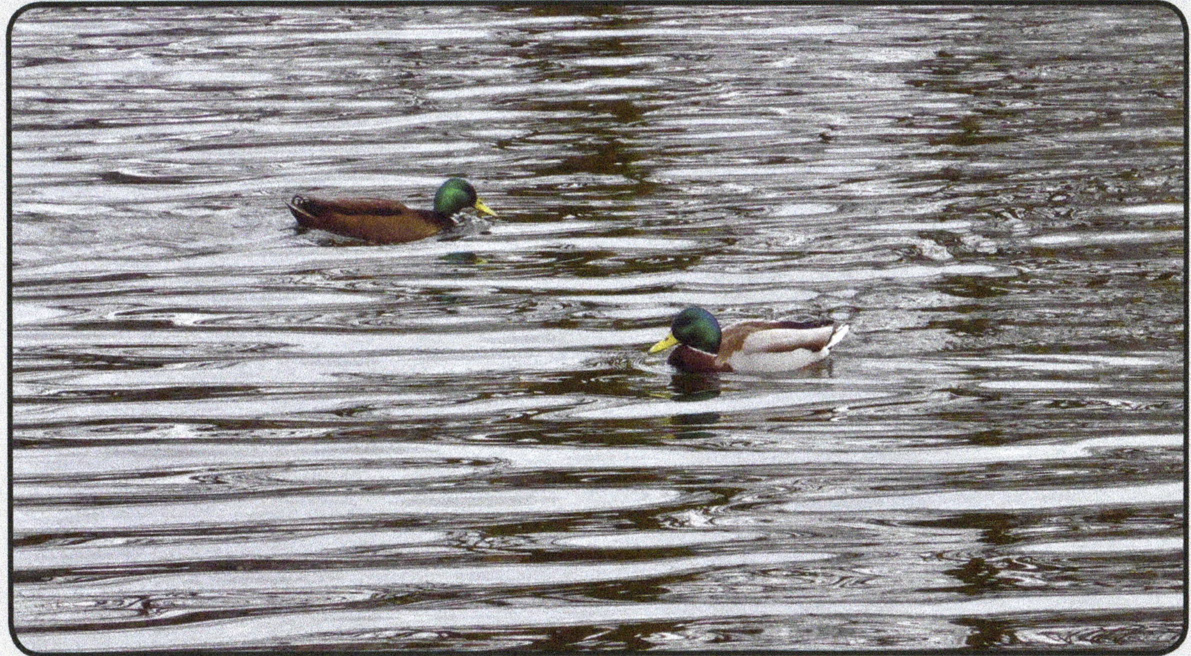

Gliding through quicksilver.

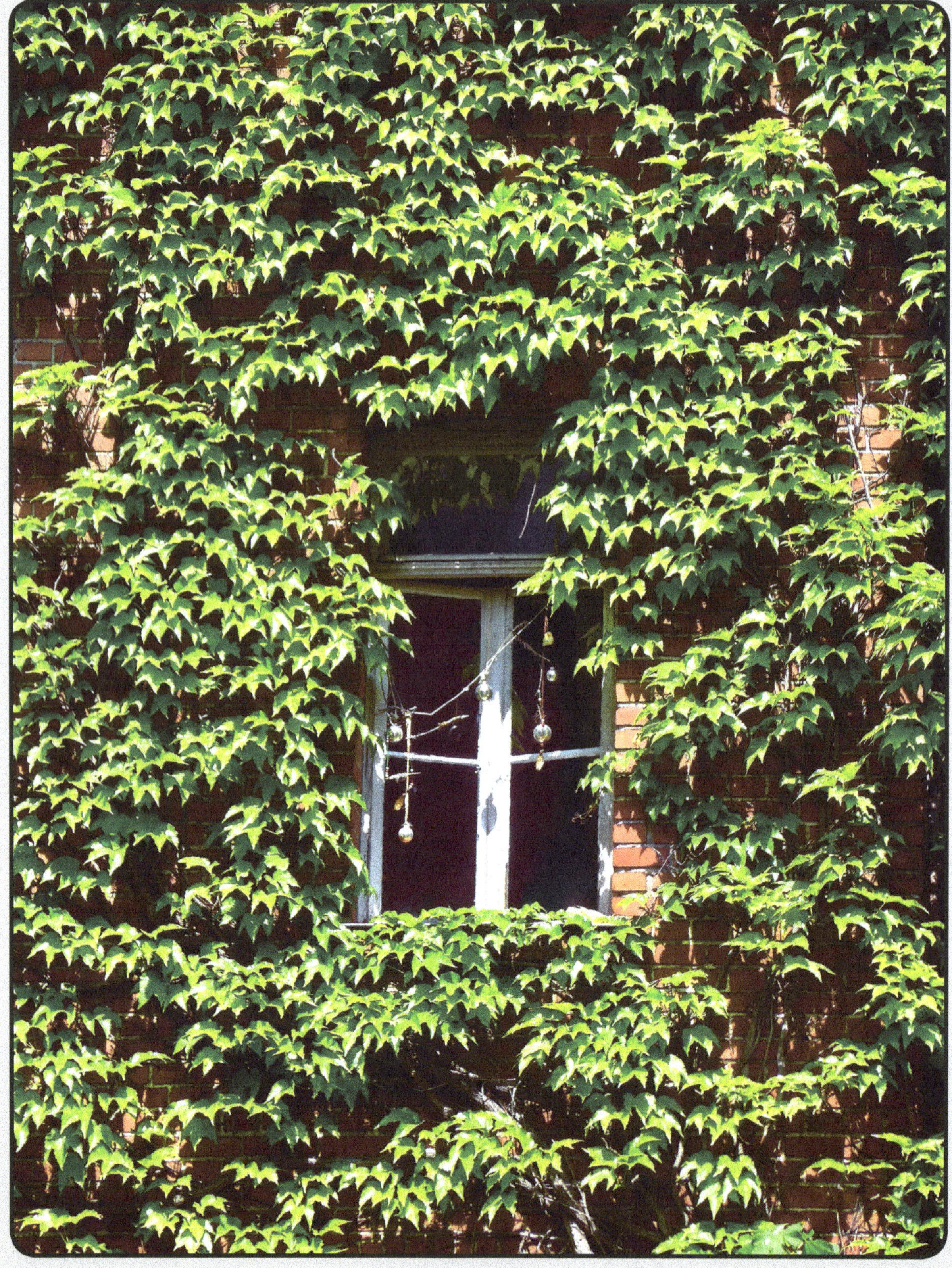

Cottage vibe.

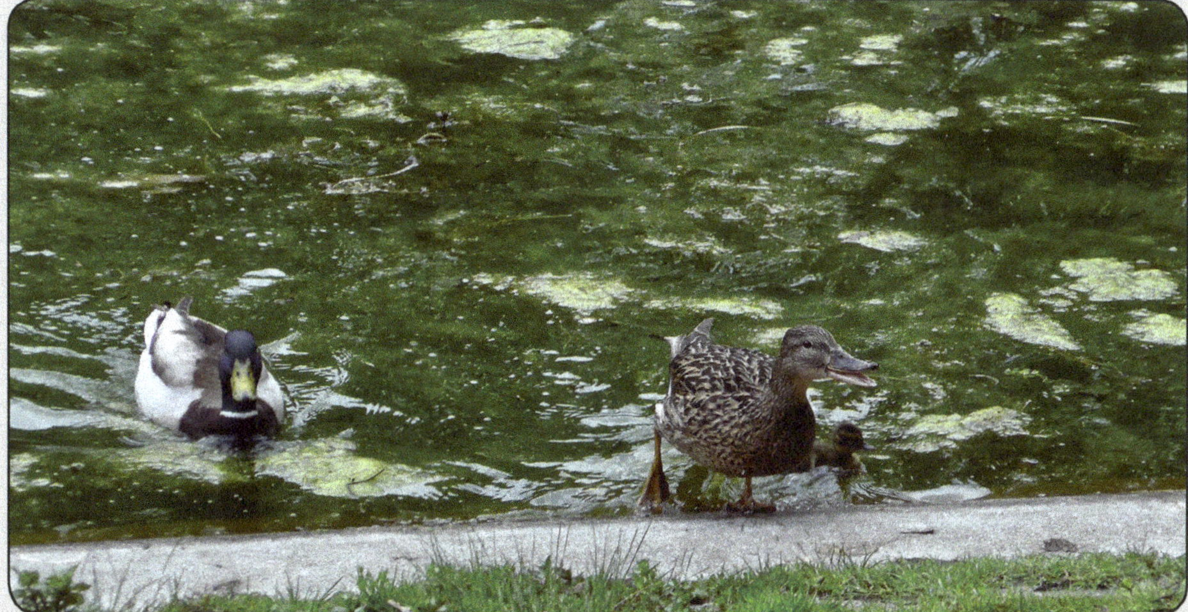

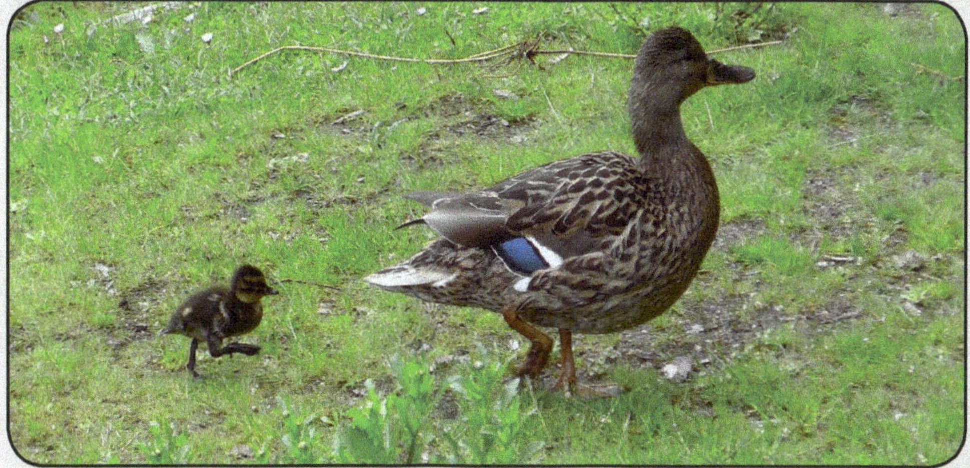

Family foray with Junior.

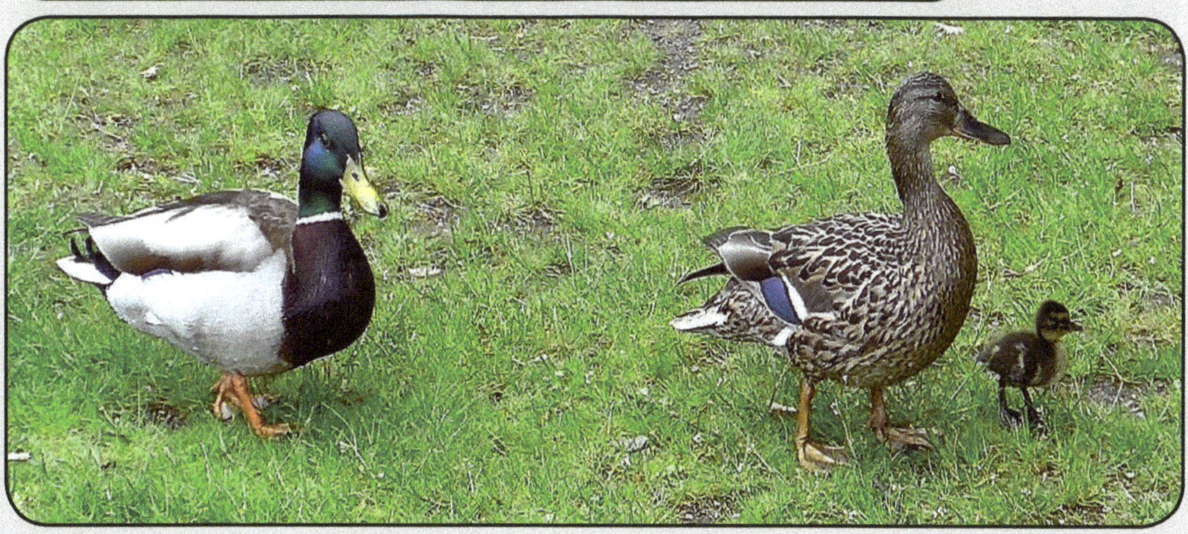

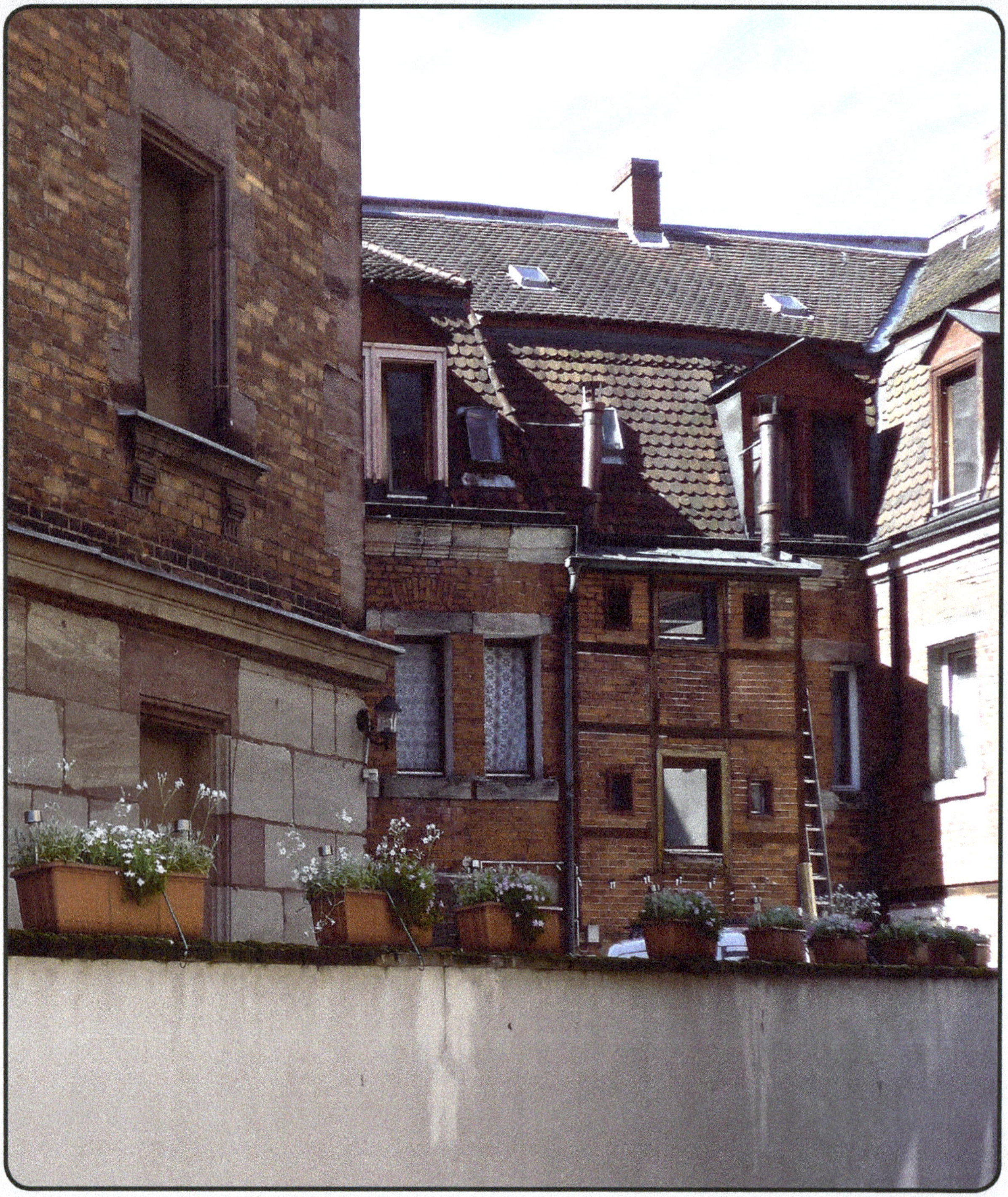

Urban jungle.

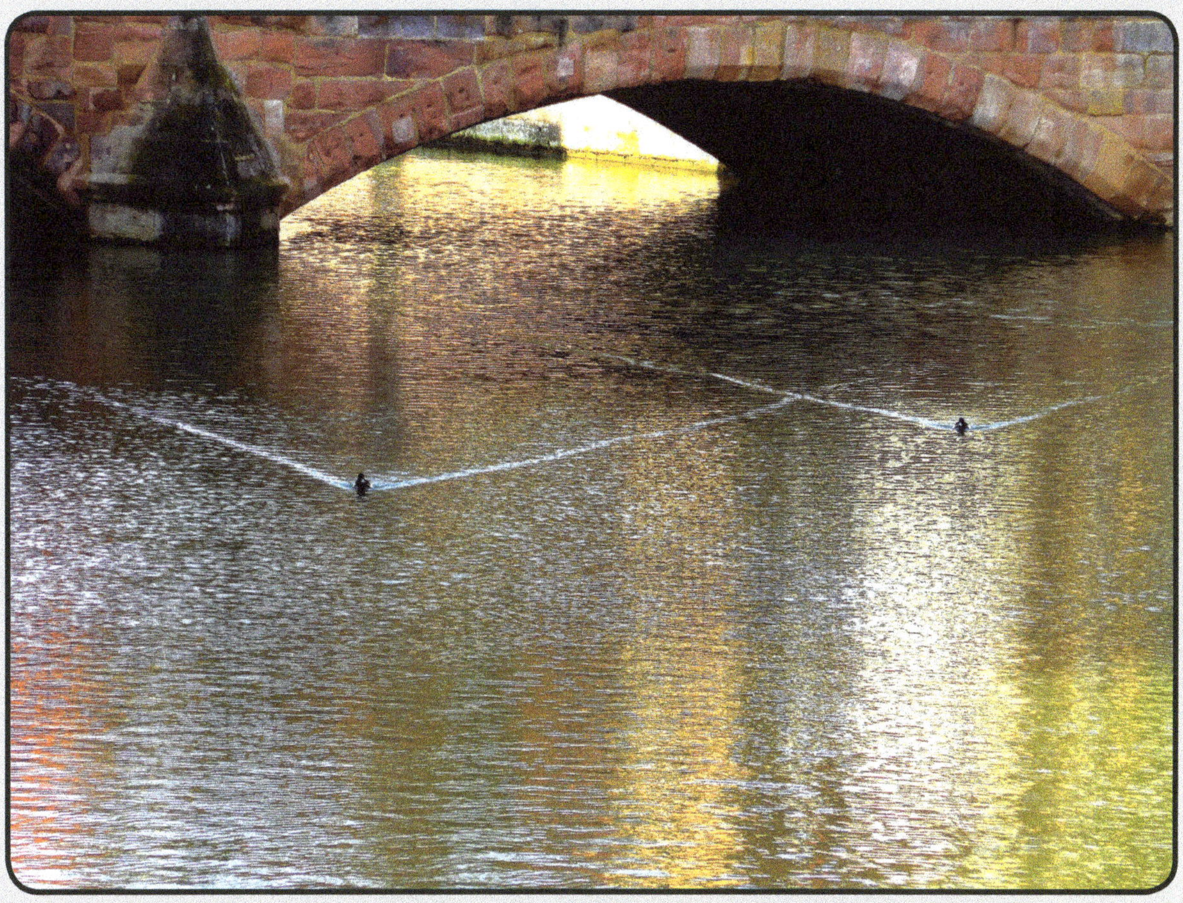

W.

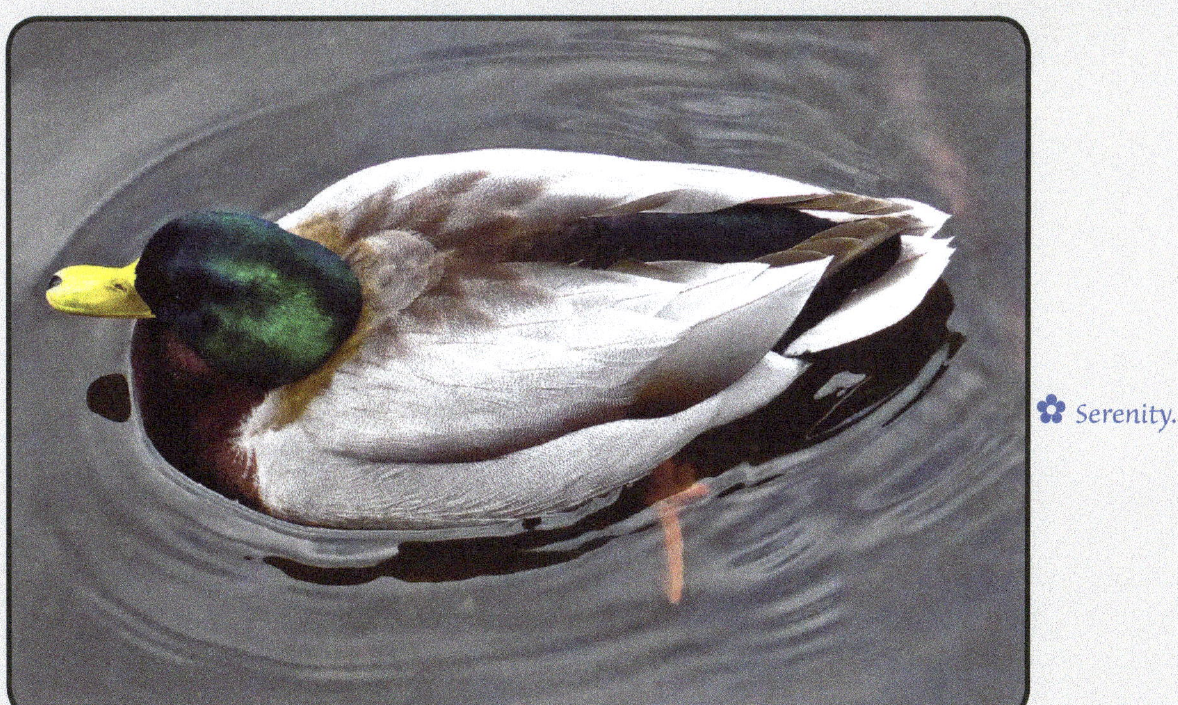

Serenity.

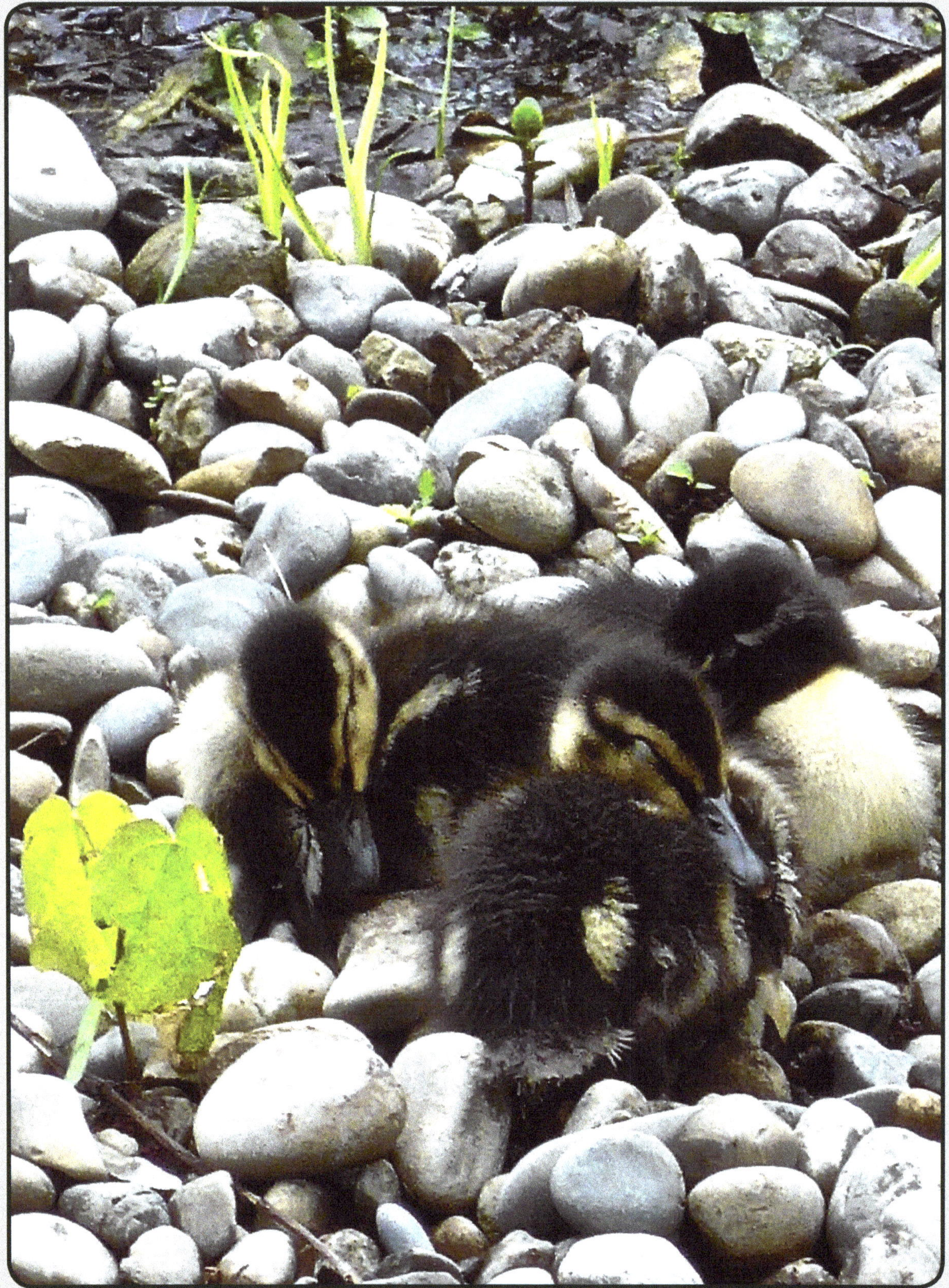

Snuggle time.

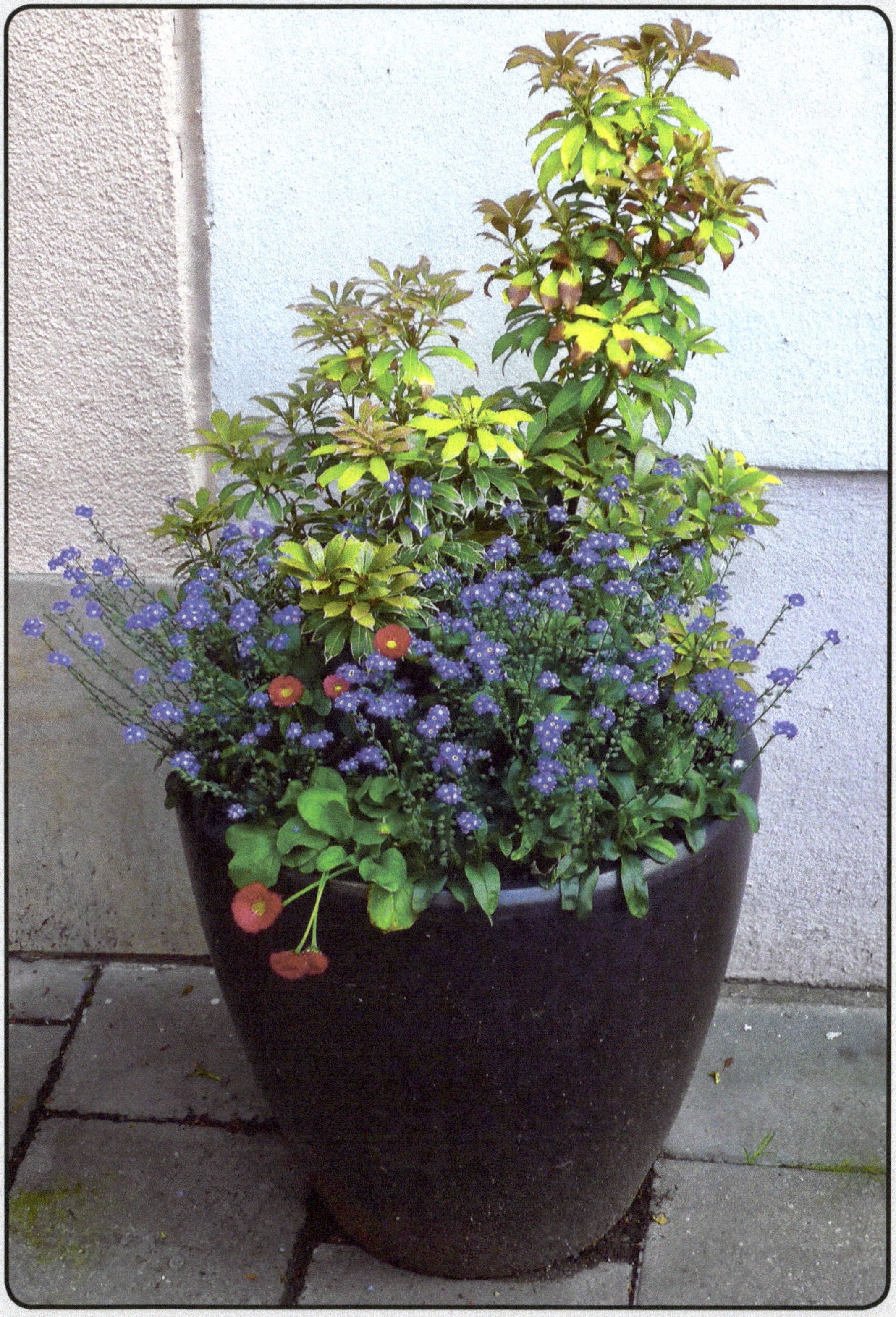

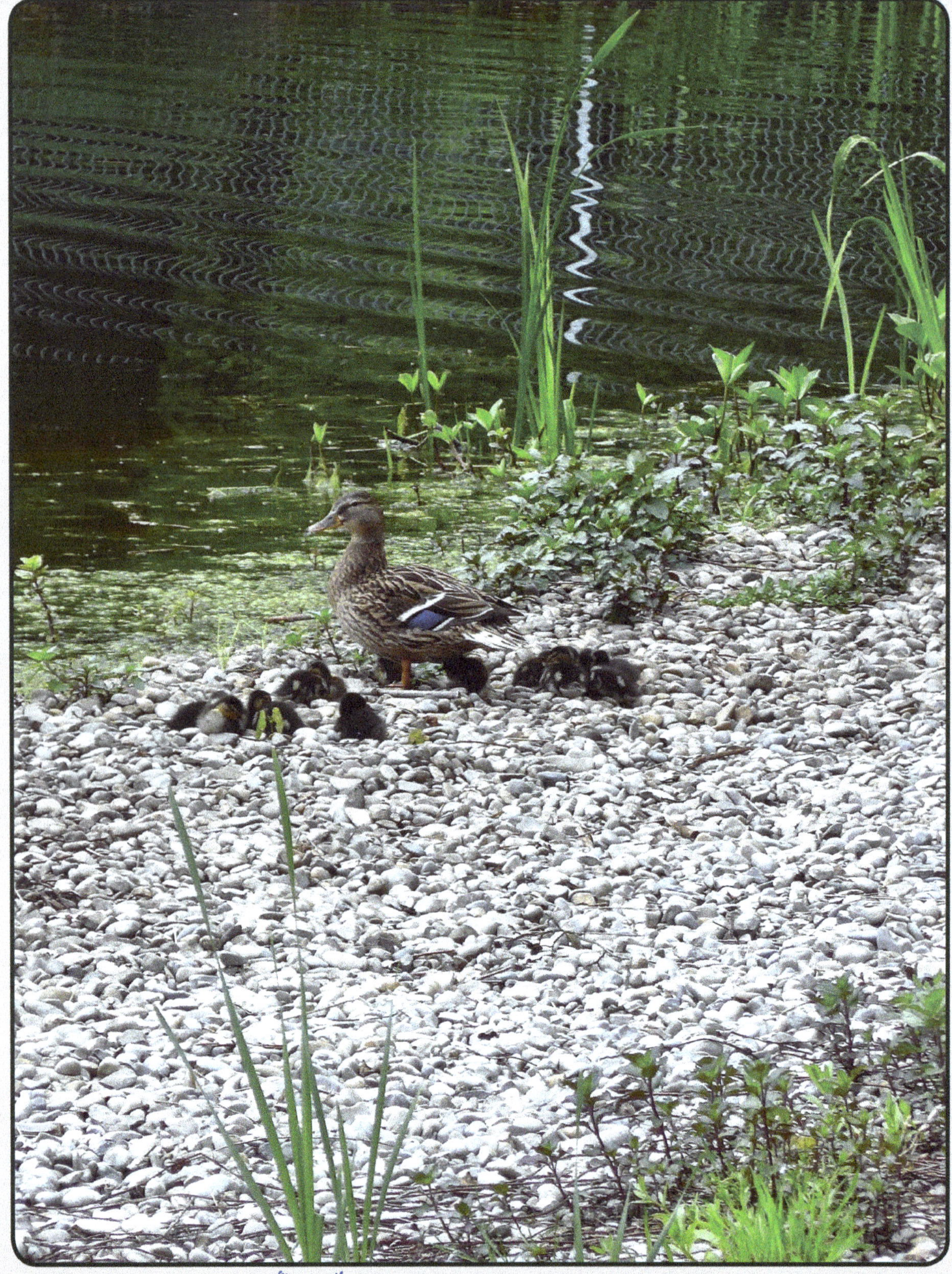

Watchful eye of Mother Duck series.

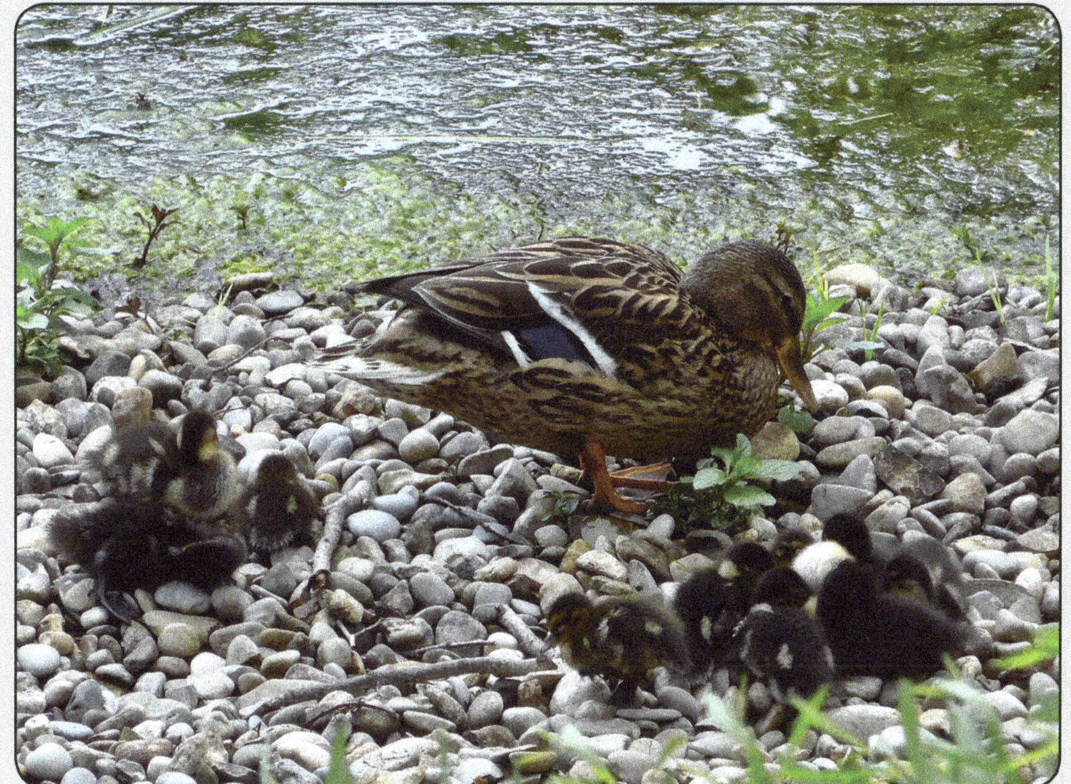

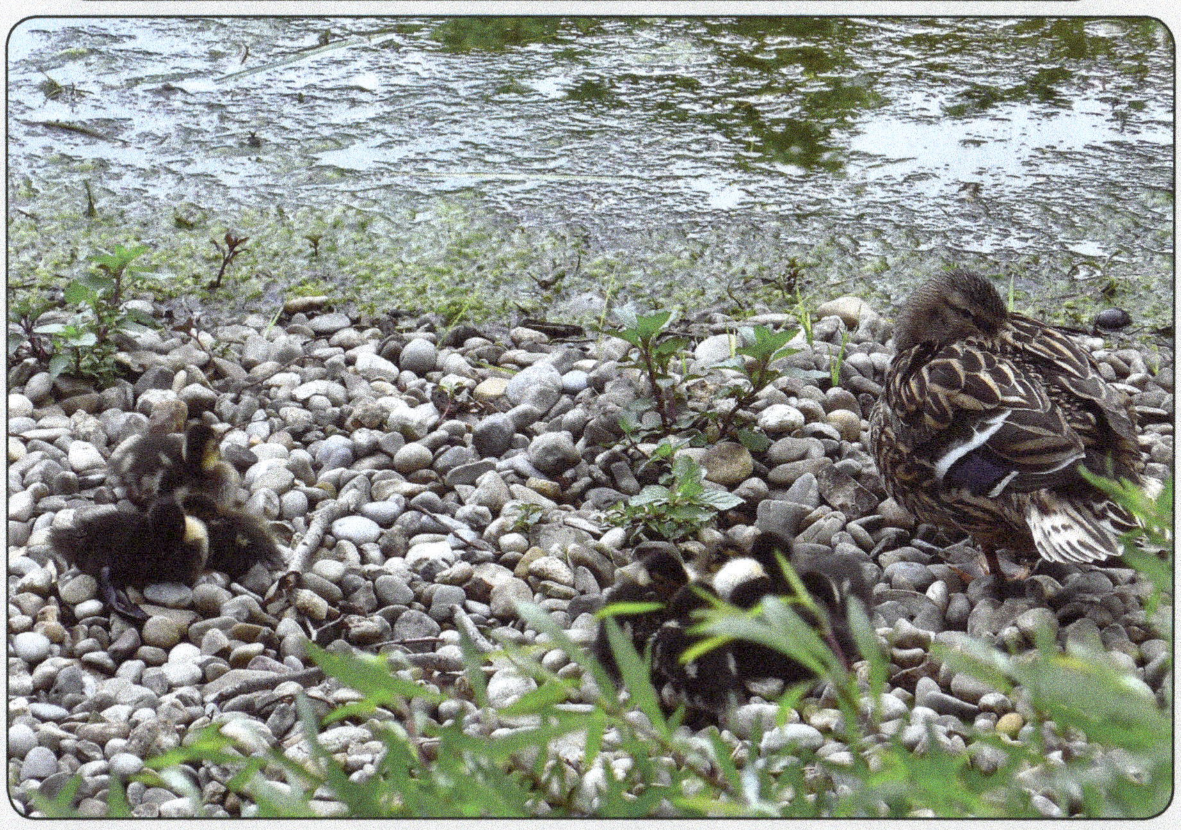

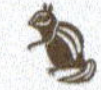

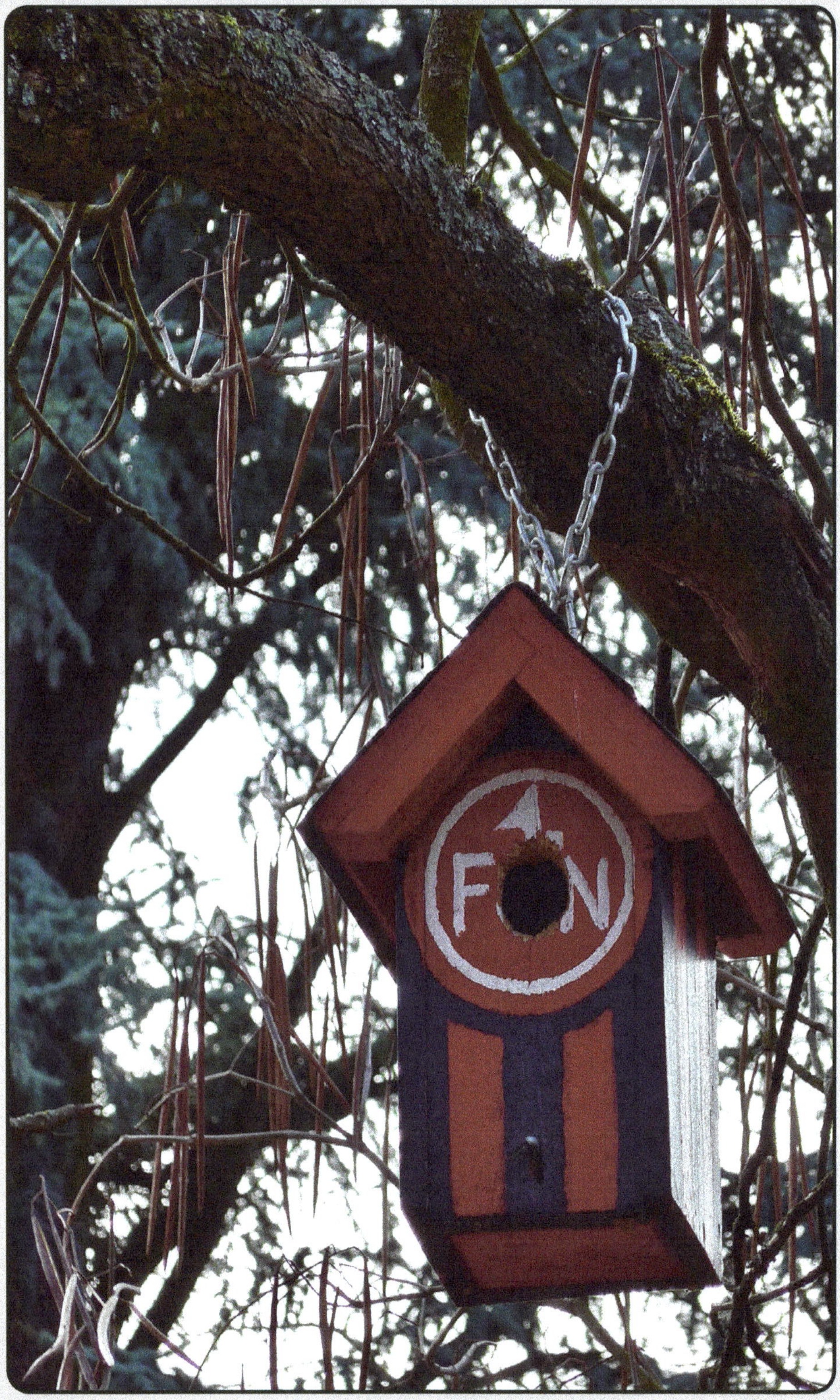

Songbird fans of FC Nürnberg soccer club.

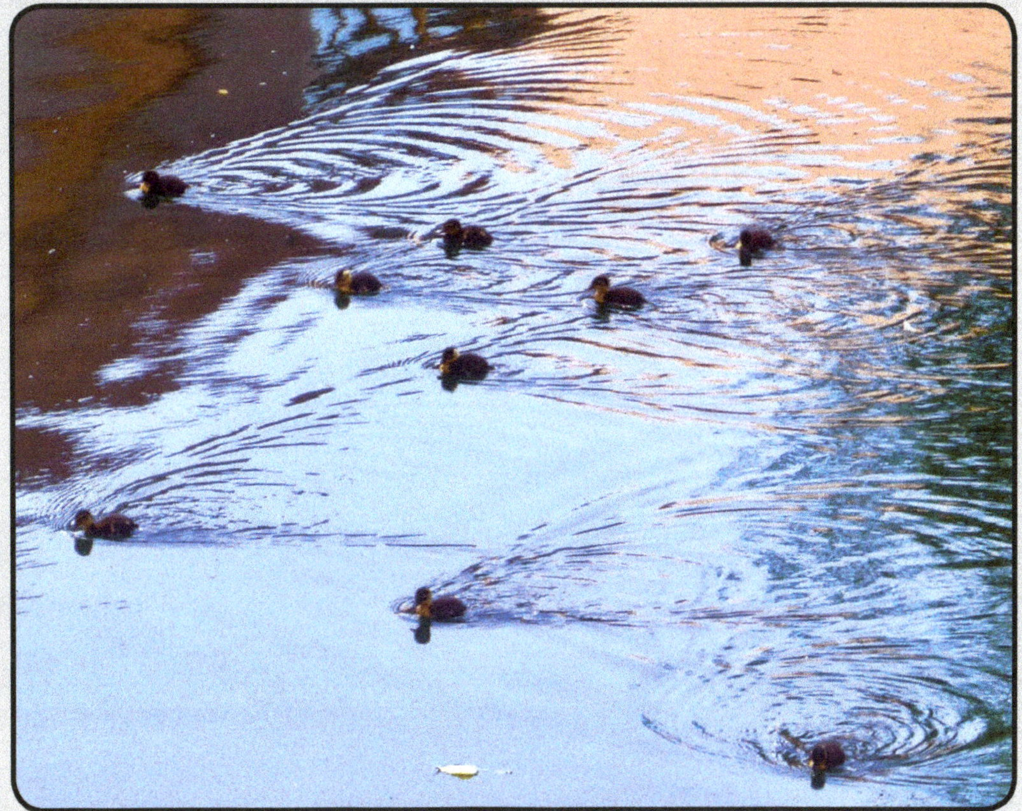

Baby beelines near a castle moat.

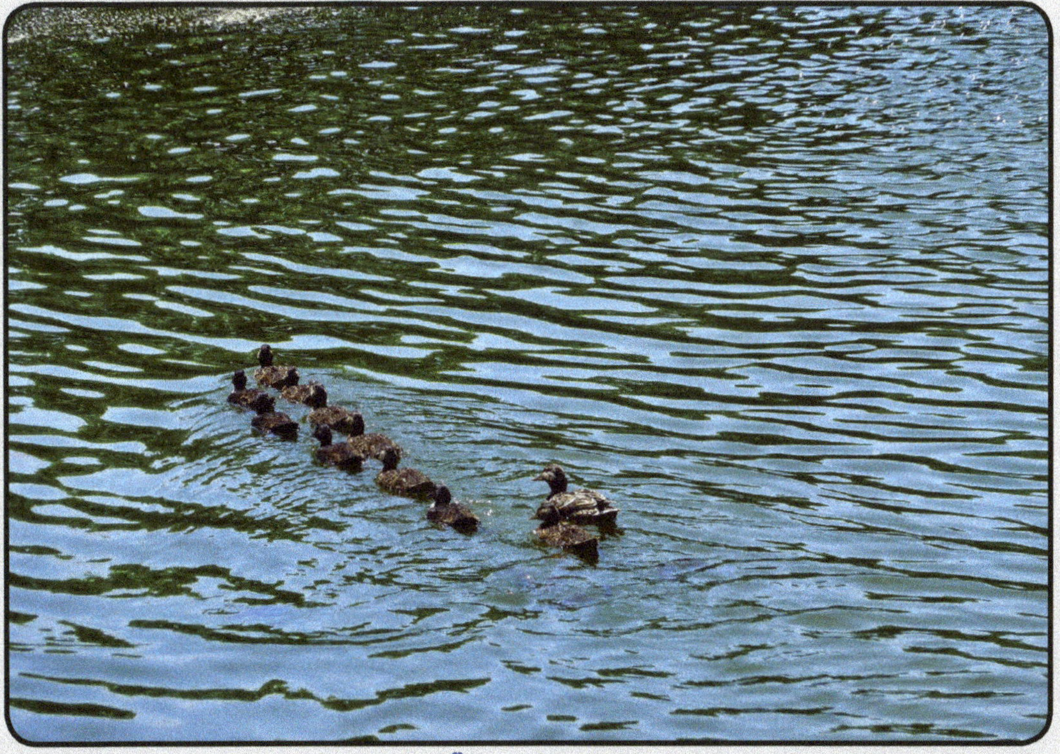

Family sailing.

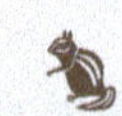

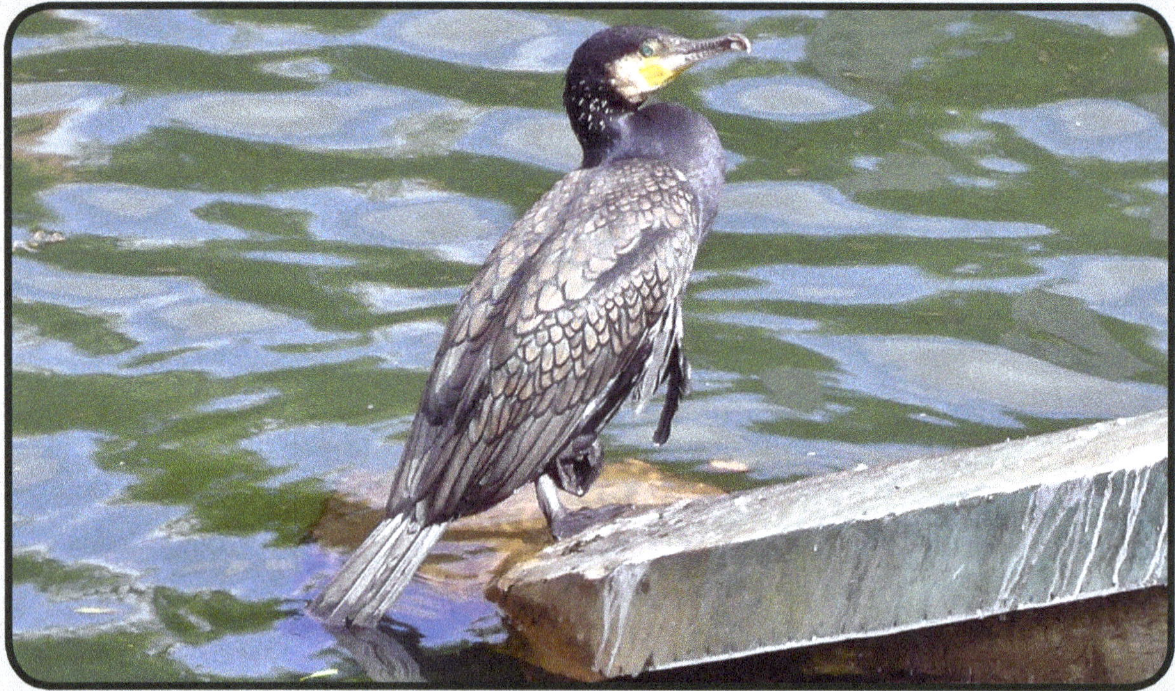

Castle cormorant.

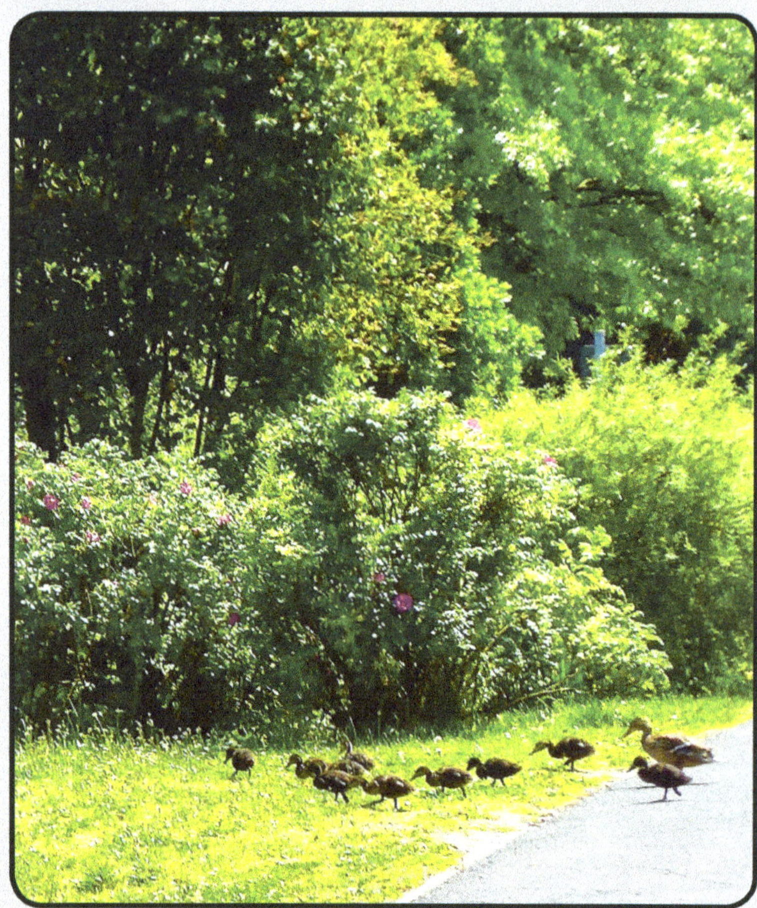

Summer picnic.

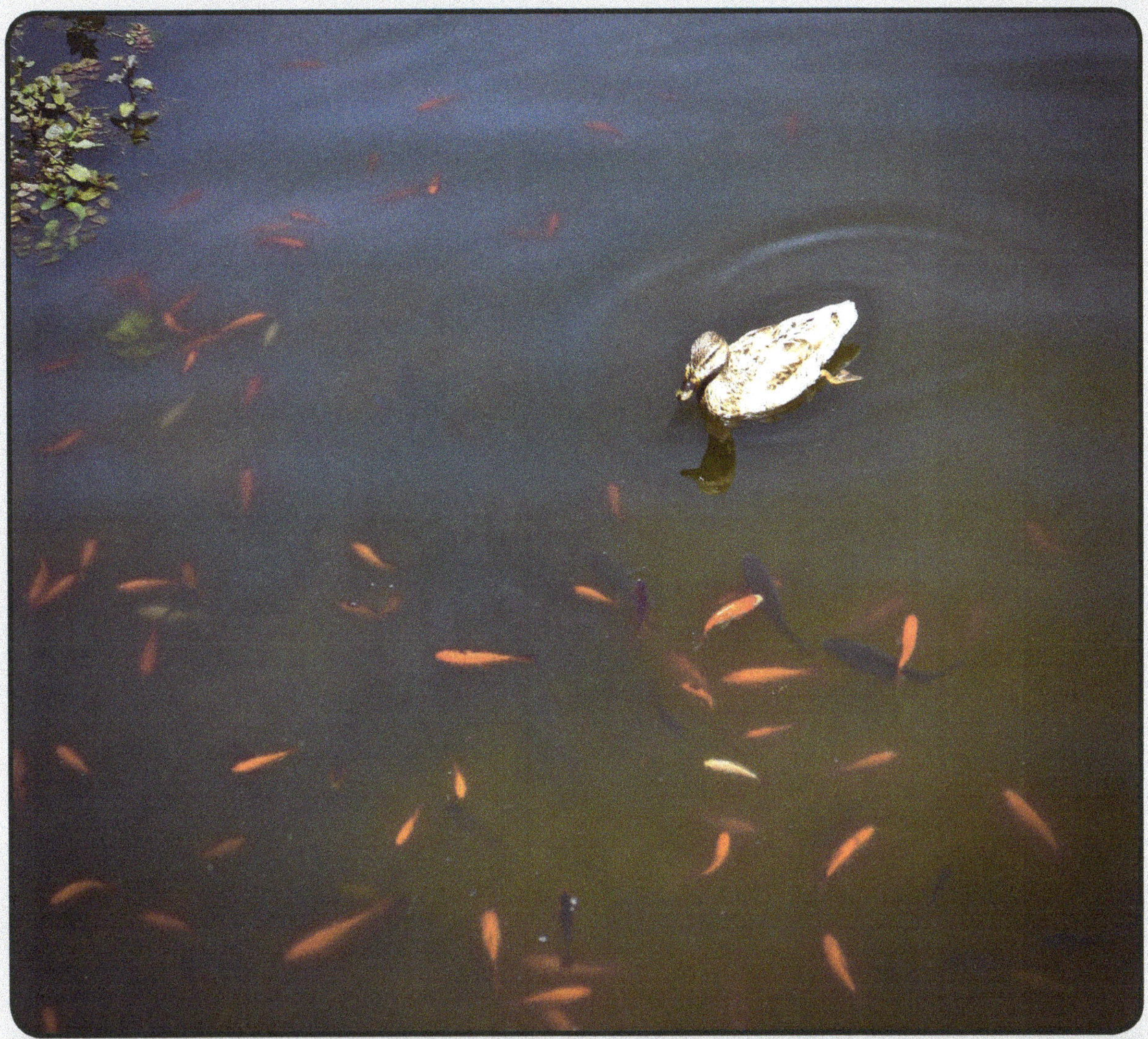

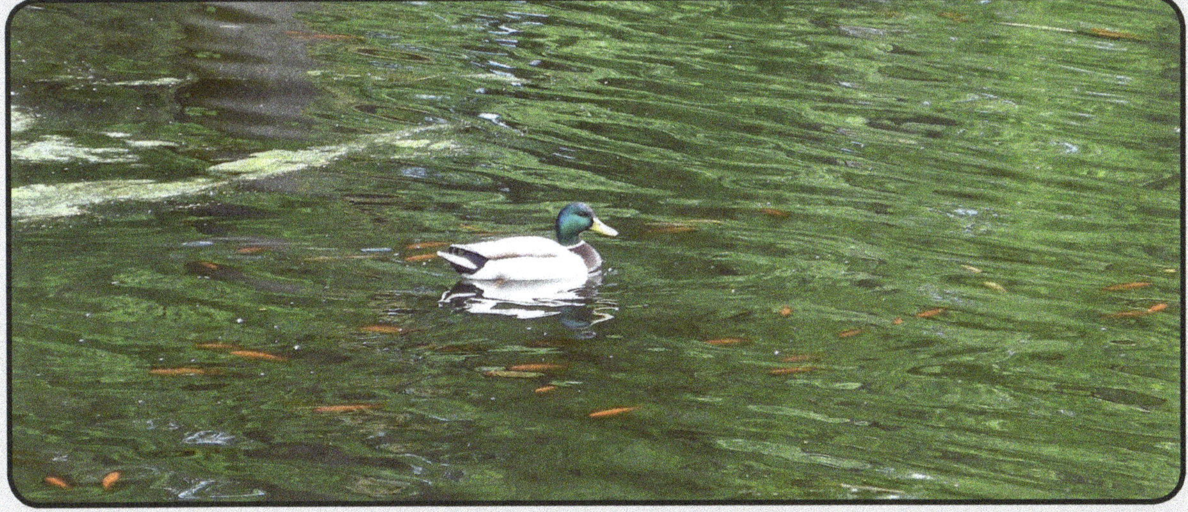

Swimming with friends series.

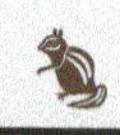

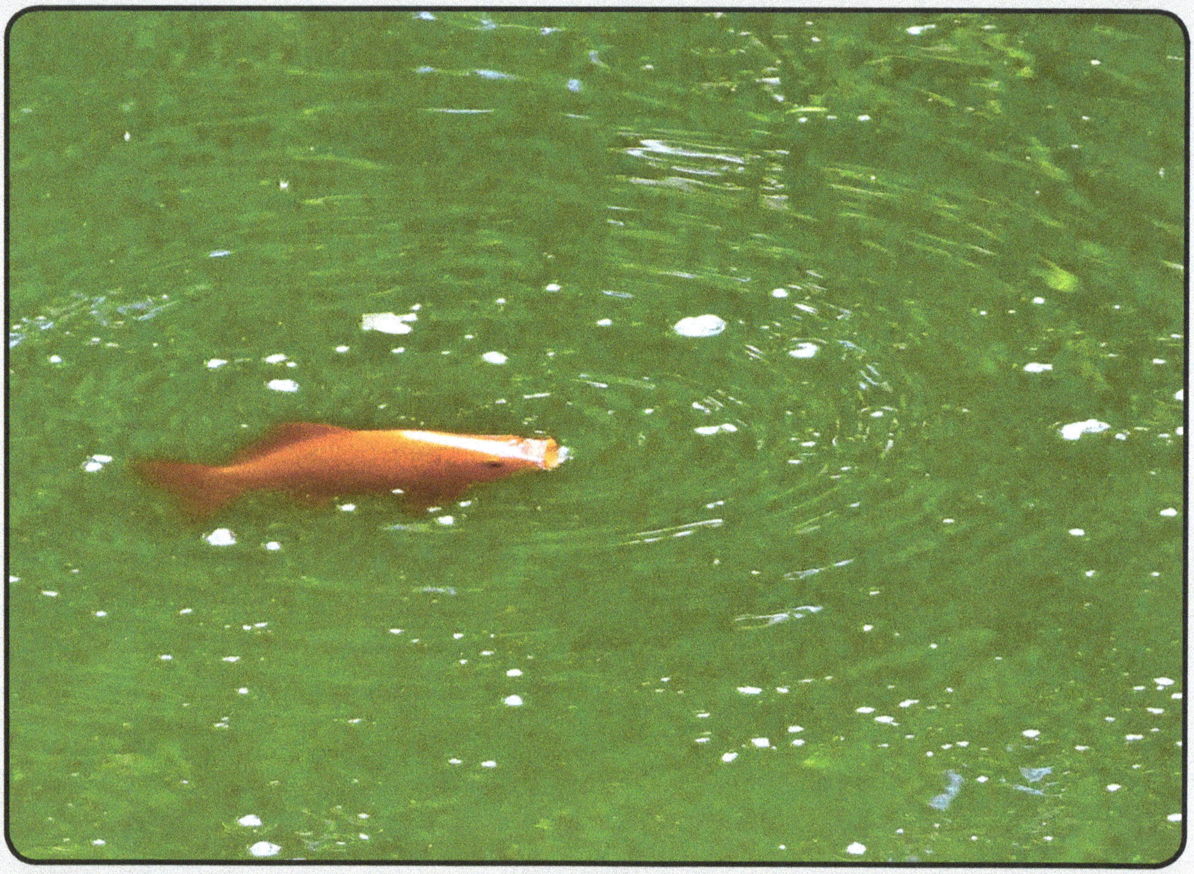

Pucker up.

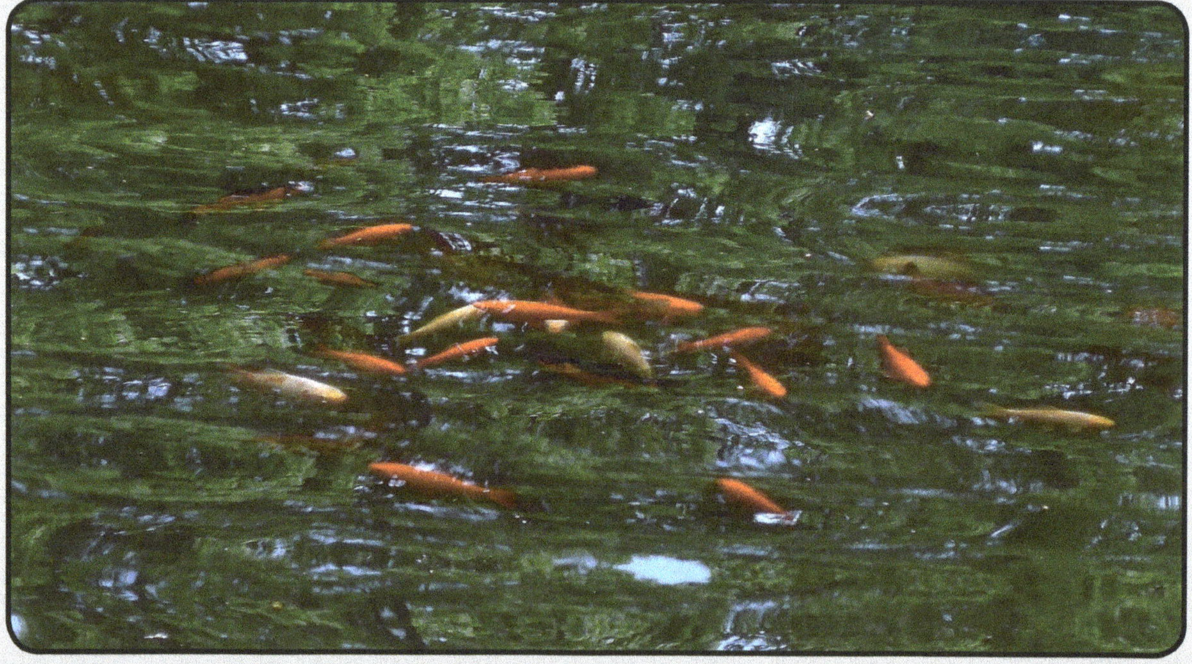

Underwater ballet.

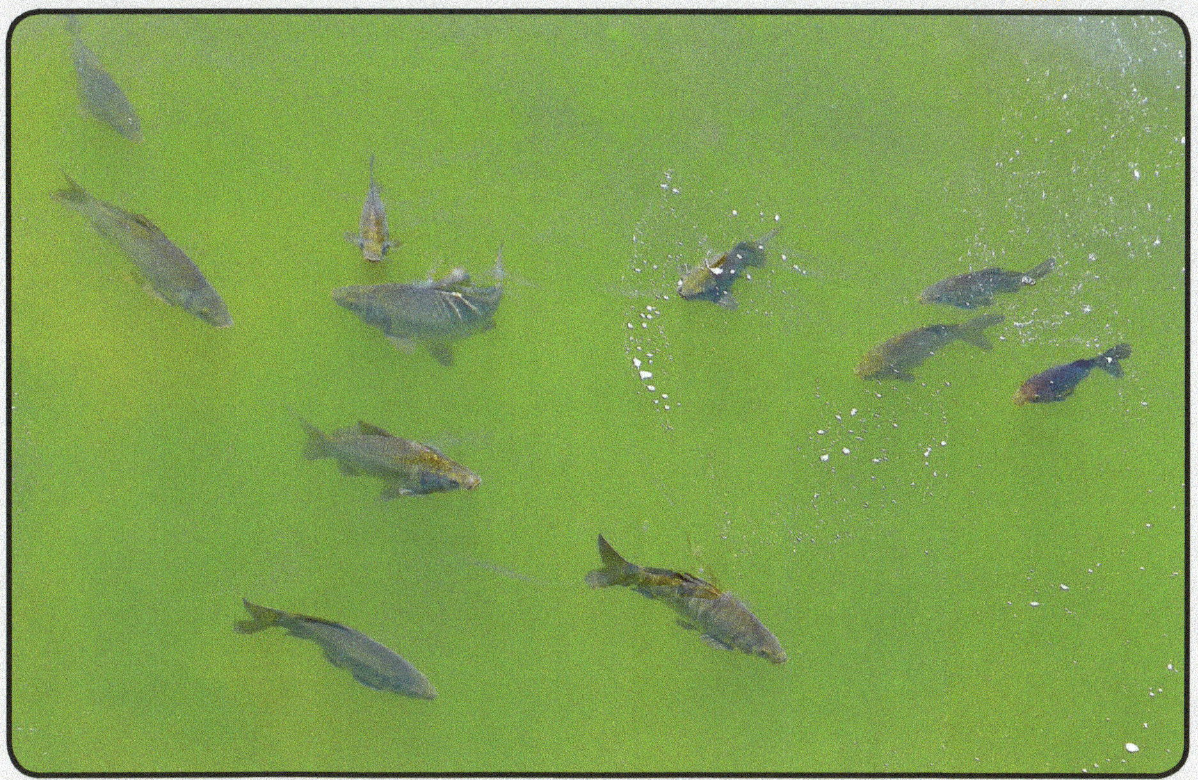

Fluidity series.

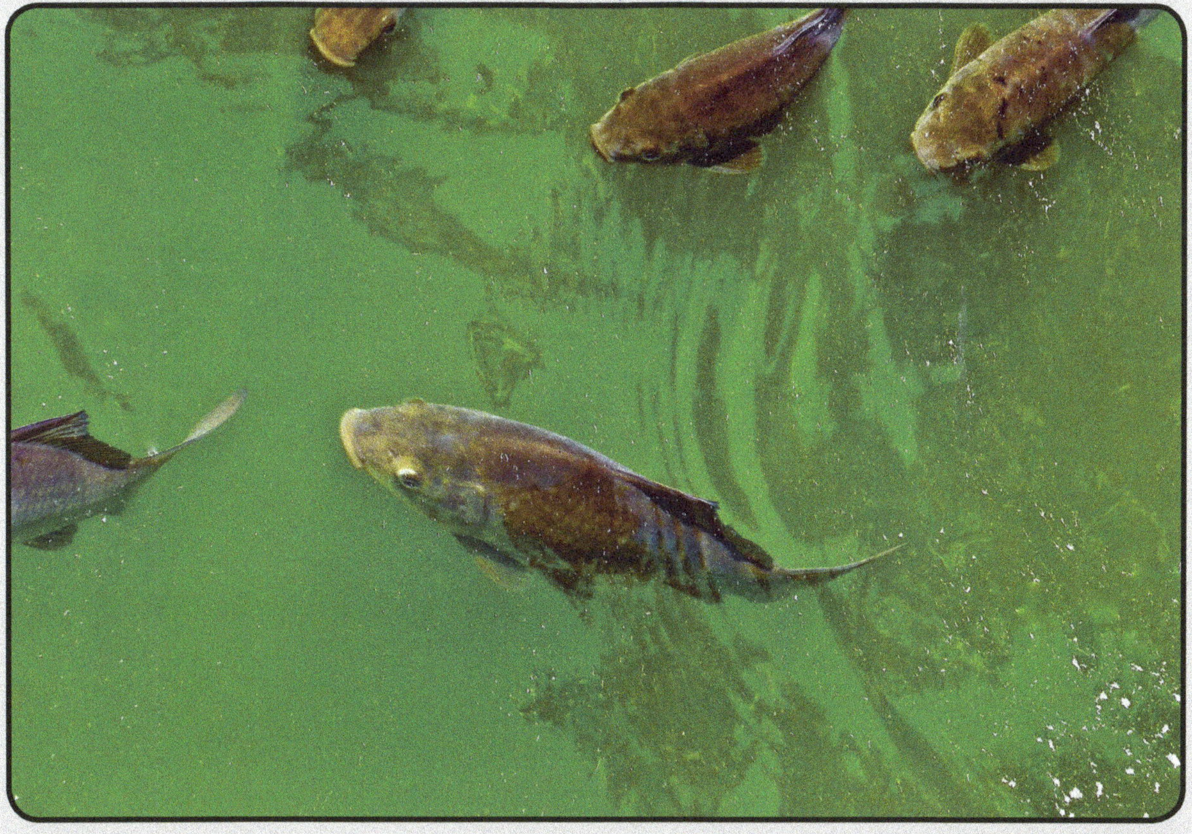

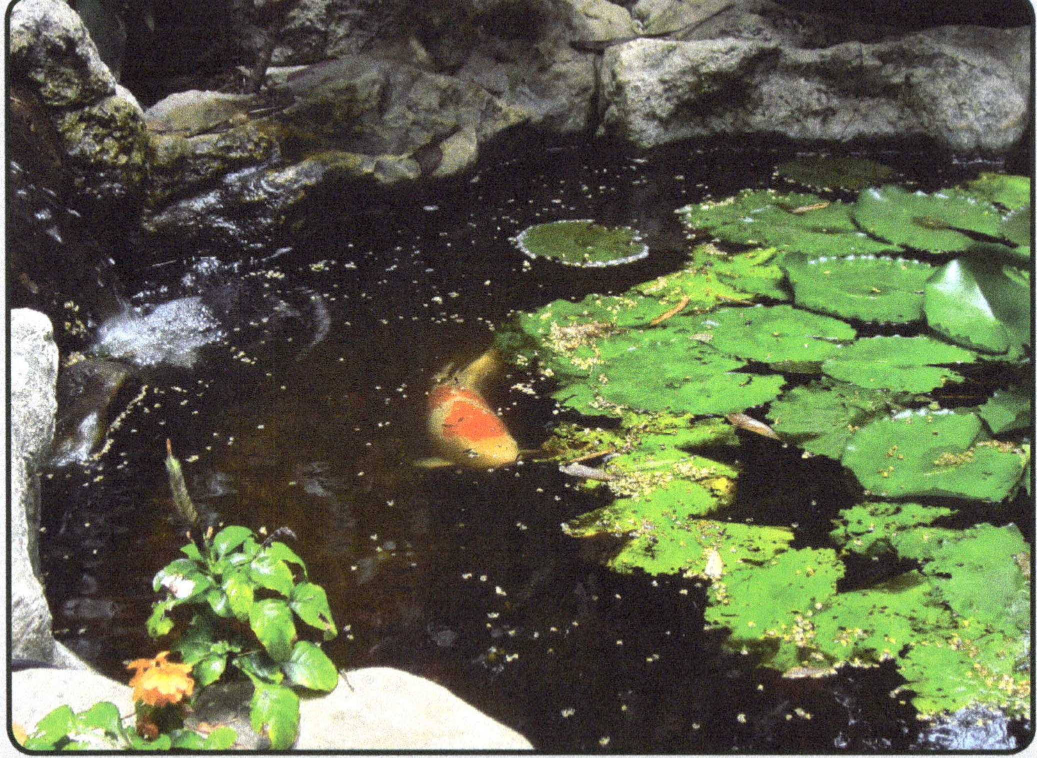

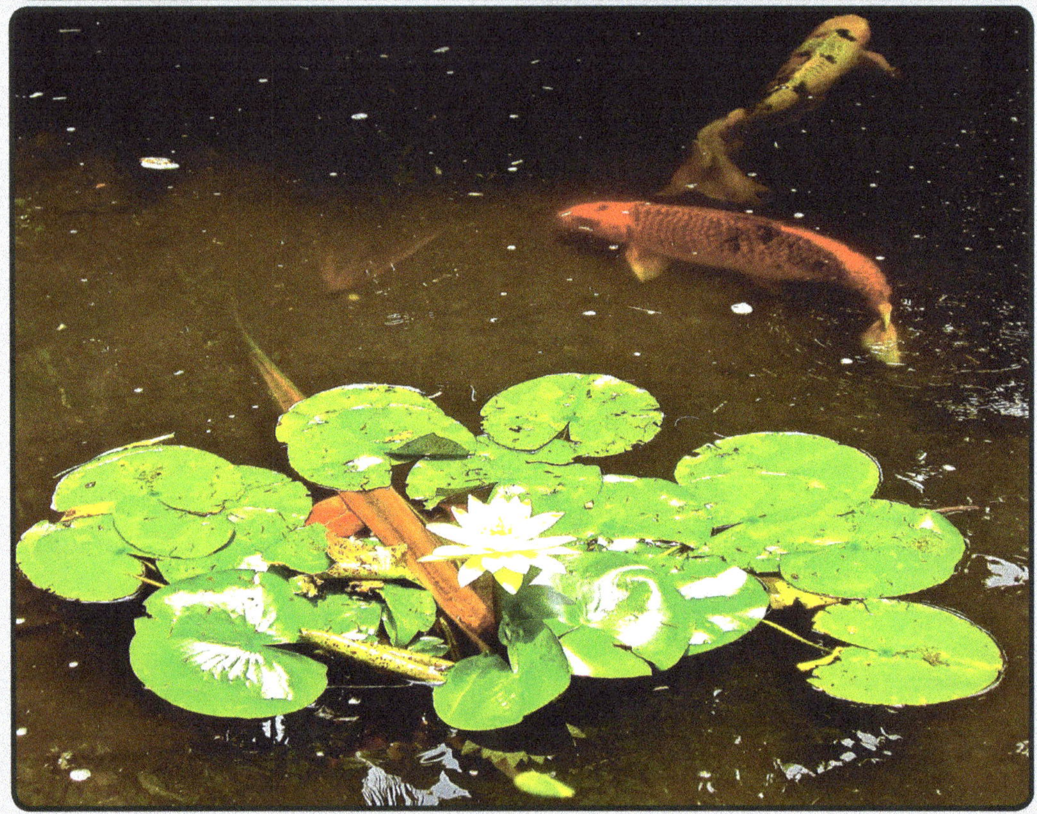

Koi series.

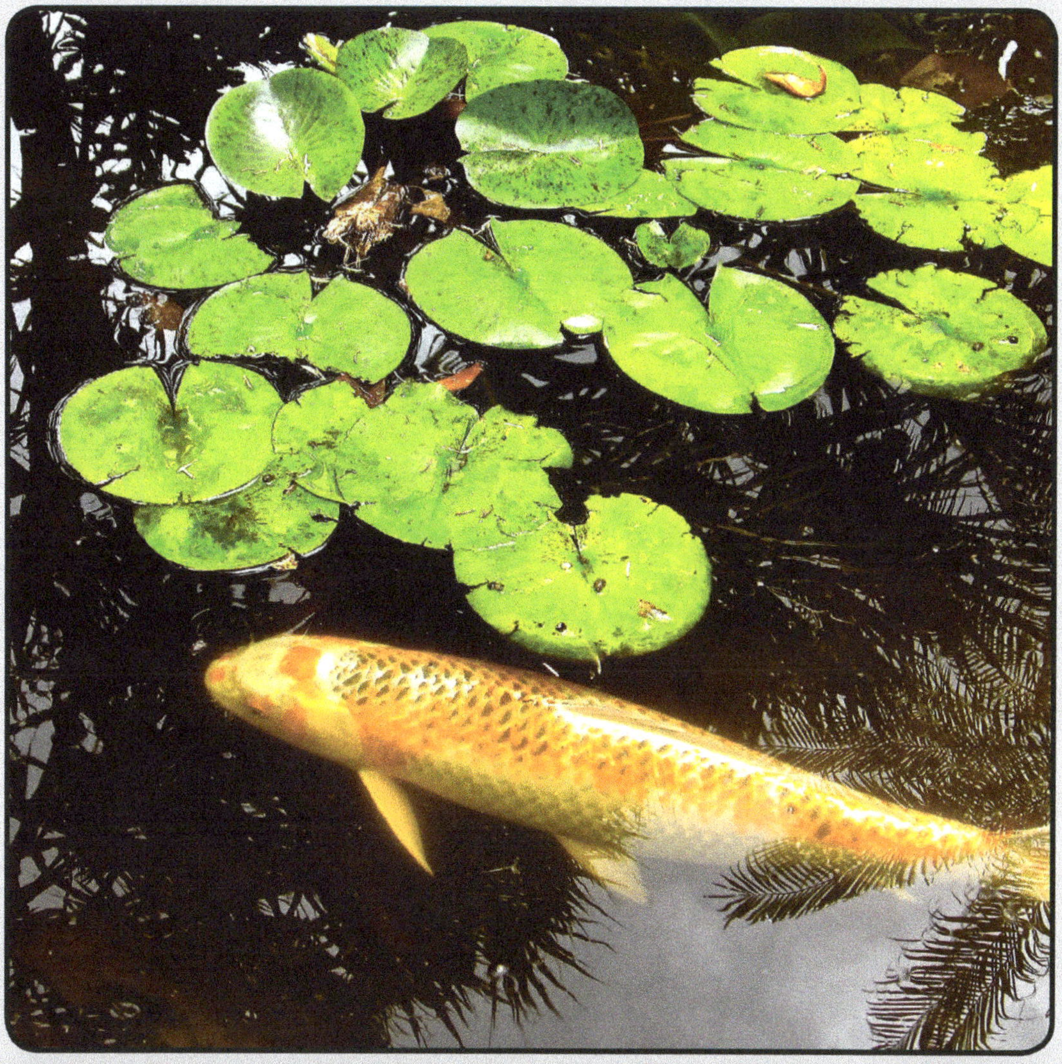

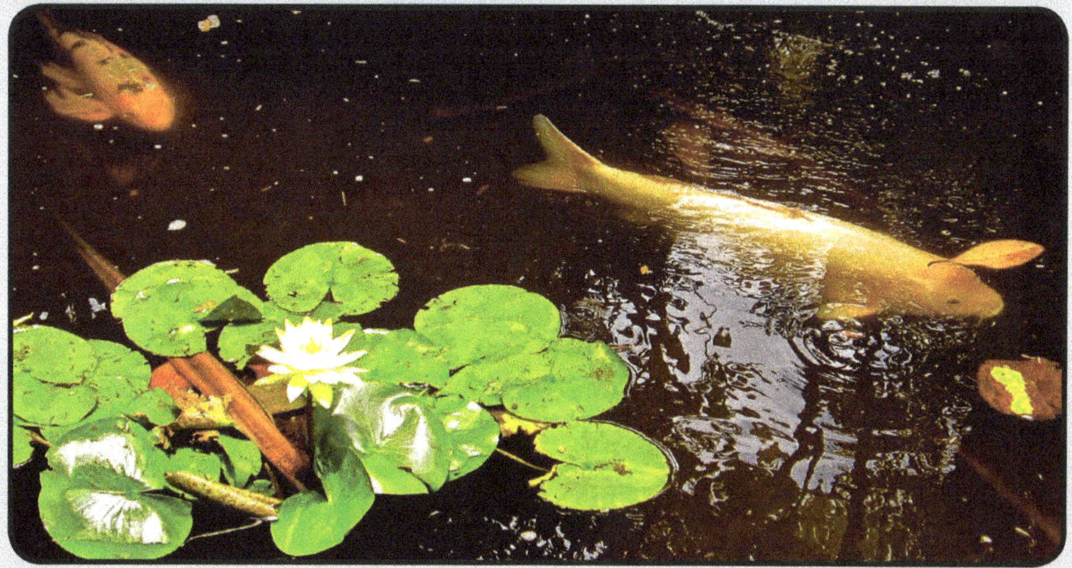

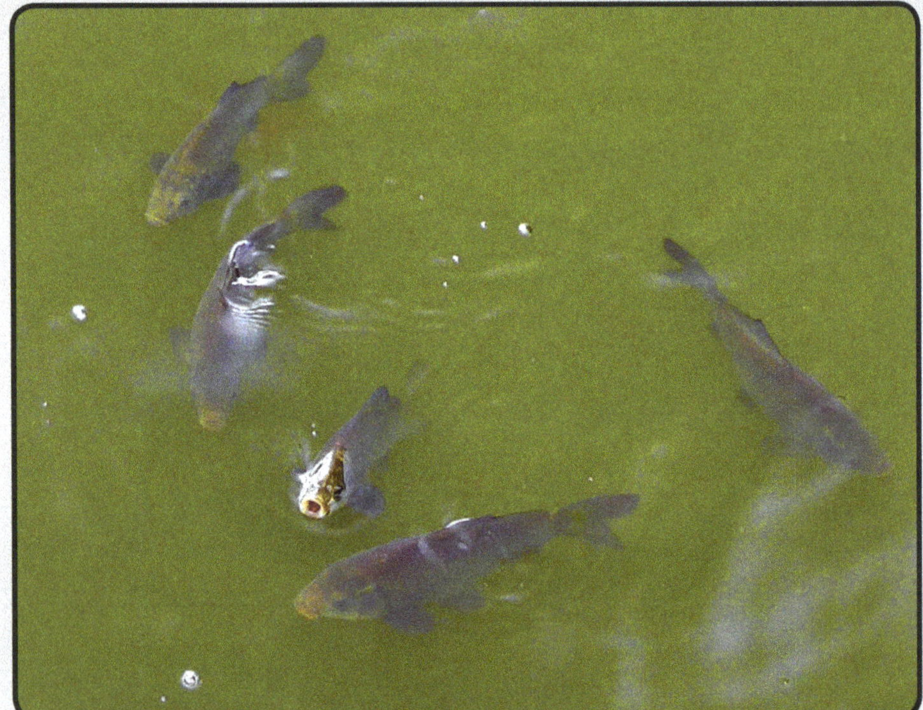

Heads up series.

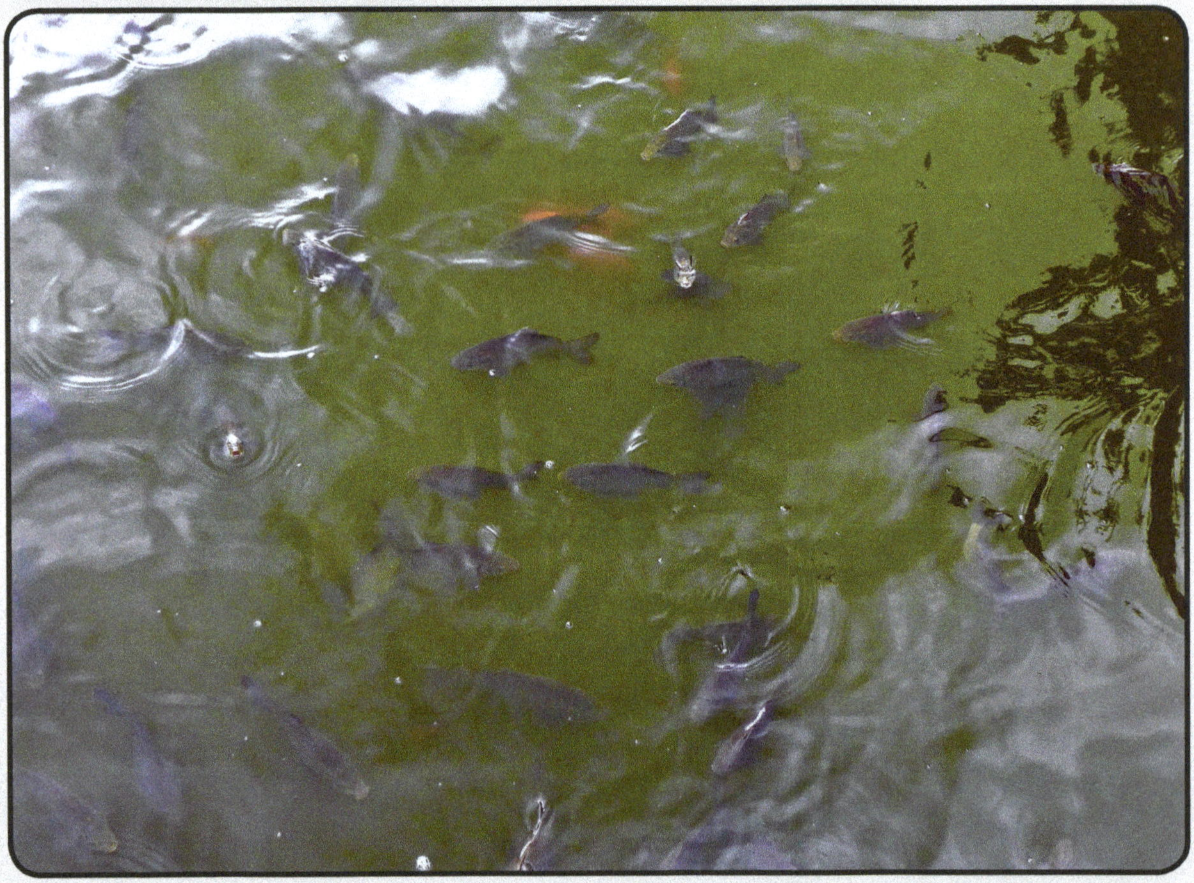

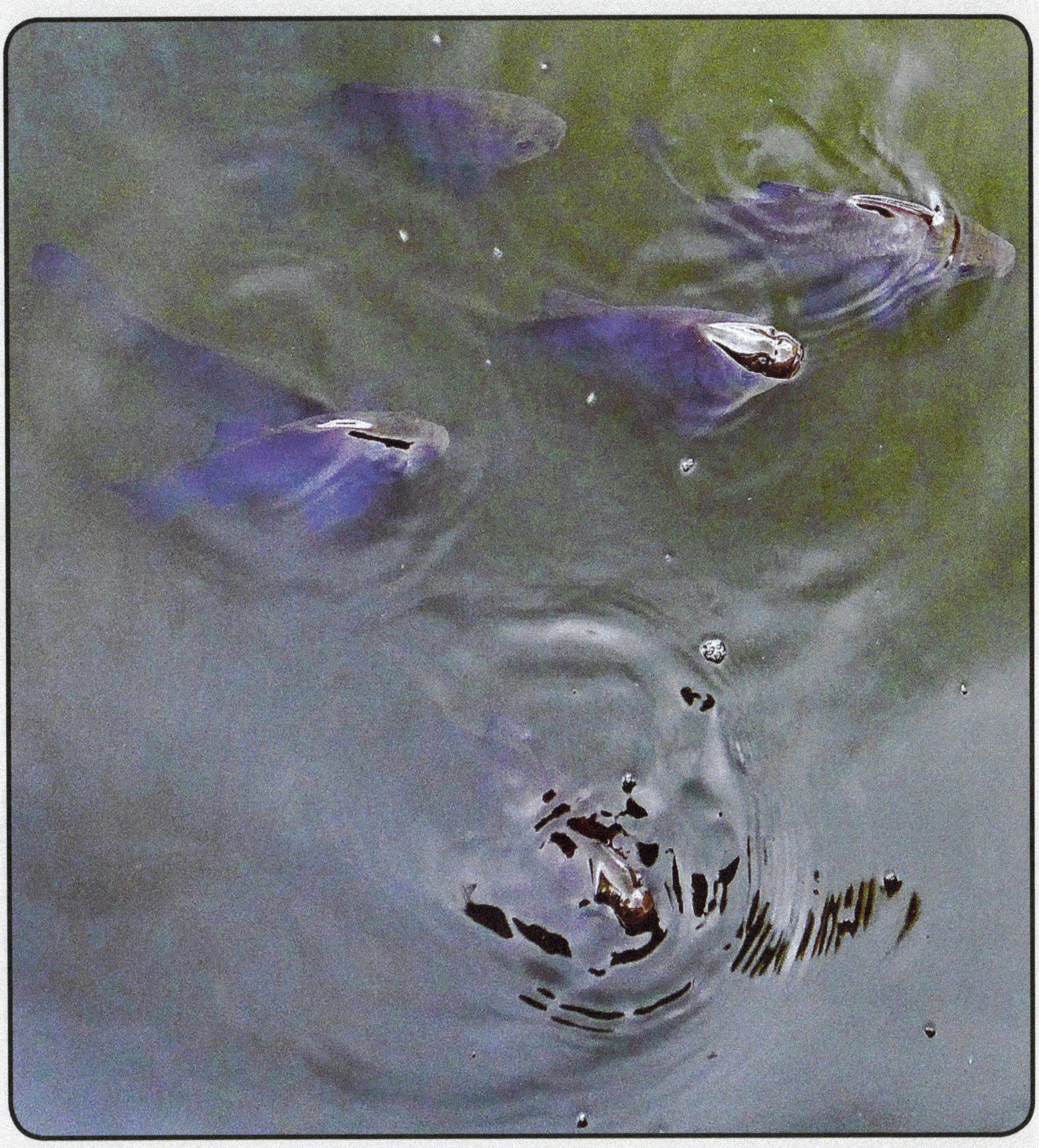

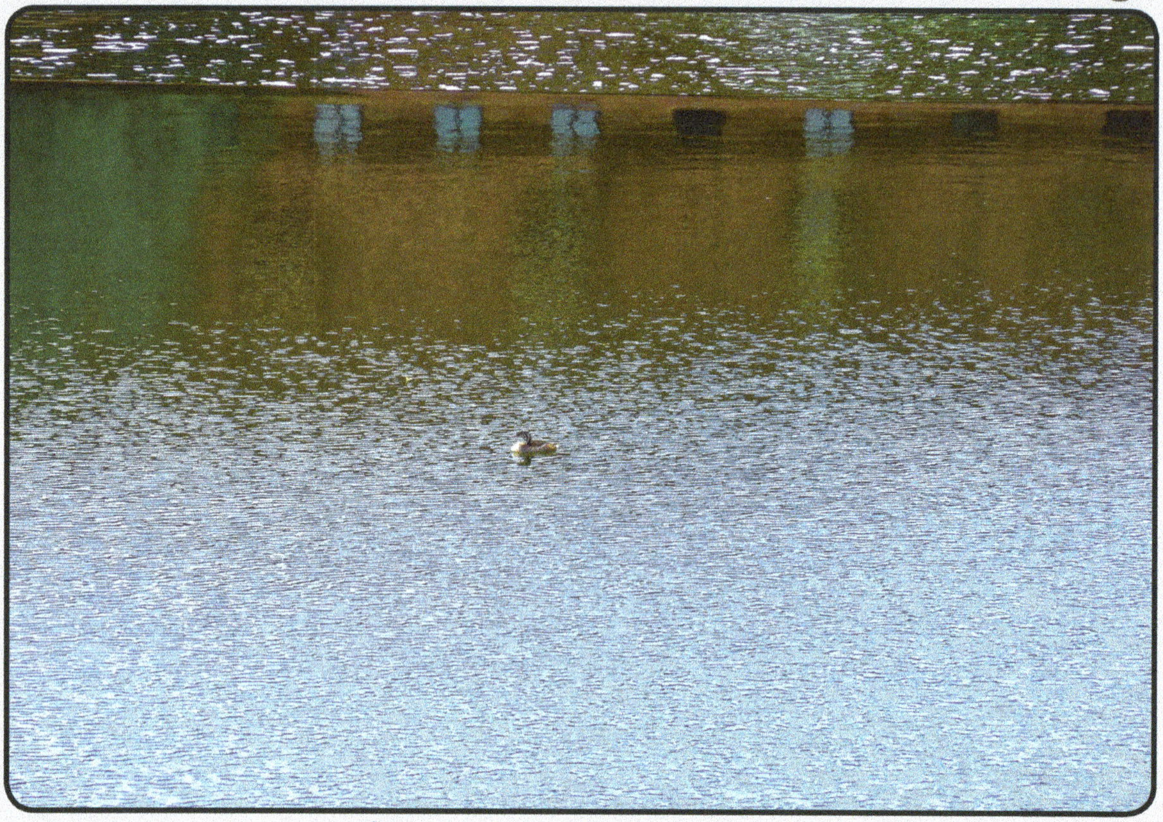

Woodblock water pattern series.

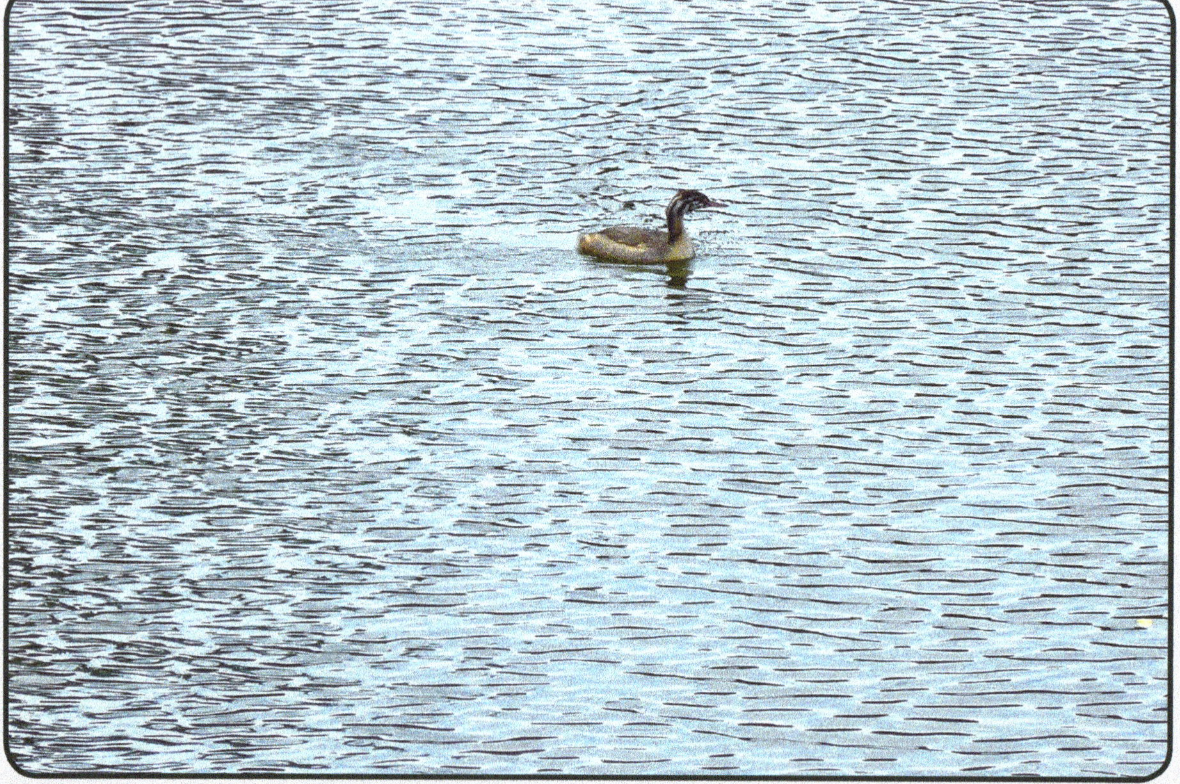

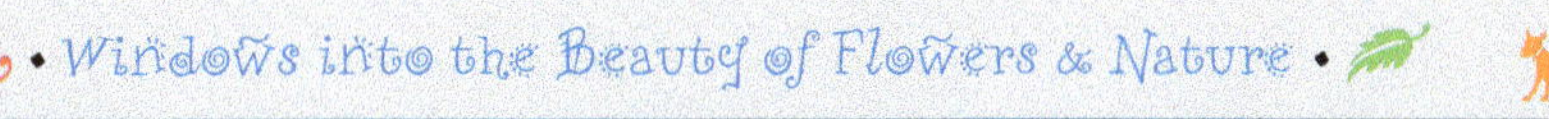

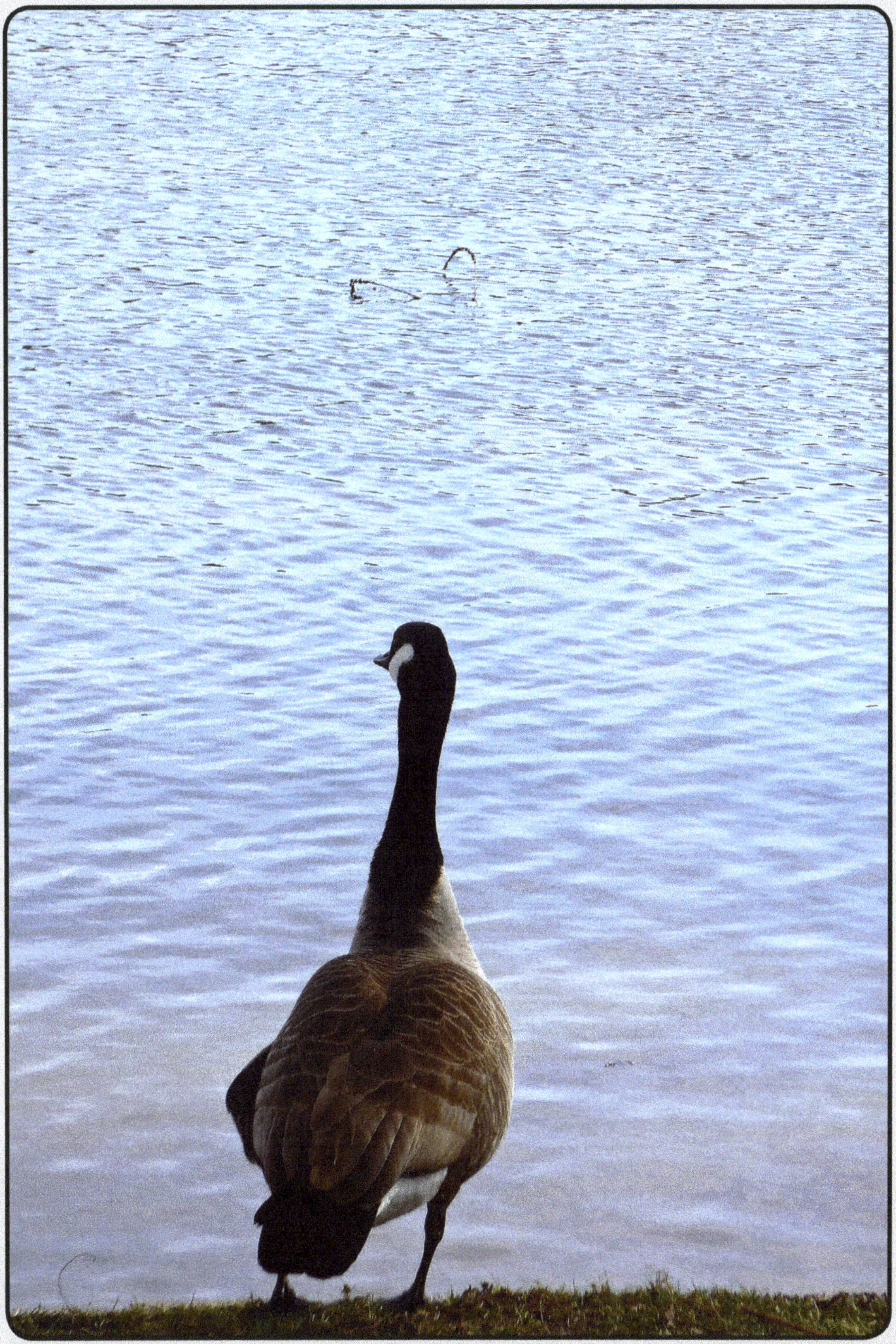

Sentry.

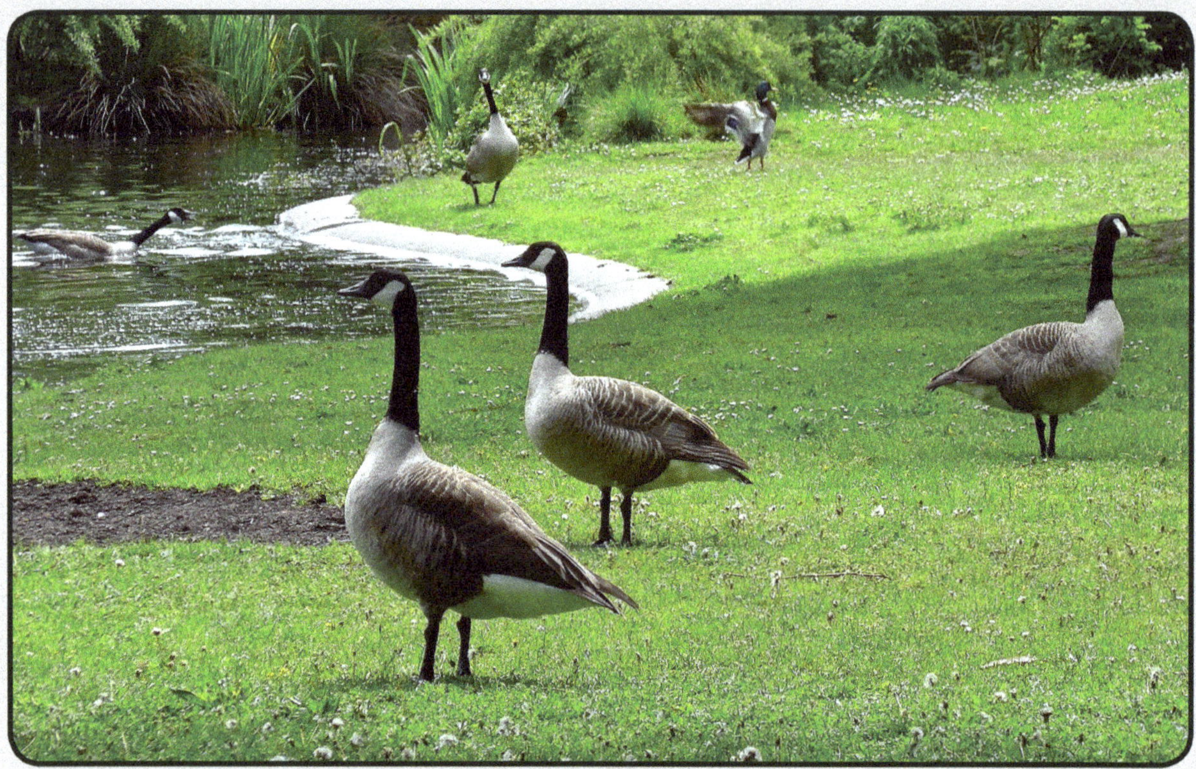

Play day.

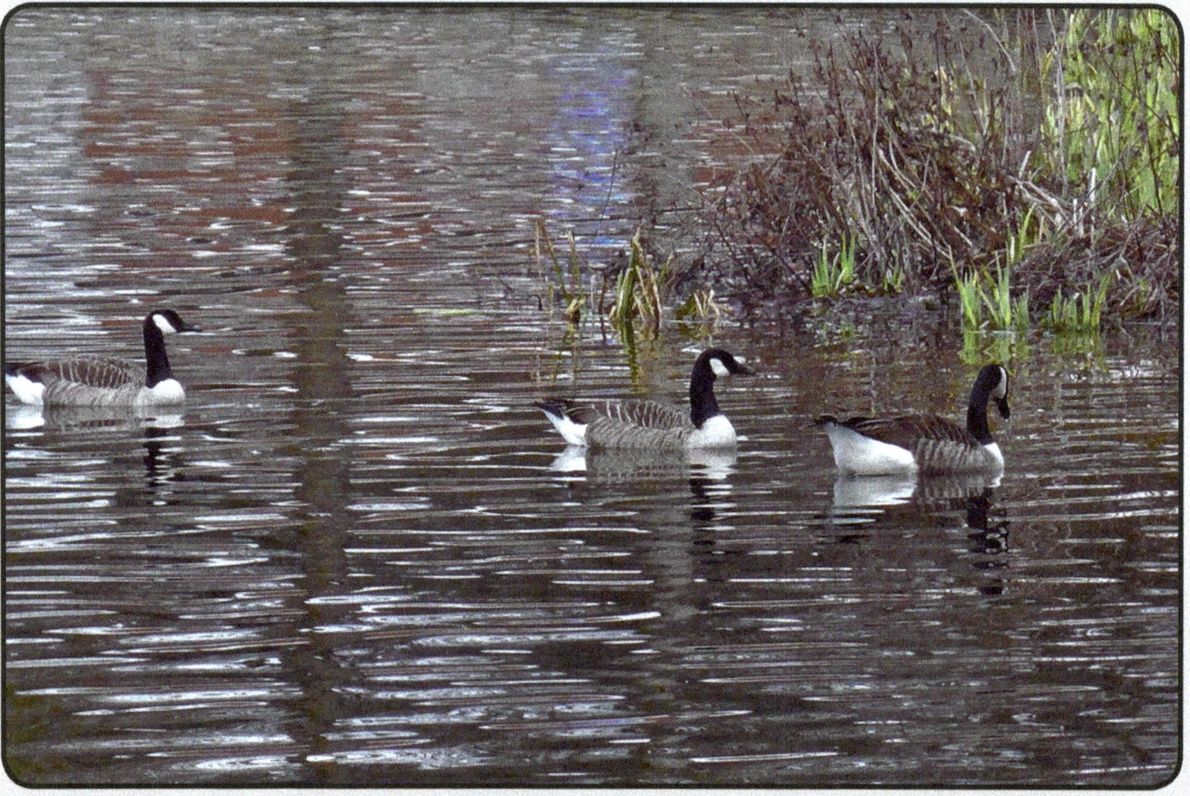

Burgundy reflections.

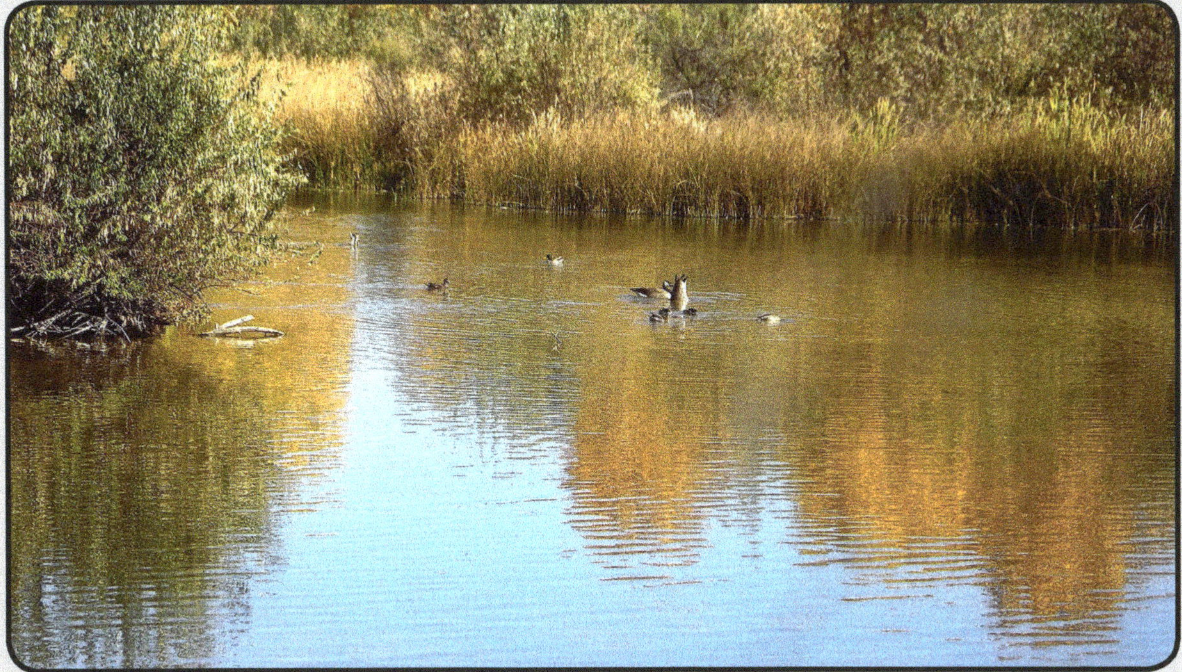

Autumn afternoon.

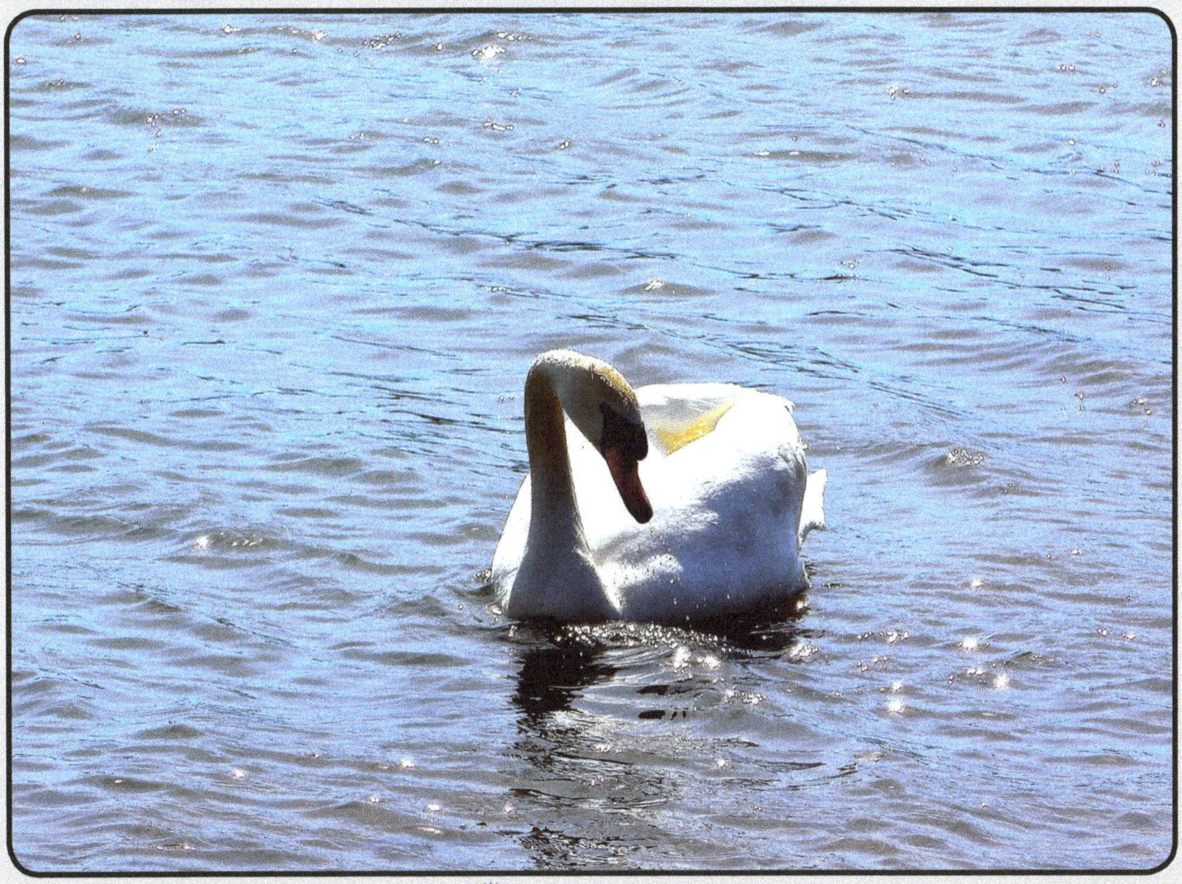

Water diamonds.

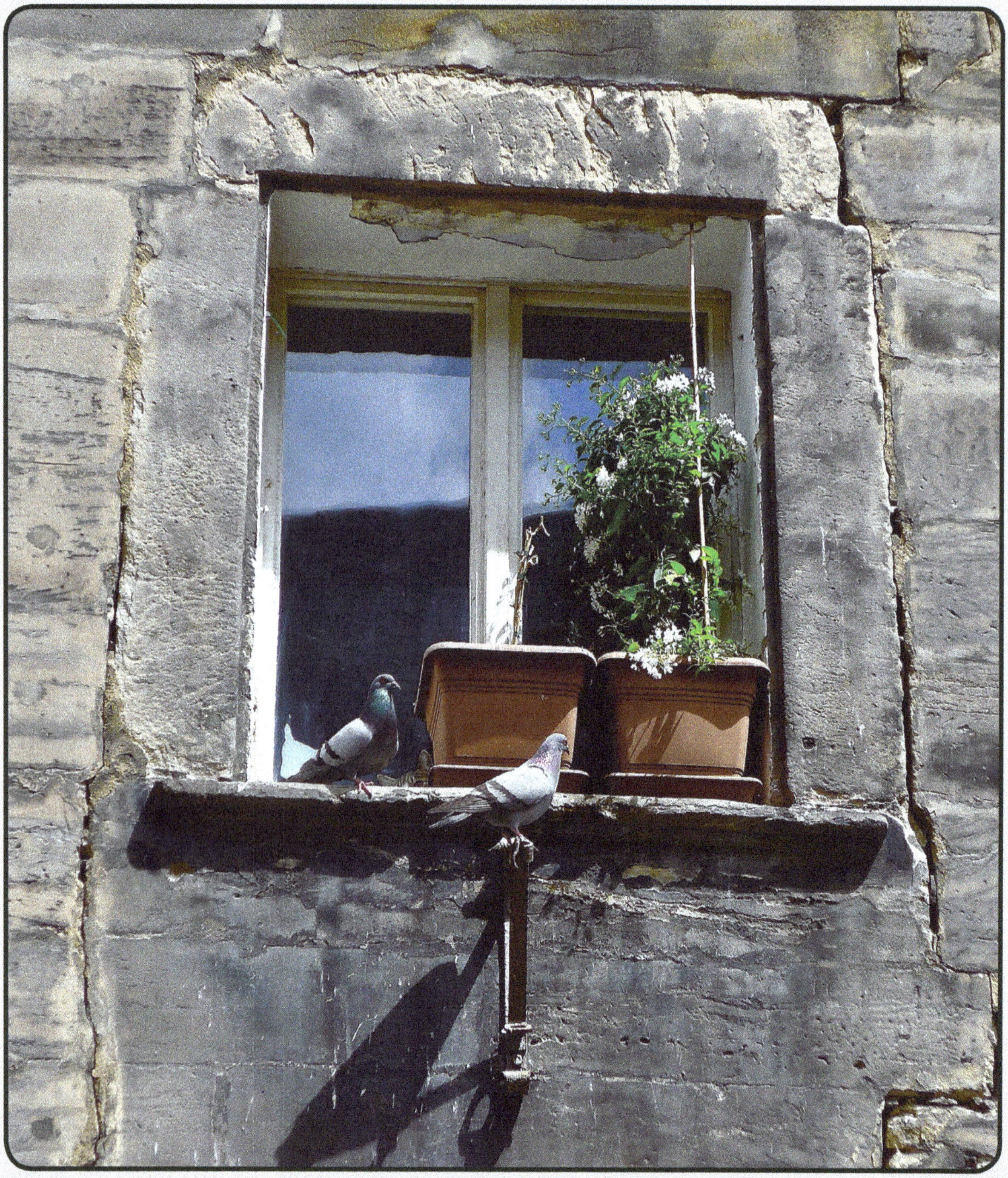

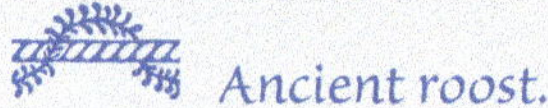

Ancient roost.

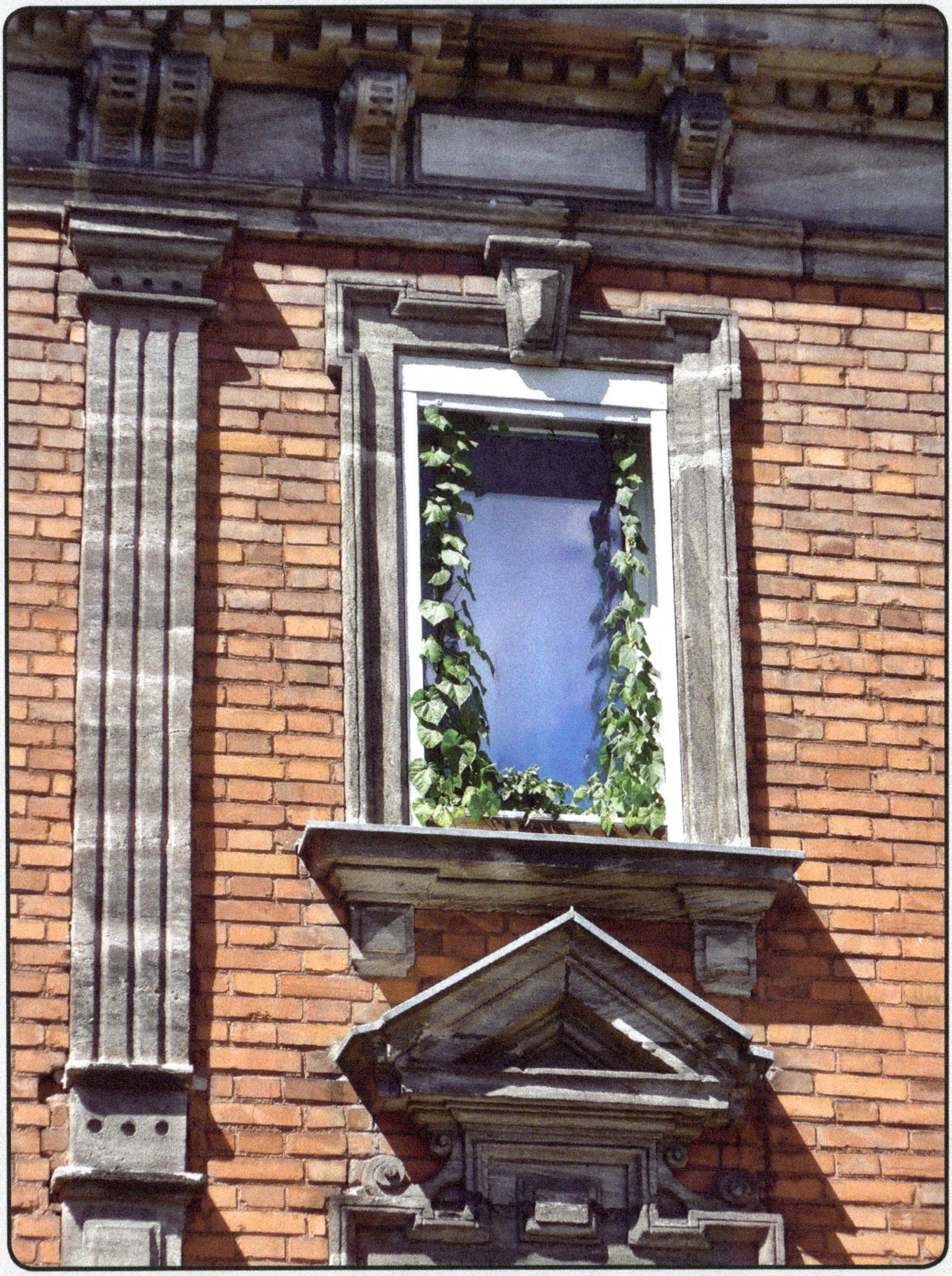

Ivy necklace.

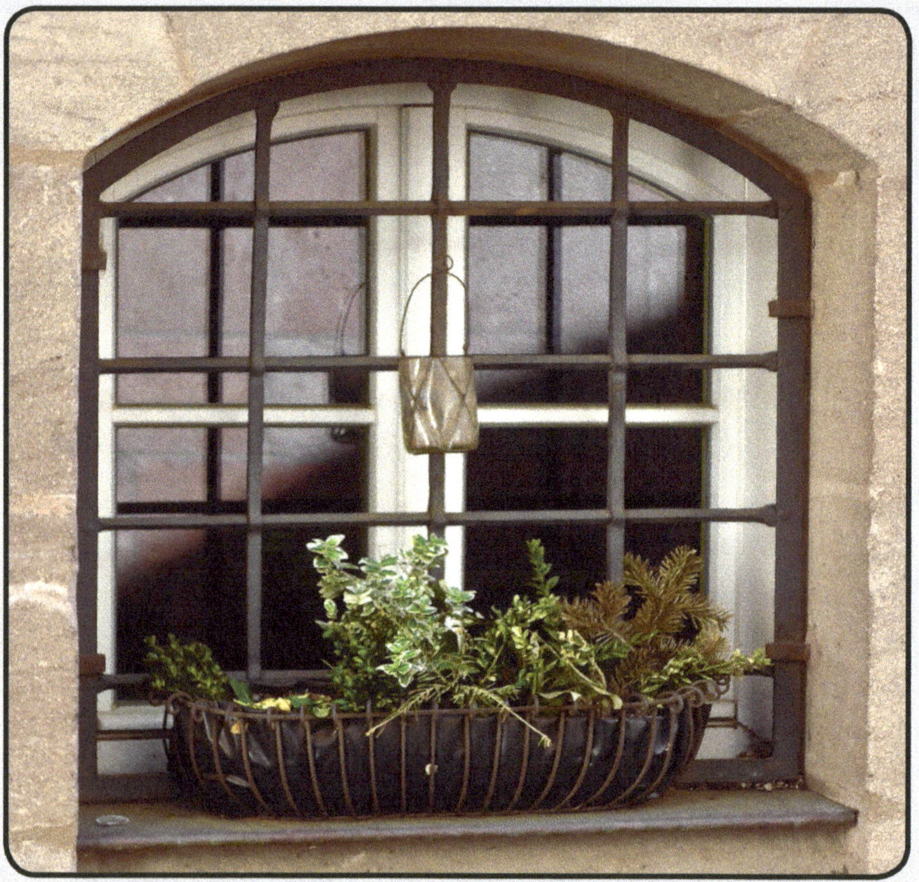

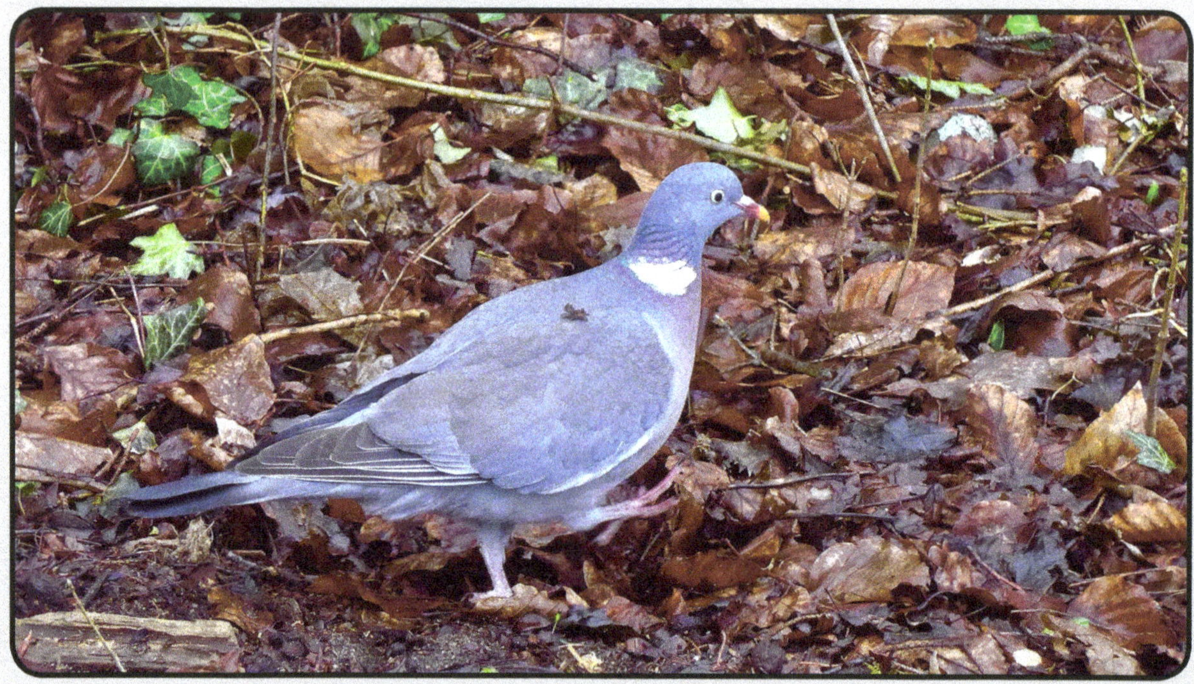

Right step...

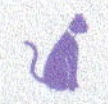

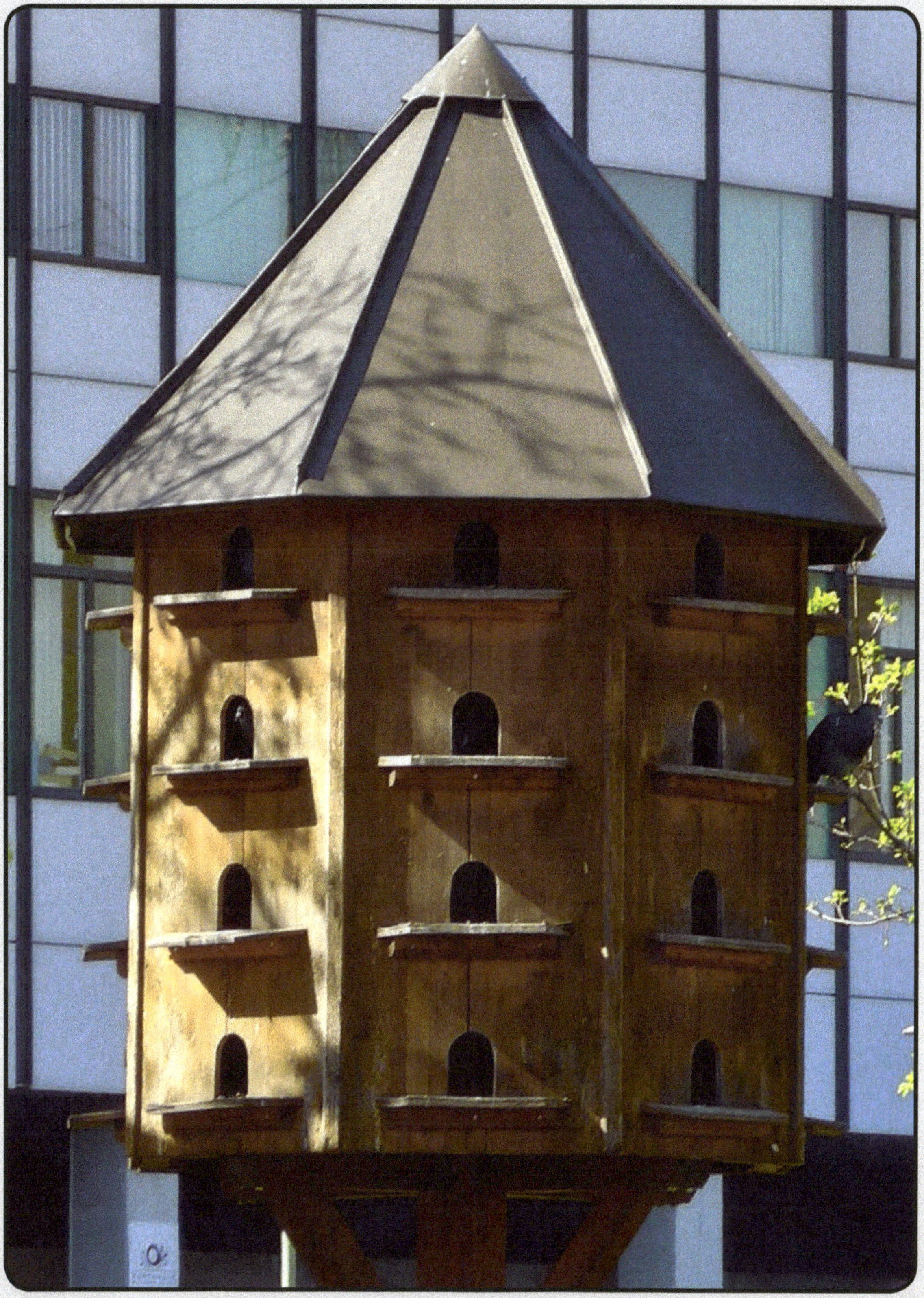

Peeking pigeon.

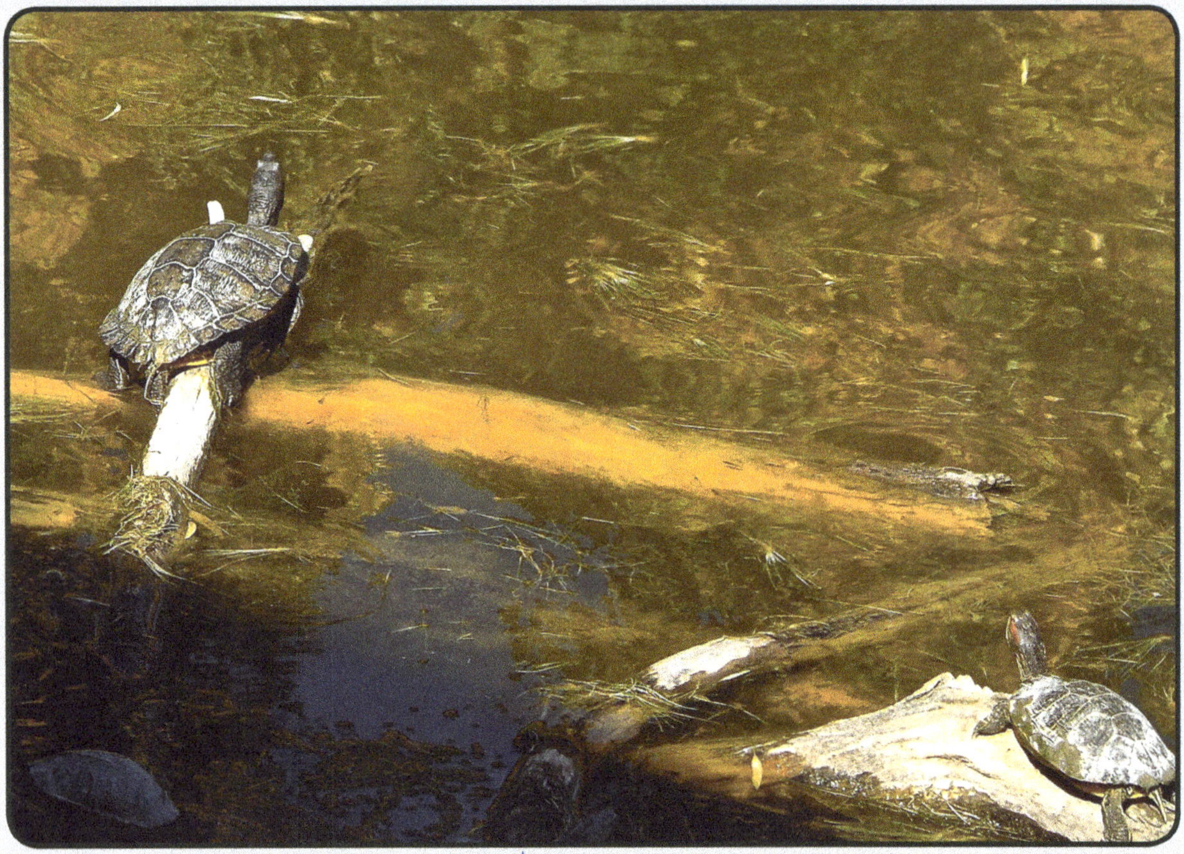

Siesta time.

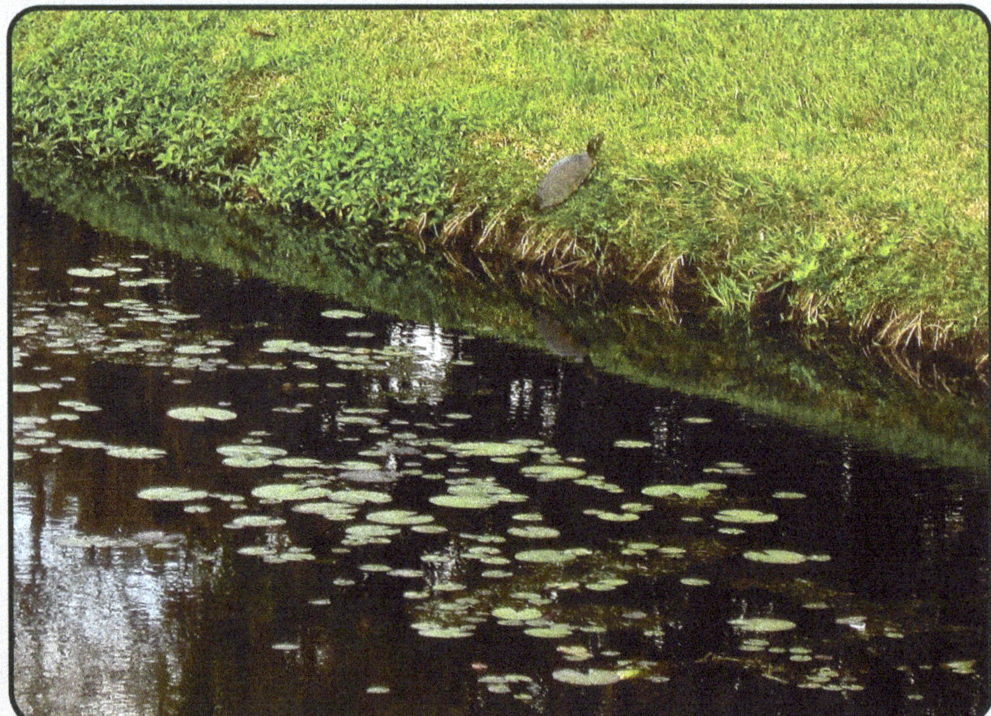

Upward climb.

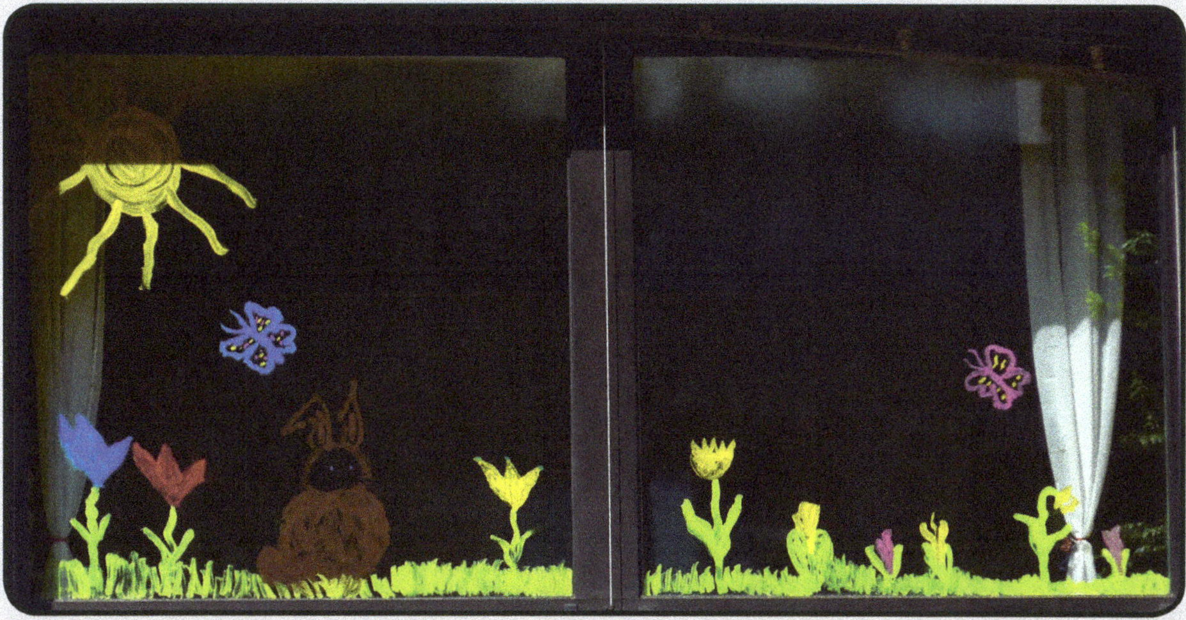

Winter outside, but springtime inside.

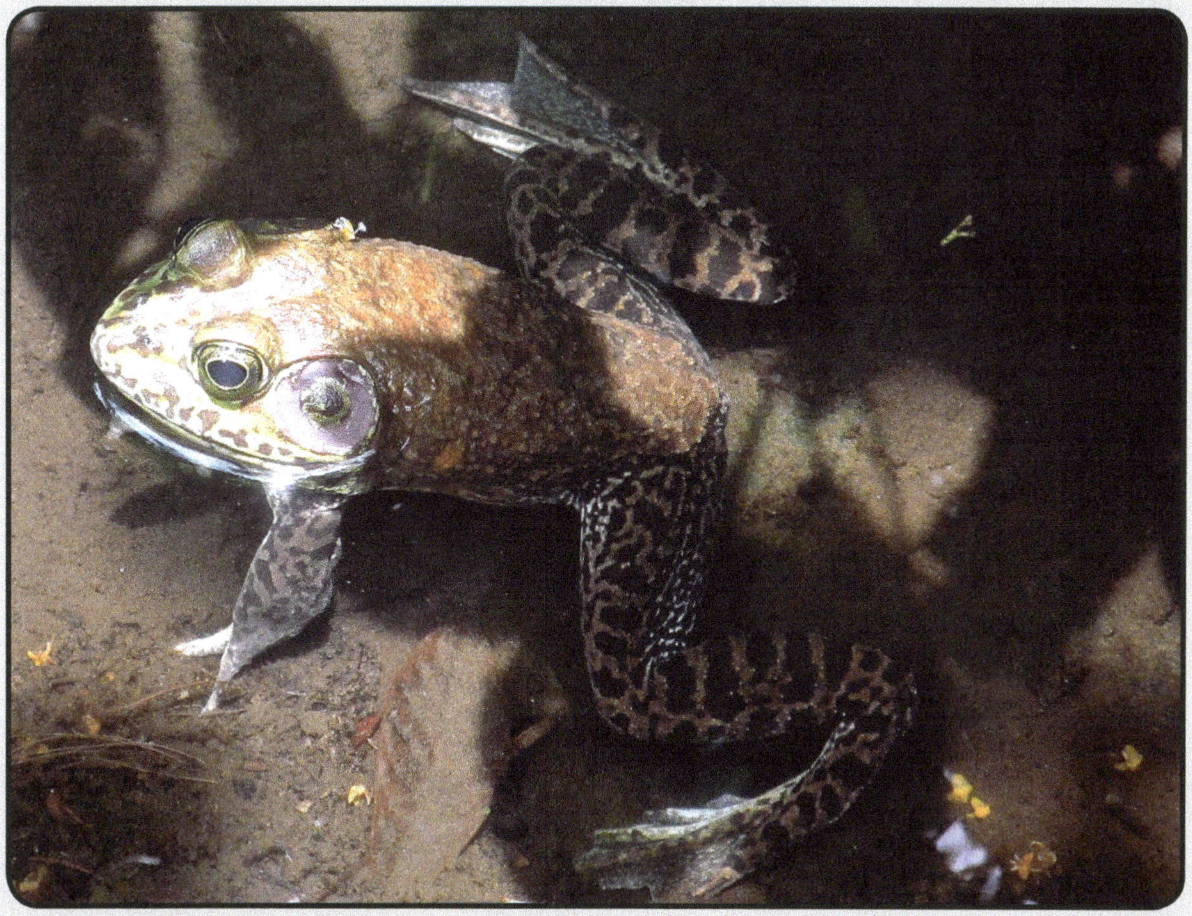

All-knowing eyes..

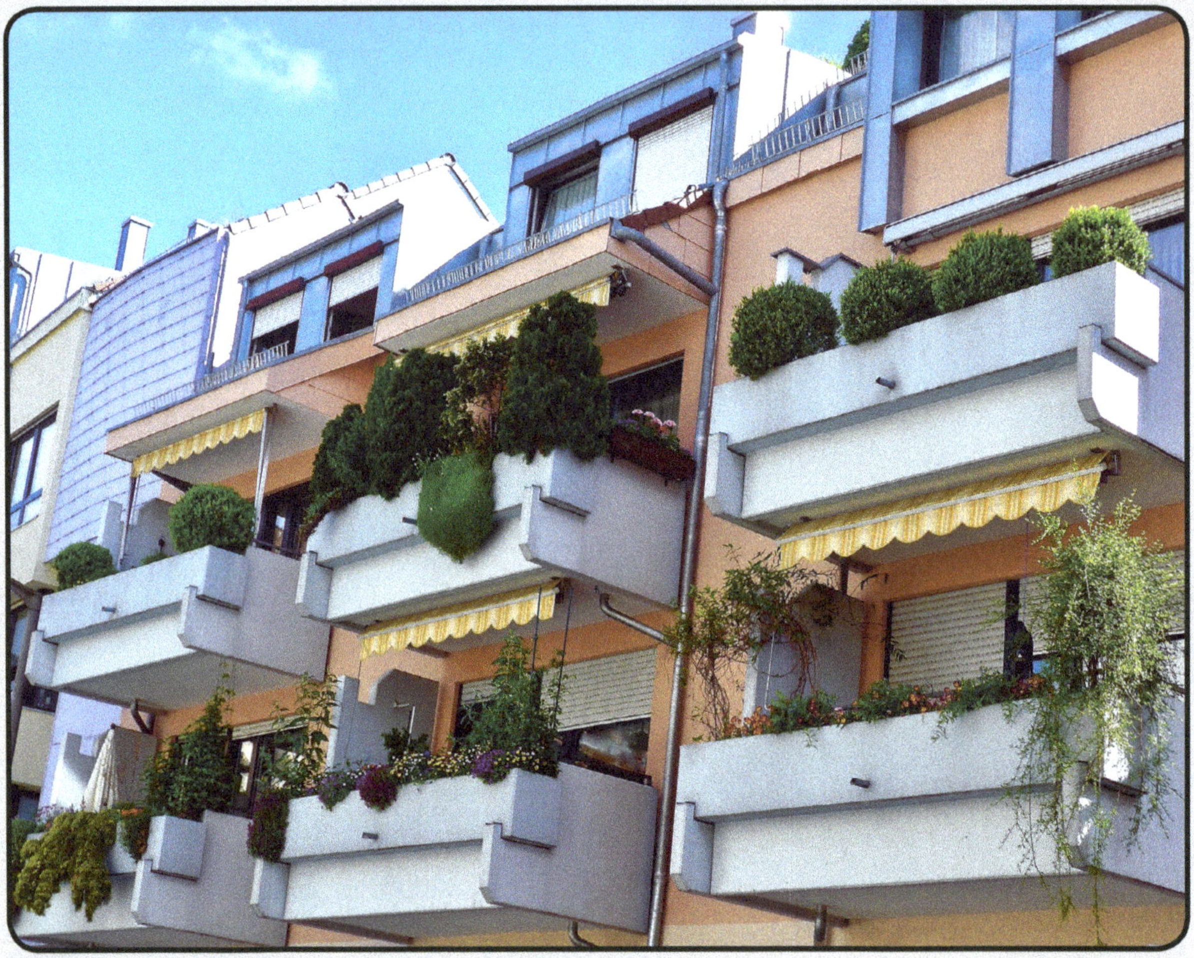

Bavarian balcony meadows.

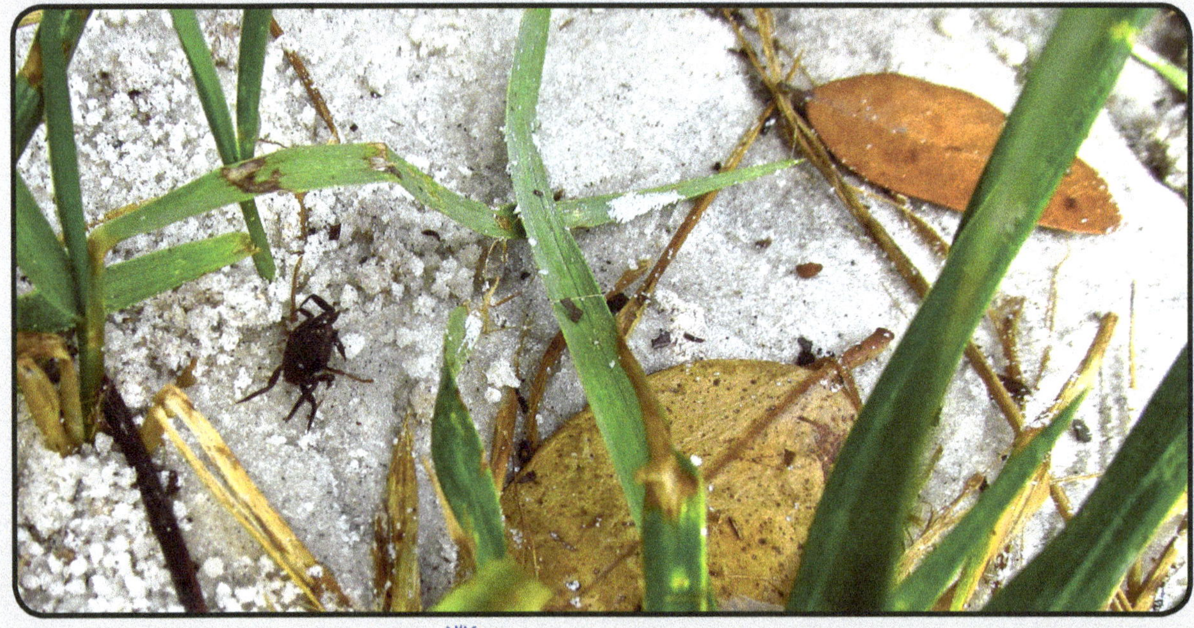

Doorstep crab in Florida.

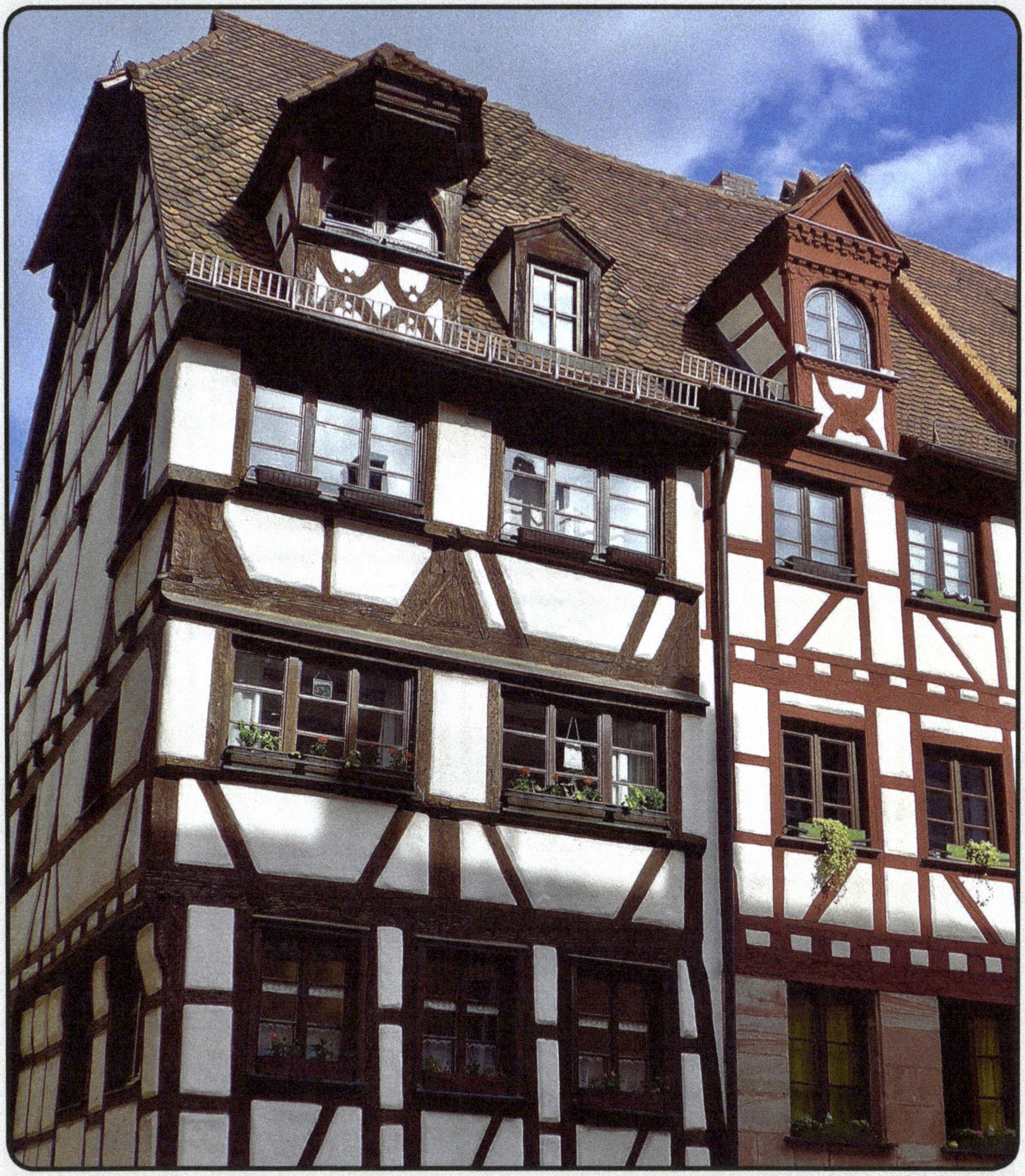

Gingerbread houses trimmed with pretty plants.

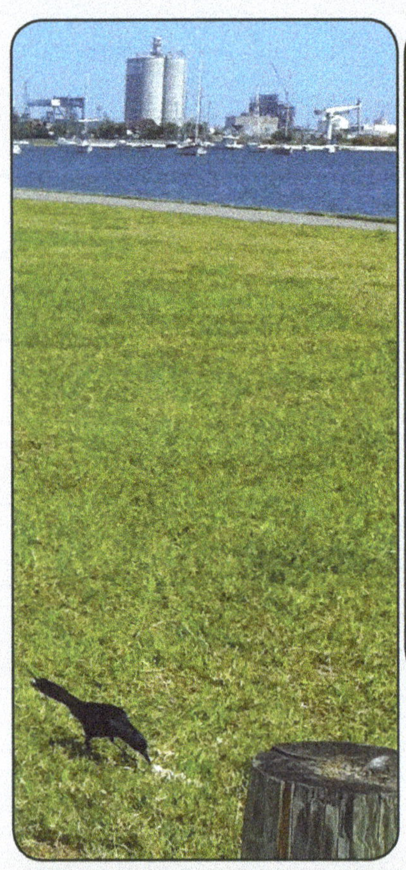

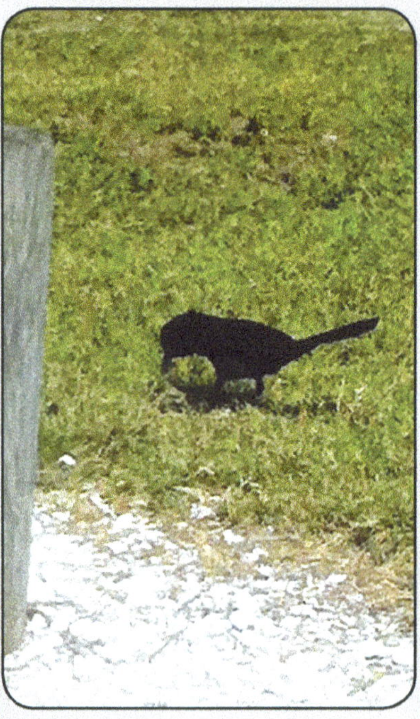

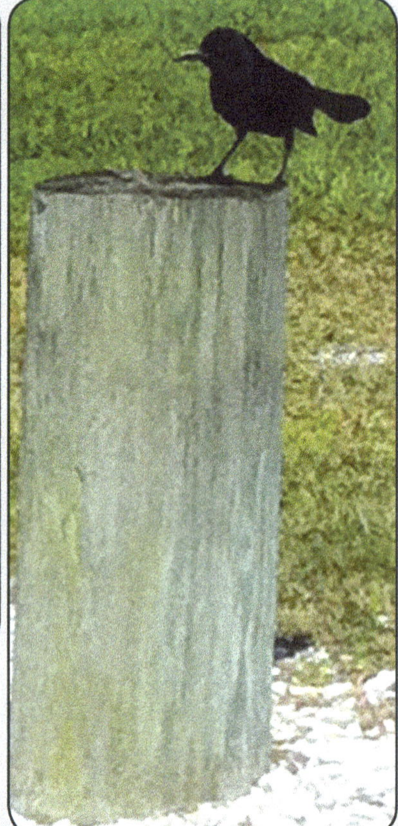

Cautious Florida island blackbird series.

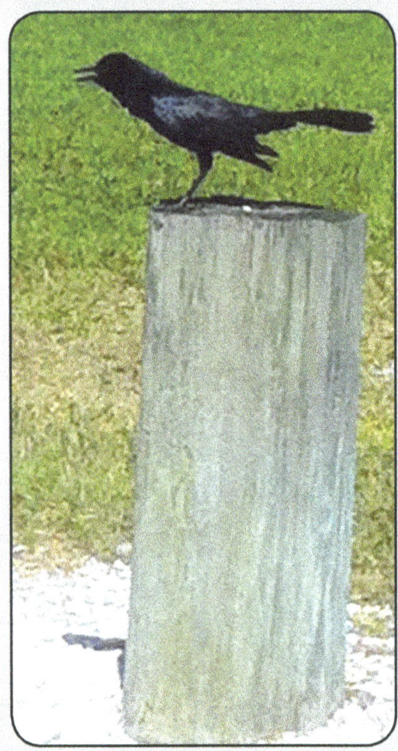

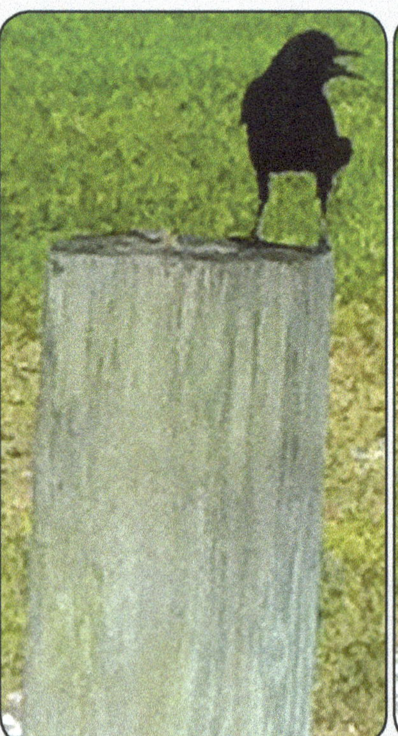

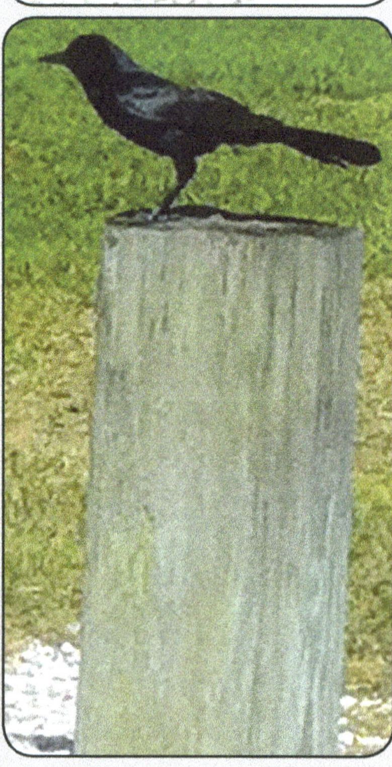

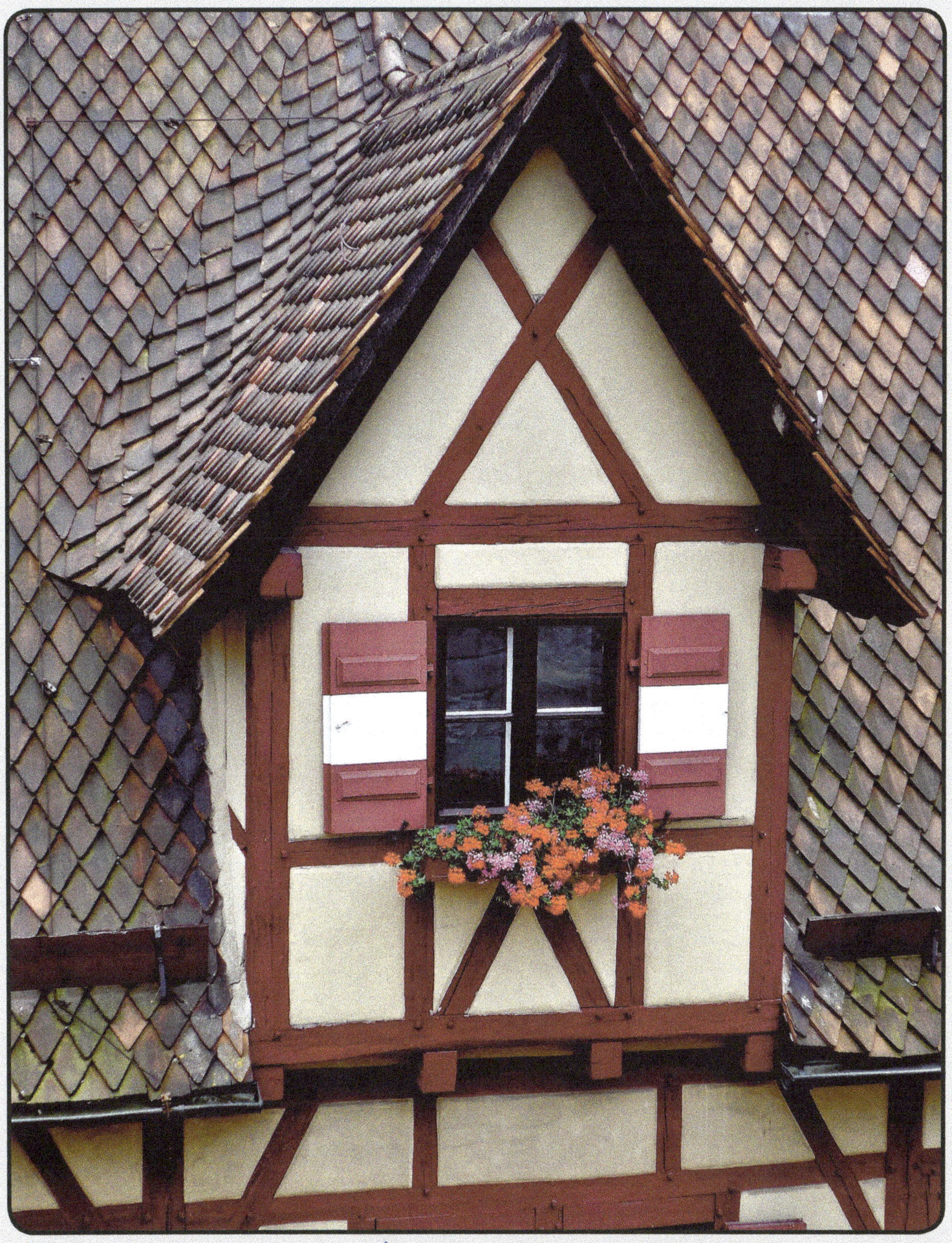

Window bouquet.

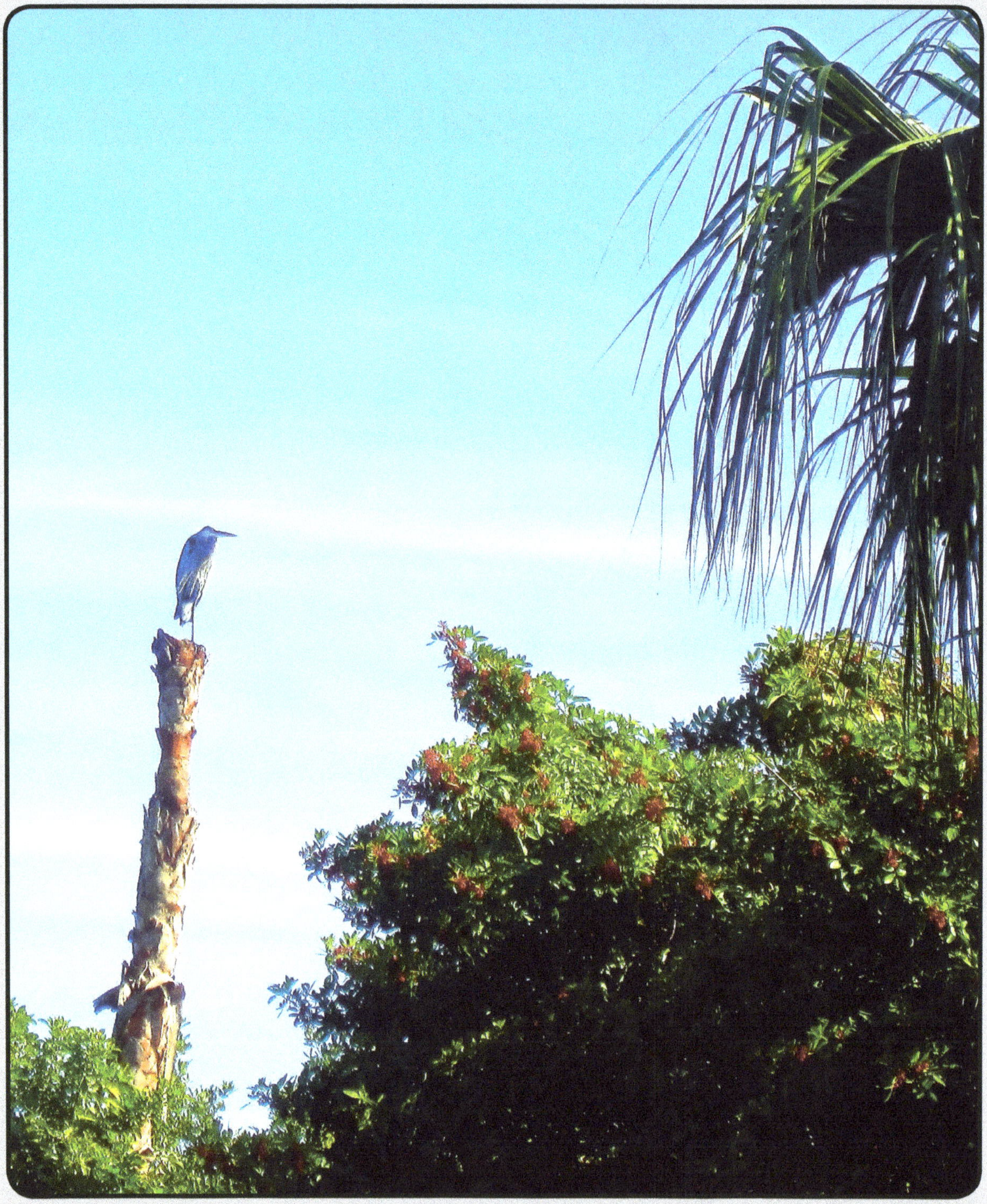

One-legged palm tree pose.

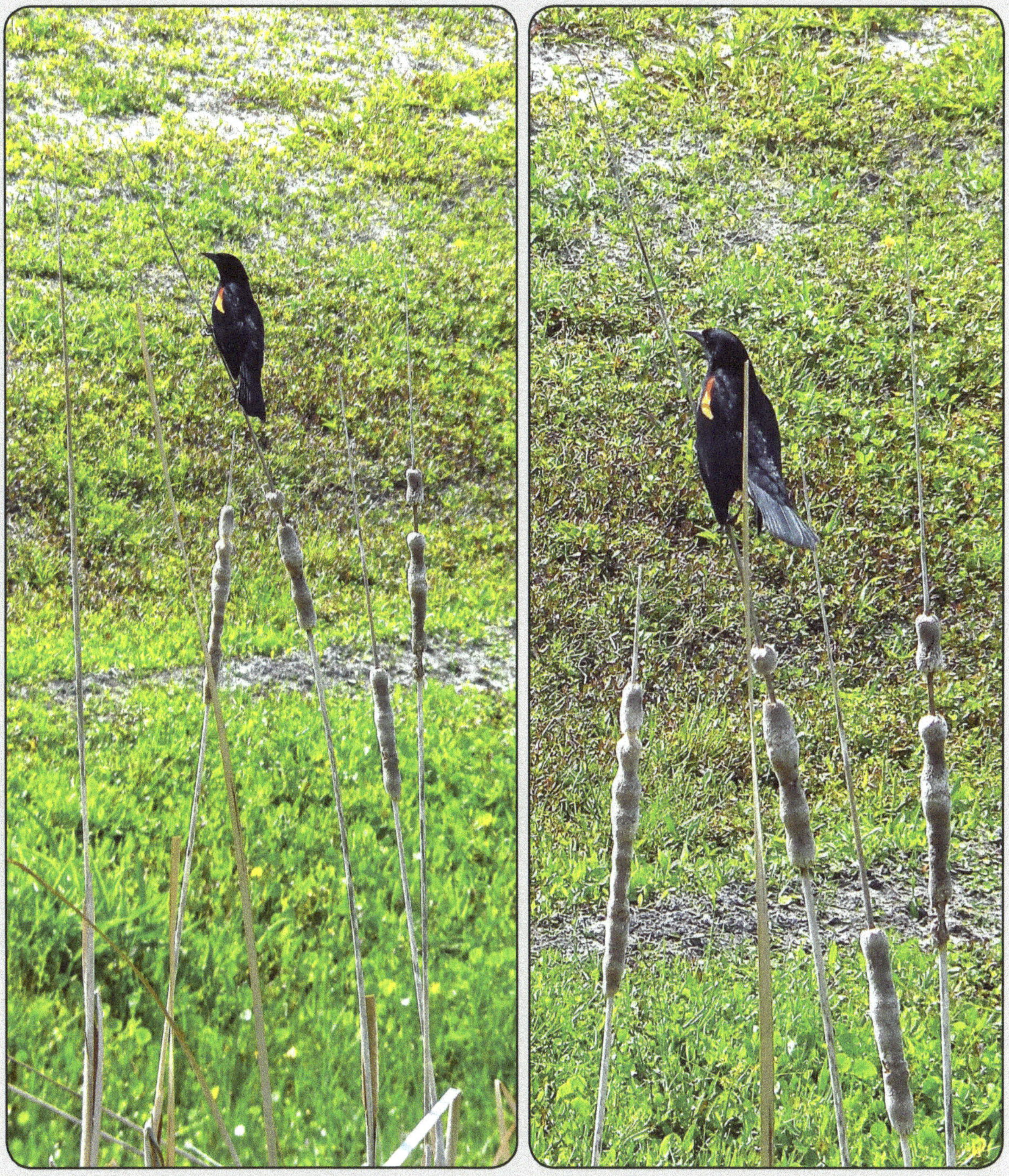

Cattail balancing series.

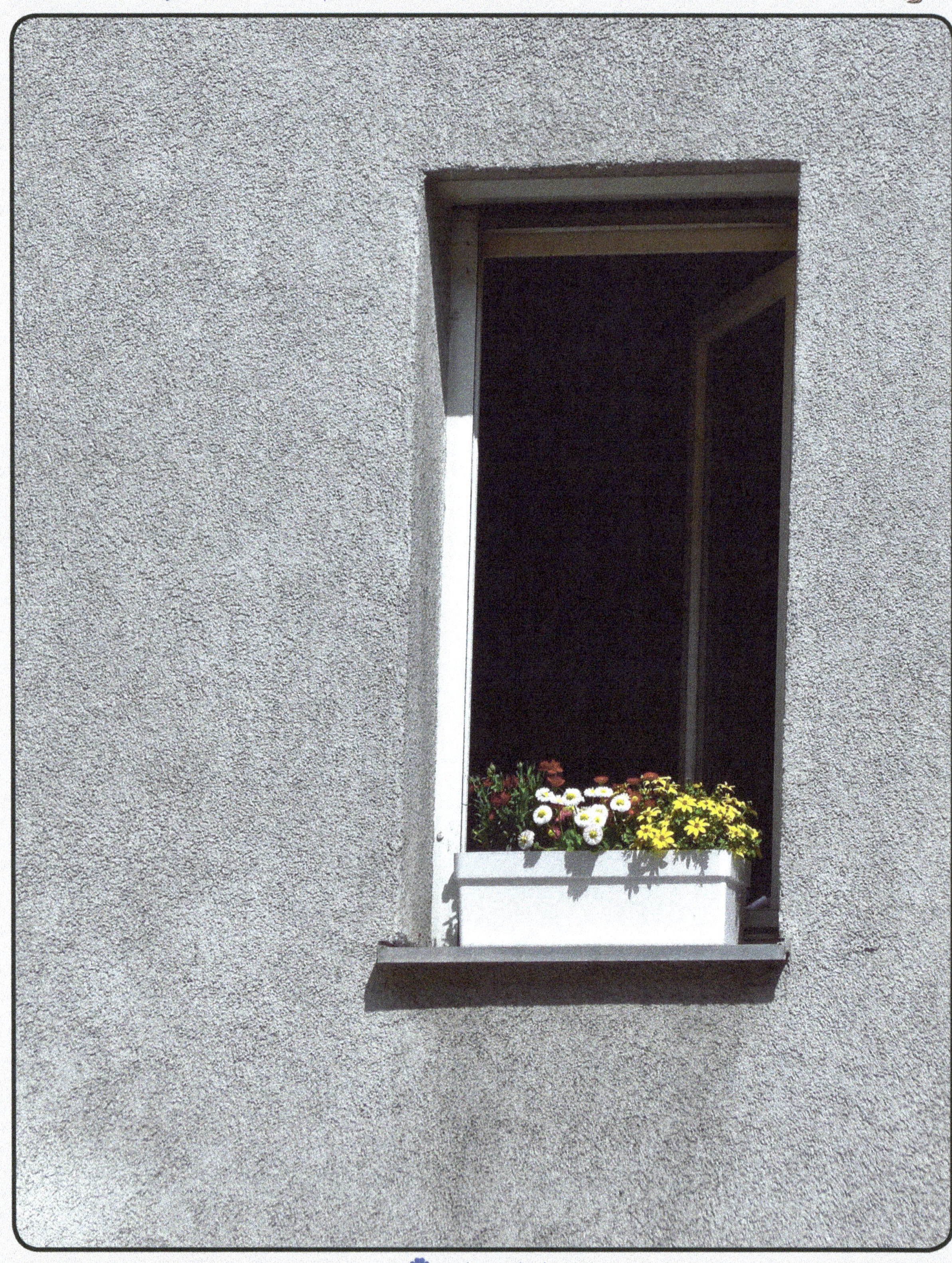

Color splash.

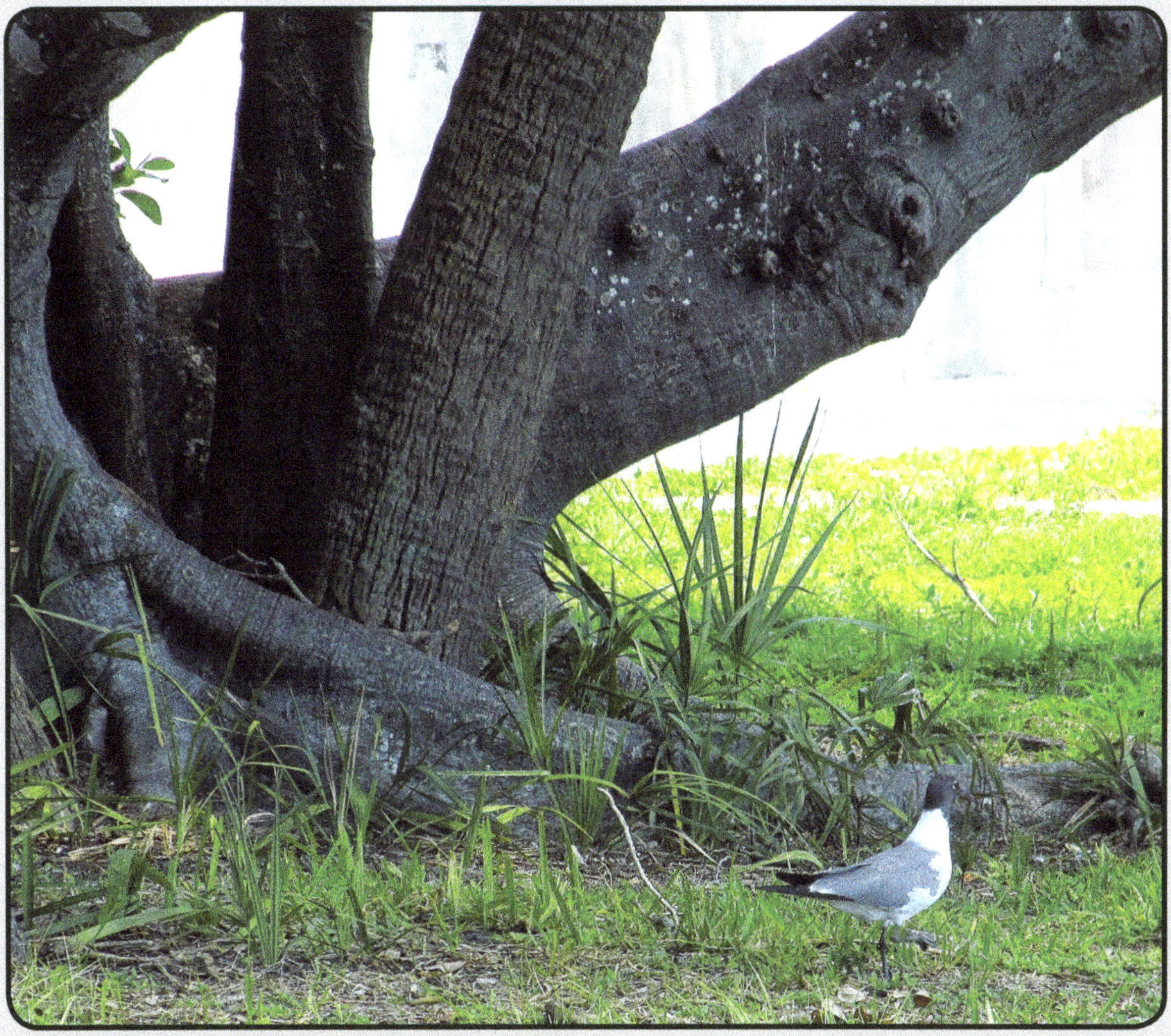

Franklin's gull on a stroll while wintering in Florida.

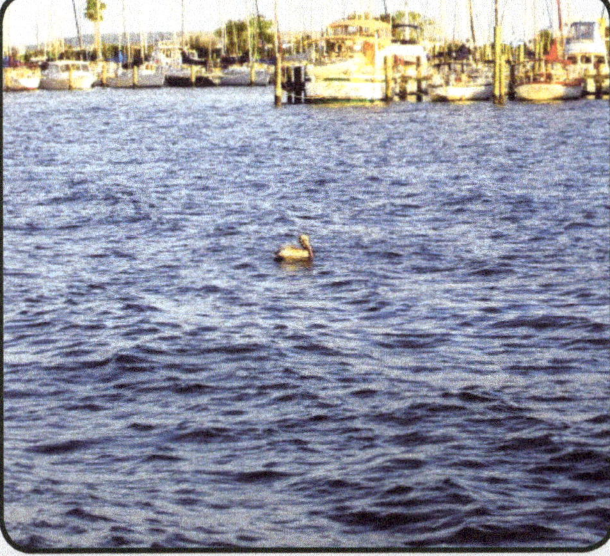

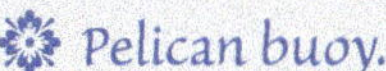

Pelican buoy.

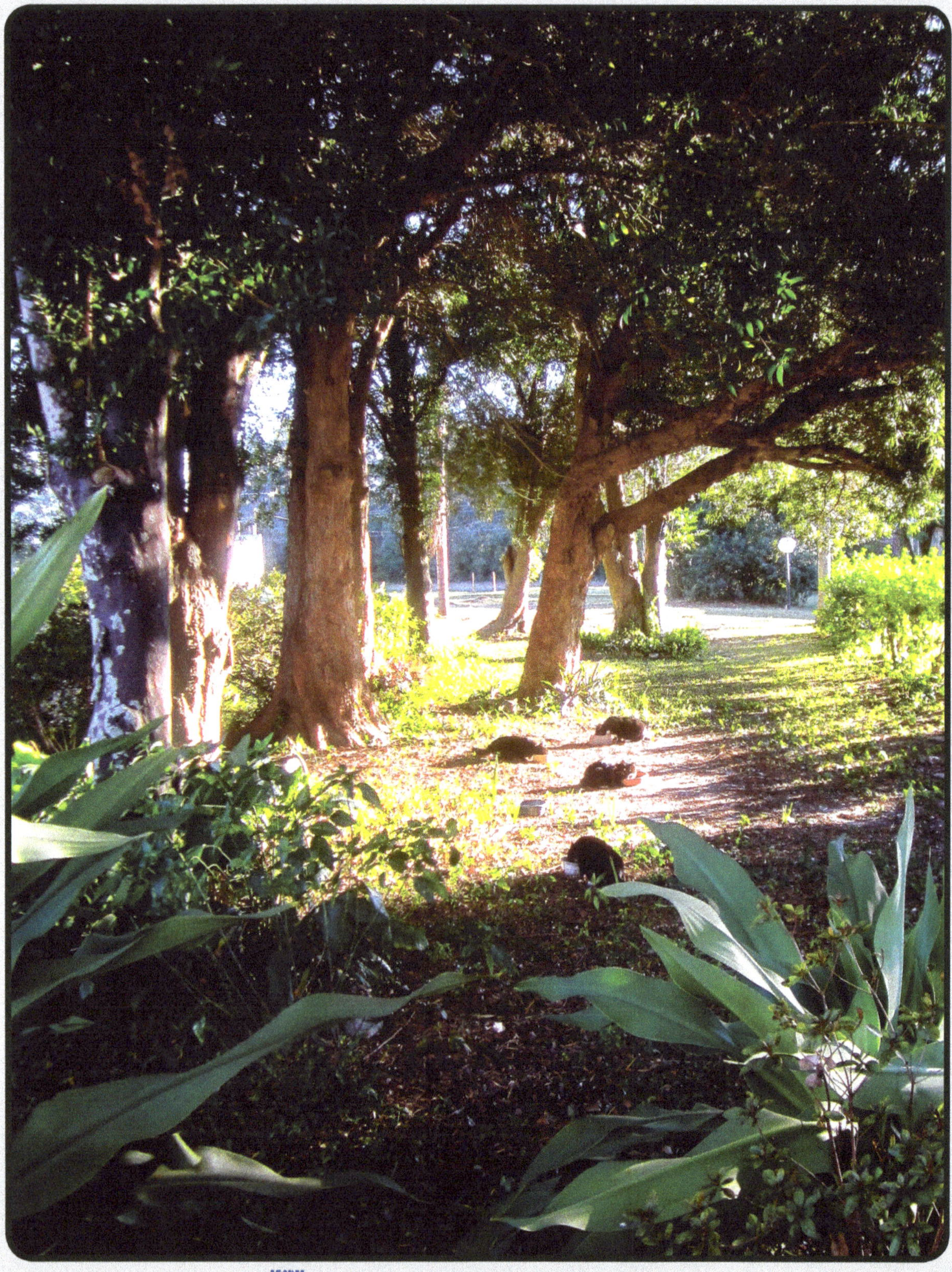

Christmas Eve supper for monastery cats.

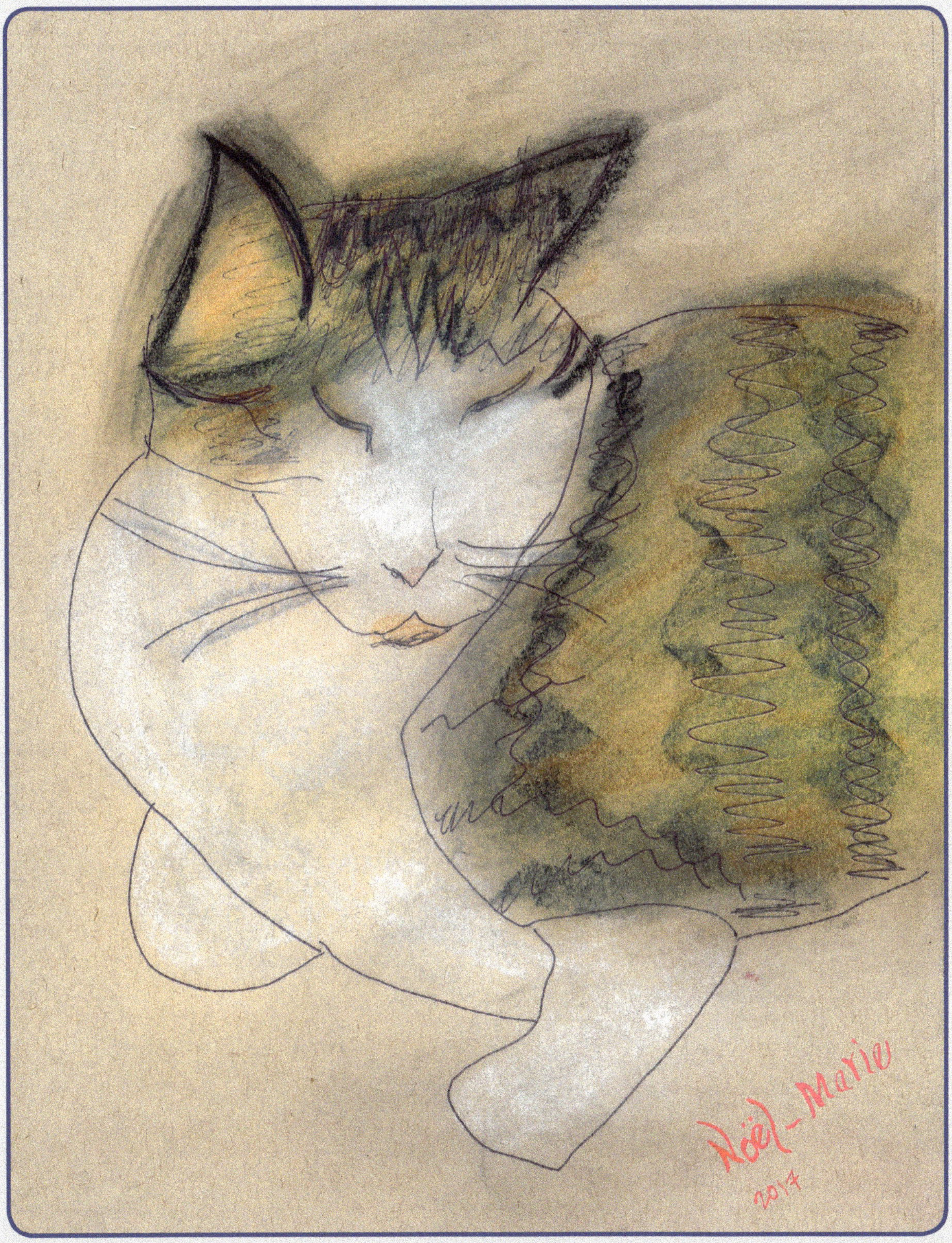

Snoozing.

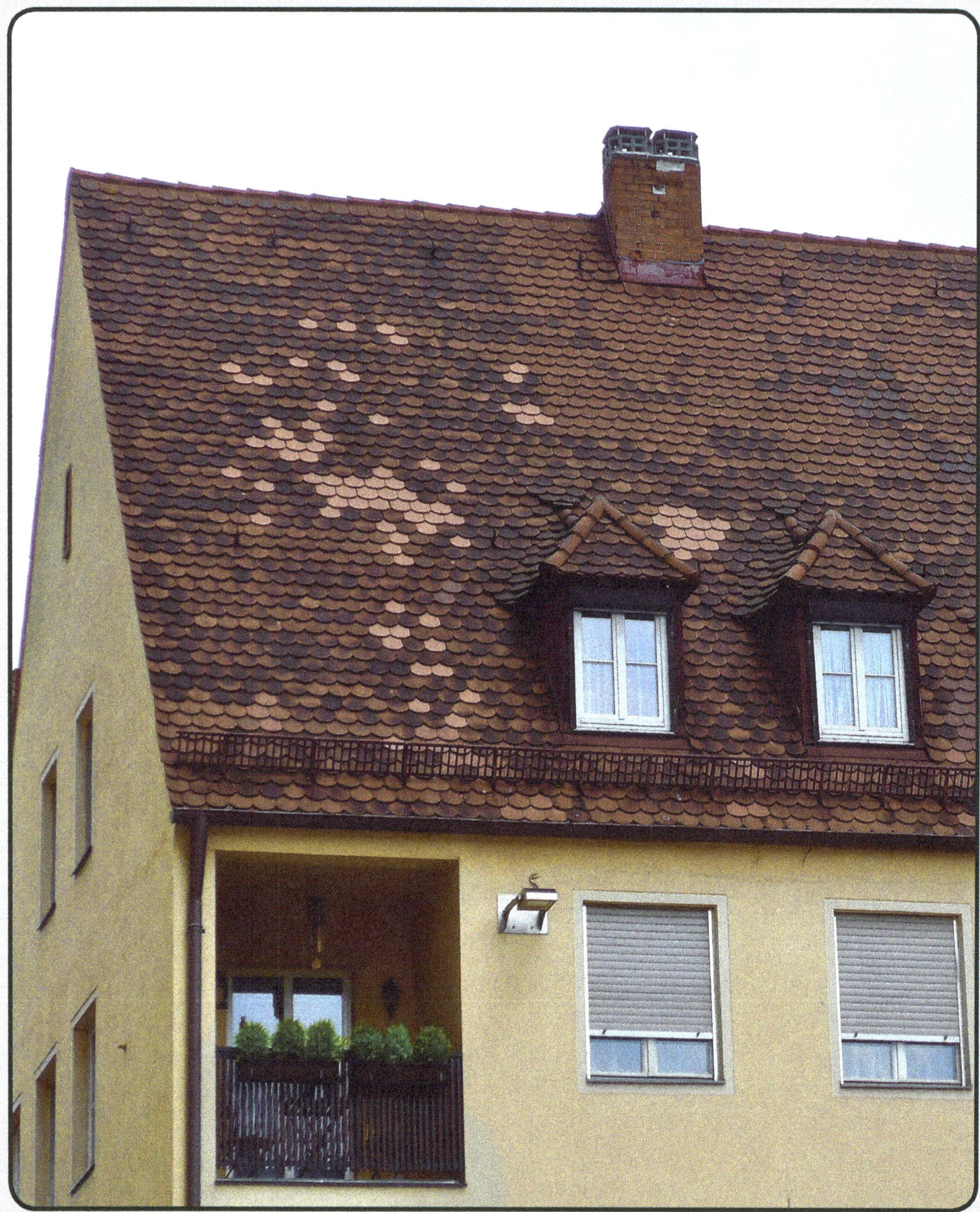

Shrub siblings.

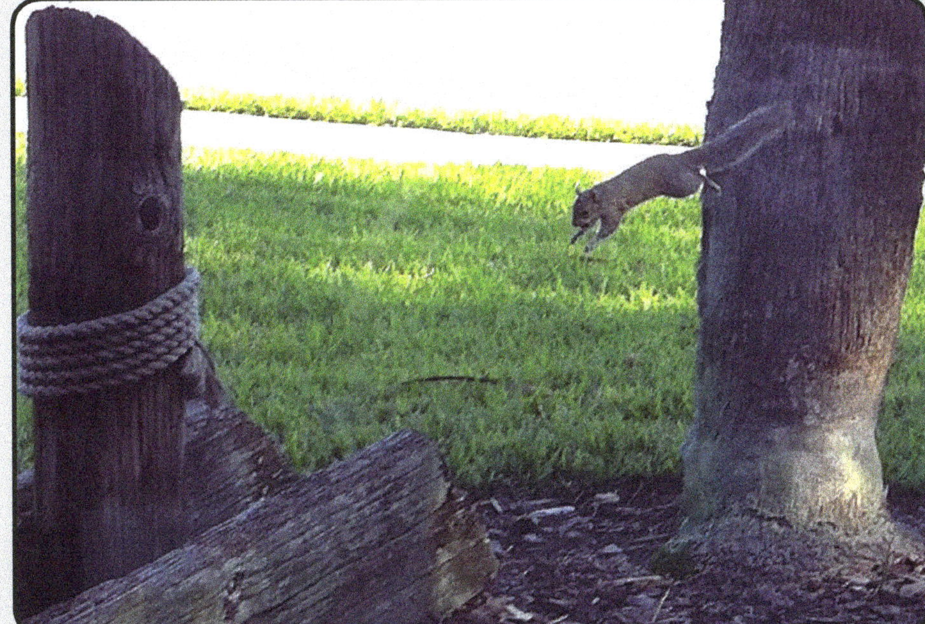

Squirrel flight.

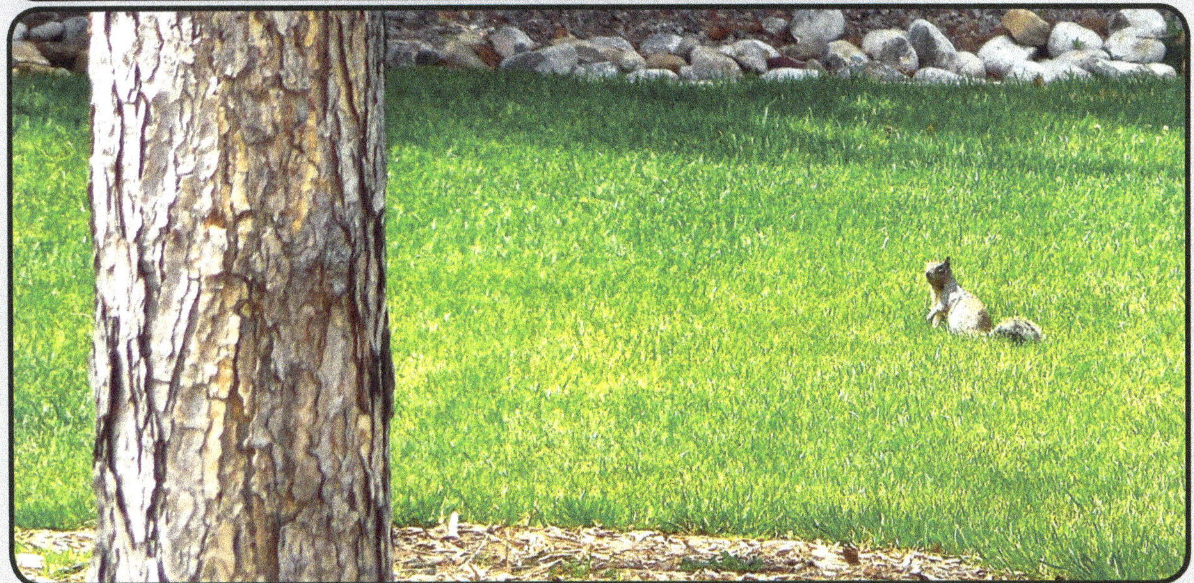

Not alone.

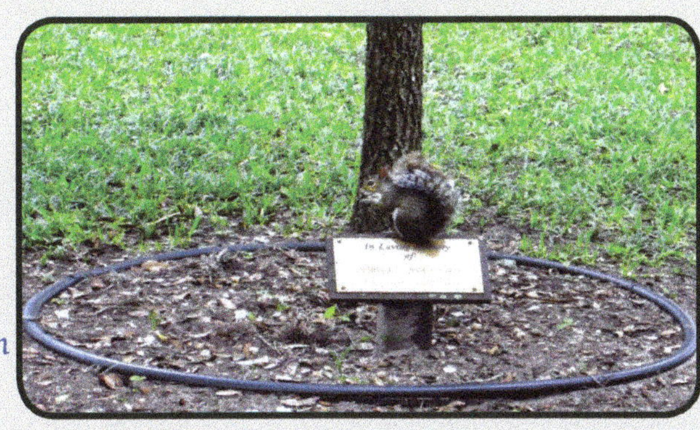

Reflections on memorial site.

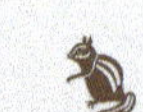

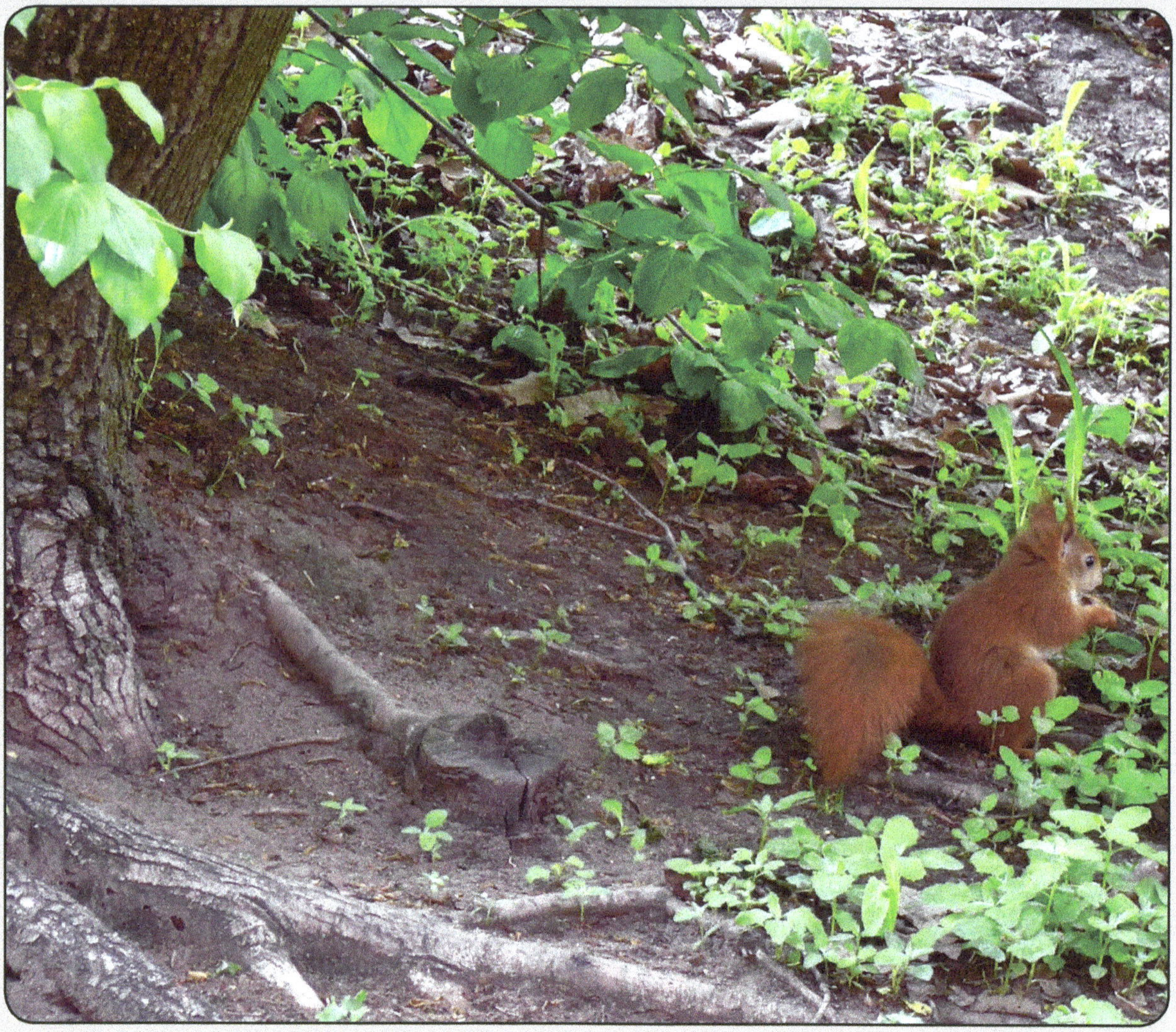

Search for buried treasure series.

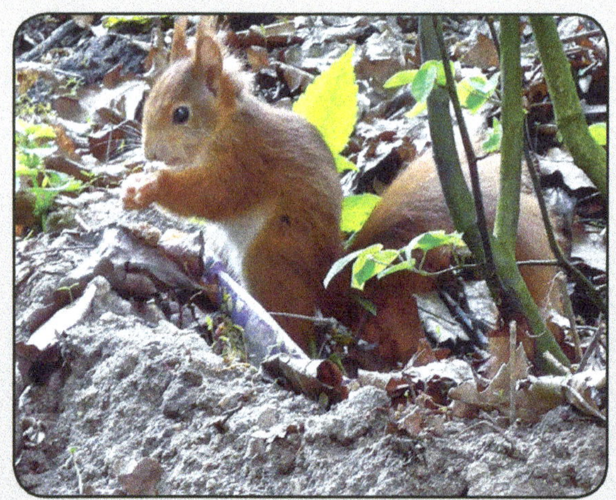

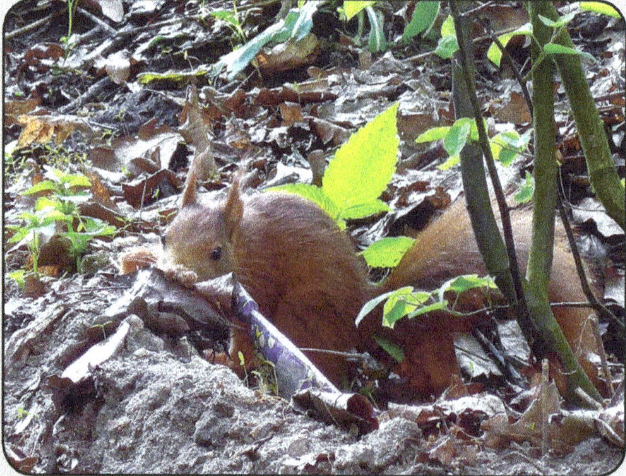

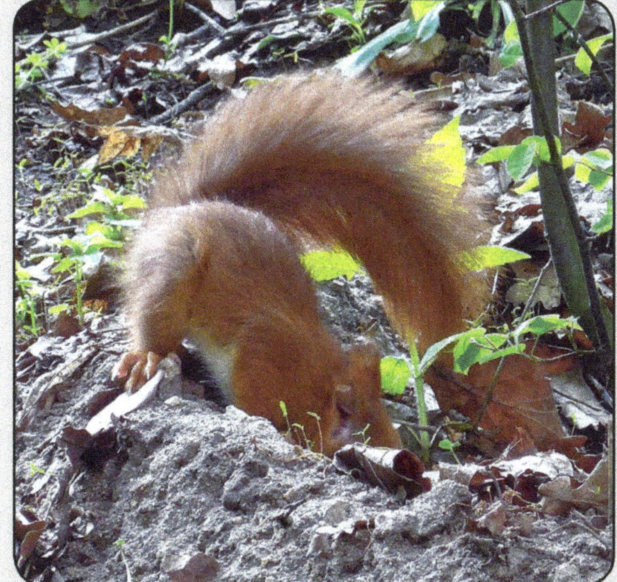

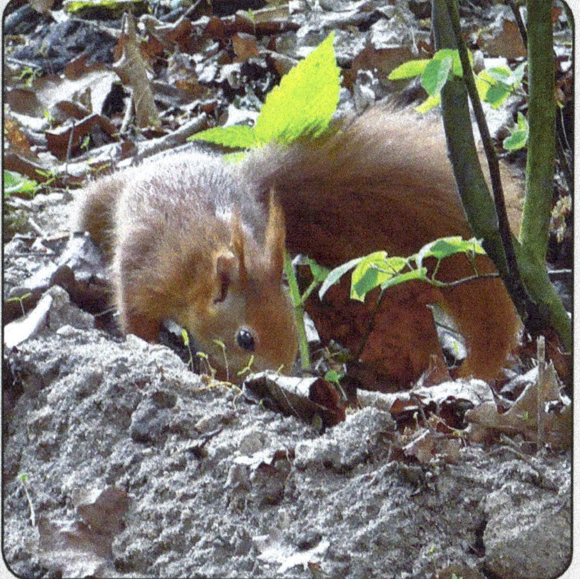

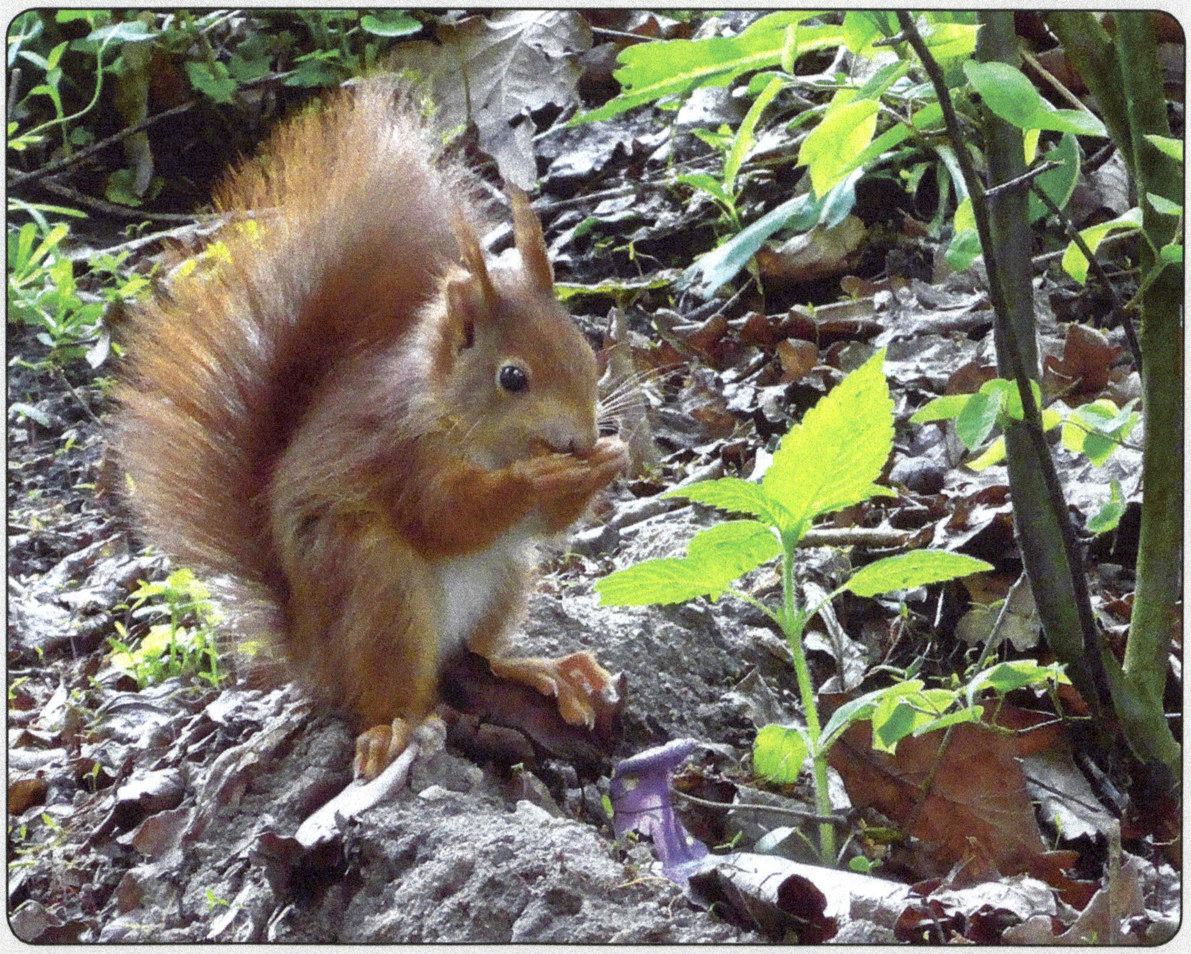

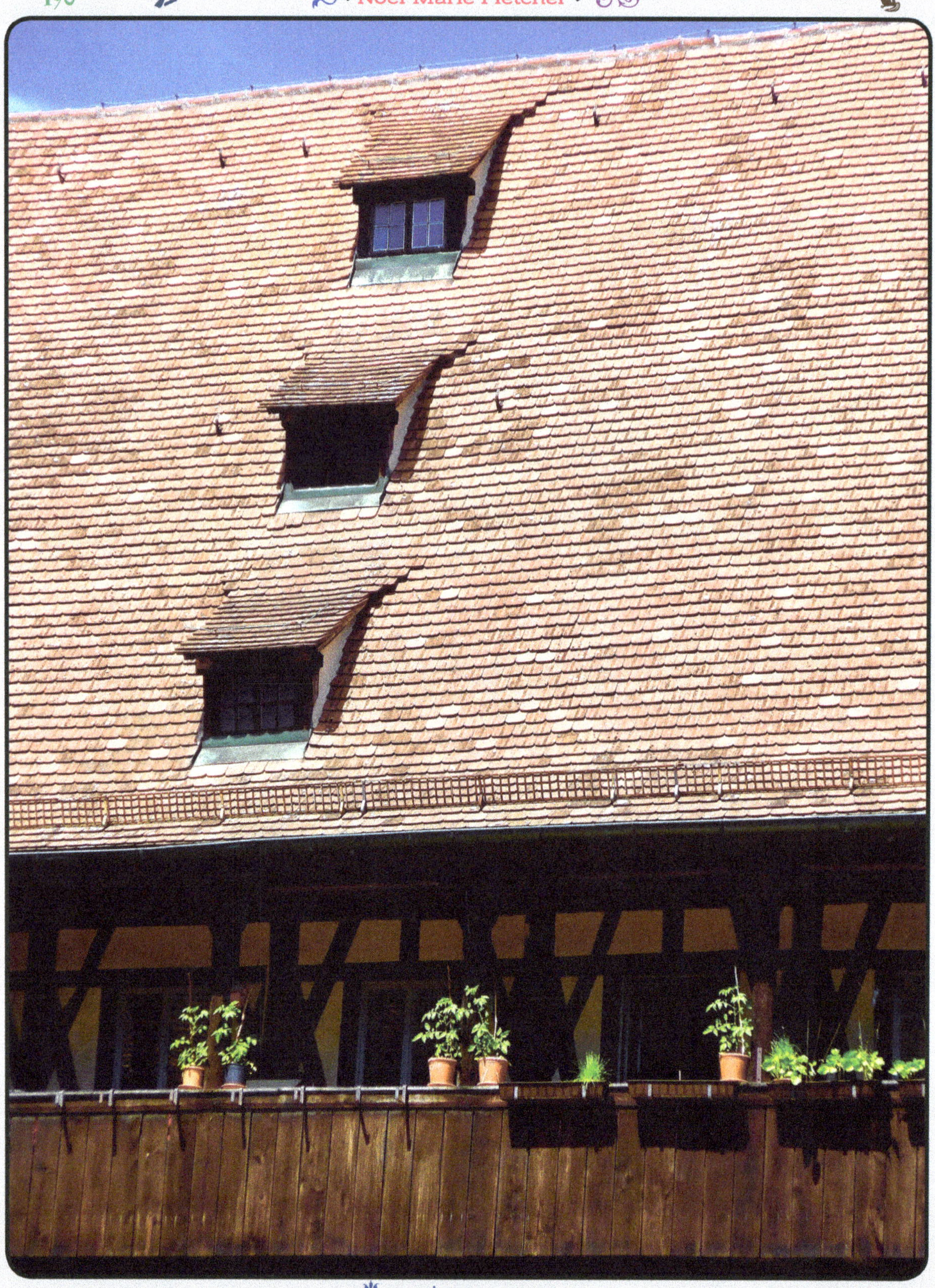

Catching some rays.

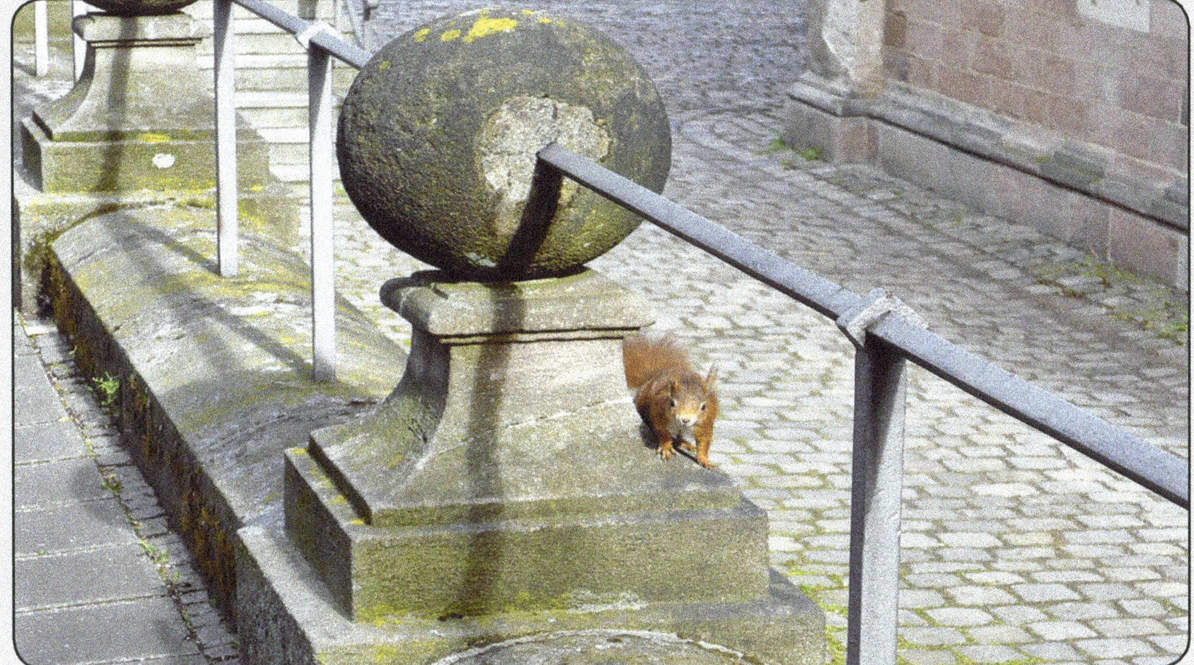

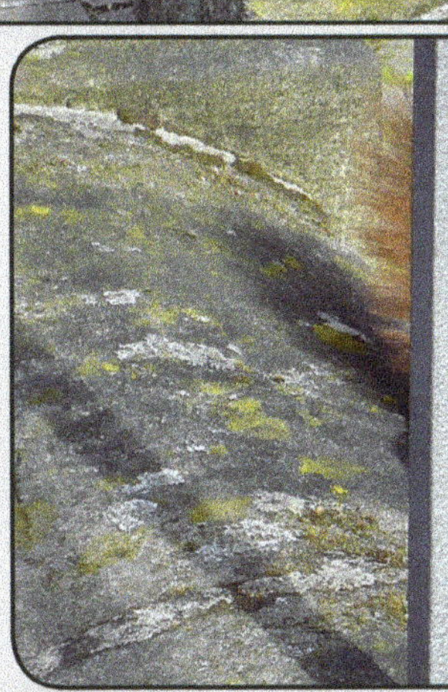

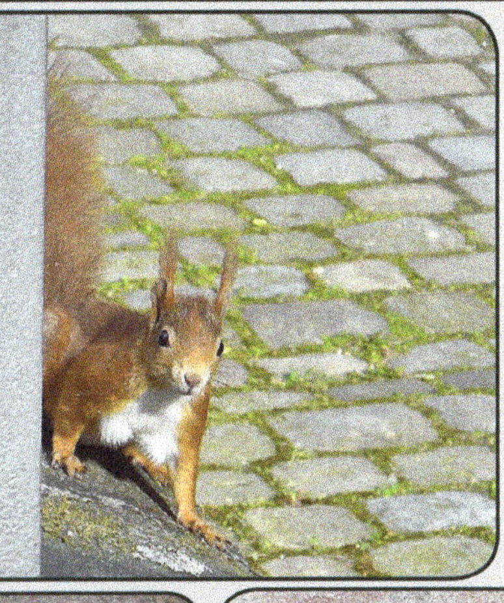

Adventures crossing the street series.

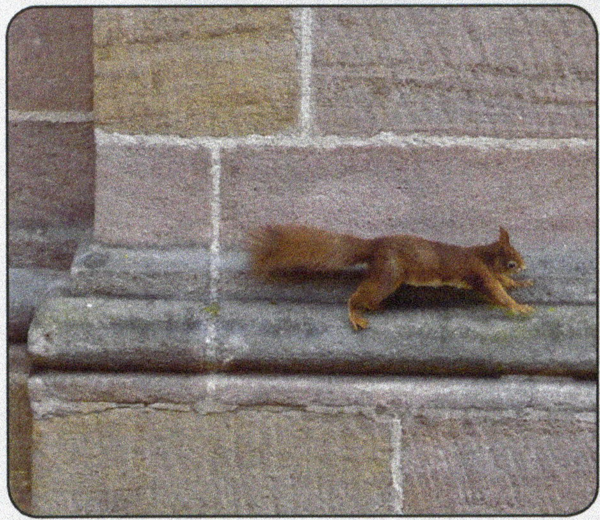

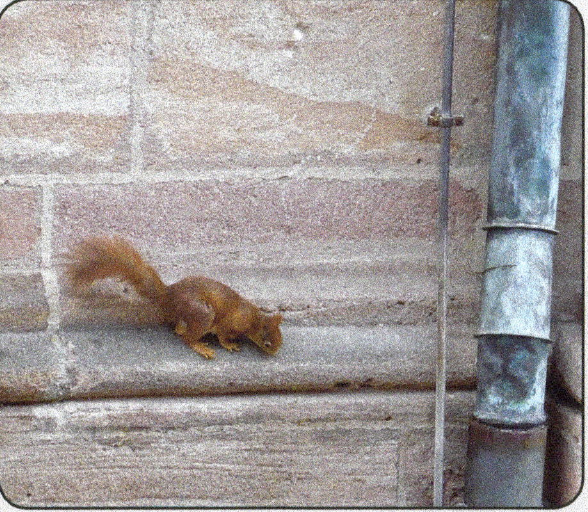

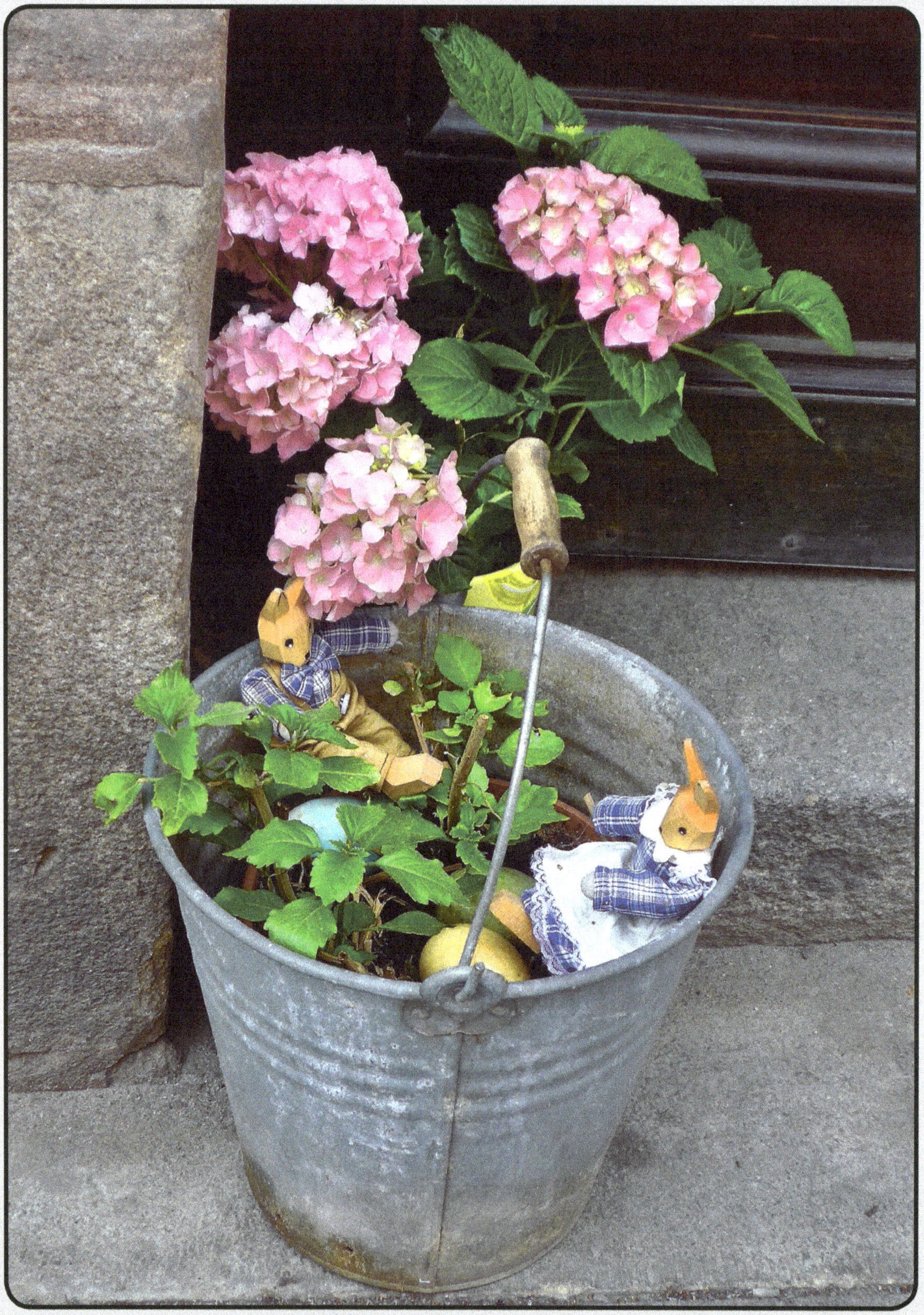

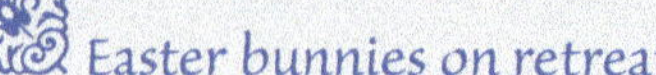

Easter bunnies on retreat.

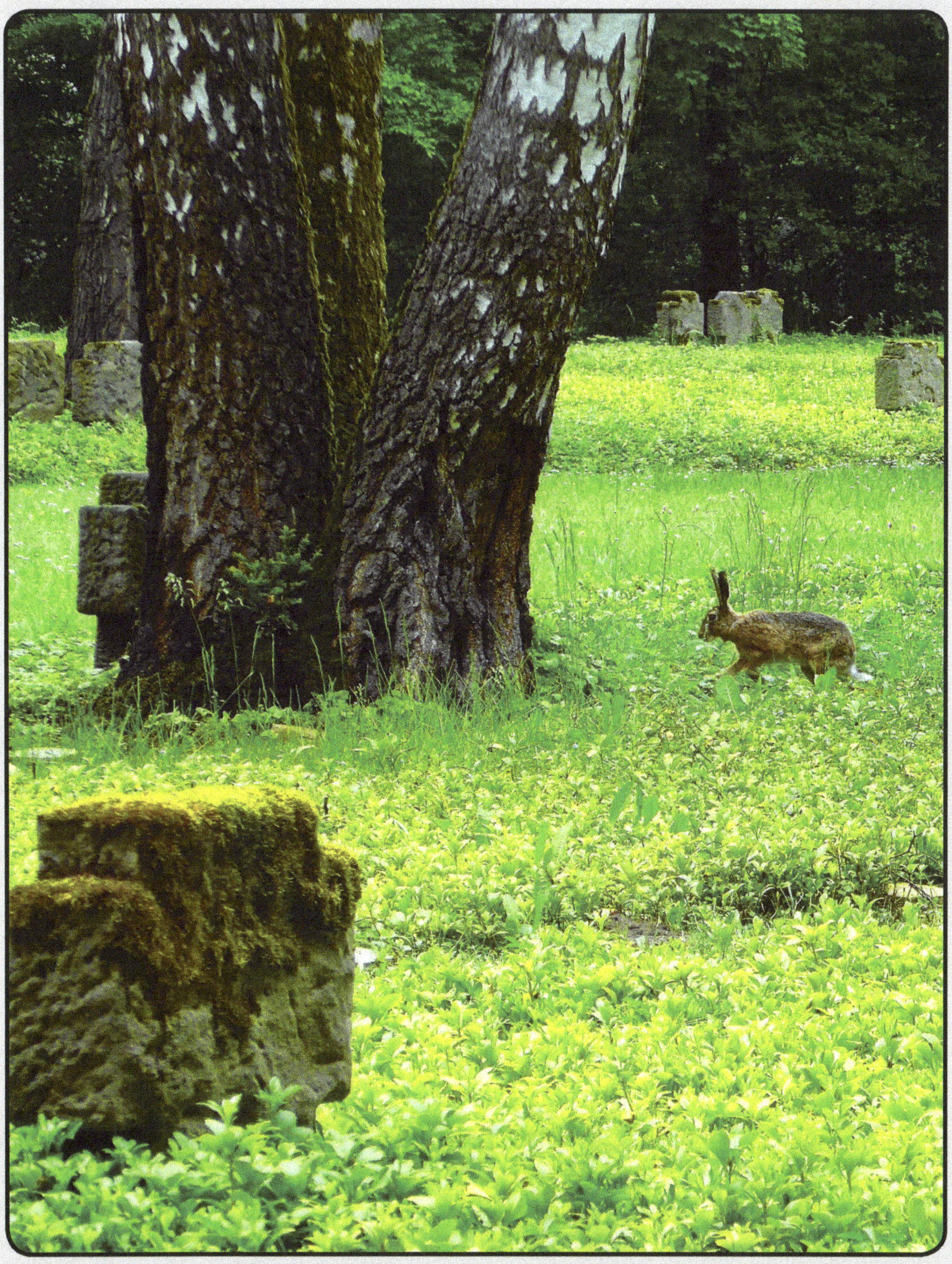

Cemetery hare tiptoes among World War I graves.

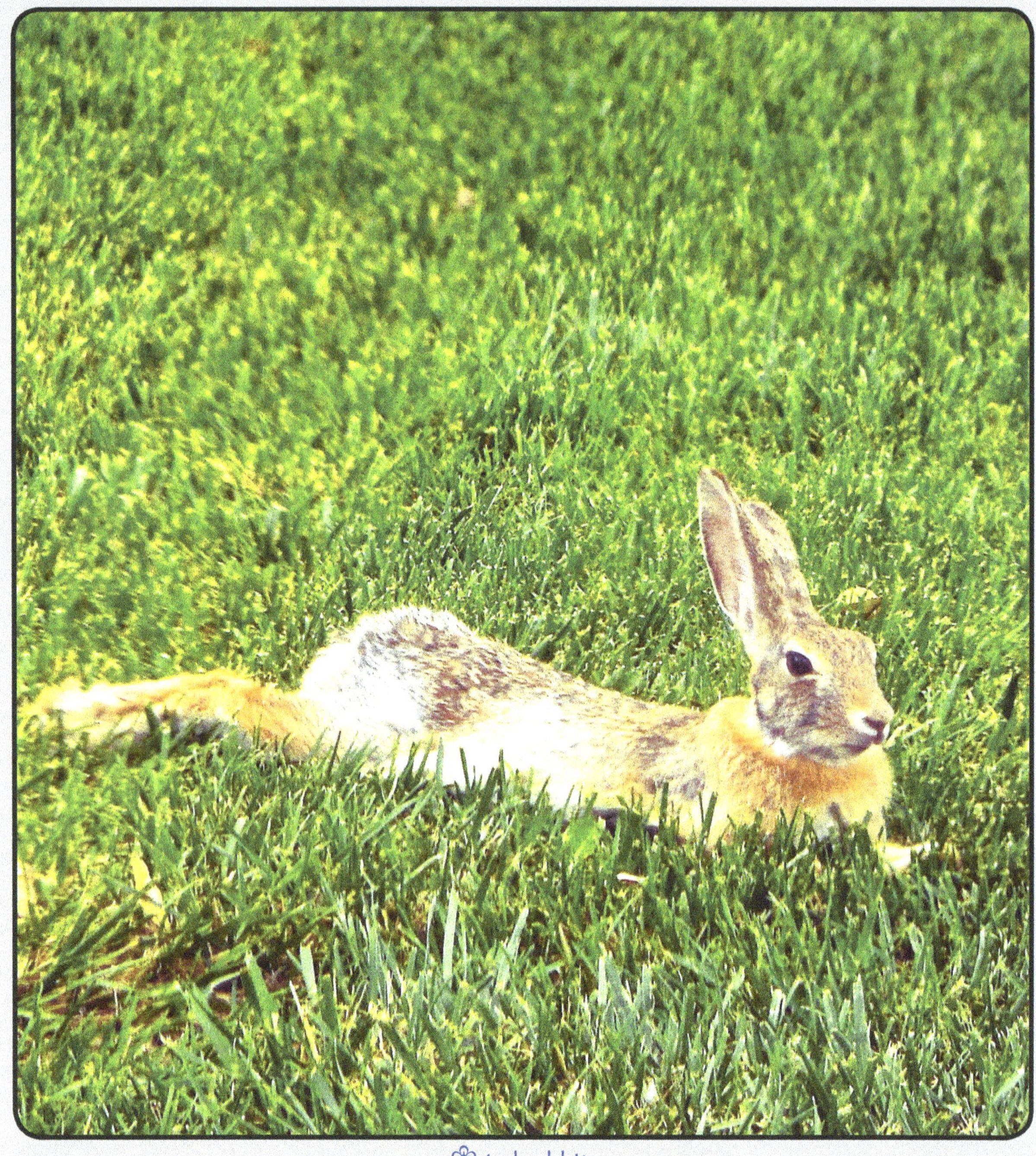

Jackrabbit.

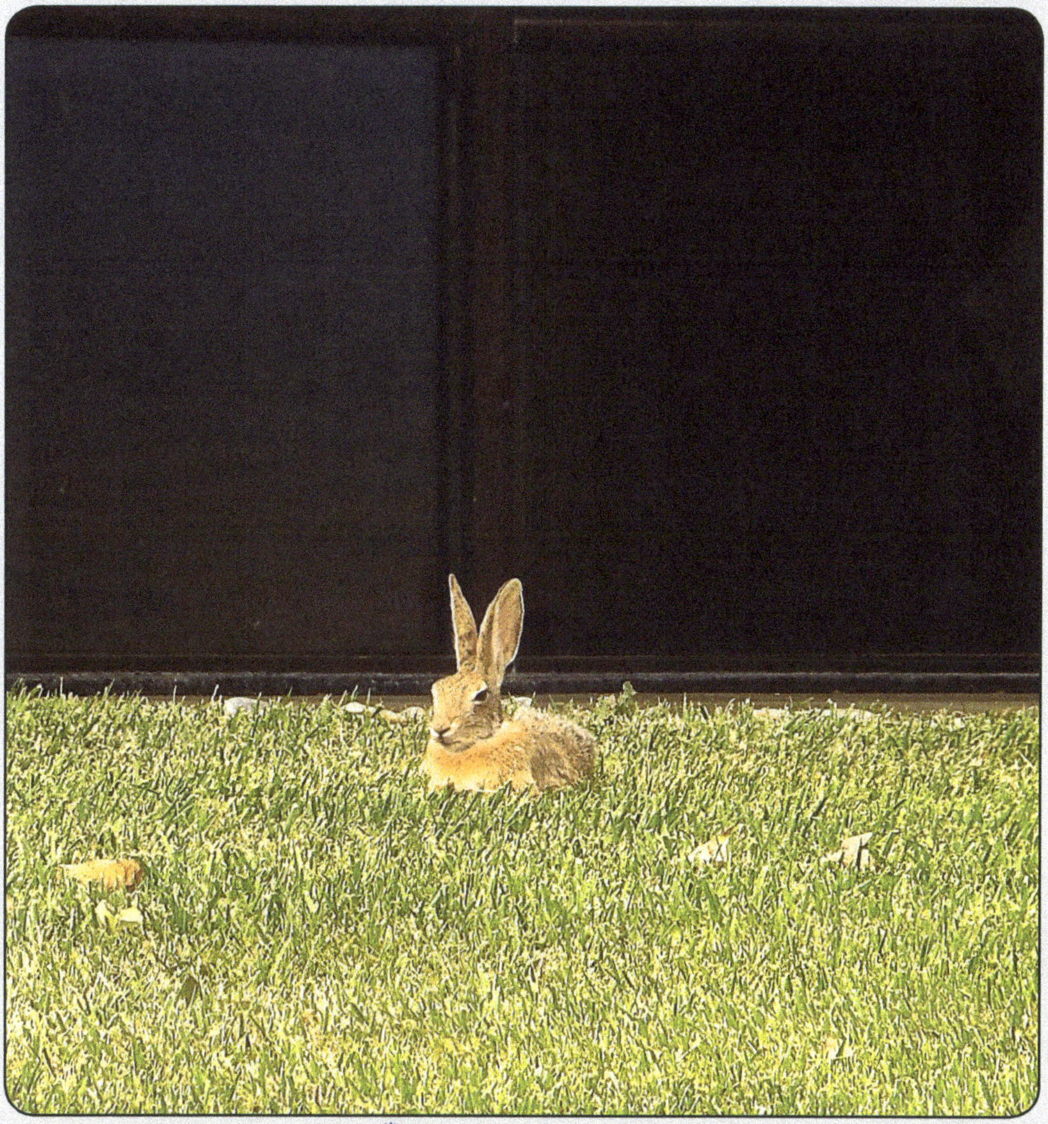

School bunnies series.

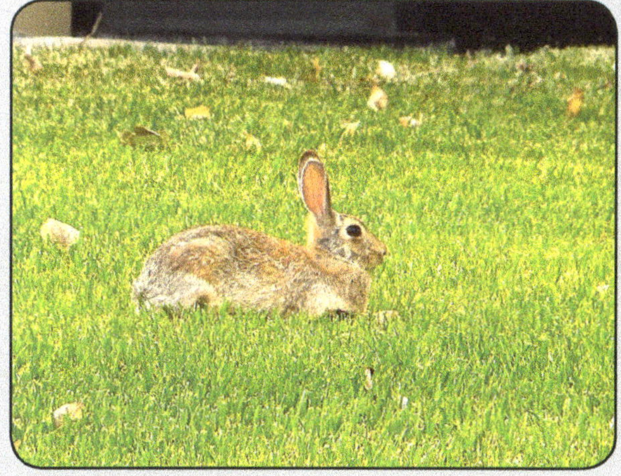

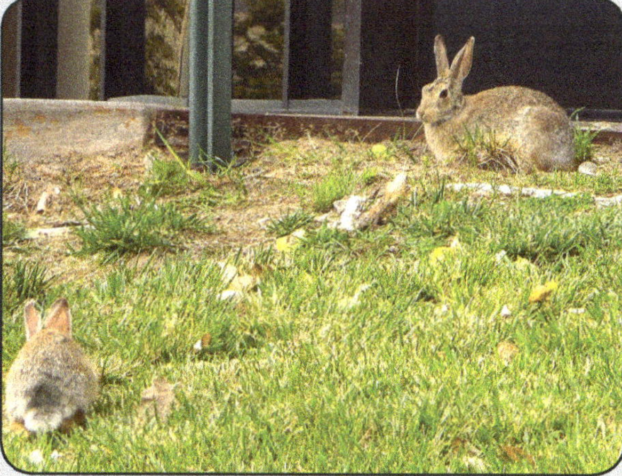

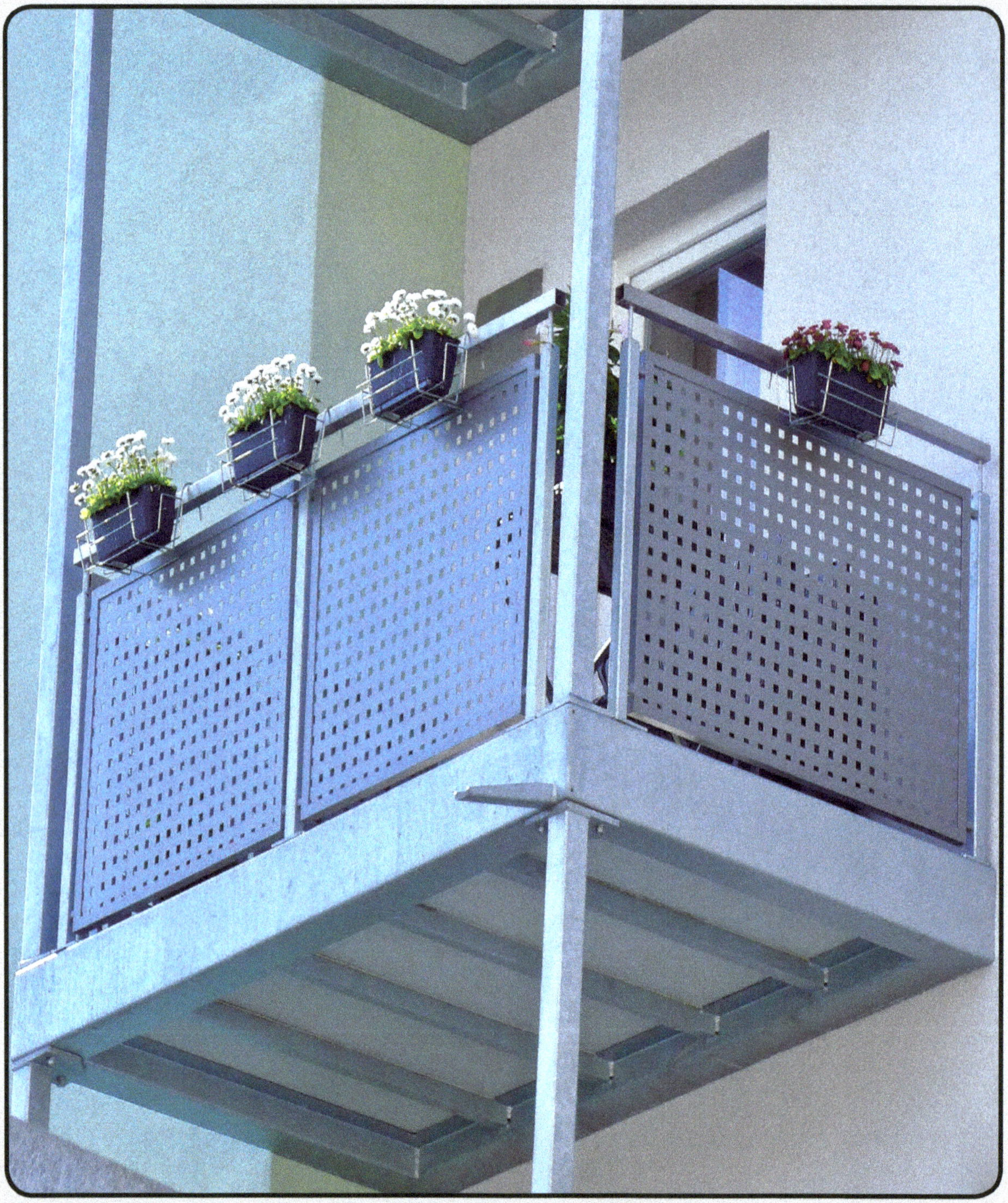

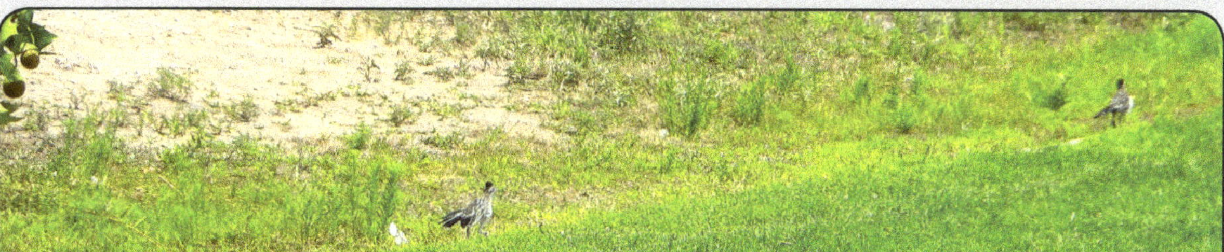

Roadrunner family stroll series.

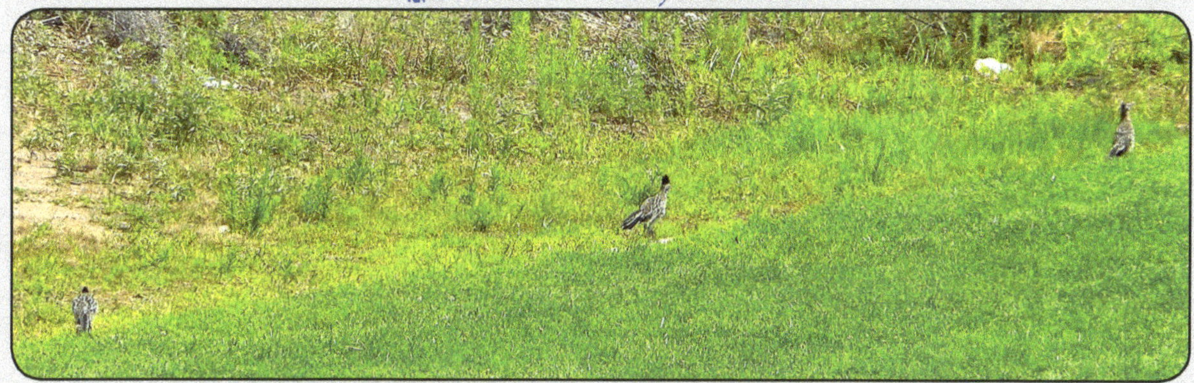

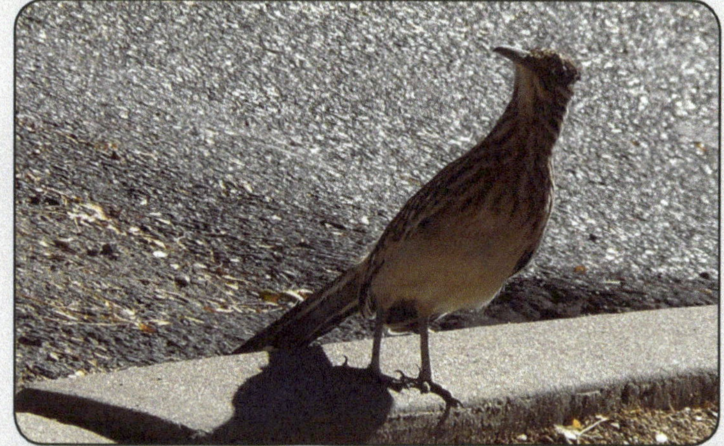

Parking lot roadrunner series.

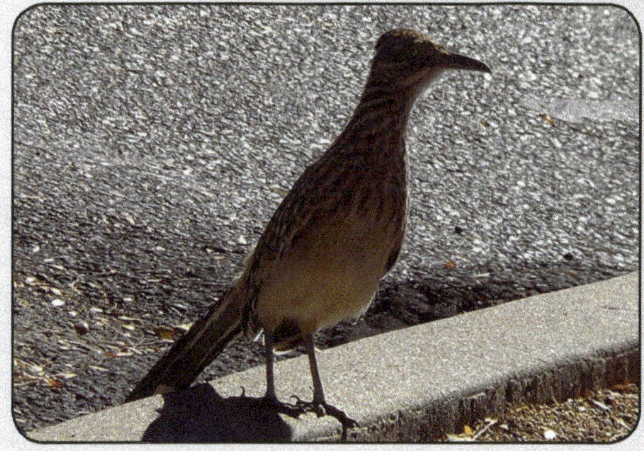

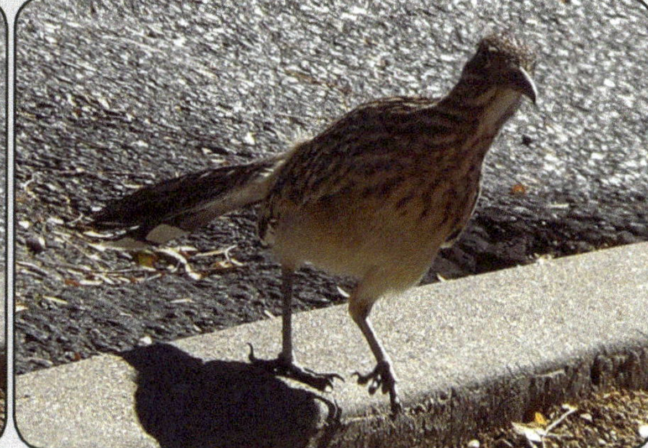

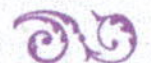

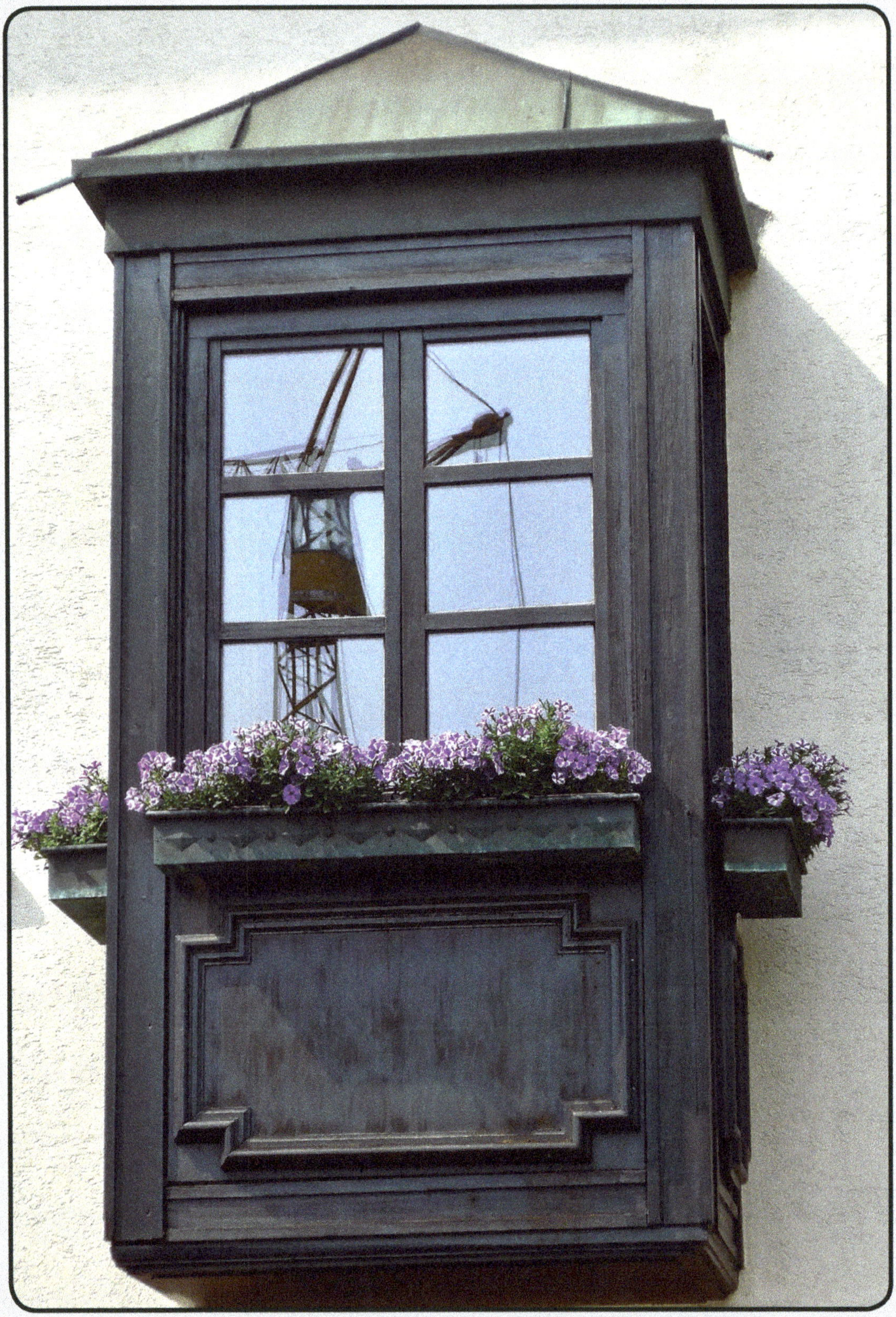

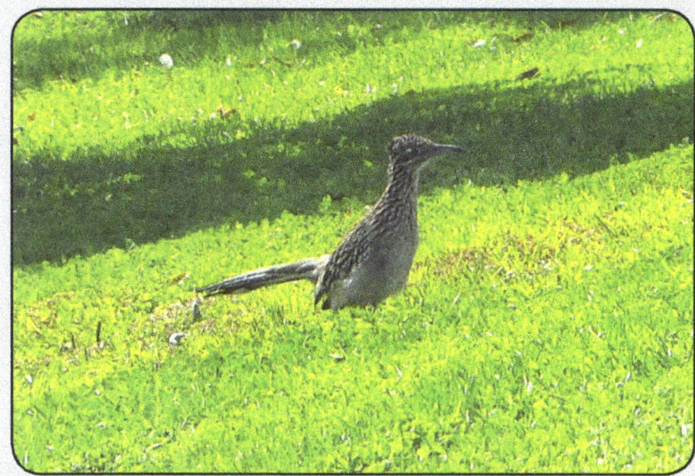

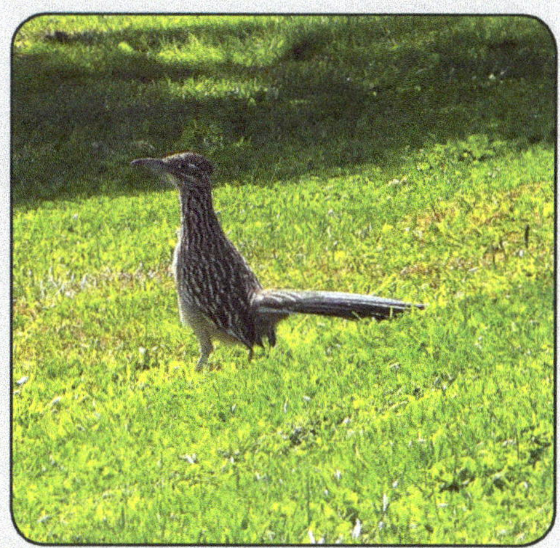

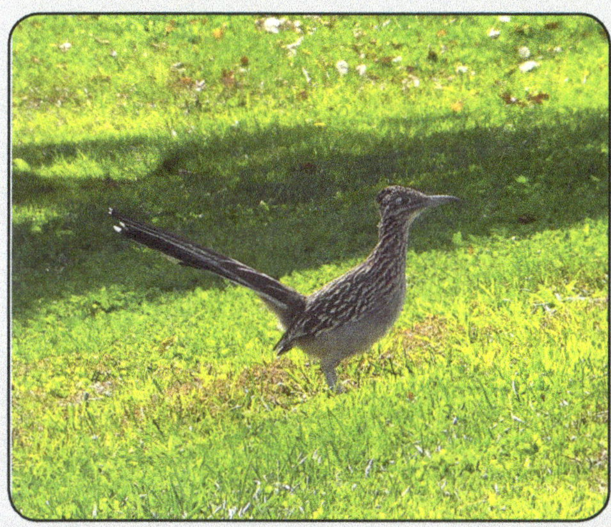

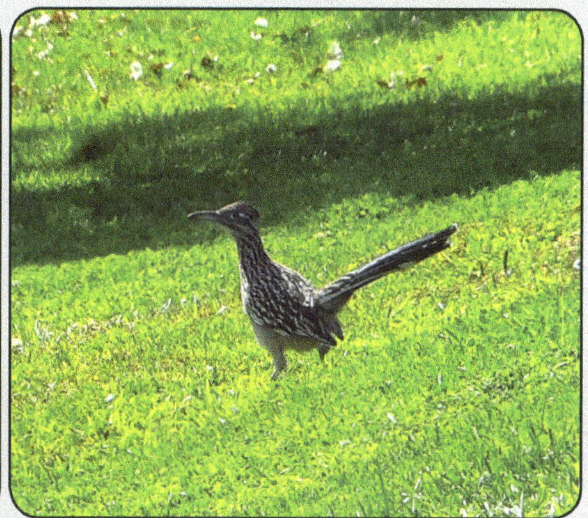

El chaparral series.

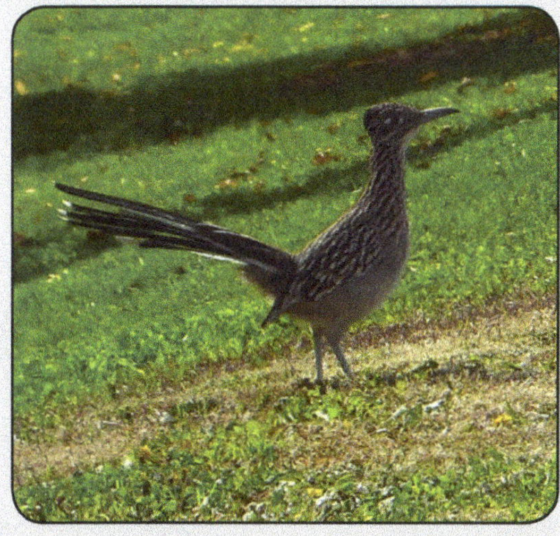

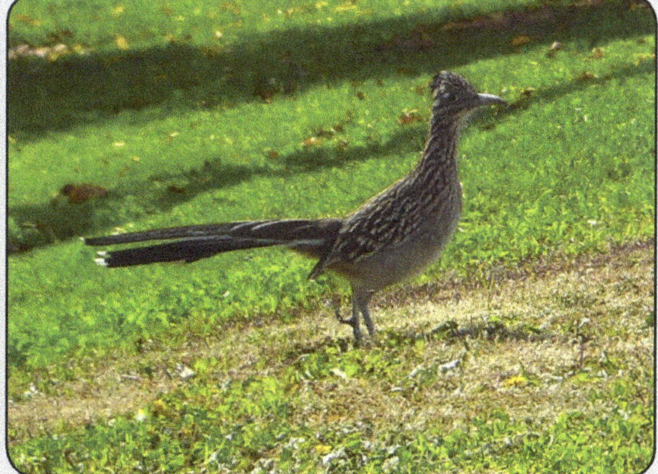

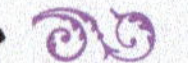

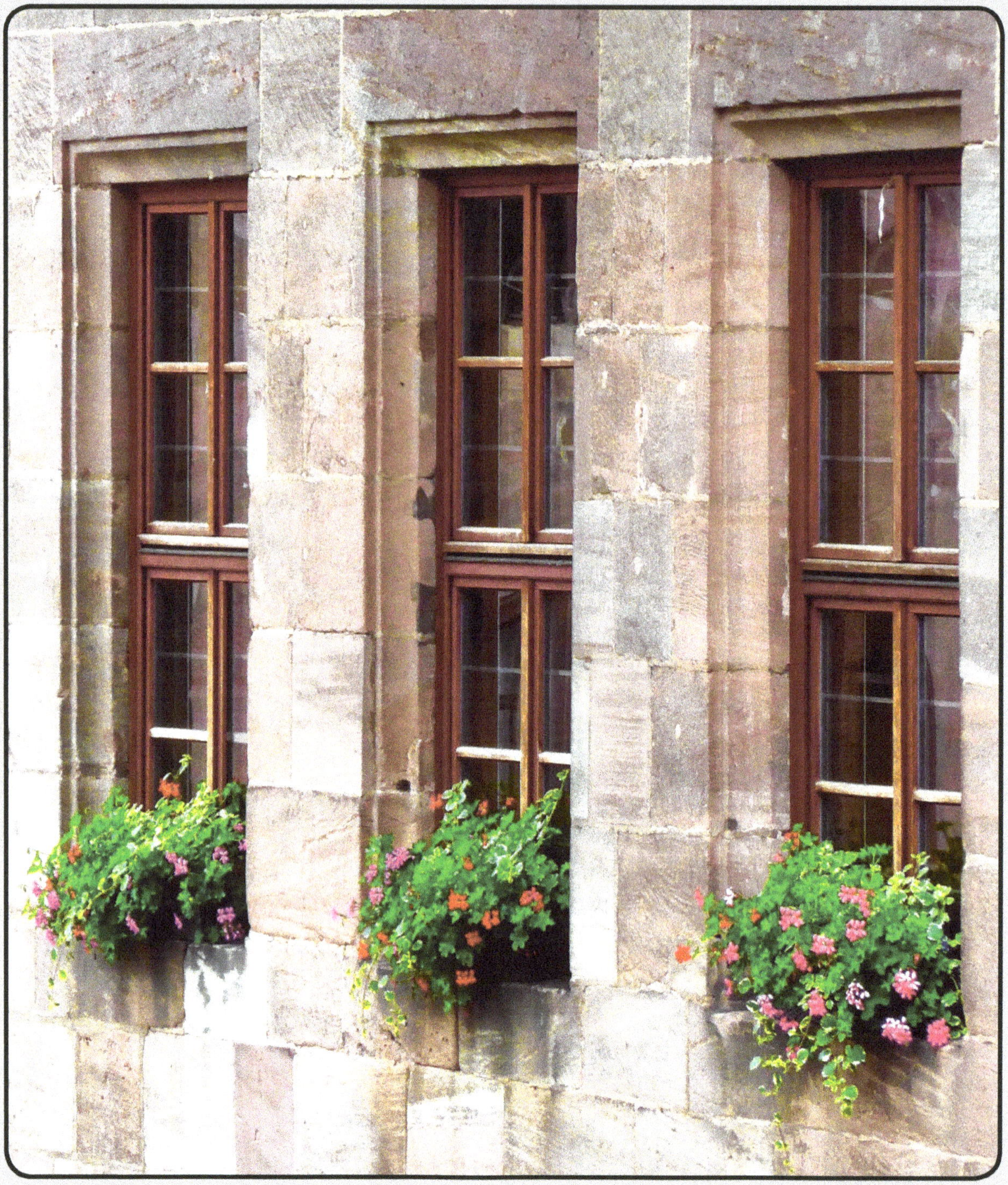

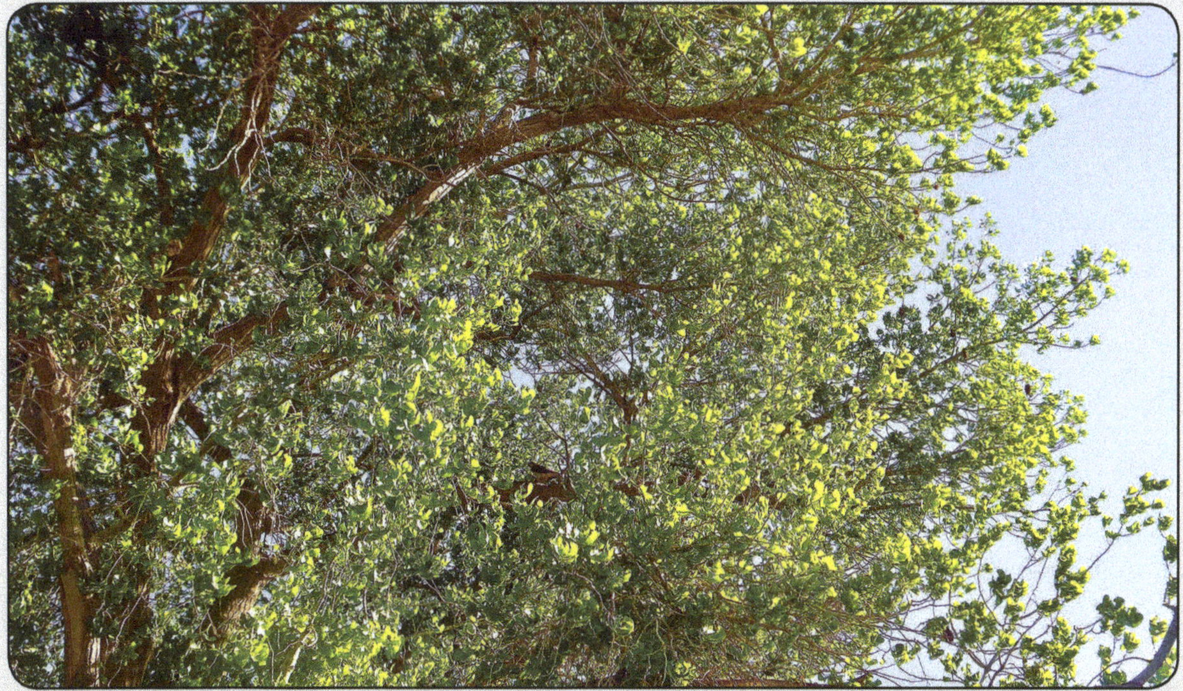

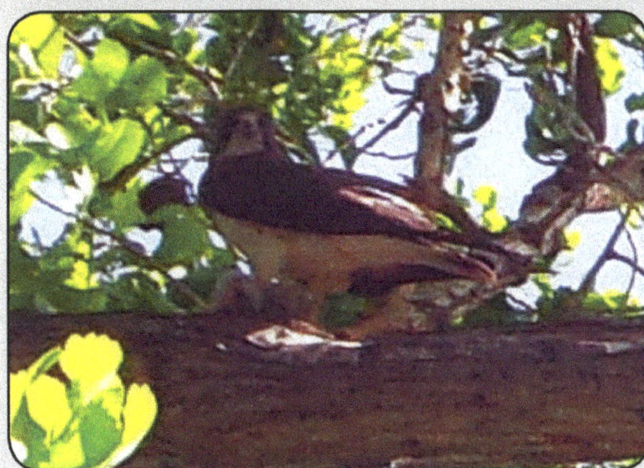

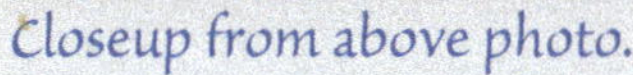

Closeup from above photo.

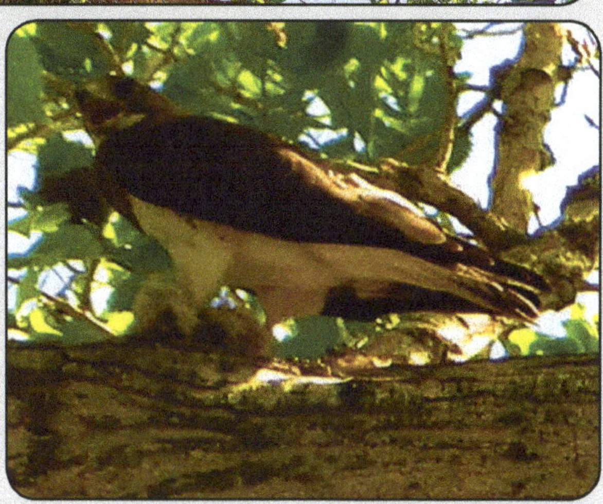

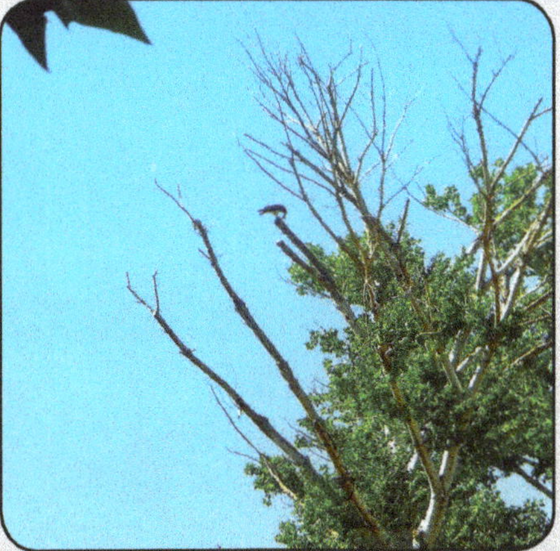

Eating prey.

Swainson's hawk parents in cottonwood trees series.

[Note: For several months I watched and photographed this pair of migratory hawks and their hatchlings.]

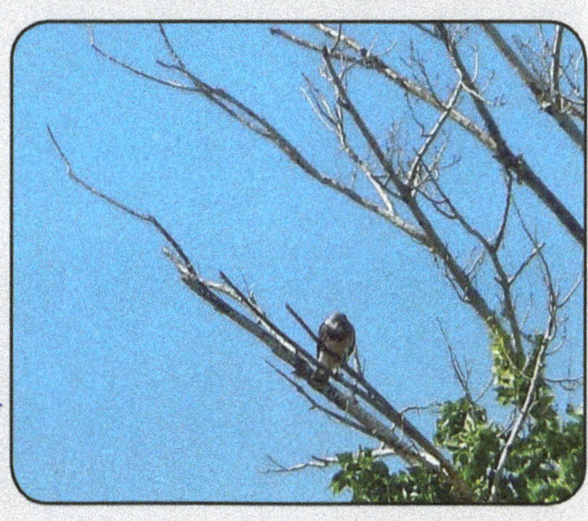

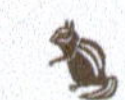

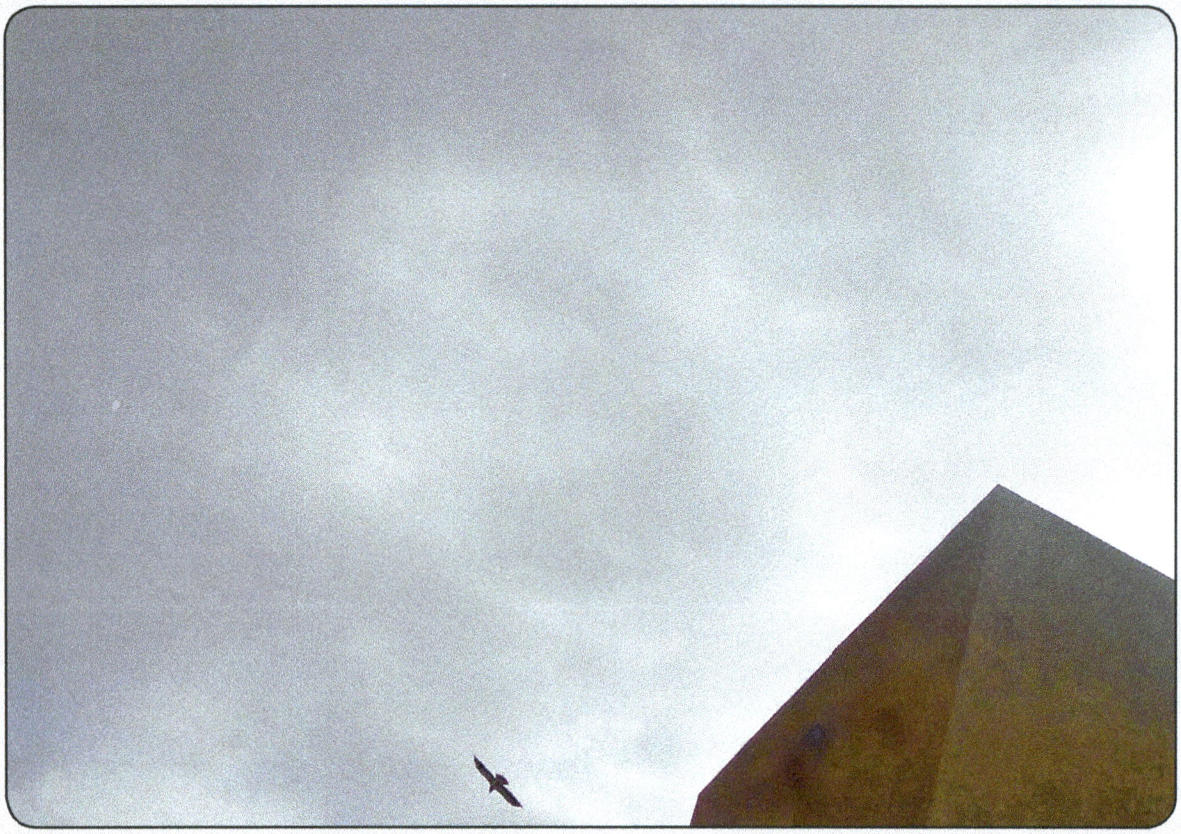

Hawk patrols near the nest.

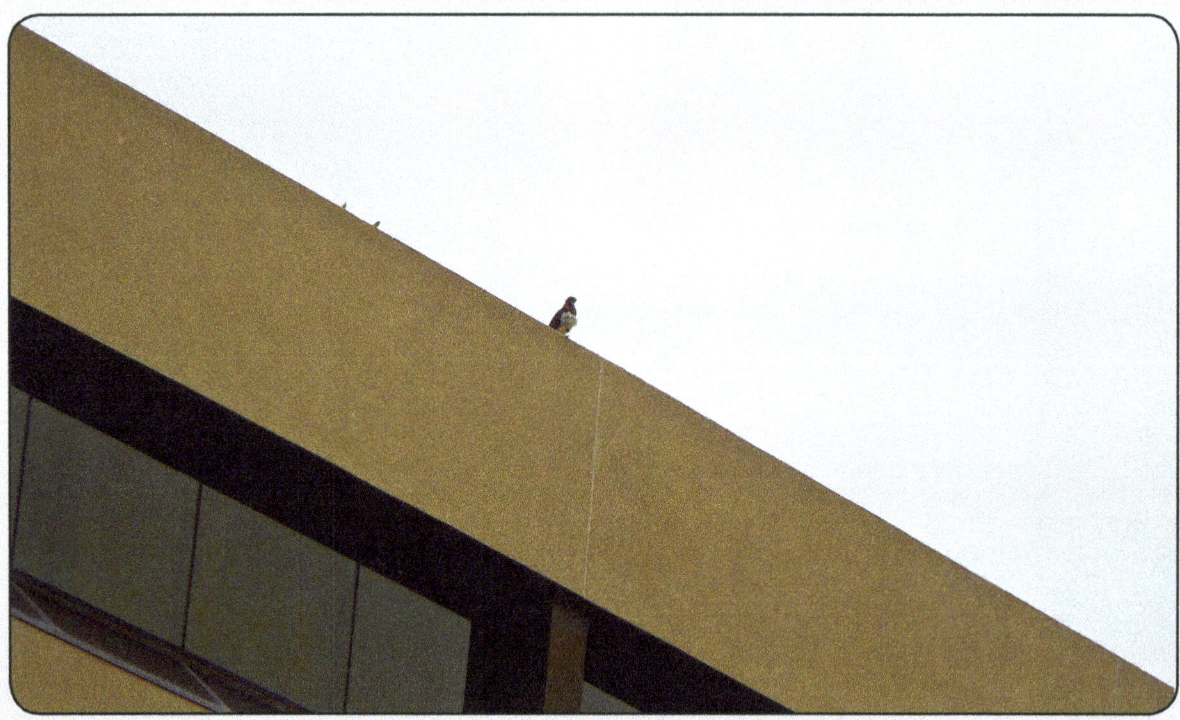

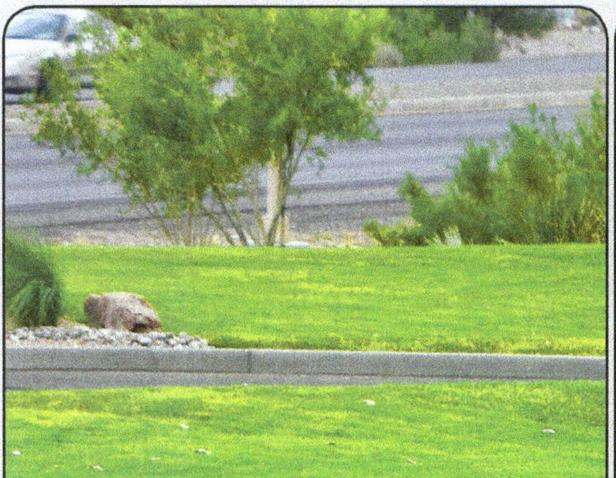

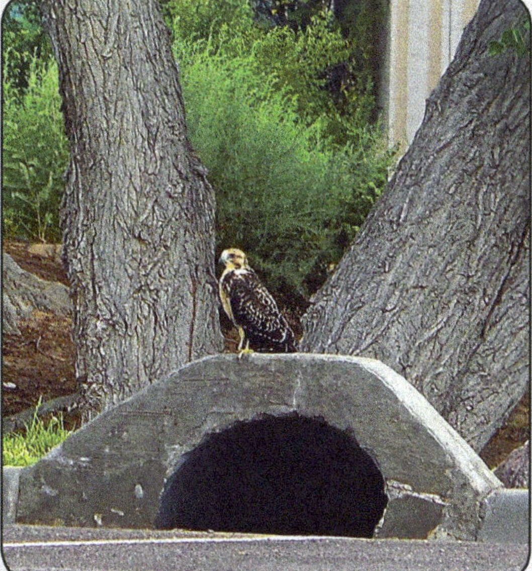

Grounded hatchling learning to fly.

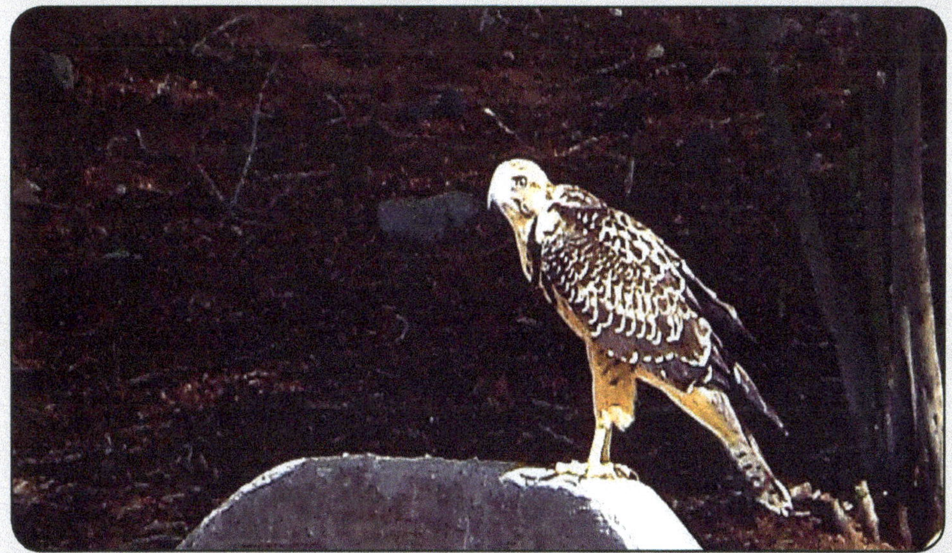

Hawk children leave nest to look in wonder at surroundings on the ground.

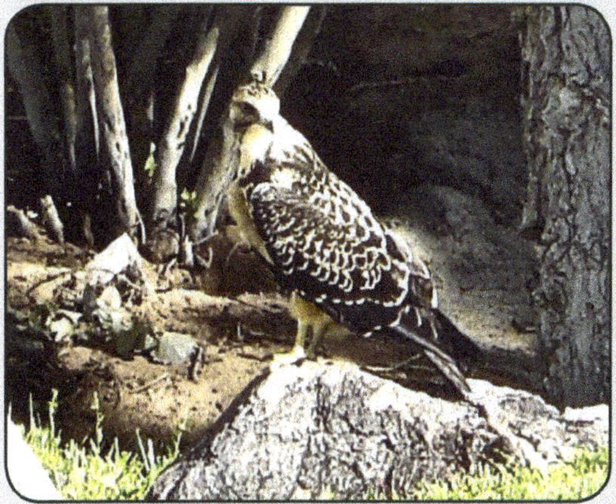

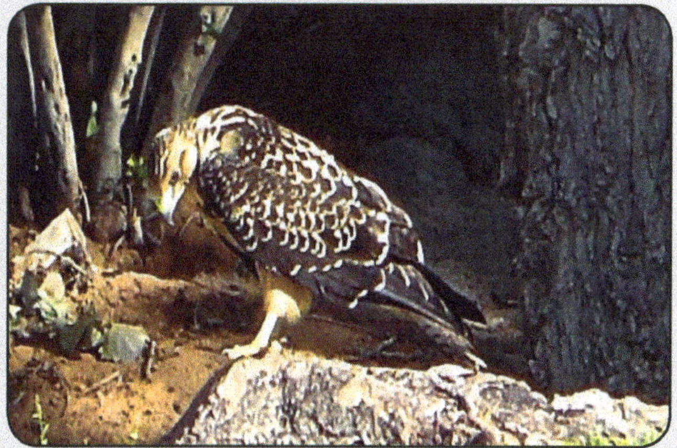

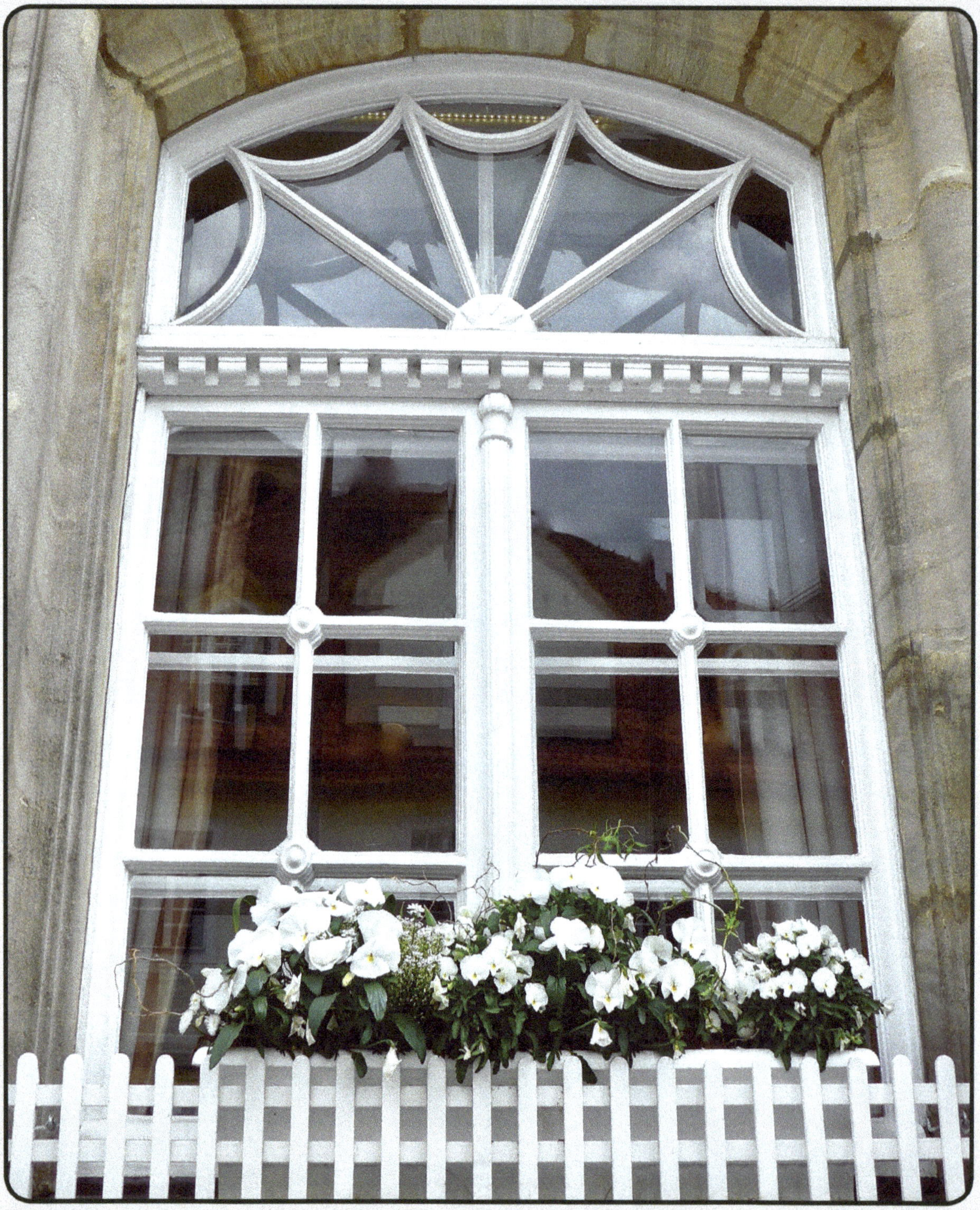

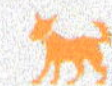

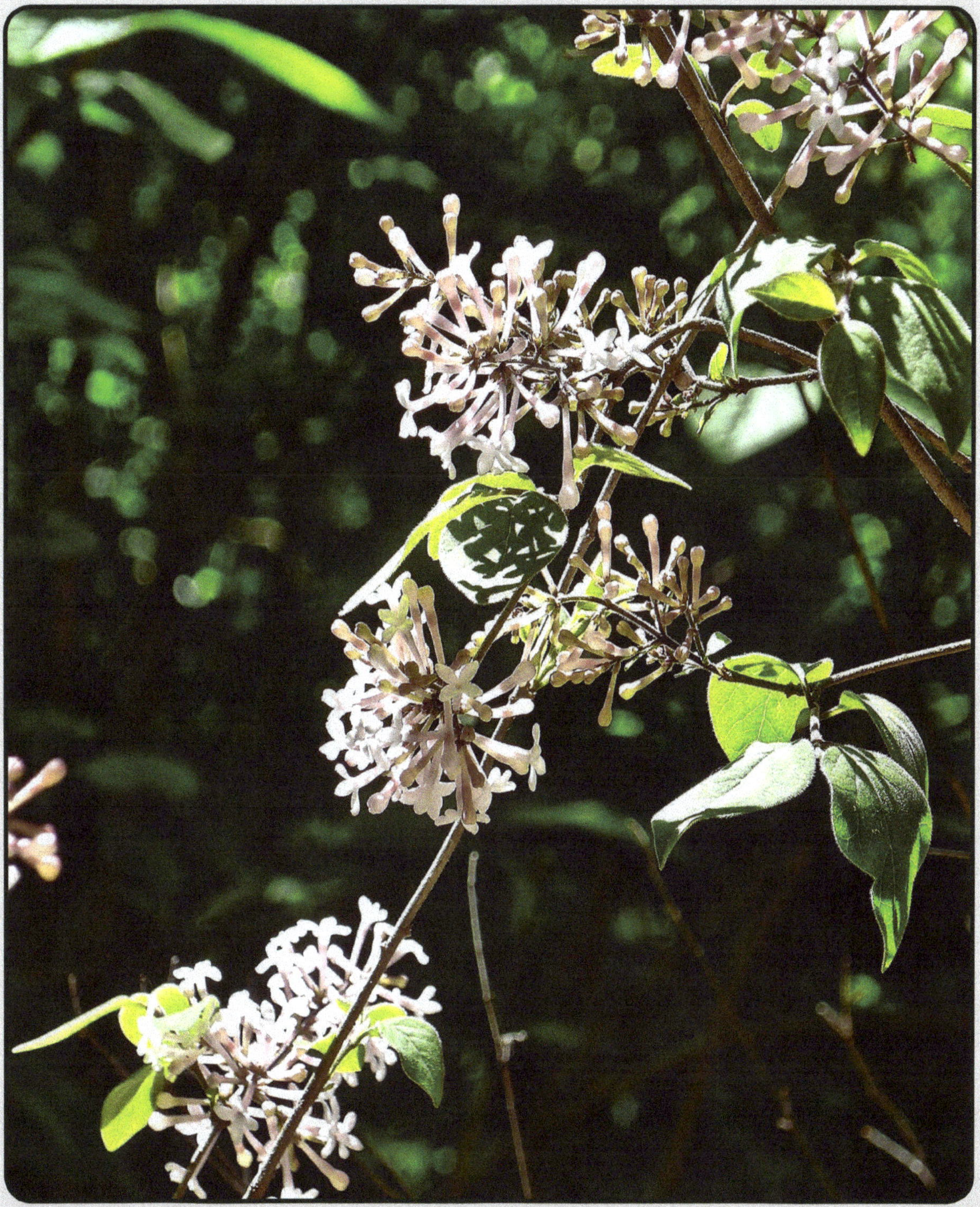

✳ Bugles rejoice.

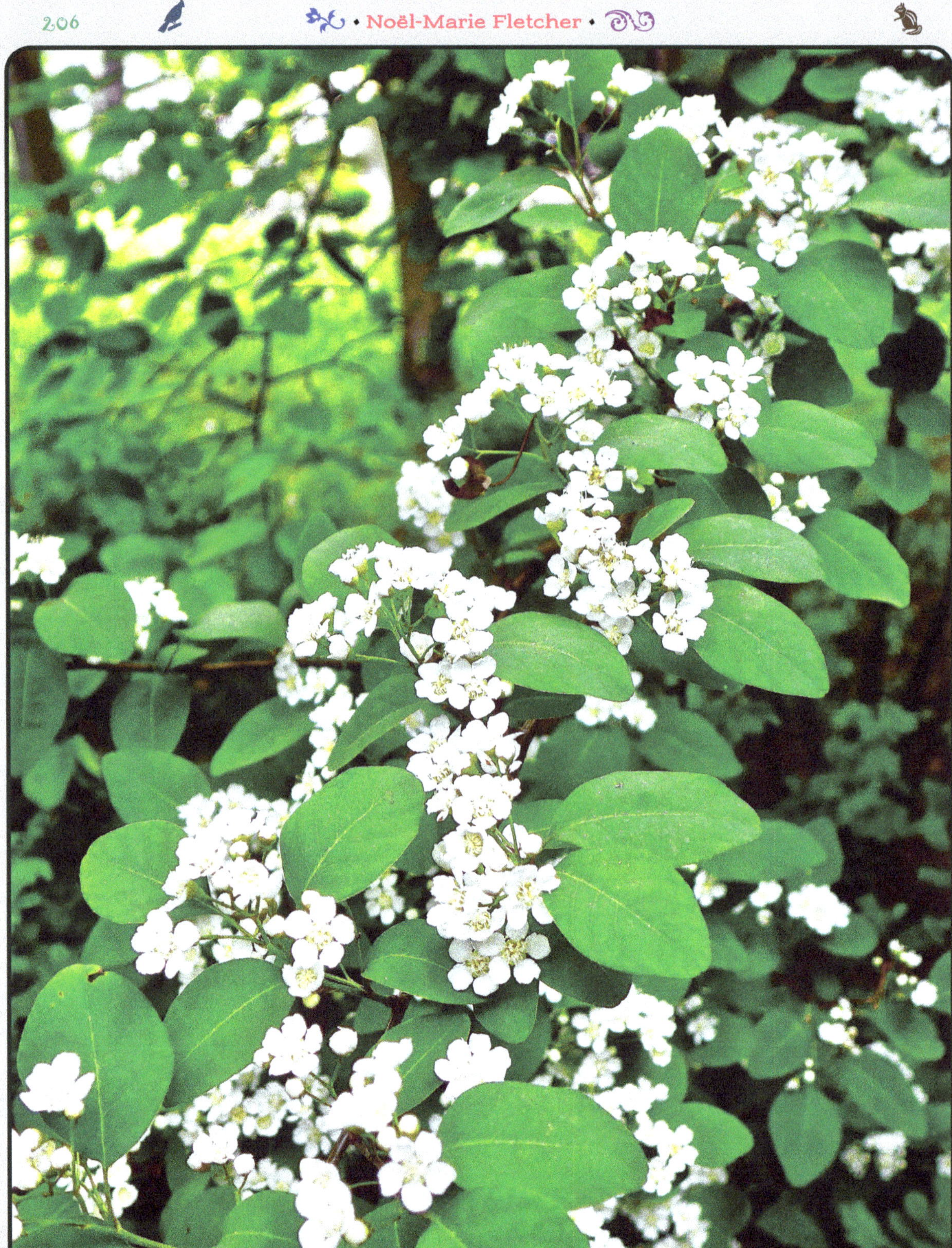

Winter whites in spring.

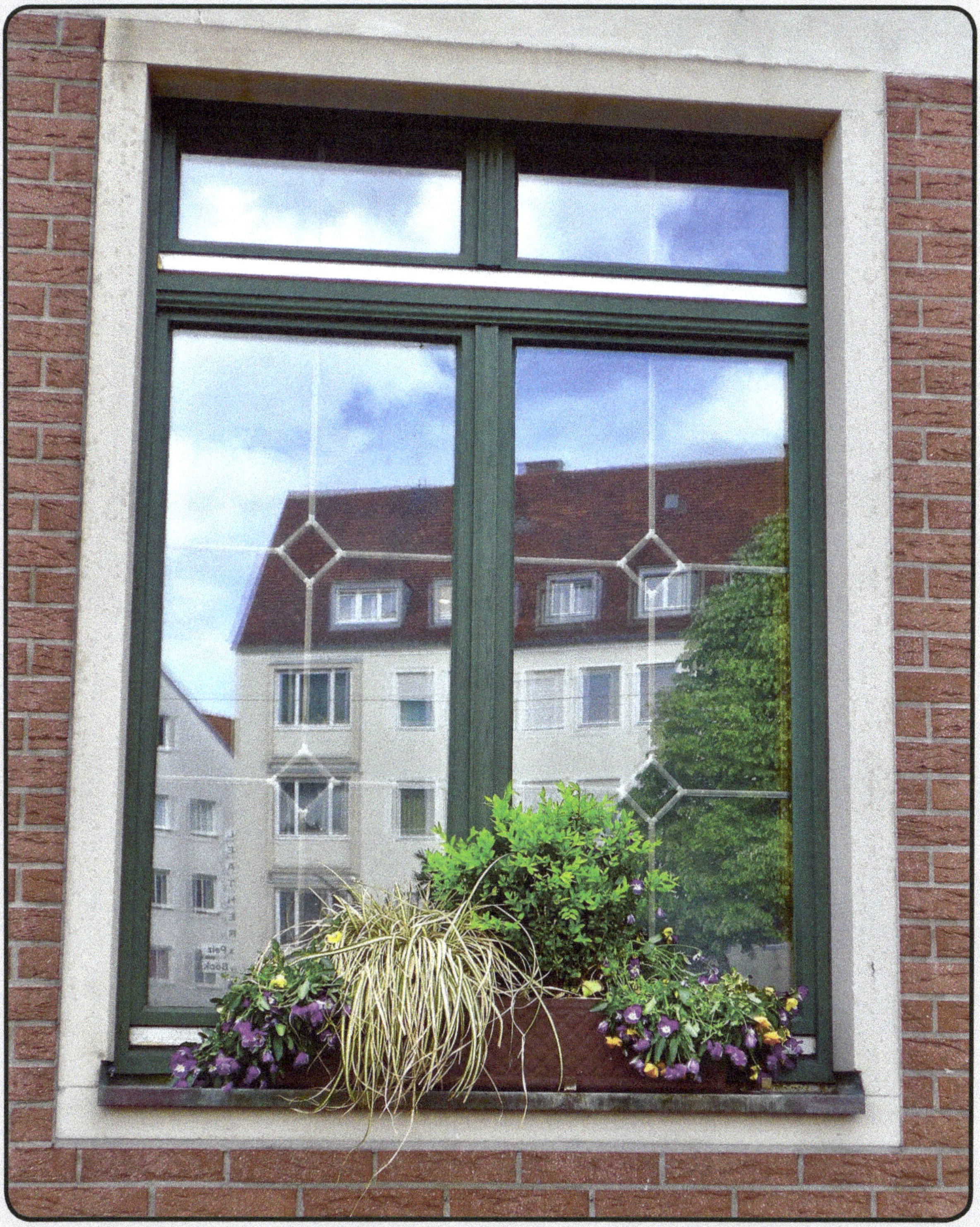

Summer afternoon.

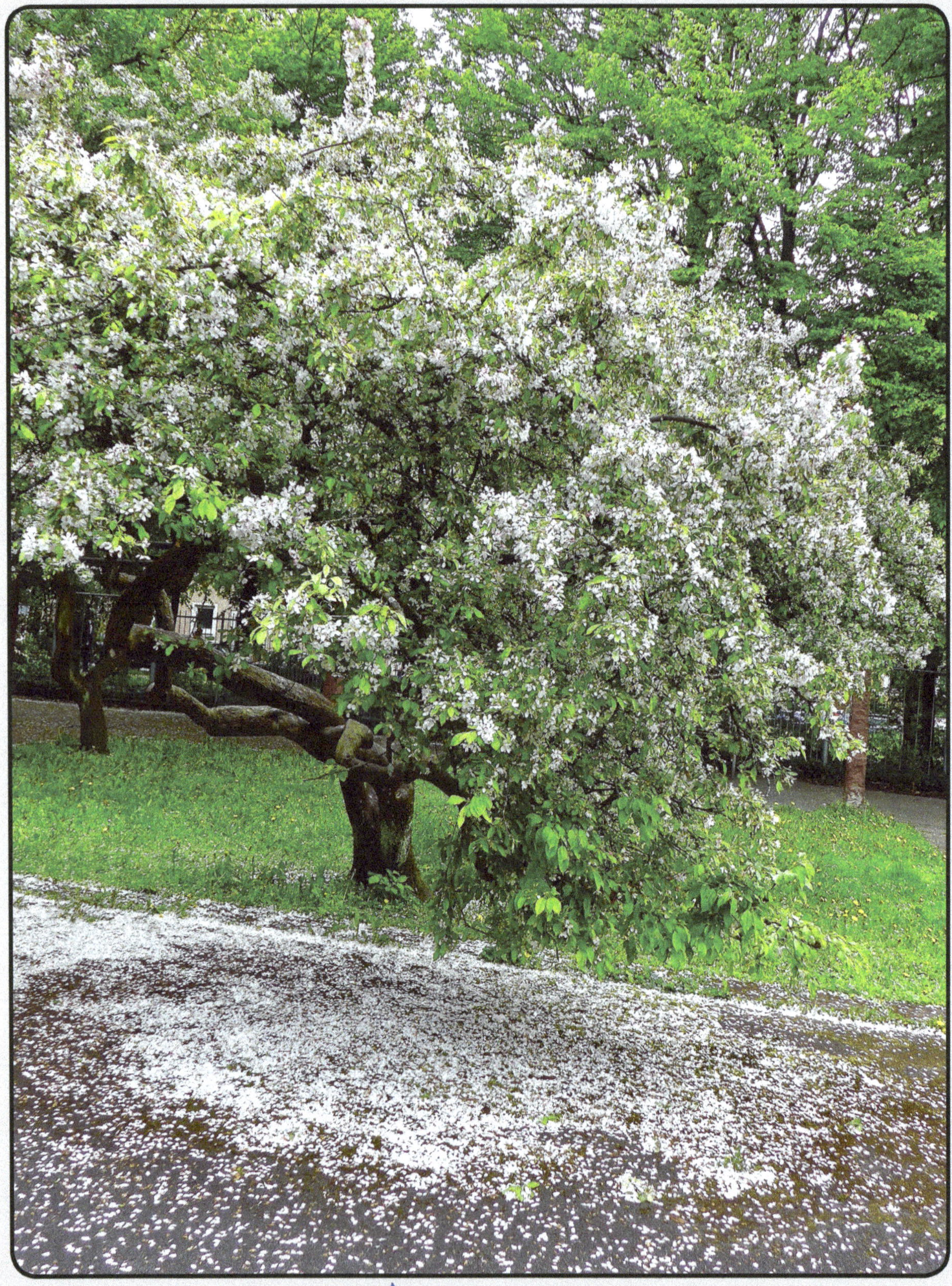

Powdered sugar.

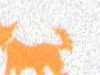

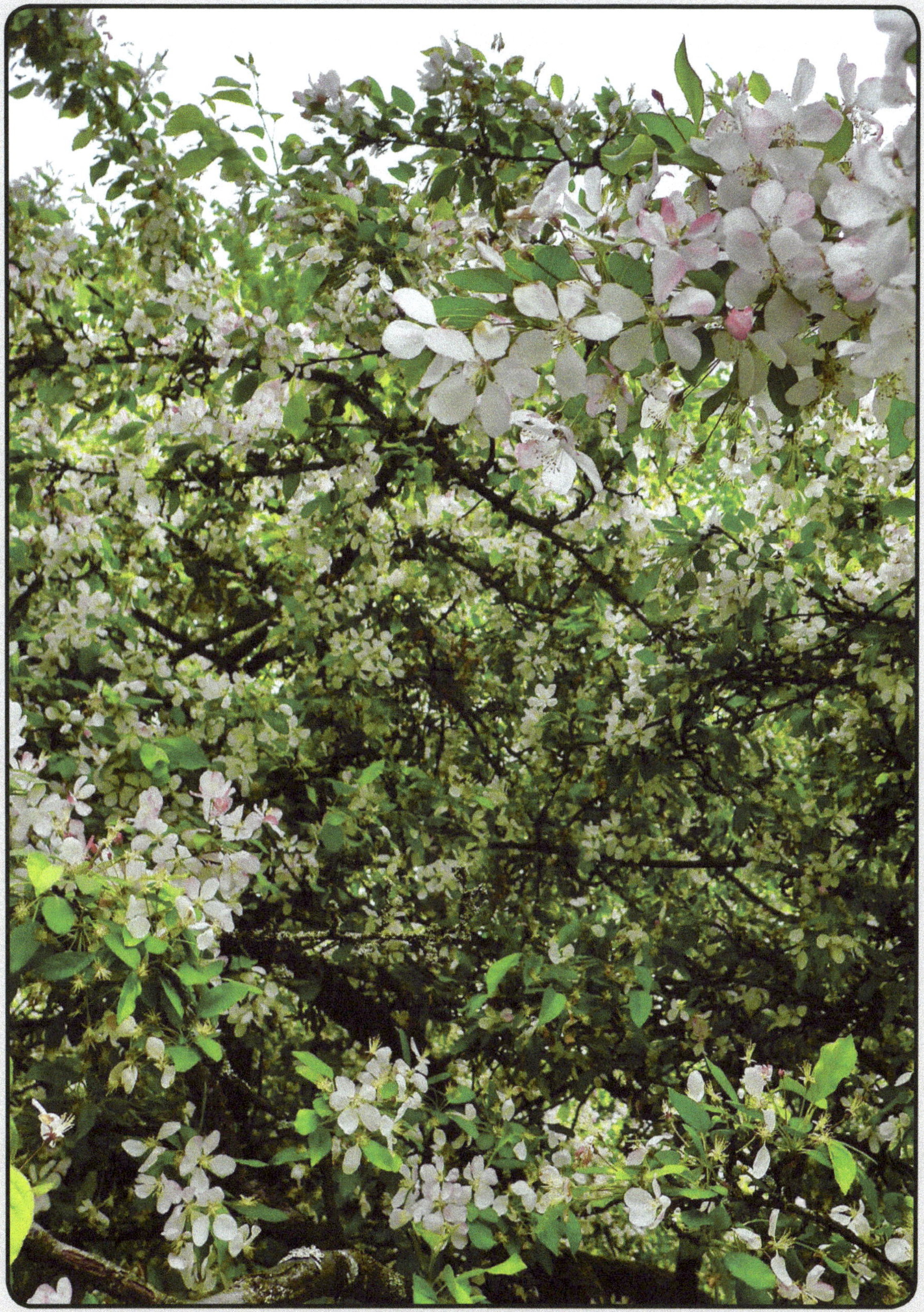

Jade shades.

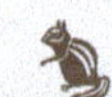

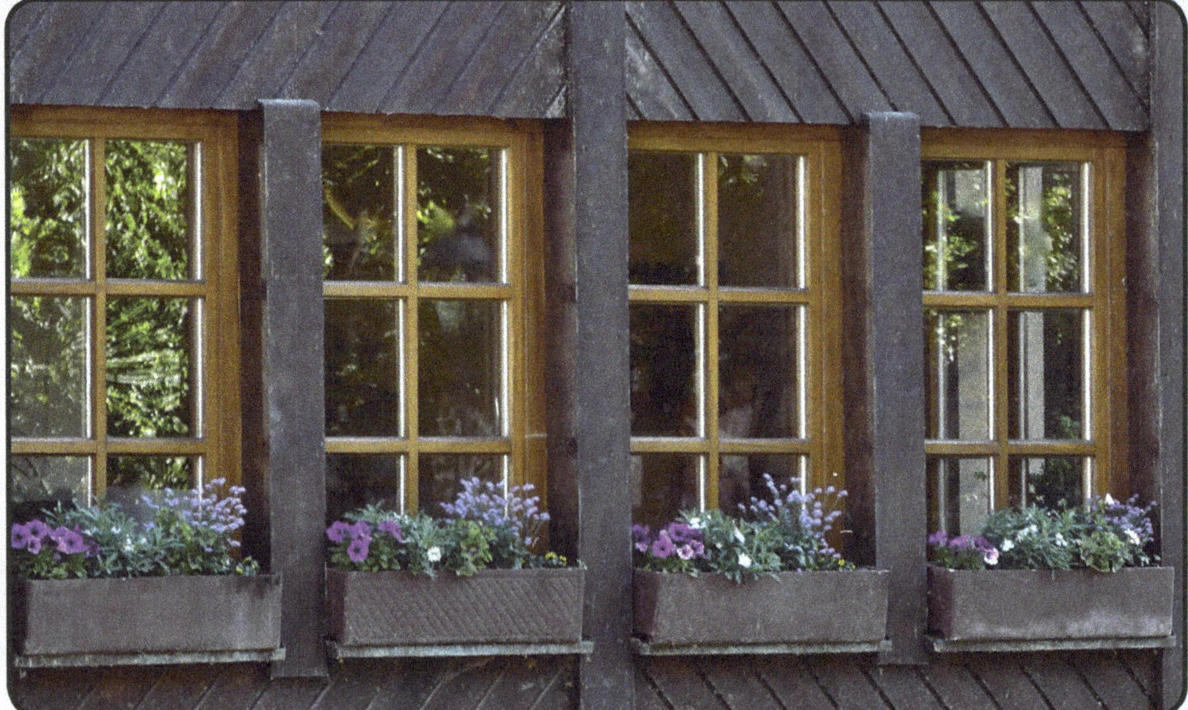

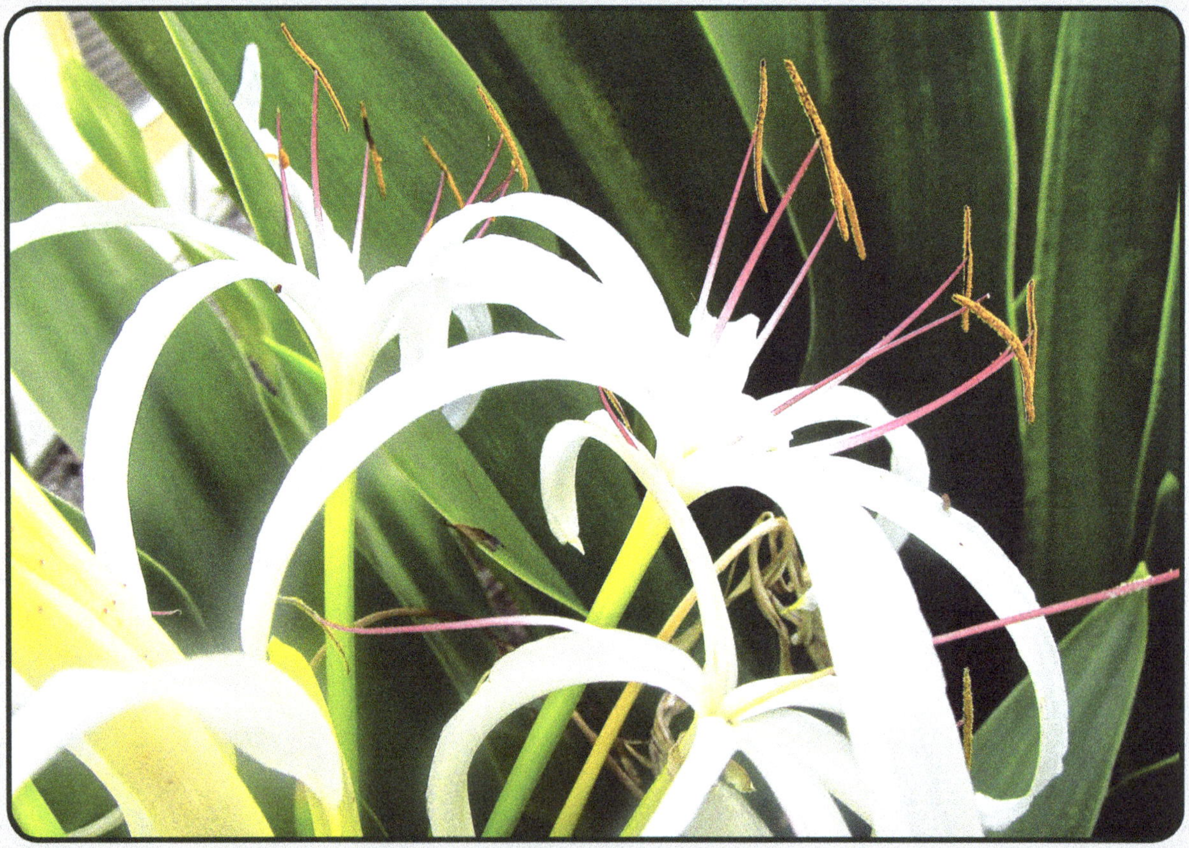

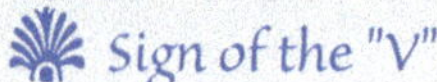

Sign of the "V".

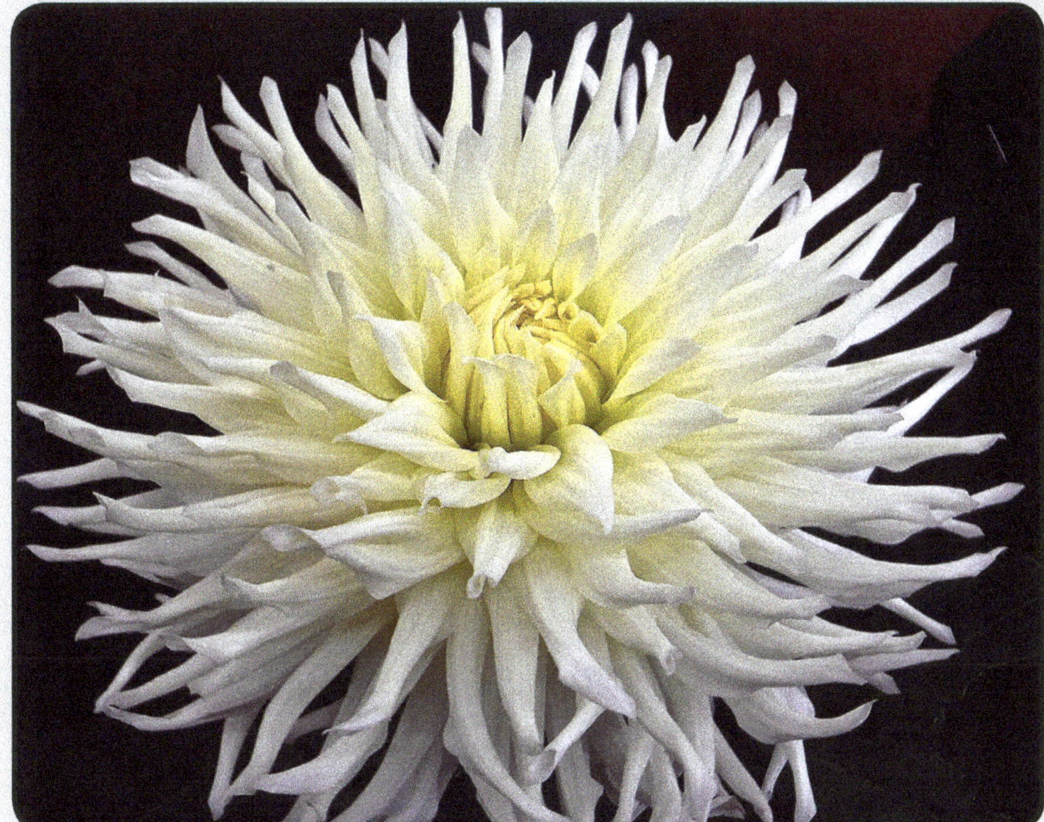

Clasping hands.

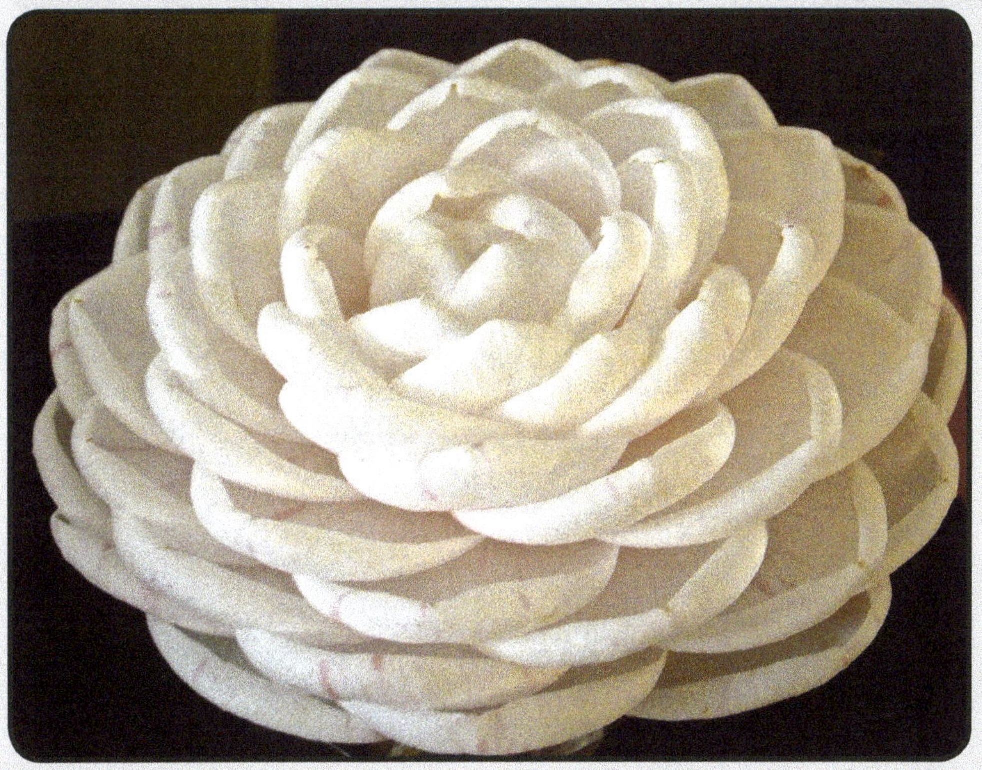

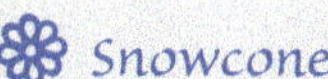

Snowcone.

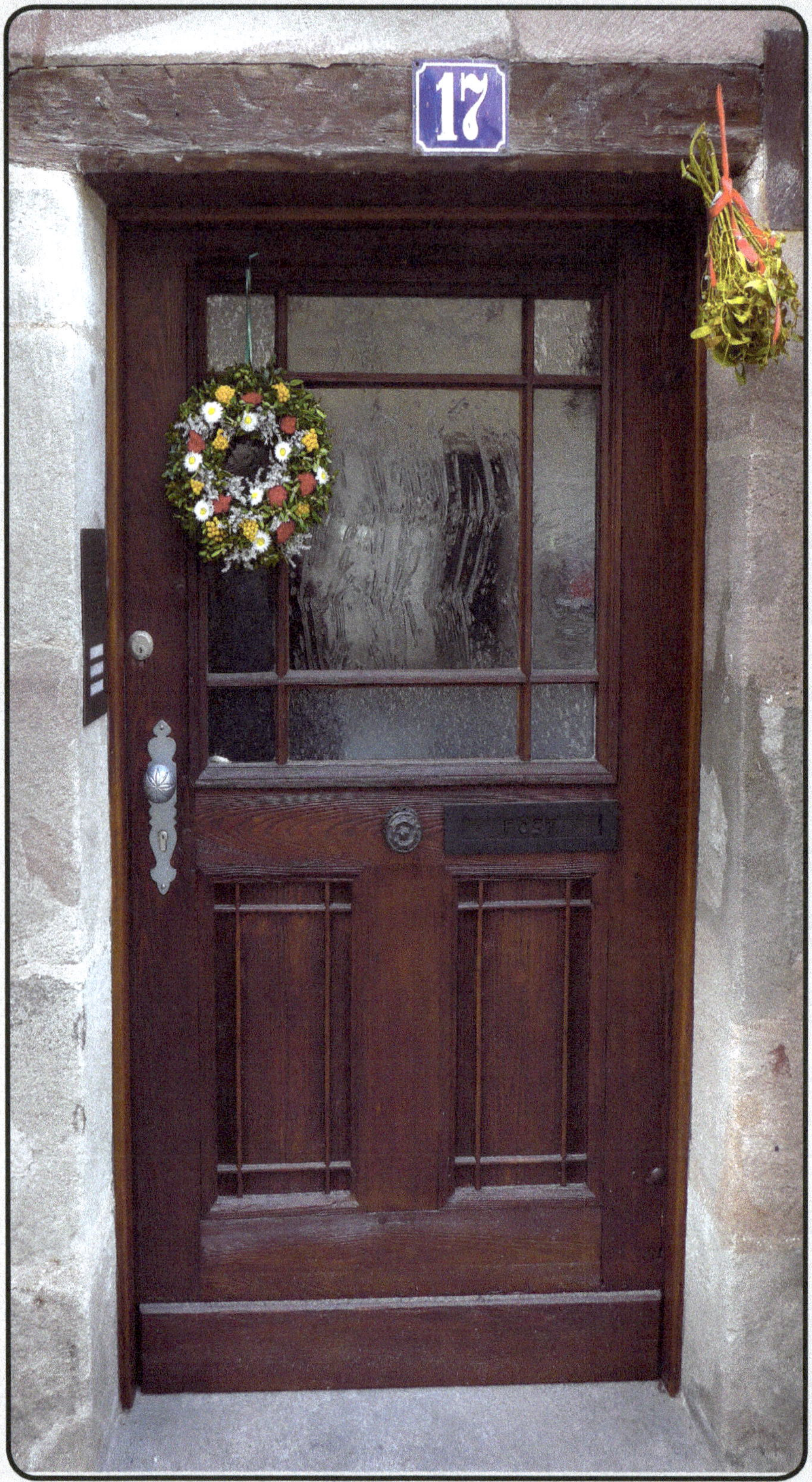

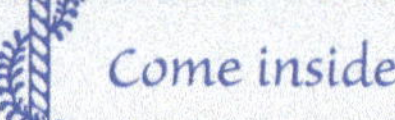

Come inside.

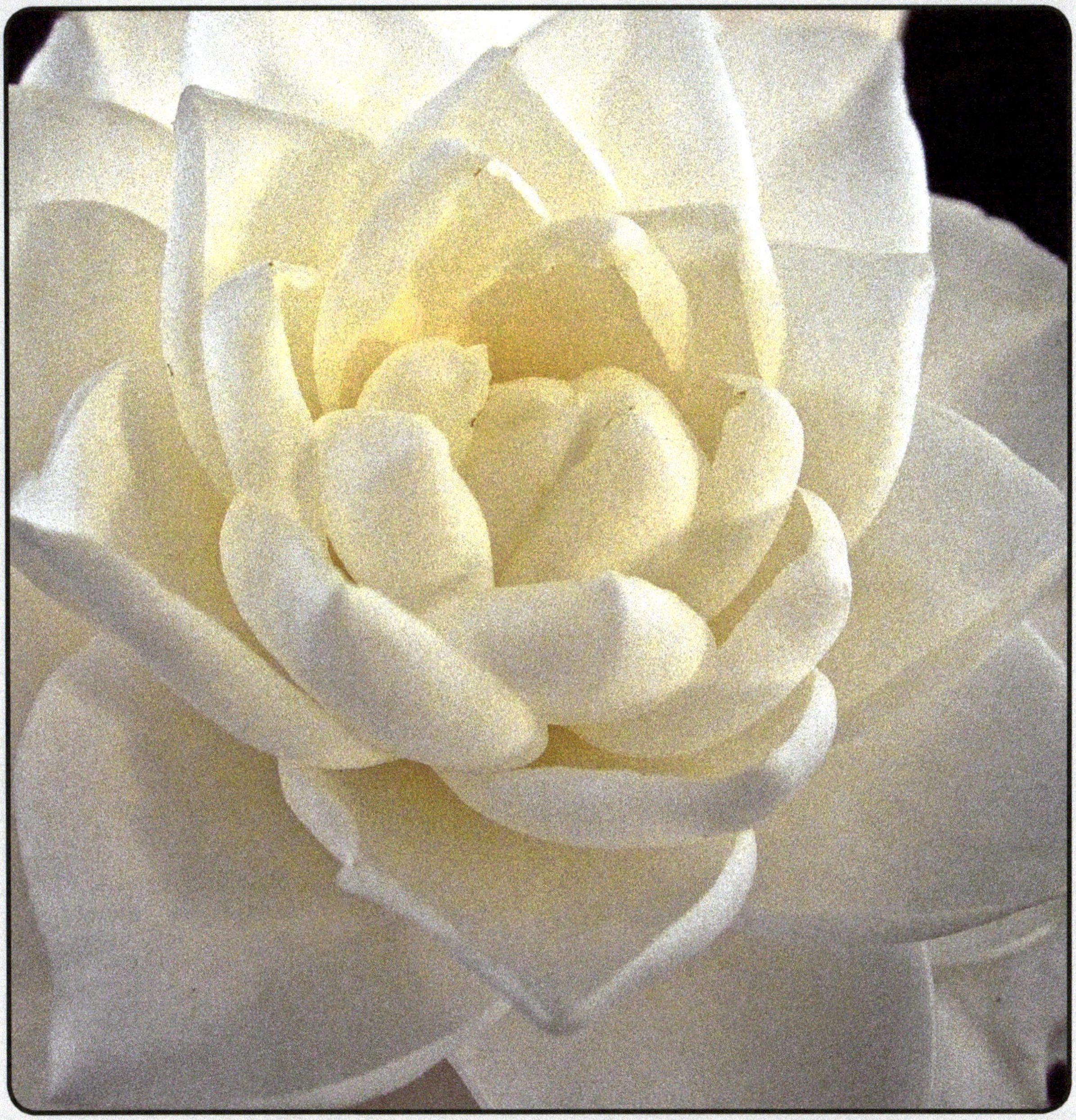

Celebration in ecru.

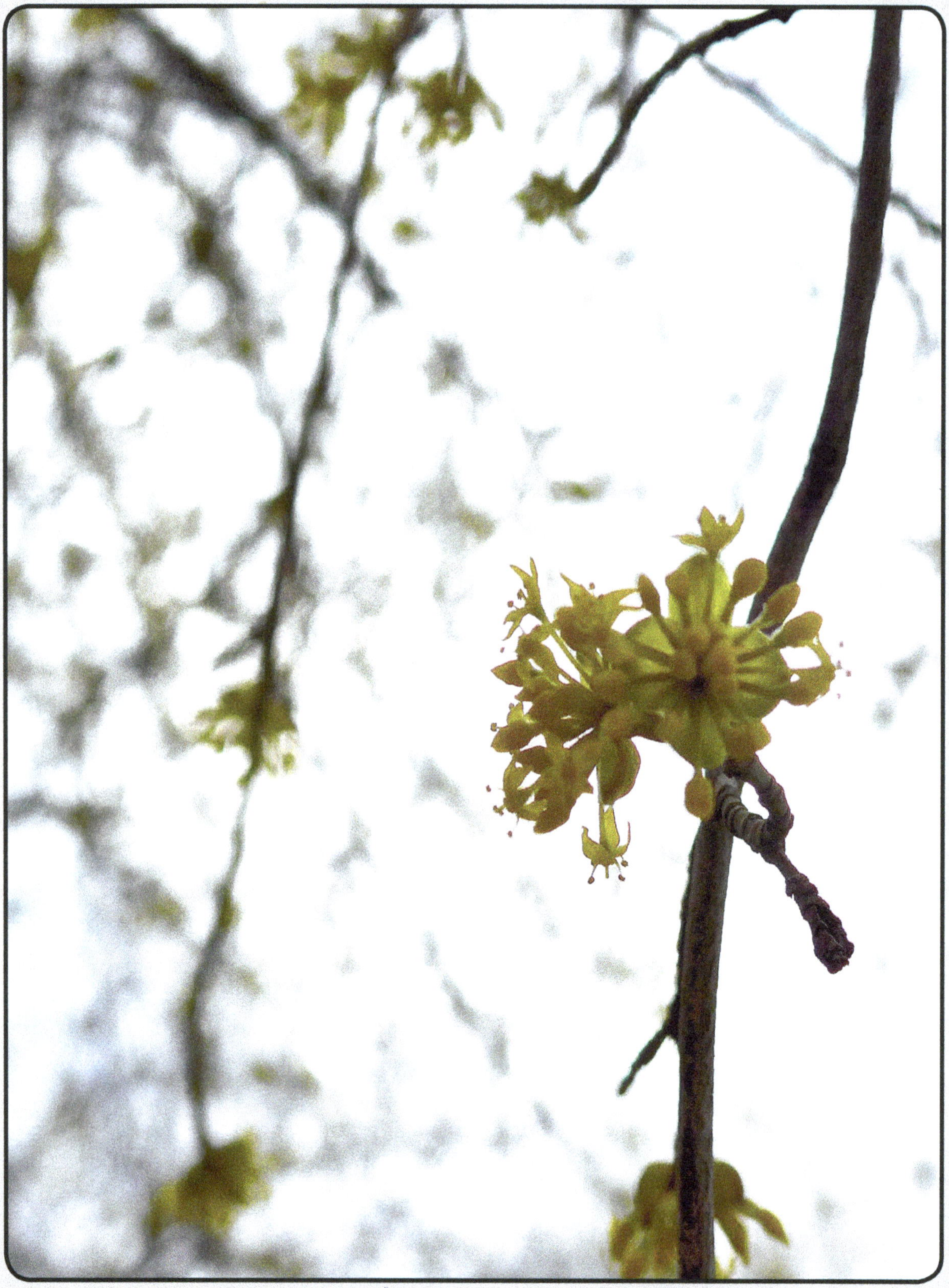

Branch offering.

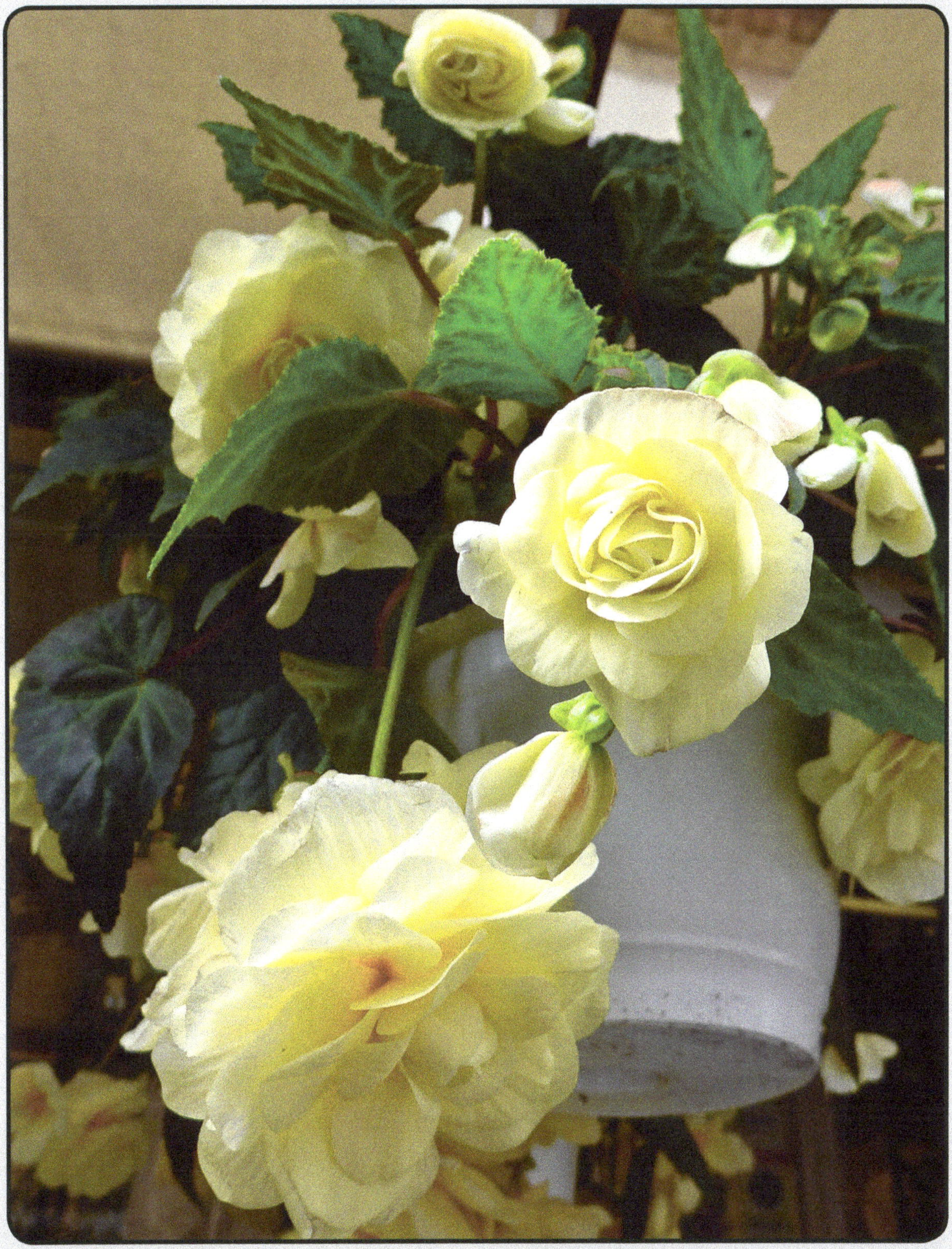

❀ Cascade in vanilla.

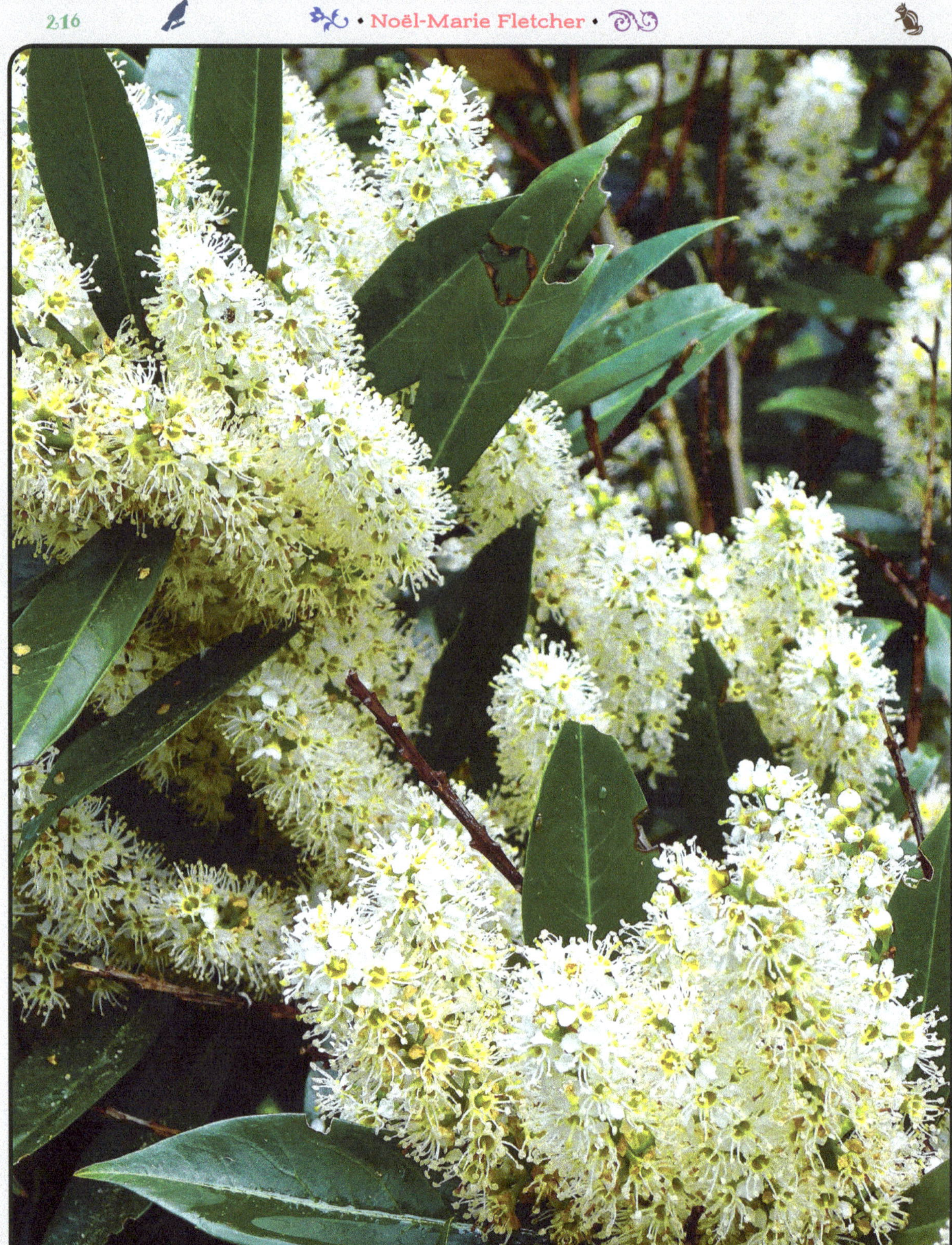

Fragrant sparklers.

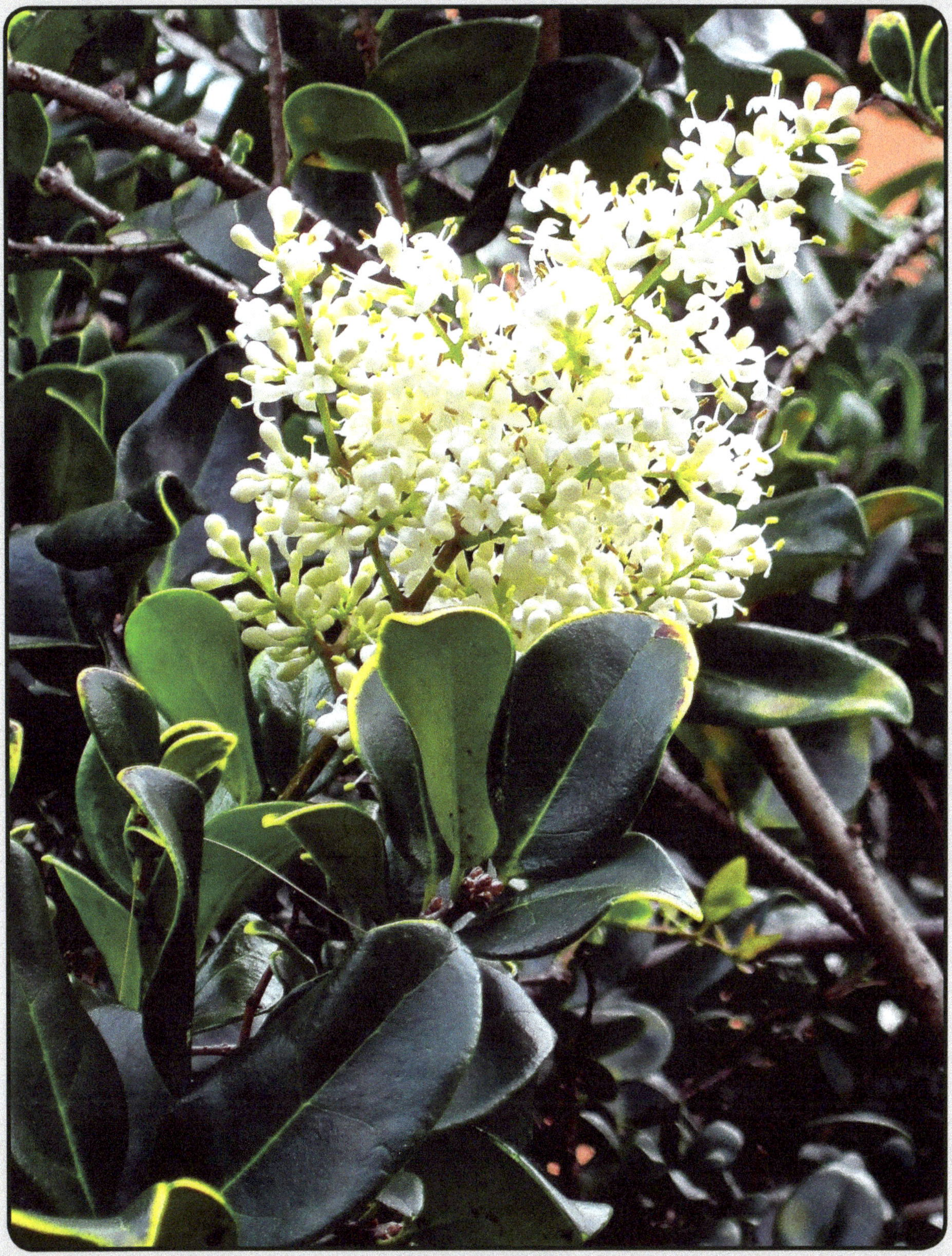

Thunderhead.

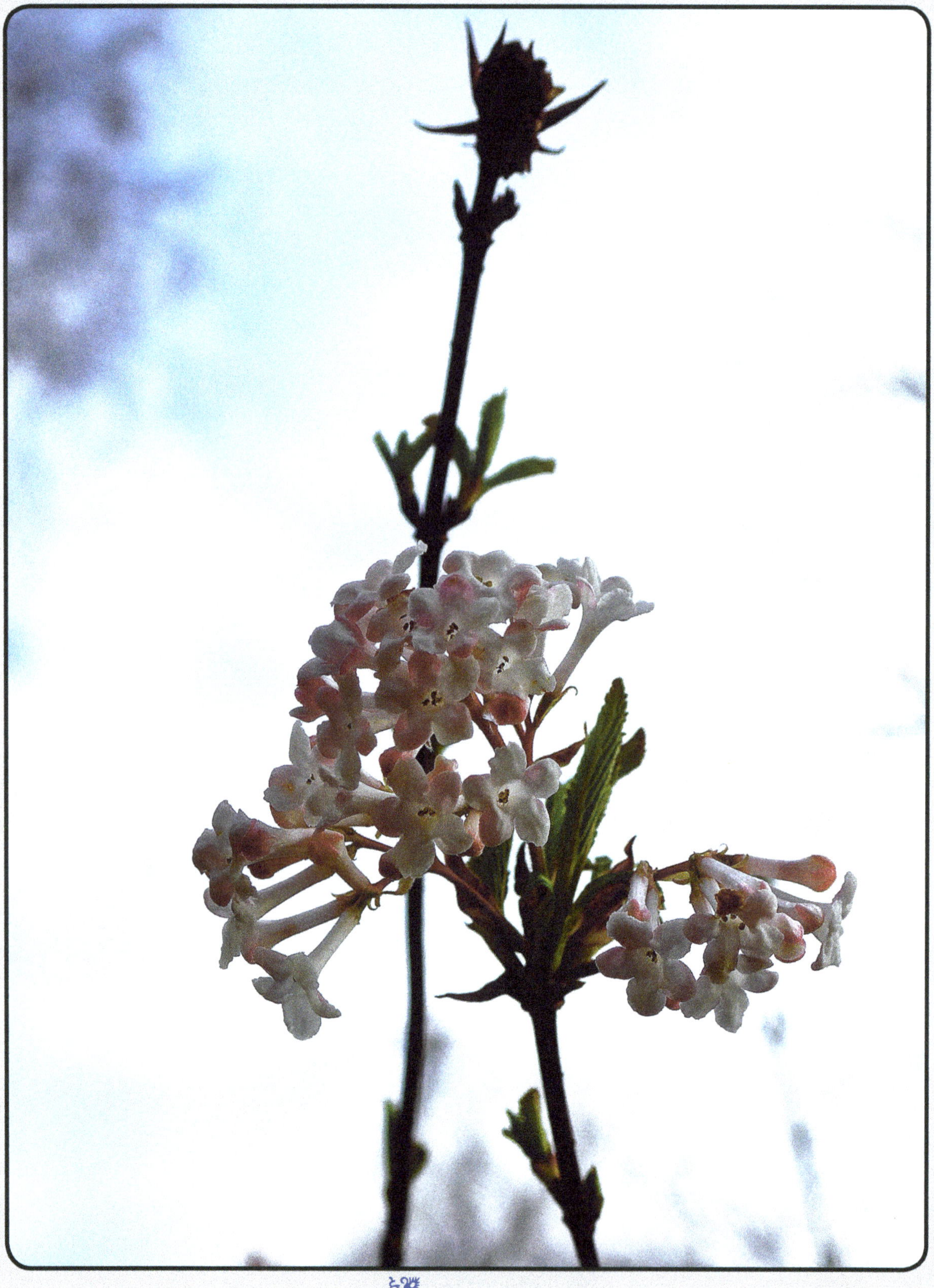

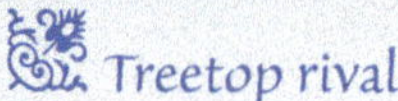

Treetop rival.

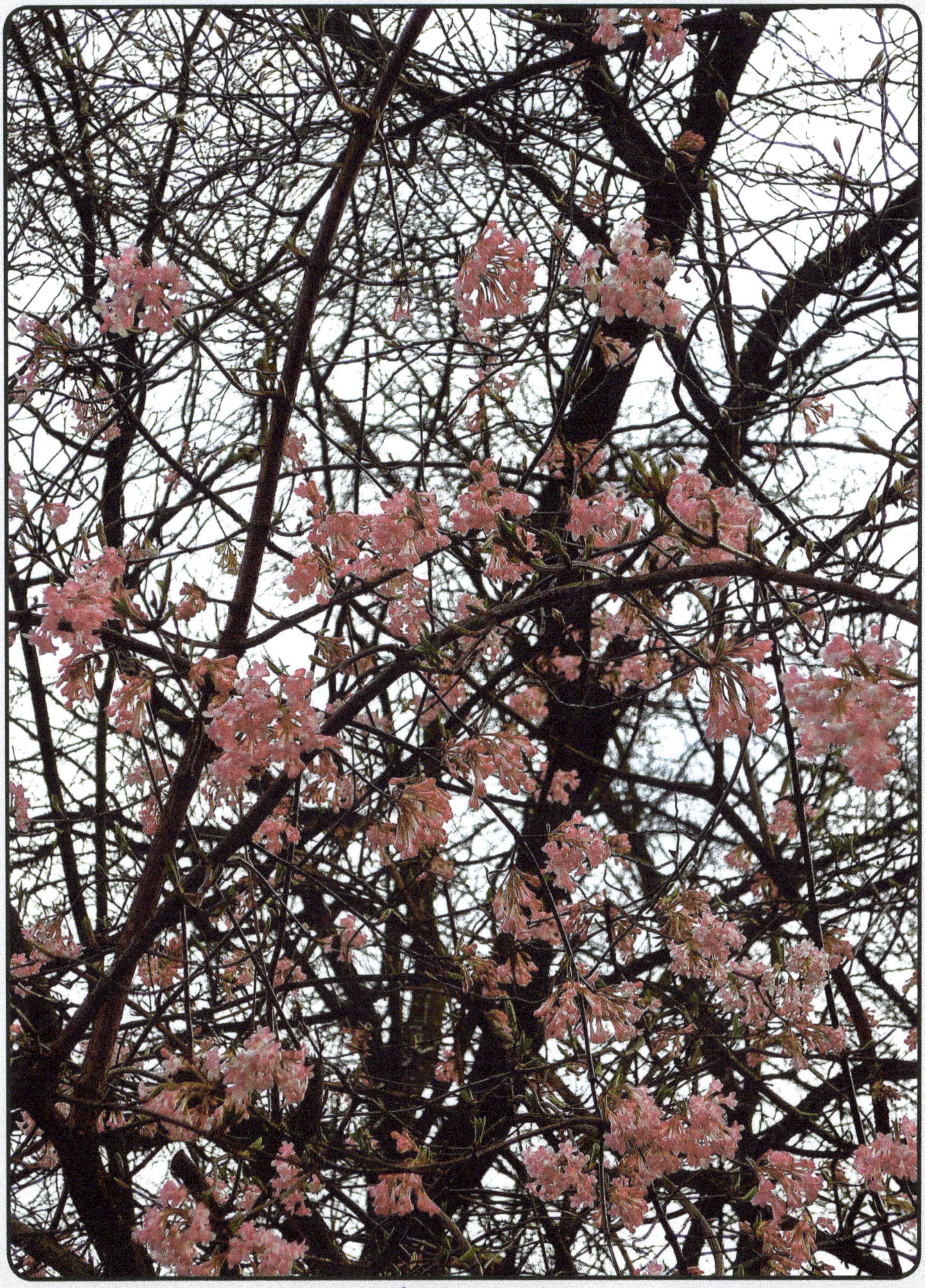

Pink on parade.

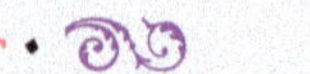

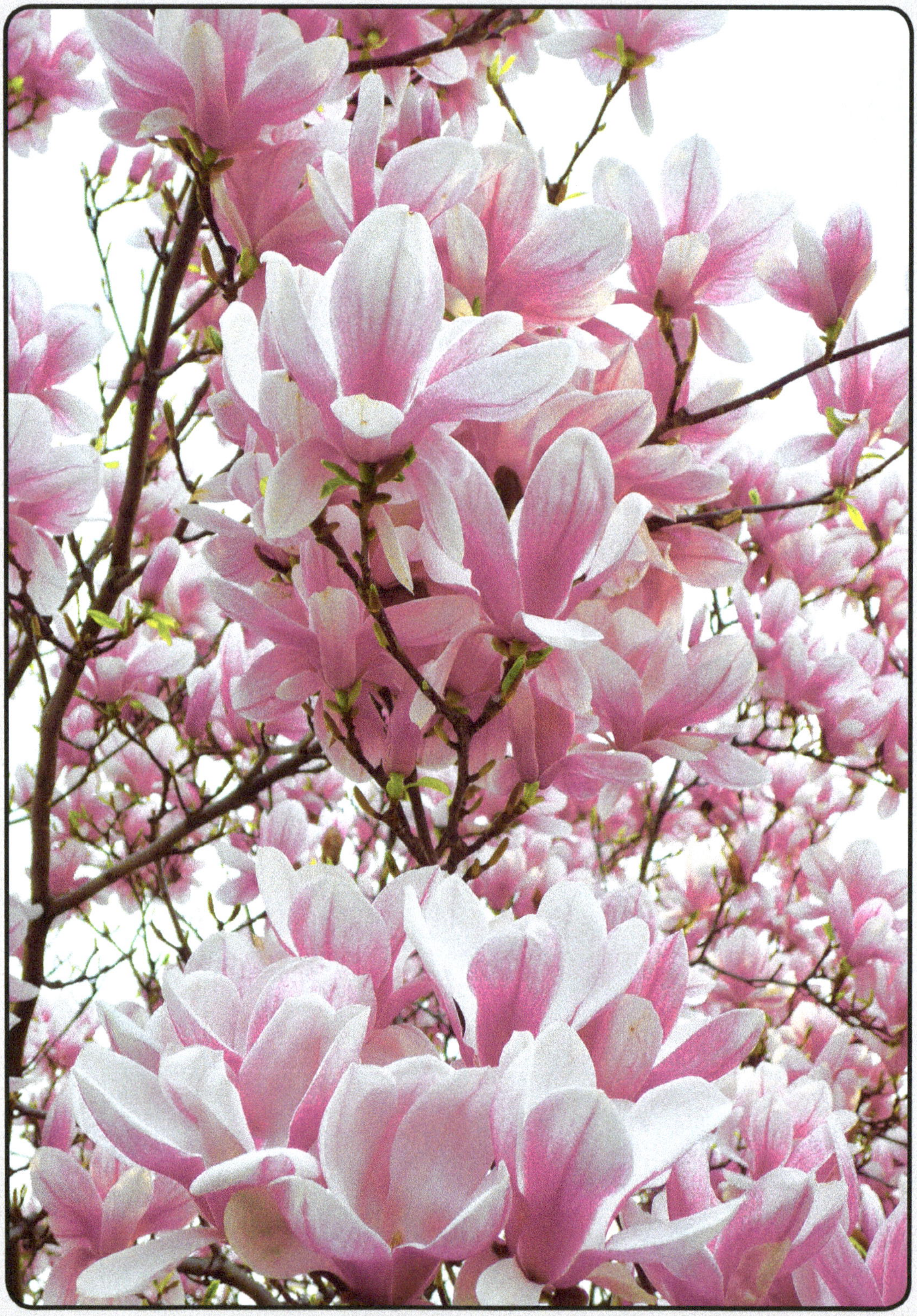

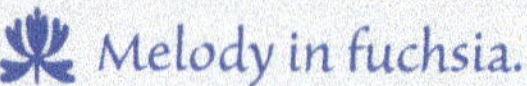

Melody in fuchsia.

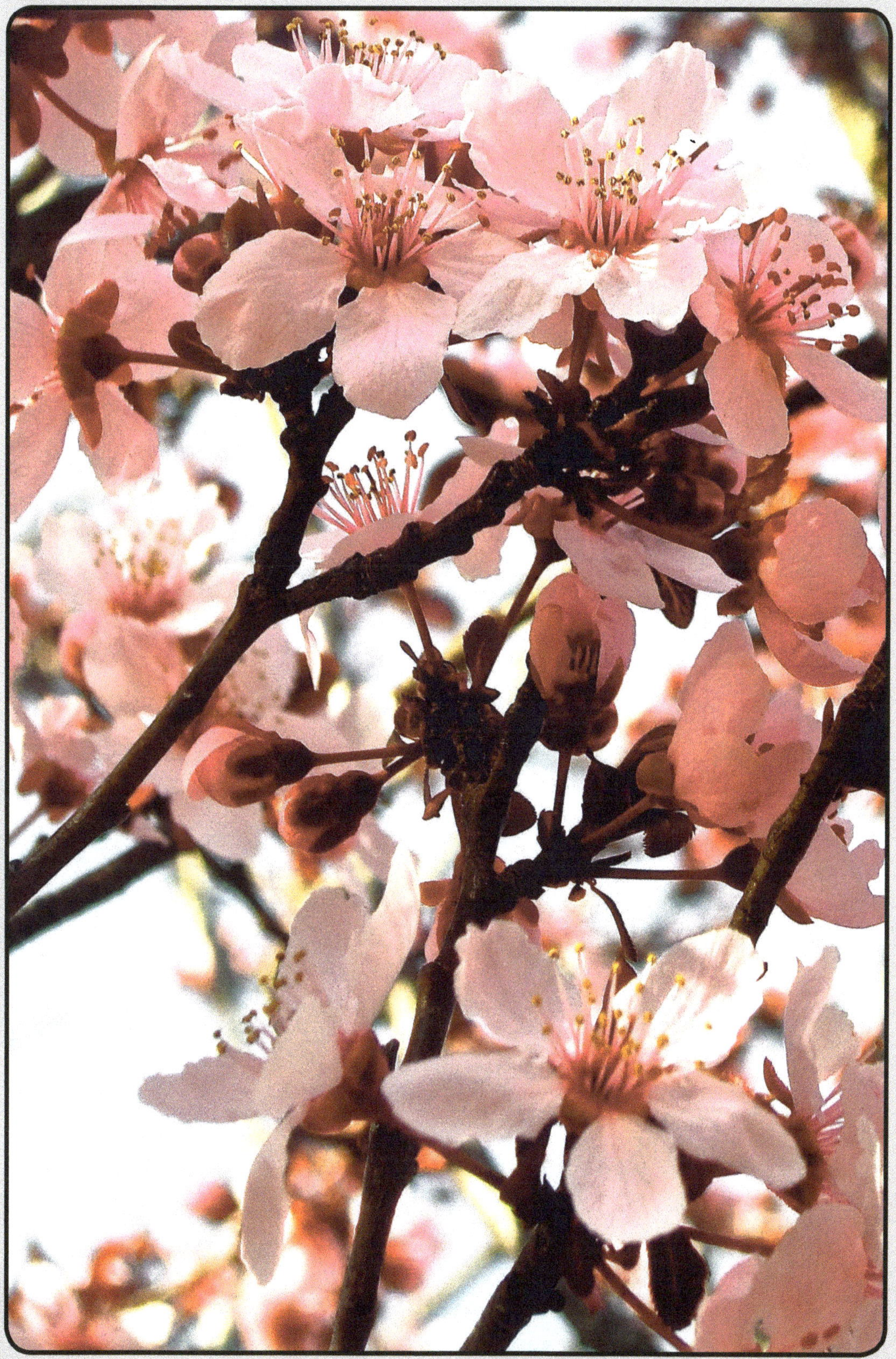

Cherry blossom time.

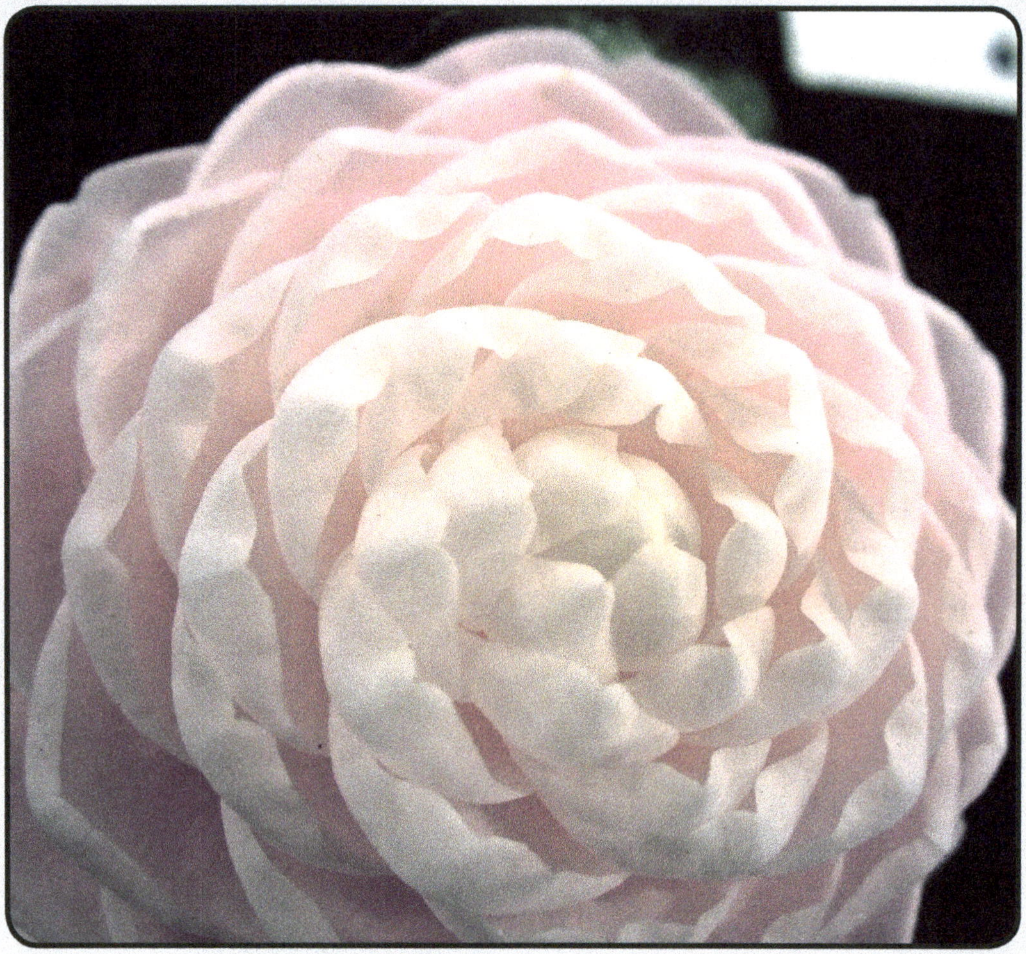

Pinwheel in lace.

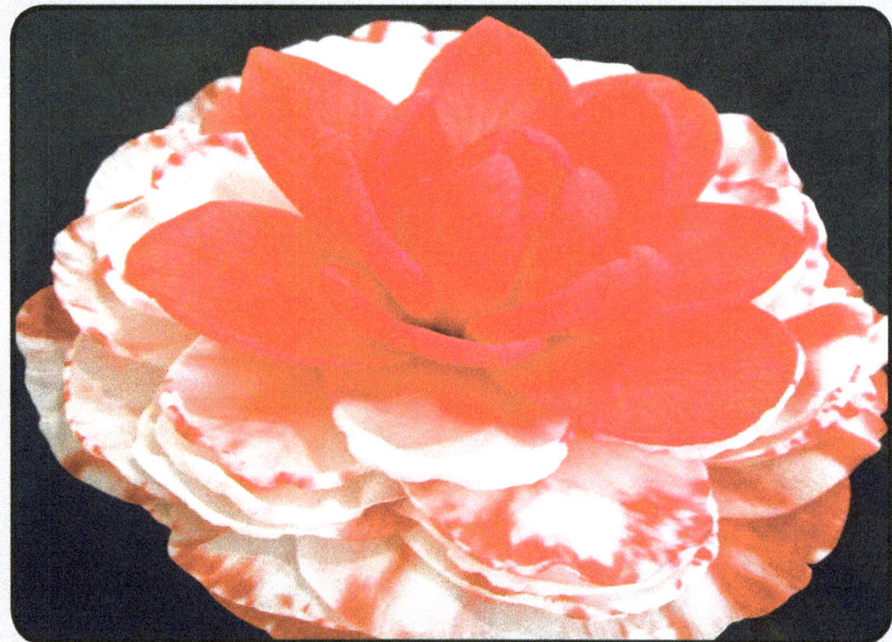

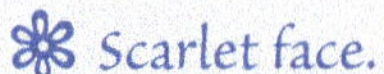

Scarlet face.

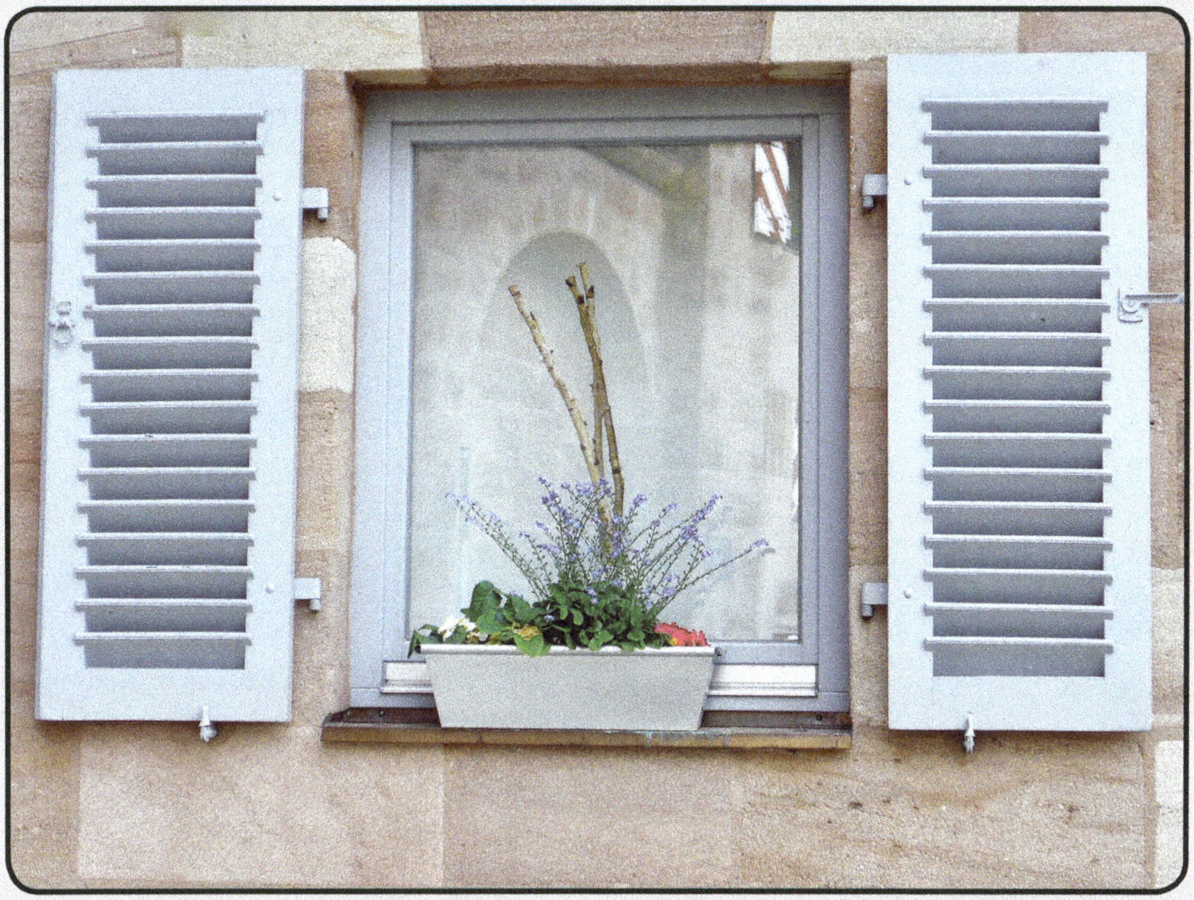

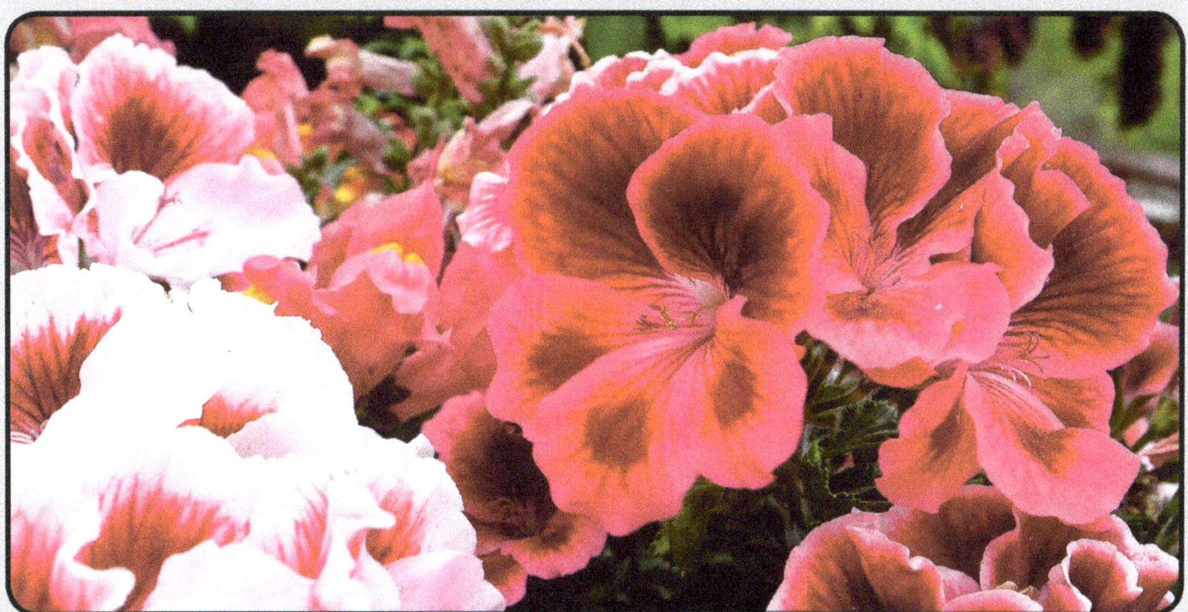

* Opposites attract.

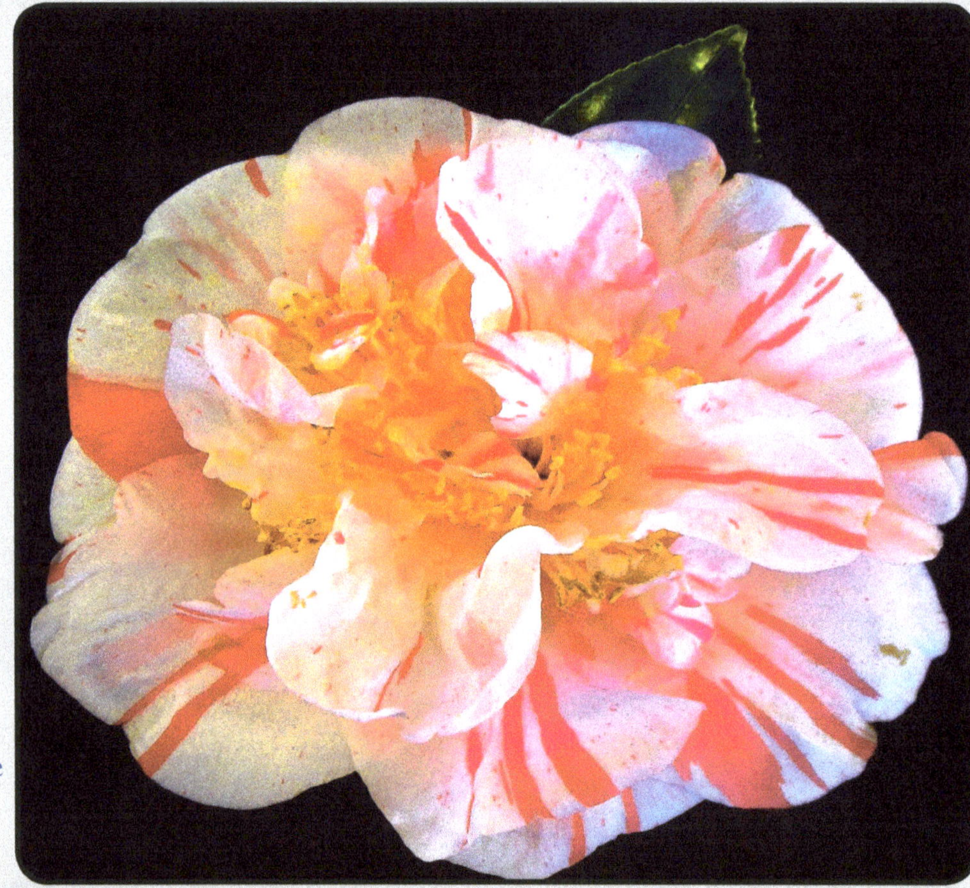

Pinstripe petals.

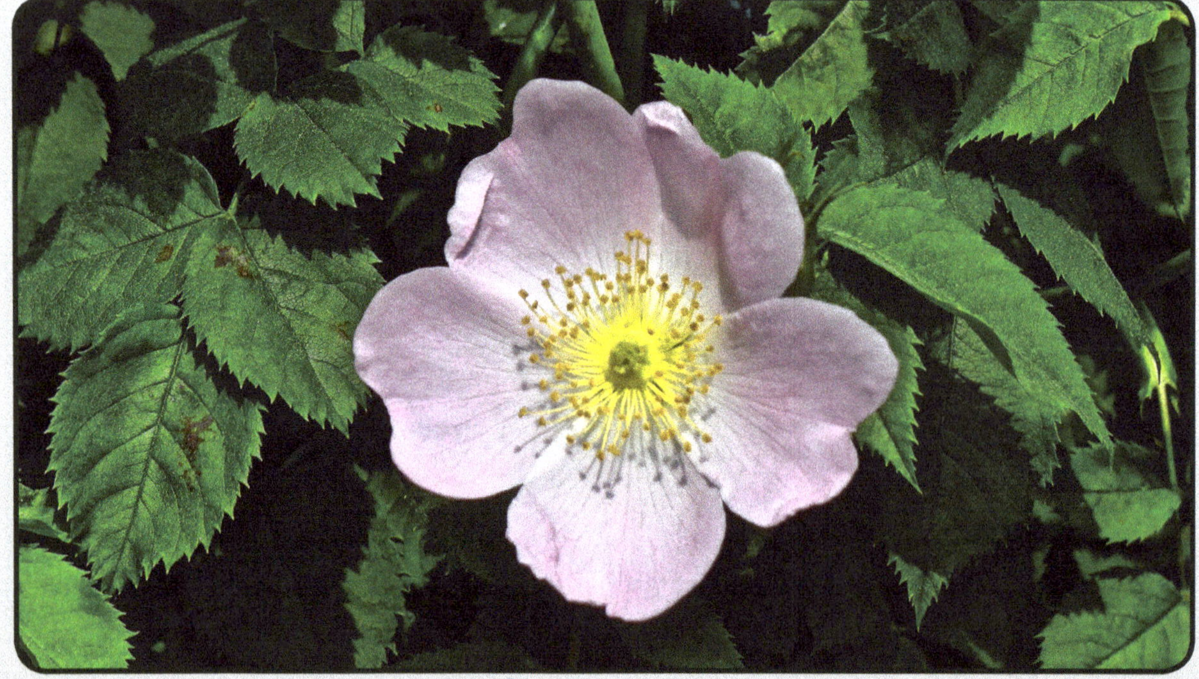

Amber brooch.

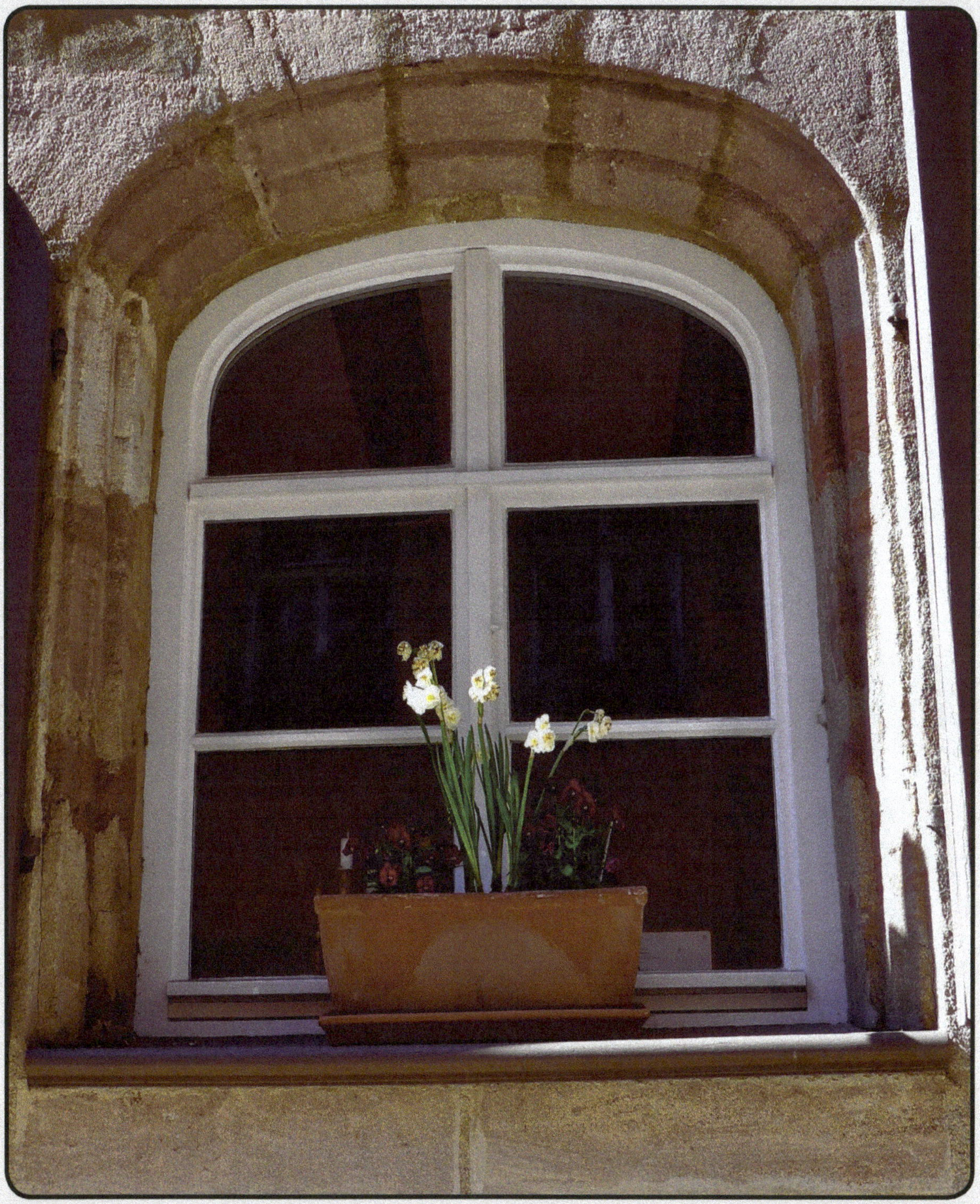

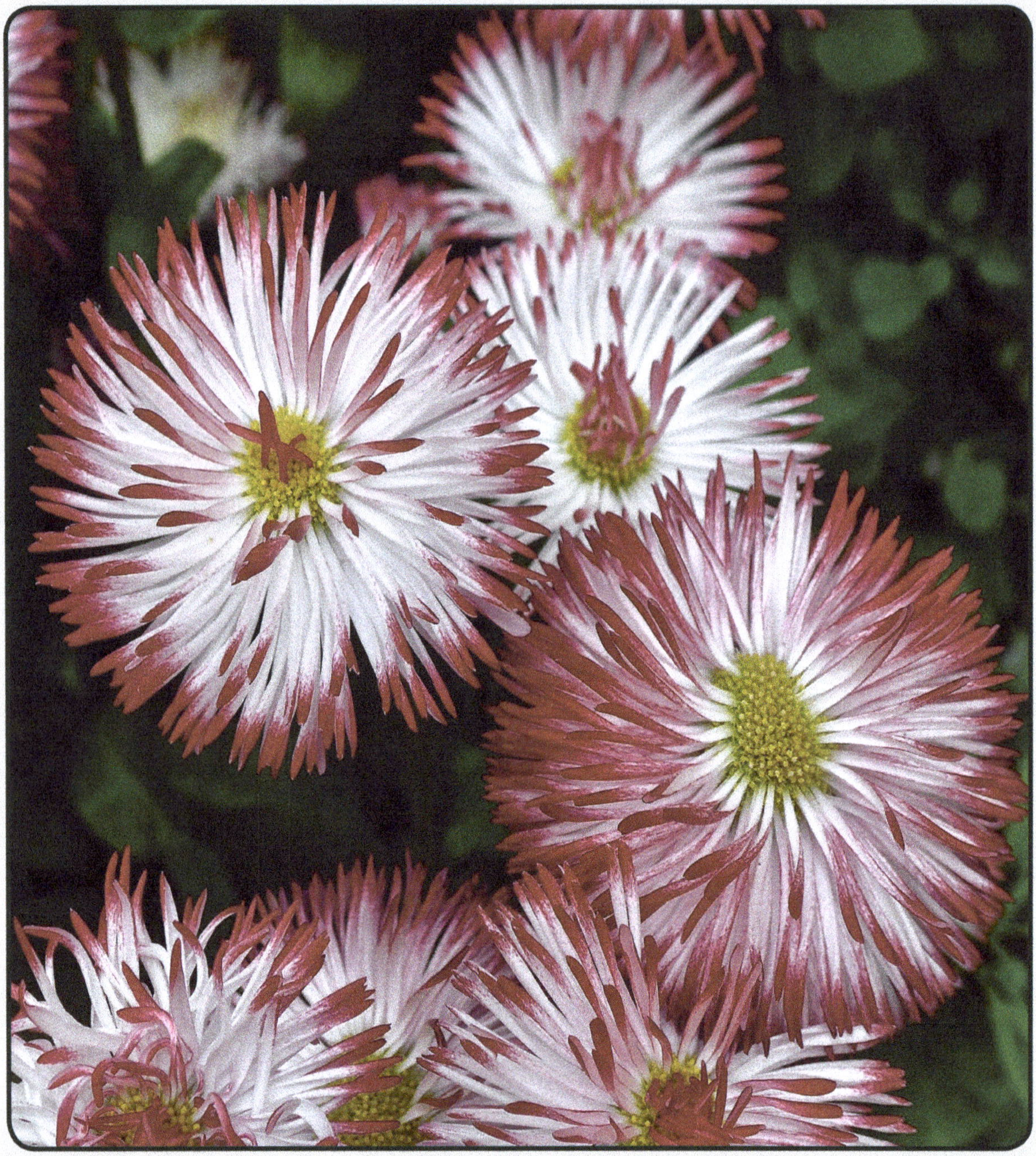

✻ Fireworks.

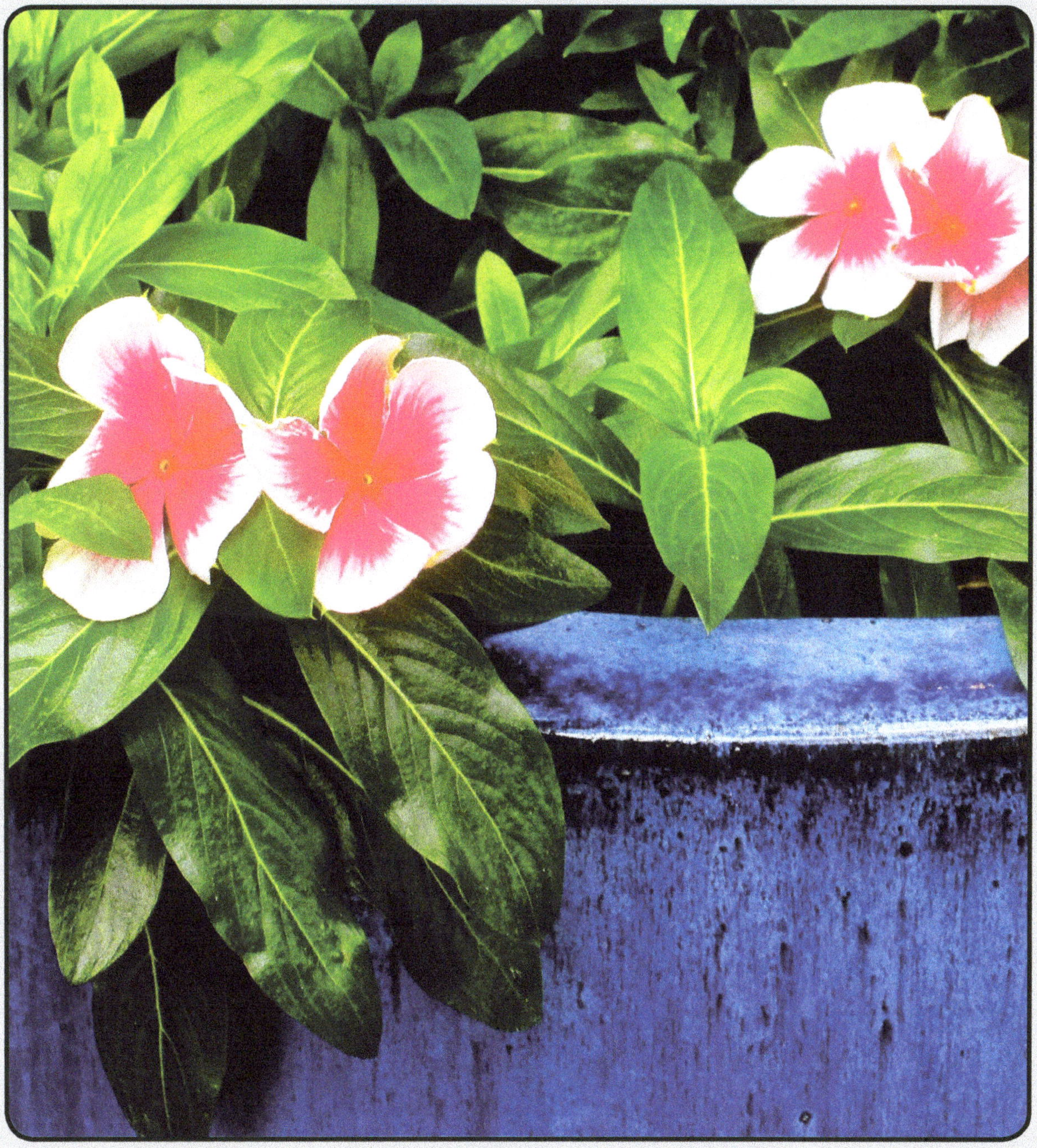

Pot of blooms.

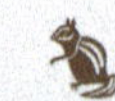

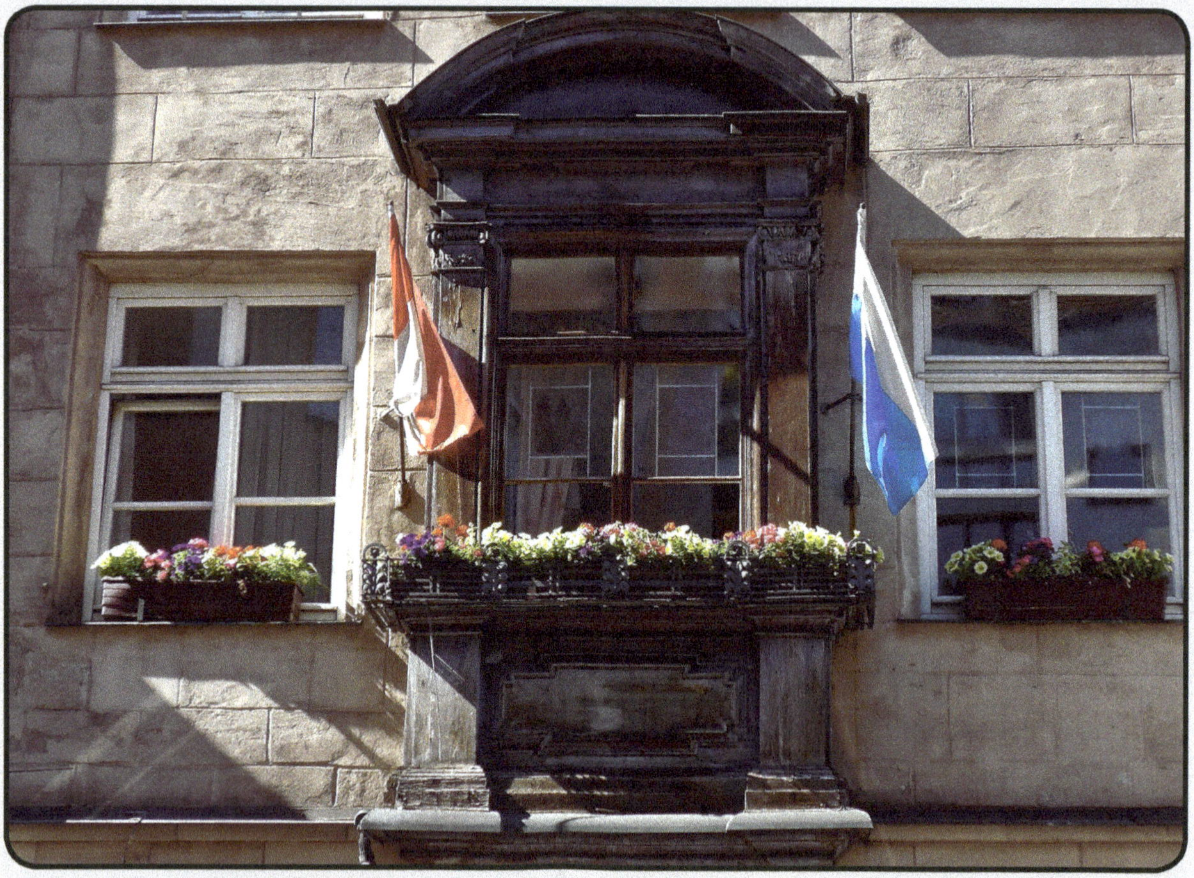

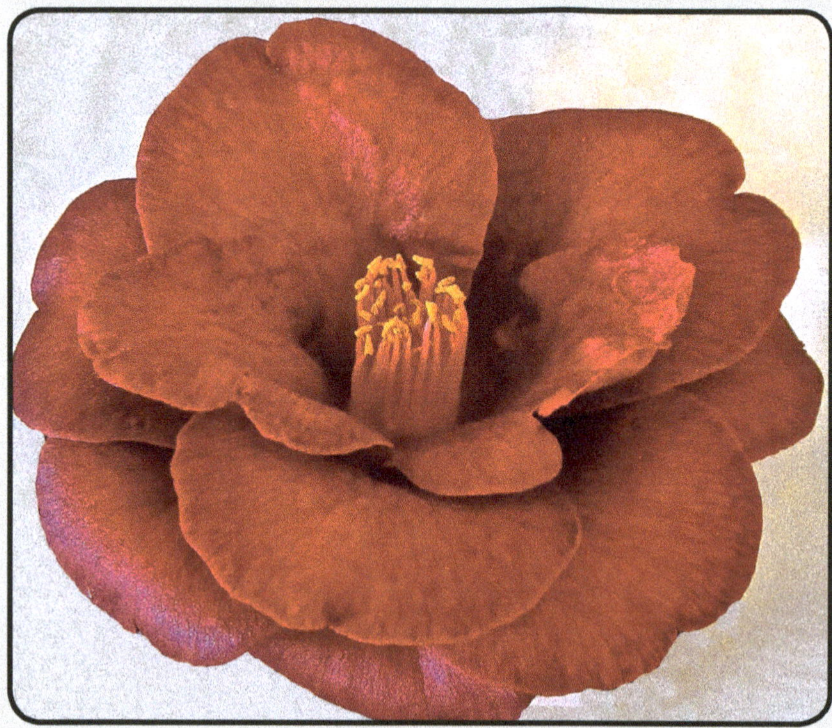

Ruby.

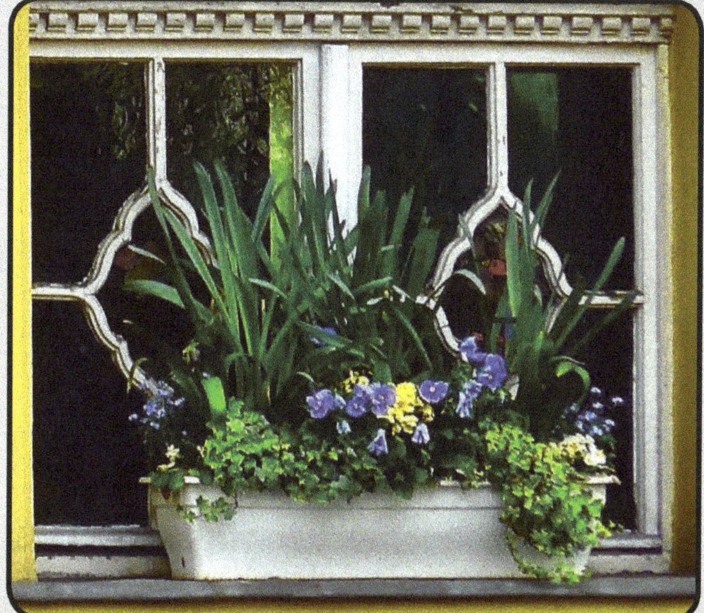

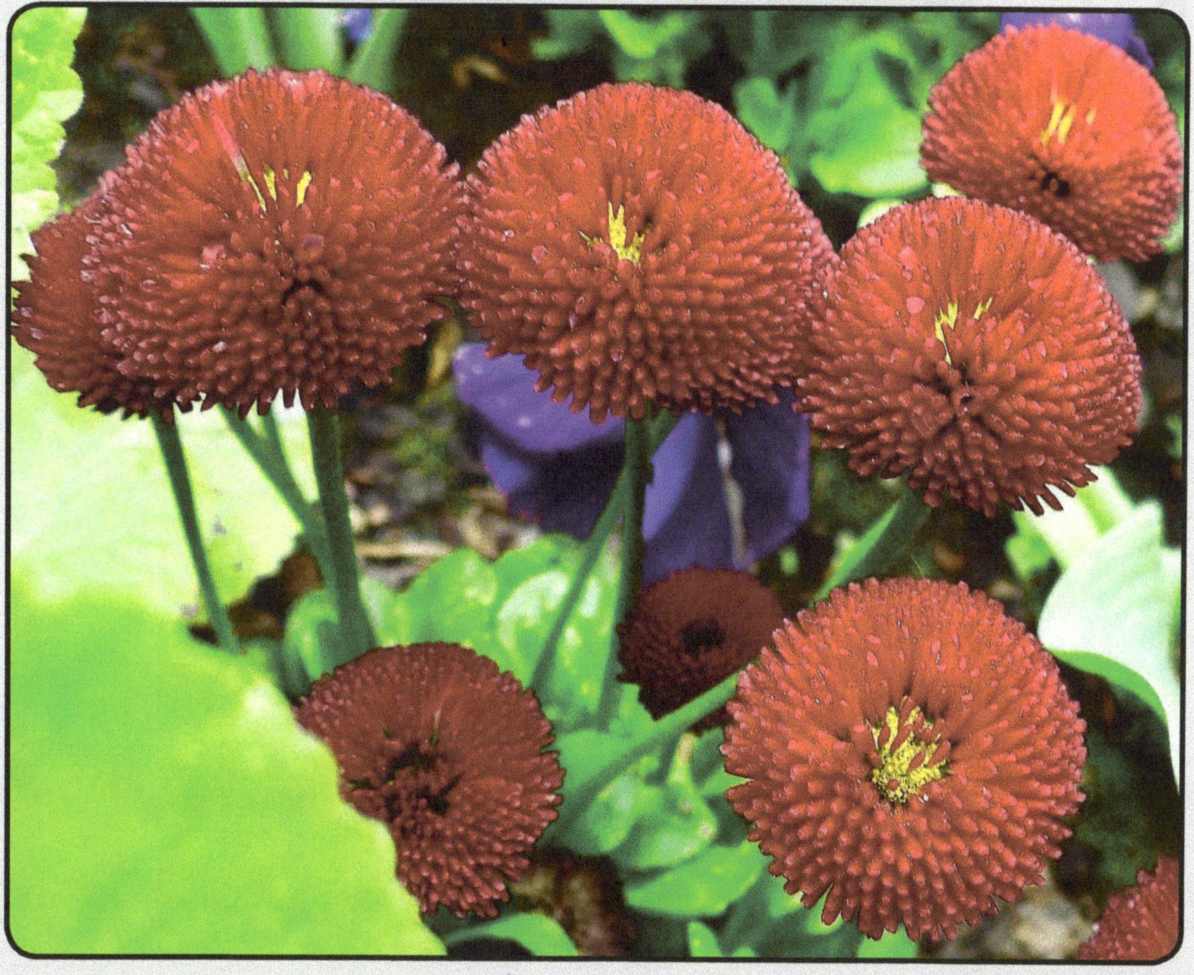

❀ Candy apples.

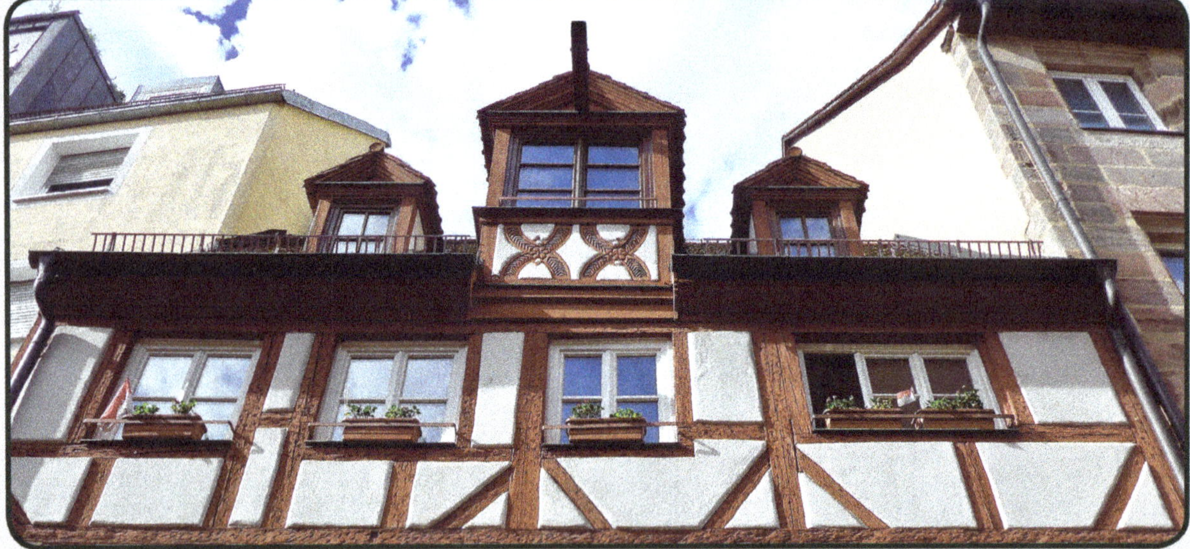

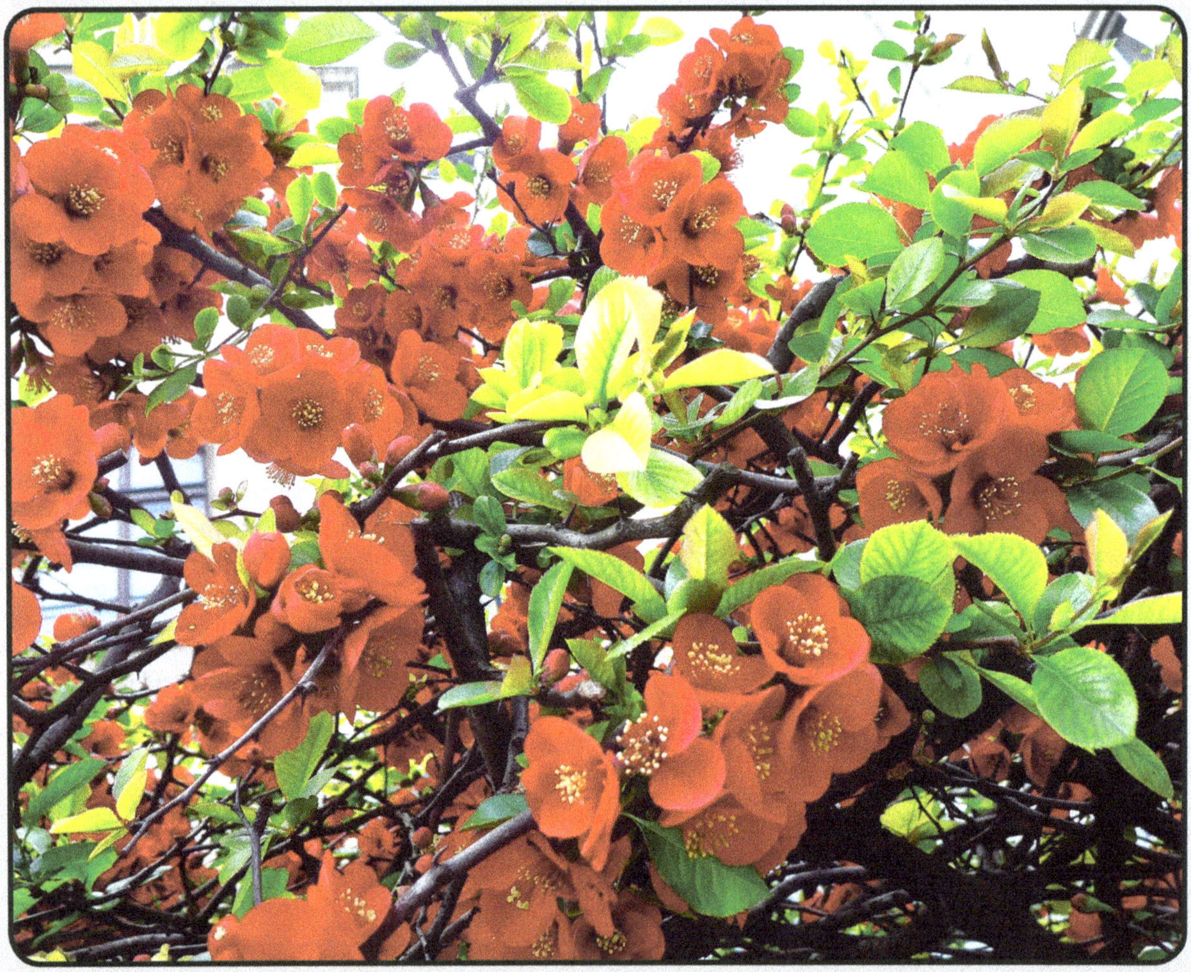

Chinese lanterns.

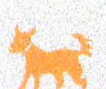

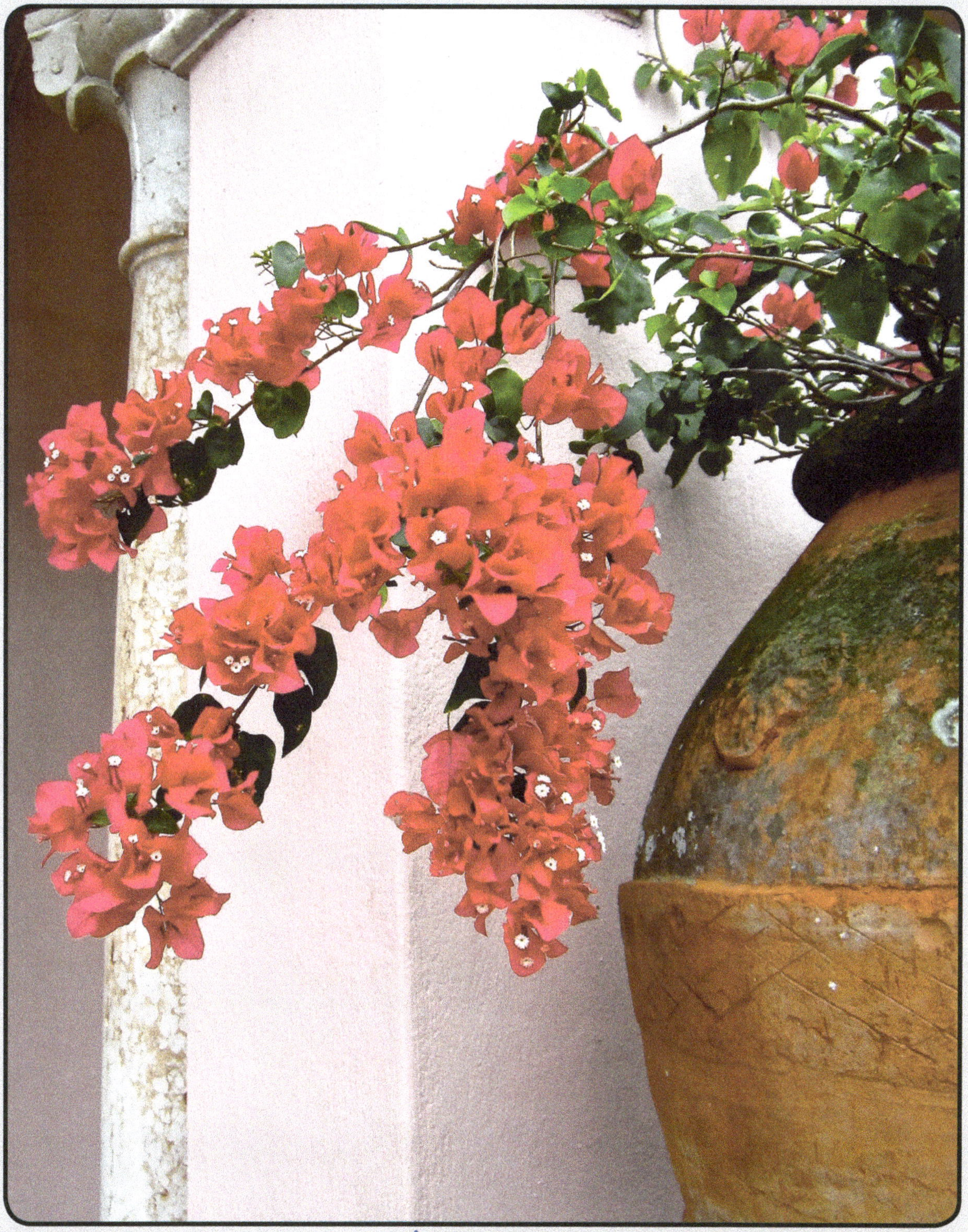

✱ Villa beauties.

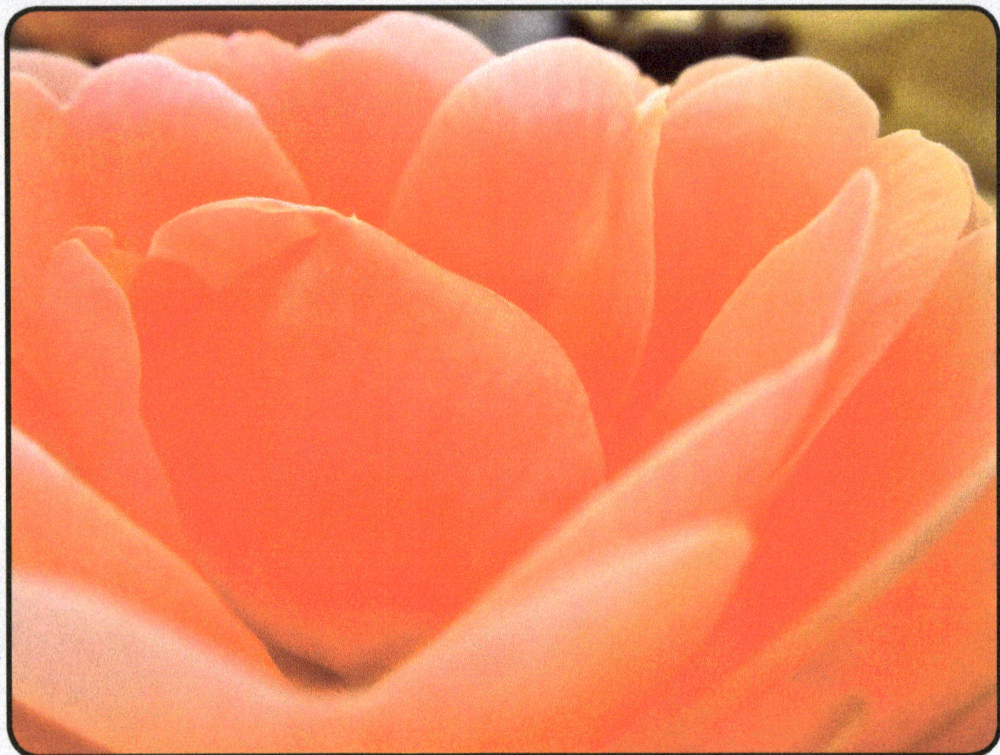

Coral corona.

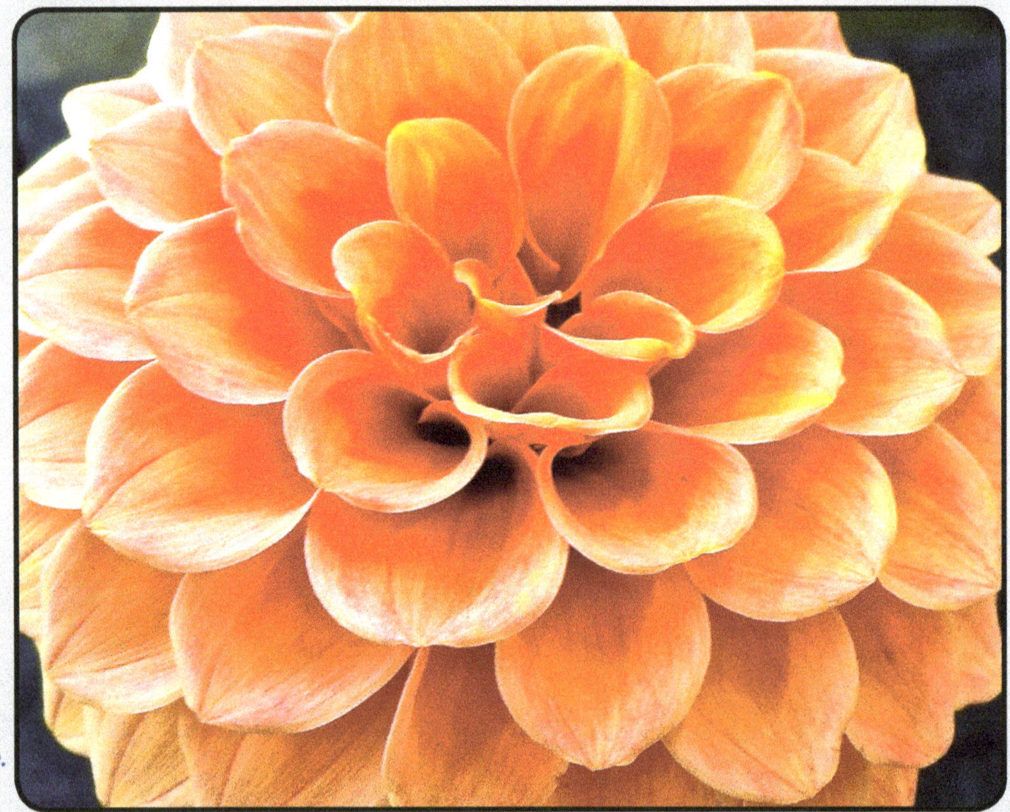

Honeycomb.

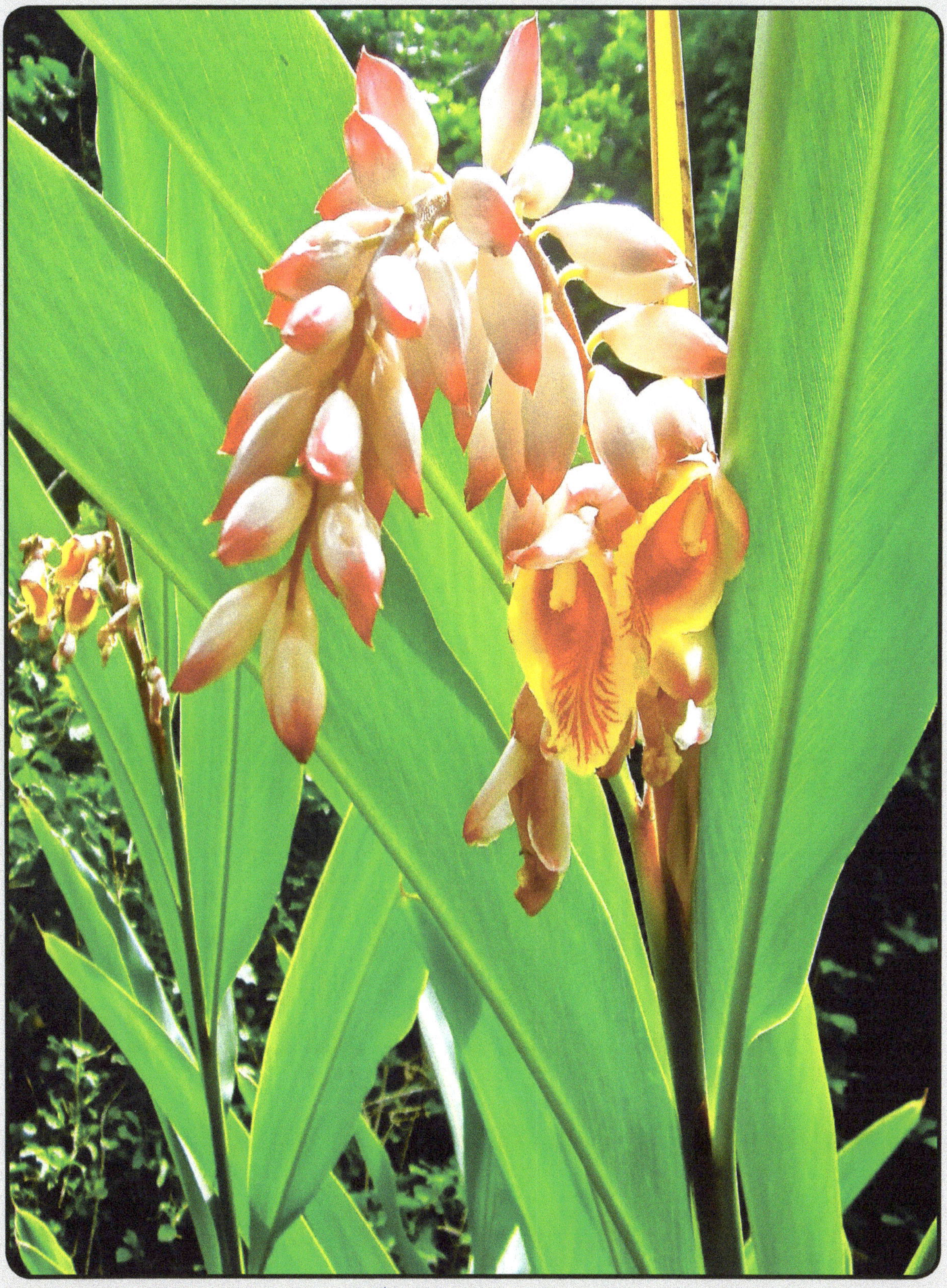

Tropical grandeur.

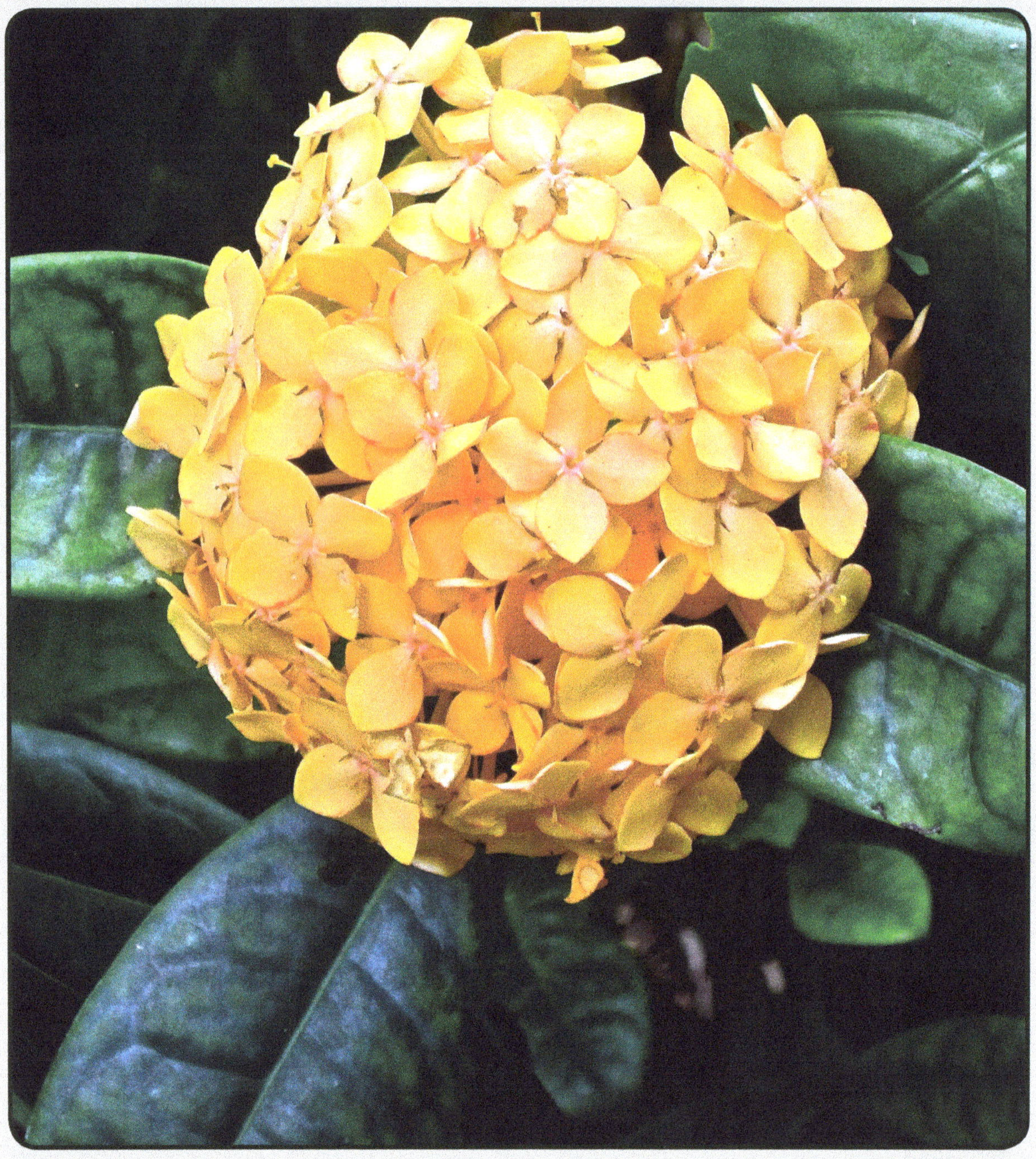

Petal prism.

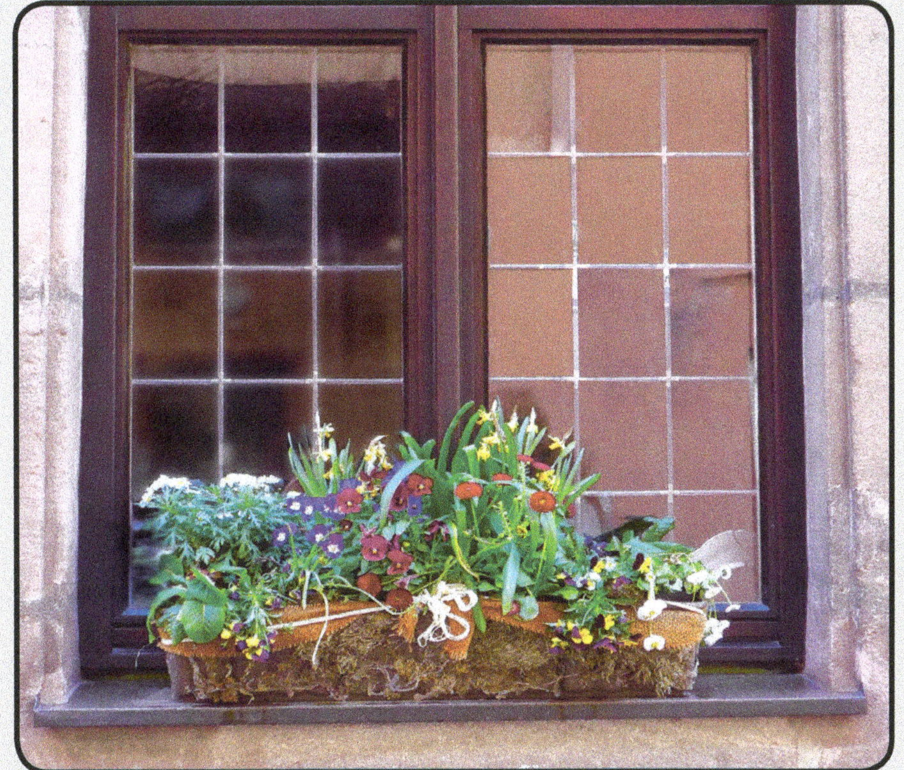

❀ Tangerine.

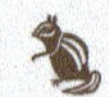

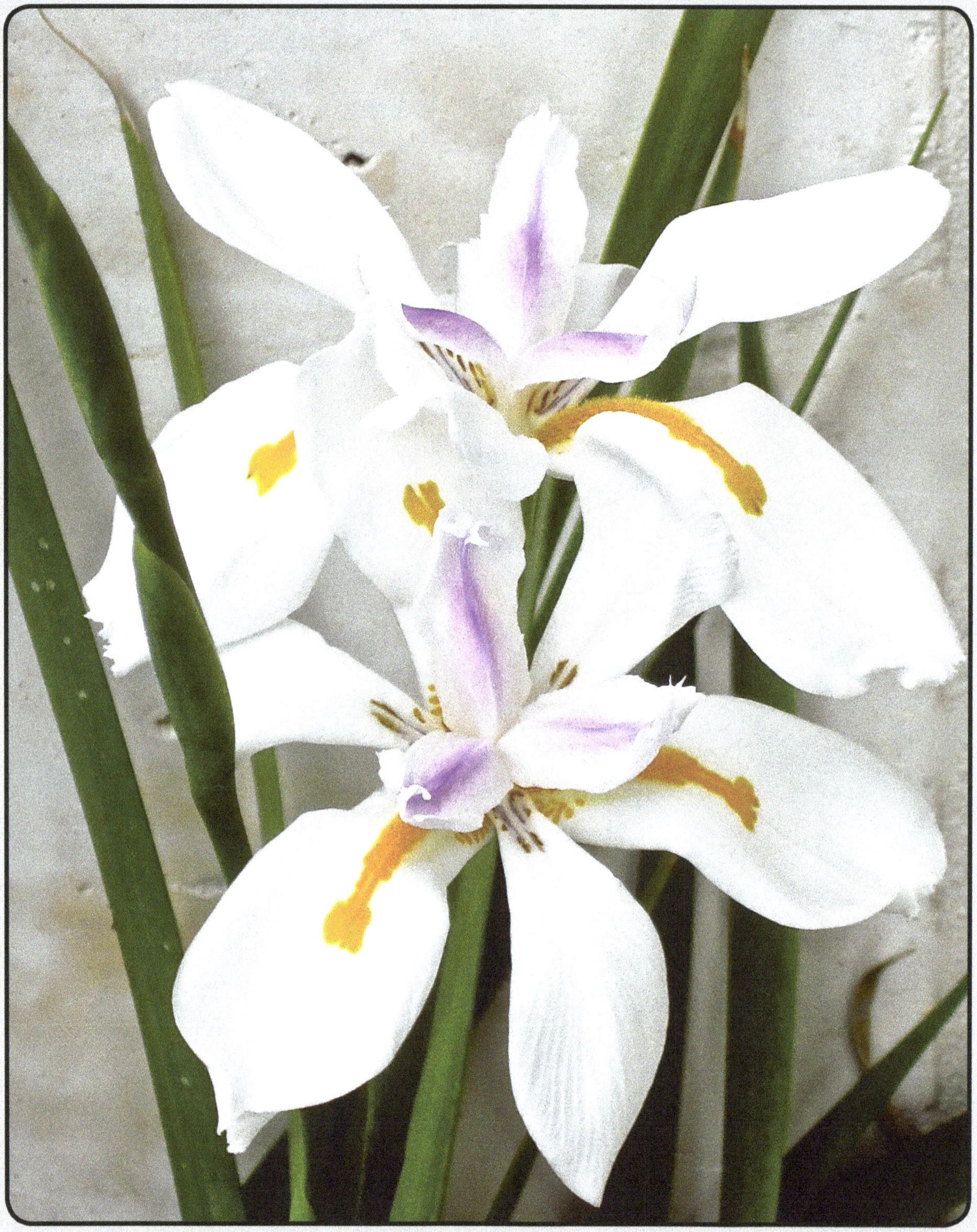

Garden starfish.

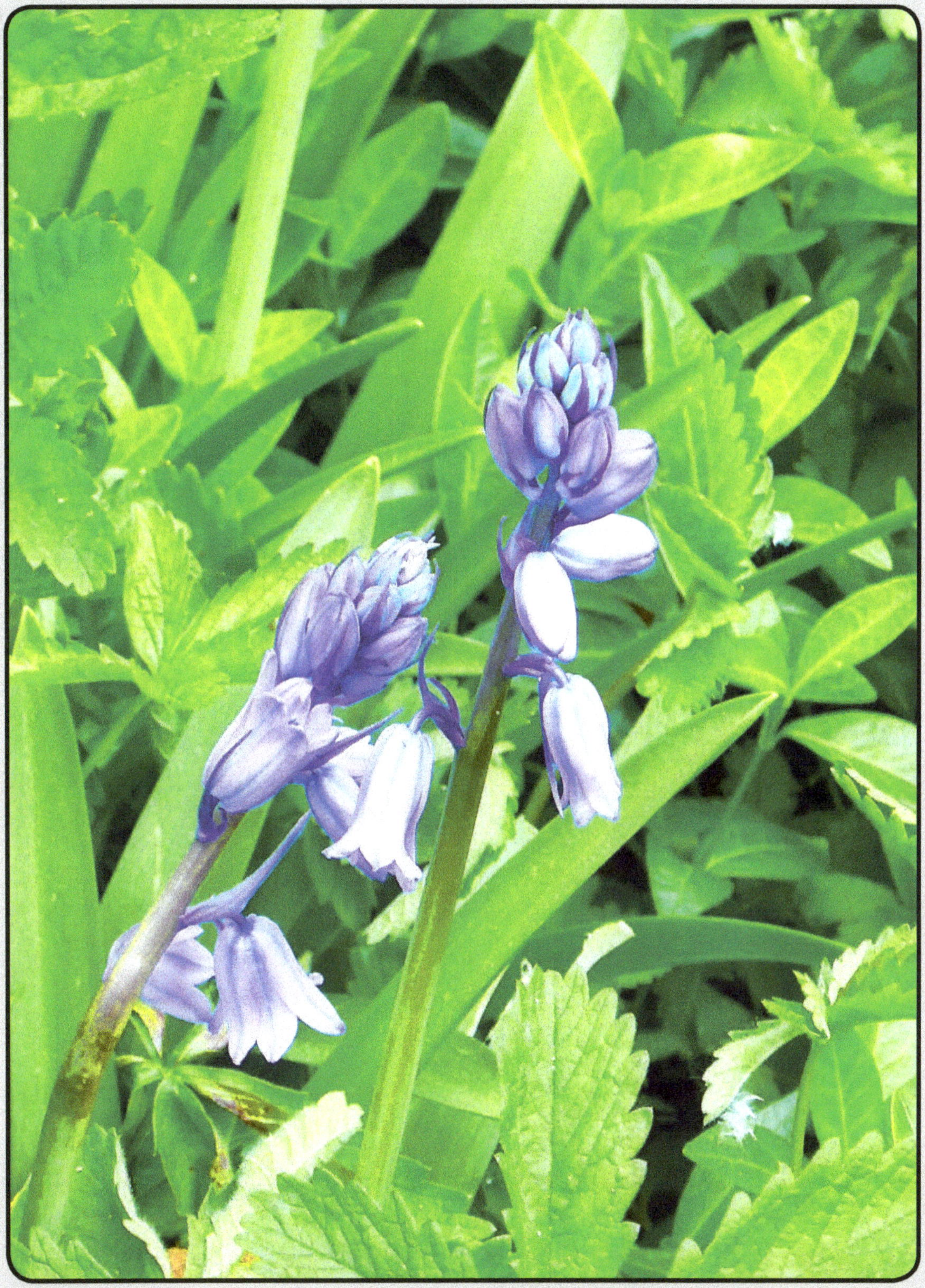

Thumbelina land.

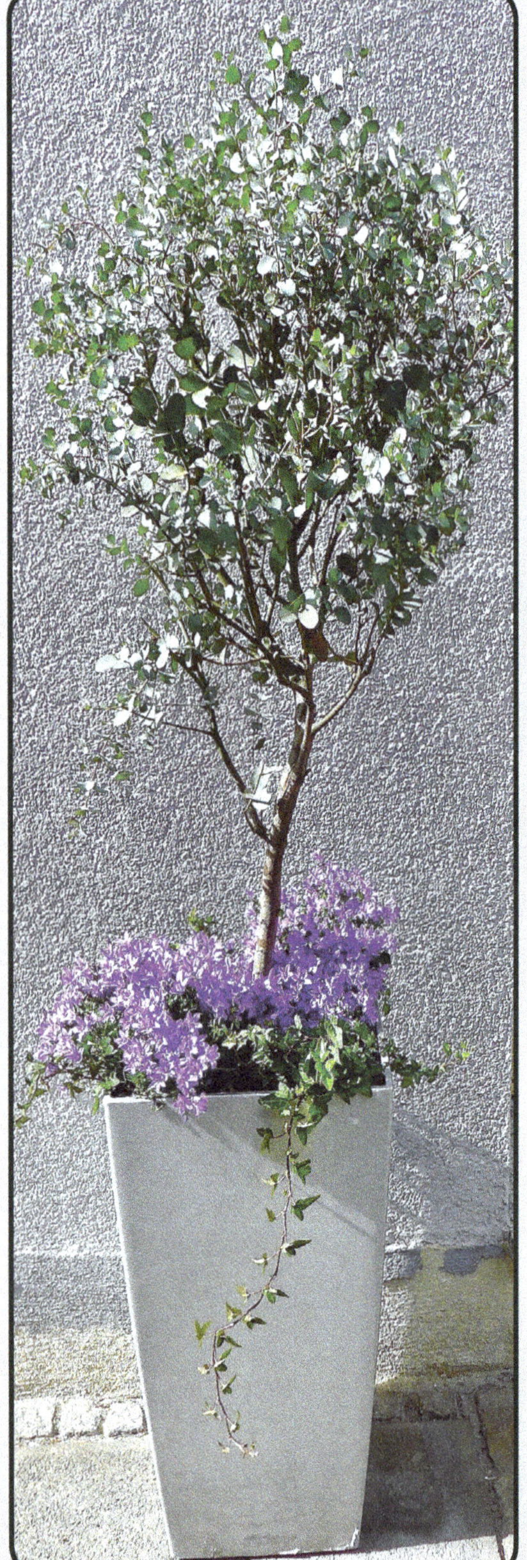

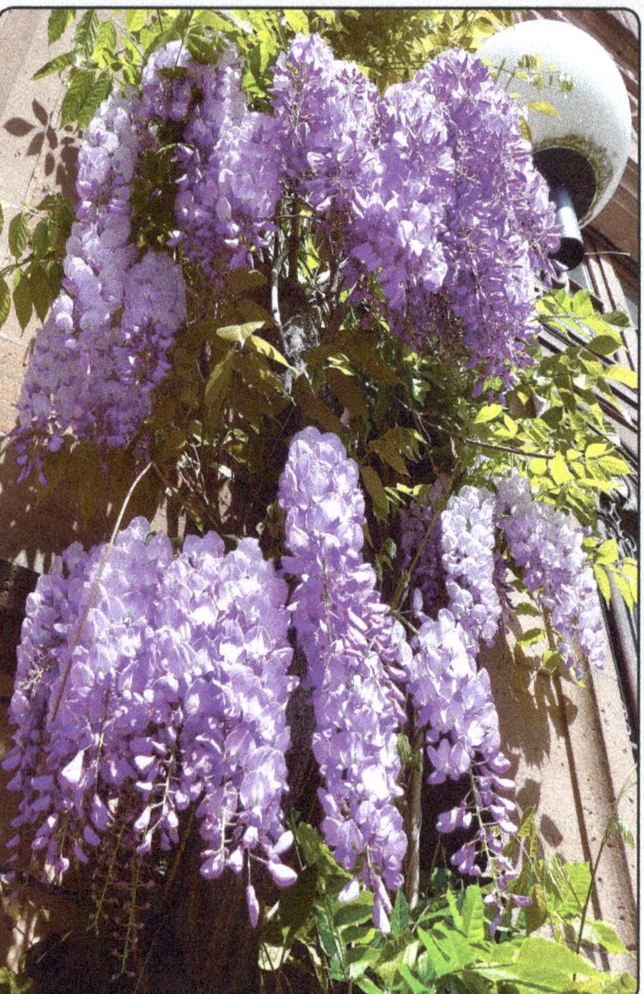

Sidewalk grapes.

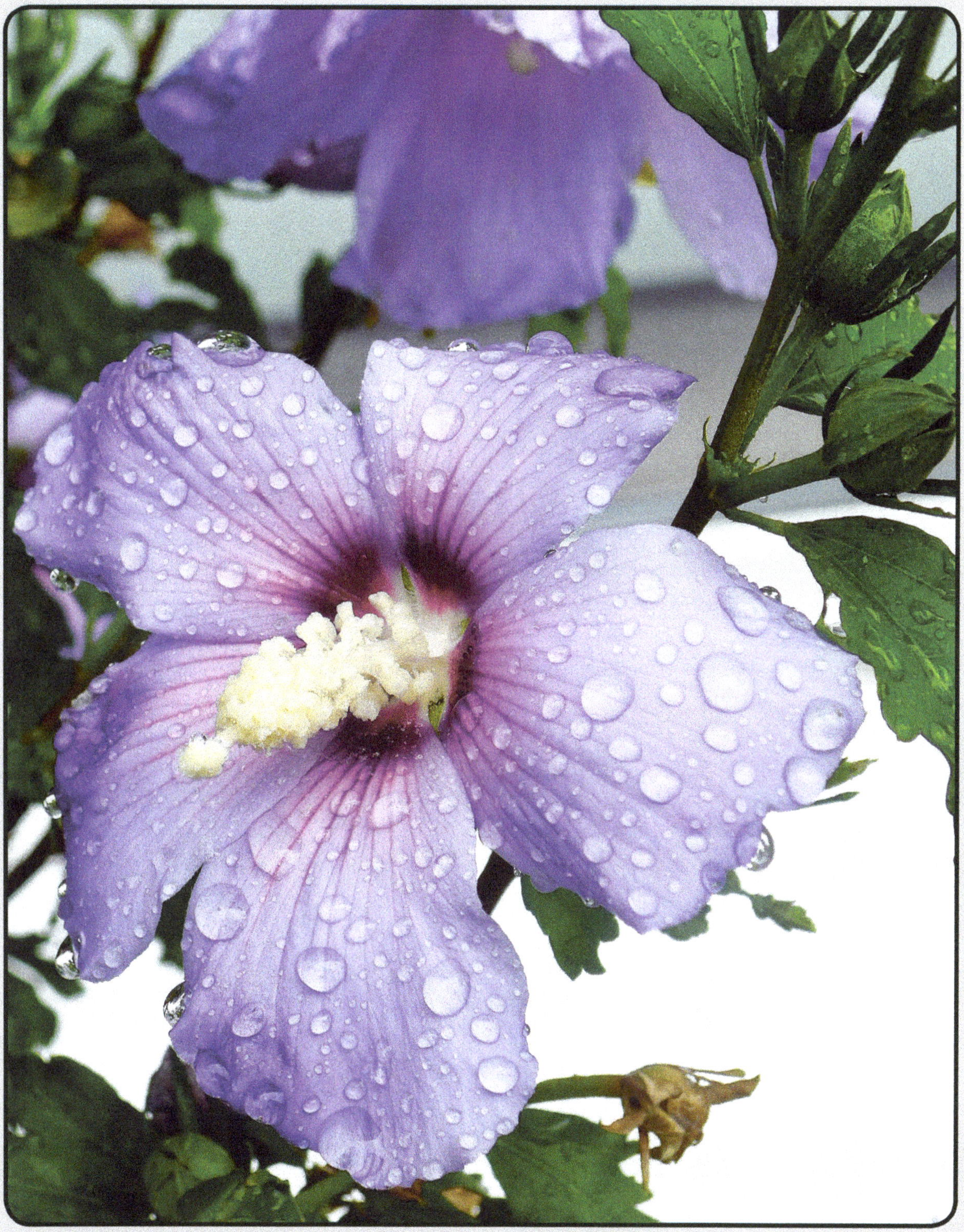

Lavender diamanté.

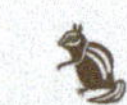

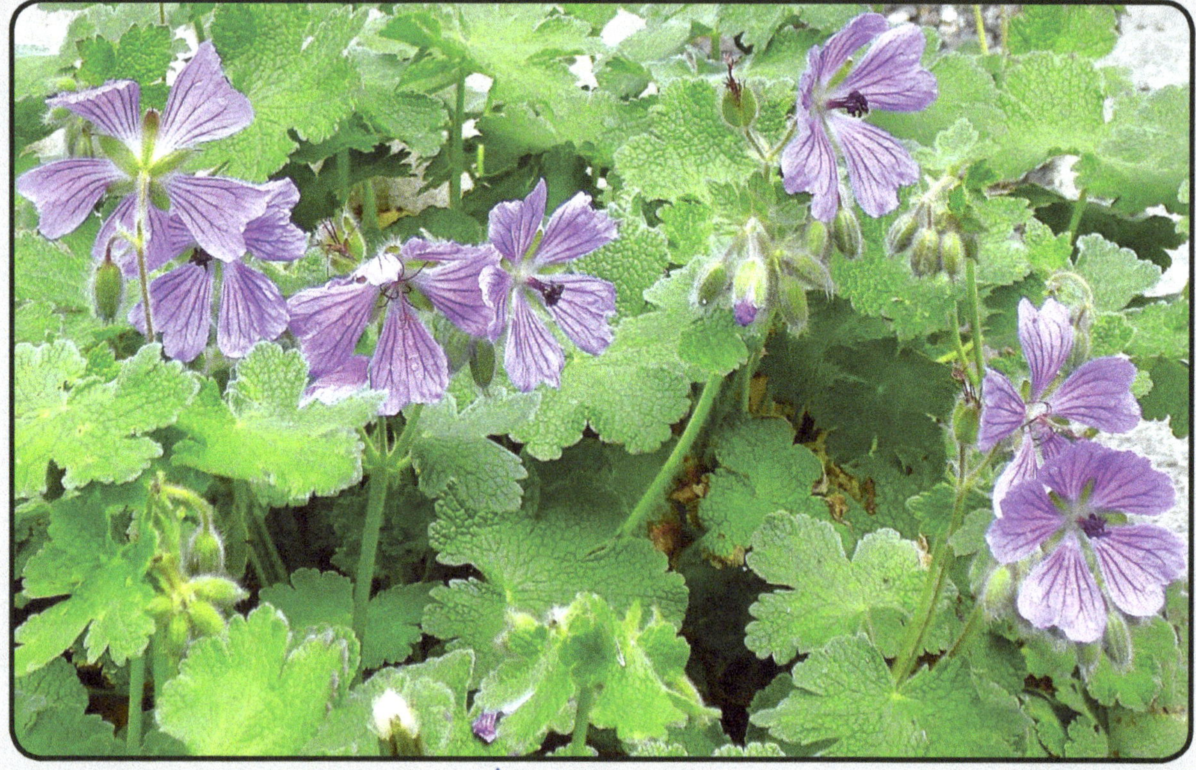

Lavender hearts.

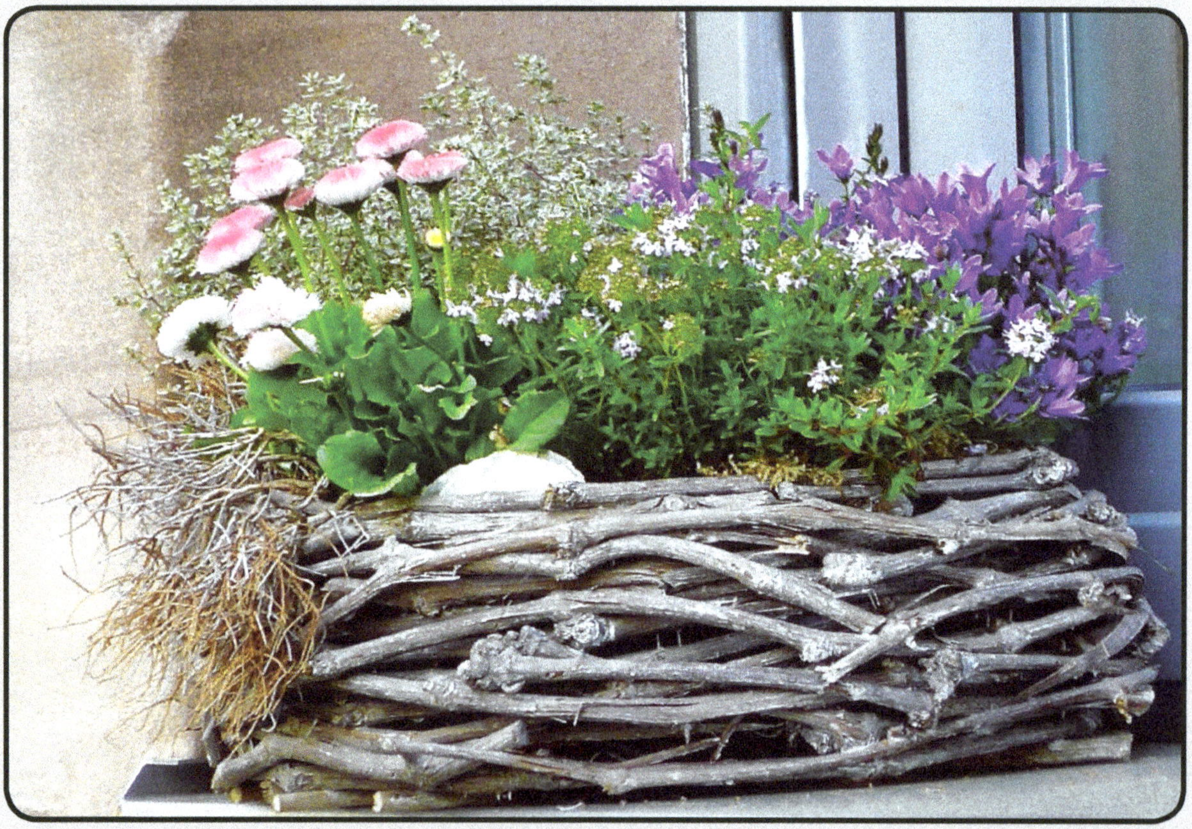

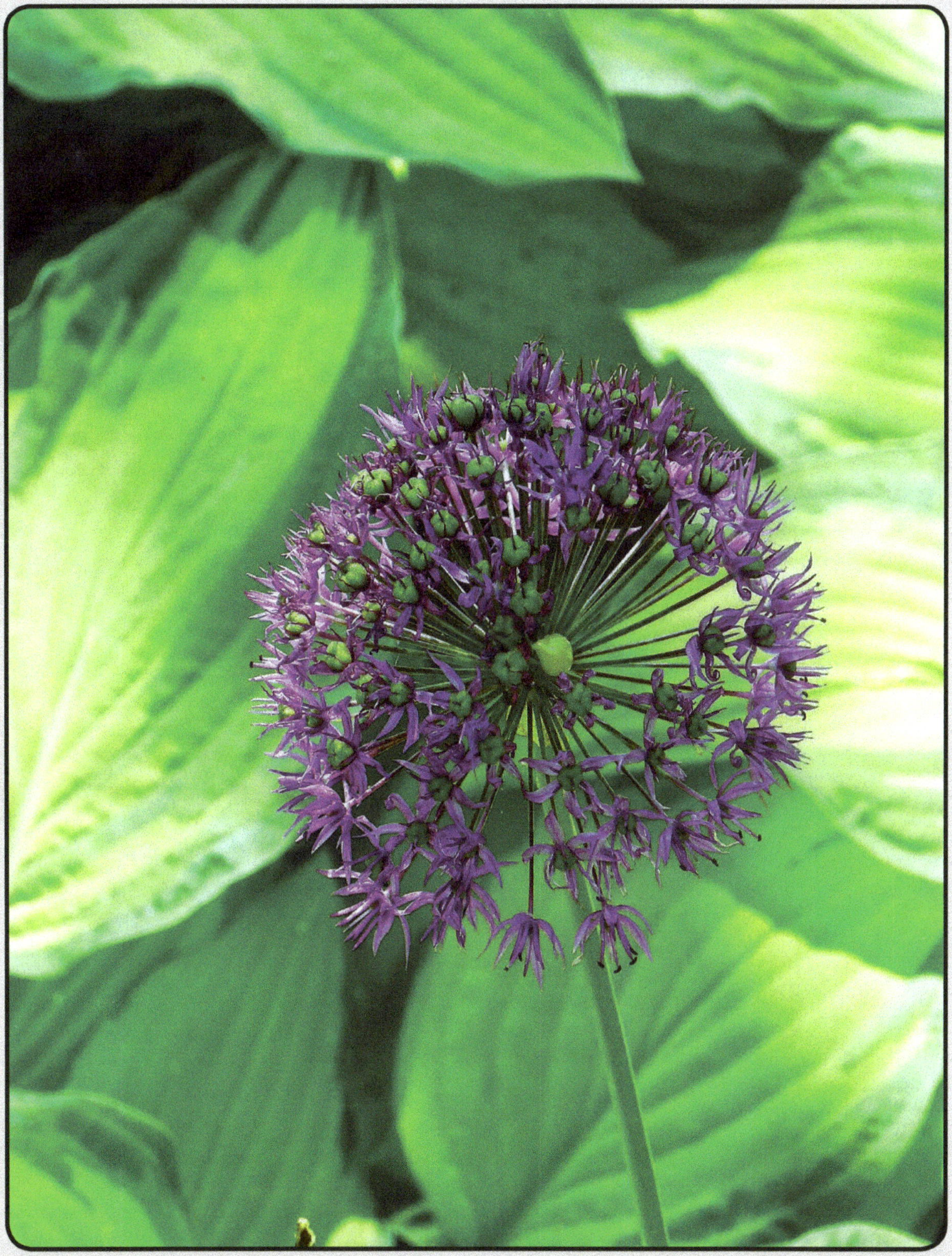

Forest wand.

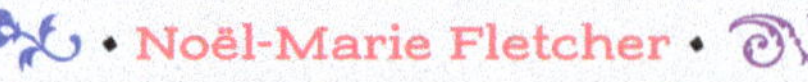

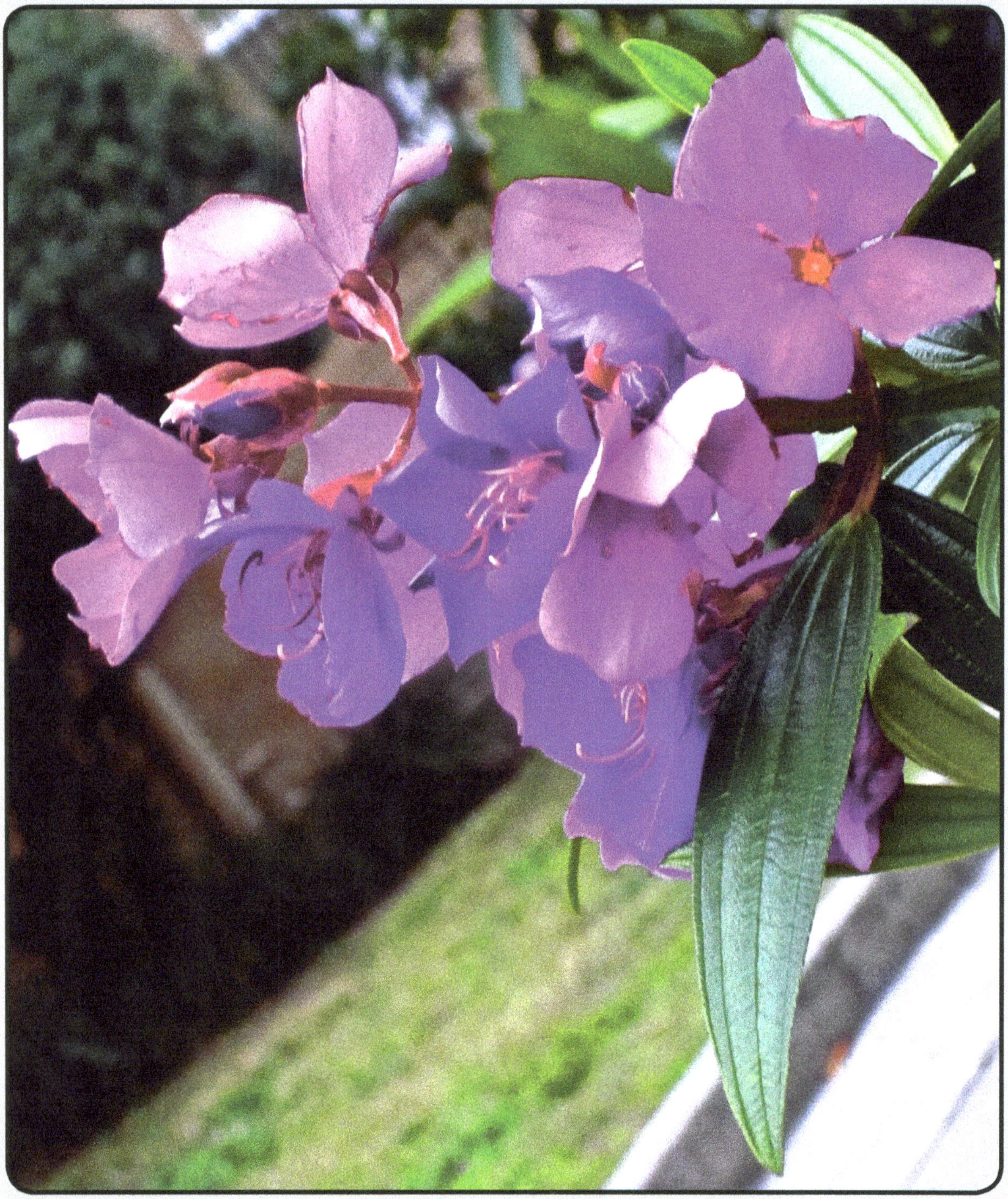

Indigo hues in origami.

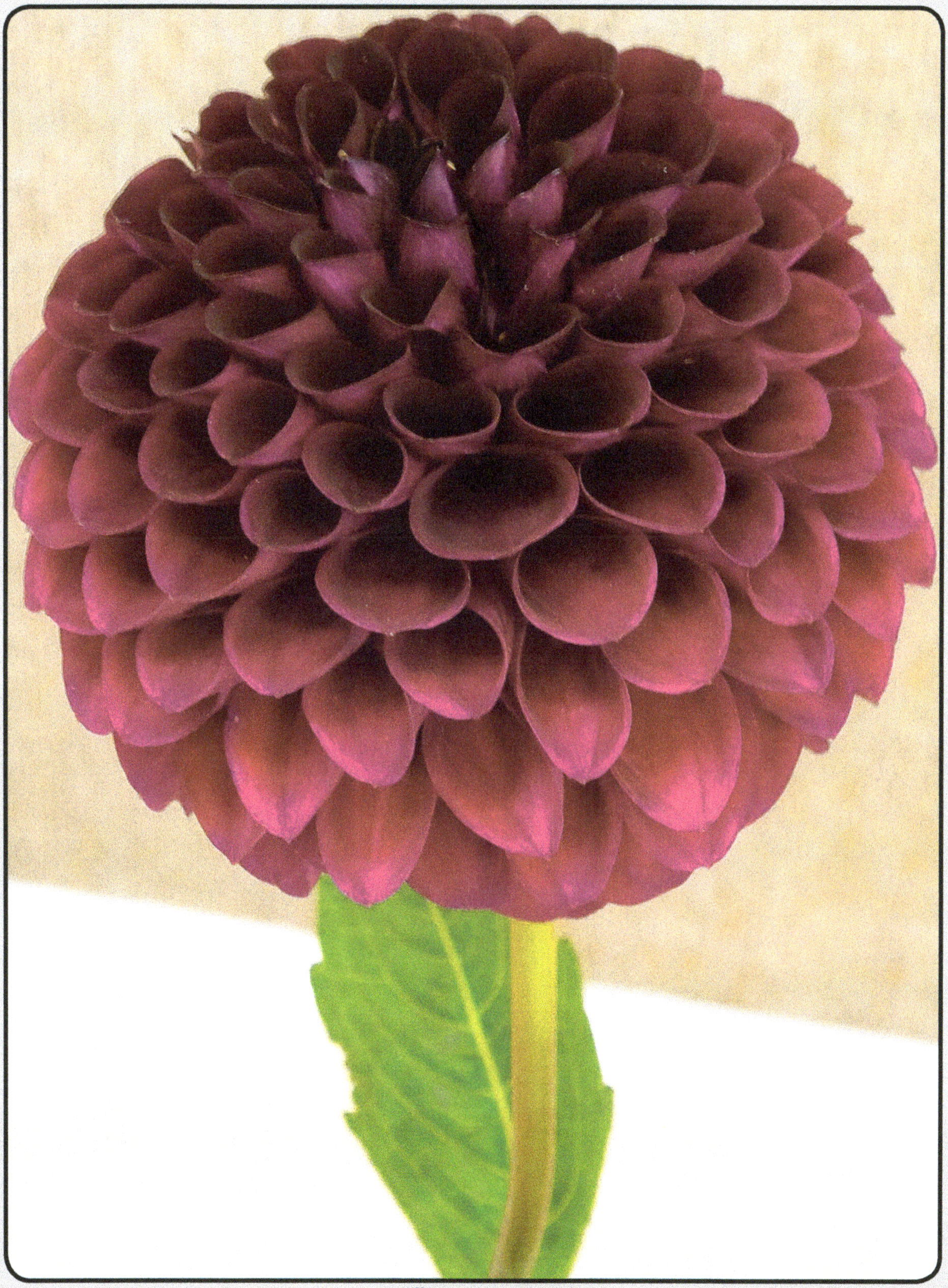

Garnet in a vase.

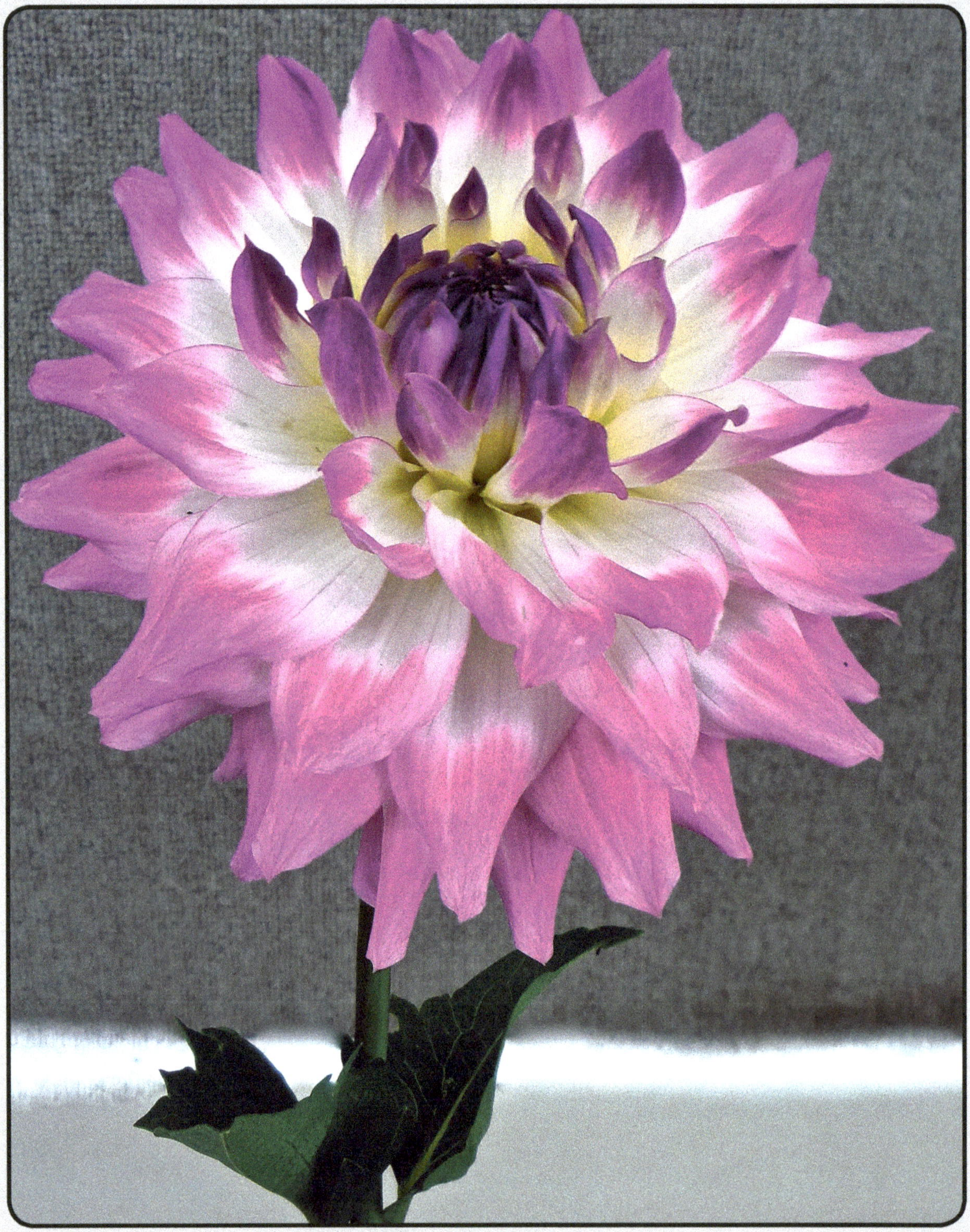

Glorious colors.

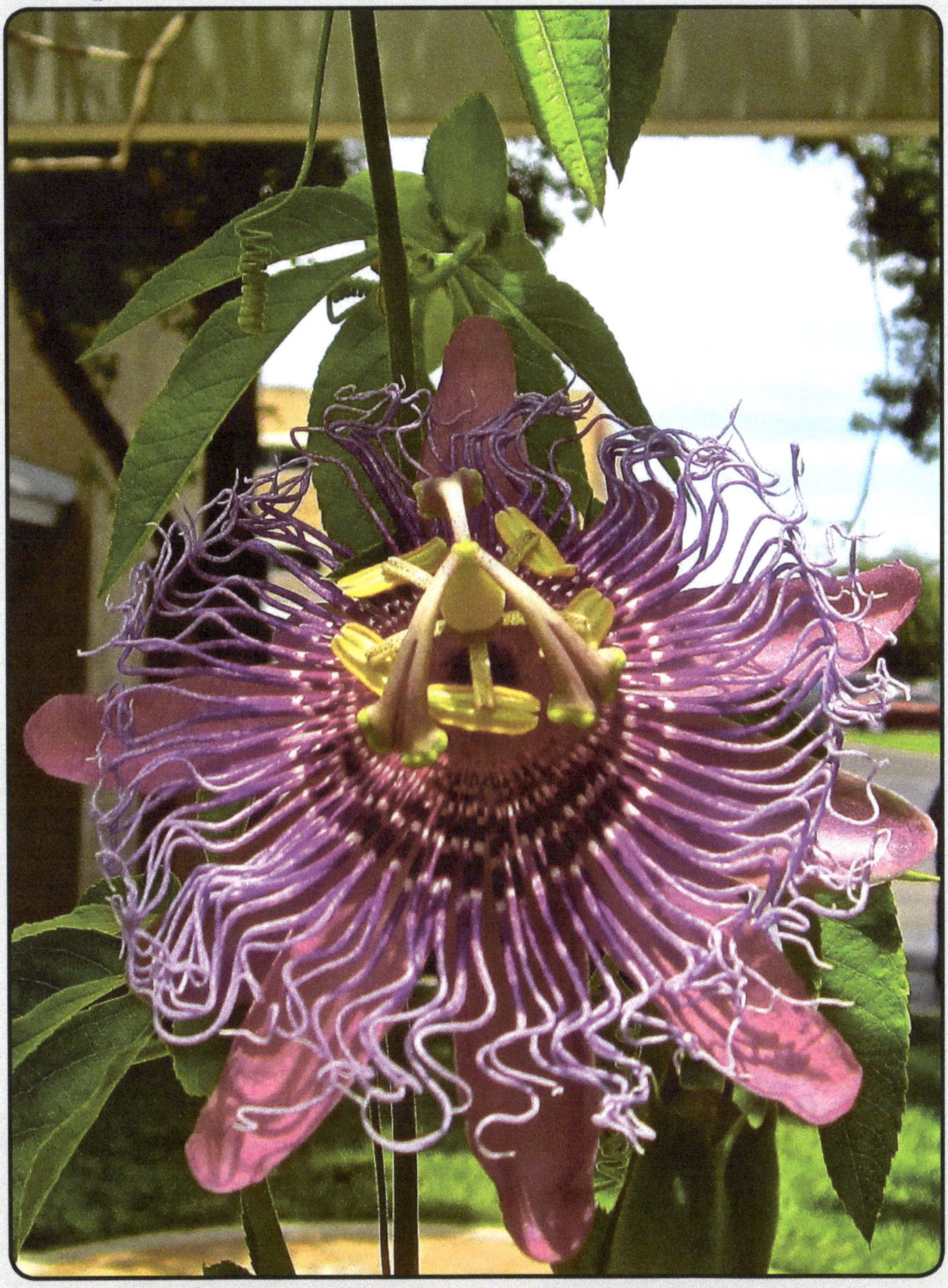

✻ Passion flower drops from a trellis outside a Florida church.

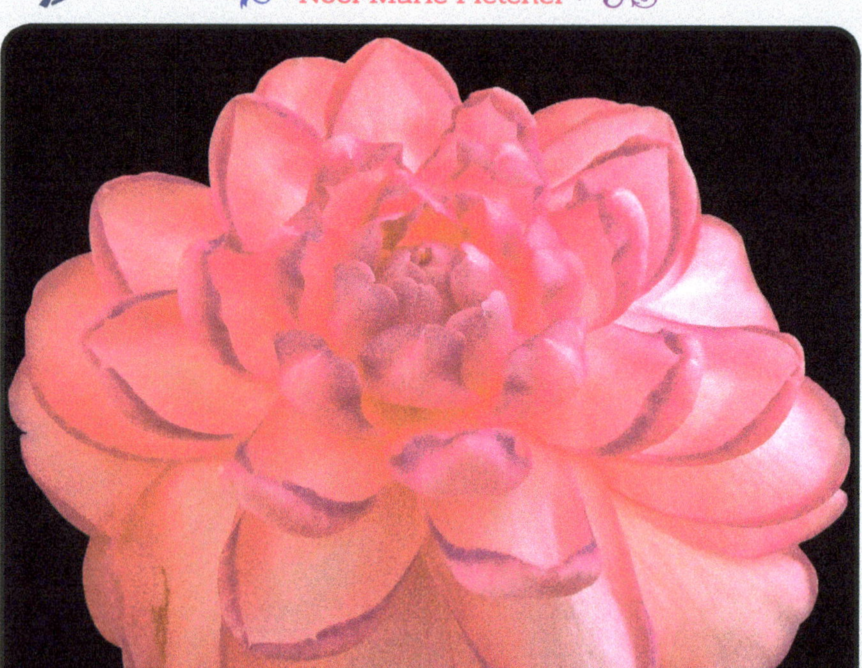

Pretties in pink series.

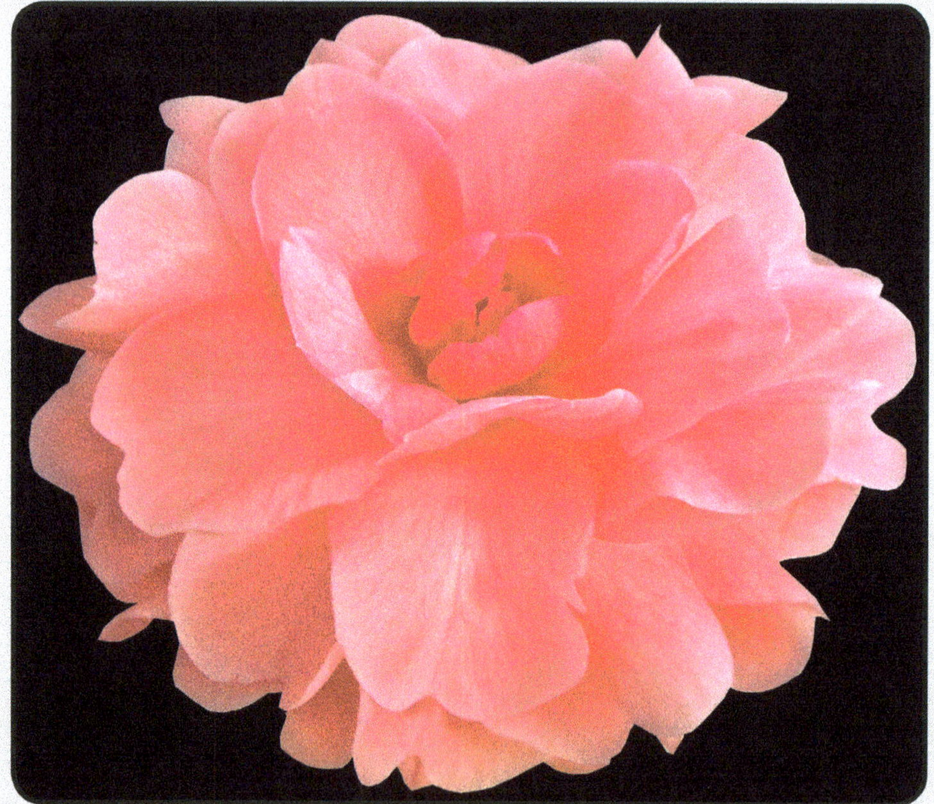

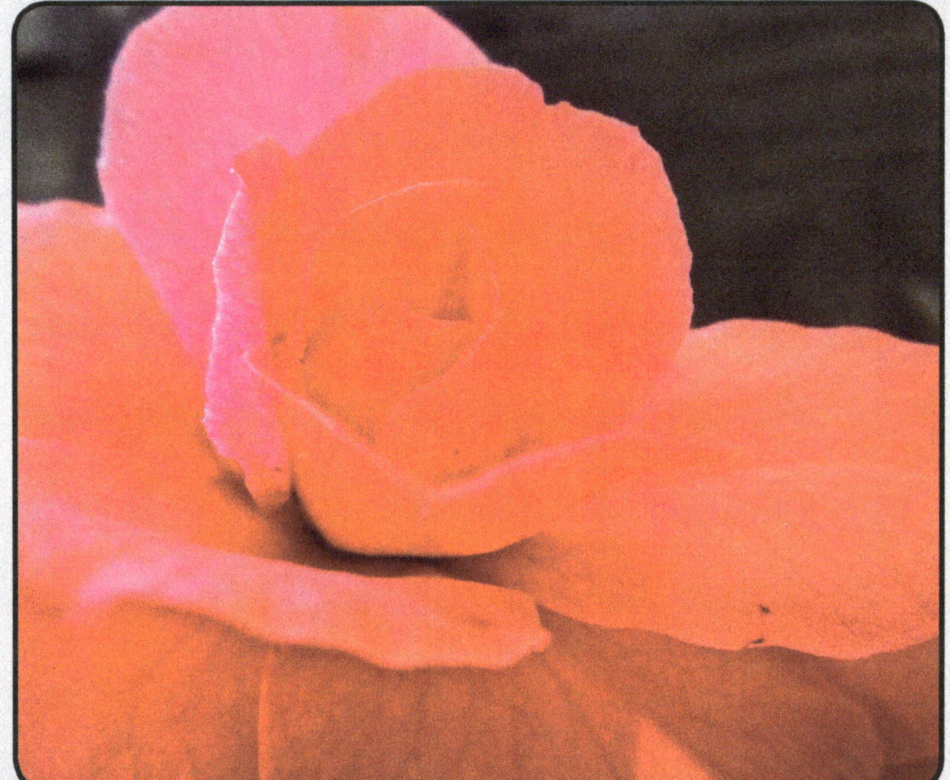

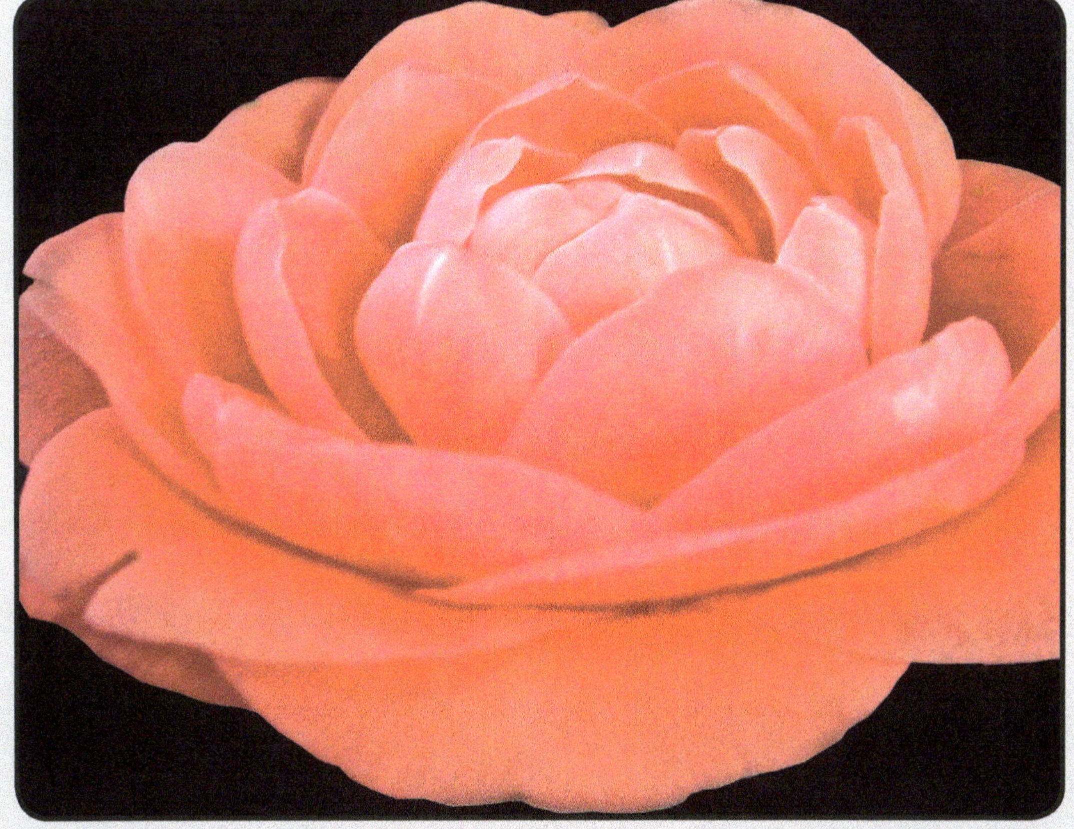

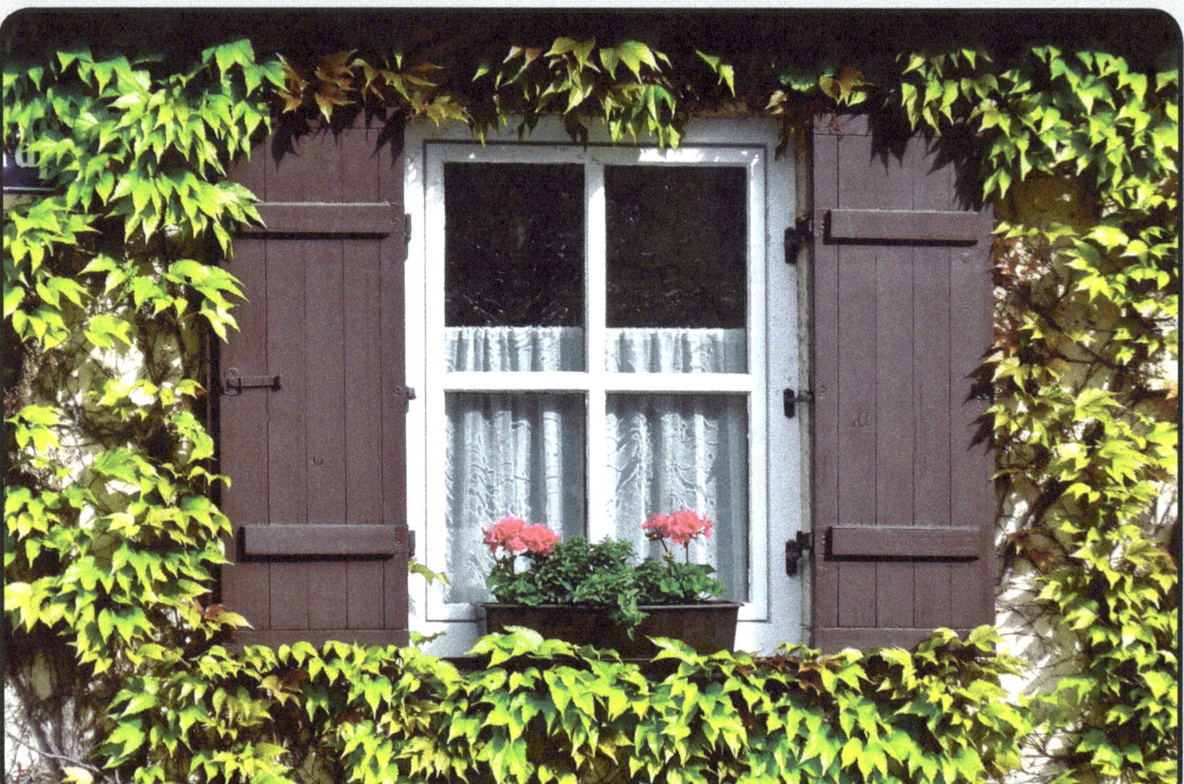

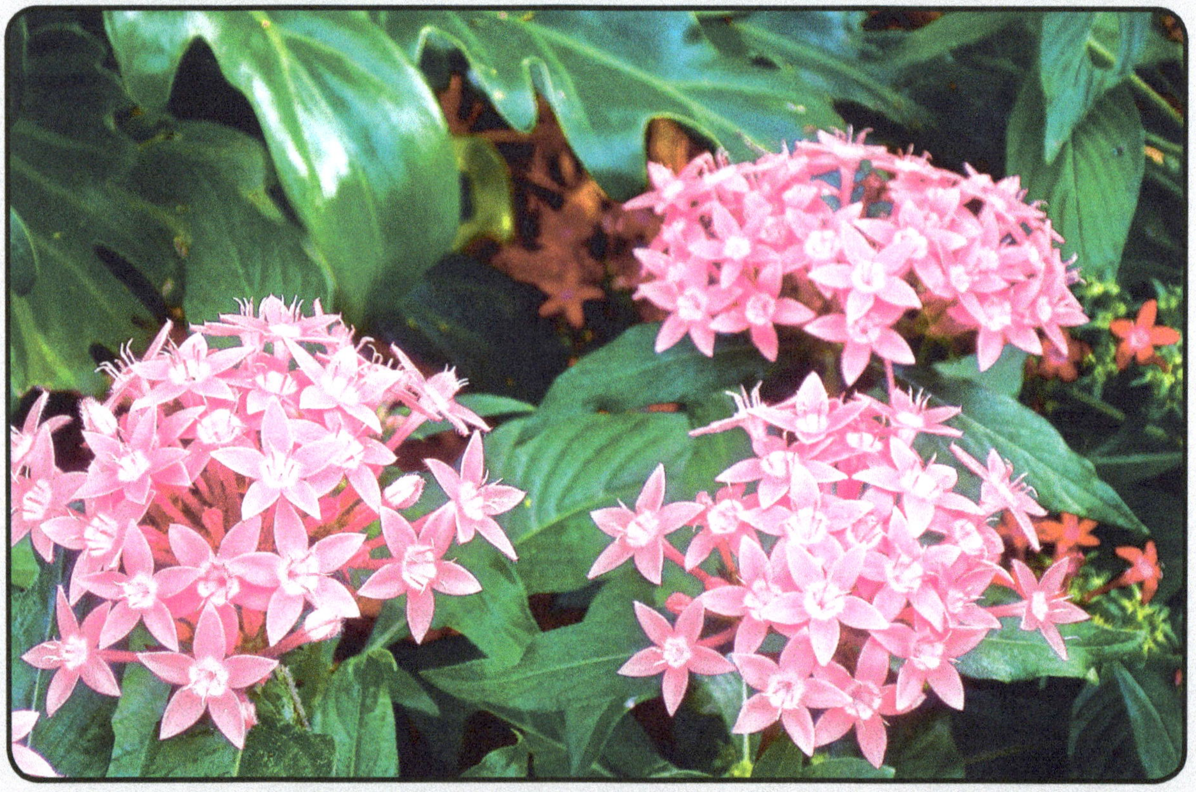

Shouts of joy.

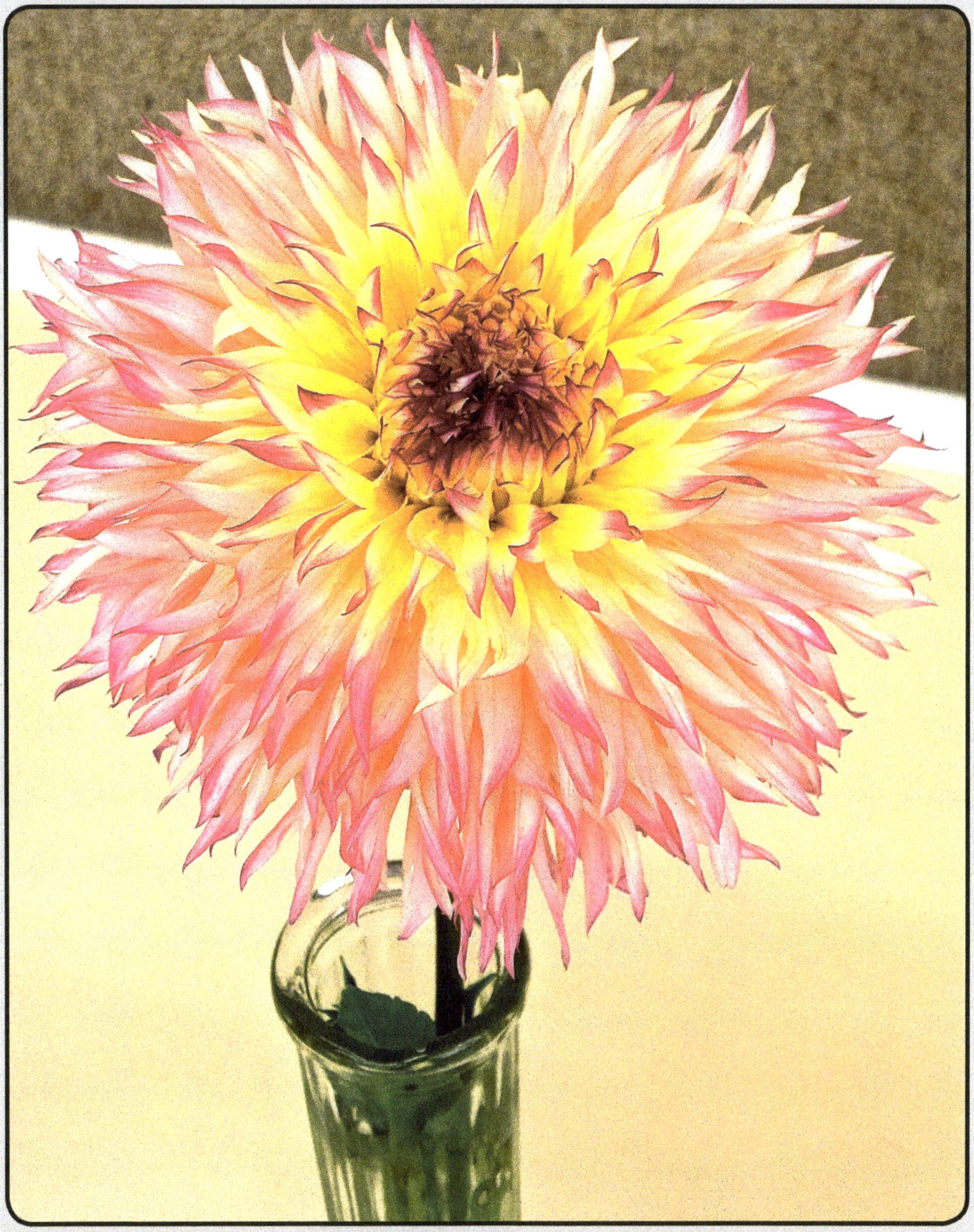

Awakening.

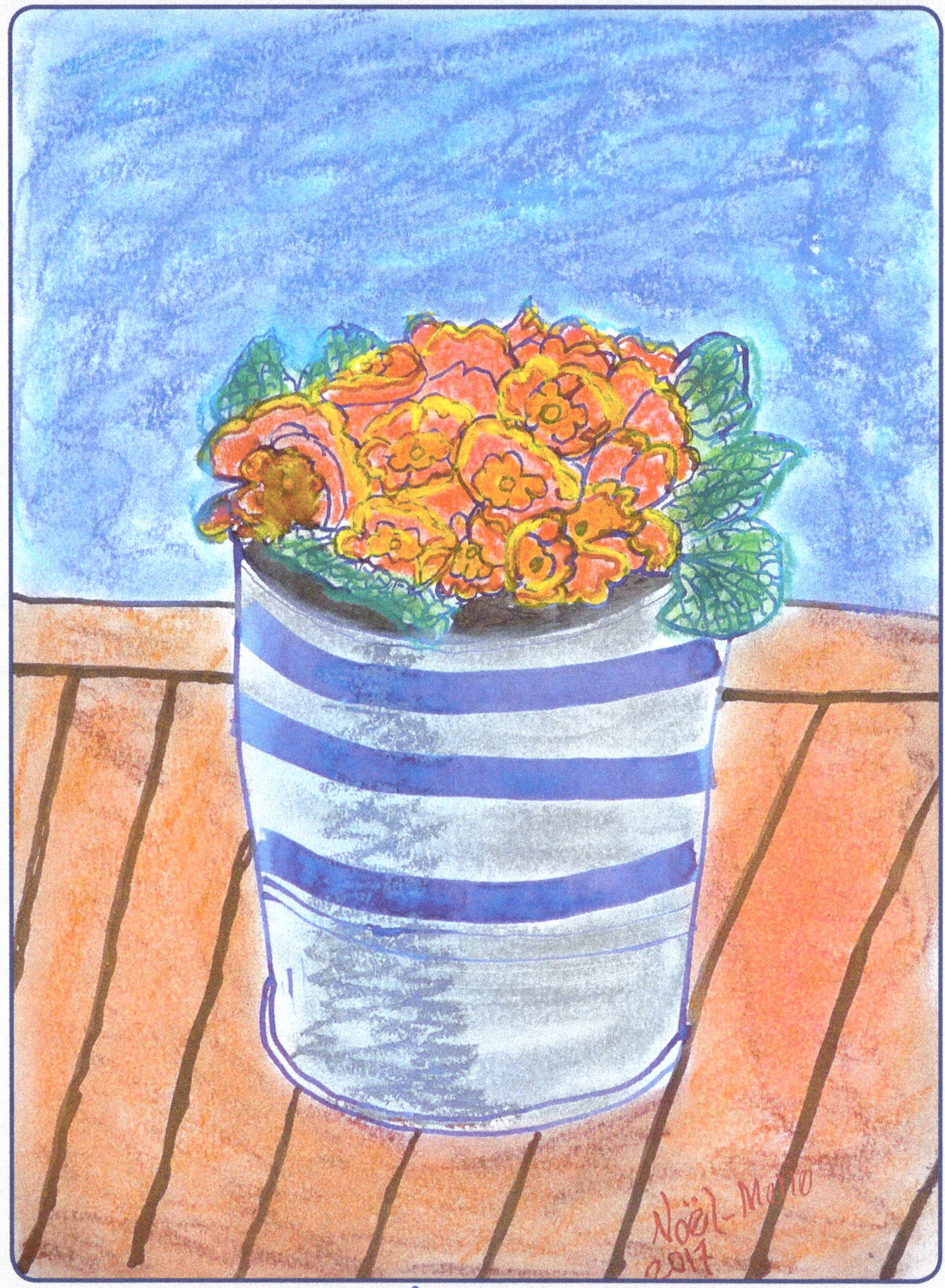


❀ Floral array.

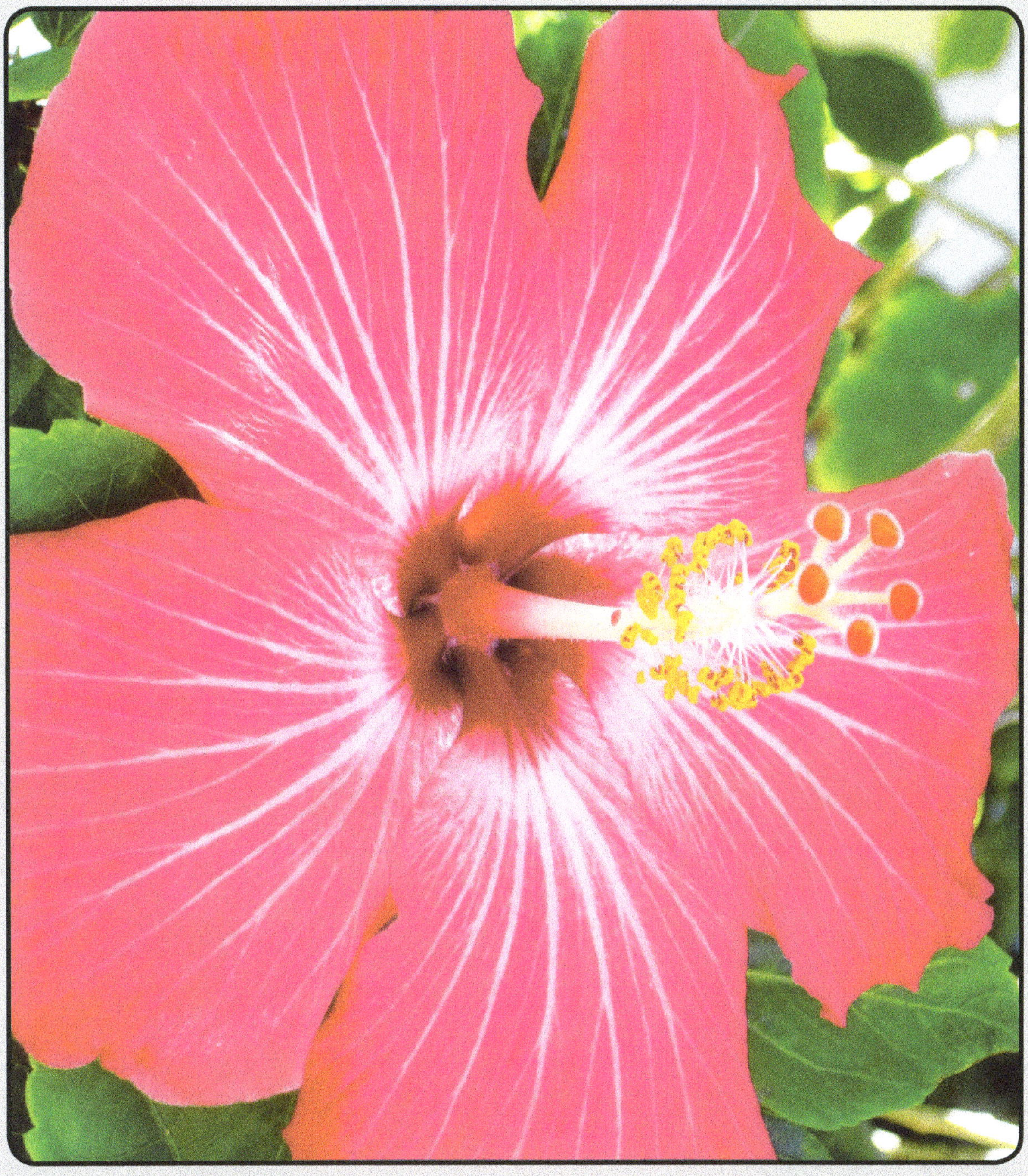

High tech.

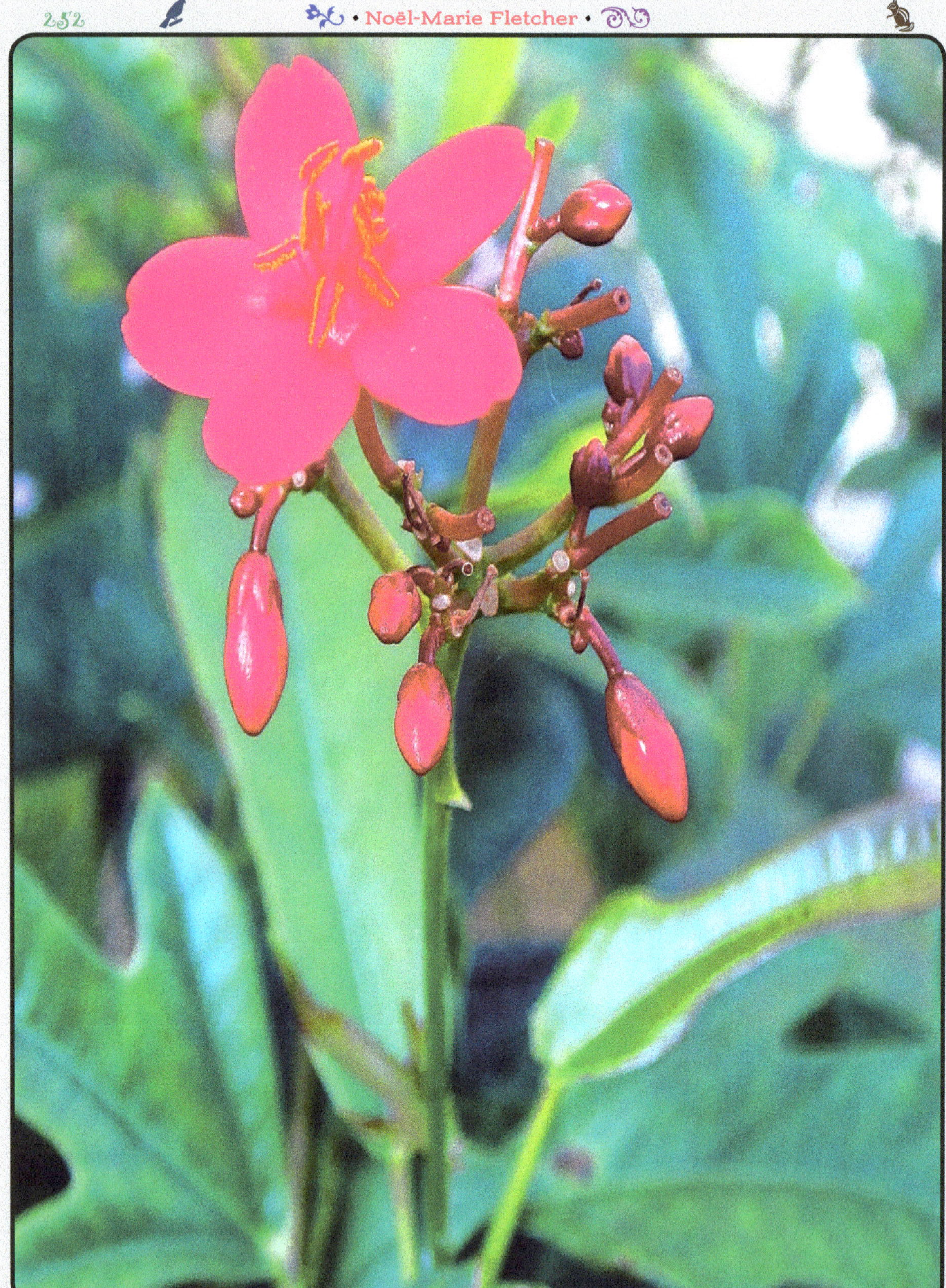

Turmeric petals.

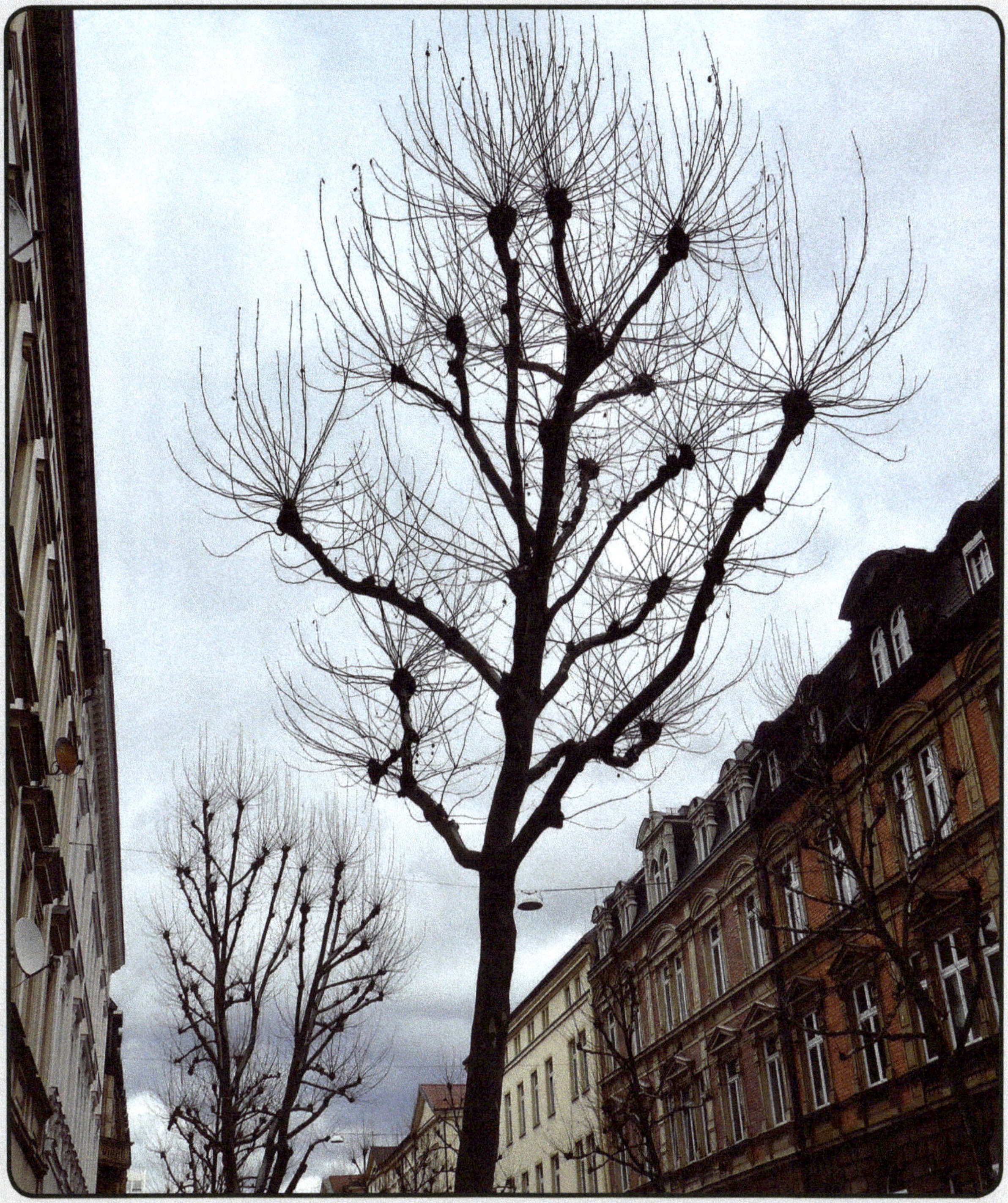

Sci-fi tree.

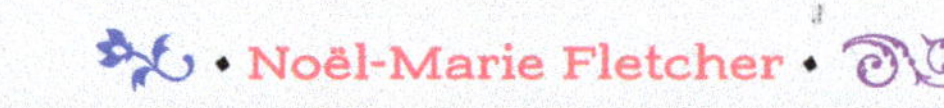

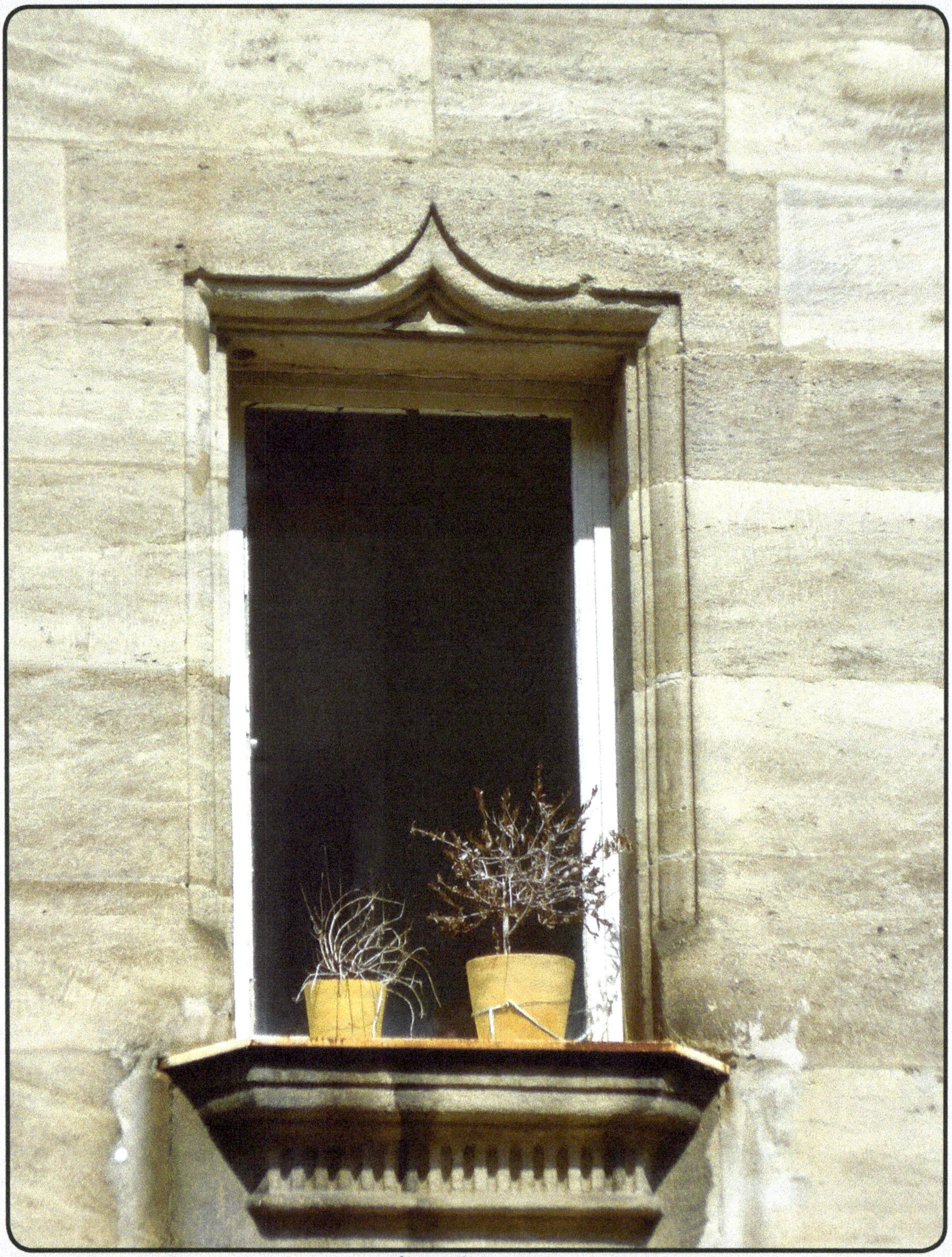

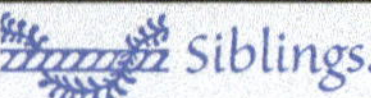

Siblings.

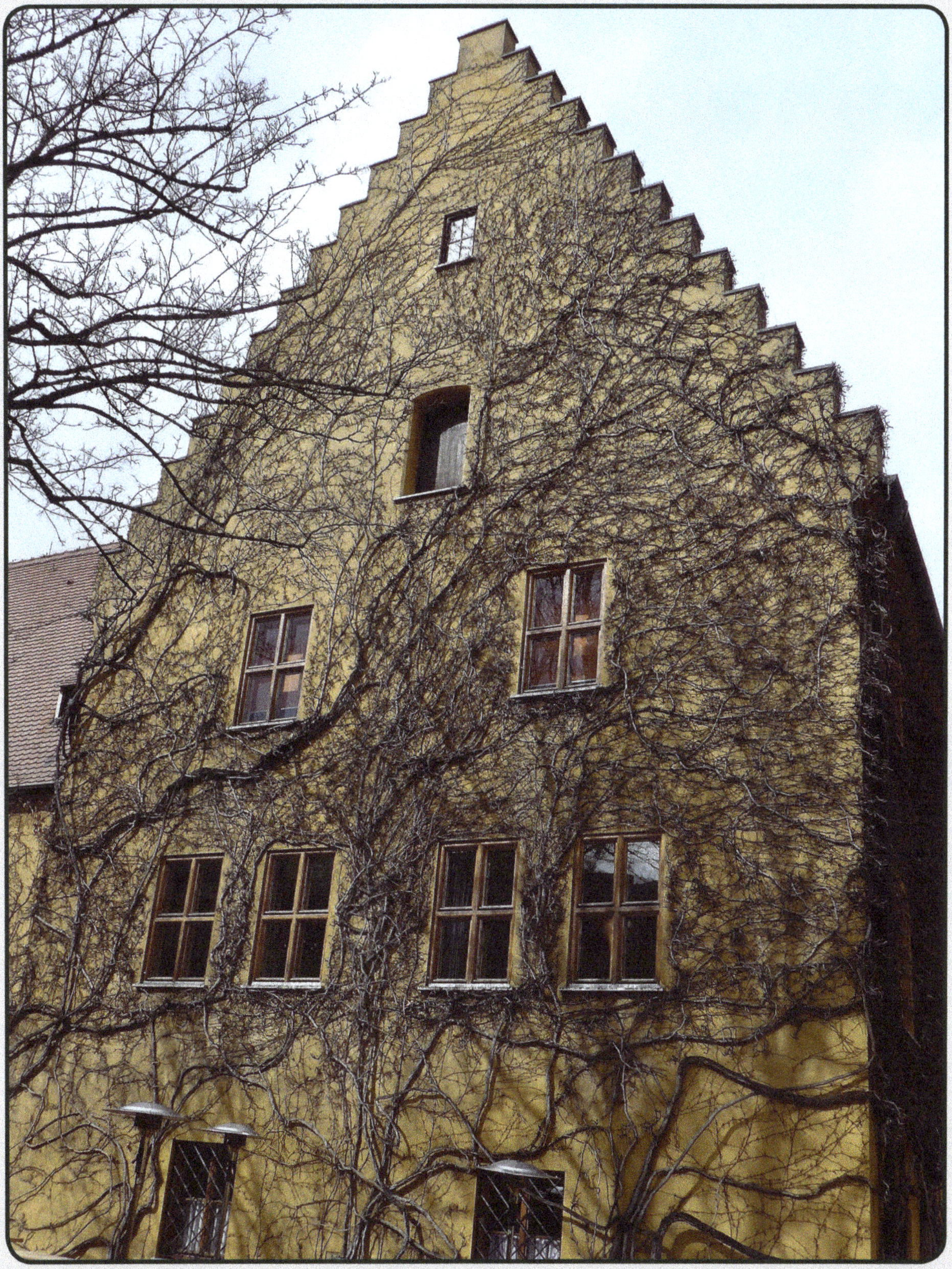

Embrace.

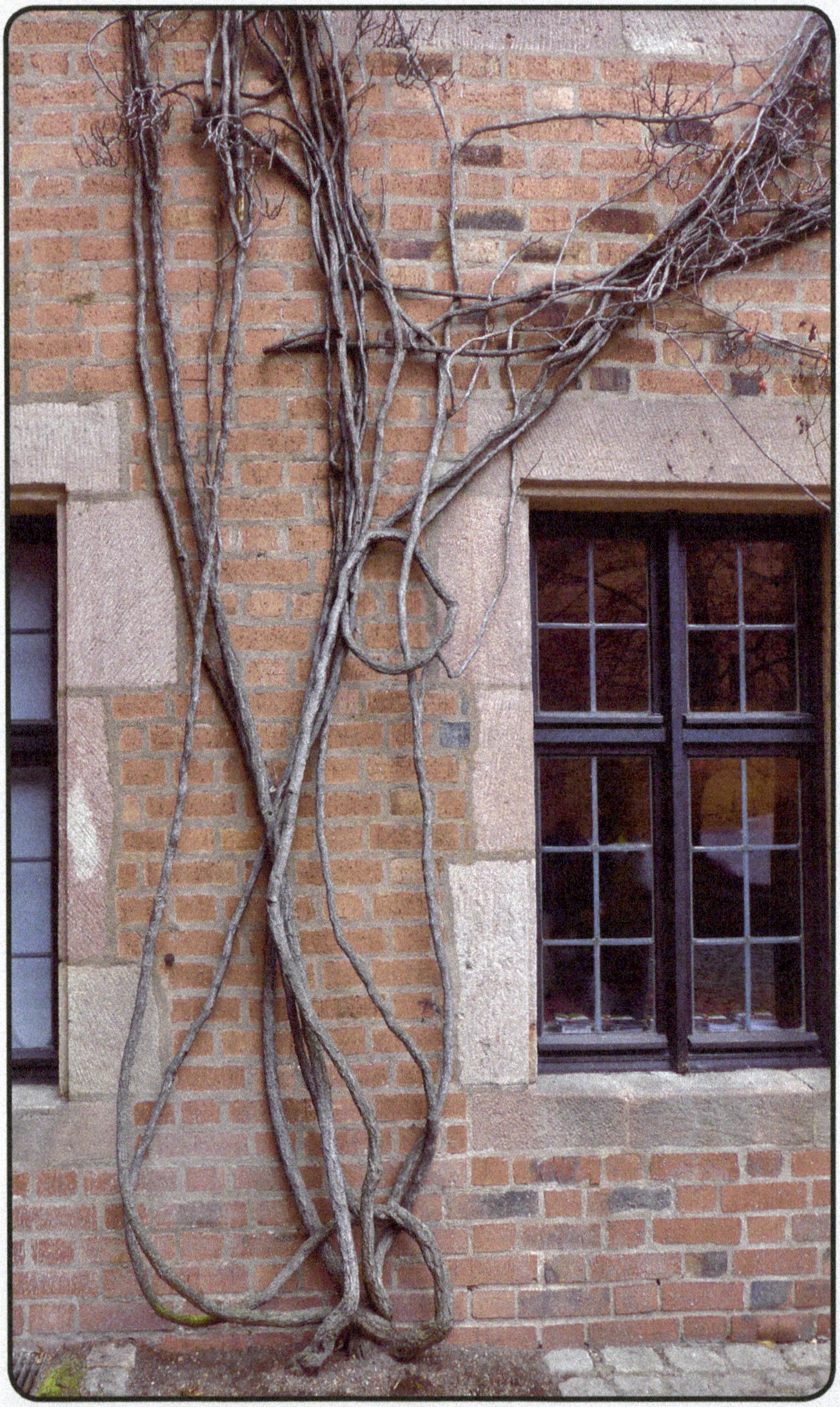

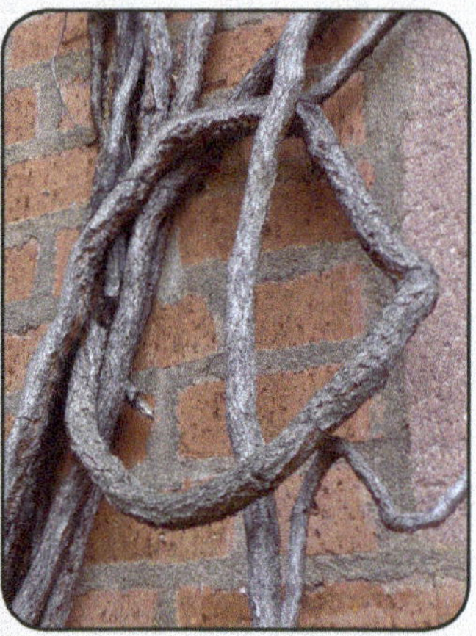

Love knot.

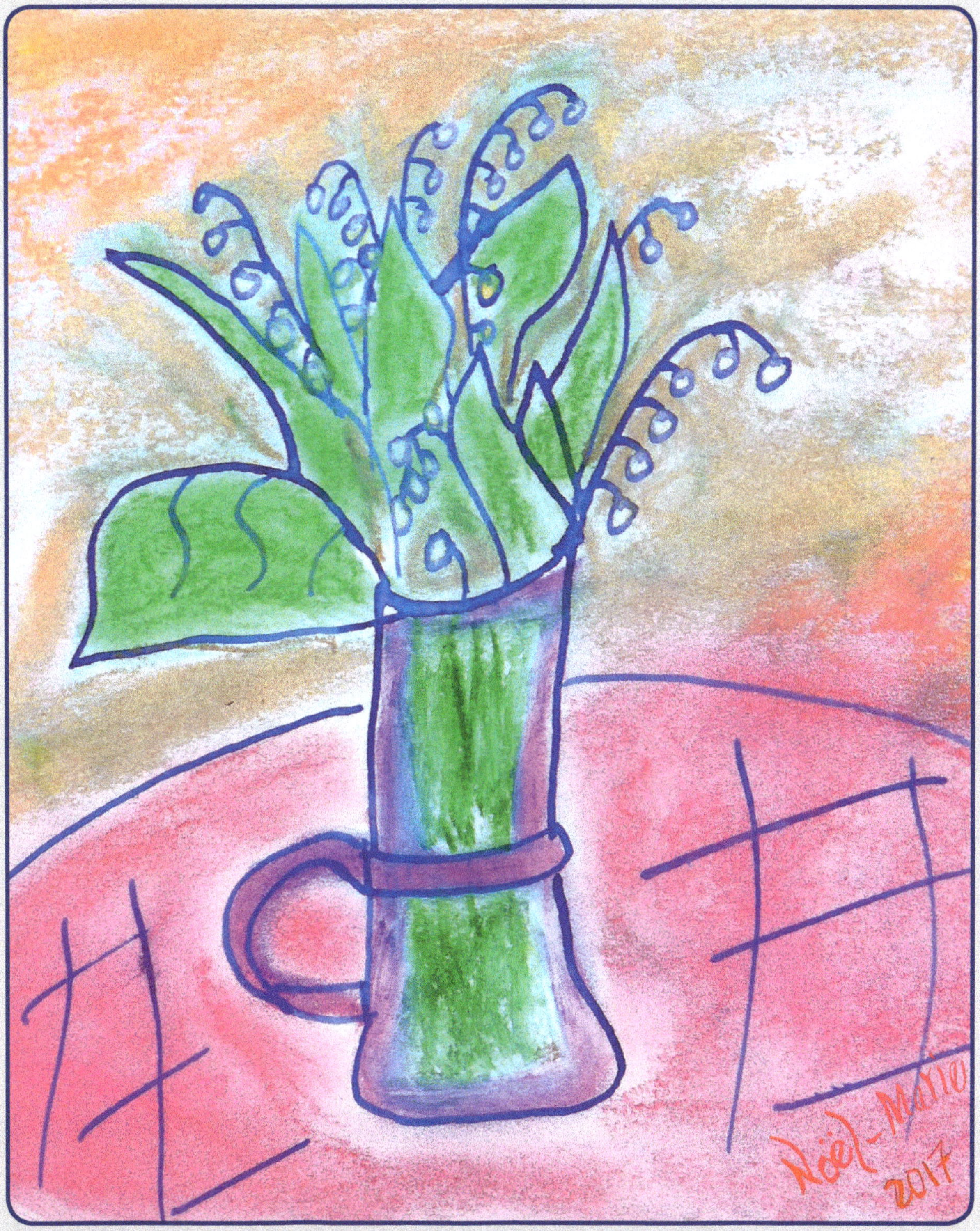

Aurora.

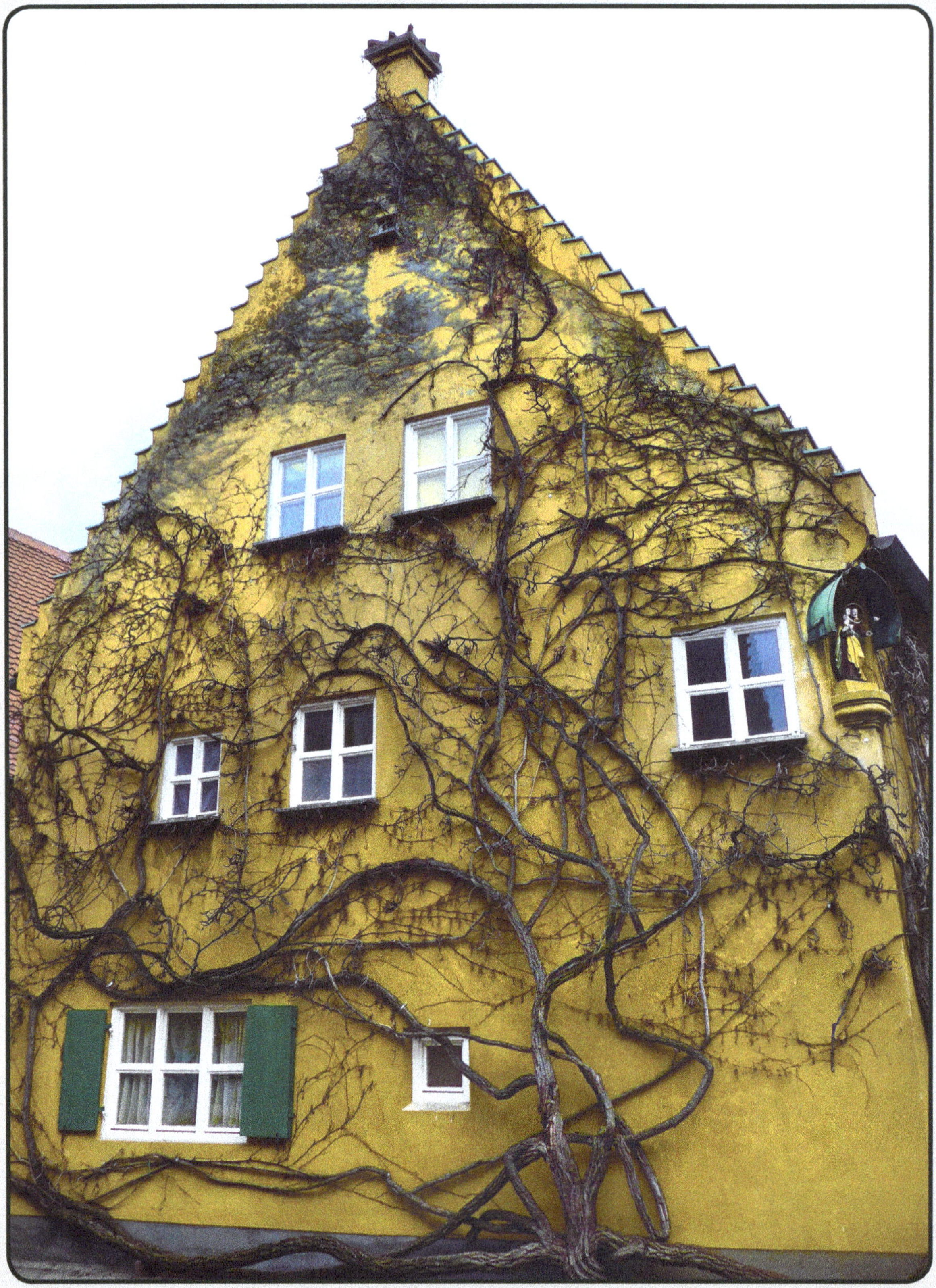

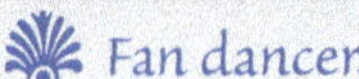
Fan dancer.

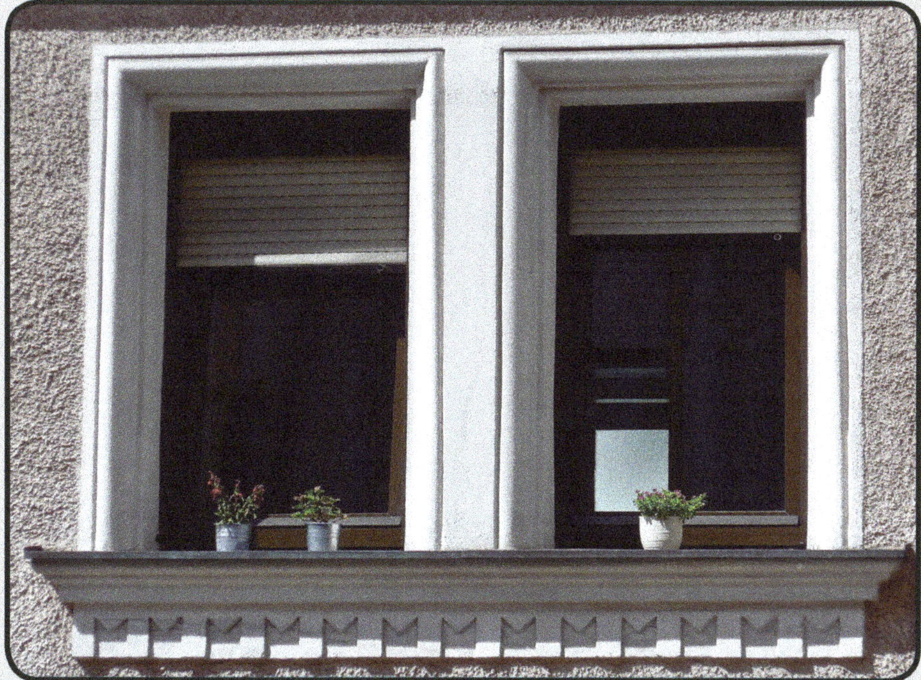

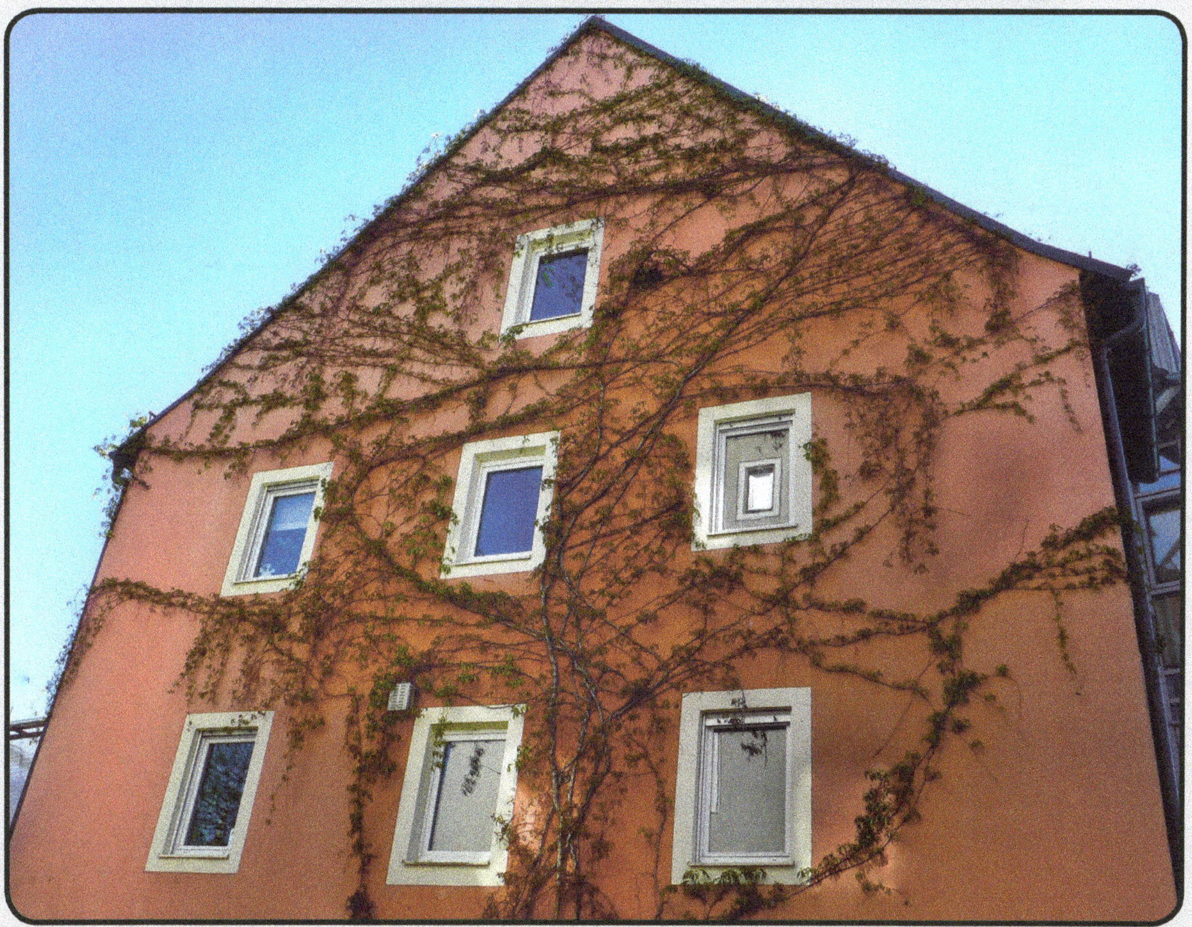

Lace handkerchief.

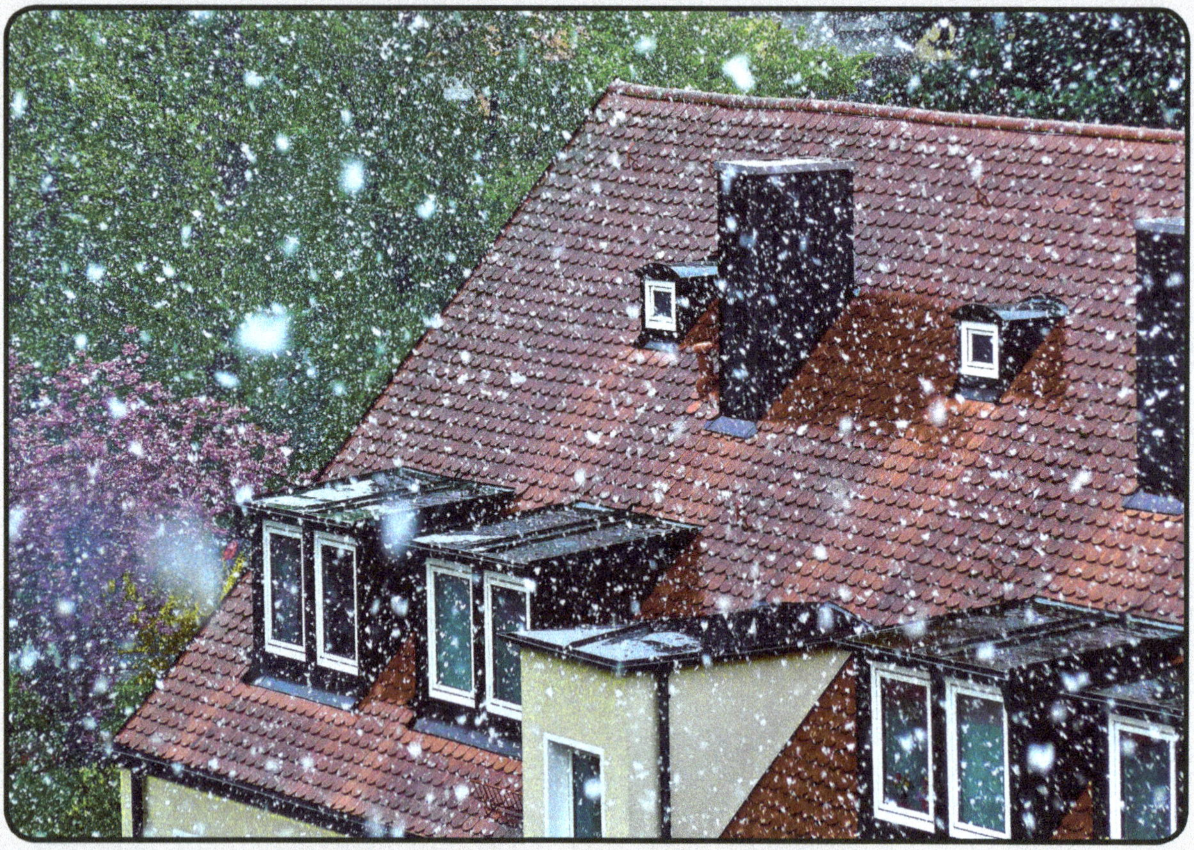

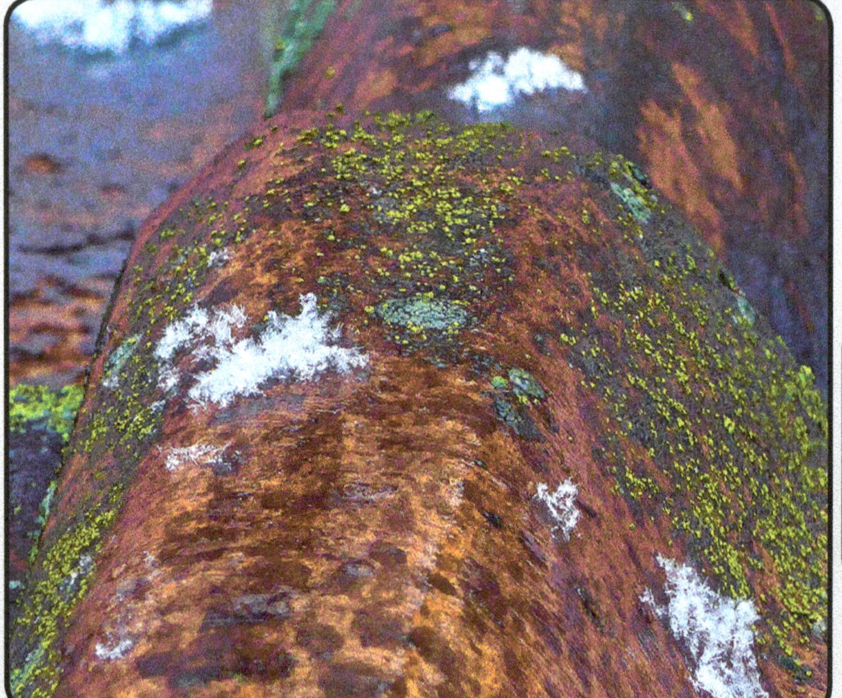

✳ Spring snow waltz series.

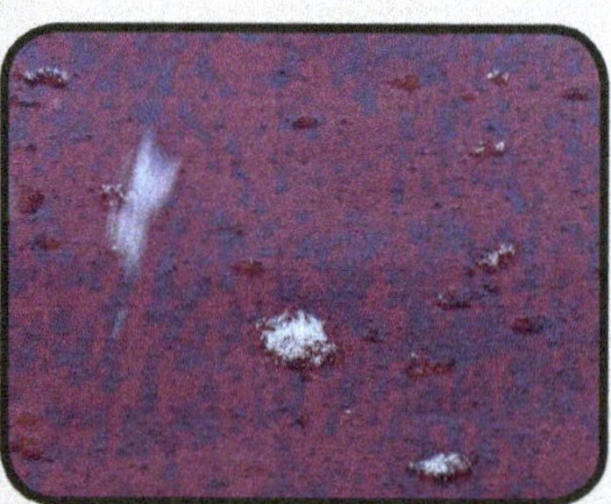

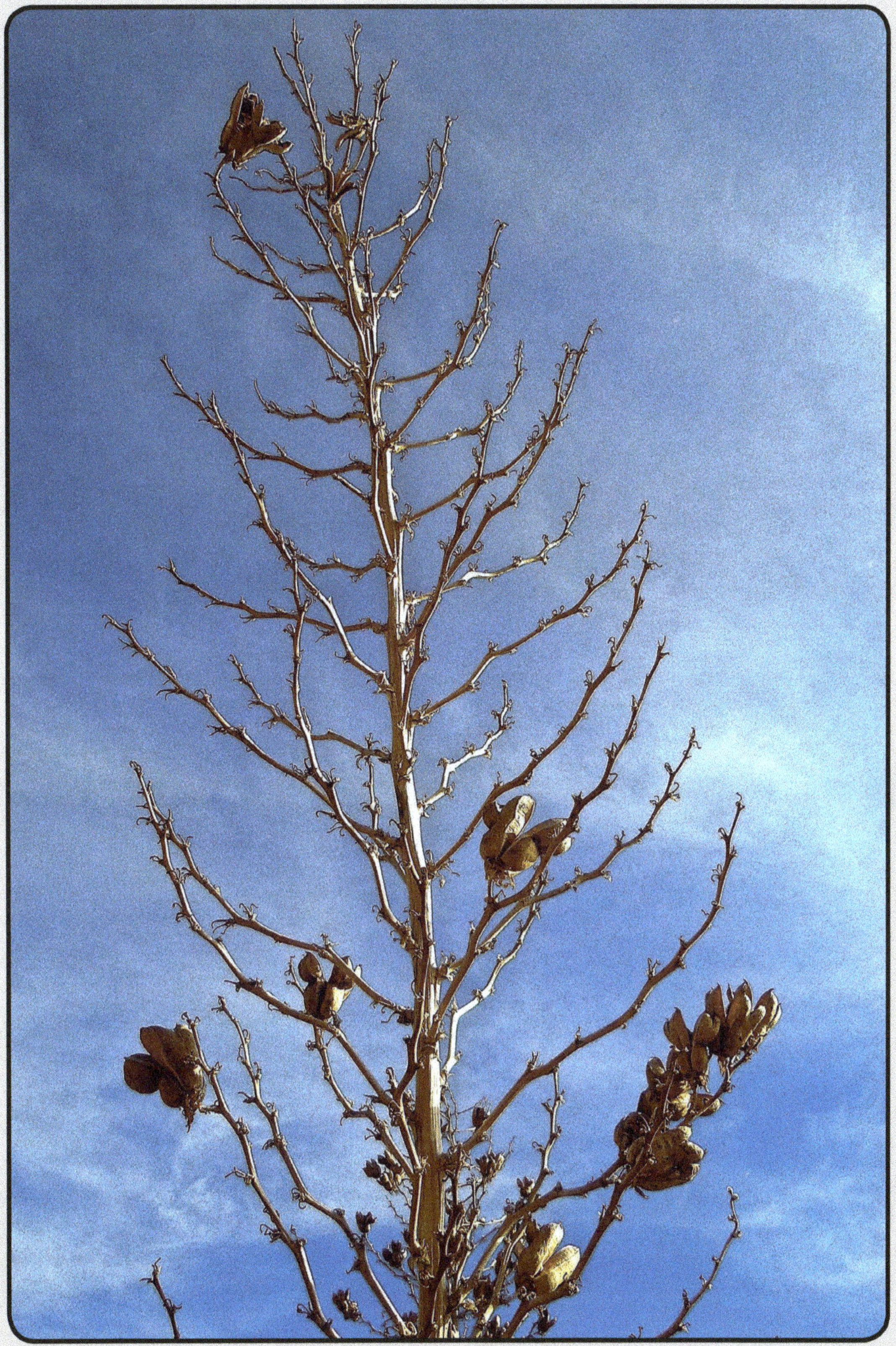

Winter isolation.

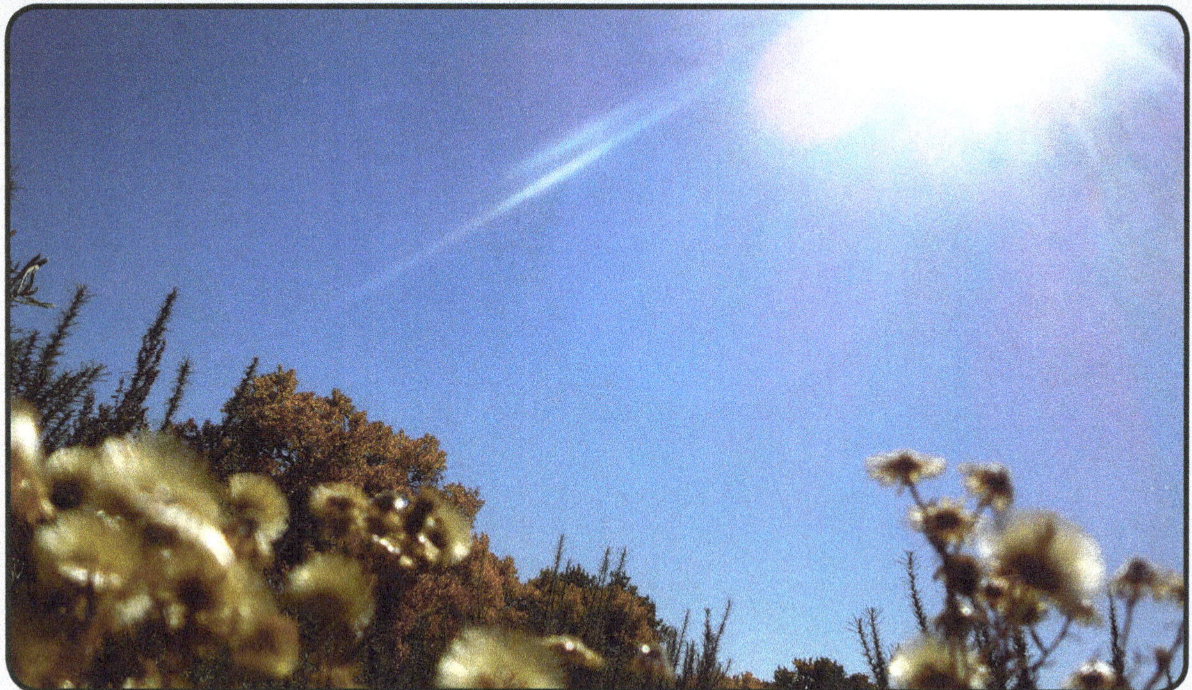

Touched by the sun's fingertips series.

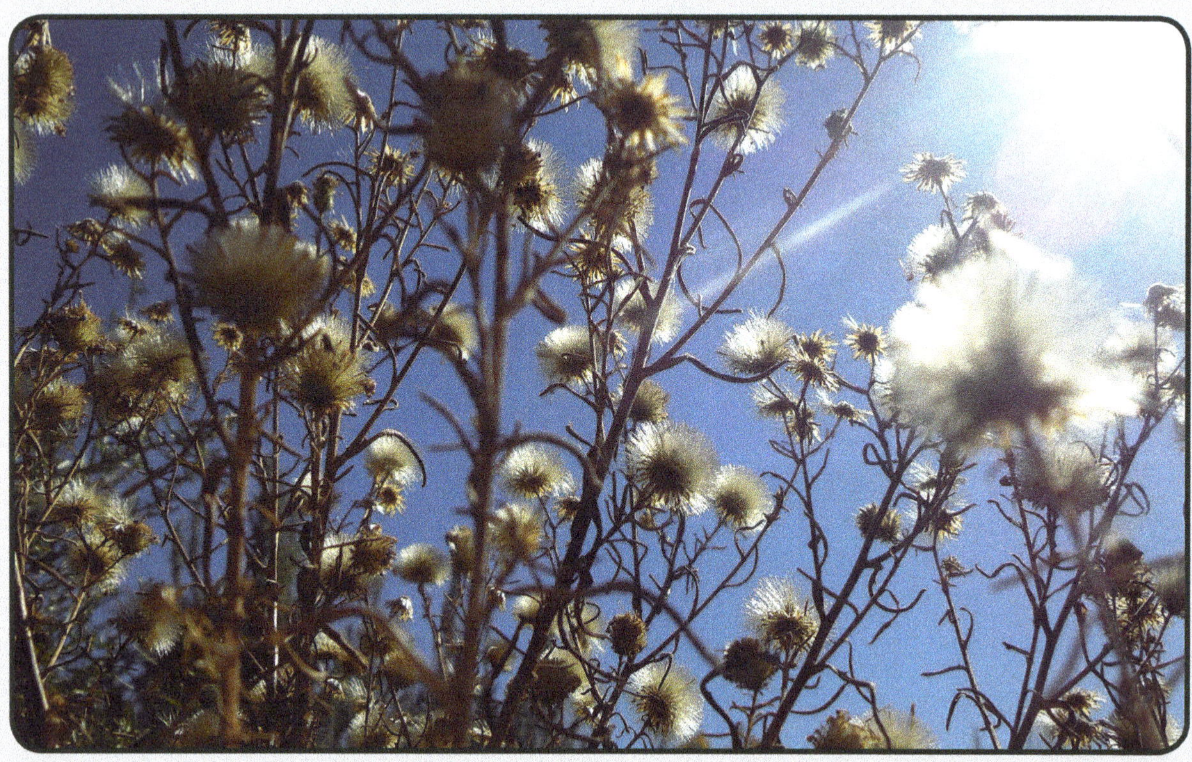

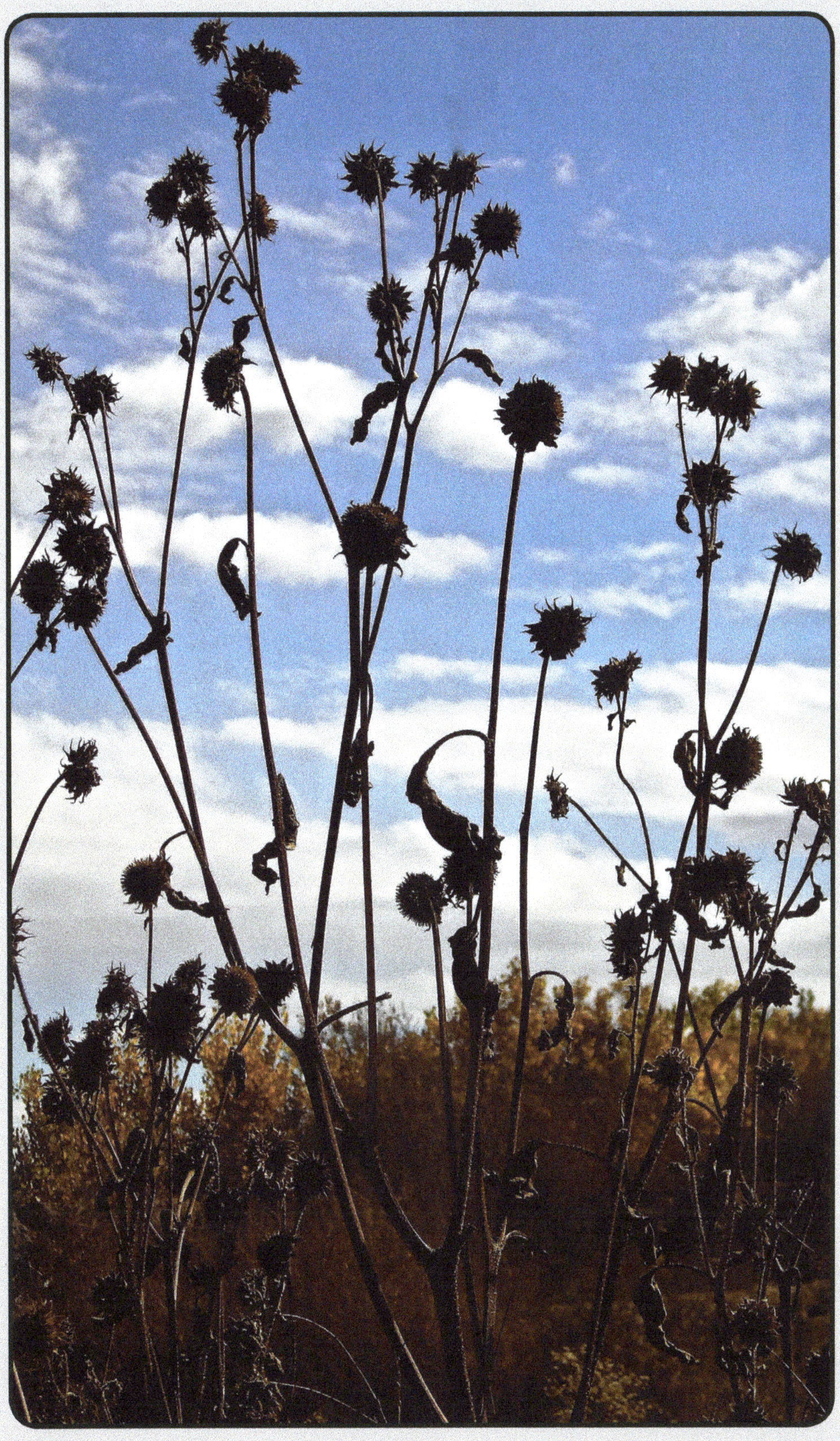

Faded but not forgotten.

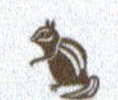

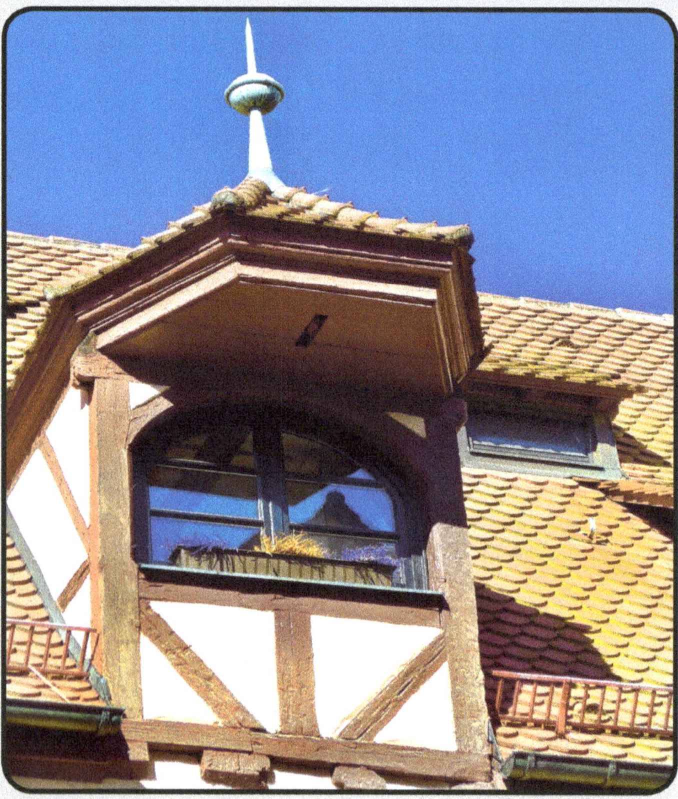

Warm vantage point.

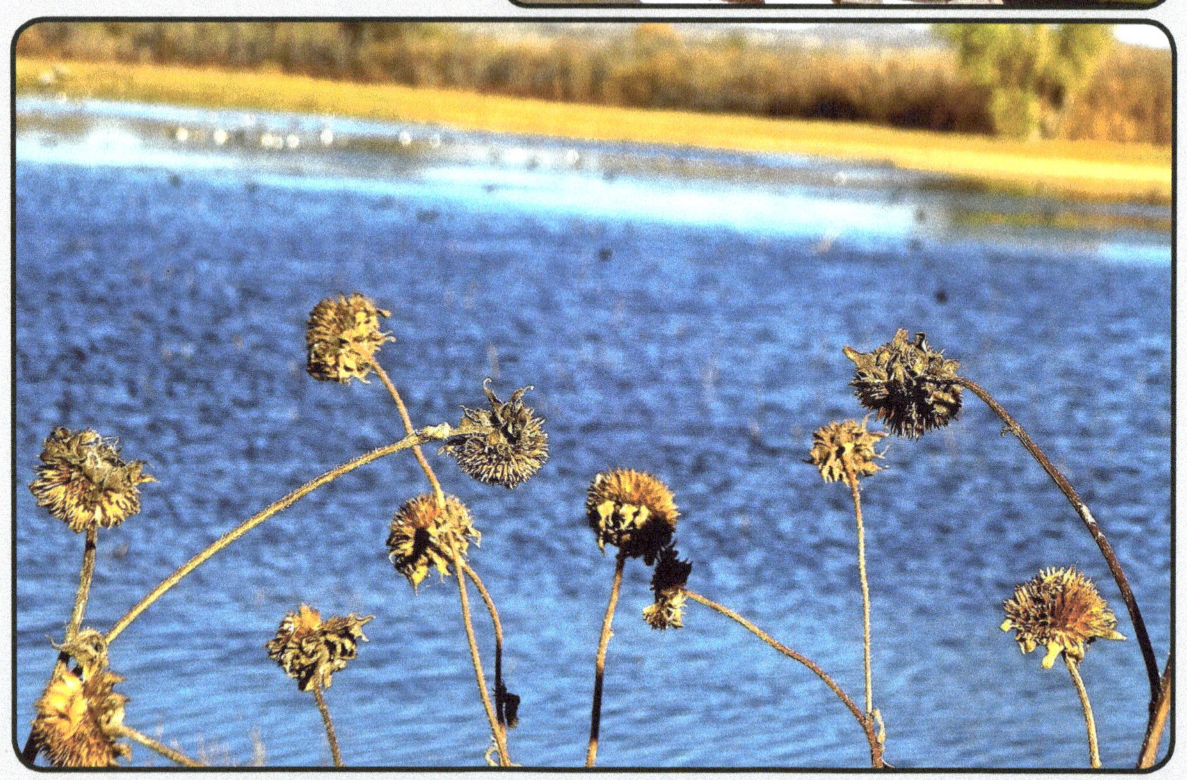

Silent spectators.

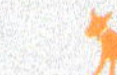

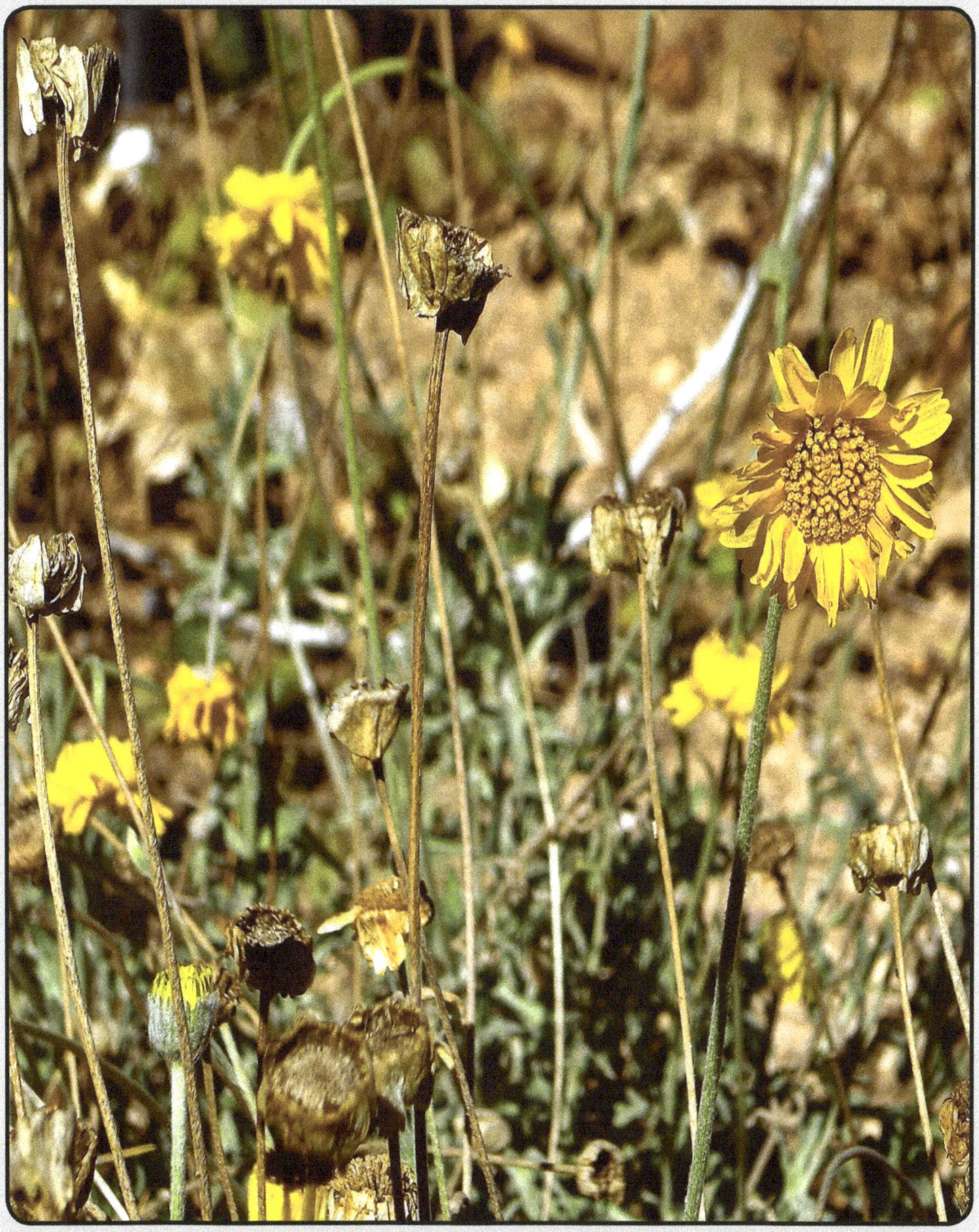

Weathered faces in the high desert.

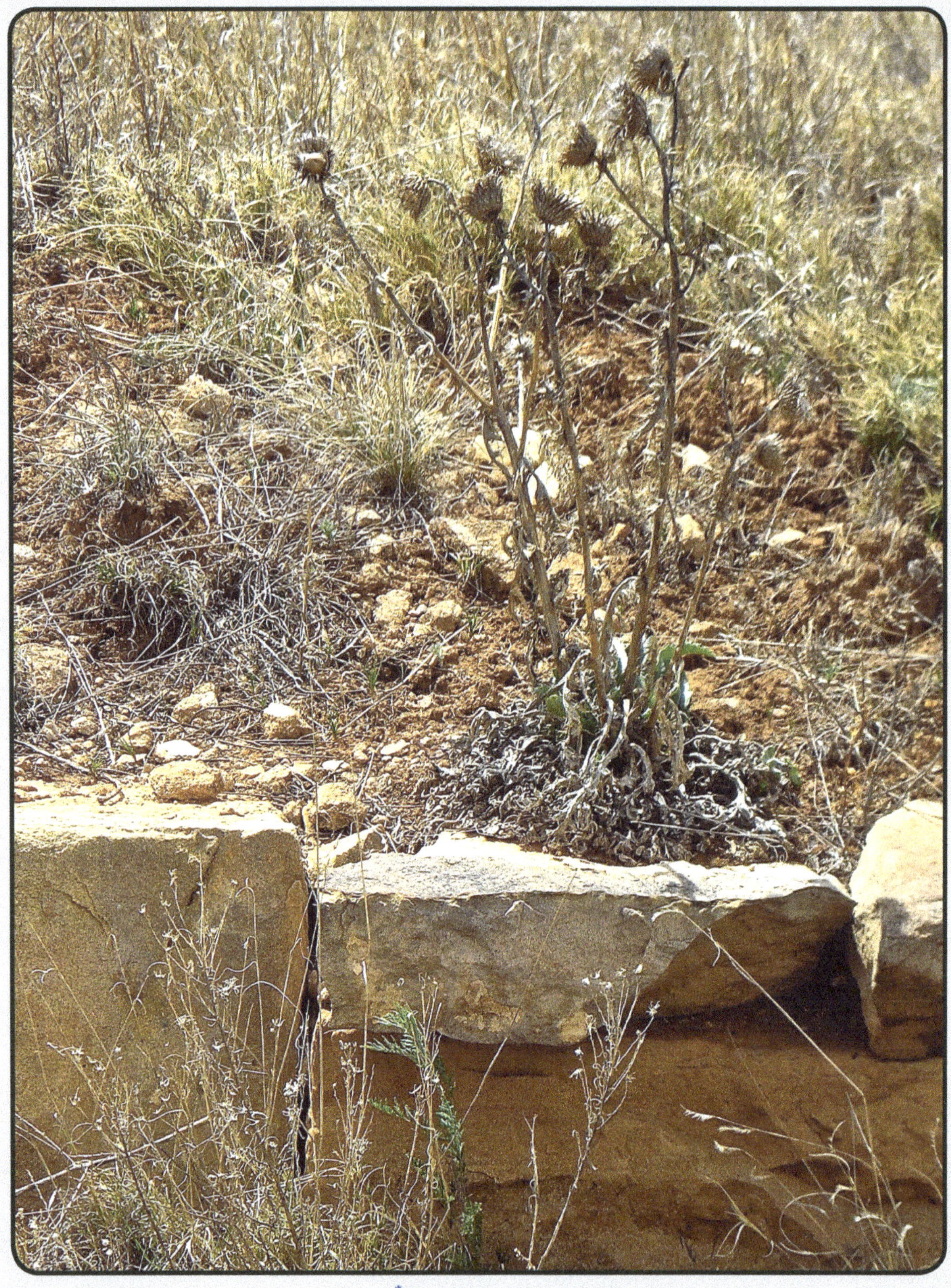

Forgotten builders.

# Chapter 8: Lizards

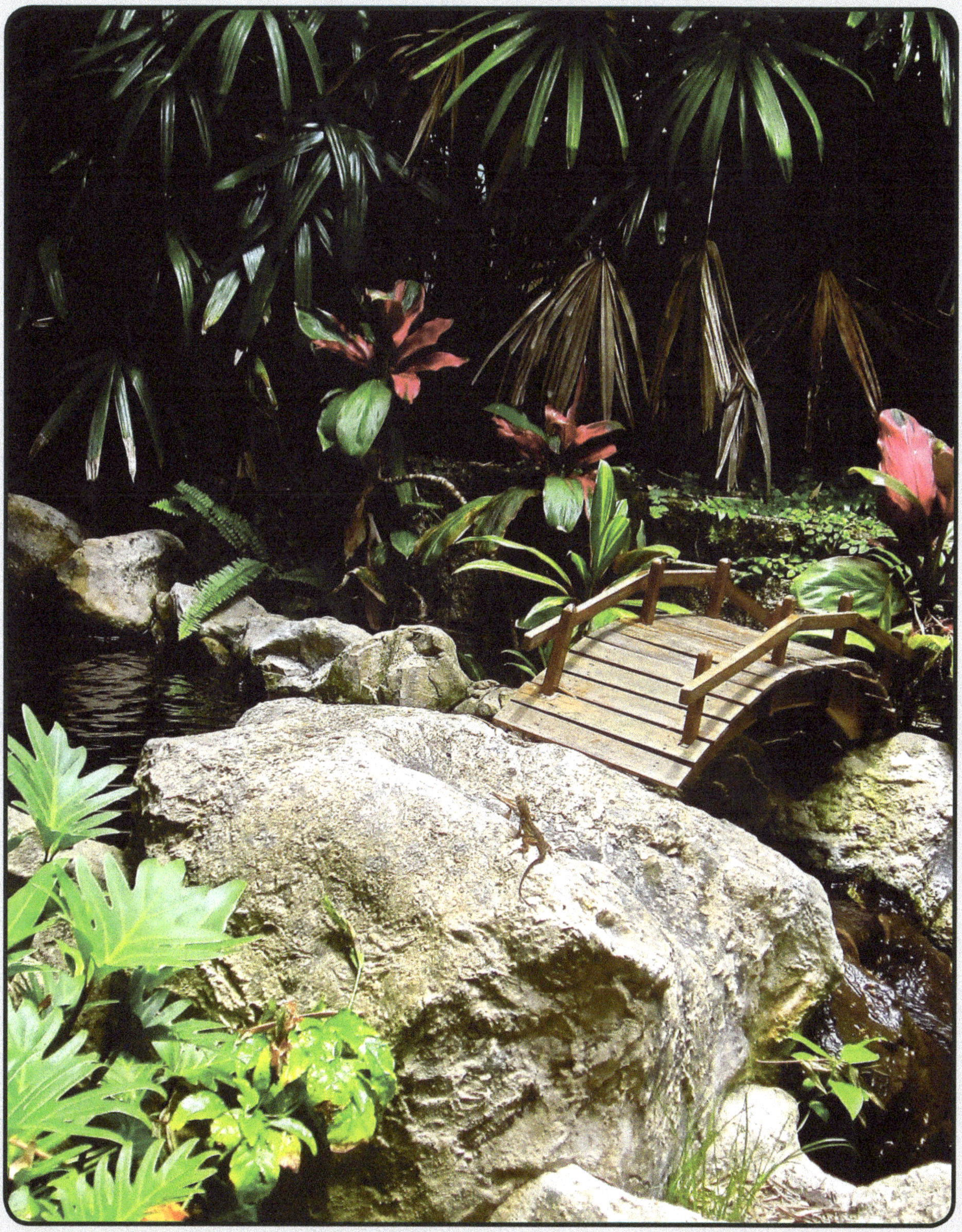

Lizard crossing.

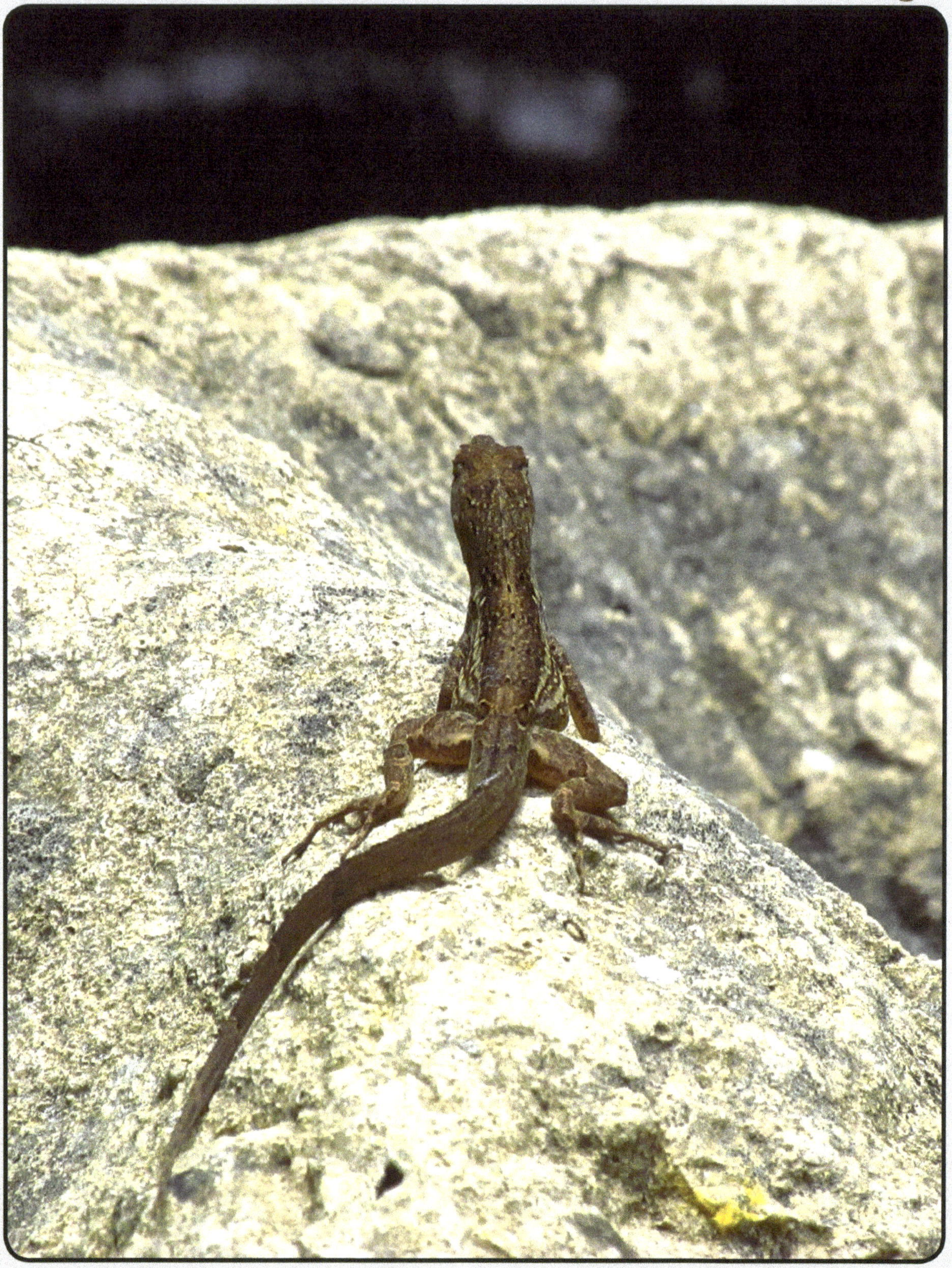

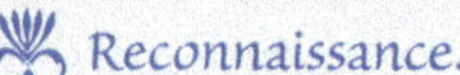

Reconnaissance.

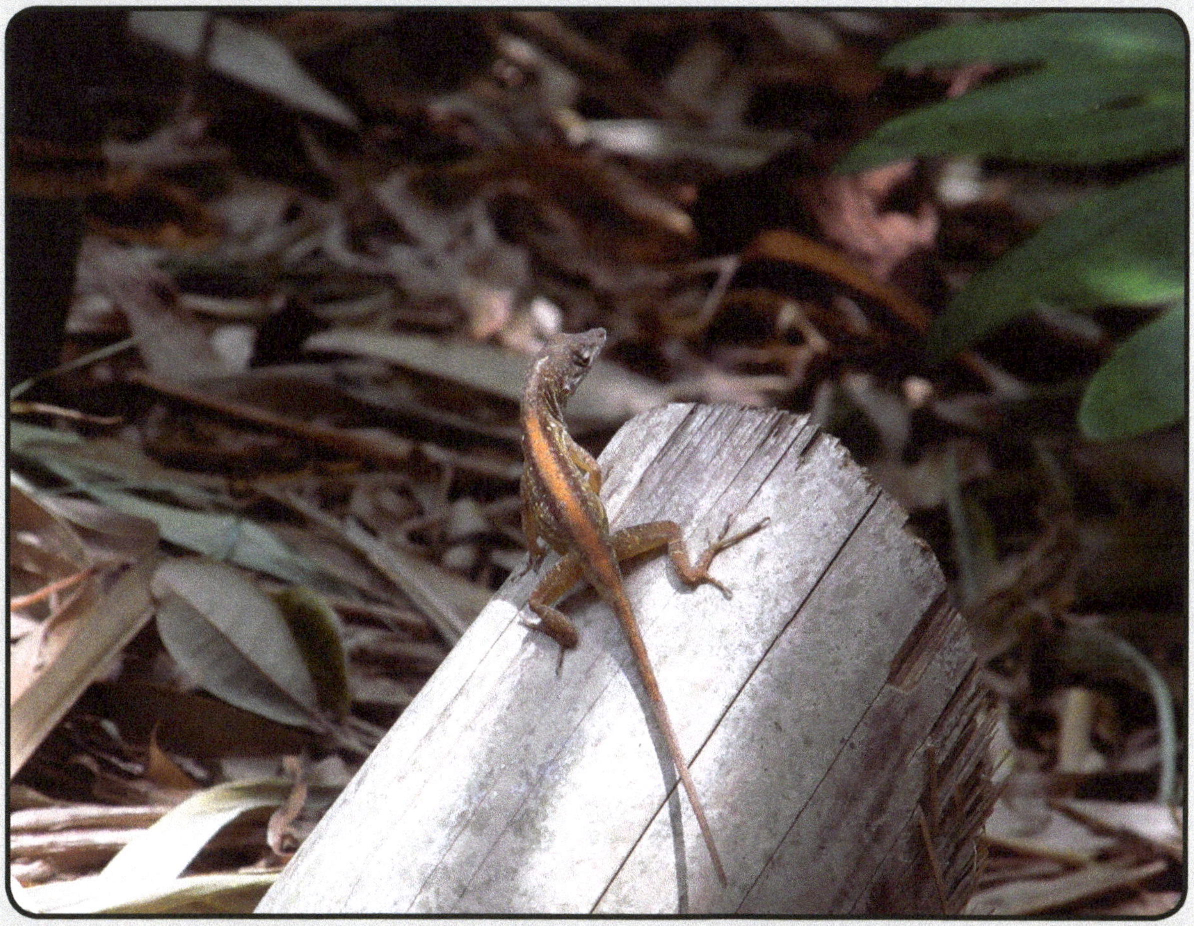

Lookout.

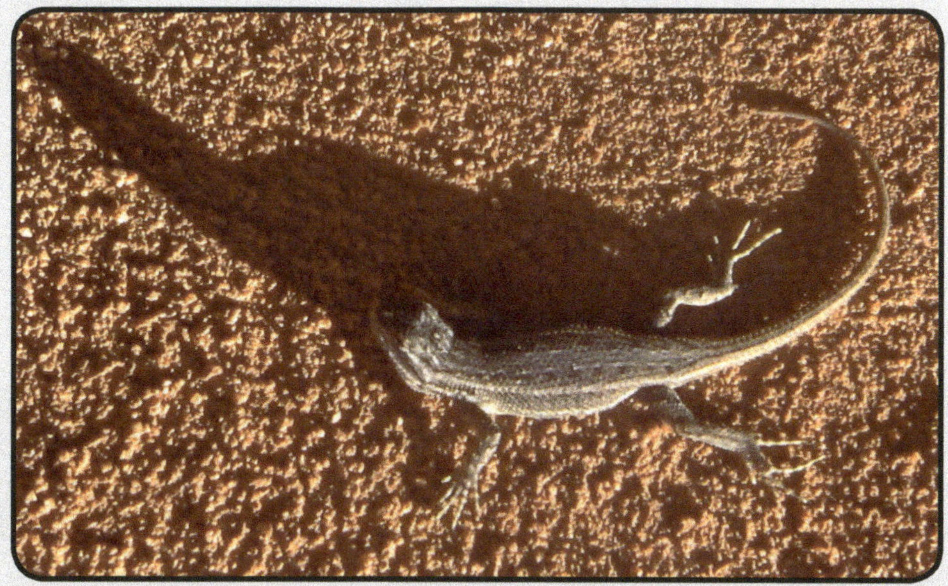

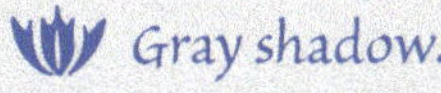
Gray shadow.

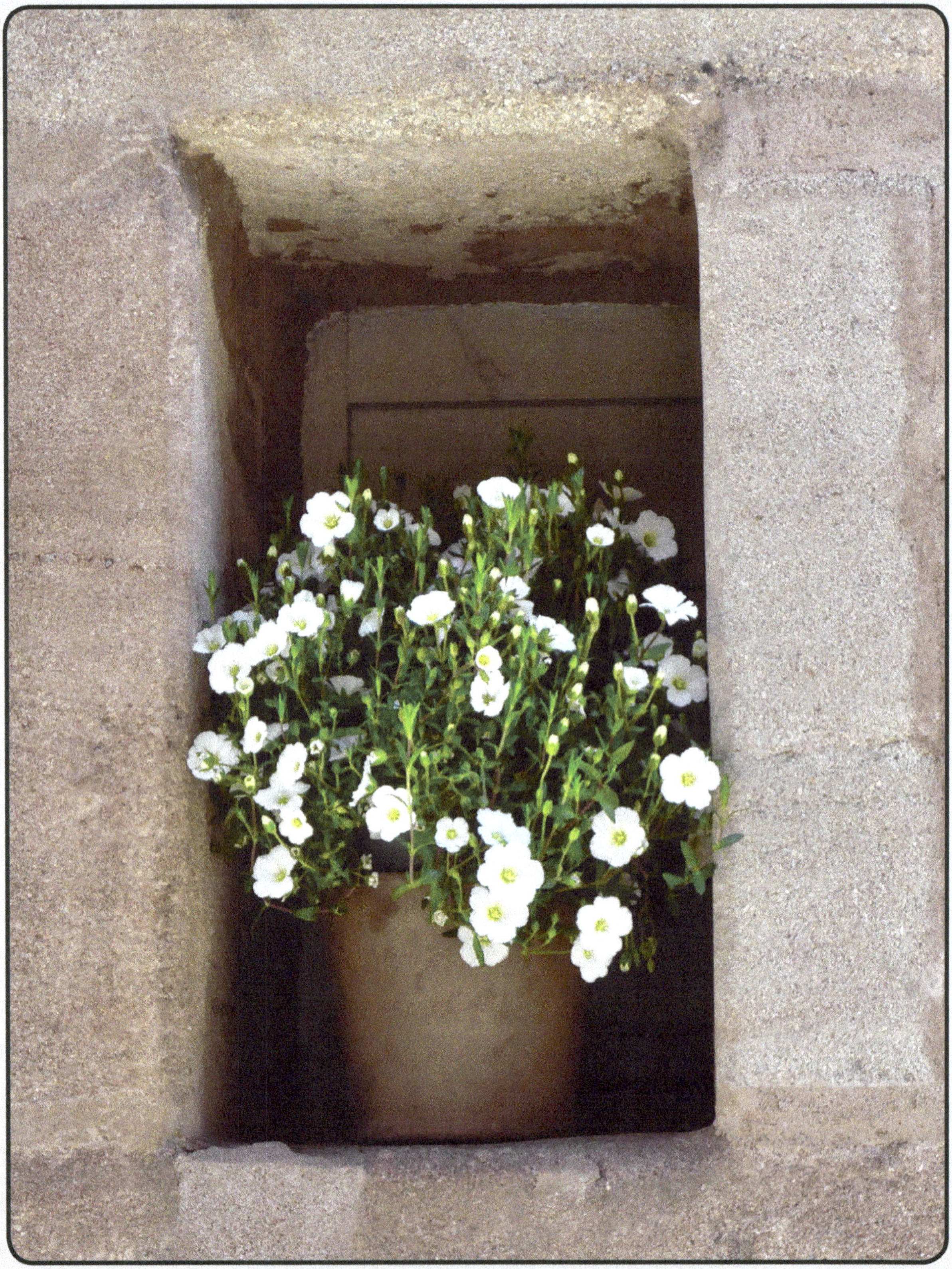

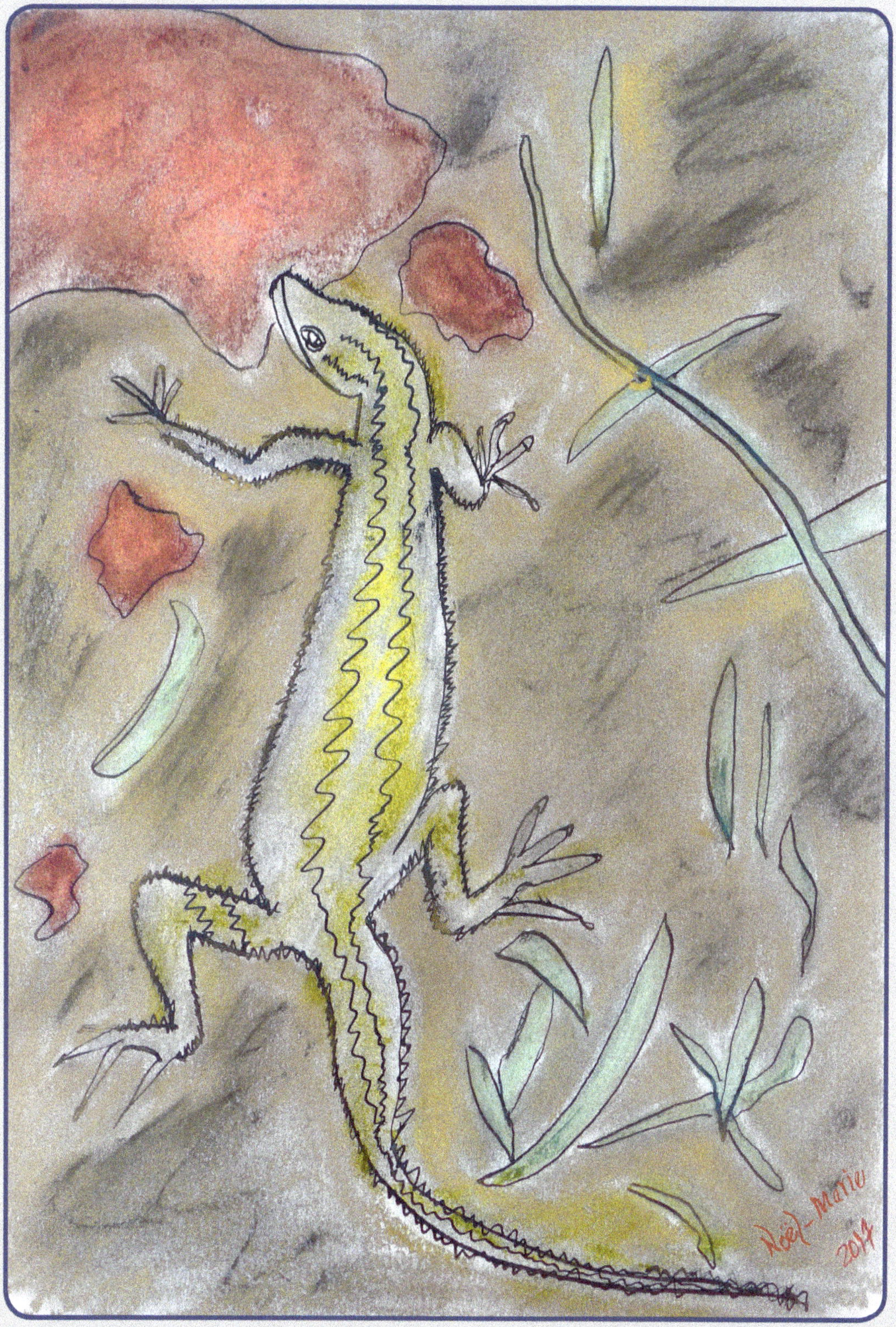

✻ Scaly hunter.

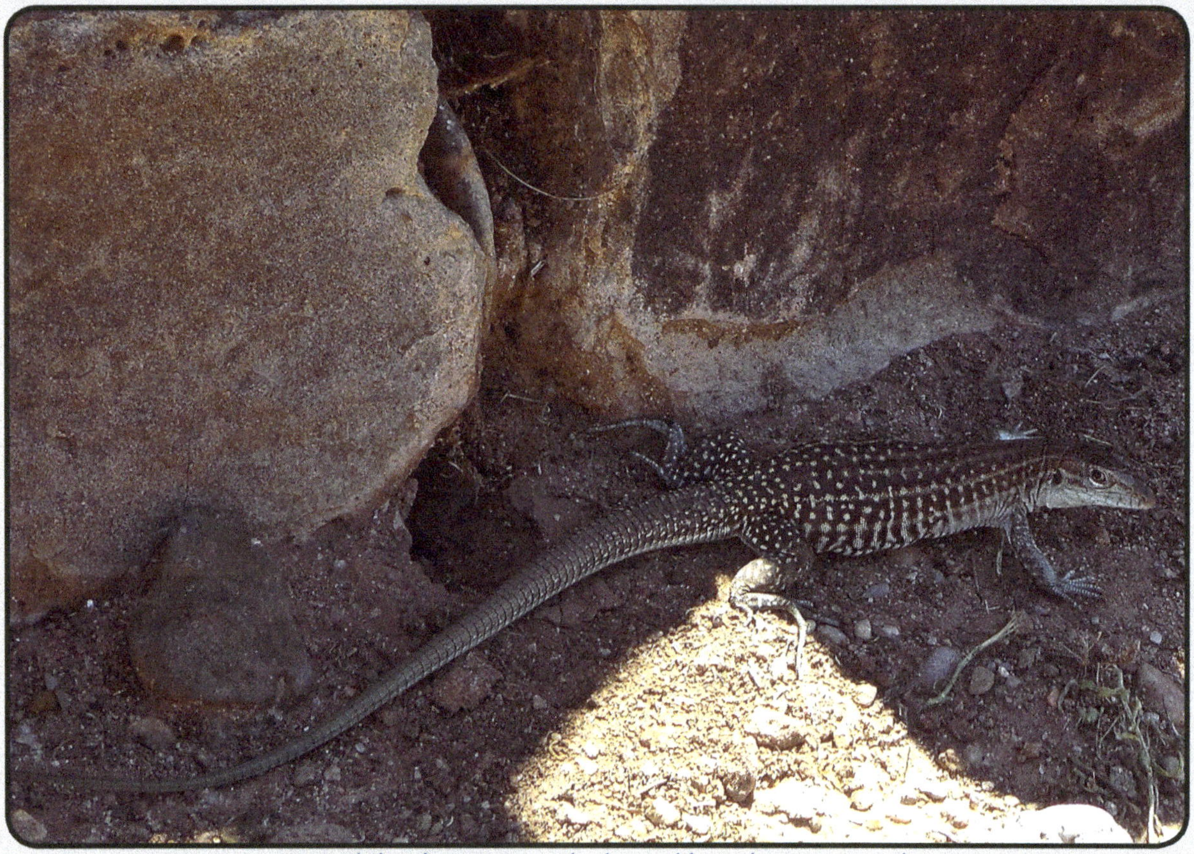

Chihuahuan spotted whiptail lizard in graveyard.

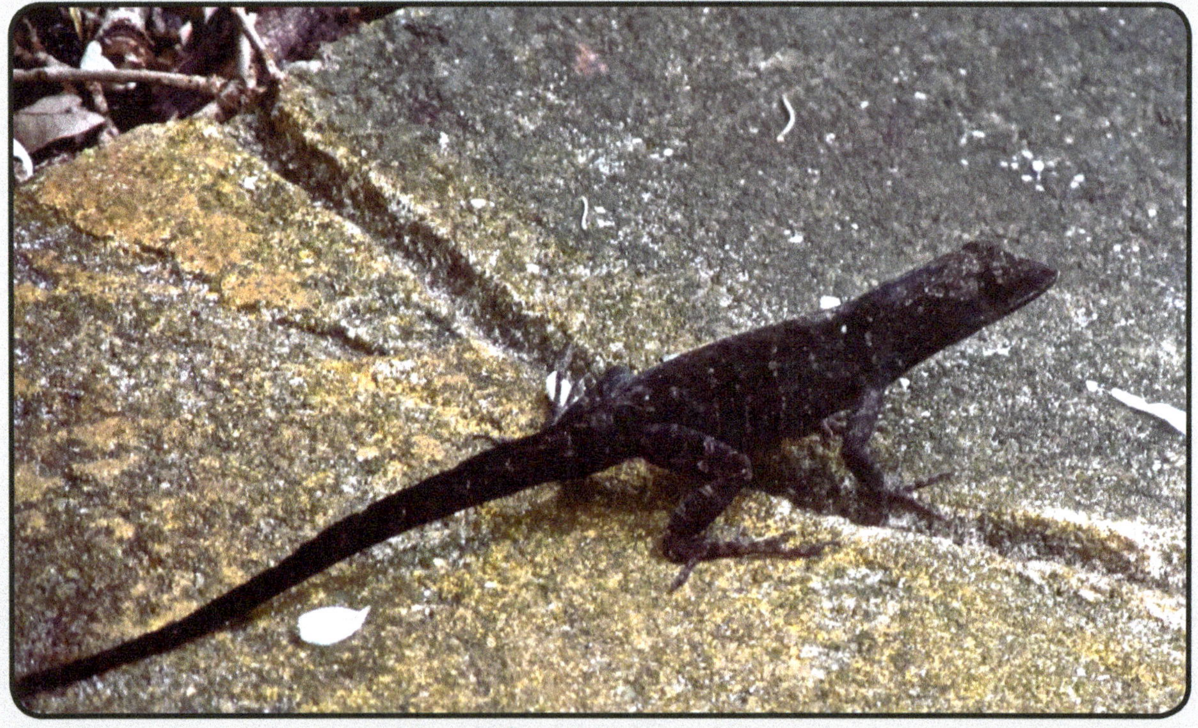

Stone faced.

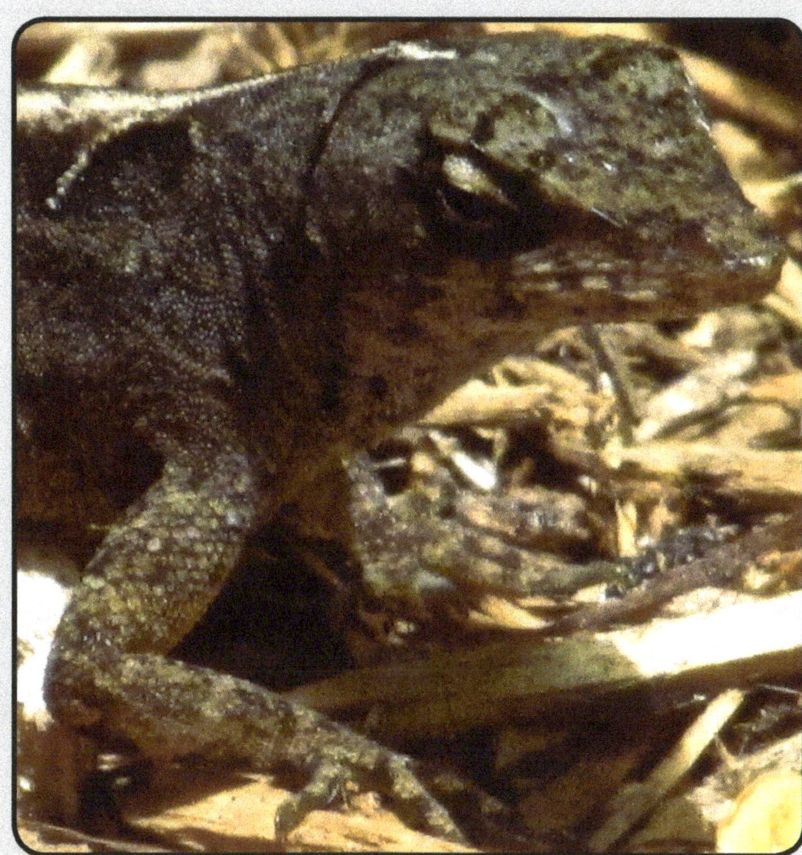

Desert dinosaur (closeup, upper right).

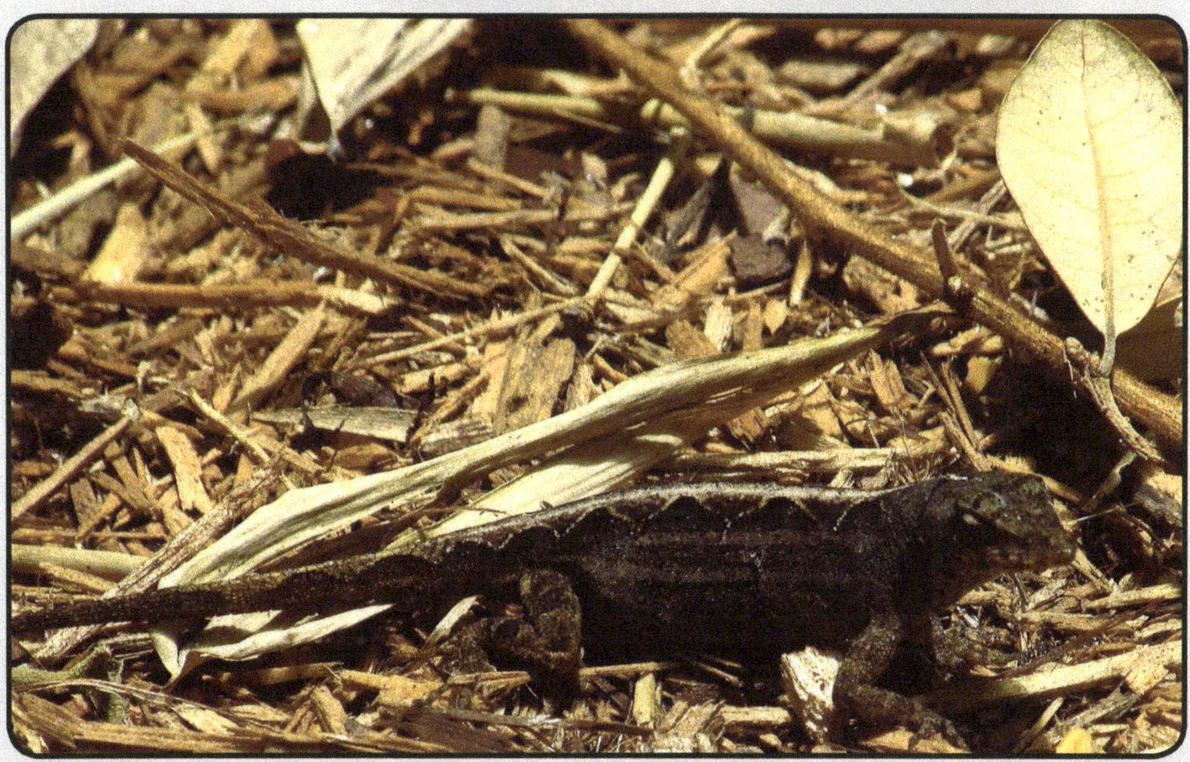

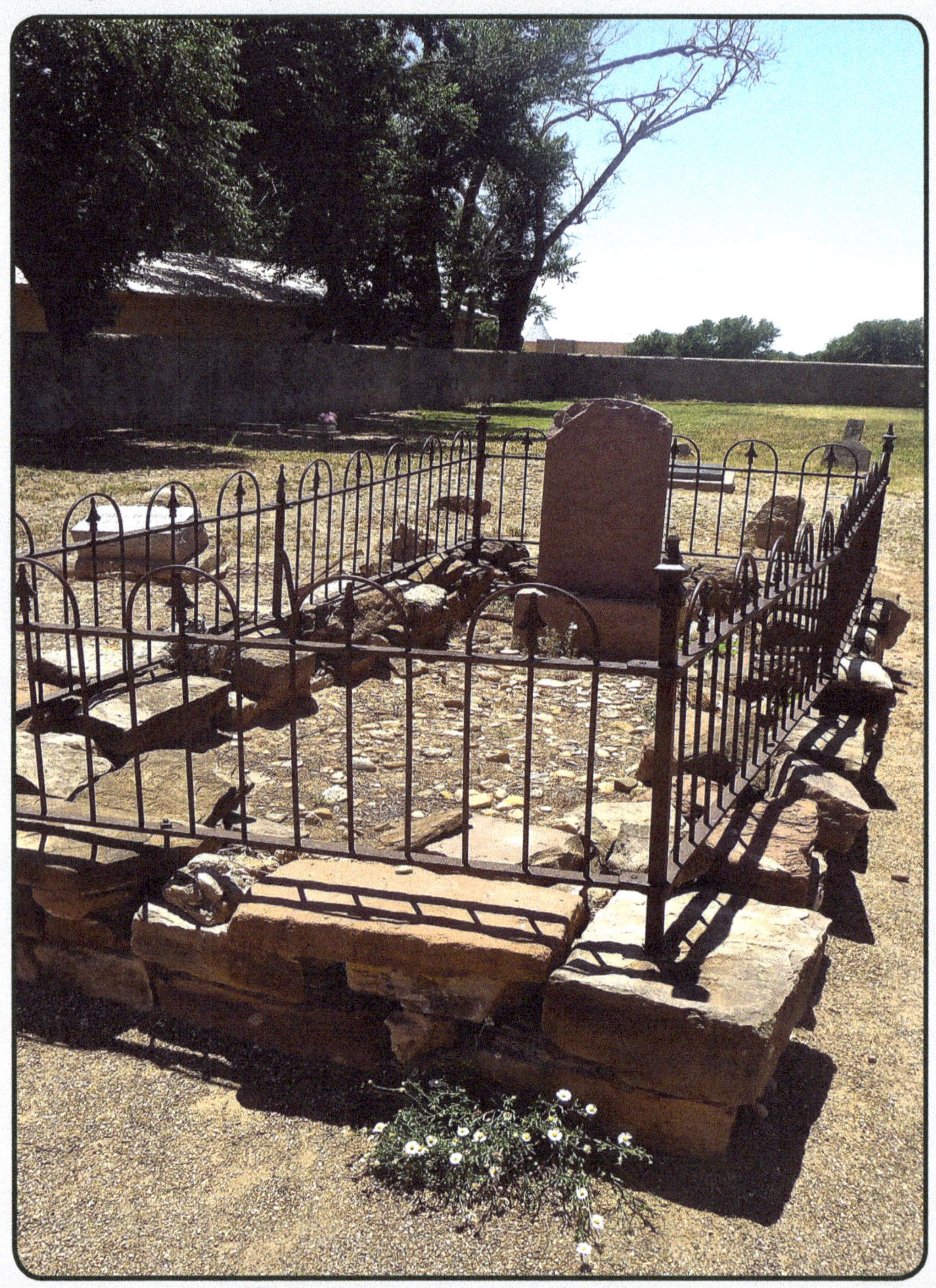

Billy the Kid graveyard lizard series.

[Note: A lizard (next pages) crawled out from the bricks (lower right) of the grave of Peter Maxwell, who died in 1898. Billy the Kid was killed in a shootout in Maxwell's bedroom in 1881. Maxwell, Billy the Kid and two of the outlaw's gang (as well as one of his victims) are all buried in this cemetery in Fort Sumner, New Mexico.]

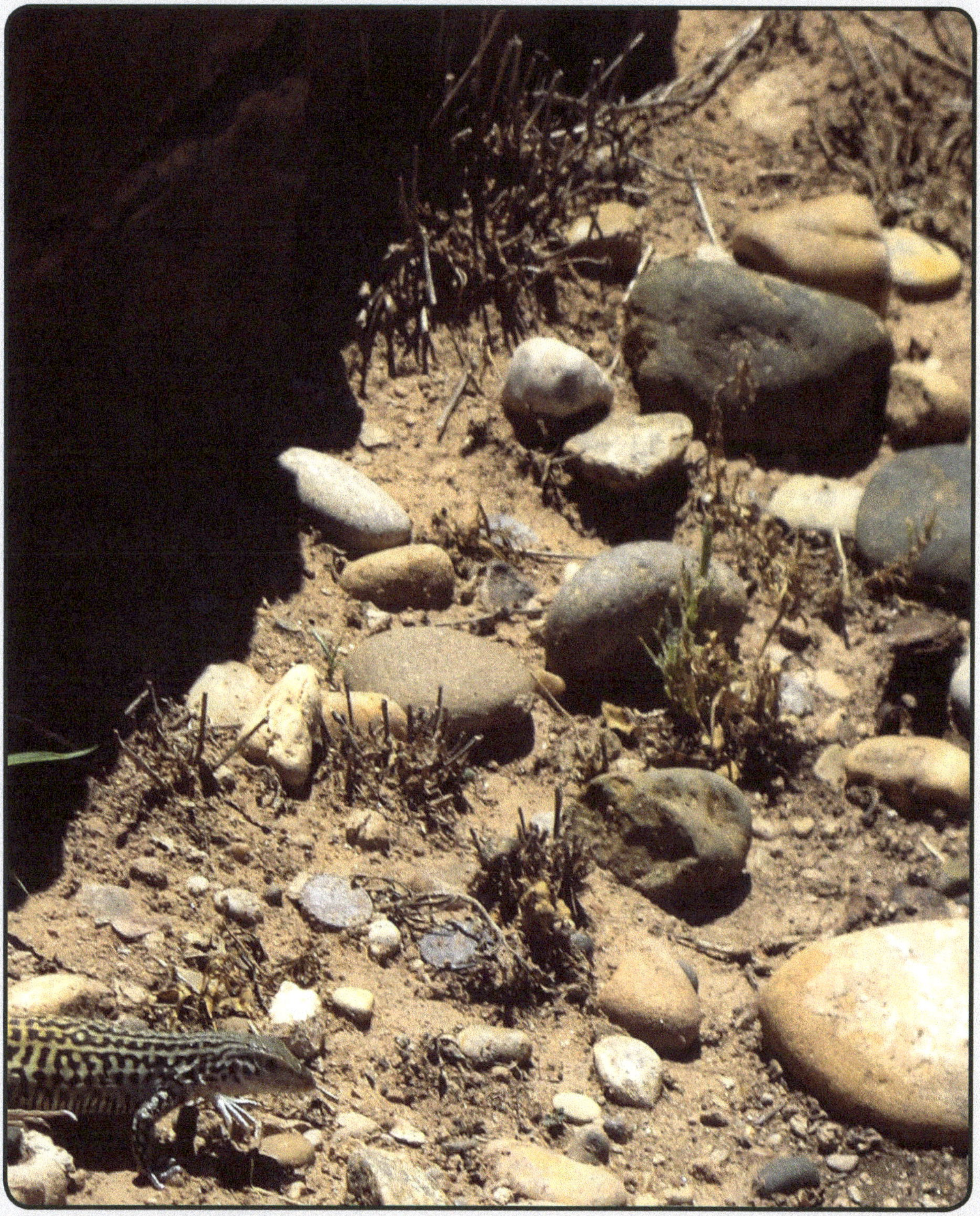

The lizard emerges from the base of Maxwell's grave.

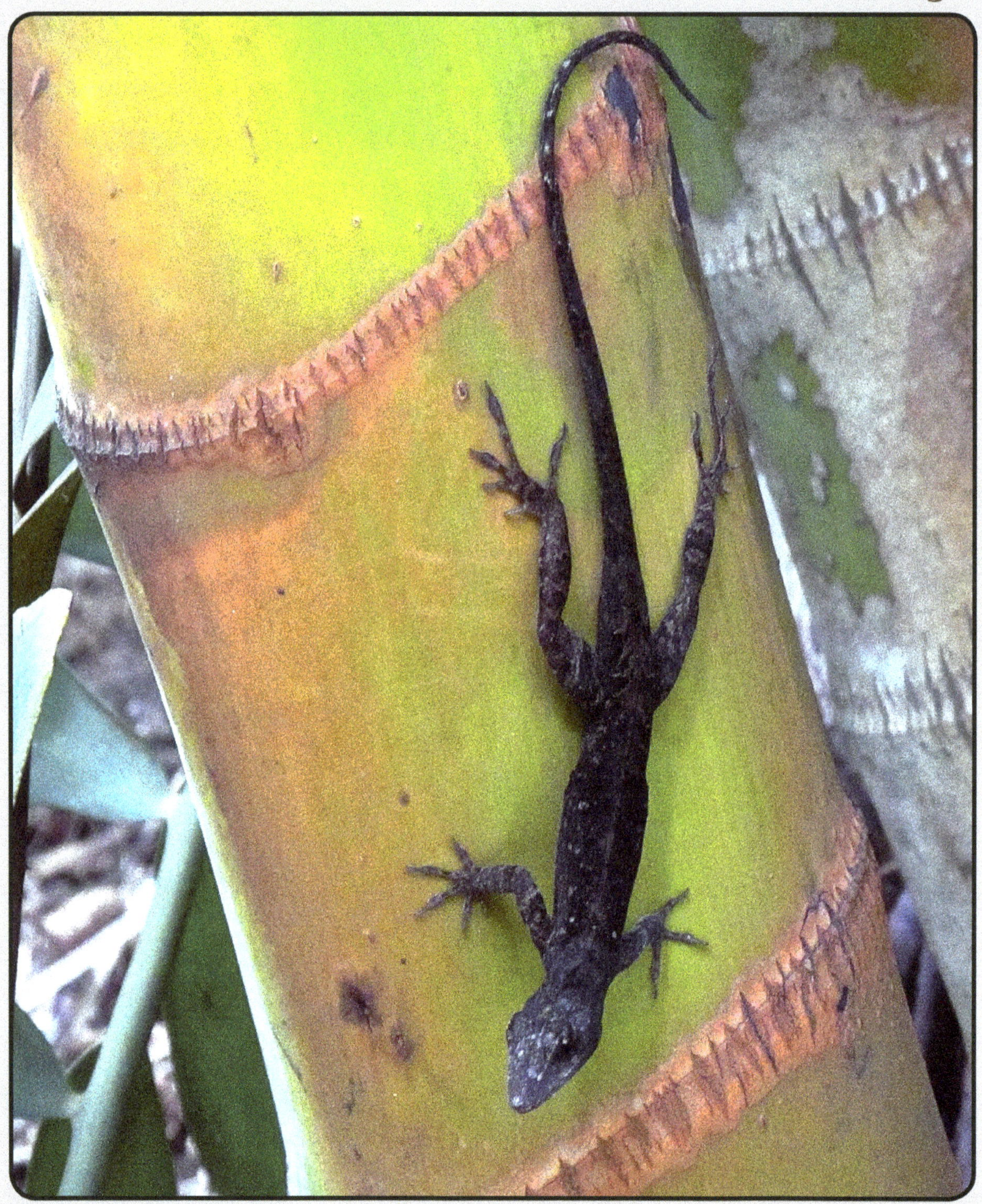

Hang ten lizard style.

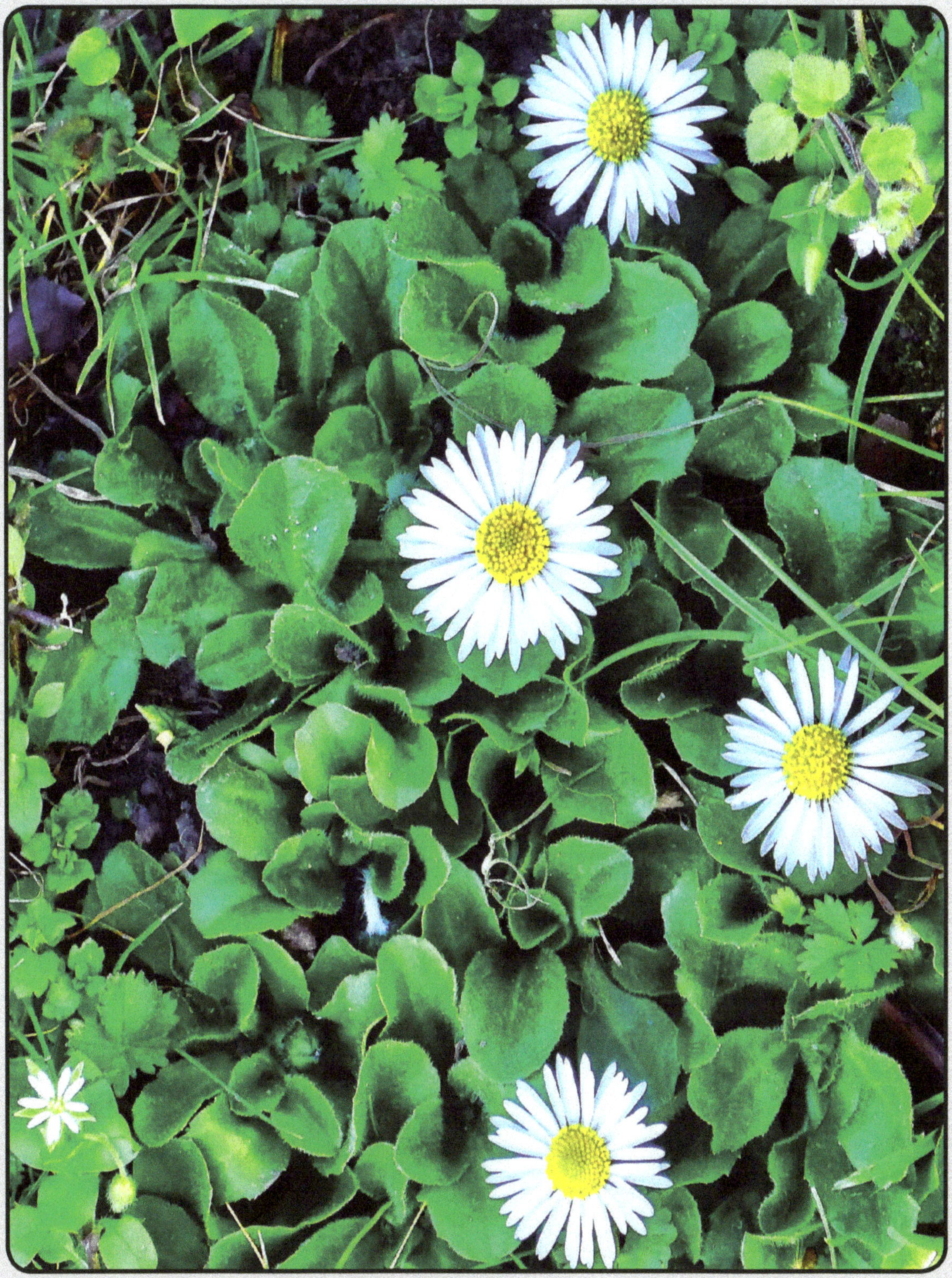

✳ Stars.

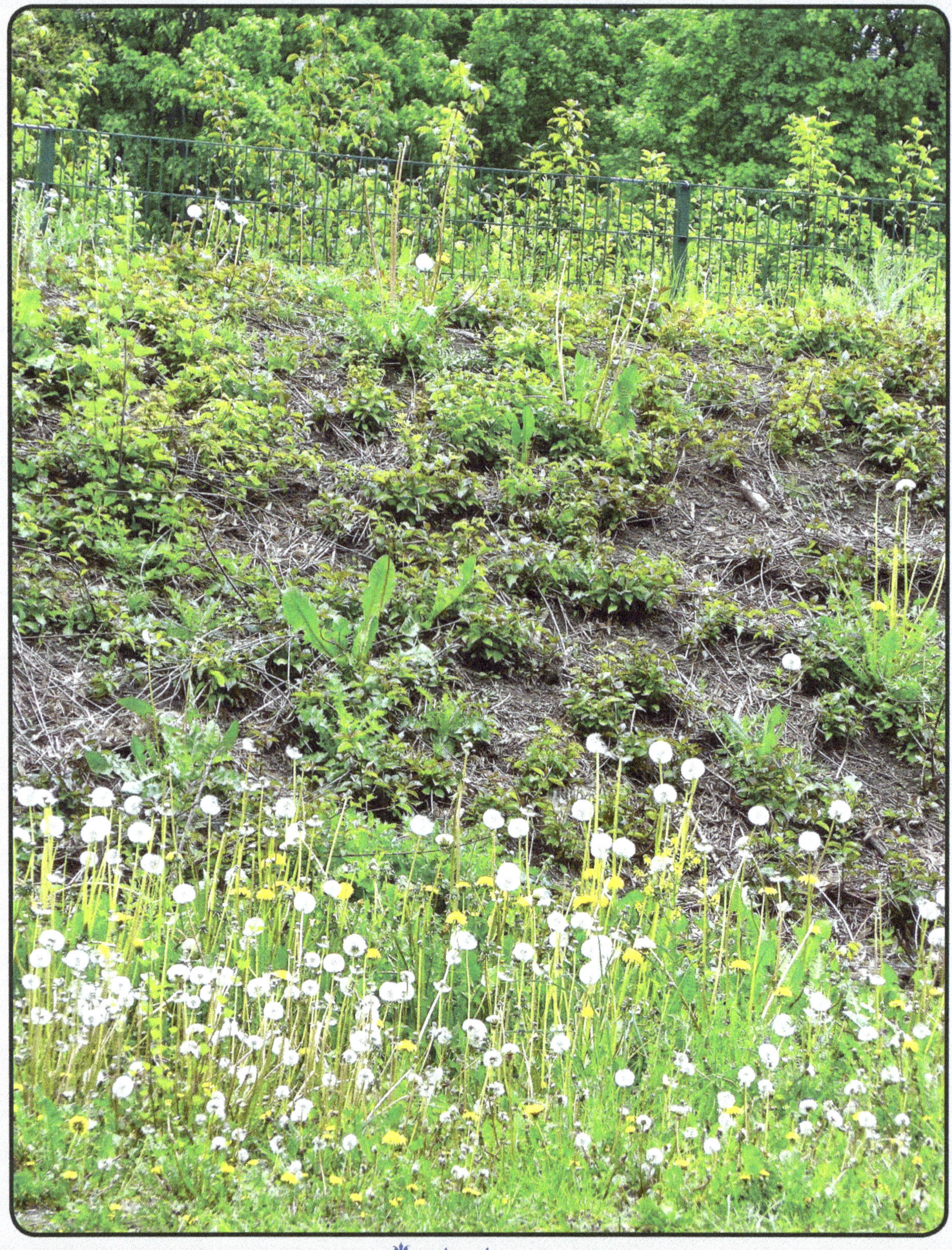

White lanterns.

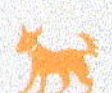

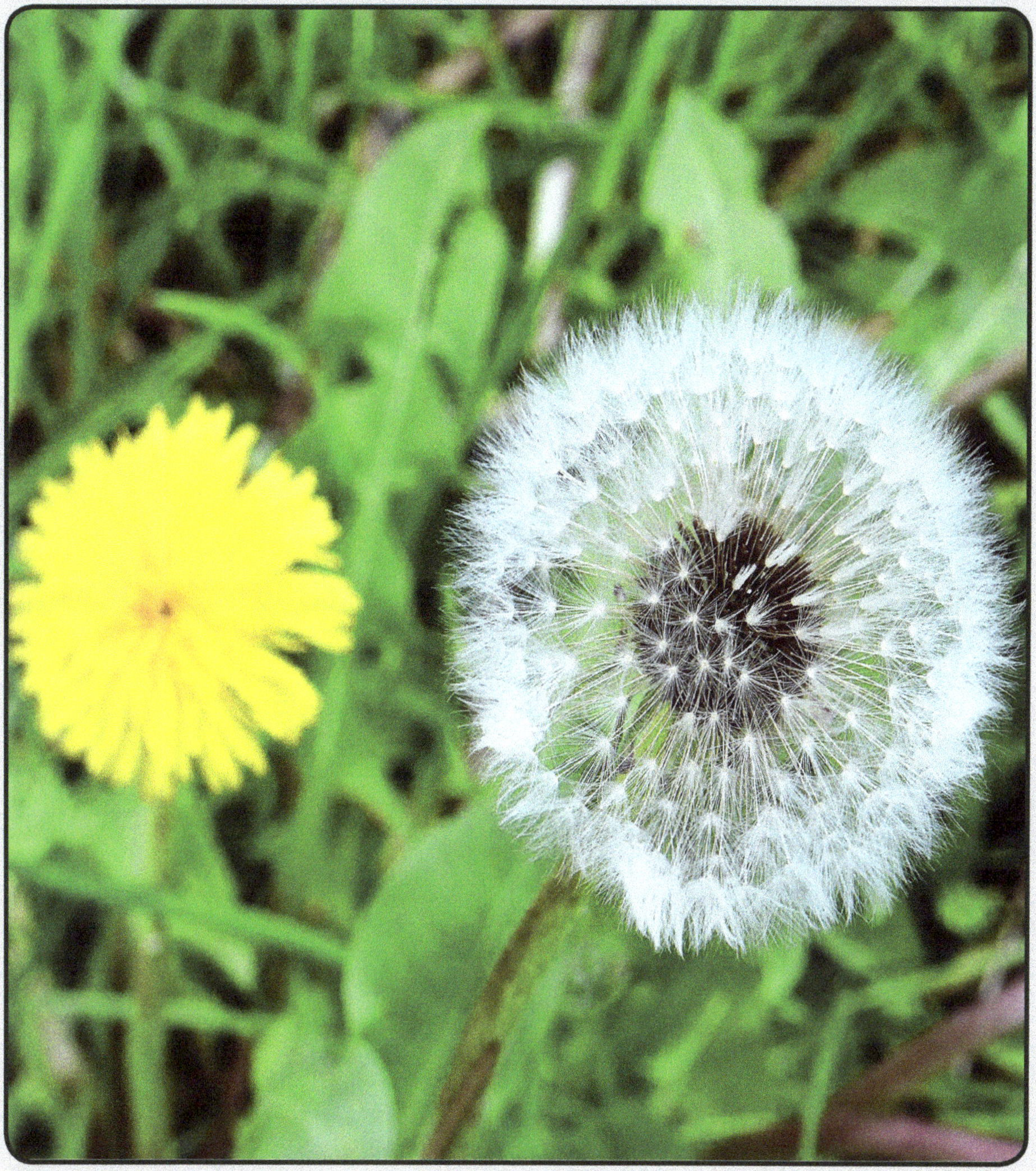

Puff.

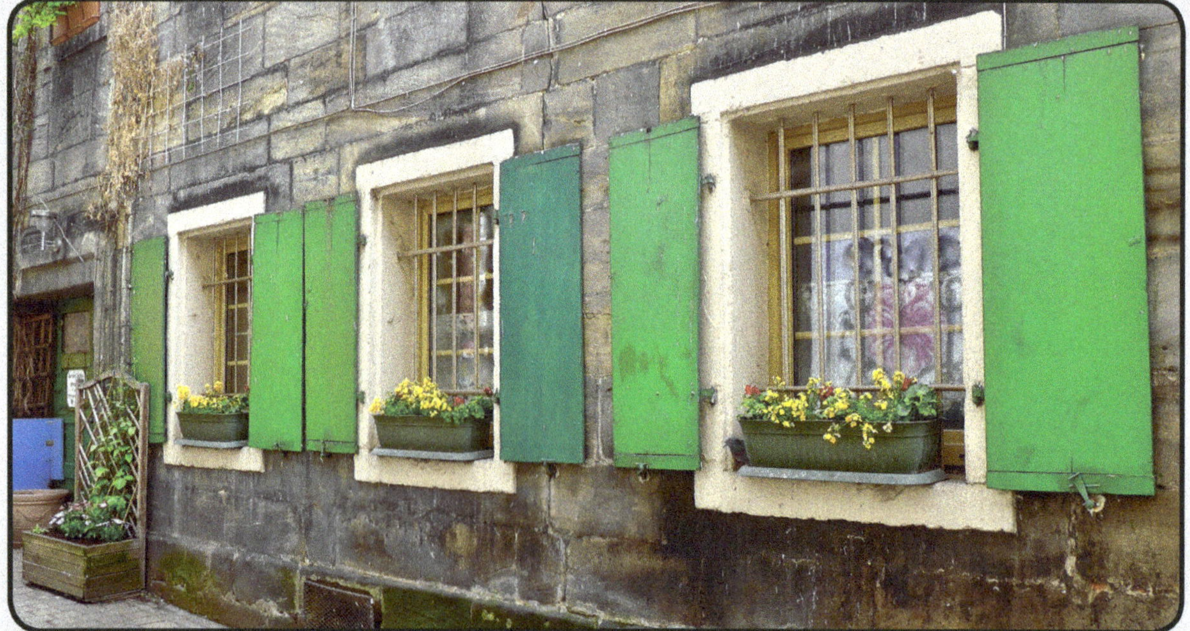

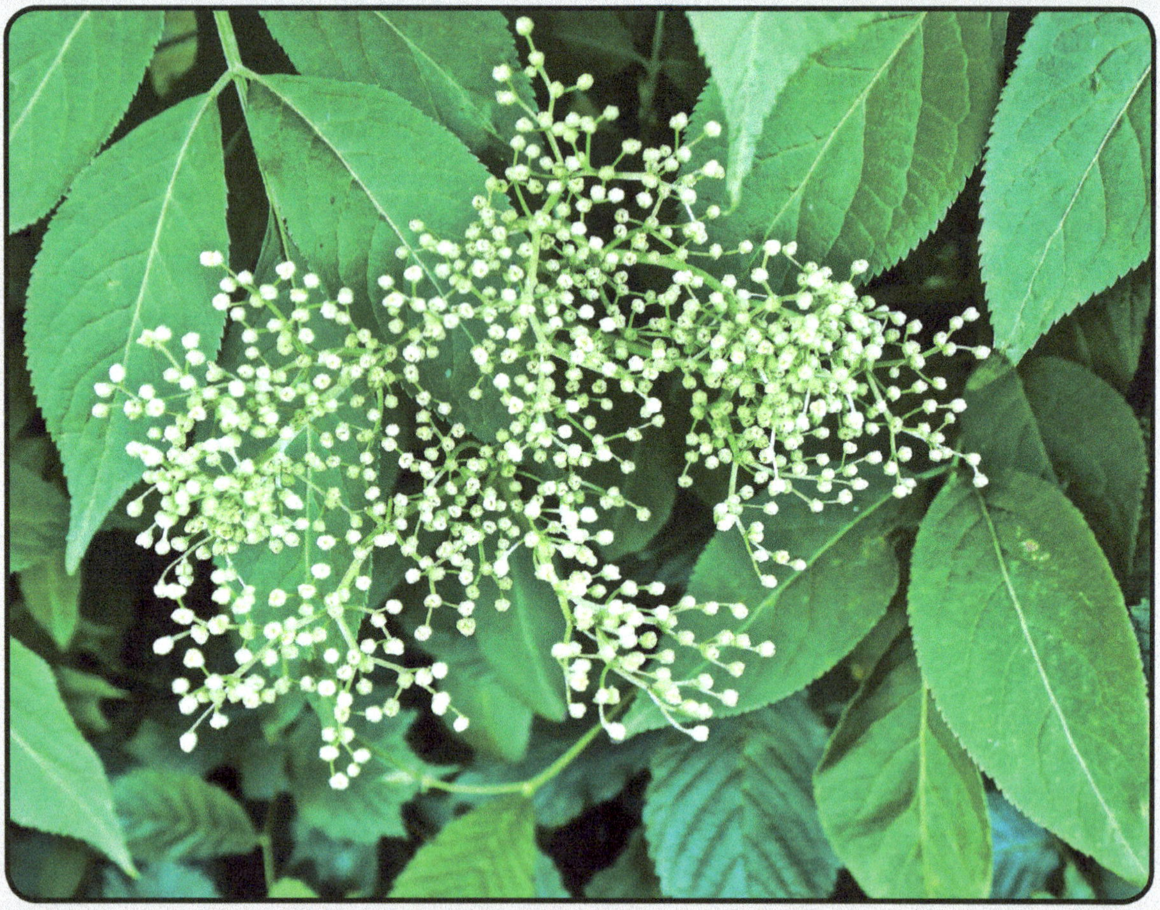

❋ Pearls and fronds.

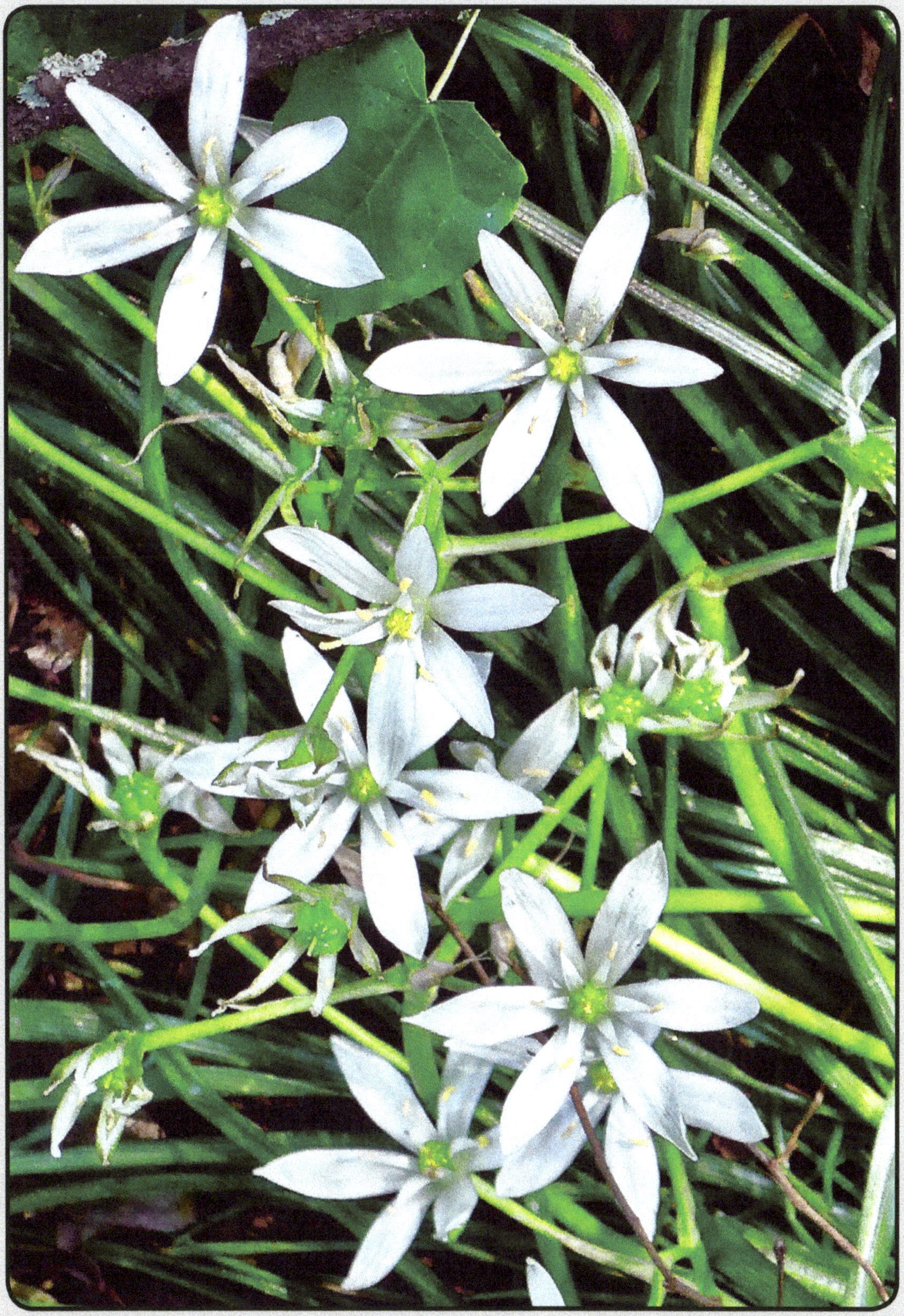

✻ Supernova duets.

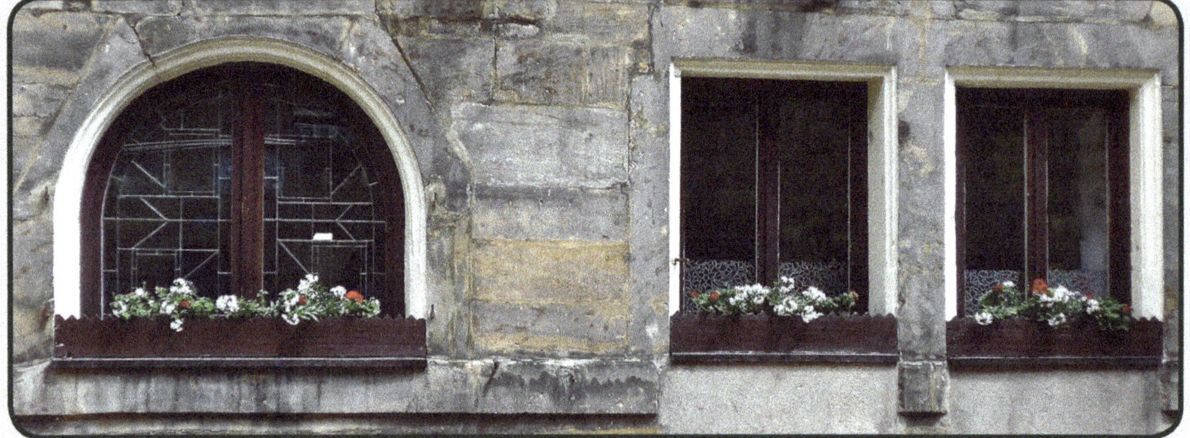

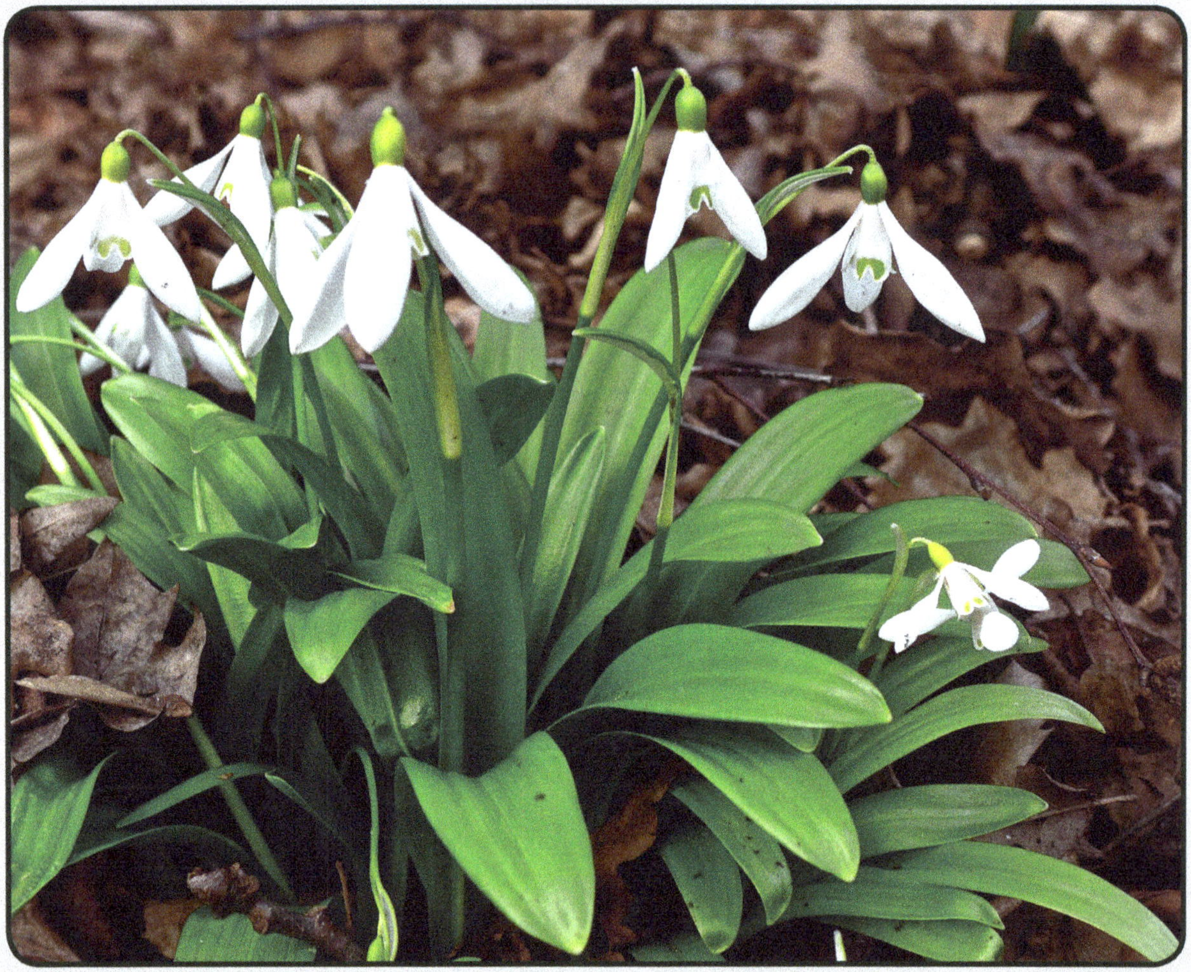

Spring bonnets.

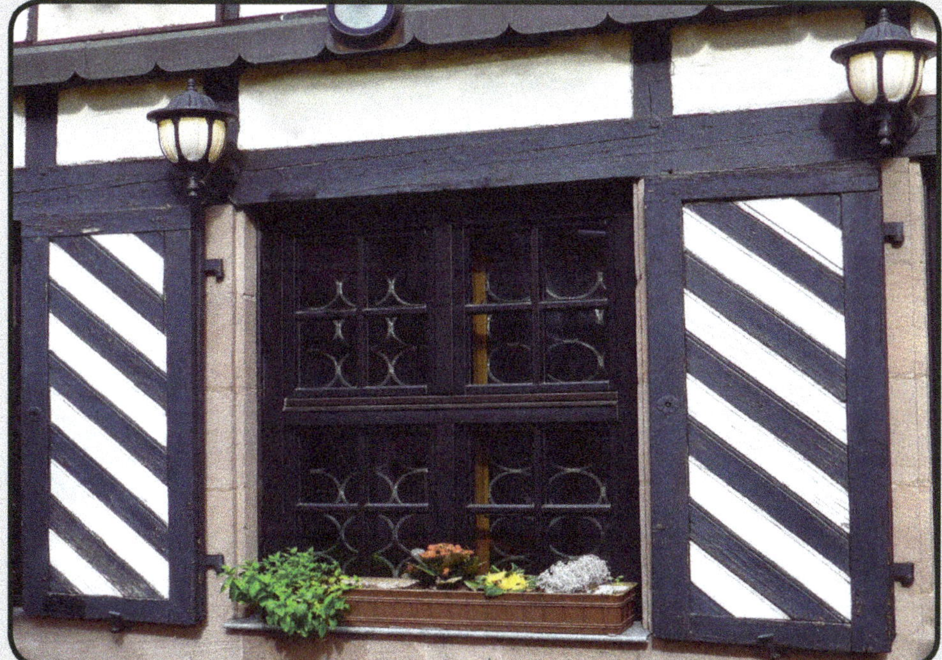

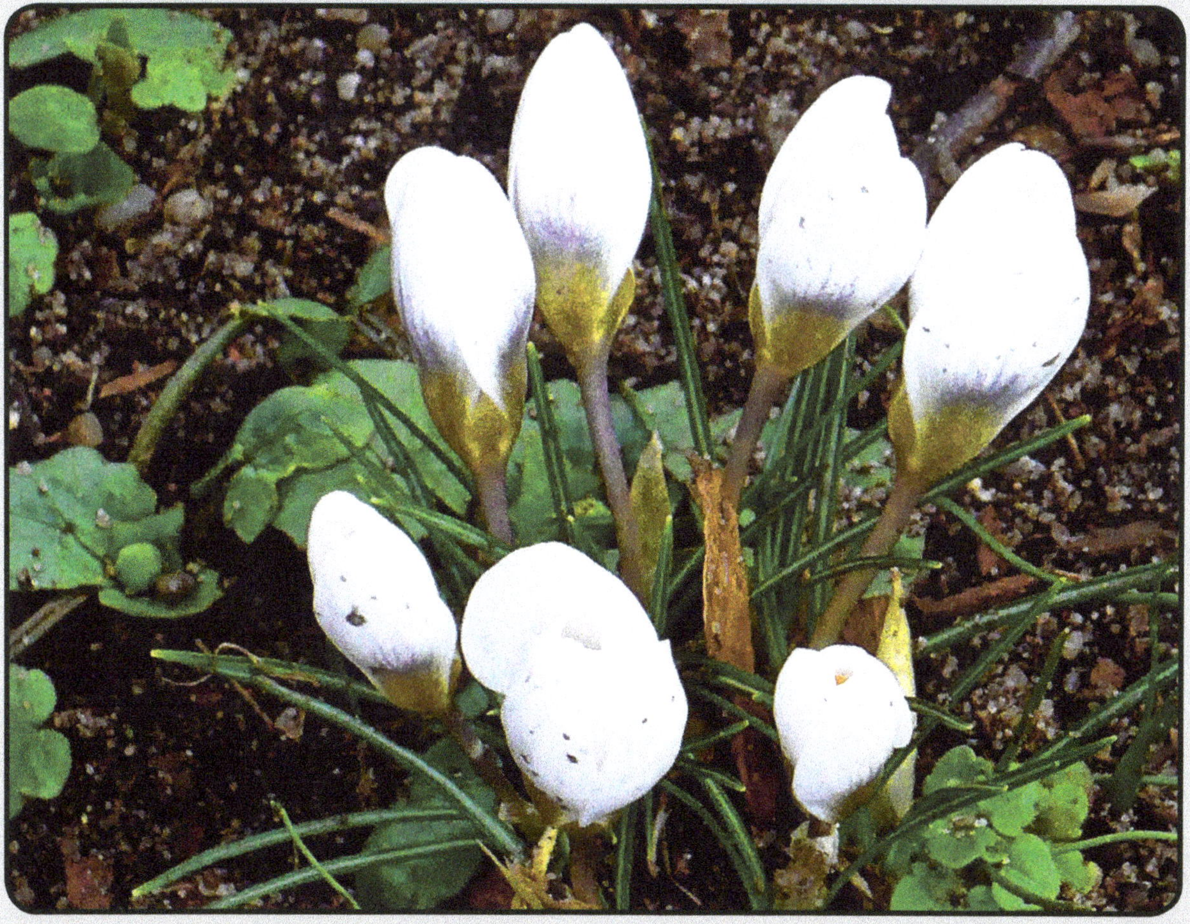

Buried treasure.

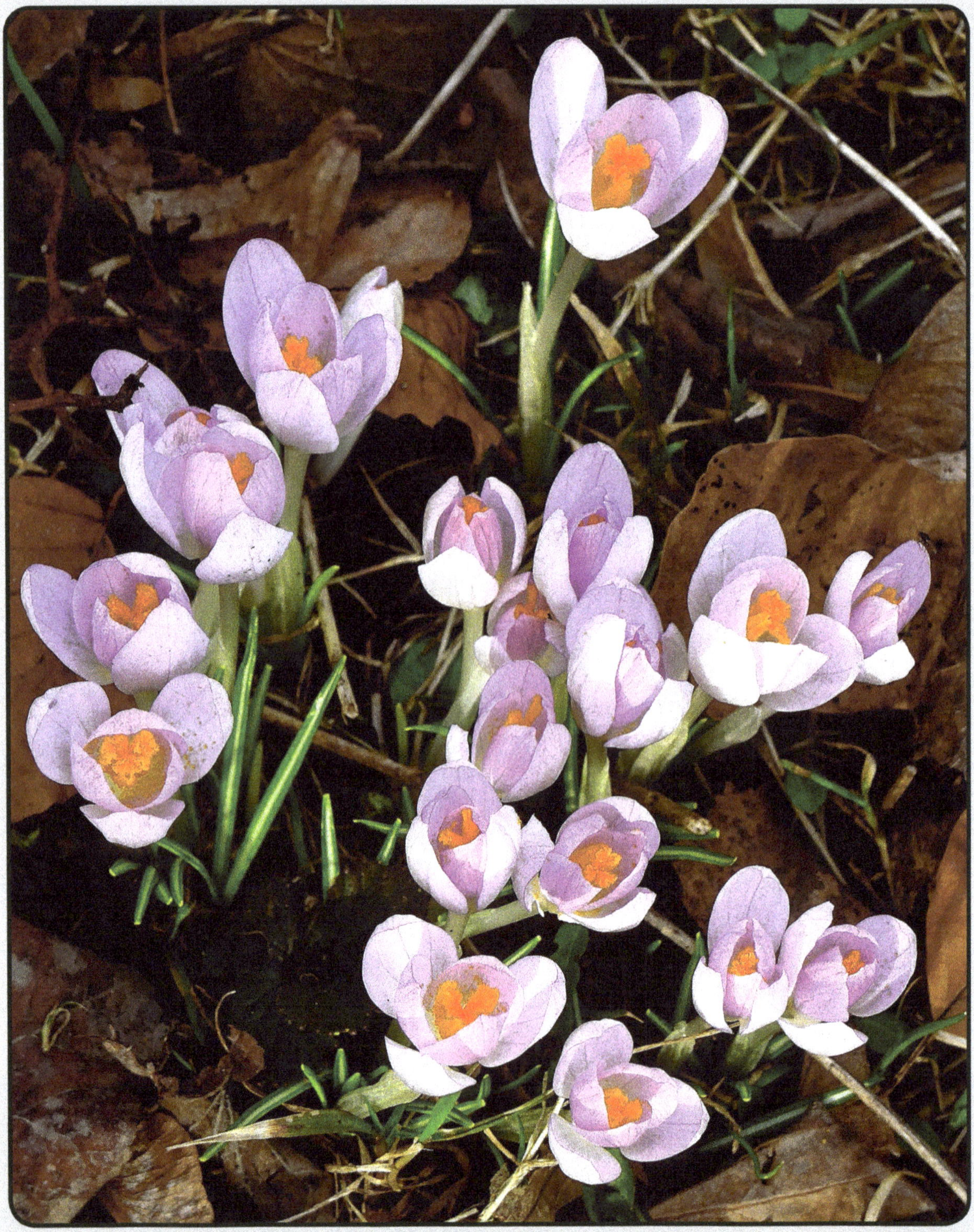

Blossoms sunny side up.

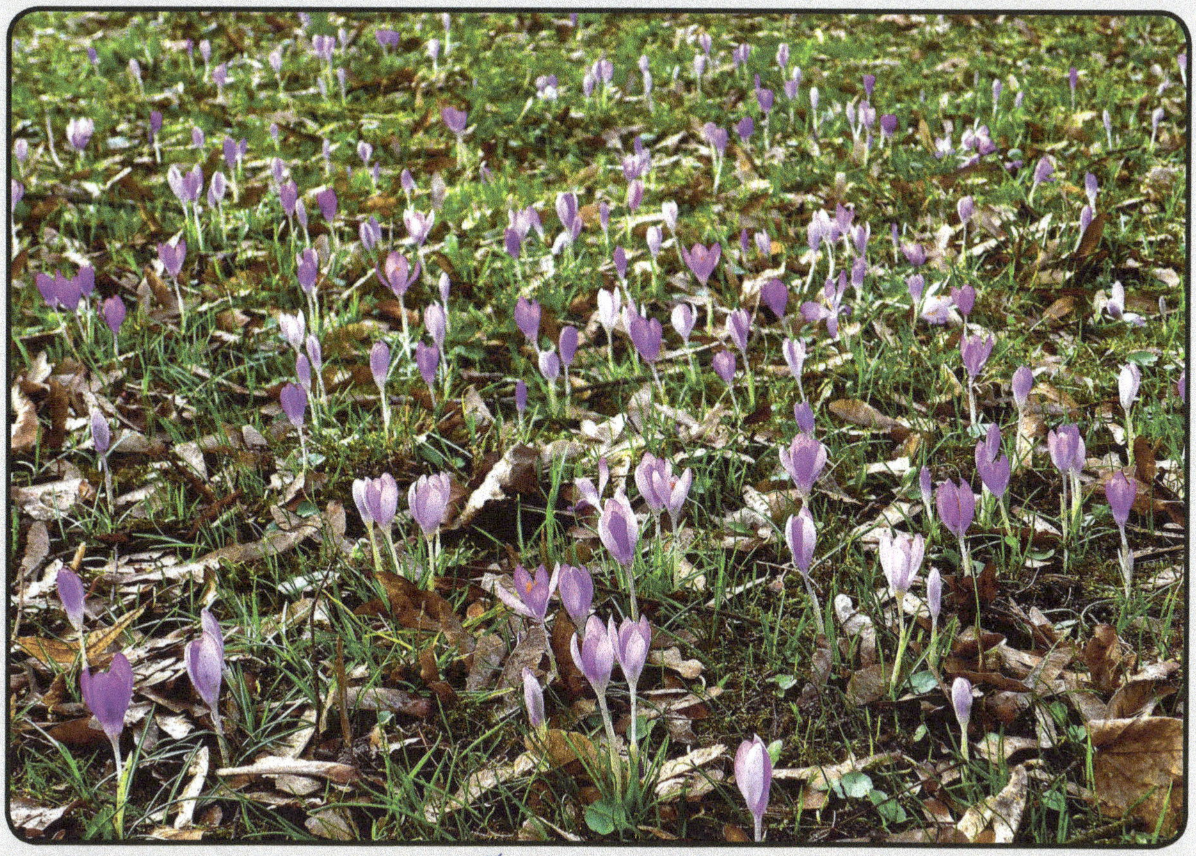

Awakening series.

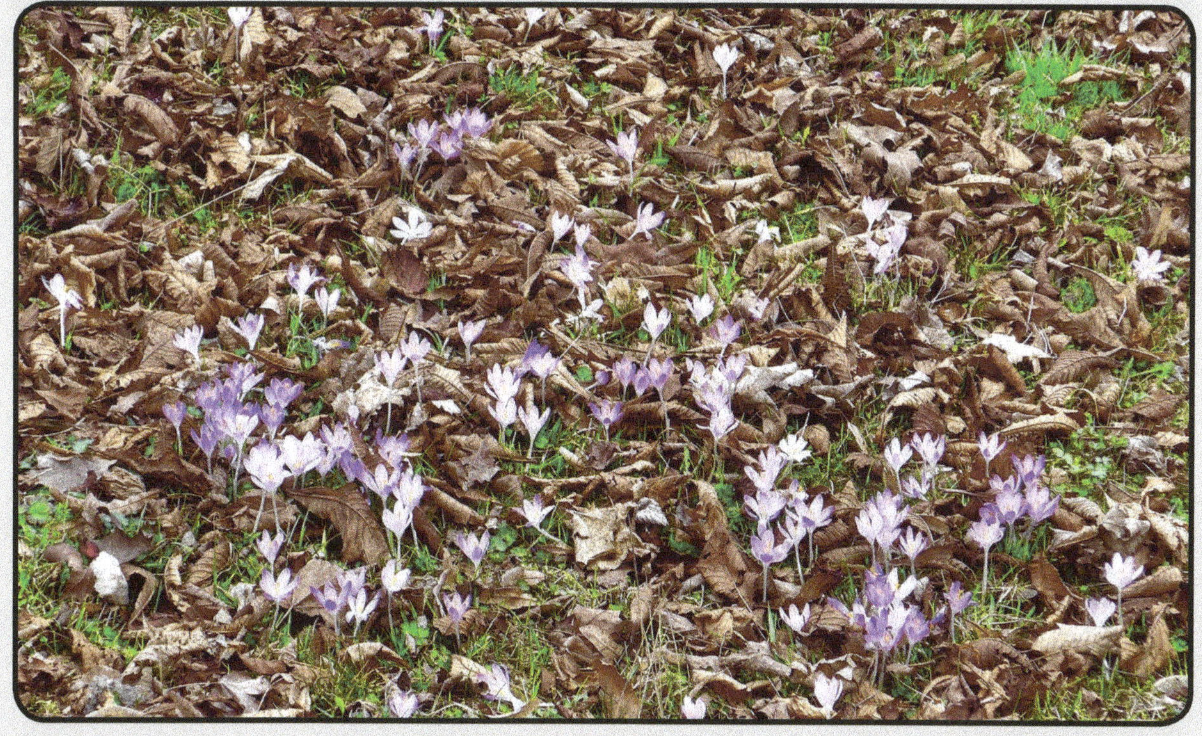

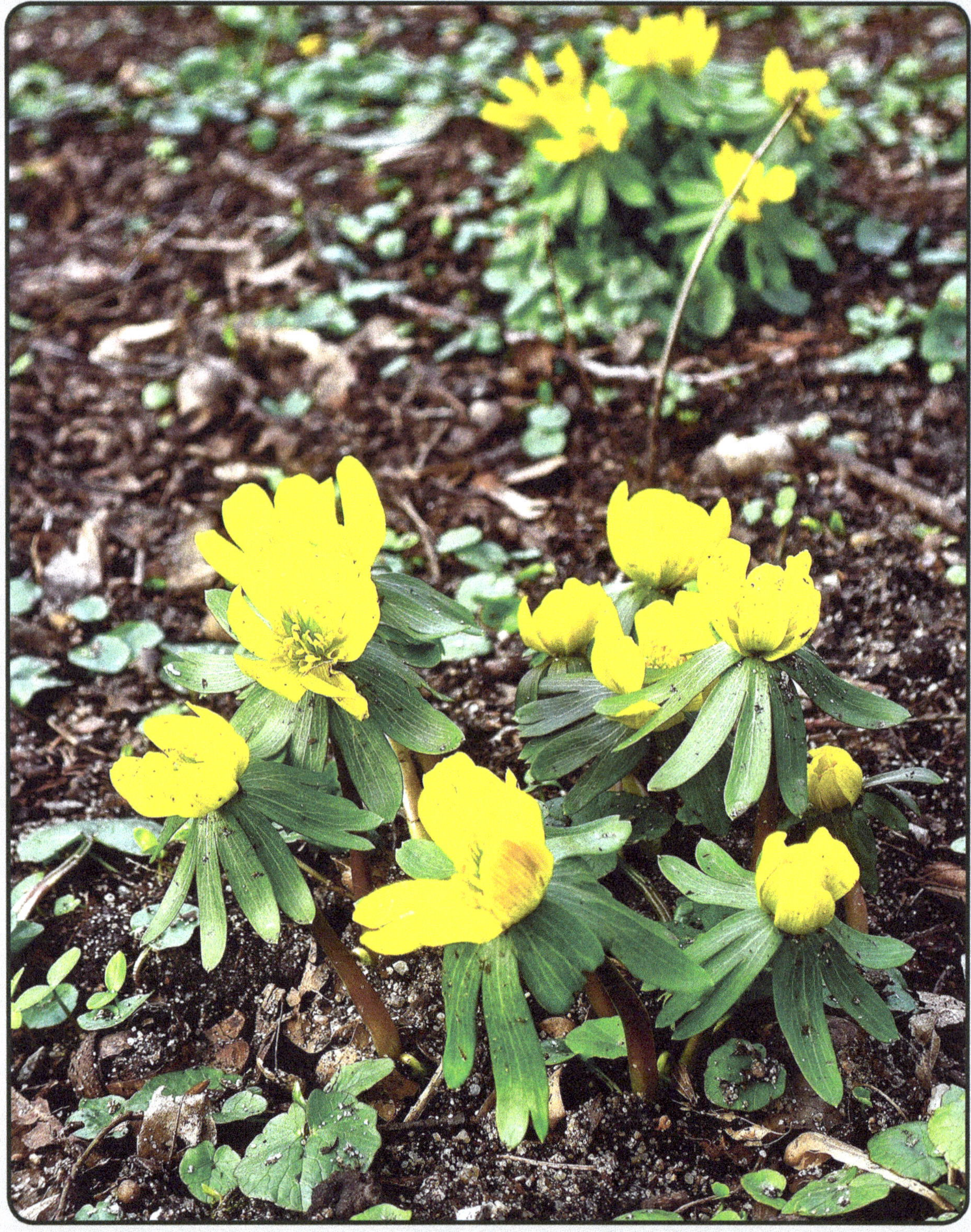

Growing up.

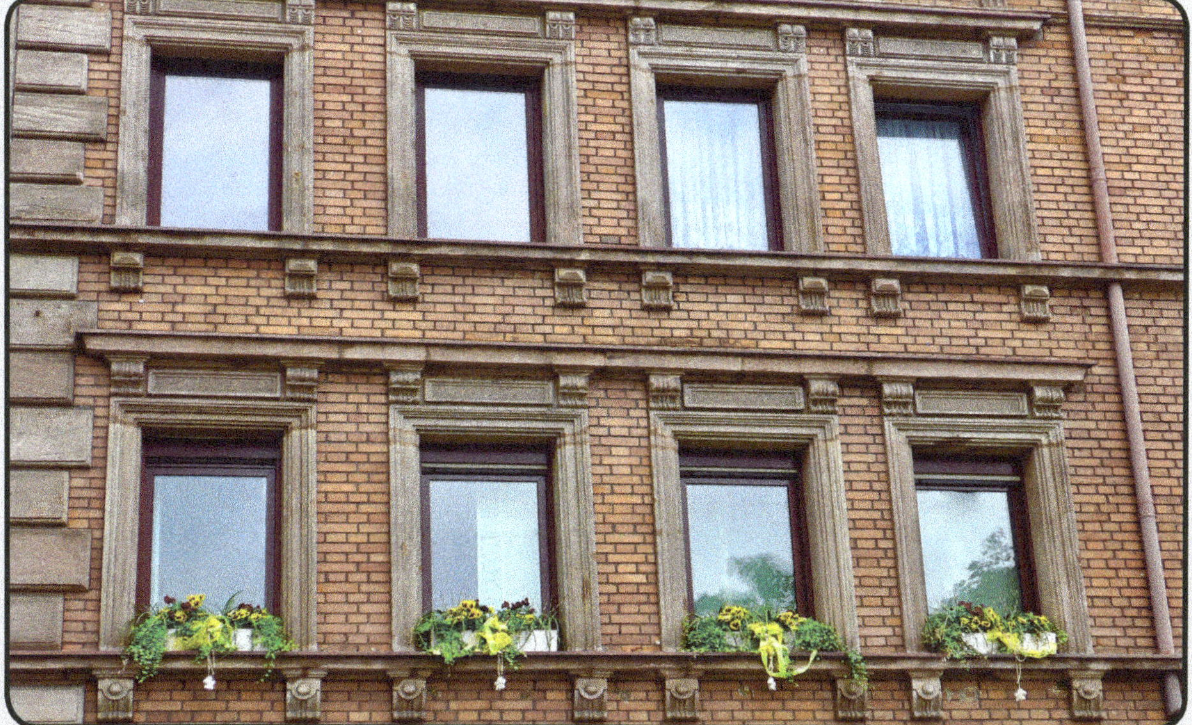

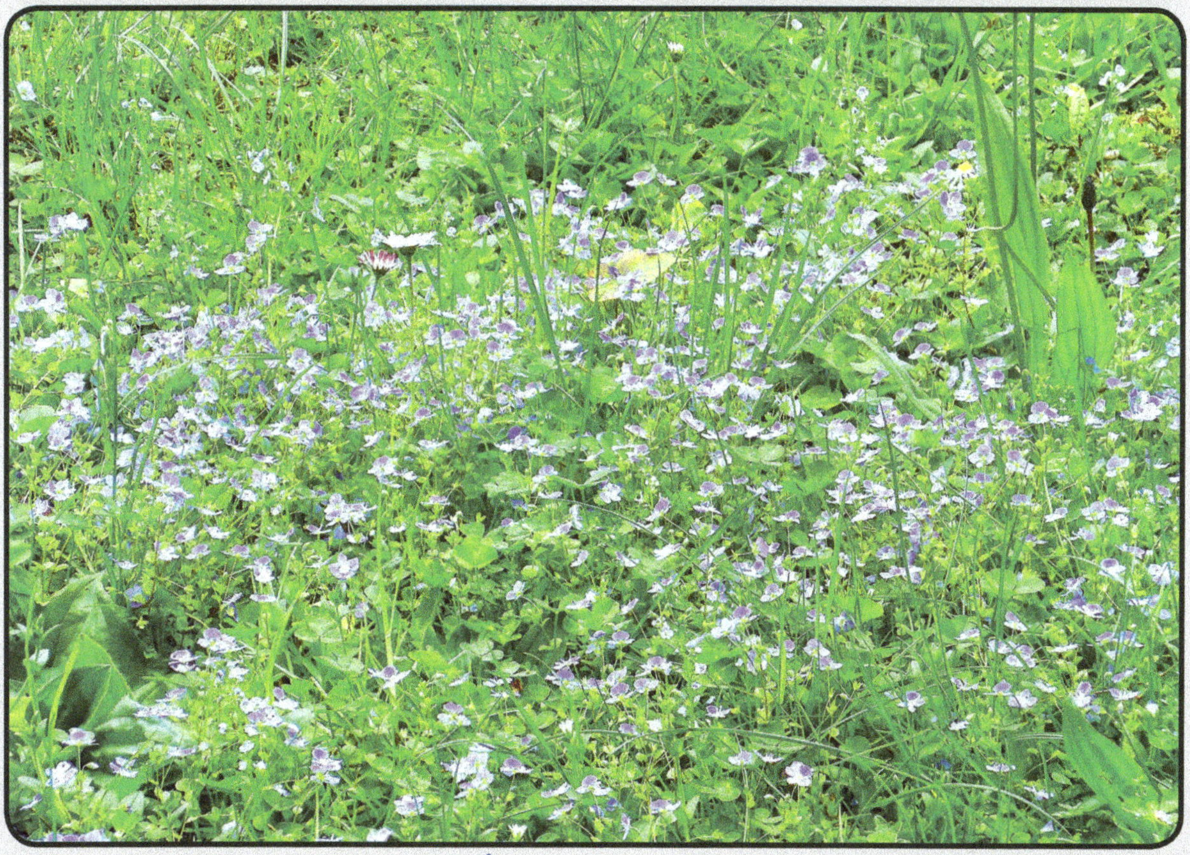

Meadow wonder.

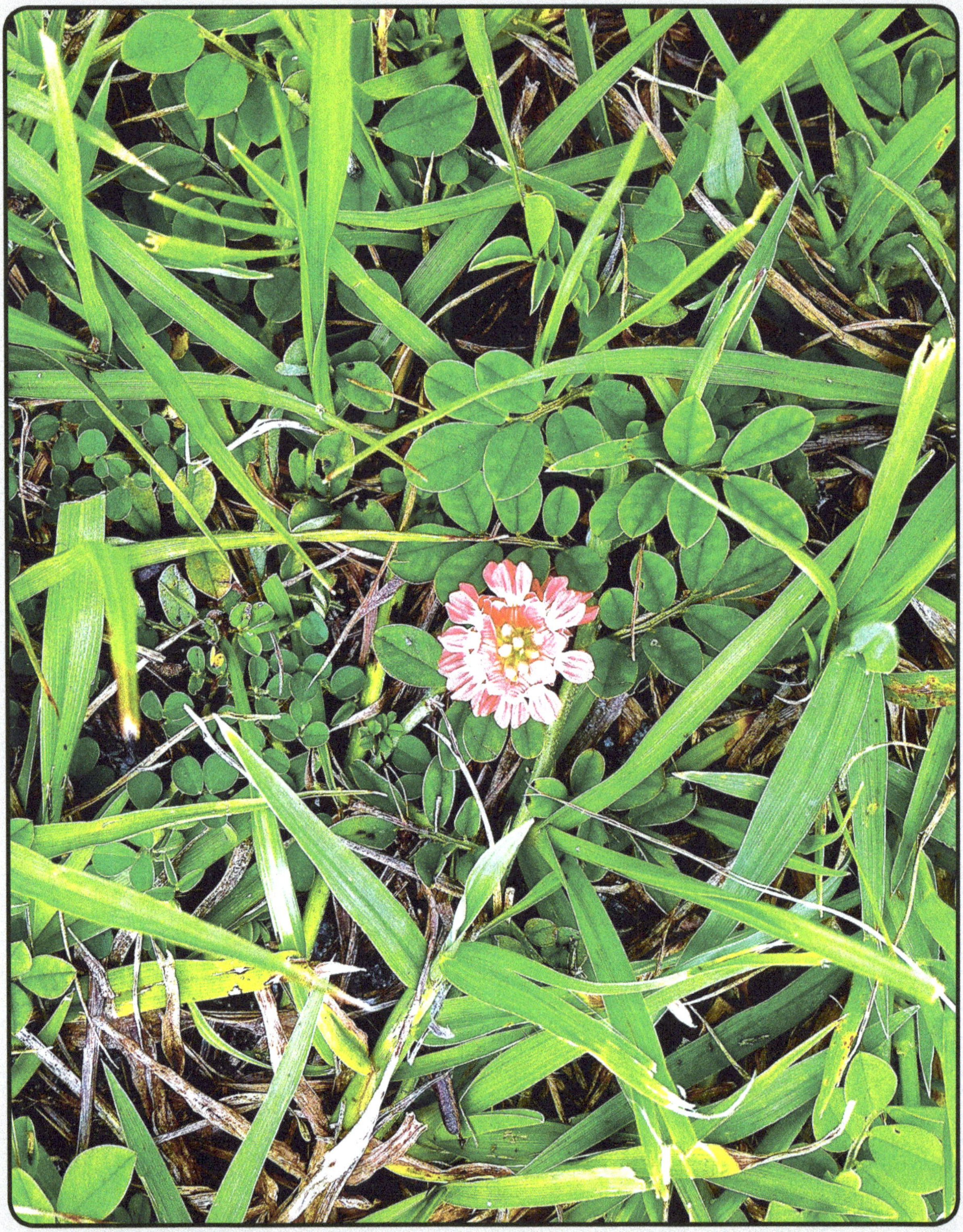

Beauty underfoot.

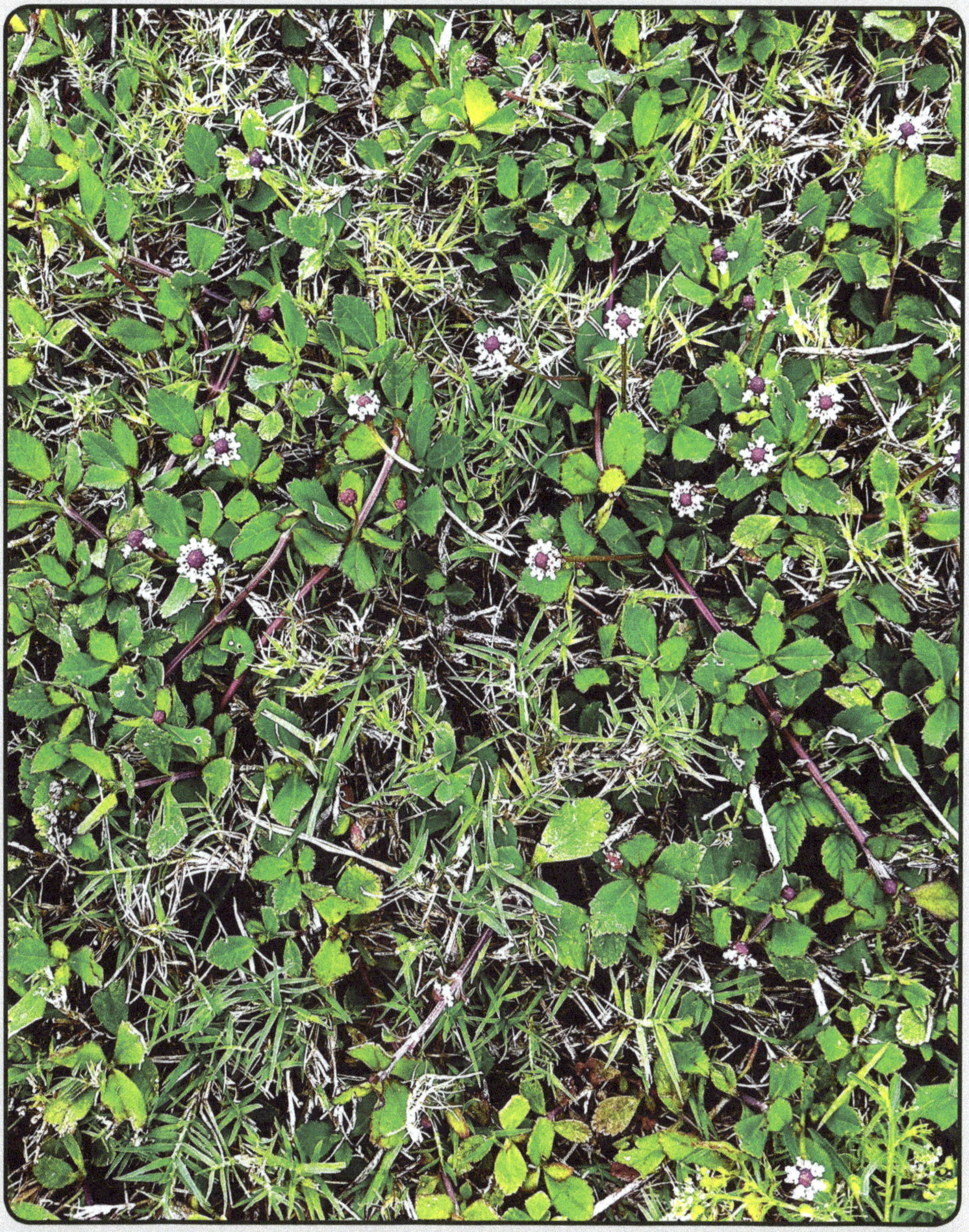

Happy faces in the grass.

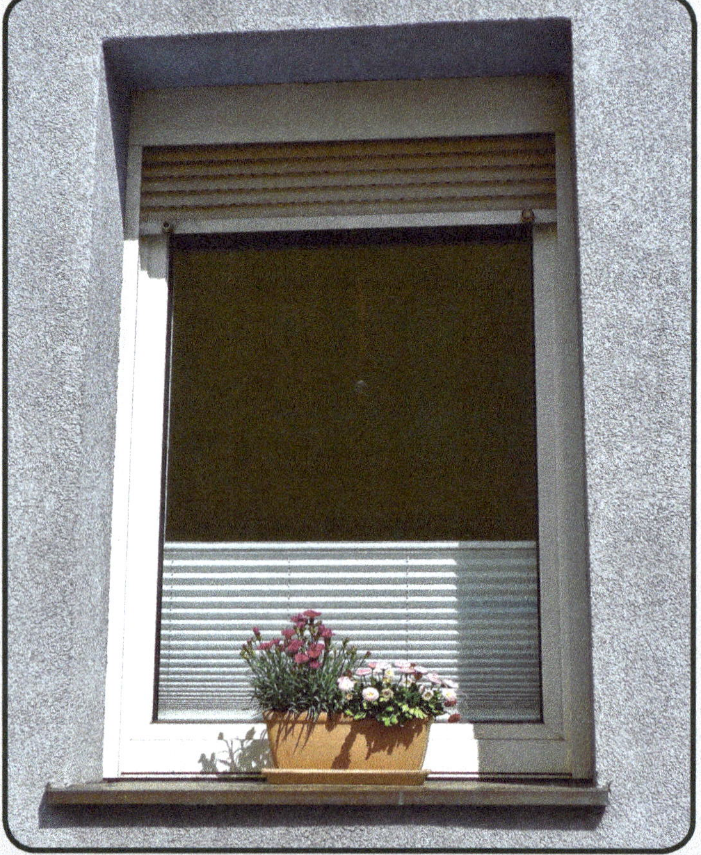

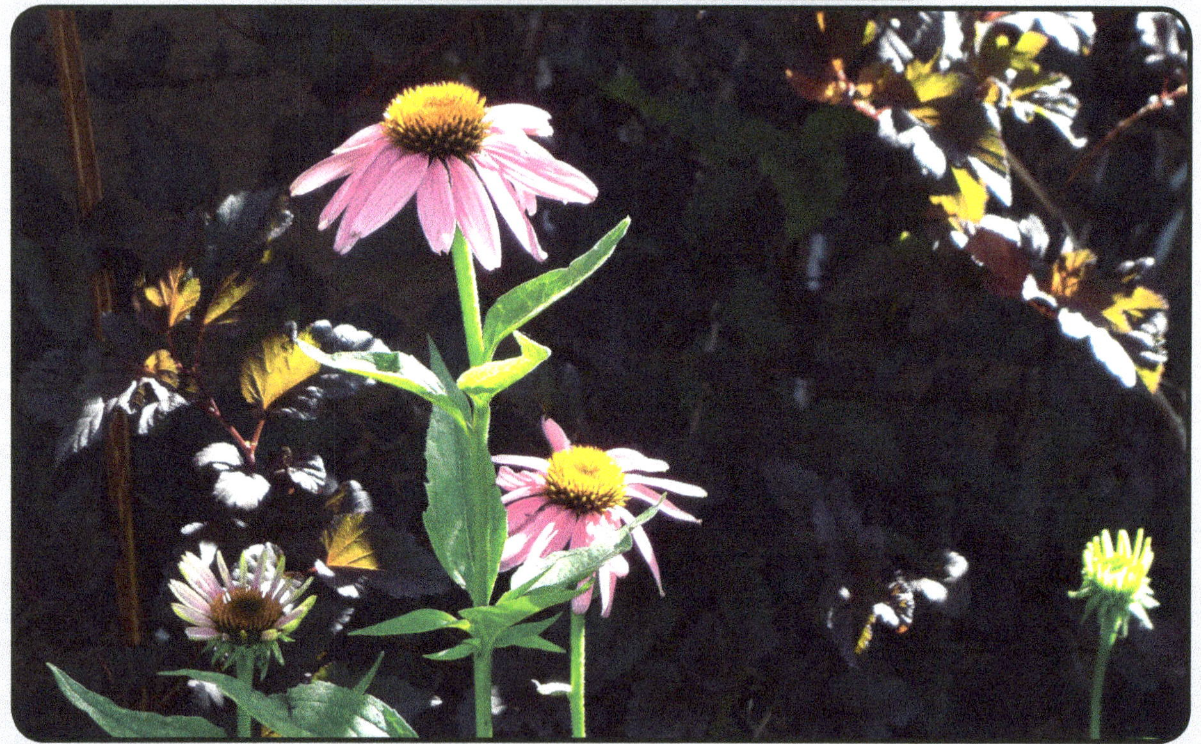

Sunray kisses.

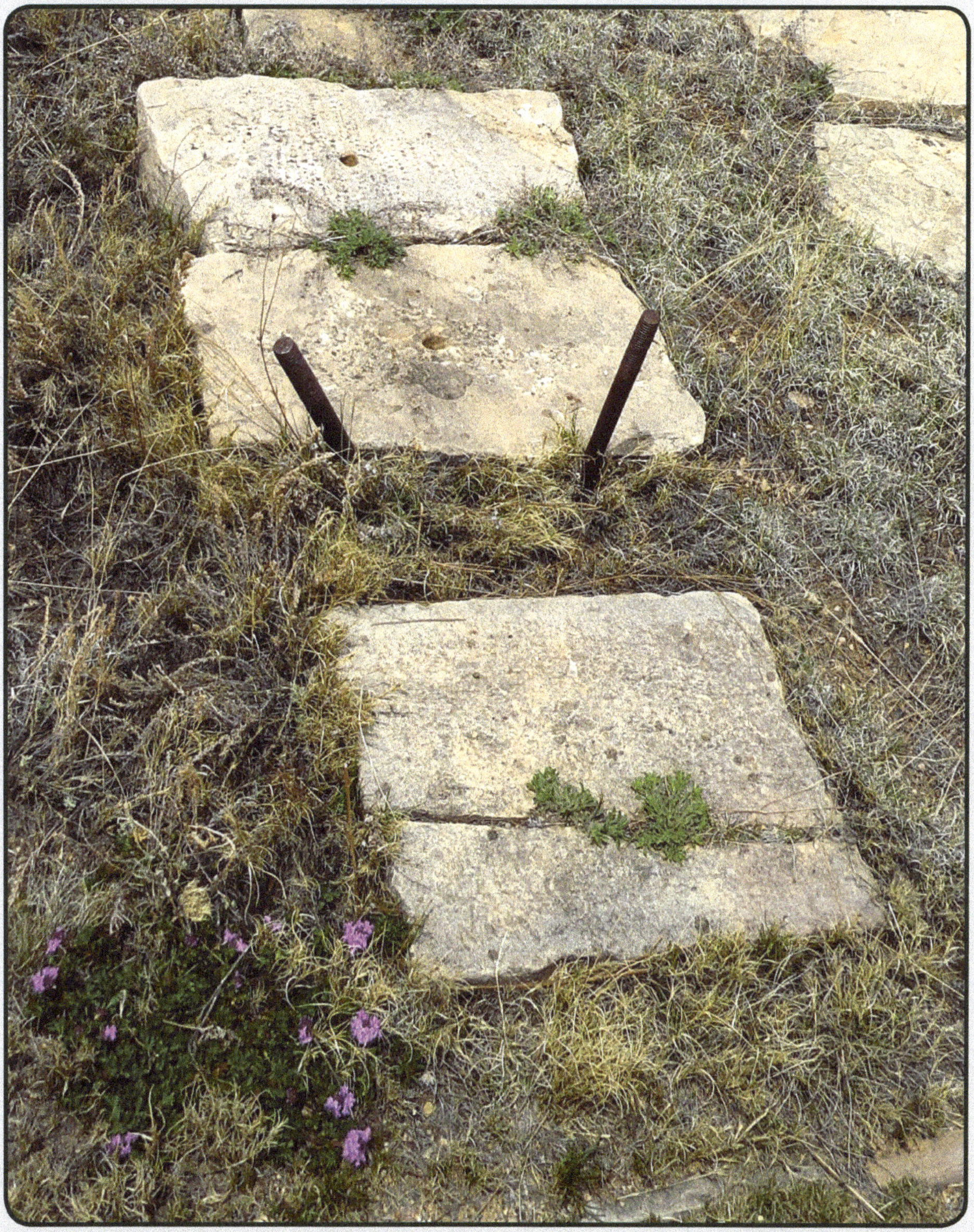

Purple blossoms light an empty pathway of Fort Union, built in 1851.

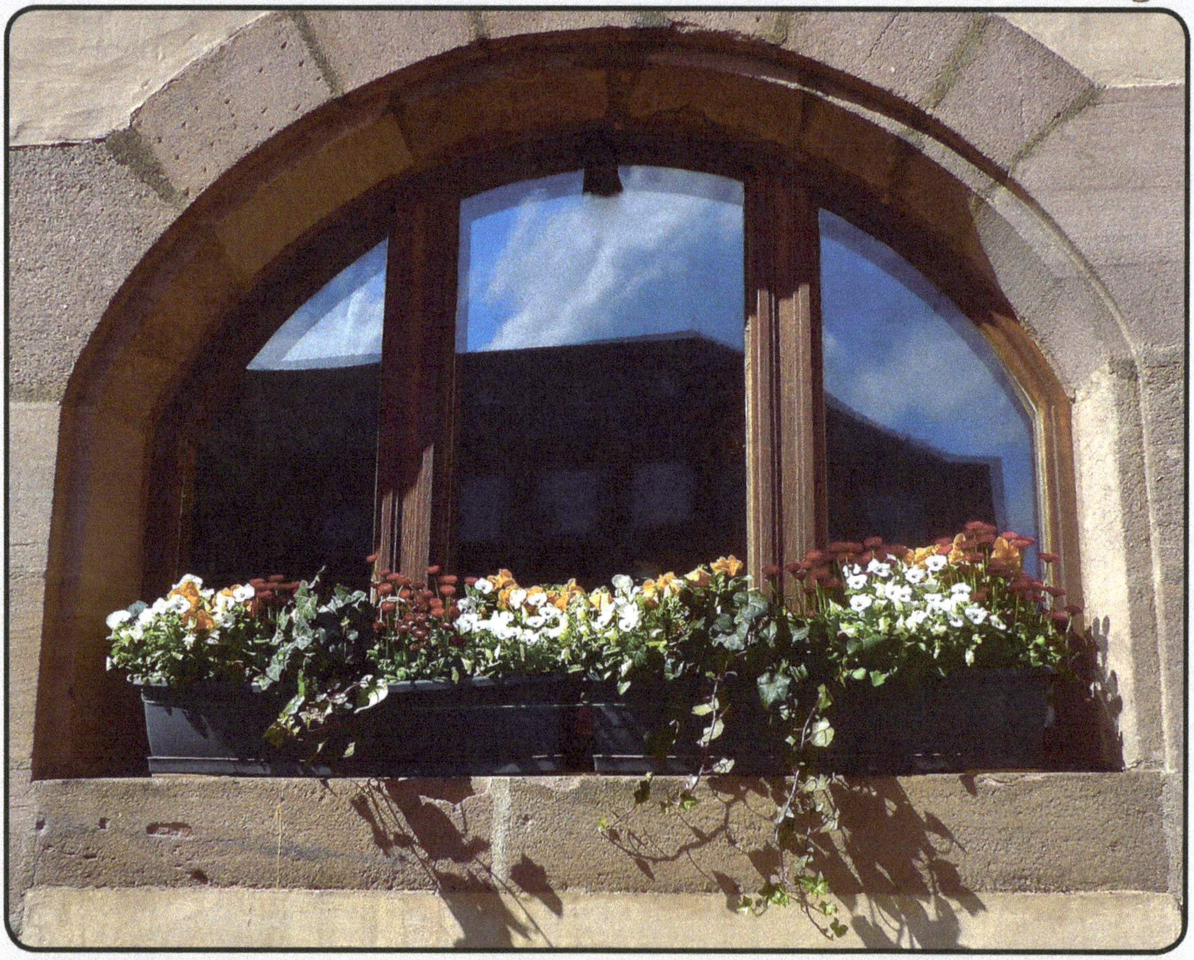

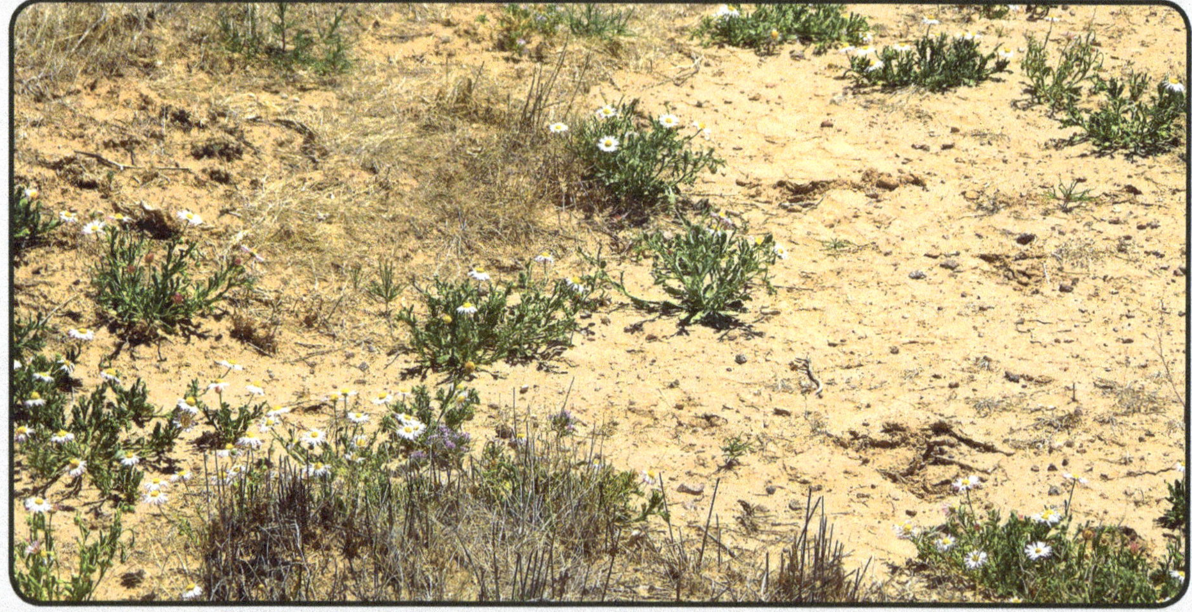

Desert flowers enliven desolate sand upon which soldiers in 1854 built Fort Craig, New Mexico.

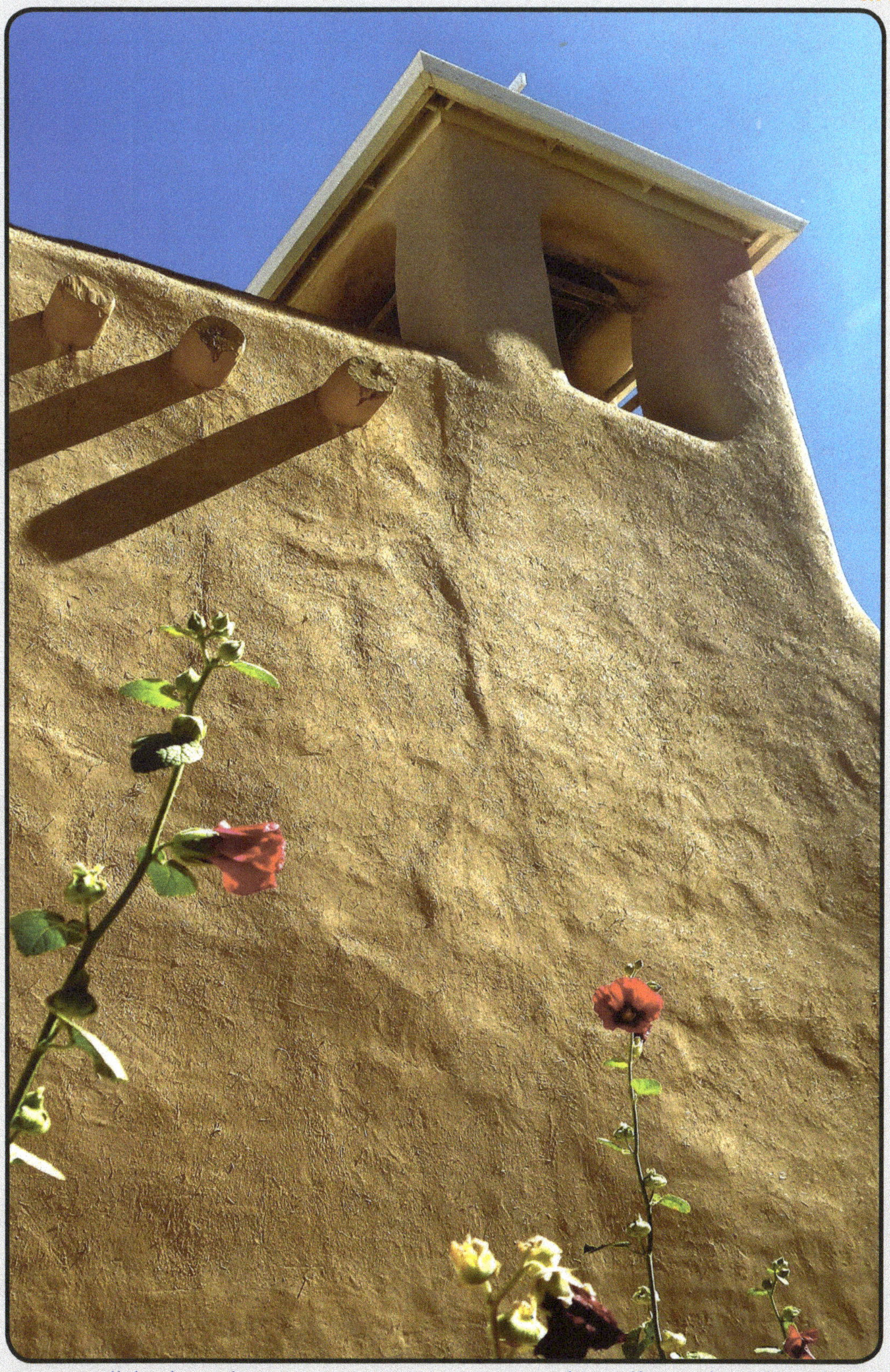

❀Las Varas de San Jose at San Francisco de Asis church.

[Note: Hollyhocks are known in New Mexico as St. Joseph's staff. I saw them throughout my life in the gardens of old Spanish adobe haciendas since this type of flower thrives in hot, arid lands.]

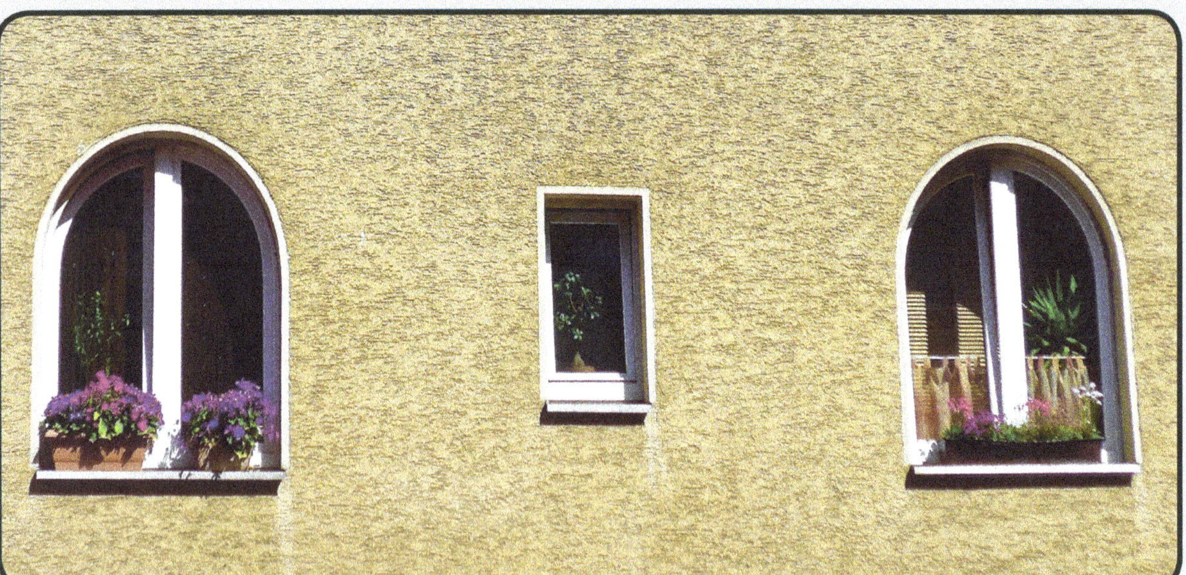

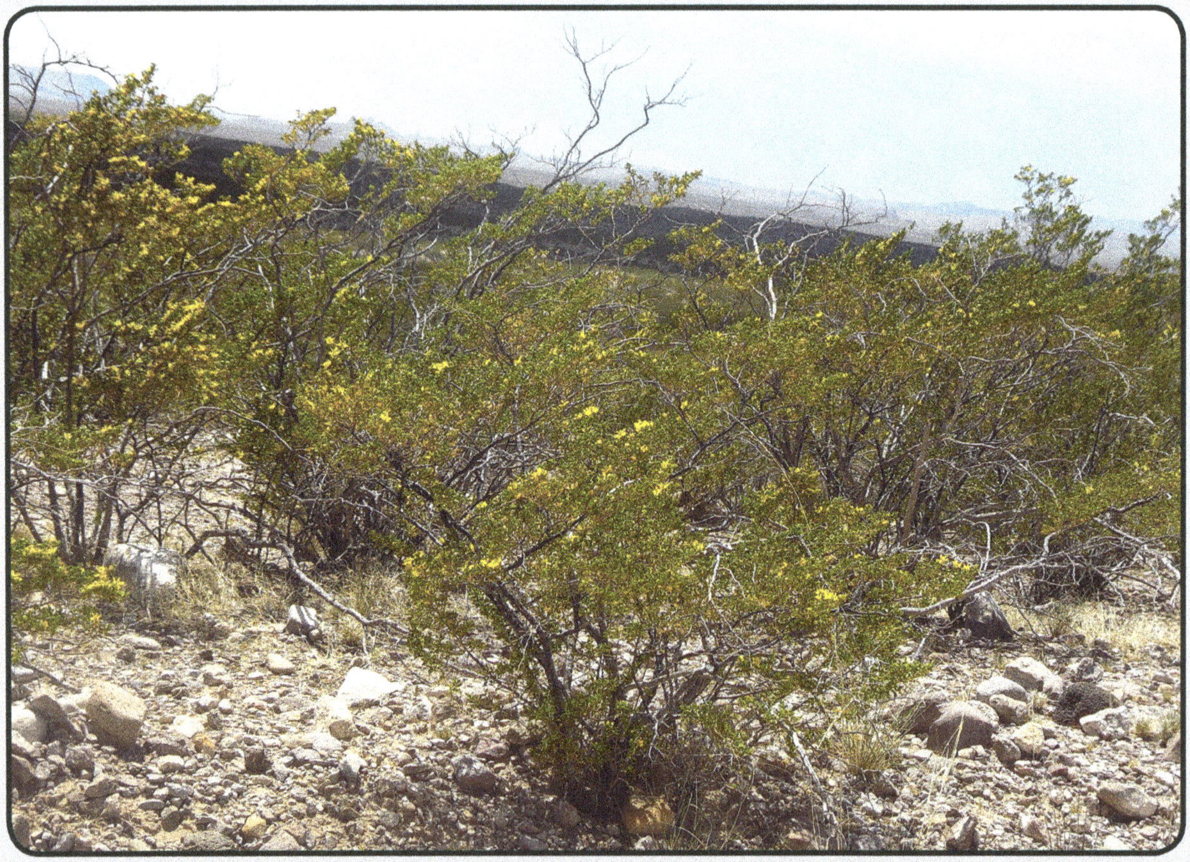

Yellow fluffs illuminate the Jornada del Muerto (Journey of Death) in New Mexico.

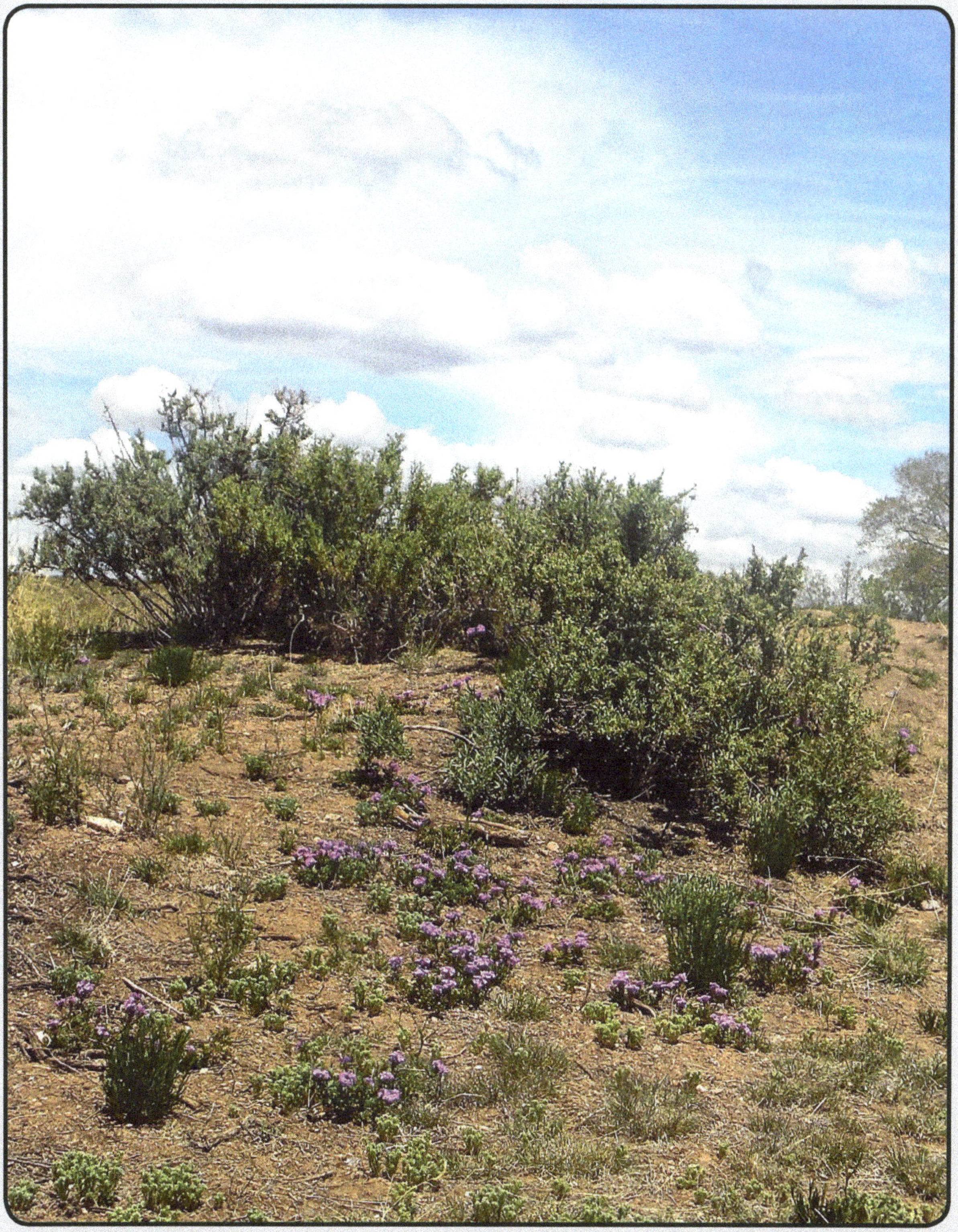

❀ Life continues where cavalry ghosts remain at the 1846 site of Fort Marcy.

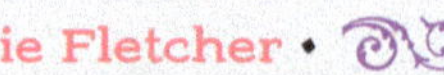

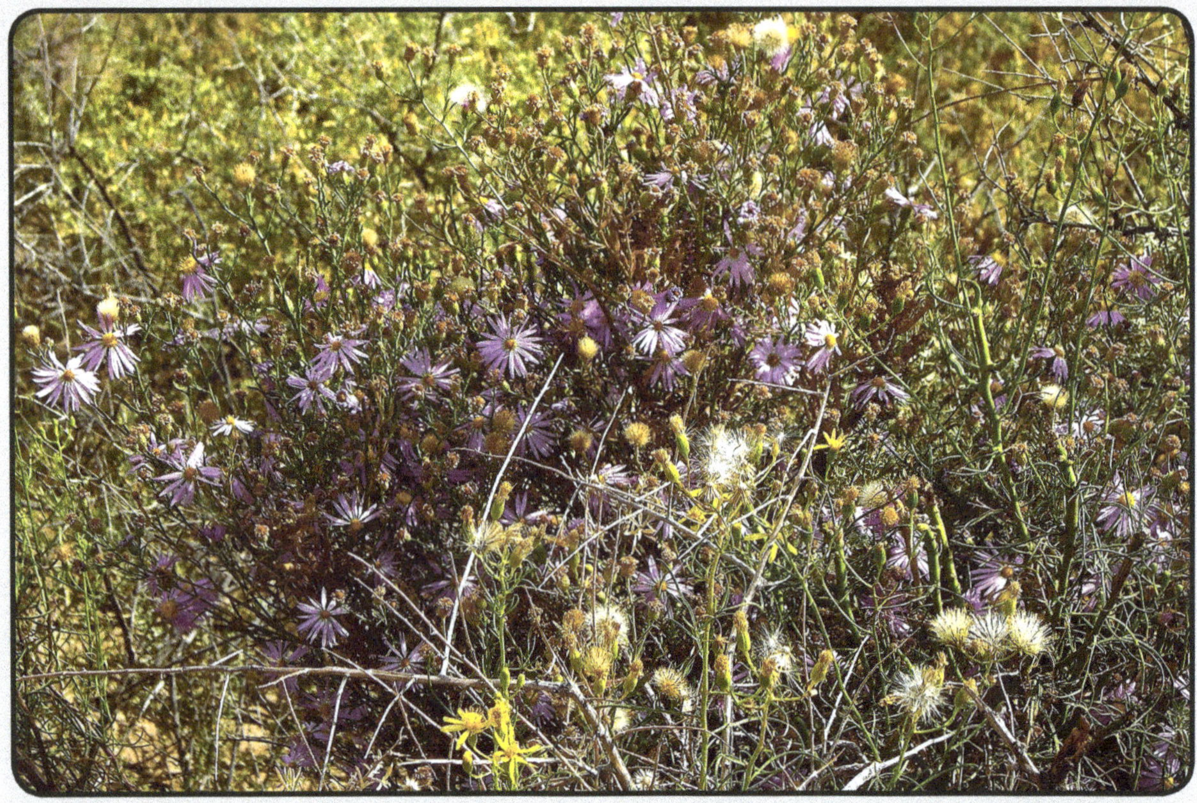

Bouquets in the wild.

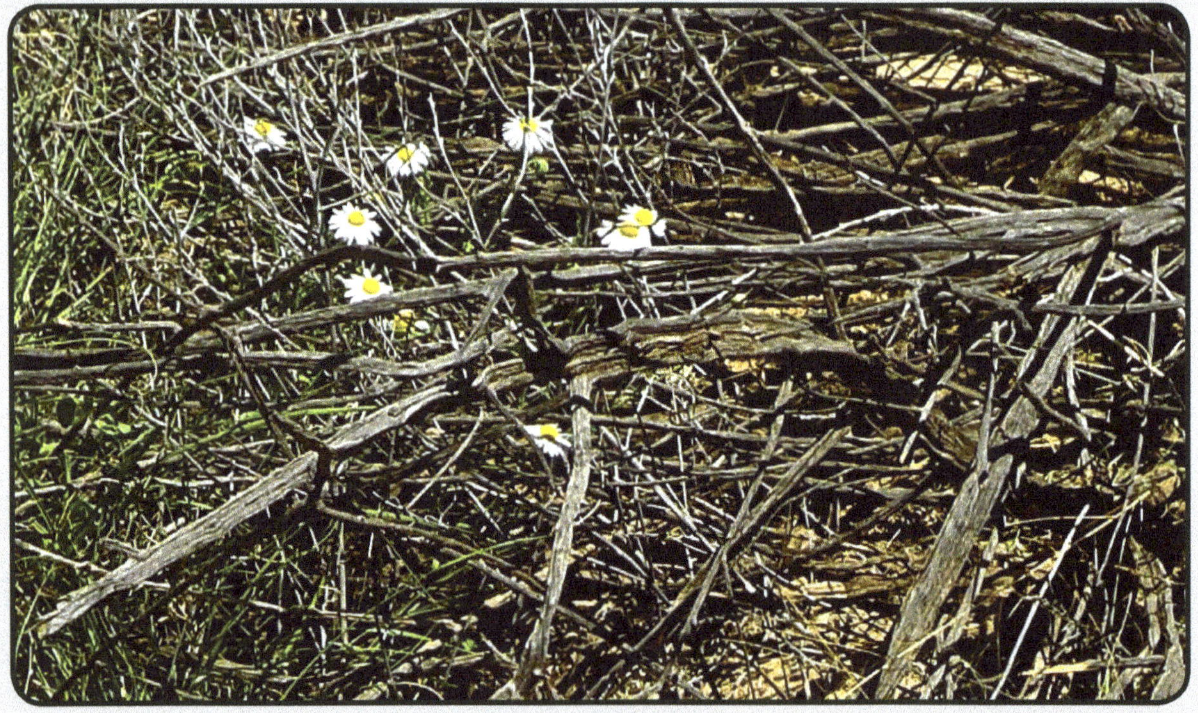

Life and death.

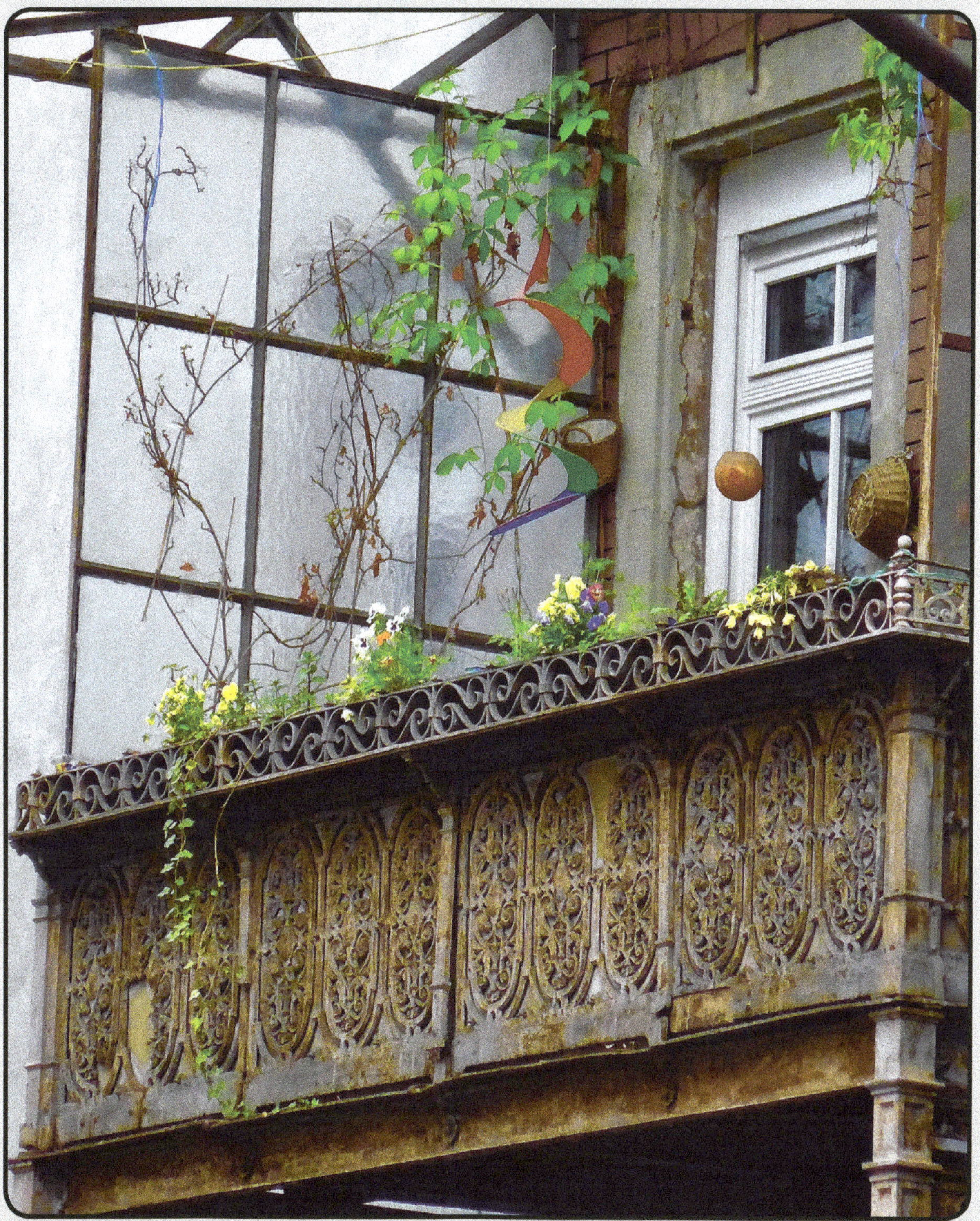

New life amid rust.

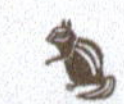

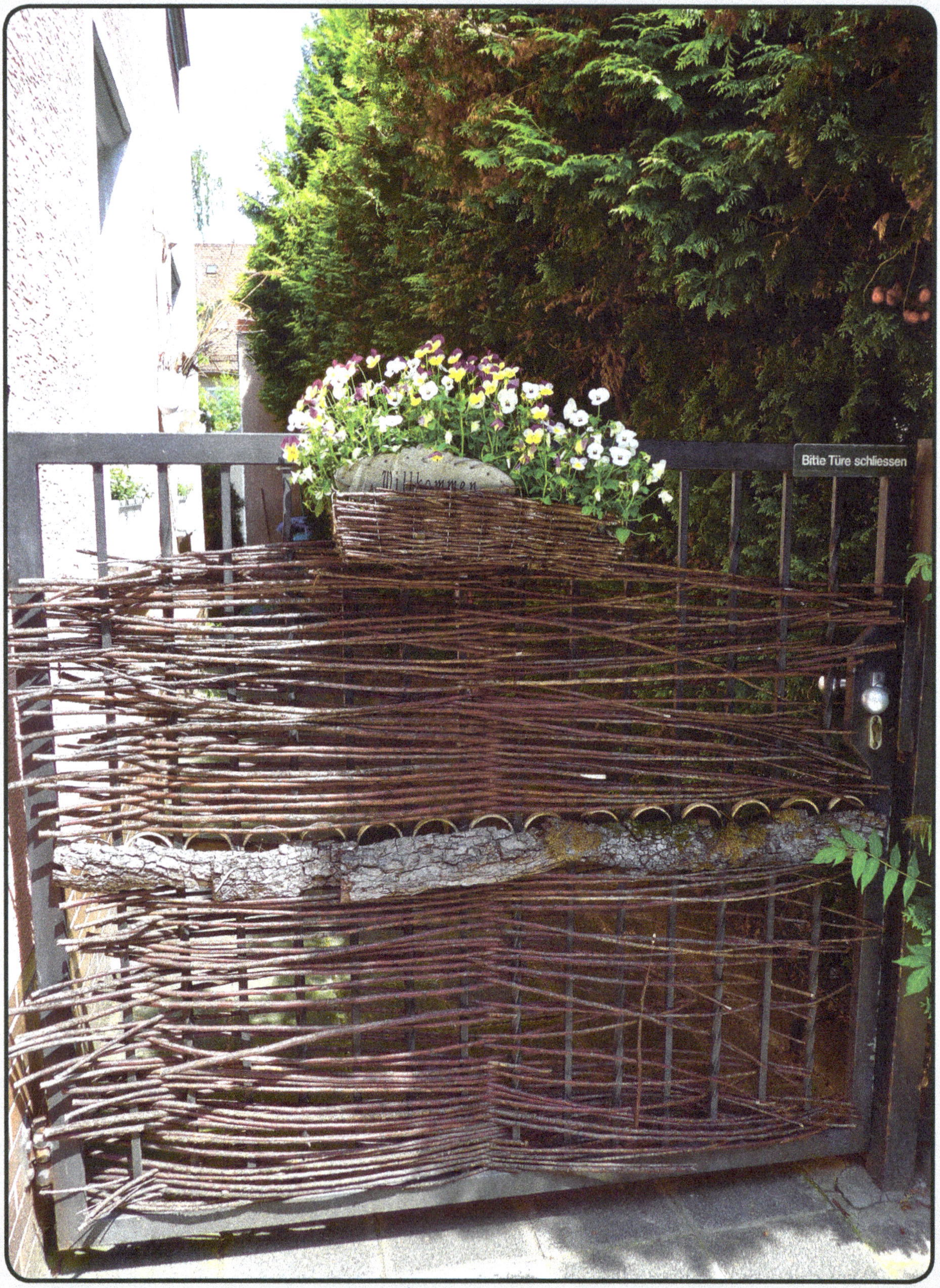

Woven gate.

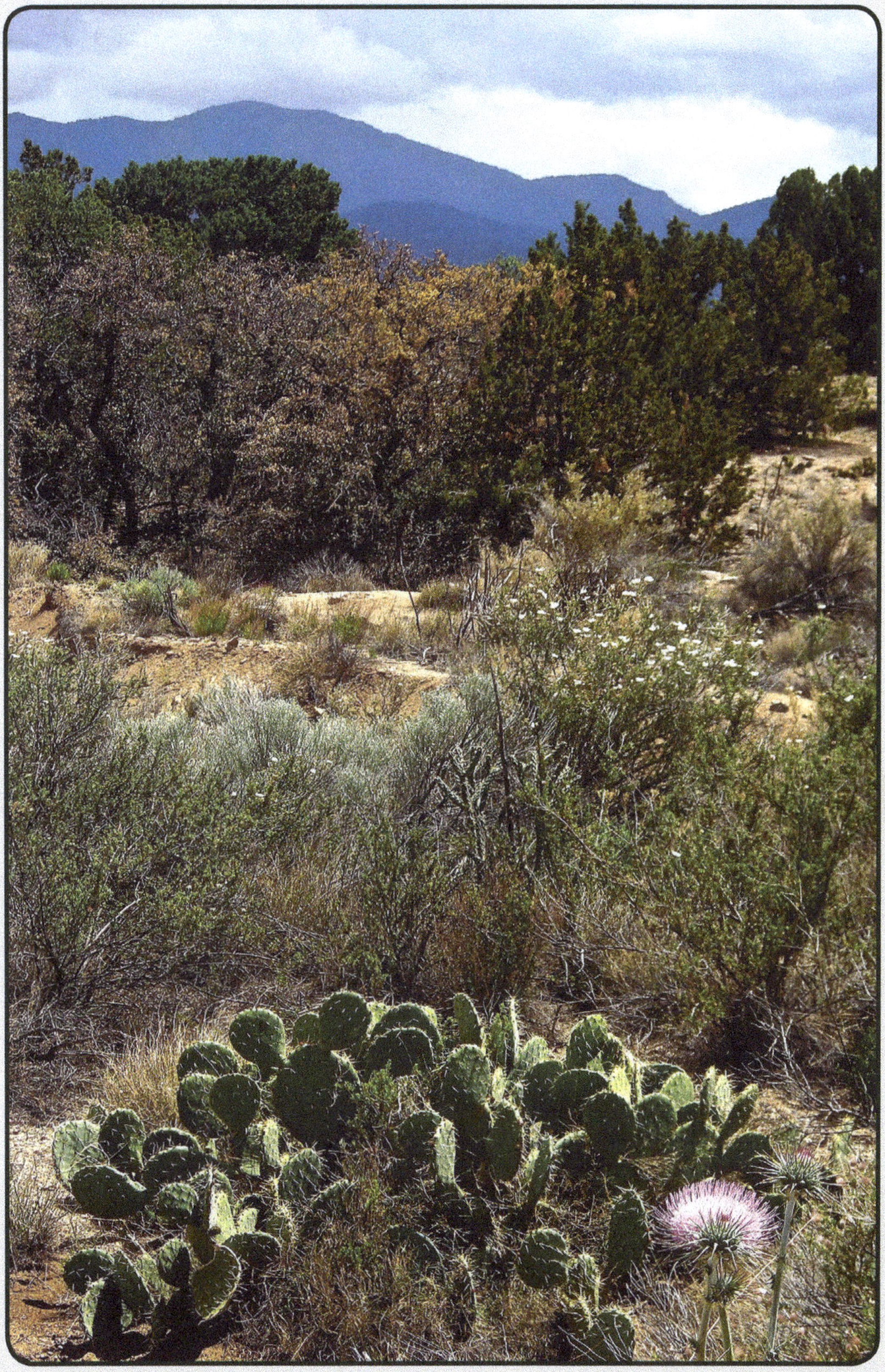

Santa Fe Trail beauty.

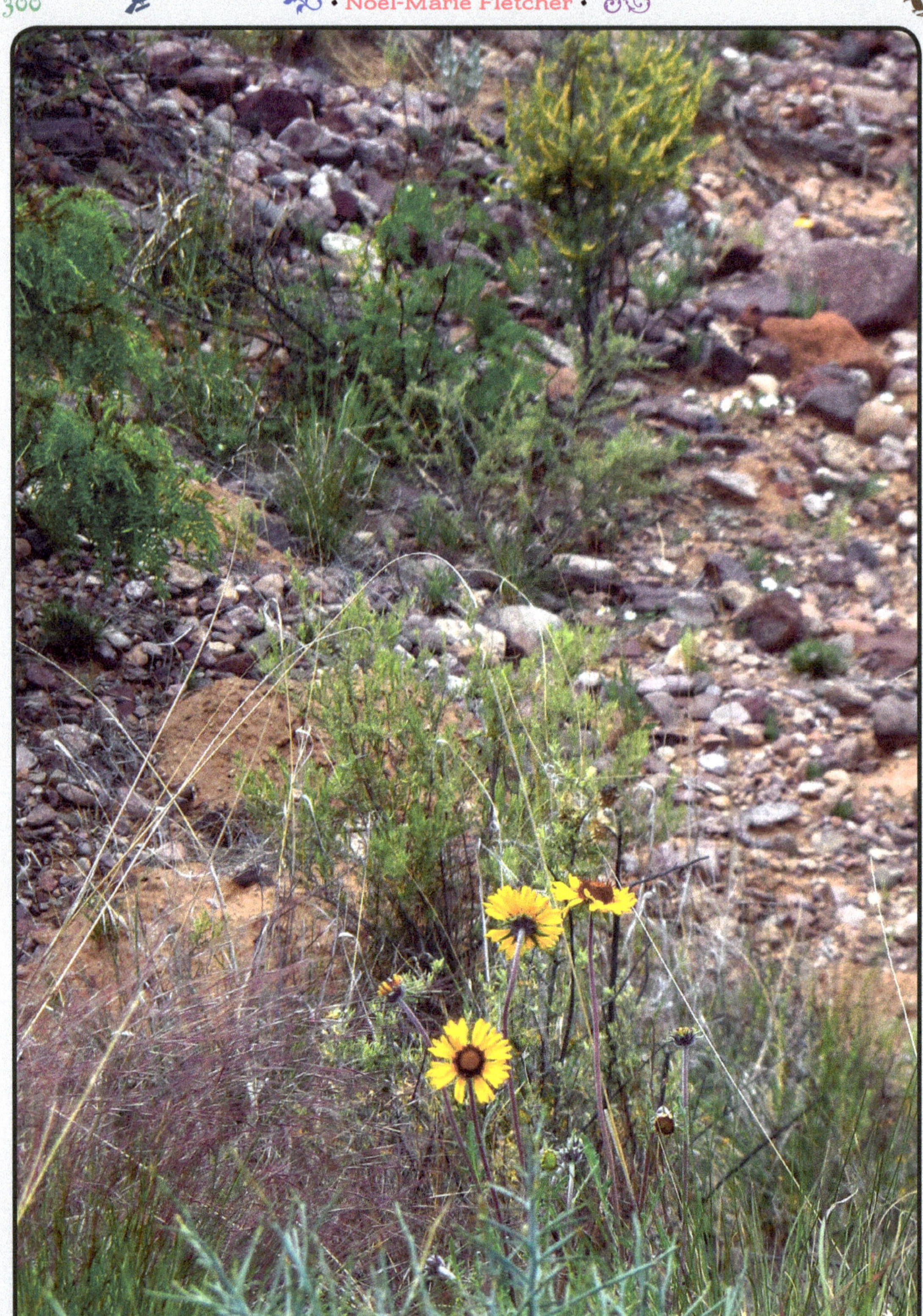

River rock blossoms.

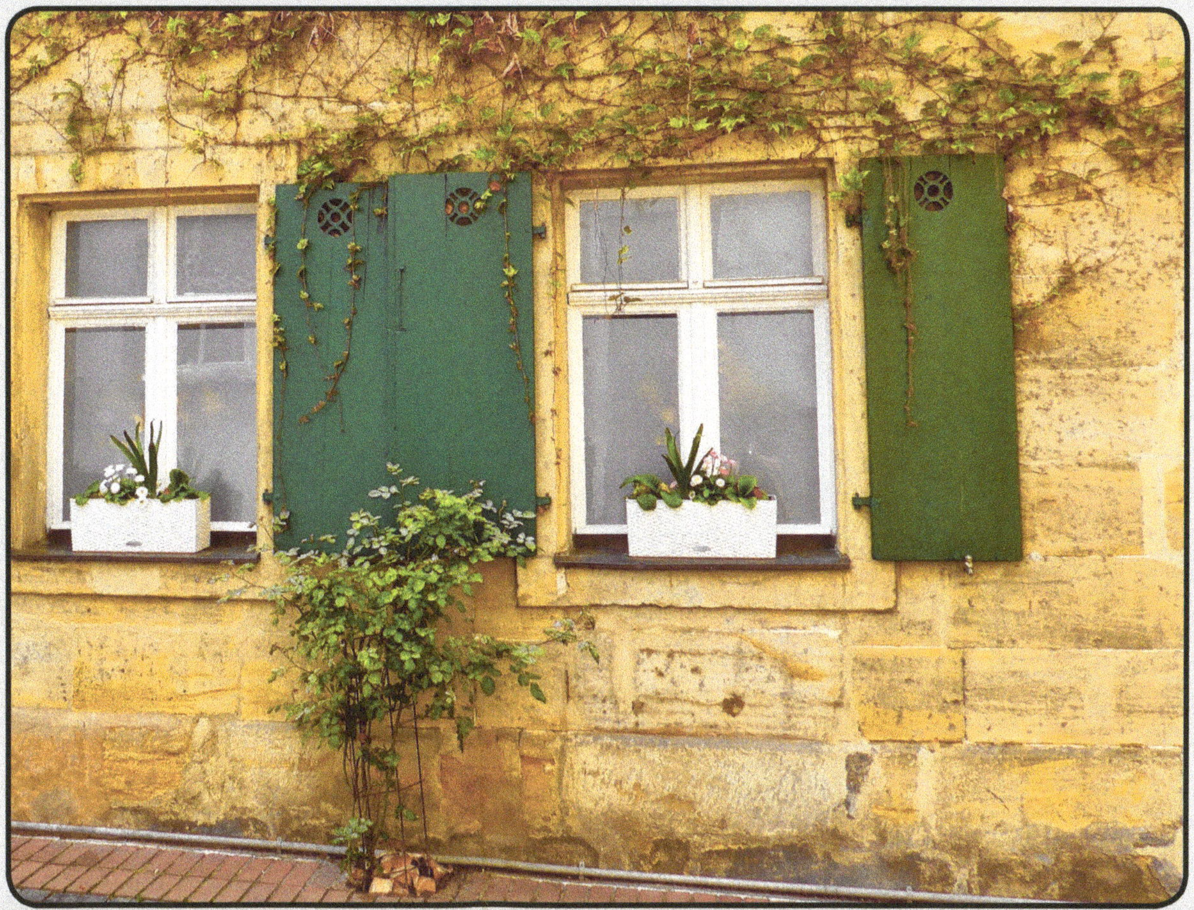

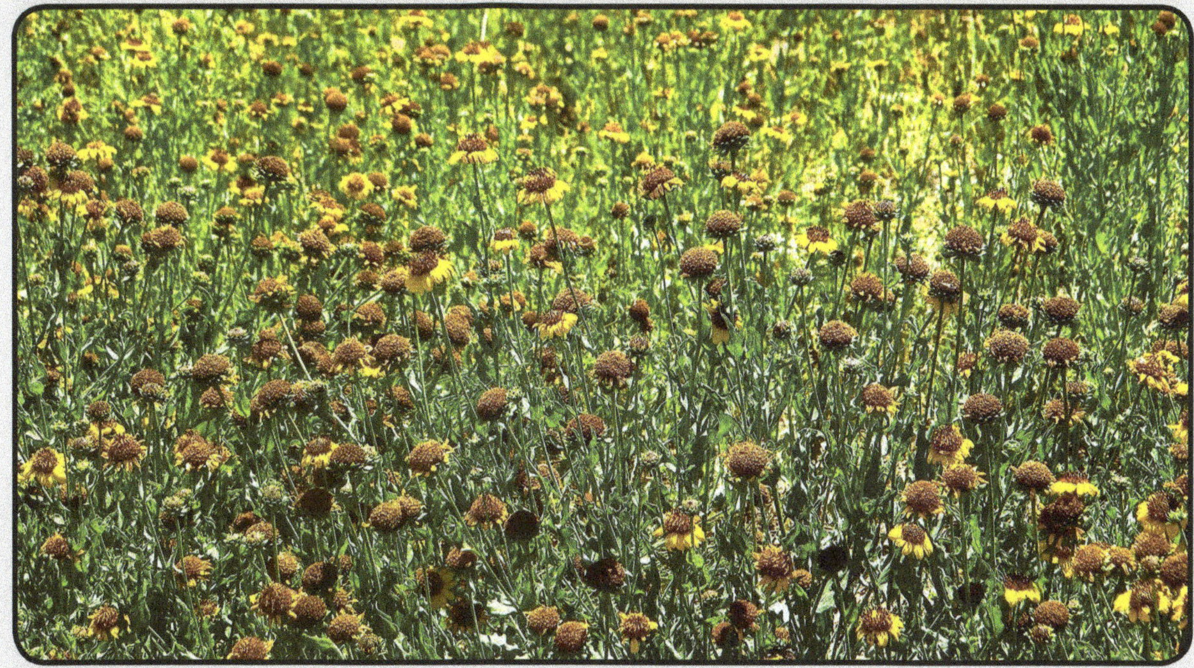

Flower villagers in Corrales, New Mexico.

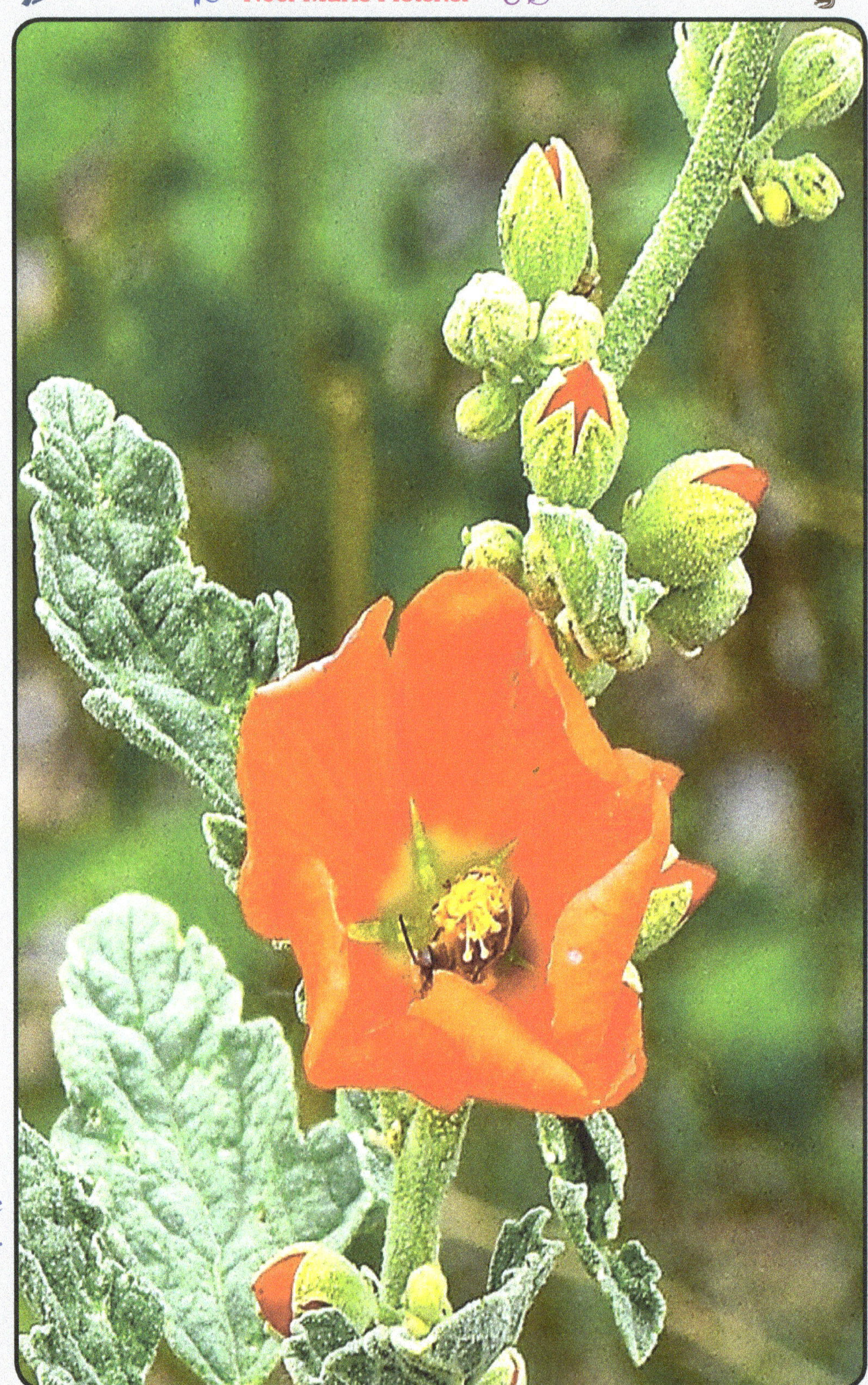

Yerba de la negrita.

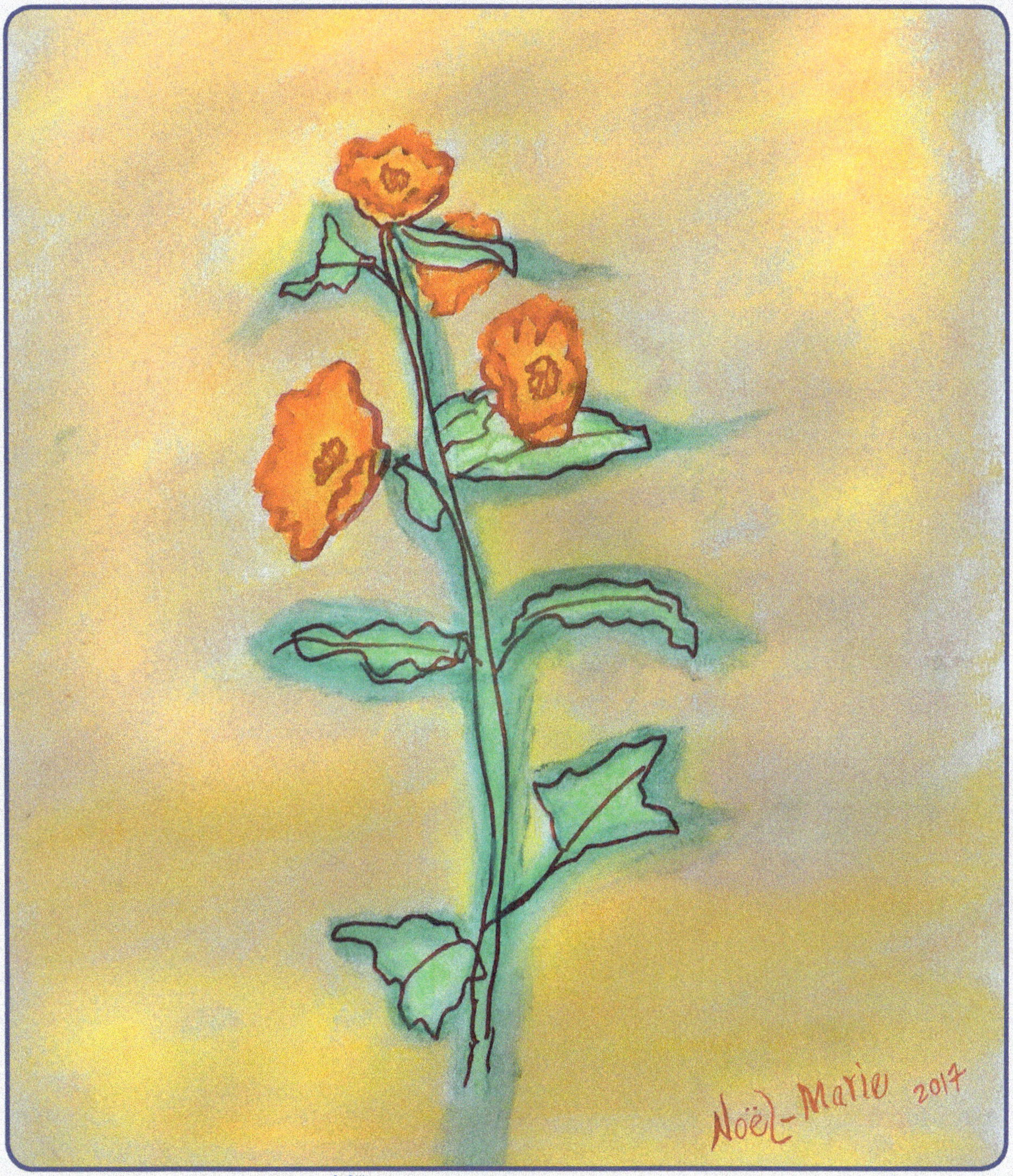

Yerba de la negrita de Noelita.

[Note: When I was young, my grandmother Desolina Perea Candelaria, told me stories about how Native Americans taught the Spaniards to make shampoo with this plant and its wondrous abilities to prevent baldness. This beautiful wildflower is a favorite of mine. Each time I see it, I can hear my grandmother's voice. Its brilliant orange flowers dot windswept sandy hills and fertile alfalfa fields throughout New Mexico.]

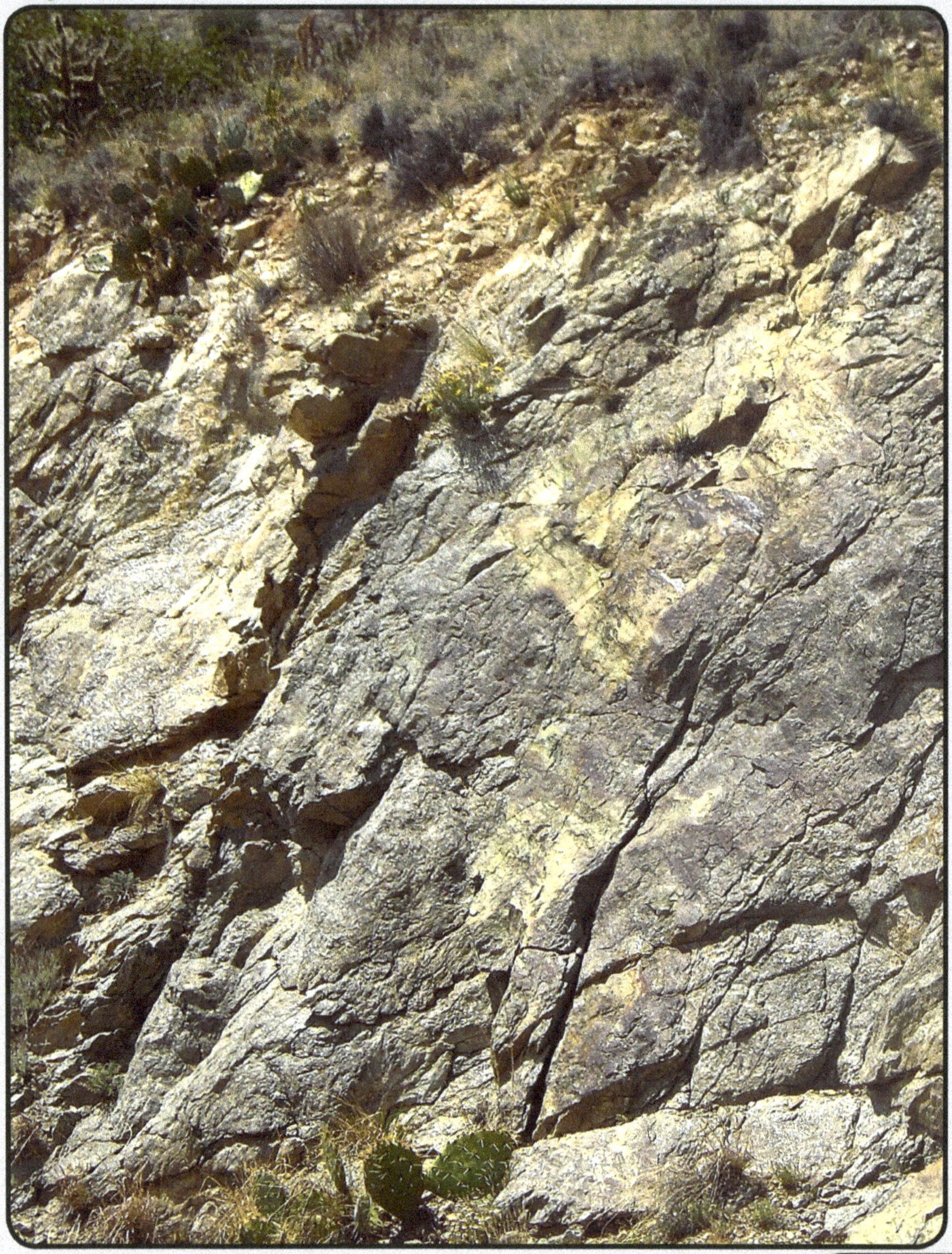

Lemon burst in granite. (Closeup below.)

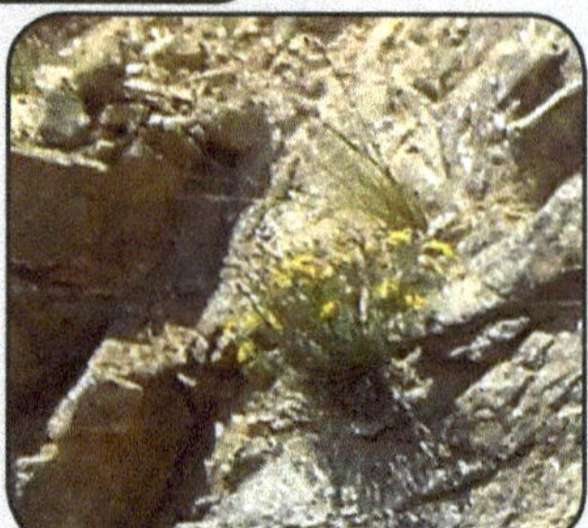

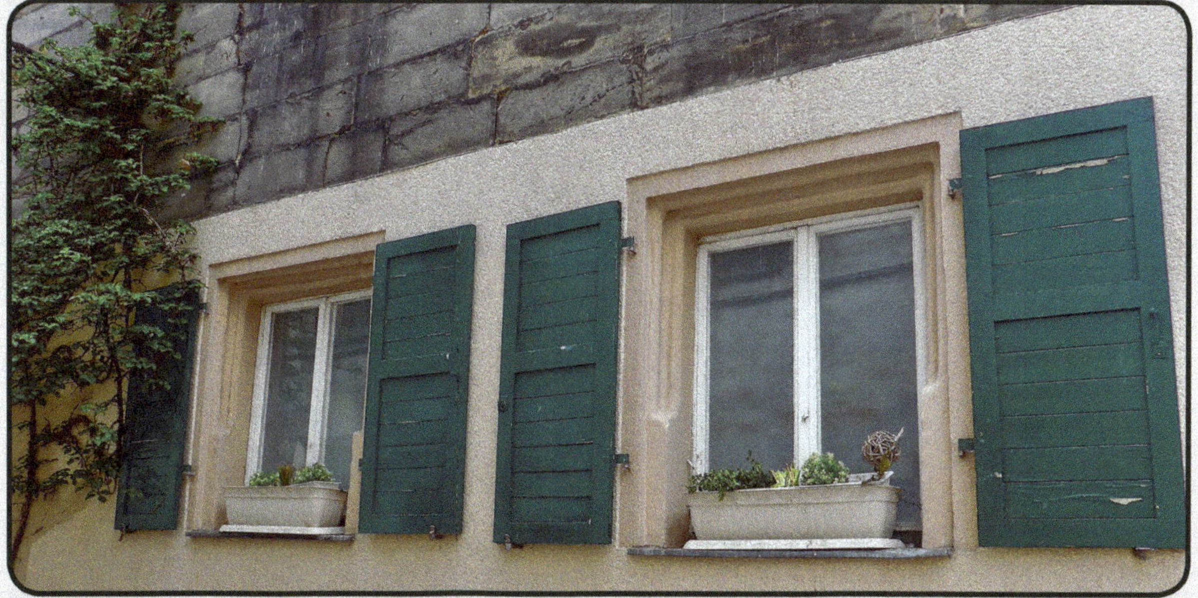

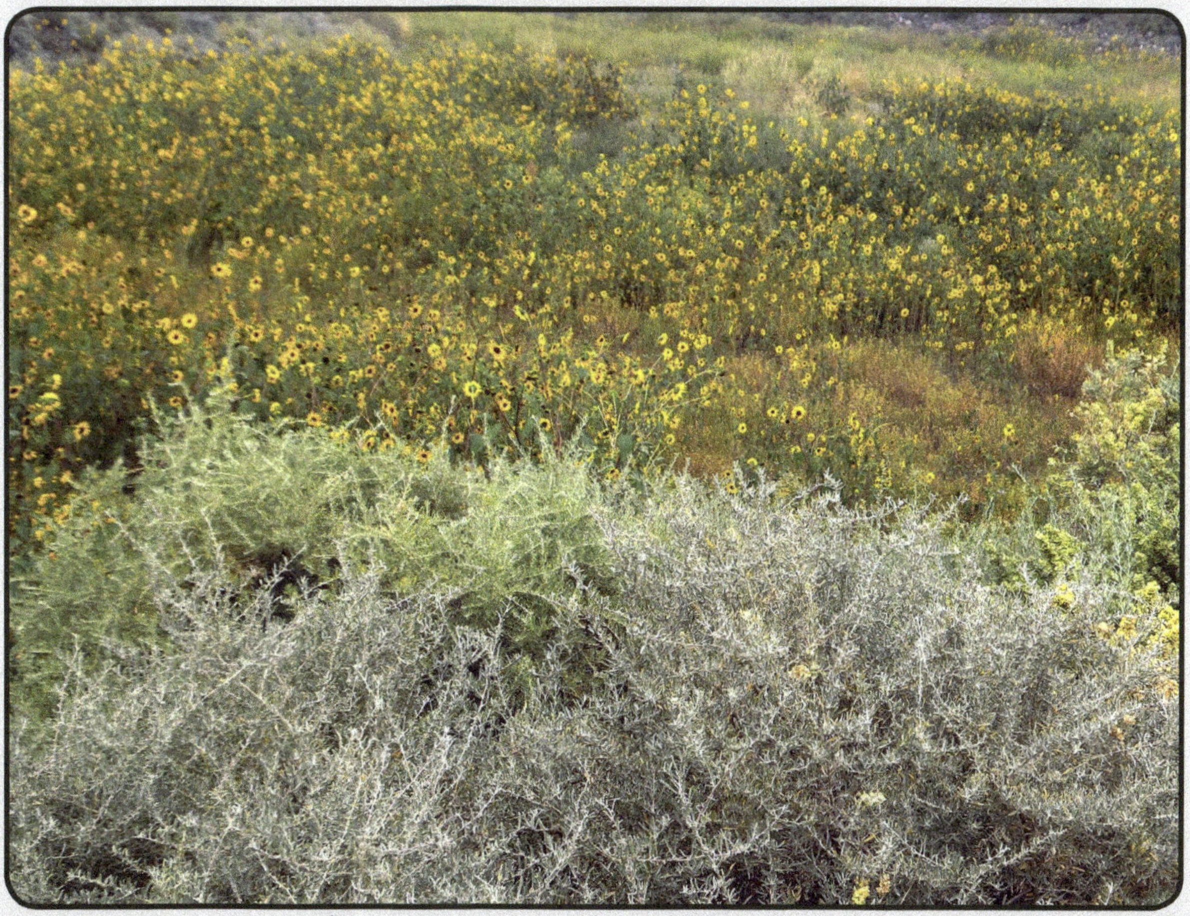

Sunflower and sagebrush at ancient volcano.

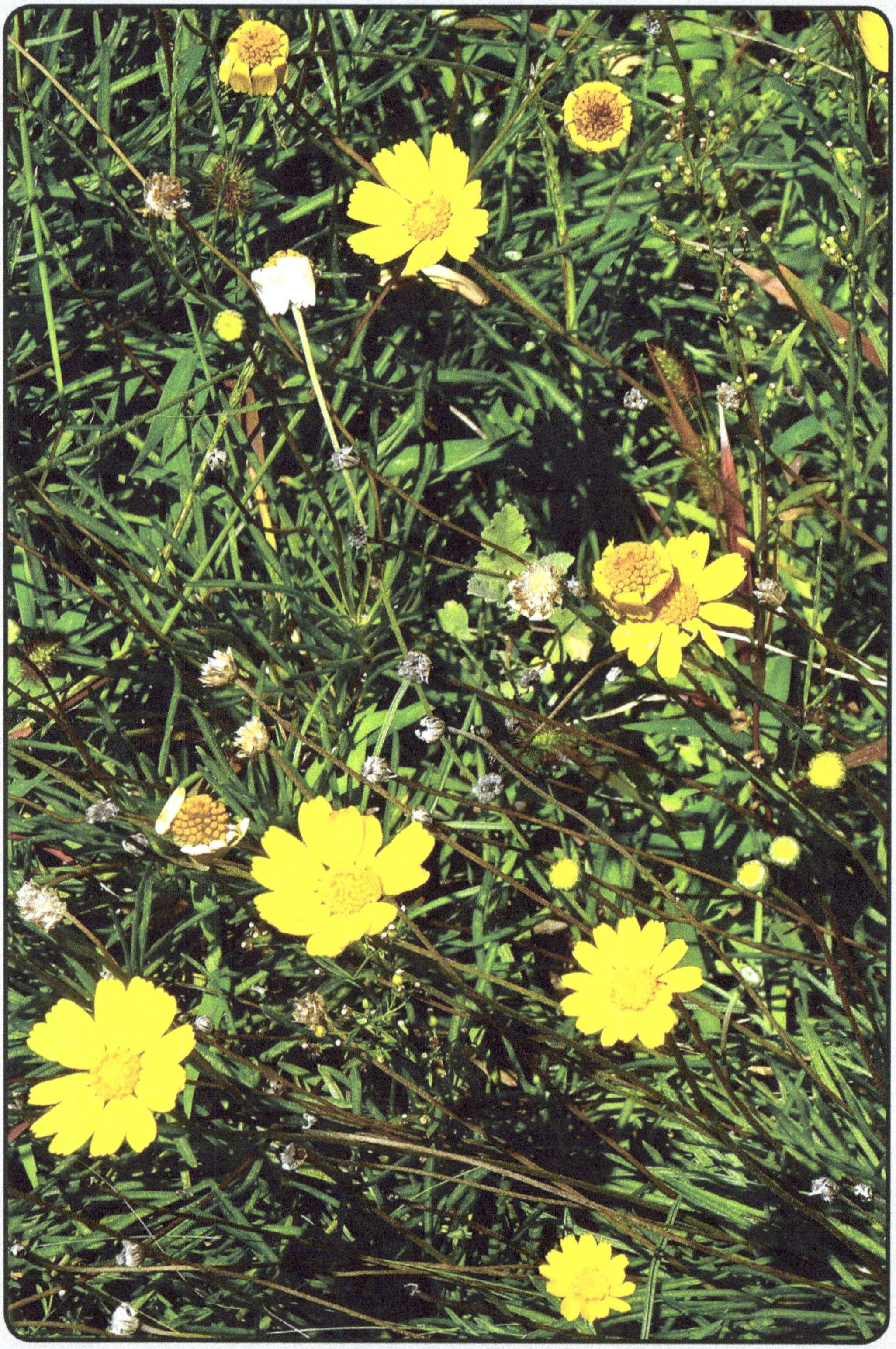

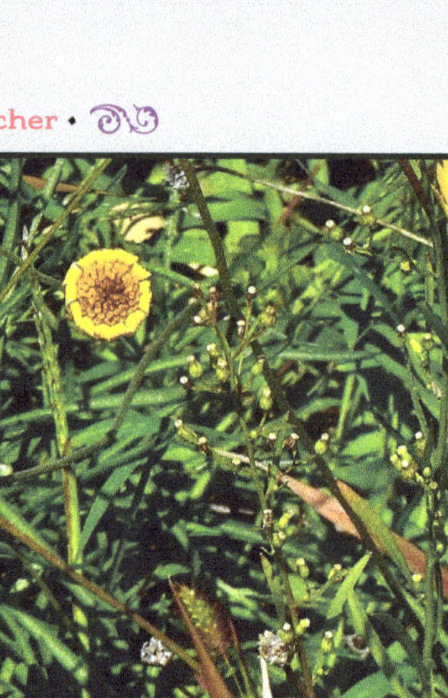

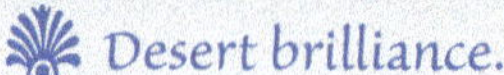

Desert brilliance.

# Chapter 10: Water Lilies

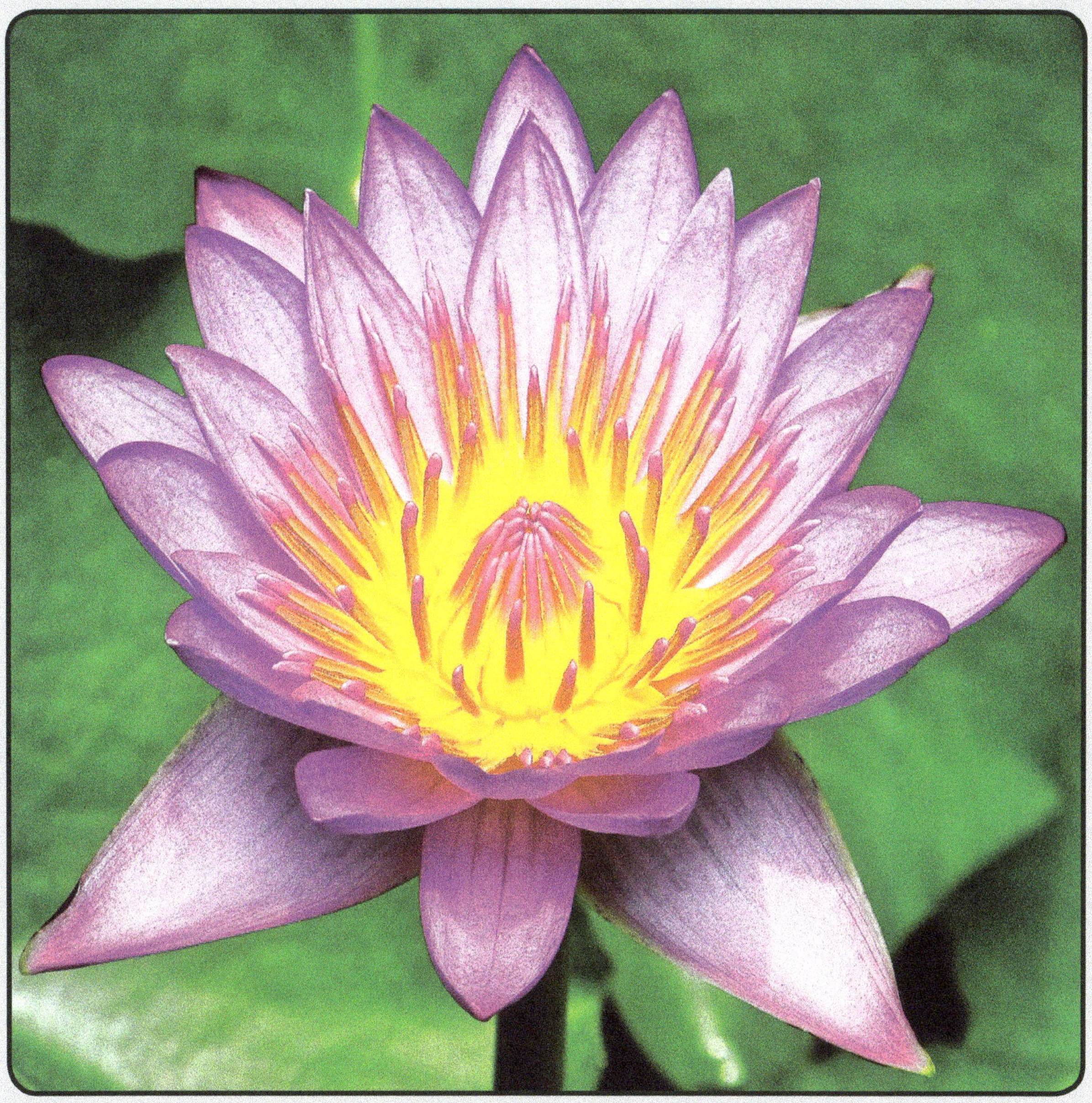

Yí Hé Yuán memories.

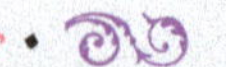

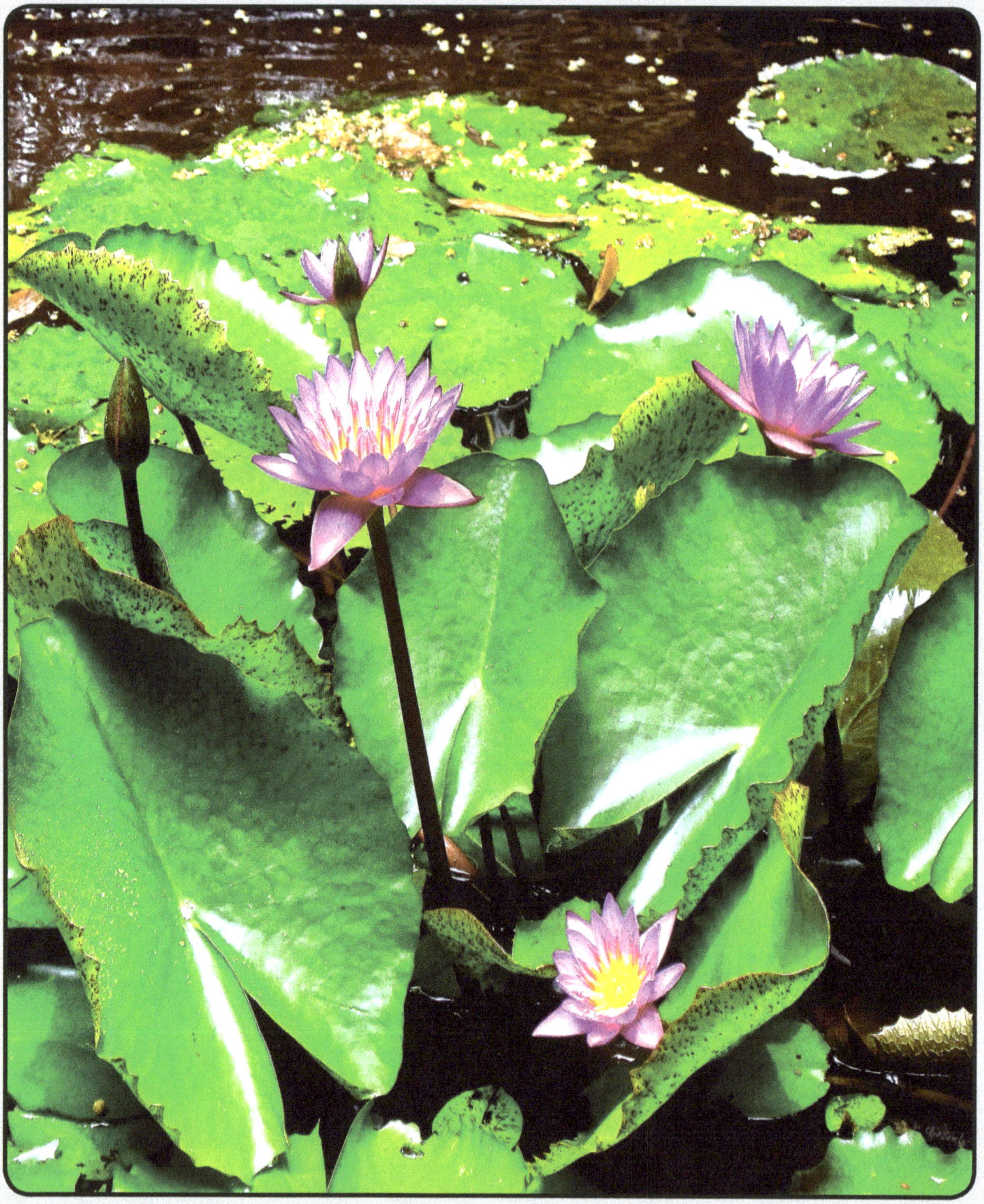

Pond scepters.

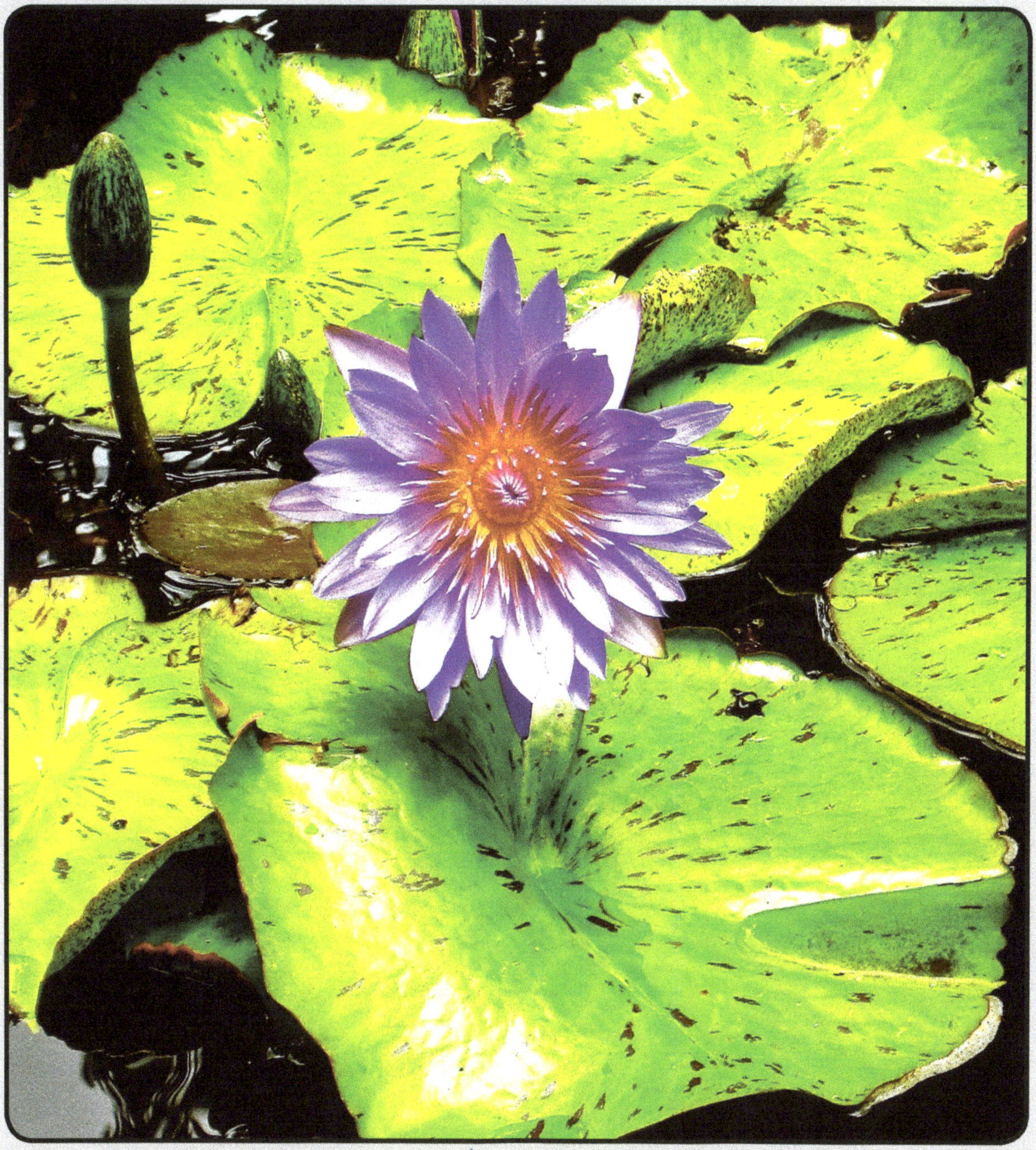

Cyclops.

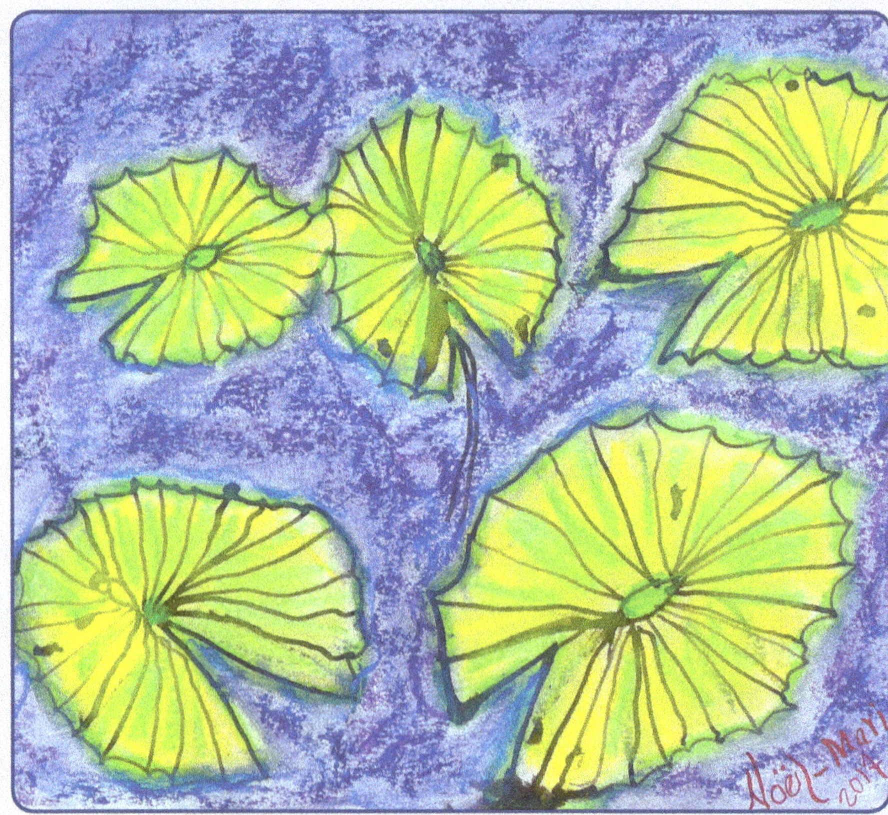


Lily pads.

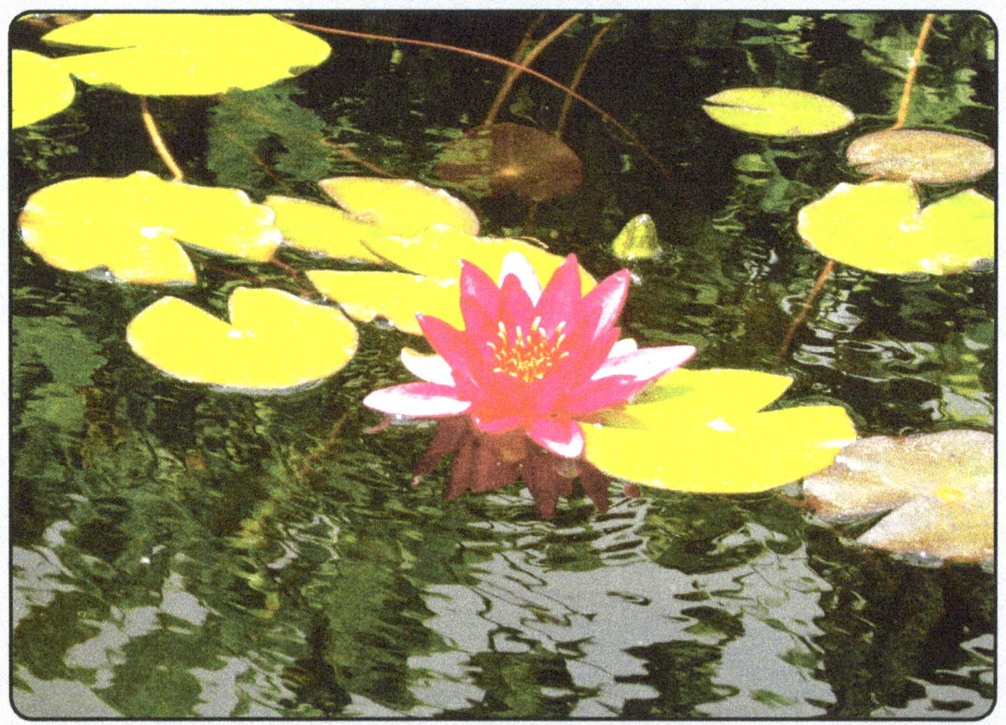

Water garnet.

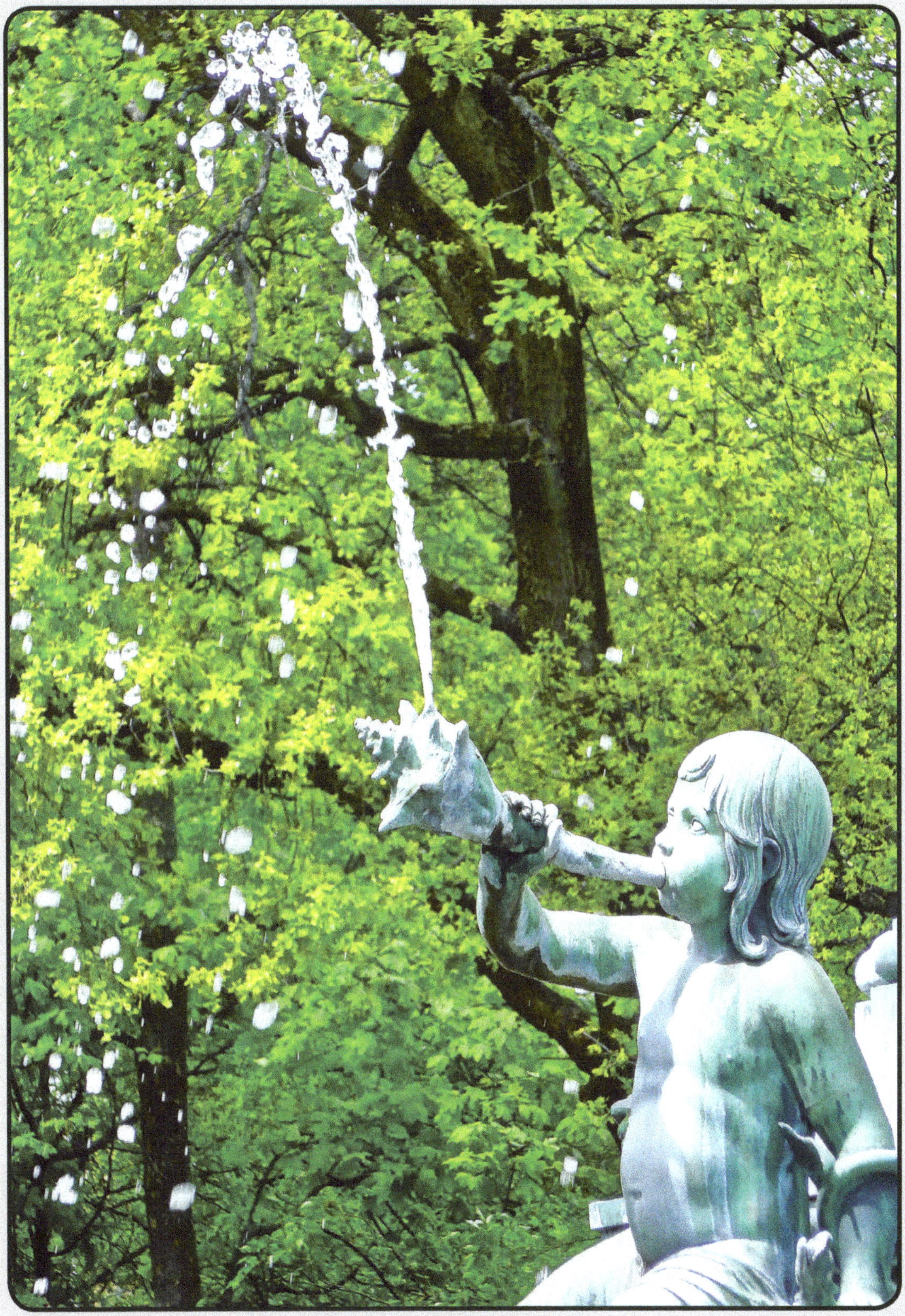

The blare of glass beads.

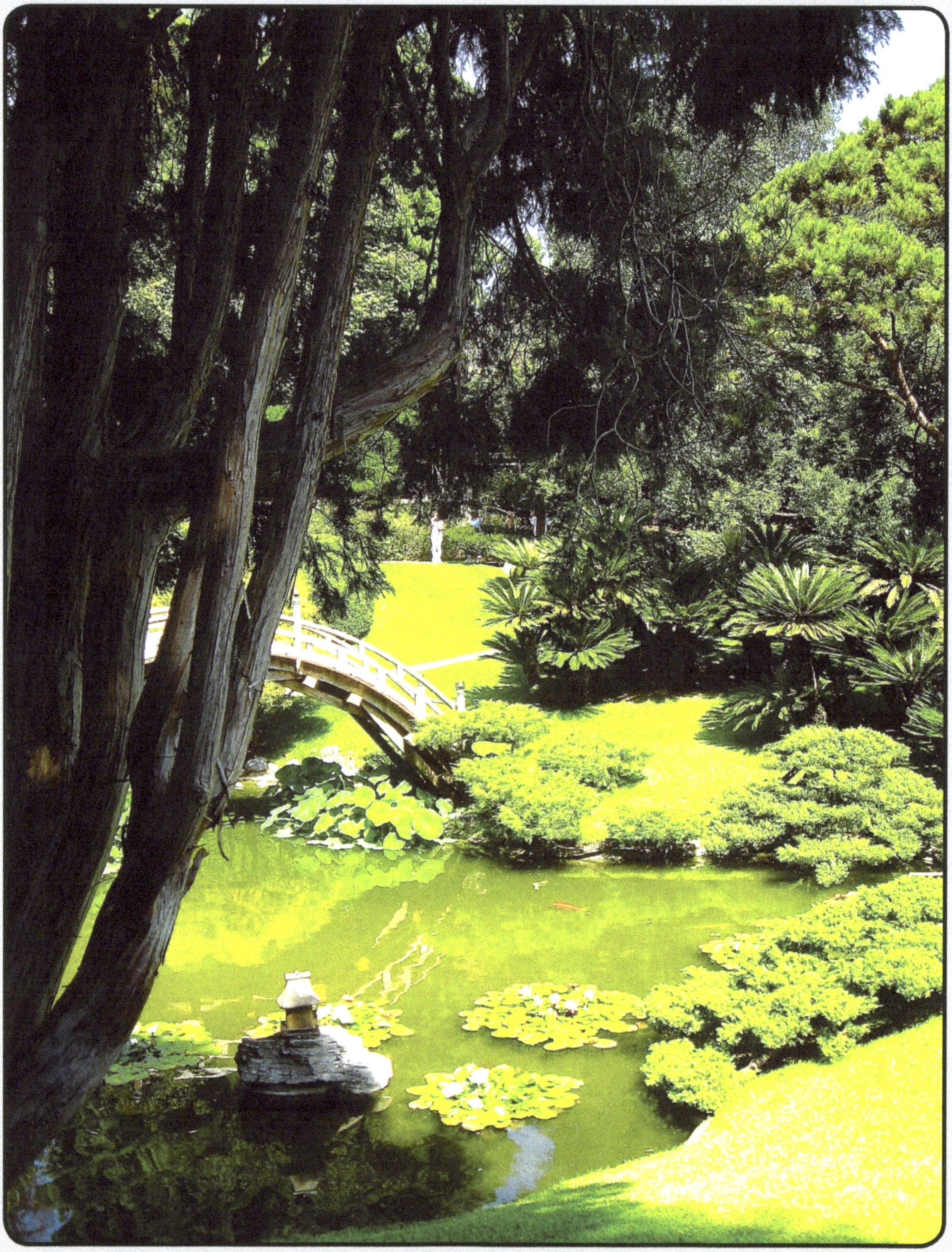

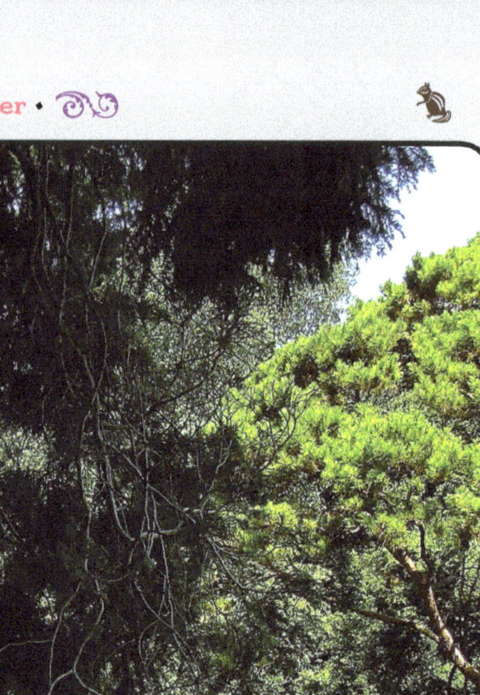

Japanese scene a la Los Angeles.

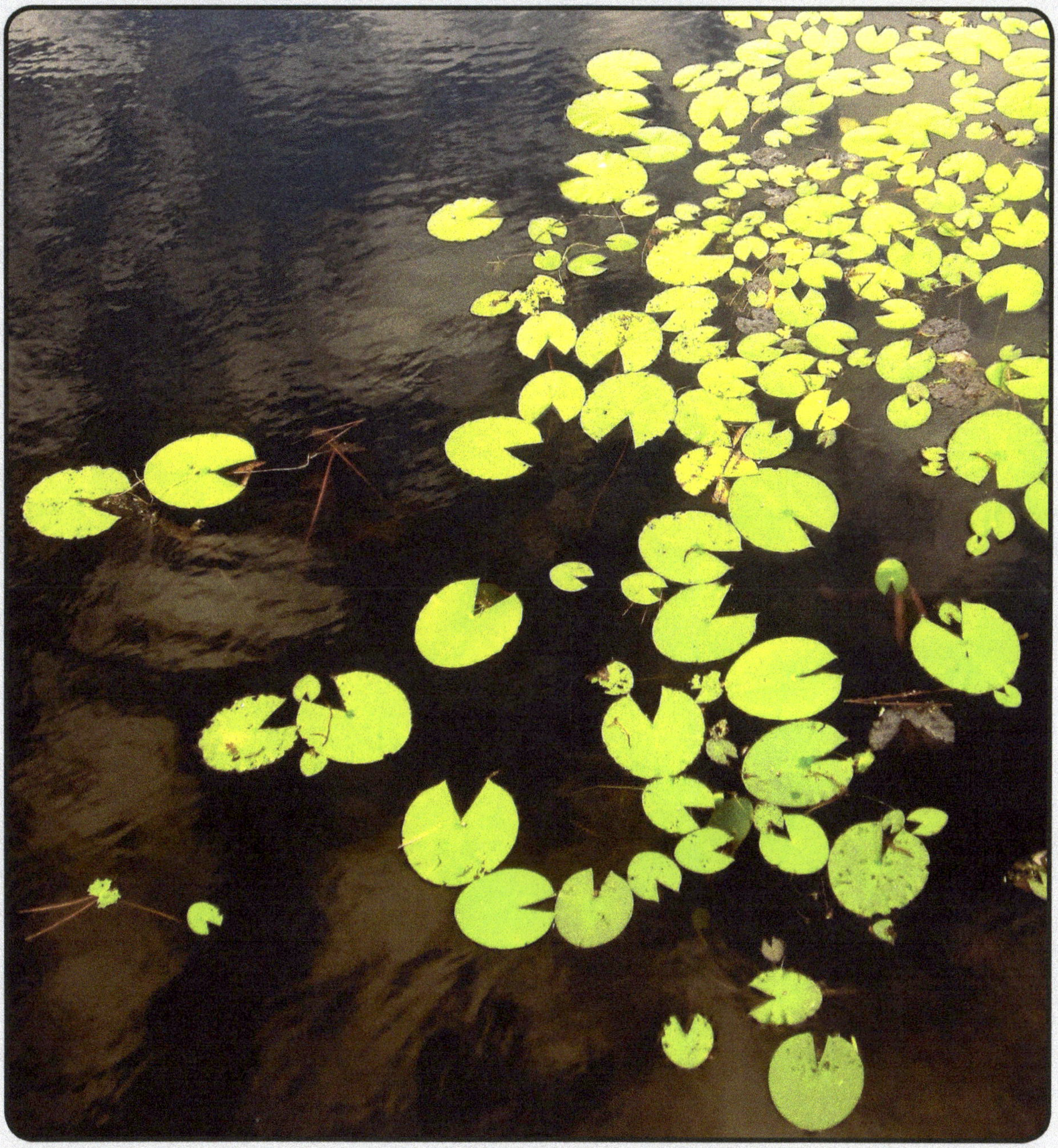

Footprints.

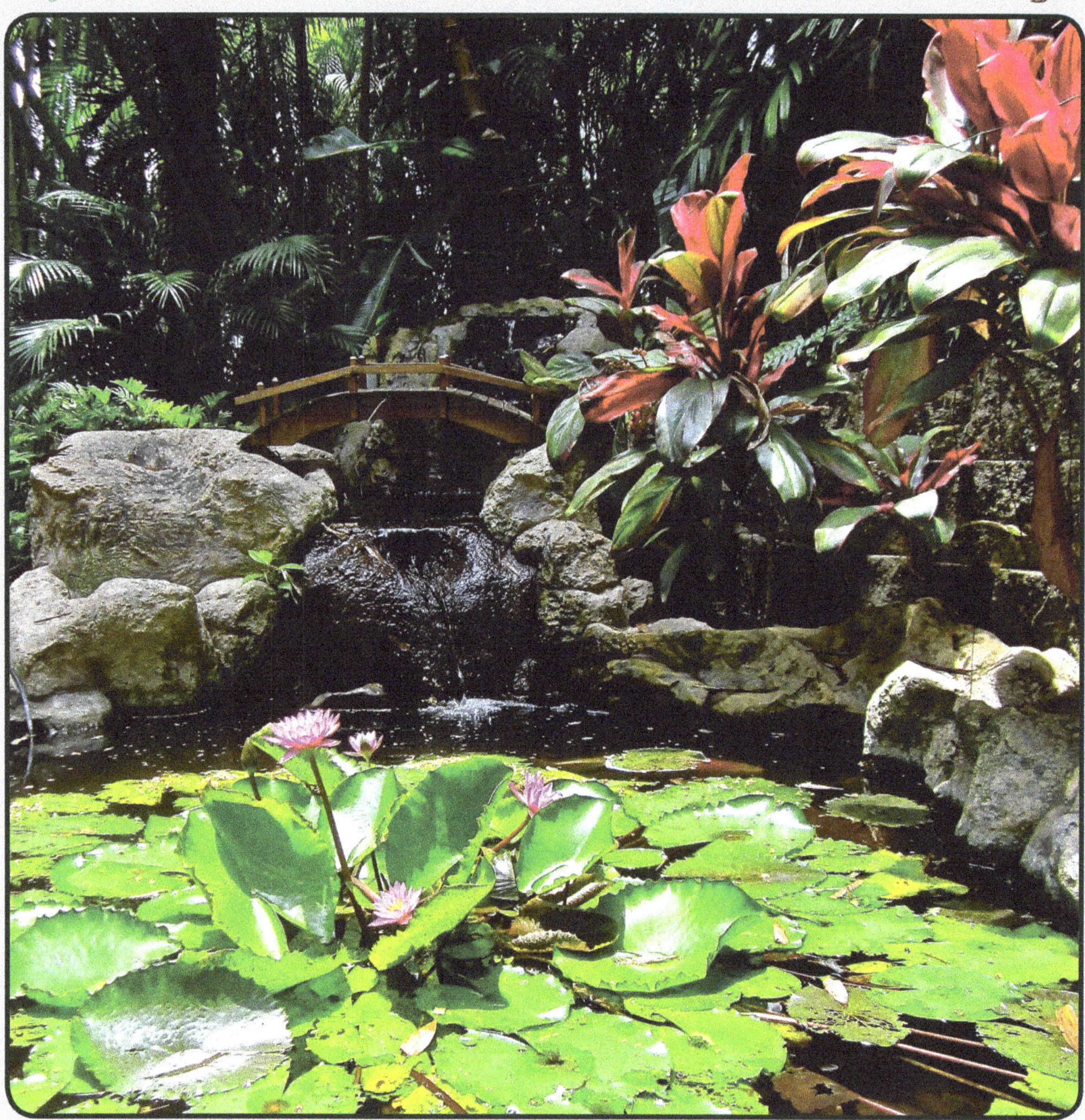

Peace pond.

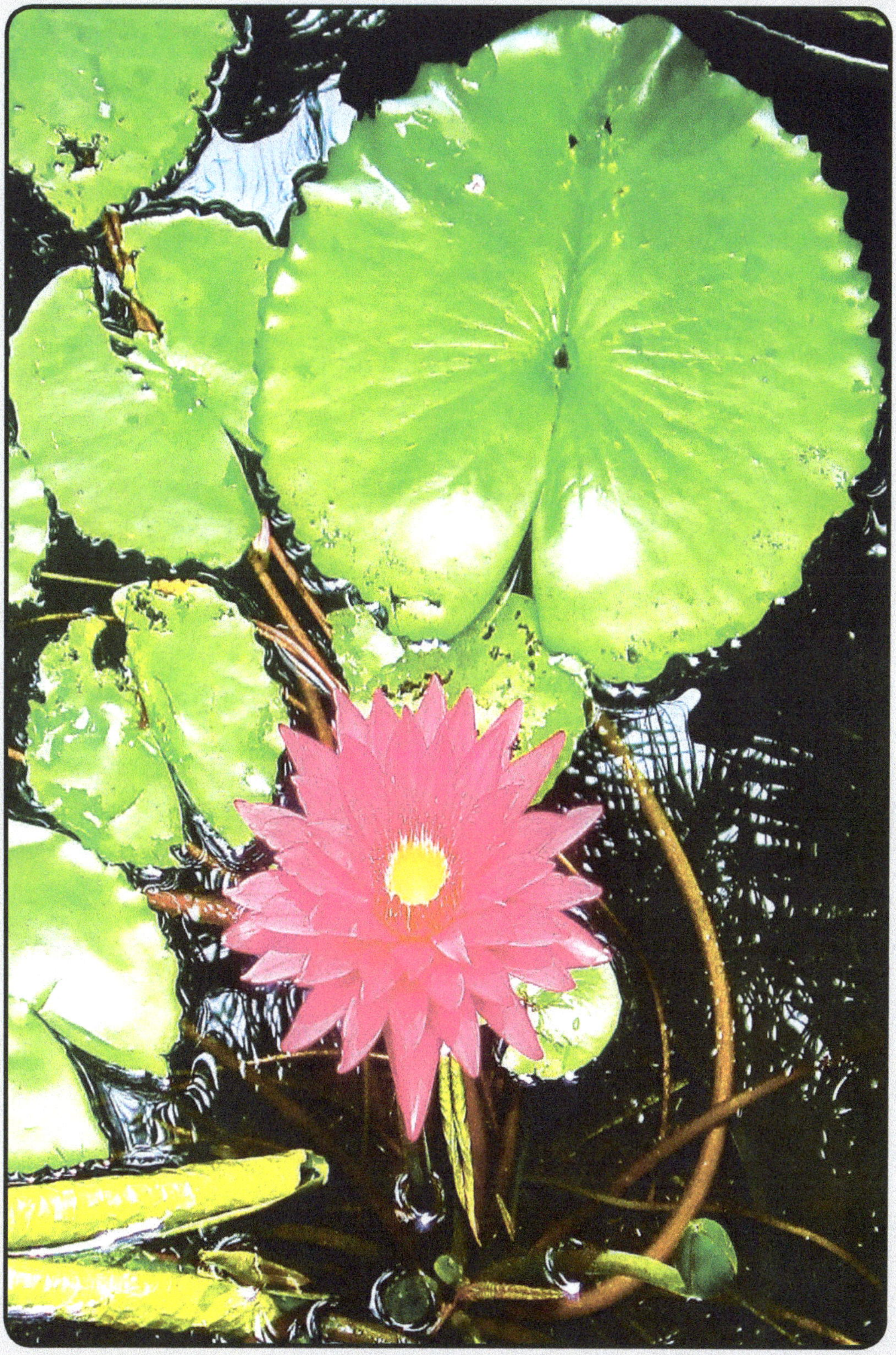

Lustrous.

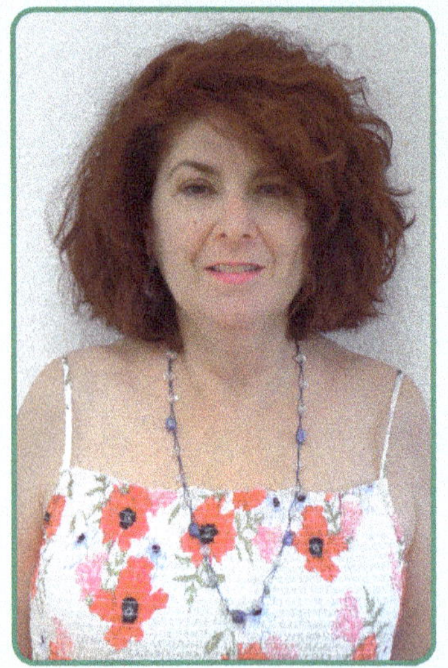

Noël-Marie Fletcher is an American journalist, communications executive, author and photographer in Europe.

Noël-Marie has established herself as an influential leader and expert in the field of communications in the United States. Her diverse experience in communication forms, including television, radio, and web, combined with her vision and leadership, solidified her position at the top of the corporate ladder, where she has managed entire external and internal communications organizations for multibillion dollar enterprises.

Noël-Marie studied the art of film as a major subject in college. She earned her degree from San Francisco State University, located in the heart of the U.S. film industry's capital. She gained expertise in all aspects of filmmaking and worked in television in the San Francisco Bay area, an environment where big business merged with creativity.

As a journalist and executive, Noël-Marie has deployed her skills at filmmaking in versatile ways with award-winning results. Her talent at composing images is demonstrated in her long track record as a photojournalist. She writes scripts and has directed video shoots.

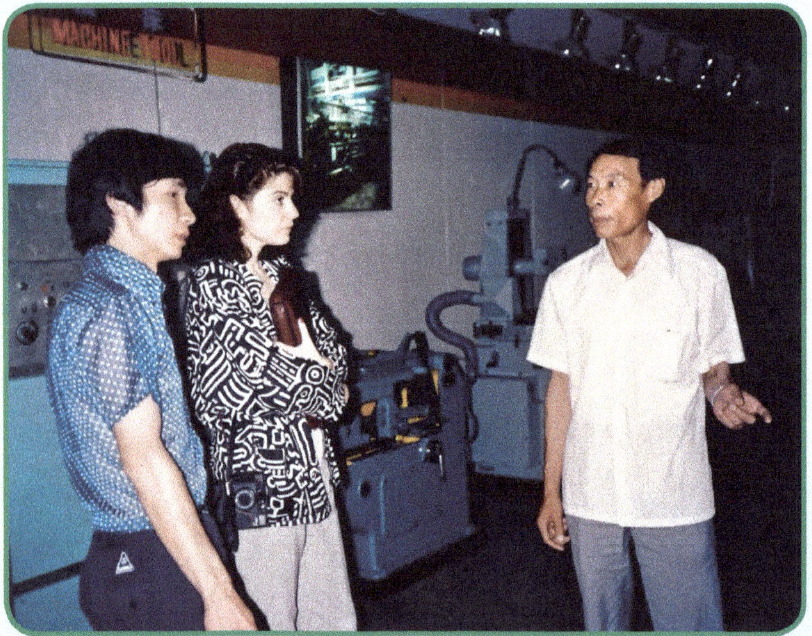


*Working as a financial foreign correspondent and photojournalist, Noël-Marie sports a camera and notebook while touring a machine tool plant in China.*

Noël-Marie has been recognized for her filmmaking prowess with diverse and numerous awards, including a Crystal Award of Excellence for a multimedia production, a Platinum Award for her video communications, and a Bronze Finalist Award from the Telly Awards, honoring outstanding productions in TV, video and film.

She has a well-established

background as a film and journalism professional and has collaborated with leaders in the film and broadcasting industry. She has written for The Hollywood Reporter and created scripts for Voice of America while working in China.

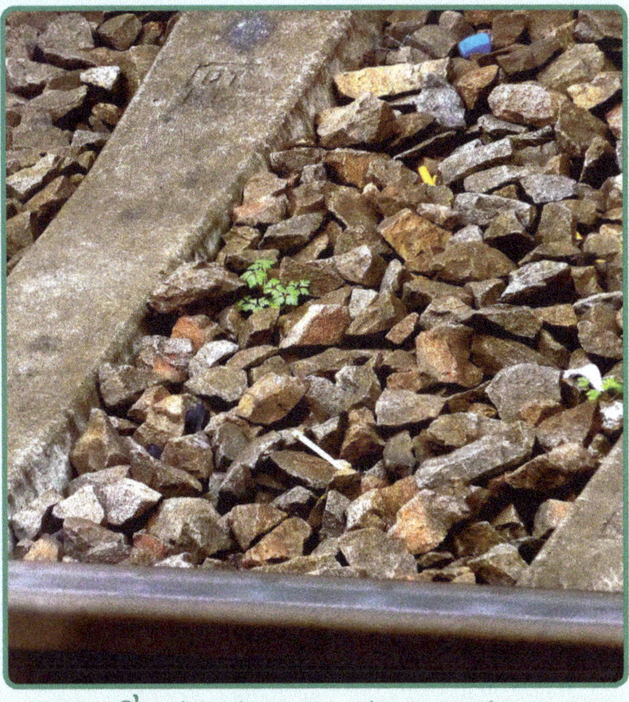
Life's whisper amid train trash.

Her writing talent, combined with her filmmaking skills, gives Noël-Marie a competitive edge. She has written books and screenplays, and continues to work in film and screenwriting.

Early in her career as a journalist, Noël-Marie began working in daily news coverage at the Desert Sun newspaper in Palm Springs. A few years later, she left on a whim to Hong Kong–with one suitcase in hand, $200, and the names of four people she'd never met–to become a foreign correspondent in Asia. Within two weeks, she landed a job at the Hongkong Standard newspaper covering the Supreme Court, a.k.a. the "High Court." She learned to navigate the British legal system by reporting on a world populated by High Court justices, barristers, and solicitors. She covered white-collar crime as well as the Court of Appeals.

Achieving the rank of foreign correspondent, Noël-Marie specialized in business and financial news and became part of an elite American press corps. Her beat was Asia.

It was here that Noël-Marie developed her wide breadth of experience in communications, business, and management on an international level. She lived and worked in China, Hong Kong, and traveled through other Asian financial powerhouses including South Korea and Singapore. She became fluent in Mandarin and traveled to Beijing as a prestigious "China correspondent," where

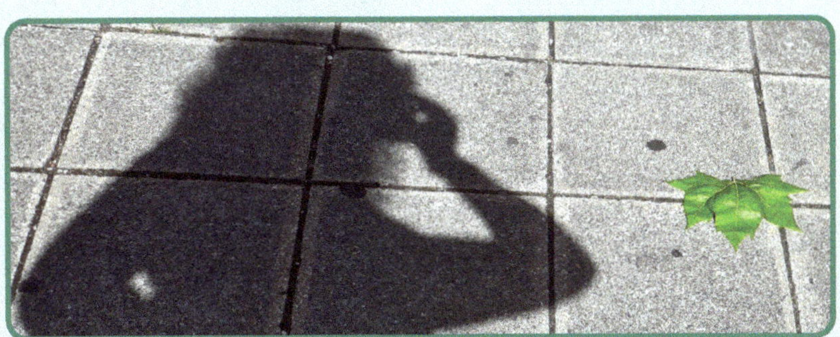
Shadow photographer and leaf.

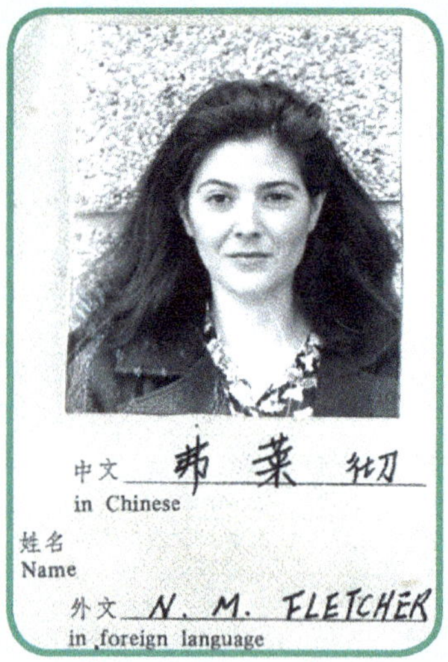

Noël-Marie's foreign correspondent credentials in Beijing.

she delved deeper into the art and culture of Asia.

She experienced a poignant chapter in China's history during the events of the Tiananmen Square Massacre, which took place a few miles from the diplomatic compound where she lived.

Returning to the U.S., Noël-Marie used her legal and communications expertise to contribute to the legislature of the State of New Mexico. She was recognized by the governor for her outstanding work.

Turning her focus to business, Noël-Marie distinguished herself with her leadership and diverse talents at communicating using writing, film, web media, and images to create change and influence behavior. She has served as the head of internal and external communications for government and privately owned companies, charged with responsibility for large enterprises. Her success has been measured by her numerous awards and achievements.

Noël-Marie comes from a long line of legislators, journalists and pioneers in diverse fields of industry. She descends from the Fletcher and Ballinger families of England, who made continuous and noteworthy contributions to the United States throughout its history, including in the fields of law, economics, journalism, and art.

Her Hispanic ancestors were the Perea family of Spanish-Arab origin, who served in government under the Spanish crown and the American acquisition and were captains of business and industry in Spain and the Southwest.

Noël-Marie established Fletcher & Co. Publishers as an outlet for creative communications. As company leader, she promotes interests in art, history, and diverse cultures. Her work as an author, artist and photographer reflect her own unique research and interests. As a publisher, she continues to blend communication in diverse forms, such as art and imagery.

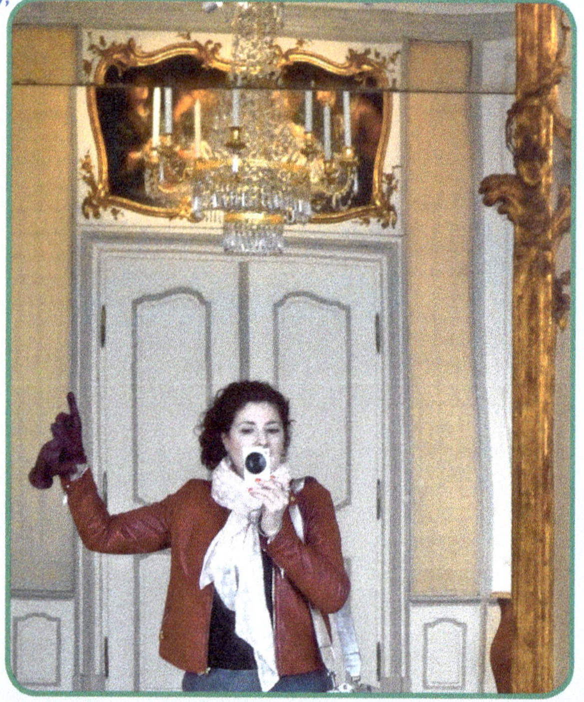
Self portrait in winter.

# Other Books by Noël-Marie Fletcher

## Captives of the Southwest *by Noël-Marie Fletcher*

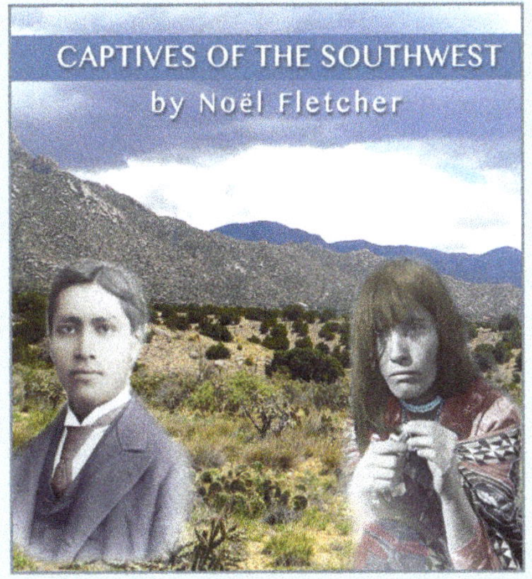


Take a journey into the lives of people who vanished in the Wild West. Explore true stories and eyewitness accounts of the kidnappings and experiences of Anglos, Hispanics, and Native Americans taken captive in New Mexico and the Southwest. Each chapter takes the reader into a unique setting alongside new casts of characters—including lost settlers, greedy prospectors, elusive desert traders, vigilante lawmen, nomadic tribesmen, courageous women and resilient children. Stunning historical and modern photographs provide vivid glimpses into the life of each captive and the environments they experienced.

Includes rich illustrations: 115 historic photos, 14 maps, 35 news articles, 40+ modern photos as well as interesting historical details and rare images of key people and places described.

Author and researcher Noël-Marie Fletcher provides a local perspective and expert analysis for events and stories A rare gem for readers of Wild West history containing gripping tales of adventure, hardship, courage.

## River of My Ancestors: The Rio Grande in Pictures *by Noël-Marie Fletcher*

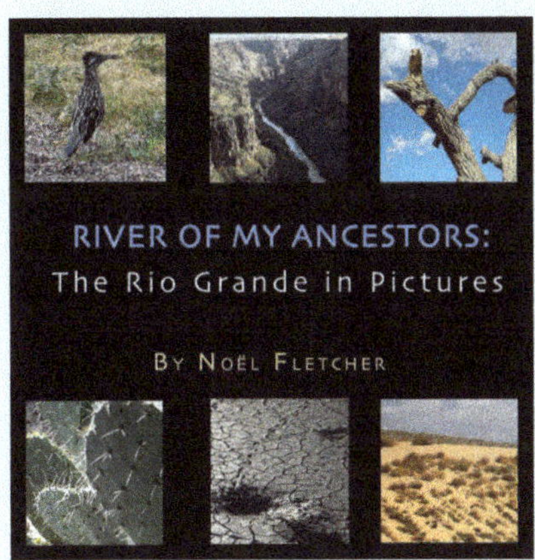


Take a journey along the wild and rugged Rio Grande. Beautiful pictures capture the essence of the famous river and its importance in the arid Southwest. Native New Mexican author and photographer Noël-Marie Fletcher provides family stories and insights about frontier life.

Follow the Rio Grande through deserts, wetlands, and rocky cliffs. Experience natural wonders, including volcanic lands and river rapids, and encounter wildlife such as snakes, wolves, cranes, and bighorn sheep.

With 180+ striking color photos, the book features:

- Author biography
- Interesting facts about New Mexico, local culture, and life along the Rio Grande
- the world's largest cottonwood forest
- Bosque del Apache National Wildlife Refuge
- Oral tradition from Spanish settlers and family stories

This captivating book combines vivid photos and the written word to tell a living history of the famous Rio Grande and the beautiful desert land of New Mexico.

## Pathways in Time: Photo Journeys *by Noël-Marie Fletcher*

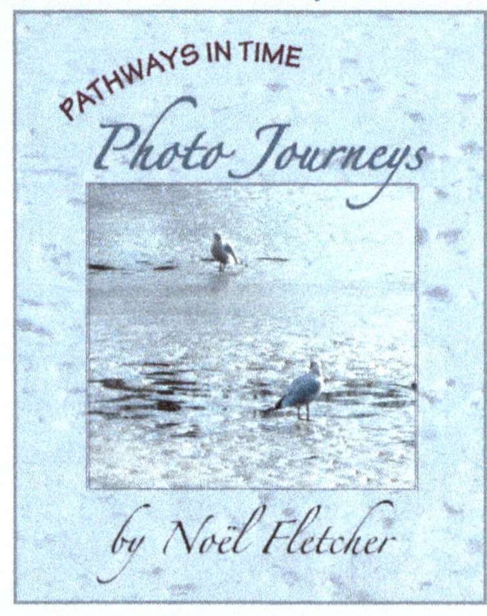


Travel along many roads and witness simple and abstract forms of beauty. Featuring over 160 photos, *"Pathways in Time: Photo Journeys"* shows the wonder of nature such as in rainbows, birds, trees, leaves, raindrops, and the earth.

It also reveals abstract views of architecture, urban settings, and found objects.

Author/photographer Noël-Marie Fletcher shows how to find beauty in ordinary life and the world that surrounds us all.

## The Strange Side of War *by* SARAH MACNAUGHTAN & *Noël-Marie Fletcher*

Take a journey across the dangerous battlefields of a world at war. Accompany Scottish novelist Sarah Macnaughtan as she volunteers alongside British humanitarian groups to alleviate the suffering in war-torn lands. Her many adventures tell unique stories of tragedy and triumph, taking readers on an unforgettable journey from the trenches of Belgium to the distant frontiers of Persia and tsarist Russia. Author/editor Noël-Marie Fletcher provides new historical context that brings Sarah's story to life and helps readers to remember the bravery and sacrifice of those who died. Illustrated with 130+ rare photos and propaganda posters from World War I, this important work features historical insights about the people and places involved in the conflict.

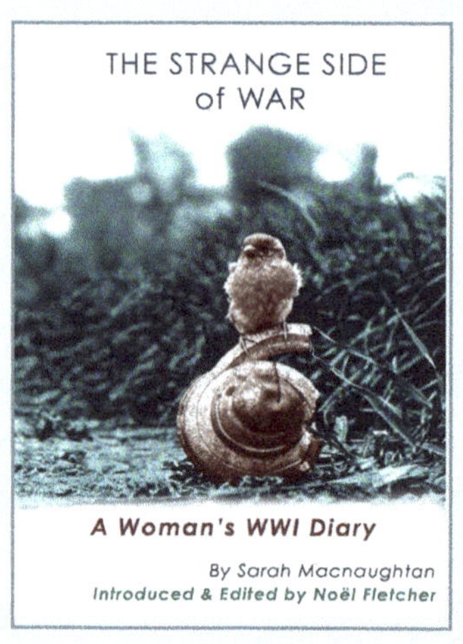


## Two Years in the Forbidden City *by* PRINCESS DER LING

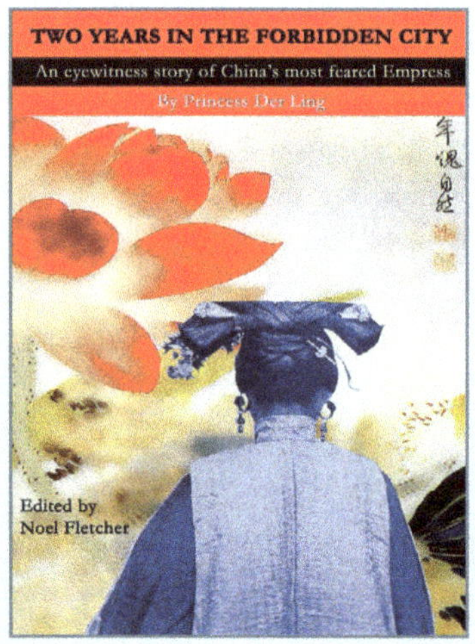


This true story was the first eyewitness account of the Imperial Court written by a Chinese aristocrat for Western readers. It provides an up-close view of the notorious Dowager Empress Tzu-hsi in her final years. Enhanced with rich imagery and additional historical notes, it includes interesting historical details and photos about China's infamous Dowager Empress, the Boxer Rebellion and the Imperial Court. It is illustrated with 100+ historical photographs, illustrations, and paintings from the late 1800s to early 1900s. Author/editor Noël-Marie Fletcher that provides context for this book in modern Chinese history.

www.ingramcontent.com/pod-product-compliance
Lightning Source LLC
LaVergne TN
LVHW060629110826
845147LV00014B/875

*9781941184172*